GLEIM®

2018 EDITION

CMA Review

Part 2

Financial Decision Making

by

Irvin N. Gleim, Ph.D., CPA, CIA, CMA, CFM

and

Dale L. Flesher, Ph.D., CPA, CIA, CMA, CFM

ii

Gleim Publications, Inc.
PO Box 12848
University Station
Gainesville, Florida 32604
(800) 87-GLEIM or (800) 874-5346
(352) 375-0772
Website: www.gleim.com
Email: admin@gleim.com

For updates to this edition of *CMA Review: Part 2*

Go To: www.gleim.com/CMAupdate

Or: Email update@gleim.com with **CMA 2 2018-1** in the subject line. You will receive our current update as a reply.

Updates are available until the next edition is published.

ISSN: 2152-6419

ISBN: 978-1-61854-140-6

First Printing: October 2017

ACKNOWLEDGMENTS

The authors are indebted to the Institute of Certified Management Accountants (ICMA) for permission to use problem materials from past CMA examinations and other ICMA exam information. Questions and unofficial answers from the Certified Management Accountant Examinations, copyright © 1982 through 2017 by the Institute of Certified Management Accountants, are reprinted and/or adapted with permission.

The authors are also indebted to The Institute of Internal Auditors, Inc., for permission to use Certified Internal Auditor Examination Questions and Suggested Solutions, copyright © 1985 through 1996 by The Institute of Internal Auditors, Inc.

The authors also appreciate and thank the American Institute of Certified Public Accountants, Inc. Material from Uniform Certified Public Accountant Examination questions and unofficial answers, copyright © 1981-2017 by the American Institute of Certified Public Accountants, Inc., is reprinted and/or adapted with permission.

Environmental Statement -- This book is printed on recyclable, environmentally friendly groundwood paper, sourced from certified sustainable forests and produced either TCF (totally chlorine-free) or ECF (elementally chlorine-free).

ABOUT THE AUTHORS

Irvin N. Gleim is Professor Emeritus in the Fisher School of Accounting at the University of Florida and is a member of the American Accounting Association, Academy of Legal Studies in Business, American Institute of Certified Public Accountants, Association of Government Accountants, Florida Institute of Certified Public Accountants, The Institute of Internal Auditors, and the Institute of Management Accountants. He has had articles published in the *Journal of Accountancy*, *The Accounting Review*, and *The American Business Law Journal* and is author/coauthor of numerous accounting books, aviation books, and CPE courses.

Dale L. Flesher is a professor, associate dean, and holder of the Roland and Sheryl Burns Chair in the School of Accountancy at the University of Mississippi and has written over 300 articles for business and professional journals, including *Management Accounting*, *Journal of Accountancy*, and *The Accounting Review*, as well as numerous books. He is a member of the IMA, AICPA, The IIA, American Accounting Association, and American Taxation Association. He is a past editor of *The Accounting Historians' Journal* and is a trustee and past president of the Academy of Accounting Historians. He is a former vice president of finance for the American Accounting Association. In 2011, he received the AICPA's highest award for educators, The Distinguished Performance in Accounting Education Award, which is a lifetime achievement award. Previously, in 1990, he received The Institute of Internal Auditors Radde Award as the Outstanding Auditing Educator worldwide.

REVIEWERS AND CONTRIBUTORS

Garrett Gleim, B.S., CPA (not in public practice), is a graduate of the Wharton School at the University of Pennsylvania. Mr. Gleim coordinated the production staff, reviewed the manuscript, and provided production assistance throughout the project.

Solomon E. Gonite, J.D., CPA, CIA, is a graduate of the Florida State University College of Law and the Fisher School of Accounting at the University of Florida. He has practiced as an auditor (in both the private and government sectors) and as a tax practitioner. Mr. Gonite provided substantial editorial assistance throughout the project.

Mark S. Modas, M.S.T., CPA, received a Bachelor of Arts in Accounting from Florida Atlantic University and a Master of Science in Taxation from Nova Southeastern University. He was the Sarbanes-Oxley project manager and internal audit department manager at Perry Ellis International, and the former Acting Director of Accounting and Financial Reporting for the School Board of Broward County, Florida. Mr. Modas provided substantial editorial assistance throughout the project.

Michael Kustanovich, M.A., CPA, is a graduate of Ben-Gurion University of the Negev in Israel. He is a Lecturer of Accountancy in the Department of Accountancy at the University of Illinois at Urbana-Champaign. He has worked in the audit departments of KPMG and PWC and as a financial accounting lecturer in the Department of Economics of Ben-Gurion University of the Negev. Mr. Kustanovich provided substantial editorial assistance throughout the project.

A PERSONAL THANKS

This manual would not have been possible without the extraordinary effort and dedication of Jacob Bennett, Julie Cutlip, Ethan Good, Blaine Hatton, Fernanda Martinez, Kelsey Olson, Bree Rodriguez, Teresa Soard, Justin Stephenson, Joanne Strong, and Elmer Tucker, who typed the entire manuscript and all revisions and drafted and laid out the diagrams, illustrations, and cover for this book.

The authors also appreciate the production and editorial assistance of Levi Bradford, Steven Critelli, Jim Harvin, Jessica Hatker, Kristen Hennen, Belea Keeney, Katie Larson, Diana León, Bernadyn Nettles, Jake Pettifor, Shane Rapp, Drew Sheppard, and Alyssa Thomas.

The author also appreciates the critical reading assistance of Felix Chen, Corey Connell, Nathan Giron, Justin Hamilton, Nichole Hyde, Andrew Johnson, Dean Kingston, Josh Lehr, Melissa Leonard, Cristian Prieto, Martin Salazar, and Yiqian Zhao.

Finally, we appreciate the encouragement, support, and tolerance of our families throughout this project.

TABLE OF CONTENTS

DETAILED TABLE OF CONTENTS

PREFACE FOR CMA PART 2 CANDIDATES

The purpose of this book is to help **you** prepare **yourself** to pass Part 2 of the two-part CMA examination. The overriding consideration is to provide an inexpensive, effective, and easy-to-use study program. This manual

- Defines the subject matter tested on Part 2 of the CMA exam.
- Covers all topics on Part 2 of the CMA exam in a concise manner to help you pass.
- Presents multiple-choice and essay questions from past CMA examinations to prepare you for questions in future CMA exams. Our signature detailed answer explanations are presented to the immediate right of each question for your convenience. Use a piece of paper to cover our explanations as you study the questions.
- Suggests exam-taking and question-answering techniques to help you maximize your exam score.

The outline format, the spacing, and the question-and-answer formats in this book are designed to facilitate readability, learning, understanding, and success on the CMA exam. Our most successful candidates use the Gleim Premium Review System*, which includes CMA Gleim Instruct, the largest test bank of multiple-choice and essay questions, expertly authored books, and the Gleim Access Until You Pass guarantee; or a group study CMA review program. This review book and all Gleim CMA Review materials are compatible with other CMA review materials and courses that are based on the ICMA's Content Specification Outlines.

To maximize the efficiency and effectiveness of your CMA review program, augment your studying with the *CMA Exam Guide* (available at www.gleim.com/PassCMA). This booklet has been carefully written and organized to provide important information to assist you in passing the CMA examination.

Thank you for your interest in our materials. We deeply appreciate all the feedback we have received from CIA, CMA, CPA, and EA candidates; accounting students; and faculty during the past 5 decades.

If you use Gleim materials, we want YOUR feedback immediately after the exam and as soon as you have received your grades. The CMA exam is NONDISCLOSED, and you must maintain its confidentiality and agree not to divulge the nature or content of any CMA question or answer under any circumstances. We ask only for information about our materials, i.e., the topics that need to be added, expanded, etc.

Please go to www.gleim.com/feedbackCMA2 to share your suggestions on how we can improve this edition.

Good Luck on the Exam,

Irvin N. Gleim
Dale L. Flesher
October 2017

PREPARING FOR AND TAKING THE CMA EXAM

READ THE GLEIM *CMA EXAM GUIDE*

Obtain a free copy of the Gleim *CMA Exam Guide* by visiting www.gleim.com/PassCMA. Then, continue to reference it throughout your studies to obtain a deeper understanding of the CMA exam and exam strategies.

OVERVIEW OF THE CMA EXAMINATION

The total exam is 8 hours of testing. It is divided into two parts, as follows:

Part 1 – Financial Reporting, Planning, Performance, and Control
Part 2 – Financial Decision Making

Each part consists of 100 multiple-choice questions and 2 essay scenarios, and testing lasts 4 hours (3 hours for the multiple-choice questions plus 1 hour for the essays). The exams are only offered during the following three testing windows: January/February, May/June, and September/ October.

The CMA exam is computerized and offered at hundreds of Prometric testing centers worldwide. The suite of Gleim products, including the Gleim CMA Review Course, CMA Mega Test Bank, and CMA Exam Rehearsal provide exact exam emulations of the Prometric computer screens and procedures so you are totally comfortable and prepared to PASS on exam day.

SUBJECT MATTER FOR PART 2

Below, we have provided the ICMA's abbreviated Content Specification Outline (CSO) for Part 2. The percentage coverage of each topic is indicated to its right. We constantly update our materials for any changes in the CSO.

Candidates for the CMA designation are expected to have a minimum level of business knowledge that transcends both examination parts. This minimum level includes knowledge of basic financial statements, time value of money concepts, and elementary statistics. Specific discussion of the ICMA's Levels of Performance (A, B, and C) is provided in Appendix C, which is a reprint of the ICMA's discussion of types and levels of exam questions.

Part 2: Financial Decision Making

Financial Statement Analysis	25%
Corporate Finance	20%
Decision Analysis	20%
Risk Management	10%
Investment Decisions	15%
Professional Ethics	10%

Appendix C contains the CSOs in their entirety as well as cross-references to the subunits in Gleim CMA Review where topics are covered. We have studied the CSOs while developing our materials and can assure you they are aligned with the most current CSOs. Accordingly, you do not need to spend time with Appendix C. Rather, it should give you confidence that Gleim CMA Review is the best review source available to help you pass the CMA exam.

LEARNING OUTCOME STATEMENTS

In addition to the CSOs, the ICMA provides Learning Outcome Statements (LOSs). The LOSs are more specific and describe in greater detail what candidates need to know and the skills they are expected to have as CMAs. Gleim materials cover these LOSs thoroughly. For your convenience, Appendix C provides a complete reproduction of the LOSs along with cross-references to the subunits in Gleim CMA Review where they are covered.

WHICH PRONOUNCEMENTS ARE TESTED?

New pronouncements are eligible to be tested on the CMA exam in the testing window beginning 1 year after a pronouncement's effective date. Rest assured that Gleim updates our materials as appropriate when any new standard is testable and will only cover what candidates need for the current CMA exam.

HOW ETHICS ARE TESTED

Ethical issues and considerations are tested from the perspectives of both the individual and the organization in Part 2. Candidates will be expected to evaluate the issues involved and make recommendations for the resolution of the situation in both the multiple-choice section and the essay section of Part 2 of the exam.

NONDISCLOSED EXAM

The CMA is a nondisclosed exam, which means that exam questions are not released to review providers or the public while they are still testable. As part of the ICMA's nondisclosure policy and to prove each candidate's willingness to adhere to this policy, a confidentiality agreement must be accepted by each candidate before each part is taken. This statement is reproduced here to remind all CMA candidates about the ICMA's strict policy of nondisclosure, which Gleim consistently supports and upholds.

> *I hereby attest that I will not divulge the content of this examination, nor will I remove any examination materials, notes or other unauthorized materials from the examination room. I understand that failure to comply with this attestation may result in invalidation of my grades and disqualification from future examinations. For those already certified by the Institute of Certified Management Accountants, failure to comply with the statement will be considered a violation of the IMA's Statement of Ethical Professional Practice and could result in revocation of the certification.*

THE ICMA'S REQUIREMENTS FOR CMA DESIGNATIONS

The CMA designation is granted only by the ICMA. Candidates must complete the following steps to become a CMA:

1. Become a member of the IMA, enter the certification program, and register for the part(s) you are going to take. The Gleim *CMA Exam Guide* contains concise instructions on the membership and certification application and registration processes as well as a useful worksheet to help you keep track of your process and organize what you need for exam day.

2. Pass both parts of the exam within 3 years.

3. Satisfy the education requirement within 2 years.

4. Satisfy the experience requirement within 2 years.

5. Comply with the IMA's *Statement of Ethical Professional Practice*.

ELIGIBILITY PERIOD

Once candidates are admitted into the Certification Program, they are required to pass both parts of the exam within 3 years. If a candidate is not able to pass both parts within this time period, the Certification Entrance Fee will have to be repaid and the passed part will have to be retaken.

MAINTAINING YOUR CMA DESIGNATION

When you have completed all requirements, you will be issued a numbered CMA certificate. This certificate is the property of the ICMA and must be returned upon request. To maintain your certificate, membership in the IMA is required. CMAs must pay the CMA Annual Fee, which covers active IMA membership and the CMA Maintenance Fee. You are also required to comply with the IMA's *Statement of Ethical Professional Practice* and all applicable state laws. The final requirement is continuing professional education (CPE).

Beginning the calendar year after successful completion of the CMA exams, 30 hours of CPE must be completed, which is about 4 days per year. Qualifying topics include management accounting, corporate taxation, statistics, computer science, systems analysis, management skills, marketing, business law, and insurance. All CMAs are required to complete 2 hours of CPE on the subject of ethics as part of their 30-hour annual requirement.

HOW TO USE THE GLEIM REVIEW SYSTEM

Gleim CMA Review is a simple three-step process, which integrates all of the review components and should be applied to each study unit (i.e., bite-sized lesson).

Step 1: Diagnostic

    a.   Multiple-Choice Quiz #1 (30 minutes, plus 10 minutes for review) – In the CMA Review Course, complete Multiple-Choice Quiz #1 in 30 minutes. This is a diagnostic quiz, so it is expected that your scores will be lower.

        1)   Immediately following the quiz, review the questions you marked and/or answered incorrectly. This step is essential to identifying your weak areas. Refer to "Learning from Your Mistakes" on page 7 for tips.

Step 2: Comprehension

    a.   Audiovisual Presentation (30 minutes) – This CMA Review Course presentation provides an overview of the study unit. Use the Gleim CMA Audio Lectures instead when you are on the go!

    b.   Gleim Instruct - CMA Video Series (30-90 minutes) – These videos are for candidates who prefer live instruction to the slide-show style of the audiovisual presentations. Gleim Instruct videos include lectures featuring professors from accredited universities, multiple-choice questions, and detailed examples.

    c.   Focus Questions (45 minutes) – Complete the Focus Questions in the CMA Review Course and receive immediate feedback.

    d.   Knowledge Transfer Outline (60-90 minutes) – Study the Knowledge Transfer Outline, particularly the troublesome areas identified from your Multiple-Choice Quiz #1 in Step 1. The Knowledge Transfer Outlines can be studied either online or in the books.

    e.   Multiple-Choice Quiz #2 (30 minutes, plus 10 minutes for review) – Complete Multiple-Choice Quiz #2 in the CMA Review Course.

        1)   Immediately following the quiz, review the questions you marked and/or answered incorrectly. This step is an essential learning activity. Refer to "Learning from Your Mistakes" on page 7 for tips.

Step 3: Application

    a.   CMA Test Prep (60 minutes, plus 20 minutes for review) – Complete two 20-question quizzes in CMA Test Prep, a component of the Mega Test Bank, using the Practice Exam feature. Spend 30 minutes taking each quiz and then spend about 10 minutes reviewing each quiz as needed.

    b.   Essay Scenario (30 minutes, plus 10 minutes for review) – Complete the essay scenario in the CMA Review Course. Budget 30 minutes to complete the scenario and spend about 10 minutes reviewing.

Additional Assistance

1.   Gleim Instruct Supplemental Videos (as needed) – These videos discuss multiple-choice questions and essay scenarios that test the topics candidates find the most difficult.

2.   Gleim Essay Bank (as needed) – For additional practice answering essays, complete scenarios from the Essay Bank, a component of the Mega Test Bank.

3.   Core Concepts – These consolidated documents provide overviews of the key points of each study unit that serve as a foundation for learning.

Final Review

1. CMA Exam Rehearsal (4 hours/240 minutes) – Take the Exam Rehearsal at the beginning of your final review stage. It contains 100 multiple-choice questions and 2 essay scenarios, just like the CMA exams. This will help you identify where you should focus during the remainder of your final review.

2. CMA Mega Test Bank (10-20 hours) – Use the Mega Test Bank to focus on your weak areas identified by your Exam Rehearsal. This software gives you access to the largest test bank of multiple-choice and essay questions so you can work on the topics and question-answering techniques you struggle with the most. Also, be sure to do a cumulative review to refresh yourself with topics you learned at the beginning of your studies. View your performance chart to make sure you are scoring 75% or higher.

The times mentioned above and on the previous page are recommendations based on prior candidate feedback and how long you have to answer questions on the actual exam. Each candidate's time spent in any area will vary depending on proficiency and familiarity with the subject matter.

GLEIM KNOWLEDGE TRANSFER OUTLINES

This edition of the CMA Part 2 Review book has the following features to make studying easier:

1. **Examples:** Longer, illustrative examples, both hypothetical and those drawn from actual events, are set off in shaded, bordered boxes.

EXAMPLE of Transaction Gains and Losses

On December 15, Year 1, Boise Co. purchased electronic components from Kinugasa Corporation. Boise must pay Kinugasa ¥15,000,000 on January 15, Year 2. The exchange rate in effect on December 15, Year 1, was $.01015 per yen, giving the transaction a value on Boise's books of $152,250 (¥15,000,000 × $.01015).

Transaction Date:

Inventory	$152,250	
Accounts payable		$152,250

The exchange rate on December 31, Year 1, Boise's reporting date, has fallen to $.01010 per yen. The balance of the payable must be adjusted in the amount of $750 [(¥15,000,000 × ($.01015 – $.01010)].

Reporting Date:

Accounts payable	$750	
Transaction gain		$750

The exchange rate on January 15, Year 2, has risen to $.01020 per yen. To settle the payable, the balance must be adjusted in the amount of $1,500 [¥15,000,000 × ($.01010 – $.01020)].

Settlement Date:

Accounts payable ($152,250 – $750)	$151,500	
Transaction loss	1,500	
Cash		$153,000

---

2. **Gleim Success Tips:** These tips supplement the core exam material by suggesting how certain topics might be presented on the exam or how you should prepare for an issue.

CMA candidates must be prepared to answer ethics questions that may be integrated with any of the other topics. Ethics may be tested in either or both the multiple-choice and essay sections. Like all other topics, ethics is eligible to be tested at all three levels of difficulty, requiring you to (1) recall aspects of the IMA's *Statement of Ethical Professional Practice* and the Foreign Corrupt Practices Act and (2) evaluate and apply the different aspects as they relate to typical business situations. In the essay format, these questions will not only require the candidate to identify the exact nature of the ethical dilemma but also how the professional facing the dilemma should resolve it. It is also important to understand the differences between illegal and unethical behavior by an organization.

TIME-BUDGETING AND QUESTION-ANSWERING TECHNIQUES FOR THE EXAM

Having a solid multiple-choice answer technique will help you maximize your score on each part of the CMA exam. Remember, knowing how to take the exam and how to answer individual questions is as important as studying/reviewing the subject matter tested on the exam. Competency in both will reduce your stress and the number of surprises you experience on exam day.

1. **Budget your time so you can finish before time expires.**

   - Spend about 1.5 minutes per question. This would result in completing 100 questions in 150 minutes to give you 30 minutes to review your answers and questions that you have marked.

2. **Answer the questions in consecutive order.**

   - Do **not** agonize over any one item or question. Stay within your time budget.
   - Never leave a multiple-choice question (MCQ) unanswered. Your score is based on the number of correct responses. You will not be penalized for answering incorrectly. If you are unsure about a question,

     - Make an educated guess,
     - Mark it for review at the bottom of the screen, and
     - Return to it before you submit the testlet as time allows. Remember, once you have selected the "End" button, you will no longer be able to review or change any answers in the MCQ section.

3. **Ignore the answer choices so that they will not affect your precise reading of the question.**

   - Only one answer option is best. In the MCQs, four answer choices are presented, and you know one of them is correct. The remaining choices are distractors and are meant to appear correct at first glance. *They are called distractors for a reason.* Eliminate them as quickly as you can.
   - In computational items, the distractors are carefully calculated to be the result of common mistakes. Be careful and double-check your computations if time permits.

4. **Read the question carefully to discover exactly what is being asked.**

   - Focusing on what is required allows you to

     - Reject extraneous information
     - Concentrate on relevant facts
     - Proceed directly to determining the best answer

   - Be careful! The requirement may be an **exception** that features a negative word.

5. **Decide the correct answer before looking at the answer choices.**

6. **Read the answer choices, paying attention to small details.**

   - Even if an answer choice appears to be correct, do not skip the remaining answer choices. Each choice requires consideration because you are looking for the best answer provided.
   - Tip: Treat each answer choice like a true/false question as you analyze it.

7. **Click on the best answer.**

   - You have a 25% chance of answering the question correctly by guessing blindly, but you can improve your odds with an educated guess.
   - For many MCQs, you can eliminate two answer choices with minimal effort and increase your educated guess to a 50/50 proposition.

LEARNING FROM YOUR MISTAKES

Learning from questions you answer incorrectly is very important. Each question you answer incorrectly is an **opportunity** to avoid missing actual test questions on your CMA exam. Thus, you should carefully study the answer explanations provided until you understand why the original answer you chose is wrong, as well as why the correct answer indicated is correct. This study technique is the difference between passing and failing for many CMA candidates.

Also, you **must** determine why you answered questions incorrectly to learn how to avoid the same errors in the future. Reasons for missing questions include

1. Misreading the requirement (stem)
2. Not understanding what is required
3. Making a math error
4. Applying the wrong rule or concept
5. Being distracted by one or more of the answers
6. Incorrectly eliminating answers from consideration
7. Not having any knowledge of the topic tested
8. Employing bad intuition when guessing

It is also important to verify that you answered correctly for the right reasons. Otherwise, if the material is tested on the CMA exam in a different manner, you may not answer it correctly.

HOW TO BE IN CONTROL WHILE TAKING THE EXAM

You have to be in control to be successful during exam preparation and execution. Control can also contribute greatly to your personal and other professional goals. Control is a process whereby you

1. Develop expectations, standards, budgets, and plans
2. Undertake activity, production, study, and learning
3. Measure the activity, production, output, and knowledge
4. Compare actual activity with expected and budgeted activity
5. Modify the activity, behavior, or study to better achieve the desired outcome
6. Revise expectations and standards in light of actual experience
7. Continue the process or restart the process in the future

Exercising control will ultimately develop the confidence you need to outperform other CMA candidates and PASS the CMA exam!

Learn how Gleim has helped more CMAs pass the CMA exam than any other course in our free *CMA Exam Guide*. You can view this booklet online at www.gleim.com/PassCMA.

IF YOU HAVE QUESTIONS ABOUT GLEIM MATERIALS

Gleim has an efficient and effective way for candidates who have purchased the Premium CMA Review System to submit an inquiry and receive a response regarding Gleim materials directly through their course. This system also allows you to view your Q&A session in your Gleim Personal Classroom.

Questions regarding the **information in this introduction and/or the Gleim *CMA Exam Guide* (study suggestions, study plans, exam specifics)** may be emailed to personalcounselor@gleim.com.

Questions concerning **orders, prices, shipments, or payments** should be sent via email to customerservice@gleim.com and will be promptly handled by our competent and courteous customer service staff.

For **technical support**, you may use our automated technical support service at www.gleim.com/support, email us at support@gleim.com, or call us at (800) 874-5346.

FEEDBACK

Please fill out our online feedback form (www.gleim.com/feedbackCMA2) immediately after you take the CMA exam so we can adapt our material based on where candidates say we need to increase or decrease coverage. Our approach has been approved by the ICMA.

STUDY UNIT ONE
ETHICS, FRAUD, AND RISK MANAGEMENT

(26 pages of outline)

Ethics for Management Accountants

Global competition and economic uncertainty place stress on accounting and finance professionals to compromise ethical principles. A report released in May 2012 by the American Institute of Certified Public Accountants and the Chartered Institute of Management Accountants (UK) found a weakened "tone from the top" and more pressure on financial professionals–especially in emerging economies–to act unethically.

Certified Management Accountants are required to be committed to the highest ethical behavior. The IMA's requirements for all members in this area are found in its *Statement of Ethical Professional Practice*. The CMA exam tests not only the contents of the *Statement* itself, but also requires the candidate to determine the best resolution to various ethical dilemmas.

This study unit deals with many elements of ethics that must be considered by management accountants and risk management. The relative weight assigned to this major topic in Part 2 of the exam is **20%** (10% for ethics and 10% for risk management).

If you are interested in reviewing more introductory or background material, go to www.gleim.com/CMAIntroVideos for a list of suggested third-party overviews of this topic. The following Gleim outline material is more than sufficient to help you pass the CMA exam; any additional introductory or background material is for your own personal enrichment.

1.1 ETHICS FOR MANAGEMENT ACCOUNTANTS

CMA candidates must be prepared to answer ethics questions that may be integrated with any of the other topics. Ethics may be tested in either or both the multiple-choice and essay sections. Like all other topics, ethics is eligible to be tested at all three levels of difficulty, requiring you to (1) recall aspects of the IMA's *Statement of Ethical Professional Practice* and the Foreign Corrupt Practices Act and (2) evaluate and apply the different aspects as they relate to typical business situations. In the essay format, these questions will not only require the candidate to identify the exact nature of the ethical dilemma but also how the professional facing the dilemma should resolve it. It is also important to understand the differences between illegal and unethical behavior by an organization.

1. **IMA's *Statement of Ethical Professional Practice***

    a. The *Statement* contains four overarching principles:

        1) Honesty
        2) Fairness
        3) Objectivity
        4) Responsibility

b. The *Statement* also contains four specific standards:

1) Competence
2) Confidentiality
3) Integrity
4) Credibility

c. The final section, **Resolution of Ethical Conflict**, is especially significant and has been the subject of many CMA examination questions over the years.

1) One of the most common questions asked deals with the individual to whom an ethical challenge should be reported.
2) The IMA has an ethics hotline for members who wish to discuss ethical conflicts. It is reached at 800-245-1383.

d. Adherence to these provisions is integral to achieving the objectives of management accounting.

1) Management accountants shall not commit acts contrary to the *Statement*, nor shall they condone the commission of such acts by others within their organization.

2. **Conflicts of Interest**

a. One of the provisions of the IMA *Statement* requires members to mitigate actual, and to avoid apparent, conflicts of interest.

1) A conflict of interest is a conflict between the personal and the official responsibilities of a person in a position of trust, sufficient to affect judgment, independence, or objectivity in conducting the affairs of the business.
2) Apparent conflicts are situations or relationships that reasonably could appear to other parties to involve a conflict of interest.

b. Examples of a conflict of interest include

1) Having a substantial financial interest in a supplier, customer, or distributor and
2) Using privileged information gained from one's official position to enter transactions for personal gain.

c. Methods for control of a conflict of interest include the following:

1) Provide a code of conduct provision applying to conflicts of interest. The code of conduct should say that employees are to refrain from engaging in any activity that would prejudice their ability to carry out their duties ethically.
2) Require full financial disclosure by all managers.
3) Require prior notification of any transaction that may raise a question about a possible conflict of interest. The code should say that all parties should be notified of the potential conflict.
4) Prohibit financial ties to any supplier, customer, or distributor.
5) Encourage adherence to strong ethical behavior in corporate actions, policies, and public communications.
6) Employees should refuse any gift, favor, or hospitality that would influence or would appear to influence their actions.

a) For example, in one case, an auditor accepted a loan from an auditee. The auditee was not trying to influence the auditor, but when it later was discovered that the auditee had committed a fraud and the auditor had not caught the fraud, the court's conclusion was that the auditor was guilty. To have refused the favor would have kept the auditor out of prison, but once he accepted the favor, there was a perception that he had allowed his judgment to be influenced.

3. **Ethics on the CMA Exam**

    a. CMA candidates should essentially memorize the entire contents of the IMA's *Statement of Ethical Professional Practice* and be able to apply its provisions in evaluating and proposing resolutions for ethical issues, such as fraudulent reporting, manipulation of financial analyses, financial statement results, and/or budgets.

IMA STATEMENT OF ETHICAL PROFESSIONAL PRACTICE

Members of IMA shall behave ethically. A commitment to ethical professional practice includes: overarching principles that express our values, and standards that guide our conduct.

PRINCIPLES

IMA's overarching ethical principles include: Honesty, Fairness, Objectivity, and Responsibility. Members shall act in accordance with these principles and shall encourage others within their organizations to adhere to them.

STANDARDS

A member's failure to comply with the following standards may result in disciplinary action.

I. COMPETENCE

Each member has a responsibility to:

1. Maintain an appropriate level of professional expertise by continually developing knowledge and skills.
2. Perform professional duties in accordance with relevant laws, regulations, and technical standards.
3. Provide decision support information and recommendations that are accurate, clear, concise, and timely.
4. Recognize and communicate professional limitations or other constraints that would preclude responsible judgment or successful performance of an activity.

II. CONFIDENTIALITY

Each member has a responsibility to:

1. Keep information confidential except when disclosure is authorized or legally required.
2. Inform all relevant parties regarding appropriate use of confidential information. Monitor subordinates' activities to ensure compliance.
3. Refrain from using confidential information for unethical or illegal advantage.

III. INTEGRITY

Each member has a responsibility to:

1. Mitigate actual conflicts of interest. Regularly communicate with business associates to avoid apparent conflicts of interest. Advise all parties of any potential conflicts.
2. Refrain from engaging in any conduct that would prejudice carrying out duties ethically.
3. Abstain from engaging in or supporting any activity that might discredit the profession.

IV. CREDIBILITY

Each member has a responsibility to:

1. Communicate information fairly and objectively.

2. Disclose all relevant information that could reasonably be expected to influence an intended user's understanding of the reports, analyses, or recommendations.

3. Disclose delays or deficiencies in information, timeliness, processing, or internal controls in conformance with organization policy and/or applicable law.

RESOLUTION OF ETHICAL CONFLICT

In applying the Standards of Ethical Professional Practice, you may encounter problems in identifying unethical behavior or in resolving an ethical conflict. When faced with ethical issues, you should follow your organization's established policies on the resolution of such conflict. If these policies do not resolve the ethical conflict, you should consider the following courses of action:

1. Discuss the issue with your immediate superior except when it appears that the supervisor is involved. In that case, present the issue to the next level. If you cannot achieve a satisfactory resolution, submit the issue to the next management level. If your immediate superior is the chief executive officer or equivalent, the acceptable reviewing authority may be a group such as the audit committee, executive committee, board of directors, board of trustees, or owners. Contact with levels above the immediate superior should be initiated only with your superior's knowledge, assuming he or she is not involved. Communication of such problems to authorities or individuals not employed or engaged by the organization is not considered appropriate, unless you believe there is a clear violation of the law.

2. Clarify relevant ethical issues by initiating a confidential discussion with an IME Ethics Counselor or other impartial advisor to obtain a better understanding of possible courses of action.

3. Consult your own attorney as to legal obligations and rights concerning the ethical conflict.

IMA Ethics Helpline Number: 800-245-1383

b. CMA candidates should be able to apply the provisions of IMA's *Statement of Ethical Professional Practice* in recommending a course of action for management accountants to follow when confronted with an ethical dilemma in the business environment.

1) A memorization of the "resolution" section of the *Statement* will enable the candidate to answer questions of this nature.

Stop and review! You have completed the outline for this subunit. Study multiple-choice questions 1 through 6 beginning on page 35.

1.2 CORPORATE ETHICS AND LEGISLATION

BACKGROUND to Foreign Corrupt Practices Act

During the Watergate investigations of 1973-74, it was brought to light that U.S. companies were in the practice of handing out bribes to government officials, politicians, and political parties in foreign countries.

The Securities and Exchange Commission (SEC) began its own investigation and, eventually, over 400 U.S. companies admitted paying out an estimated total of over $300 million from secret "slush funds." The most notable firm involved was the aerospace giant Lockheed, which was found to have paid bribes in West Germany, Italy, Japan, the Netherlands, and Saudi Arabia since the late 1950s to ensure purchase by those governments of the company's fighter planes and passenger jets.

The Foreign Corrupt Practices Act (FCPA) was passed by Congress in 1977 in response to these disclosures.

1. **Foreign Corrupt Practices Act of 1977 (FCPA)**

   a. The FCPA contains two sets of provisions:

      1) Accounting

         a) Books and Records

            i) Issuers are required to make and keep books, records, and accounts that properly reflect transactions and dispositions of assets.

         b) Internal Control

            i) All issuers must devise and maintain a system of internal accounting control sufficient to ensure management's control, authority, and responsibility over assets, regardless of whether they have foreign operations.

               • This provision has a particular impact on internal and external auditors.

      2) Anti-Bribery

         a) No concern or person subject to the FCPA's anti-bribery provisions may offer or authorize corrupt payments to any foreign official, foreign political party or official thereof, or candidate for political office in a foreign country.

            i) Subject to the FCPA's anti-bribery provisions are

               • Domestic concerns, including any person acting on a concern's behalf, whether or not doing business overseas and whether or not registered with the SEC;

               • Issuers, both U.S. and foreign companies, including any person acting on an issuer's behalf, that have a class of securities traded at a U.S. stock exchange or are otherwise required to file reports with the SEC; and

               • Any person, including both concerns and individuals other than domestic concerns or issuers, and including foreign nationals and foreign non-issuing companies acting corruptly while in the U.S.

            ii) Note that only payments to foreign officials and politicians are prohibited; commercial bribery, such as payments to foreign business owners, corporate officers, or domestic U.S. officials, are not addressed by the FCPA.

   b. **Corrupt payments** are payments intended to improperly influence the recipient to act or refrain from acting with the mere goal to obtain or retain business.

      1) The FCPA prohibits a mere offer or promise of a bribe, even if it is not consummated.

         a) The act prohibits payment of anything of value; de minimis gifts and tokens of hospitality are acceptable.

         b) Passive bribery, i.e., receiving or accepting a bribe, is not prohibited by the FCPA.

      2) Payments are prohibited if the person making them knew or should have known that some or all of them would be used to improperly influence a governmental official.

      3) Individuals found in violation of the FCPA are subject to both fines and imprisonment. A corporation may be assessed a fine as well.

         a) Fines imposed upon individuals may not be paid directly or indirectly by an employer.

    c.   The FCPA contains an unusual provision that reflects the culturally determined nature of ethics.

        1)   During the various investigations leading to passage of the FCPA, it became clear that some of the bribes had been distributed, not to gain unfair advantage, but simply to compete at all.

            a)   In some countries, government officials expect to be paid by foreign companies just to perform the duties that would be considered a routine part of their job in the U.S.

            b)   Congress became convinced that being prohibited from making such payments would put U.S. firms at a disadvantage.

            c)   The anti-bribery section of the FCPA therefore contains a provision that permits facilitation or "grease" payments when the purpose is to get paperwork processed, secure a license, receive utility service, etc.

        2)   The accounting and internal control provisions of the FCPA work hand-in-hand with the anti-bribery provision. A company with an adequate accounting system and internal controls would not be able to pay a bribe without reporting "Bribe Expense" on its income statement.

    d.   Financial institutions must also watch out for money laundering and terrorist financing under the requirements of the FCPA.

  2. **FCPA Examples**

    a.   Royal Philips Electronics

        1)   In 2013, the SEC charged the Dutch electronics and health care company with FCPA violations related to improper payments made by employees of a Polish subsidiary to healthcare officials–qualifying as government officials–in Poland, in order to ensure and quicken the sale of Philips products. Philips settled the charges with the SEC by paying more than $4.5 million.

        2)   Note that Philips, a Netherlands-based company, could be charged by the SEC even though the bribery took place outside the U.S. and no U.S. citizens or concerns were involved. Just by being listed on a U.S. stock exchange, Philips became subject to the FCPA.

    b.   SAP SE

        1)   A former SAP SE executive was charged in 2015 for violating the FCPA by bribing Panamanian government officials to ensure the sale of software licenses. The SAP executive settled the case and agreed to return the received kickbacks with interest.

        2)   Note that not only companies are subject to the FCPA, but also people acting on behalf of the company.

BACKGROUND to the Sarbanes-Oxley Act

About 25 years after the passage of the FCPA, business ethics were even more in the news than in the mid-1970s. In late 2001 and early 2002, a wave of improper practices came to light. The following table summarizes some of the more prominent ones:

Scandal Became Public	Company	Details	How Practices Came to Light
Oct 2001	Enron	Hid debt of over $1 billion in improper off-the-books partnerships	Whistleblower
Nov 2001	Arthur Andersen	Shredded documents related to audit of scandal-plagued client Enron	Enron investigation by SEC
Feb 2002	Global Crossing	Inflated revenues, shredded accounting-related documents	Whistleblower
Feb 2002	Qwest	Inflated revenues	Whistleblower
Mar 2002	WorldCom	Booked operating expenses as capital expenses; large off-the-books payments to founder	Internal audit
Apr 2002	Adelphia	Booked operating expenses as capital expenses; hid debt	Voluntary disclosure
Jun 2002	Xerox	Inflated revenues	Whistleblower

3. **Sarbanes-Oxley Act of 2002 (SOX)**

   a. In response to the scandals described on the previous page, SOX imposed extensive new responsibilities on issuers of publicly traded securities and their auditors.

   b. The most significant provision of SOX regarding ethics is Section 406(a), which requires any company issuing securities

   > *...to disclose whether or not, and if not, the reason therefor, such issuer has adopted a **code of ethics for senior financial officers**, applicable to its principal financial officer and comptroller or principal accounting officer, or persons performing similar functions.*

   c. Section 406(c) defines "code of ethics" as

   > *...such standards as are reasonably necessary to promote (1) honest and ethical conduct, including the ethical handling of actual or apparent conflicts of interest between personal and professional relationships; (2) full, fair, accurate, timely, and understandable disclosure in the periodic reports required to be filed by the issuer; and (3) compliance with applicable governmental rules and regulations.*

   d. Note that SOX does not define "ethics" itself; it simply takes an understanding of the concept for granted. This reflects the difficulty of legislating a sense of ethics.

Stop and review! You have completed the outline for this subunit. Study multiple-choice questions 7 through 11 beginning on page 36.

1.3 CORPORATE RESPONSIBILITY FOR ETHICAL BEHAVIOR

The IMA's Statement on Management Accounting, "Values and Ethics: From Inception to Practice," published in 2008, is a useful document for understanding ethical concepts in an organizational context. Quotations from this document are integrated into the outline below and on the following pages.

1. The **organization has a responsibility** to foster a sense of ethics in its employees and agents. All organizations need a code of conduct.

   > *If no defined code of conduct and ethical behavior is developed, employees will act on their own beliefs and values, or they will observe and emulate the behavior they see around them on a daily basis. . . .*

   > *[O]rganizational behavior needs to be defined and deployed in a way that drives the individual behavior of employees in a manner consistent with defined expectations of the wider organization. (II. Introduction)*

2. A pervasive sense of ethical values can **benefit an organization**.

   > *In the past, quality compliance and industrially-engineered output expectations helped exert a high level of control over direct-production employees . . .*

   > *In today's service economy, control often involves developing management systems that include the flowcharting, mapping, and documentation of processes, activities, and tasks so that individuals know what to do "on the job." This works well when everything proceeds as anticipated, but what does an employee do when unplanned events occur? What reference does an individual look to for help in making decisions? To take a phrase from the pioneering work done in process management by Geary Rummler and Alan Brache (1995), what does one do "in the white spaces"? In most cases, an organization relies on the judgment of the individual and/or direct supervisor to develop a course of action that they feel represents the "policy" of the organization. This is why it is important to have a defined set of organizational values and code of ethics — they create the "touchstone" against which every unanticipated decision must be judged. Failure to have every individual in the organization know and understand these values and ethical code leads to inconsistency and, in the worst cases, unethical or fraudulent behavior. (IV. Values, Ethics, and Accounting)*

3. A sense of ethics requires an ability to **distinguish between ethical and merely legal behavior**.

    Ethical behavior is not about abiding by the law. Individuals and organizations can act legally and still be acting unethically. Ethical behavior is driven by compliance with a set of values that acts as the touchstone for situational decisions where rules may not exist to cover every alternative. Ethics is about the integrity of the decision-making process that is used to resolve any number of issues. . . .

    Many individuals at the center of corporate scandals [of the late 20th and early 21st Century] have professed the belief that they were innocent of any wrongdoing, including Kenneth Lay of Enron or Conrad Black of Hollinger. The problem is that these individuals did not define their behavior by what most of society would see as "reasonable," but rather they followed their own particular code—in some cases, limiting the definition of ethical behavior to require compliance with the law and nothing more. When laws may have been broken, it falls to the courts to decide if an act was illegal and to assess penalties. In situations that may be unethical but are not illegal, however, there is no legal remedy. The only course of action for society is to either pressure the government to enact more rules or to decide not to do business or develop relationships with unethical companies and individuals. (II. Introduction)

4. **"Leadership by example,"** or "tone at the top," plays an important role in determining an organization's ethical environment.

    Ethical behavior is not something that applies to someone else — every single individual is responsible for behaving ethically. Nowhere is this more important than the demonstration of ethical behavior that managers and supervisors exhibit in the way they execute their day-to-day work . . .

    Many of us in today's workforce have seen organizations operating with a lack of ethical commitment. As a result, there often is a high level of skepticism toward what is said by those in management and leadership positions: People tend to believe what they see rather than what they are told in the company "pep talk." In order for a code of ethics to be effective, its application must be demonstrated by those in positions of power and leadership. Leaders must be seen living and managing by the code of ethics. (VI. Leadership by Example)

5. **The concept of "human capital"** is important to an organization in creating a climate where "doing the right thing" is expected.

    In most organizations today, labor costs constitute the majority of operating expenses. Efforts to reduce overhead have led to decentralization of operating decisions and the slimming down of supervision. The result is that employees cannot be watched and controlled in every aspect of their work, and an organization must, to a great degree, trust that its employees are acting in its best interests. Human "capital" is a critical asset. Humans create the innovation that generates new products or services and finds unique ways to undertake work in more cost-effective ways. They bring knowledge to the workplace and share it with coworkers. People develop relationships with each other and with suppliers, clients, and others on whom the organization depends. Top leadership in particular creates a climate and culture in which such productive applications of human skills can be optimized to the highest level. . . .

If hiring decisions and employee orientation and training fail to address the alignment of individual values and ethics with organizational expectations, the result can be an equal, if not greater, negative impact on an organization's performance. Unmotivated employees can poison the atmosphere and reduce the teamwork and cooperation required for knowledge transfer and innovation, and they can have a significant negative impact on relationships with suppliers and customers.

Understanding and acting on this aspect of human behavior has potential far beyond compliance with legal or regulatory requirements. Effective development and deployment of a values-based ethical culture becomes the cornerstone of an optimized and productive knowledge-based organization. (IV. Values, Ethics, and Accounting)

An organizational code of ethics must therefore be used as a benchmark for hiring decisions. This ensures candidates have a personal code that aligns with the organizational expectations. (VI. Leadership by Example)

6. An **organization's culture** impacts its behavioral values.

    Every organization already has a culture. In smaller companies — particularly family-owned businesses — the culture reflects the personal values and business methods of the owners and primary operators. In larger companies, it is more difficult to convey the proper culture from the top. One of the most significant risks in very large organizations, in fact, is that the culture (and, by definition, the values and ethics) that the board of directors and senior management believe to exist within the company may be different from the actual culture experienced by employees, clients, and suppliers. In other words, upper management's perception of the culture is not reality. . . .

    Step one in establishing an ethical culture must be an assessment of the existing organizational values and culture and the development of a set of statements that define the principles the organization believes in and should act upon. These statements and principles can be developed by the shareholders, the board, or a governing body within the organization. (V. Defining and Developing the Organization's Behavioral Values)

7. **Employee training** is important to maintaining an ethical organizational culture.

    Although orientation must be provided to every employee at the time of hiring, it is not enough to maintain awareness and commitment to the application of a code of ethics in the workplace. Every existing member of staff should receive ongoing training, starting at the board level and cascading down throughout the organization . . . Ethics training for employees should focus on covering ethical concepts, the organization's code, and compliance. To achieve this, training should include:

    • Ethical concepts and thinking: What is "behind" the issue of ethical action?
    • The organization's code of ethics and any supporting "rules"
    (VIII. Practical Application: Converting Intent into Operational Reality)

8. **Two methods for monitoring** ethical compliance are

    a. **Human performance feedback loop**

        Performance review and development systems must be fully aligned with the requirements for ethical conduct. Competencies, job descriptions, and objectives should include ethical expectations, and the regular employee review systems (conducted on an annual basis at minimum) must assess employees against the same criteria. If the code of ethics dictates that employees treat all others with dignity and respect, then the review process must include 360° input — including both internal and external responses — in order to assess whether that is truly happening. Key Performance Indicators (KPIs) must include tracking of employees against ethical training requirements. Examples include:

        - *The number of new hires and percentage who completed orientation within required time frame*
        - *Percentage of employees who completed annual refresher training on ethical conduct*
        - *Number of employees scoring "achieved" and "exceeded" on annual reviews in ethics criteria*
        - *Number of employees given an award for noted ethical conduct*

        (IX. Measuring and Improving Ethical Compliance)

    b. **Survey tools**

        Ongoing surveys are very valuable tools for assessing ethical performance, especially in areas such as management and leadership. Surveys can be created using the organization's code of ethics and asking employees to rate how well the organization is following the contents. . .

        Respondents can be asked to rate each statement on a scale of 1 through 5 or from "Strongly Disagree" to "Strongly Agree." The results become the basis for developing ongoing compliance indicators and can be used to stimulate dialogue with employees about their concerns and the possible courses of action that could be taken to improve ethical compliance. This turns the company into learning and developing organization. (IX. Measuring and Improving Ethical Compliance)

9. A **whistleblowing framework** (e.g., an ethics helpline) is an important component in maintaining an ethical organizational culture.

    An effective feedback system includes having a confidential framework for employees to report possible violations of the organization's code of ethics and to receive advice on the ethical aspects of challenging decisions. Statistics show that a large number of occupational fraud cases are detected through an employee "hotline" or other reporting method . . .

    Whichever approach an organization chooses, the collection, analysis, and summarization of ethics issues can provide insight into the operation of its code of ethics and the degree to which employees are following it. In addition, tracking and monitoring issues raised through a whistleblowing framework creates opportunities to enhance and improve internal controls. Management accountants need to ensure that such processes are in place, that they operate on a fully confidential basis, and that they are capable of generating statistical or event-based reporting through which insight into ethical practice can be created. (IX. Measuring and Improving Ethical Compliance)

    a. SOX mandates that U.S. companies registered with the SEC have a whistleblowing hotline available.

10. Organizations face particular challenges in applying their values and ethical standards **internationally**.

   When groups share the same cultural background, they tend to share the same values as well. Consequently, the basis for decision making and actions, including alignment with a code of ethical conduct, will be similar. When immigration combines groups from dissimilar countries or backgrounds, the impact can be significant, and the values and decision making processes may not be the same. It has nothing to do with a person being "good" or "bad," but rather is a matter of differing "norms" of behavior based on the society in which that person grew up. This situation is also observable when individuals go abroad to receive an education. . . .

   The challenge of conflicting values becomes greatest in cases where a society has, for example, a limited separation of "state and religion." While most of the Western world professes to maintain a barrier between church and state, a number of countries in other parts of the world have a far greater integration of the two. In many cases, this creates national conflict when the two find themselves in disagreement on various issues.

   All of these changes lead to a melting pot of personal values within societies and organizations, creating profound challenges for leaders and resulting in a new aspect of risk management for organizations. If organizations fail to make the effort to clearly define their expectations of ethical behavior and provide support and encouragement for complying with them, then the vacuum that is left will lead to unpredictable results. (II. Introduction)

11. A comprehensive framework of corporate **ethical behavior** is a prerequisite for an effective system of **internal control**.

   CEOs and CFOs have to place their own integrity on the line by attesting to compliance with an adequate level of internal controls (as well as all other certifications). Creating a thorough, integrated system for developing, implementing, sustaining, and monitoring ethical performance within the organization will allow executives to make such declarations with confidence that a code of ethics is the foundation of the organization's culture and is fully integrated into the thinking process of every employee and business partner. (IX. Measuring and Improving Ethical Compliance)

12. **Three tools** can be used to identify process controls related to ethical and behavioral issues:

   - *Business Process Reengineering (BPR), which became popular in the 1990s, provides a structured view of organizational processes and reveals the existence of tasks and activities that are carried out in order to transform inputs into outputs. At each task and activity level, there are potential risks that the management accountant will want to consider. In all cases, however, the behavioral aspects must provide a context for the risk and its control.*

   - *Quality Management provides another view of process management that can provide management accountants with an excellent variety of options that assist in creating greater visibility on process performance and risk. In fact, quality management and management accounting have much in common. The quality manager seeks to ensure that a process achieves "zero defects" by avoiding unplanned mistakes and costly rework. This includes ensuring that any potential risks that can lead to mistakes occurring or not being identified are assessed and evaluated — goals shared by management accountants . . .*

Using this tool and considering risk from a behavioral aspect can assist in identifying what types of controls should be in place and where they would be best provided. Rather than relying on traditional accounting approaches such as control batch totals, authorization and security levels, etc., this approach uses the perspective of behavioral deviation from an anticipated norm.

- **Continual Process Improvement** *(CPI) is the third area that can significantly contribute to identifying process controls related to ethical and behavioral issues. This concept relates to the development of a "learning organization" — where continual monitoring and assessment of process performance leads to the identification of potential process management and control issues . . . As an organization progresses — hiring new employees or adapting itself to competitive pressures — the business environment changes. These changes have the potential to make current internal controls ineffective or unacceptable. For example, as the workforce changes, the traditional reliance on the behavior of experienced staff may no longer be sufficient; new staff may not behave in a way that achieves the desired outcomes — especially if there is an inadequate approach to ethical hiring, leadership, and compliance. (VII. Ethics and Internal Controls)*

Stop and review! You have completed the outline for this subunit. Study multiple-choice questions 12 through 14 beginning on page 38.

1.4 FRAUD AND THE FRAUD RISK MODEL (FRAUD TRIANGLE)

1. **Types of Fraud**

   a. Fraudulent Financial Reporting

      1) Fraudulent financial reporting is most often committed **by management** to deceive financial statement users.
      2) It is the focus of external auditors and the concern of regulatory bodies, such as the Public Company Accounting Oversight Board and the SEC.

   b. Misappropriation of Assets

      1) Misappropriation of assets is most often committed **by employees** and results from theft, embezzlement, or defalcation.
      2) Although misappropriation of assets can cause the financial statements to be materially misstated, these frauds typically create internal problems rather than external ones.

         a) Once discovered, the effects of the material misappropriation of assets should be accounted for in the financial statements.
         b) Management is expected to create controls to mitigate exposure to this fraud and to deal effectively with it when discovered.

2. **The Fraud Risk Model (Fraud Triangle)**

   a. There are three characteristics of fraud:

      1) Opportunity
      2) Rationalization
      3) Pressure (motivation)

b. Even when **no** characteristics are observed, the risk of fraud cannot be completely excluded.

   1) The fraud triangle appears as follows:

Figure 1-1

   2) Some practitioners like to view the fraud model as a trio of overlapping circles, such as the following:

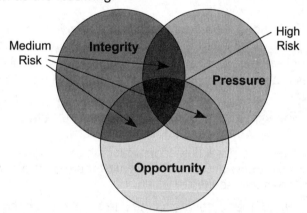

Figure 1-2

   3) Characteristics may be present but hidden from the accountant. For example, financial pressure on an employee is not likely to be noticed by an auditor unless bill collectors are harassing the employee at the office.

c. **Opportunity** relates to the ability of a person not only to perpetrate but also to conceal fraud.

   1) Opportunity is created by an absence of oversight, inadequate internal controls, or the lack of enforcement of those controls.

   2) Opportunity is the **only** characteristic of fraud that can be controlled by management or the organization.

      a) Management typically institutes internal controls to mitigate opportunity, but breakdowns in internal controls do happen.

d. **Rationalization** is a person's ability to justify actions as consistent with his or her personal code of ethics.

   1) Levels of ethical principles and integrity vary greatly among individuals; thus, Certified Management Accountants should assume that anyone can justify the commission of fraud.

      2) Various rationalizations that have been expressed by past perpetrators include the following:

          a) Thoughts of being underpaid or overworked
          b) Feeling that "everybody else is doing it"
          c) Belief that rank in the company has its privileges
          d) Low self-esteem or morale
          e) A desire to seek revenge
          f) Conviction that taking assets is only a loan and will be paid back
          g) Assumption that nobody will get hurt

      3) Rationalization is likely the most difficult characteristic to appraise.

          a) It is difficult to gain insight into another person's ethical principles without intimate knowledge about the person.

          b) Many frauds result from the belief by those in oversight positions that the perpetrator was honest.

  e. **Pressure (motivation)** is a person's reason or need for committing fraud.

      1) Pressure for misappropriation of assets is typically motivated by the need for cash.

          a) Few individuals are motivated to steal just to have the assets. A need or perceived need for cash creates the pressure to steal.

      2) Although motives for fraudulent financial reporting often include the expectation of reward, the relationship between the fraud and the reward is not always so direct.

          a) The expectation of reward may be other than monetary (e.g., continued employment, respect, or admiration).

          b) When the reward is economic gain, managers may feel pressured to manipulate financial reporting if the managers' compensation is tied to financial results.

              i) Other motivations include meeting debt covenants, budgets, or other financial goals.

              ii) Probably the biggest motivation for management is to meet or exceed earnings targets.

              iii) For larger public companies, the need to meet or exceed analysts' forecasts is a major motivator.

3. **Red Flags or Risk Factors Indicating Potential Fraud**

  a. Fraudulent Financial Reporting

      1) Performances too bad or too good to be true
      2) Threat of imminent bankruptcy, foreclosure, or hostile takeover
      3) High turnover of senior management, counsel, or board members
      4) Nonfinancial management's excessive participation in selecting accounting principles or determining estimates
      5) Strained relationship with the auditor
      6) Known history of securities laws violations
      7) Industry or market declines
      8) Poor cash flows
      9) Significant related party transactions not in the ordinary course of business
      10) Highly complex transactions
      11) Transactions in tax-haven jurisdictions
      12) Unrealistic sales or profitability incentives
      13) Unusually rapid growth
      14) Pressures to meet analysts' earnings expectations

    b.   Misappropriation of Assets

        1)   Missing documentation for transactions

        2)   Large amounts of cash on hand

        3)   High-valued, small-sized inventories or other assets

        4)   Unexplained budget variances

        5)   Failure of certain employees to take vacations

        6)   Unusual write-offs of receivables

        7)   Failure to follow up on past-due receivables

        8)   Shortages in delivered or received goods

        9)   Poor supervision

       10) Products or services purchased in excess of needs

       11) Payroll checks with a second endorsement

       12) Employees on the payroll who do not sign up for benefits

       13) Undocumented petty cash expenditures

       14) Common addresses on payables, refunds, or payments

       15) Addresses or telephone numbers of employees that match with suppliers or others

       16) Complaints by customers

4.   **Investigative Resources and Techniques**

    a.   Documents

        1)   Documents provide a key source of evidence in most investigations.

           a)   The accountant should search the most likely locations and files for evidence-related documents and also should check other locations, such as trash bins, dumpsters, and shredders.

           b)   The accountant should be alert for altered documents.

               i)   An altered document often is evidence that fraud occurred.

           c)   Documents can be altered in various ways, such as by erasure or forgery.

               i)   Handwriting, particularly signatures, lends itself to identification. Handwriting examinations, which involve the comparison of known writing from a person with the questioned writing of another, can be used to detect forgeries. Experts will likely be needed to provide testimony.

              ii)   Photocopies should be examined for authenticity of the original. Photocopies of supposed originals often can be recognized by the notation of "trash marks," extraneous marks that appear on the copy.

             iii)   Torn, smudged, faded, burned, etc., documents also should be examined for authenticity.

    b.   Public searches of information

        1)   Public records may be important in discovering the motives of, or the pressures on, a fraudster. Searches may uncover records for the following types of information:

           a)   Civil and criminal actions

           b)   Bankruptcy records

           c)   Marriage licenses and divorces

           d)   Property records

           e)   Litigation history

        2)   Social media is another potential source of information.

        3)   Privacy concerns restrict the release of certain records by government and certain other organizations. These include the following:

           a)   Medical records
           b)   Banking records
           c)   Trust records
           d)   Telephone records
           e)   Passenger lists
           f)   Stock ownership

c.   Commercial online services

        1)   Numerous commercial online services provide information about legal, financial, personal, and business activities for a fee.

d.   Electronic evidence

        1)   Accountants may need to consider electronic evidence; however, it is important to note that it may be difficult to determine who created it, and it is easily changed or deleted.

           a)   Erased files may be retrievable even when they appear to have been purged.

        2)   Considerations for electronic evidence include who created it, when it was created, who has the ability to change it, whether it has been changed since it was created, and how and where it is maintained and stored.

           a)   Documentation is often the key to answering these concerns and establishing credibility for evidence. Experts may be useful.

e.   Interviews

        1)   An interview is one of the most efficient and useful evidence collection techniques.
        2)   An experienced interviewer can quickly gather information that might not be available in any other form.
        3)   In general, interviews should

           a)   Be of sufficient length and depth to uncover relevant facts
           b)   Exclude irrelevant or useless facts
           c)   Be objective and impartial
           d)   Be conducted on a timely basis
           e)   Allow flow of information from subject to interviewer, not vice versa

        4)   Determining whether a person is lying is difficult. However, although the signs are often unclear, those not telling the truth frequently exhibit physiological behaviors during the interview, such as

           a)   Shaking of the head rather than a verbal response
           b)   Responding to the interviewer with a question
           c)   Sweating
           d)   Denying an assertion while providing inconsistent nonverbal cues
           e)   Looking down rather than at the interviewer
           f)   Shifting and fidgeting
           g)   Delaying responses to questions

        5)   Care must always be taken when drawing conclusions from an interview concerning what is and is not truthful.

           a)   The stress of the interview or cultural differences could produce false positives.

Stop and review! You have completed the outline for this subunit. Study multiple-choice questions 15 through 20 beginning on page 39.

1.5 MANAGING THE RISK OF FRAUD

1. A system of control is established to stop fraud and error from occurring or at least to address and fix issues as they happen.

    a. Internal controls are designed to, among other things, prevent or detect fraud. However, because of the concealment aspects of fraudulent activity, the controls cannot give absolute assurance that material fraud will be prevented or detected.

2. **Types of Controls**

    a. **Primary Controls**

        1) Preventive controls deter the occurrence of unwanted events.

            a) Storing petty cash in a locked safe and segregation of duties are examples of this type of control.

            b) IT examples include (1) designing a database so that users cannot enter a letter in the field that stores a Social Security number and (2) requiring the number of invoices in a batch to be entered before processing begins.

        2) Detective controls alert the proper people after an unwanted event. They are effective when detection occurs before material harm occurs.

            a) For example, a batch of invoices submitted for processing may be rejected by the computer system. A detective control provides for automatic reporting of all rejected batches to the accounts payable department.

            b) Hash totals are commonly used to detect data entry errors but may also be used to test for completeness.

            c) A burglar alarm is another example.

        3) Corrective controls correct the negative effects of unwanted events.

            a) An example is a requirement that all cost variances over a certain amount be justified.

        4) Directive controls cause or encourage the occurrence of a desirable event.

            a) Policy and procedure manuals are common examples.

    b. **Secondary Controls**

        1) Compensatory (mitigative) controls may reduce risk when the primary controls are ineffective. However, they do not, by themselves, reduce risk to an acceptable level.

            a) An example is supervisory review when segregation of duties is not feasible.

        2) Complementary controls work with other controls to reduce risk to an acceptable level.

            a) For example, separating the functions of accounting for and custody of cash receipts is complemented by obtaining deposit slips validated by the bank.

3. **Segregation of Duties**

    a. The **segregation of accounting duties** can enhance systems security. Segregation of duties involves the separation of the functions of authorization, recordkeeping, and asset custody so as to minimize the opportunities for a person to perpetrate and conceal errors or fraud in the normal course of his or her duties.

    b. Compensating controls replace normal controls, such as segregation of duties when the latter cannot be feasibly implemented.

4.   **Independent Checks and Verification**

    a.   At a certain point in the control process, a reconciliation between recorded amounts and assets must be performed by a part of the organization that is either (1) unconnected with the original transaction or (2) without custody of the assets involved.

        1)   A comparison revealing that assets do not agree with recorded amounts should be investigated, as it could indicate fraud or error.

            a)   Inquiries should be made into the cause of the discrepancy, and appropriate action should be taken.

        2)   The frequency of such comparisons for the purpose of safeguarding assets depends on the nature and amount of the assets involved and the cost of making the comparison.

            a)   The costs should not outweigh the benefits.

    b.   Prenumbered forms can assist in reconciliation because it is easier to establish a complete record of prenumbered forms, which can then all be reconciled.

5.   **Safeguarding Controls**

    a.   Safeguarding controls limit access of an organization's assets to authorized personnel, including both physical access and access to documents and records.

        1)   Examples include a lockbox system.

Stop and review! You have completed the outline for this subunit. Study multiple-choice questions 21 through 26 beginning on page 40.

1.6 RISK MANAGEMENT

1.   **The Evolution of Risk Management**

    a.   In previous decades, businesses addressed risk management with a "stovepipe" approach. The IMA's Statement on Management Accounting, "Enterprise Risk Management: Frameworks, Elements, and Integration," describes it this way:

> . . . the treasury function focused on risks emanating from foreign currencies, interest rates, and commodities--so called financial risks. An organization's insurance group focused on hazard risks such as fire and accidents. Operating management looked after various operational risks, and the information technology group was concerned with security and systems risks. The accounting and internal audit function focused on risks caused by inadequate internal controls and trends in performance indicators. The general assumption was that executive management had their eye on the big picture of strategic risks facing the enterprise in the short term and over the life of the strategic plan.

    b.   This fragmented approach to risk management is unsuitable to the complex and interconnected business environment of the 21st century. The concept of enterprise risk management (ERM) arose to address the current need.

    c.   ERM approaches risk from an enterprise-wide perspective. Its goal is

> to create, protect, and enhance shareholder value by managing the uncertainties that could either negatively or positively influence achievement of the organization's objectives.

2. **Five Types of Risk**

    a.   **Hazard risks** are insurable risks. Examples include natural disasters, the incapacity or death of senior officers, sabotage, impairment of physical assets, and terrorism.

    b.   **Financial risks** encompass interest-rate risk, exchange-rate risk, commodity risk, credit risk, liquidity risk, and market risk.

    c.   **Operational risks** are related to the enterprise's ongoing, everyday operations. Operational risk is the risk of loss from inadequate or failed internal processes, people, and systems.

        1)   These failures can relate to human resources (e.g., inadequate hiring or training practices), business processes (poor internal controls), technology, product failure (customer ill will, lawsuits), occupational safety and health incidents, environmental damage, and business continuity (power outages, natural disasters).

        2)   Operational risk includes legal risk (making the enterprise subject to civil or criminal penalties) and compliance risk (the risk that processes will not be carried out in accordance with best practices).

        3)   Operational risk can be managed with adequate internal controls, business process reengineering, and business continuity planning.

    d.   **Strategic risks** include global economic risk, political risk, regulatory risk, and risks related to global market conditions. Also included are reputation risk, leadership risk, brand risk, and changing customer needs.

    e.   **Business risk** is the risk that a company will have lower than anticipated profits or will incur a loss.

3. **Volatility and Time**

    a.   Any time uncertainty increases, risk increases. Thus, as the volatility or duration of a project or investment increases, so does the associated risk.

4. **Key Steps in the Risk Management Process**

    a.   **Step 1 – Identify risks.** Every risk that could affect the success of the organization must be considered. Note that this does not mean every single risk that is possible, only those that have could have an impact on the organization.

        1)   Risk identification must be performed for the entire organization, down to its lowest operating units. Some occurrences may be inconsequential for the enterprise as a whole but disastrous for an individual unit.

    b.   **Step 2 – Assess risks.** Every risk identified must be assessed as to its probability and potential impact (item 5.a. on the next page).

        1)   Quantitative risk assessment techniques include benchmarking and scenario analysis.

        2)   Not all assessments need to be made in quantitative terms. Qualitative terms (e.g., high, medium, low) are often useful.

    c.   **Step 3 – Prioritize risks.** In large and/or complex organizations, top management may appoint an ERM committee to review the risks identified by the various operating units and create a coherent response plan.

        1)   The committee must include persons who are competent to make these judgments and are in a position to allocate the resources for adequate risk response (i.e, chief operating officer, chief audit officer, chief information officer).

d.   **Step 4 – Formulate risk responses.** The ERM committee proposes adequate response strategies (item 7. below and on the next page).

1)   Personnel at all levels of the organization must be made aware of the importance of the risk response appropriate to their levels.

e.   **Step 5 – Monitor risk responses.** The two most important sources of information for ongoing assessments of the adequacy of risk responses (and the changing nature of the risks themselves) are

1)   Those closest to the activities themselves. The manager of an operating unit is in the best position to monitor the effects of the chosen risk response strategies.

2)   The audit function. Operating managers may not always be objective about the risks facing their units, especially if they had a stake in designing a particular response strategy. Analyzing risks and responses are among the normal duties of internal auditors.

5.   **Probabilities of Risk Exposures**

a.   Risk can be quantified as a combination of two factors: the severity of consequences and the likelihood of occurrence. The expected value of a loss due to a risk exposure can thus be stated numerically as the product of the two factors.

1)   EXAMPLE: A company is assessing the risks of its systems being penetrated by hackers.

Event	Potential Monetary Loss		Likelihood		Expected Loss
Minor penetration	$ 1,000,000	×	95%	=	$ 950,000
Unauthorized viewing of internal databases	50,000,000	×	35%	=	17,500,000
Unauthorized alteration of internal databases	2,000,000,000	×	1%	=	20,000,000

a)   The company considers it almost inevitable that a minor penetration of its systems will take place. However, the expected monetary loss is sustainable.

b)   By contrast, the other two levels of incident are much less likely but would have a disastrous impact on the firm.

b.   Obviously, neither the probabilities nor the dollar amounts in an expected loss calculation are precise. If a disastrous penetration of the company's systems did occur, it might induce a loss of more than $2 billion.

1)   The **unexpected loss or maximum possible loss** is the amount of potential loss that exceeds the expected amount.

6.   **Risk Appetite**

a.   The degree of willingness of upper management to accept risk is termed the organization's risk appetite.

1)   If top management has a low appetite for risk, the risk response strategies adopted will be quite different from those of an organization whose management is willing to accept a high level of risk.

7.   **Strategies for Risk Response**

a.   **Risk avoidance** ends the activity from which the risk arises. For instance, the risk of having a pipeline sabotaged in an unstable region can be avoided by simply selling the pipeline.

b.   **Risk retention** is the organization's acceptance of the risk of an activity. This term is becoming synonymous with the phrase "self insurance."

   c.   **Risk reduction** (mitigation) is the act of lowering the level of risk associated with an activity. For instance, the risk of systems penetration can be reduced by maintaining a robust information security function within the organization.

   d.   **Risk sharing** transfers some loss potential to another party. Common examples are the purchase of insurance policies, engaging in hedging operations, outsourcing an activity, and entering into joint ventures. It is synonymous with risk transfer.

   e.   **Risk exploitation** is the deliberate courting of risk in order to pursue a high return on investment. Examples include the wave of Internet-only businesses that crested in the late 1990s and cutting-edge technologies, such as genetic engineering.

8.   **Cost-Benefit Analysis**

   a.   In deciding among risk responses, management must consider the costs and benefits of each risk response. A risk response should be ignored if its costs exceed its benefits.

   b.   The costs associated with a risk response include both direct and indirect costs. Such costs include the costs incurred to design, implement, and maintain the risk response. Management should also consider the opportunity costs associated with each risk response.

   c.   The costs and related benefits of each risk response can be measured quantitatively or qualitatively.

9.   **Residual Risk vs. Inherent Risk**

   a.   Residual risk is the risk of an activity remaining after the effects of any risk responses.

   b.   Inherent risk is the risk of an activity that arises from the activity itself. For example, uranium prospecting is inherently riskier than retailing.

10.   **Benefits of Risk Management**

   a.   Efficient use of resources. Only after risks are identified can resources be directed toward those with the greatest exposure.

   b.   Fewer surprises. After a comprehensive, organization-wide risk assessment has been performed, the odds that an incident that has never been considered will arise are greatly reduced.

   c.   Reassuring investors. Corporations with strong risk management functions will probably have a lower cost of capital.

11.   **Liability and Hazard Insurance**

   a.   An insurance policy is a contract that shifts the risk of financial loss caused by certain specified occurrences from the insured to the insurer in exchange for a periodic payment called a premium.

      1)   Liability insurance provides an organization with financial protection against damage caused to consumers by faulty products or injury to persons suffered on the organization's premises.

      2)   Hazard insurance is the same as homeowner's or automobile driver's insurance. It protects the organization against damage caused to its facilities by accident or natural disaster.

12.   **Financial Risk Management Methods**

   a.   An extremely common form of financial risk management is called hedging. **Hedging** is the process of using offsetting commitments to minimize or avoid the impact of adverse price movements.

      1)   A person who would like to sell an asset in the future has a long position in the asset because (s)he benefits from a rise in value of the asset. To protect against a decline in value, the owner can enter into a short hedge, i.e., obtain an instrument whose value will rise if the asset's value falls.

        2)   A person who would like to buy an asset in the future has a short position in the asset because (s)he benefits from a fall in value of the asset. To protect against a rise in value, the party can enter into a long hedge, i.e., obtain an instrument whose value will rise if the asset's value rises.

        3)   Instruments for hedging include options, futures contracts, and swaps.

  b.   Financial risk can also be addressed through more conventional methods.

        1)   For instance, an organization can lower the risk that it will be unable to meet maturing bond obligations by establishing a sinking fund.

        2)   Similarly, the risk of being unable to meet maturing short-term obligations can be mitigated. The establishment of policies regarding the terms of short-term investment instruments can ensure that funds will be available when they are needed (a practice called maturity matching).

13. Qualitative Risk Assessment Tools

  a.   Precise numeric quantification of risk is not necessarily required to have a sound risk management structure. Qualitative tools are crucial for upper and operational management to describe the risks they face.

        1)   Risk identification, the very first step in the process, does not lend itself to quantitative techniques. Intuitive and thought-provoking methods are required to identify all the areas of organizational vulnerability.

            a)   The first round of risk identifications can begin with a simple question to management at all levels: What aspects of the organization keep you up at night?

            b)   A list of generic risk areas can be distributed to inspire managers about possible points of vulnerability in their domains (foreign exchange risk, supply chain risk, regulatory risk, competitive risk, computer hacker risk, etc.).

            c)   A brainstorming session among managers is a simple technique to get the risk identification process started.

        2)   Risk ranking is also necessarily an intuitive process. Managers have a "feel" for how much risk a given vulnerability presents to their domains.

        3)   **Risk mapping** is a visual tool for depicting relative risks. The probabilities of the identified events can be graphed on one axis and the severity of the consequences on the other.

14. The COSO ERM Framework

  a.   *Enterprise Risk Management – Integrated Framework* describes a model that incorporates the earlier COSO control framework while extending it to the broader subject of ERM. The purpose is to provide a basis for coordinating and integrating all of the entity's risk management activities.

        1)   ERM is based on key concepts applicable to many types of organizations. The emphasis is on (a) the objectives of a specific entity and (b) establishing a means for evaluating the effectiveness of ERM.

  b.   The COSO Framework defines ERM as follows:

> *Enterprise risk management is a process, effected by an entity's board of directors, management, and other personnel, applied in strategy setting and across the enterprise, designed to identify potential events that may affect the entity, and manage risk to be within its risk appetite, to provide reasonable assurance regarding the achievement of entity objectives.*

15. **ERM Concepts**

   a.   Risk is the possibility that an event will occur and negatively affect the achievement of objectives.

   b.   Inherent risk is the risk in the absence of a risk response.

   c.   Residual risk is the risk after a risk response.

   d.   Risk appetite is the amount of risk an entity is willing to accept in pursuit of value. It reflects the entity's risk management philosophy and influences the entity's culture and operating style.

   e.   Risk tolerance is the acceptable variation relative to the achievement of an objective.

   f.   An opportunity is the possibility that an event will occur and positively affect the achievement of objectives by creating or preserving value.

   1)   Management plans to exploit opportunities, subject to the entity's objectives and strategies.

   g.   Risk management, at any level, consists of (1) identifying potential events that may affect the entity and (2) managing the associated risk to be within the entity's risk appetite.

   1)   Risk management should provide **reasonable assurance** that entity objectives are achieved.

16. **ERM Capabilities**

   a.   ERM allows management to optimize stakeholder value by coping effectively with uncertainty and the risks and opportunities it presents. ERM helps management to

   1)   Reach objectives,
   2)   Prevent loss of reputation and resources,
   3)   Report effectively, and
   4)   Comply with laws and regulations.

   b.   The following are the capabilities of ERM:

   1)   Consideration of risk appetite and strategy

   a)   Risk appetite should be considered in

   i)   Evaluating strategies,
   ii)   Setting objectives, and
   iii) Developing risk management methods.

   2)   Risk response decisions

   a)   ERM permits identification and selection of such responses to risk as

   i)   Avoidance,
   ii)   Reduction,
   iii) Sharing, and
   iv)   Acceptance.

   3)   Reduction of operational surprises and losses

   a)   These are reduced by an improved ability to anticipate potential events and develop responses.

   4)   Multiple and cross-enterprise risks

   a)   Risks may affect different parts of the entity. ERM allows

   i)   Effective responses to interrelated effects and
   ii)   Integrated responses to multiple risks.

   5)   Response to opportunities

   a)   By facilitating the identification of potential events, ERM helps management respond quickly to opportunities.

      6)   Use of capital

         a)   The risk information provided by ERM permits

            i)   Assessment of capital needs and
           ii)   Better capital allocation.

17. **ERM Components**

   a.   The components ordinarily are addressed in the order below:

      1)   The **internal environment** reflects the entity's (a) risk management philosophy, (b) risk appetite, (c) integrity, (d) ethical values, and (e) overall environment. It sets the tone of the entity.

      2)   **Objective setting** precedes event identification. ERM ensures that (a) a process is established and (b) objectives are consistent with the mission and the risk appetite. The following categories of objectives apply to all entities:

         a)   <u>S</u>trategic objectives are consistent with and support the entity's mission.
         b)   <u>O</u>perations objectives address effectiveness and efficiency.
         c)   <u>R</u>eporting objectives concern reliability.
         d)   <u>C</u>ompliance objectives relate to adherence to laws and regulations.

            i)   Memory aid: <u>S</u>tudying <u>O</u>bsessively <u>R</u>eally <u>C</u>ounts

      3)   **Event identification** relates to internal and external events affecting the organization that may create opportunities or risks.

         a)   Event identification techniques include the following:

            i)   Event inventories. Identify events by reviewing a detailed listing of potential events that are common to the organization's industry.

           ii)   Internal analysis. Identify events by performing an internal analysis on information obtained from stakeholders (e.g., customers, suppliers, or other business divisions, units, or subsidiaries) or relevant subject matter experts.

          iii)   Escalation or threshold triggers. Identify events through triggers that alert the organization when current transactions or events vary from established criteria.

          iv)   Facilitated workshops and interviews. Identify events through structured discussions with management, staff, and other stakeholders.

           v)   Process flow analysis. Identify events by analyzing the components of a process (inputs, tasks, and outputs) and the responsibilities associated with each component.

          vi)   Leading event indicators. Identify events by monitoring data correlated to events. For example, given a correlation between late loan payments and loan default, a financial institution would monitor for late loan payments to mitigate the risk of loan defaults.

      4)   **Risk assessment** considers likelihood and impact as a basis for risk management. The assessment considers inherent risk and residual risk.

      5)   **Risk responses** reduce the impact or likelihood of adverse events. They include control activities. They should be consistent with the entity's risk tolerances and appetite.

      6)   **Control activities** are policies and procedures to ensure the effectiveness of risk responses, for example, segregation of duties.

      7)   The **information and communication** component identifies, captures, and communicates relevant and timely information.

      8)   **Monitoring** involves ongoing management activities or separate evaluations. The full ERM process is monitored.

b. These distinct categories overlap. They apply to different needs, and different managers may be assigned responsibility for them.

 1) **Safeguarding of resources** is another category that may be appropriate for some entities.

c. The achievement of strategic and operational matters is affected by external events that the entity may not control. Thus, ERM should provide reasonable assurance that management and the board receive timely information about whether those objectives are being achieved.

d. Reporting and compliance are within the entity's control. Accordingly, ERM should provide reasonable assurance of achieving those objectives.

18. **ERM Matrix**

a. The matrix is a cube with rows, slices, and columns.

 1) The rows are the eight components, the slices are the four categories of objectives, and the columns are the organizational units of the entity.

b. The entity should make the appropriate response at each intersection of the matrix, such as control activities for achieving reporting objectives at the division level.

COSO ERM Framework

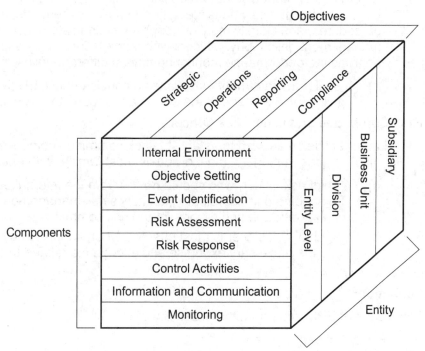

Figure 1-3

c. The **components** should be present and functioning effectively. Consequently, the components are criteria for the effectiveness of ERM.

 1) No material weaknesses should exist, and risk should be within the risk appetite.

 2) When ERM is effective regarding all **objectives**, the board and management have reasonable assurance that (a) reporting is reliable, (b) compliance is achieved, and (c) the extent of achievement of strategic and operations objectives is known.

 3) The components operate differently in different organizations. For example, they may be applied in a less formal way in smaller organizations.

19. **Responsibilities**

    a. **Board of Directors**

        1) The board has an **oversight role**. It should determine that risk management processes are in place, adequate, and effective.

        2) Directors' attitudes are a key component of the internal environment. They must possess certain qualities to be effective.

            a) A majority of the board should be outside directors.

            b) Directors generally should have years of experience either in the industry or in corporate governance.

            c) Directors must be willing to challenge management's choices. Complacent directors increase the chances of adverse consequences.

    b. **Senior Management**

        1) The CEO sets the **tone at the top** of the entity and has ultimate responsibility for ERM.

        2) Senior management should ensure that sound risk management processes are functioning.

        3) Senior management also determines the entity's risk management philosophy. For example, officers who issue definitive policy statements, insist on written procedures, and closely monitor performance indicators have one type of risk management philosophy. Officers who manage informally and take a relaxed approach to performance monitoring have a different philosophy.

            a) If senior management establishes a consistent risk management philosophy, all parts of the entity can respond to risk appropriately.

    c. **Risk Committee and Chief Risk Officer**

        1) Larger entities may wish to establish a risk committee composed of directors that also includes managers, the individuals most familiar with entity processes.

            a) A chief risk officer, who should **not** be from the internal audit function, may be appointed to coordinate the entity's risk management activities. (S)he is a member of, and reports to, the risk committee.

            b) The chief risk officer is most effective when supported by a specific team with the necessary expertise and experience related to organization-wide risk.

20. **ERM Limitations**

    a. Limitations of ERM arise from the possibility of

        1) Faulty human judgment,
        2) Cost-benefit considerations,
        3) Simple errors or mistakes,
        4) Collusion, and
        5) Management override of ERM decisions.

Stop and review! You have completed the outline for this subunit. Study multiple-choice questions 27 through 30 beginning on page 42.

QUESTIONS

1.1 Ethics for Management Accountants

1. The controller is responsible for directing the budgeting process. In this role, the controller has significant influence with executive management as individual department budgets are modified and approved. For the current year, the controller was instrumental in the approval of a particular line manager's budget without modification, even though significant reductions were made to the budgets submitted by other line managers. As a token of appreciation, the line manager in question has given the controller a gift certificate for a popular local restaurant. In considering whether or not to accept the certificate, the controller should refer to which section of IMA's *Statement of Ethical Professional Practice*?

    A. Competence.

    B. Confidentiality.

    C. Integrity.

    D. Credibility.

Answer (C) is correct.
    REQUIRED: The ethical standard relevant to the controller's acceptance of a gift from a line manager.
    DISCUSSION: The integrity standard requires an IMA member to "refrain from engaging in any conduct that would prejudice carrying out duties ethically."
    Answer (A) is incorrect. The competence standard pertains to an IMA member's responsibility to maintain his or her professional skills and knowledge. It also pertains to the performance of activities in accordance with relevant standards. Answer (B) is incorrect. The confidentiality standard concerns an IMA member's responsibility not to disclose or use the firm's confidential information. Answer (D) is incorrect. Credibility is the fourth standard of IMA's *Statement of Ethical Professional Practice*. It requires that information be communicated "fairly and objectively," and that all information that could reasonably influence users be disclosed.

2. In accordance with IMA's *Statement of Ethical Professional Practice*, a member who fails to perform professional duties in accordance with relevant standards is acting contrary to which one of the following standards?

    A. Competence.

    B. Confidentiality.

    C. Integrity.

    D. Credibility.

Answer (A) is correct.
    REQUIRED: The ethical standard violated by a management accountant who fails to perform professional duties in accordance with relevant standards.
    DISCUSSION: One of the responsibilities of an IMA member under the competence standard is to "maintain an appropriate level of professional expertise by continually developing knowledge and skills." (S)he must also "perform professional duties in accordance with relevant laws, regulations, and technical standards." The third requirement under this standard is to "provide decision support information and recommendations that are accurate, clear, concise, and timely."
    Answer (B) is incorrect. The confidentiality standard concerns an IMA member's responsibility not to disclose or use the firm's confidential information. Answer (C) is incorrect. The integrity standard pertains to conflicts of interest, avoidance of acts discreditable to the profession and refraining from activities that prejudice the ability to carry out duties ethically. Answer (D) is incorrect. Credibility is the fourth standard of IMA's *Statement of Ethical Professional Practice*. It requires that information be communicated "fairly and objectively," and that all information that could reasonably influence users be disclosed.

3. According to IMA's *Statement of Ethical Professional Practice*, a member has a responsibility to recognize professional limitations. Under which standard of ethical conduct would this responsibility be included?

    A. Competence.

    B. Confidentiality.

    C. Integrity.

    D. Credibility.

Answer (A) is correct.
    REQUIRED: The standard of ethical conduct related to the responsibility to recognize professional limitations.
    DISCUSSION: The competence standard pertains to an IMA member's responsibility to "recognize and communicate professional limitations or other constraints that would preclude responsible judgment or successful performance of an activity."
    Answer (B) is incorrect. The confidentiality standard concerns an IMA member's responsibility not to disclose or use the firm's confidential information. Answer (C) is incorrect. The integrity standard deals with conflicts of interest, avoidance of acts discreditable to the profession and refraining from activities that prejudice the ability to carry out duties ethically. Answer (D) is incorrect. Credibility is the fourth standard of IMA's *Statement of Ethical Professional Practice*. It requires that information be communicated "fairly and objectively," and that all information that could reasonably influence users be disclosed.

4. If an IMA member has a problem in identifying unethical behavior or resolving an ethical conflict, the first action (s)he should normally take is to

A. Consult the board of directors.

B. Discuss the problem with his or her immediate superior.

C. Notify the appropriate law enforcement agency.

D. Resign from the company.

Answer (B) is correct.
REQUIRED: The proper ethical behavior by an IMA member.
DISCUSSION: IMA's *Statement of Ethical Professional Practice* states that the member should first discuss an ethical problem with his or her immediate superior. If the superior is involved, the problem should be taken initially to the next higher managerial level.
Answer (A) is incorrect. The board would be consulted initially only if the immediate superior is the chief executive officer and that person is involved in the ethical conflict. Answer (C) is incorrect. An IMA member should keep information confidential except when disclosure is authorized or legally required. Answer (D) is incorrect. Resignation is a last resort.

5. If an IMA member discovers unethical conduct in his or her organization and fails to act, (s)he will be in violation of which of IMA's ethical standard(s)?

A. "Refrain from engaging in any conduct that would prejudice carrying out duties correctly."

B. "Communicate information fairly and objectively."

C. "Disclose all relevant information that could reasonably be expected to influence an intended user's understanding of reporting analyses or recommendations."

D. All of the answers are correct.

Answer (D) is correct.
REQUIRED: The ethical standard(s) violated by failure to disclose unethical behavior.
DISCUSSION: An IMA member displays his or her competence and credibility and maintains integrity by taking the appropriate action within the organization to resolve an ethical problem. All of these activities should be a part of an IMA member's normal job processes.

6. IMA's *Statement of Ethical Professional Practice* requires an IMA member to follow the established policies of the organization when faced with an ethical conflict. If these policies do not resolve the conflict, the member should

A. Consult the board of directors immediately.

B. Discuss the problem with the immediate superior if (s)he is involved in the conflict.

C. Communicate the problem to authorities outside the organization.

D. Contact the next higher managerial level if initial presentation to the immediate superior does not resolve the conflict.

Answer (D) is correct.
REQUIRED: The proper action when organizational policies do not resolve an ethical conflict.
DISCUSSION: In these circumstances, the problem should be discussed with the immediate superior unless (s)he is involved. In that case initial presentation should be to the next higher managerial level. If the problem is not satisfactorily resolved after initial presentation, the question should be submitted to the next higher level.
Answer (A) is incorrect. This course of action would be appropriate only for the chief executive officer or for his or her immediate subordinate when the CEO is involved in the conflict. Answer (B) is incorrect. The proper action would be to present the matter to the next higher managerial level. Answer (C) is incorrect. Such action is inappropriate unless legally prescribed.

1.2 Corporate Ethics and Legislation

7. The Foreign Corrupt Practices Act prohibits

A. Bribes to all foreigners.

B. Small bribes to foreign officials that serve as facilitating or grease payments.

C. Bribery only by corporations and their representatives.

D. Bribes to foreign officials to improperly influence official acts.

Answer (D) is correct.
REQUIRED: The action prohibited by the Foreign Corrupt Practices Act.
DISCUSSION: The Foreign Corrupt Practices Act (FCPA) prohibits any U.S. firm from making bribes to foreign officials to improperly influence official acts. The businesses subject to the FCPA include corporations, partnerships, limited partnerships, business trusts, and unincorporated organizations. Violations of the FCPA are federal felonies. The penalties are up to 5 years in prison or up to a $100,000 fine or both for an officer, director, or shareholder who helps make the bribe.
Answer (A) is incorrect. Bribes to all foreigners is not covered by the provisions in the FCPA. Answer (B) is incorrect. Small bribes to foreign officials that serve as facilitating or grease payments is not covered by the provisions in the FCPA. Answer (C) is incorrect. All U.S. firms are subject to the anti-bribery provisions.

8. A major impact of the Foreign Corrupt Practices Act of 1977 is that registrants subject to the Securities Exchange Act of 1934 are now required to

A. Keep records that reflect the transactions and dispositions of assets and to maintain a system of internal accounting controls.

B. Provide access to records by authorized agencies of the federal government.

C. Prepare financial statements in accord with international accounting standards.

D. Produce full, fair, and accurate periodic reports on foreign commerce and/or foreign political party affiliations.

Answer (A) is correct.

REQUIRED: The major impact of the Foreign Corrupt Practices Act of 1977.

DISCUSSION: The main purpose of the Foreign Corrupt Practices Act of 1977 is to prevent bribery by firms that do business in foreign countries. A major ramification is that it requires all companies that must register with the SEC under the Securities Exchange Act of 1934 to maintain adequate accounting records and a system of internal accounting control.

Answer (B) is incorrect. Authorized agents of the federal government already have access to records of SEC registrants. Answer (C) is incorrect. Although some international accounting standards have been promulgated, they are incomplete and have not gained widespread acceptance. Answer (D) is incorrect. There are no requirements for providing periodic reports on foreign commerce or foreign political party affiliations.

9. Which of the following is **not** an aspect of the Foreign Corrupt Practices Act of 1977?

A. It subjects management to fines and imprisonment.

B. It prohibits bribes to foreign officials.

C. It requires the establishment of independent audit committees.

D. It requires an internal control system to be developed and maintained.

Answer (C) is correct.

REQUIRED: The false statement with respect to the Foreign Corrupt Practices Act.

DISCUSSION: The Foreign Corrupt Practices Act of 1977 prohibits bribes to foreign officials and requires firms to have adequate systems of internal control. Violation of the act subjects individual managers to fines and/or imprisonment. The act does not specifically require the establishment of audit committees, but many firms have established audit committees as one means of dealing with the internal control provisions of the act.

10. Firms subject to the reporting requirements of the Securities Exchange Act of 1934 are required by the Foreign Corrupt Practices Act of 1977 to maintain satisfactory internal control. The role of the independent auditor relative to this act is to

A. Report clients with unsatisfactory internal control to the SEC.

B. Provide assurances to users as part of the traditional audit attest function that the client is in compliance with the present legislation.

C. Express an opinion on the sufficiency of the client's internal control to meet the requirements of the Act.

D. Attest to the financial statements.

Answer (D) is correct.

REQUIRED: The role of the independent auditor relative to the Foreign Corrupt Practices Act.

DISCUSSION: Whether a client is in conformity with the Foreign Corrupt Practices Act is a legal question. Auditors cannot be expected to provide clients or users of the financial statements with legal advice. The role of the auditor is to assess control risk in the course of an engagement to attest to the fair presentation of the financial statements.

Answer (A) is incorrect. The auditor is not required to report violations of the act to the SEC, although a duty to disclose outside the client may exist in some circumstances; e.g., the client's failure to take remedial action regarding an illegal act may constitute a disagreement that it must report on Form 8-K (AU 317). Answer (B) is incorrect. The traditional attest function does not involve compliance auditing. Answer (C) is incorrect. The FCPA contains no requirement that an auditor express an opinion on internal control.

11. The requirement of the Foreign Corrupt Practices Act of 1977 to devise and maintain adequate internal control is assigned in the act to the

A. Chief financial officer.

B. Board of directors.

C. Director of internal auditing.

D. Company as a whole with no designation of specific persons or positions.

Answer (D) is correct.

REQUIRED: The person in a company responsible for compliance with the FCPA.

DISCUSSION: The accounting requirements apply to all public companies that must register under the Securities Exchange Act of 1934. The responsibility is thus placed on companies, not individuals.

Answer (A) is incorrect. Compliance with the FCPA is not the specific responsibility of the chief financial officer. Answer (B) is incorrect. Compliance with the FCPA is not the specific responsibility of the board of directors. Answer (C) is incorrect. Compliance with the FCPA is not the specific responsibility of the director of internal auditing.

1.3 Corporate Responsibility for Ethical Behavior

12. Which one of the following is a **true** statement regarding organizational ethics?

A. As long as officer and employee behavior meet the requirements of the law, the organization can be considered to have a functioning system of ethical behavior.

B. A strong sense of ethics on the part of employees who are in the best position to appropriate cash and other assets is the most vital part of a functioning system of ethical behavior.

C. If an organization has a strong code of ethical conduct in place, the role of employee training can be downplayed.

D. Paying attention to "whistleblowers" plays a significant role in maintaining an effective ethical atmosphere.

Answer (D) is correct.
    REQUIRED: The true statement regarding organizational ethics.
    DISCUSSION: "Values and Ethics: From Inception to Practice" states, in part, "A whistleblowing framework (e.g., an ethics helpline) is an important component in maintaining an ethical organizational culture. An effective feedback system includes having a confidential framework for employees to report possible violations of the organization's code of ethics and to receive advice on the ethical aspects of challenging decisions. Statistics show that a large number of occupational fraud cases are detected through an employee "hotline" or other reporting method . . . " (IX. Measuring and Improving Ethical Compliance.)
    Answer (A) is incorrect. A sense of ethics requires an ability to distinguish between ethical and merely legal behavior. "Values and Ethics: From Inception to Practice" states, in part, "Many individuals at the center of corporate scandals [of the late 20th and early 21st Century] have professed the belief that they were innocent of any wrongdoing, including Kenneth Lay of Enron or Conrad Black of Hollinger. The problem is that these individuals did not define their behavior by what most of society would see as 'reasonable,' but rather they followed their own particular code—in some cases, limiting the definition of ethical behavior to require compliance with the law and nothing more." (II. Introduction.) Answer (B) is incorrect. "Values and Ethics: From Inception to Practice" states, in part, "Ethical behavior is not something that applies to someone else—every single individual is responsible for behaving ethically. Nowhere is this more important than the demonstration of ethical behavior that managers and supervisors exhibit in the way they execute their day-to-day work. . . " This phenomenon is referred to as the "tone at the top." (VI. Leadership by Example.) Answer (C) is incorrect. Employee training is important to maintaining an ethical organizational culture. "Values and Ethics: From Inception to Practice" states, in part, "Every existing member of staff should receive ongoing training, starting at the board level and cascading down throughout the organization . . . Ethics training for employees should focus on covering ethical concepts, the organization's code, and compliance. To achieve this, training should include: ethical concepts and thinking: What is 'behind' the issue of ethical action?; [and] the organization's code of ethics and any supporting 'rules.'" (VIII. Practical Application: Converting Intent into Operational Reality.)

13. IMA's Statement on Management Accounting, "Values and Ethics: From Inception to Practice," recommends a defined code of conduct and ethical behavior for all organizations. One advantage of having such a code is that it

A. Provides employees with guidance for handling unfamiliar situations.

B. Ensures ethical behavior by all employees.

C. Shields the organization from liability in cases of loss of stockholder value due to fraud.

D. Eases the investigative process performed by police and prosecutors in cases of suspected fraud.

Answer (A) is correct.
    REQUIRED: The advantage to the organization of having a code of conduct.
    DISCUSSION: "Values and Ethics: From Inception to Practice" states, in part, ". . . what does an employee do when unplanned events occur? What reference does an individual look to for help in making decisions? . . . This is why it is important to have a defined set of organizational values and code of ethics – they create the "touchstone" against which every unanticipated decision must be judged. Failure to have every individual in the organization know and understand these values and ethical code leads to inconsistency and, in the worst cases, unethical or fraudulent behavior." (IV. Values, Ethics, and Accounting.)
    Answer (B) is incorrect. A code of conduct cannot guarantee ethical behavior by employees. Answer (C) is incorrect. A code of conduct cannot guarantee that an organization will be shielded from liability in cases of fraud. Answer (D) is incorrect. A code of conduct does not ease law enforcement's investigative process.

14. Which one of the following is a **true** statement regarding organizational ethics?

A. A comprehensive framework of corporate ethical behavior is a prerequisite for an effective system of internal control.

B. An effective system of internal control is a prerequisite for corporate ethical behavior.

C. If a functioning system of ethical behavior is in place, an organization is able to devote fewer resources to developing human capital.

D. "Organizational culture" is determined mostly by the industry(ies) in which the firm operates.

Answer (A) is correct.
    REQUIRED: The true statement regarding organizational ethics.
    DISCUSSION: A comprehensive framework of corporate ethical behavior is a prerequisite for an effective system of internal control. "Values and Ethics: From Inception to Practice" states, in part, "CEOs and CFOs have to place their own integrity on the line by attesting to compliance with an adequate level of internal controls (as well as all other certifications). Creating a thorough, integrated system for developing, implementing, sustaining, and monitoring ethical performance within the organization will allow executives to make such declarations with confidence that a code of ethics is the foundation of the organization's culture and is fully integrated into the thinking process of every employee and business partner." (IX. Measuring and Improving Ethical Compliance.)
    Answer (B) is incorrect. It is more nearly true to state the opposite. Answer (C) is incorrect. The concept of "human capital" is important to an organization in creating a climate where "doing the right thing" is expected. In most organizations today, labor costs constitute the majority of operating expenses. "Values and Ethics: From Inception to Practice" states, in part, " . . . an organization must, to a great degree, trust that its employees are acting in its best interests. Human 'capital' is a critical asset . . . Unmotivated employees can poison the atmosphere and reduce the teamwork and cooperation required for knowledge transfer and innovation, and they can have a significant negative impact on relationships with suppliers and customers." (IV. Values, Ethics, and Accounting.) Answer (D) is incorrect. "Values and Ethics: From Inception to Practice" states, in part, "Every organization already has a culture . . . Step one in establishing an ethical culture must be an assessment of the existing organizational values and culture and the development of a set of statements that define the principles the organization believes in and should act upon. These statements and principles can be developed by the shareholders, the board, or a governing body within the organization." (V. Defining and Developing the Organization's Behavioral Values.)

1.4 Fraud and the Fraud Risk Model (Fraud Triangle)

15. Misappropriation of assets is **most** often perpetrated by

A. Employees.

B. Customers.

C. Suppliers.

D. Auditors.

Answer (A) is correct.
    REQUIRED: Whom misappropriated assets are most often perpetrated by.
    DISCUSSION: Employees who have fiduciary responsibilities for assets are most likely to steal them.
    Answer (B) is incorrect. Customers may misappropriate assets, but most businesses are more vulnerable to misappropriation by employees. Answer (C) is incorrect. Suppliers may misappropriate assets, but most businesses are more vulnerable to misappropriation by employees. Answer (D) is incorrect. Independent auditors have little opportunity or motive to misappropriate assets.

16. Inappropriate earnings management is typically considered one form of

A. Embezzlement.

B. Fraudulent financial reporting.

C. Theft of assets.

D. Misappropriation of assets.

Answer (B) is correct.
    REQUIRED: What inappropriate earnings management is typically considered a form of.
    DISCUSSION: Inappropriate earnings management has been defined as the purposeful intercession in the financial reporting process.
    Answer (A) is incorrect. Embezzlement is a form of misappropriation of assets. Answer (C) is incorrect. Theft is a form of misappropriation of assets. Answer (D) is incorrect. Misappropriation of assets is one of the two main classifications of employee fraud.

17. When none of the three fraud risk factors are present, an accountant

    A. Can rule out the presence of fraud.

    B. Should consider the likelihood of fraud to be high.

    C. Should not rule out the presence of fraud completely.

    D. Will likely search more diligently for fraud.

Answer (C) is correct.
    REQUIRED: What an accountant could do when none of the three fraud risk factors are present.
    DISCUSSION: Even when no factors are observed, an accountant cannot completely exclude the risk of fraud. Factors may be present but hidden from the accountant.
    Answer (A) is incorrect. The accountant would need more solid evidence to rule out the presence of fraud. Answer (B) is incorrect. When all three factors are present, fraud risk is high. Answer (D) is incorrect. When fraud risk factors are present, the accountant will likely search more diligently for fraud.

18. Management is often able to rationalize the commission of fraud by

    A. Blaming it on others.

    B. Forcing staff to perpetrate it.

    C. Hiding it.

    D. Reasoning that it is in the best interests of the company.

Answer (D) is correct.
    REQUIRED: How management often rationalizes the commission of fraud.
    DISCUSSION: Rationalization is a person's ability to justify actions as consistent with his or her personal code of ethics. A person may rationalize a fraud by believing that the misdeed is to help the company to prosper or survive. Thus, a person may believe that the ends justify the means.
    Answer (A) is incorrect. Blaming does not relate to rationalization. Answer (B) is incorrect. Forcing staff to perpetuate a fraud does not rationalize it. Answer (C) is incorrect. Hiding a fraud does not rationalize it.

19. High risk of employee fraud is **most** likely when there is pressure, rationalization, and

    A. Opportunity.

    B. Internal control.

    C. Personal integrity.

    D. Limited responsibility.

Answer (A) is correct.
    REQUIRED: The third factor that most likely indicates a high risk of employee fraud.
    DISCUSSION: Opportunity creates risk of employee fraud.
    Answer (B) is incorrect. Internal control mitigates the risk of employee fraud. Answer (C) is incorrect. Personal integrity mitigates the risk of employee fraud. Answer (D) is incorrect. Limited employee responsibility mitigates the risk of employee fraud.

20. The fraud risk factor that may be mitigated by internal controls is

    A. Rationalization.

    B. Motive.

    C. Pressure.

    D. Opportunity.

Answer (D) is correct.
    REQUIRED: The fraud risk factor that may be mitigated by internal control.
    DISCUSSION: The opportunity for individuals to perpetrate a fraud can be mitigated by proper controls. Examples are appropriate oversight, segregation of duties, and the audit process itself.
    Answer (A) is incorrect. Rationalization cannot be affected by controls because it is a mental state of a potential perpetrator of a fraud. Answer (B) is incorrect. Like rationalization, motive is a mental state that cannot be mitigated by controls. Answer (C) is incorrect. Pressure relates to motive and cannot be mitigated by controls.

1.5 Managing the Risk of Fraud

21. A proper segregation of duties requires that an individual

    A. Authorizing a transaction records it.

    B. Authorizing a transaction maintain custody of the asset that resulted from the transaction.

    C. Maintaining custody of an asset be entitled to access the accounting records for the asset.

    D. Recording a transaction not compare the accounting record of the asset with the asset itself.

Answer (D) is correct.
    REQUIRED: The item required by proper segregation of duties.
    DISCUSSION: One person should not be responsible for all phases of a transaction, i.e., for authorization, recording, and custodianship of the related assets. These duties should be performed by separate individuals to reduce the opportunities for any person to be in a position of both perpetrating and concealing errors or fraud in the normal course of his or her duties. For instance, an employee who receives and lists cash receipts should not be responsible for comparing the recorded accountability for cash with existing amounts.
    Answer (A) is incorrect. Authorization and recordkeeping should be separate. Answer (B) is incorrect. Authorization and asset custody should be separate. Answer (C) is incorrect. Recordkeeping and asset custody should be separate.

22. The frequency of the comparison of recorded accountability with assets (for the purpose of safeguarding assets) should be determined by

A. The amount of assets independent of the cost of the comparison.

B. The nature and amount of the asset and the cost of making the comparison.

C. The cost of the comparison and whether the susceptibility to loss results from errors or fraud.

D. The auditor in consultation with client management.

Answer (B) is correct.
REQUIRED: The factor(s) determining the frequency of comparing recorded accountability with assets.
DISCUSSION: Assets should be compared with the recorded accountability as frequently as the nature and amount of the assets require, within the limits of acceptable costs of comparison. The costs of safeguarding assets should not exceed the expected benefits.
Answer (A) is incorrect. The costs of controls should be considered when making the comparison. Answer (C) is incorrect. Whether the susceptibility to loss arises from errors or fraud should have little bearing on the frequency of the comparison. Answer (D) is incorrect. Management, not the auditor, has responsibility for internal control.

23. An adequate system of internal controls is **most** likely to detect a fraud perpetrated by a

A. Group of employees in collusion.

B. Single employee.

C. Group of managers in collusion.

D. Single manager.

Answer (B) is correct.
REQUIRED: The fraud most likely to be detected by an adequate system of internal controls.
DISCUSSION: Segregation of duties and other control procedures serve to prevent or detect a fraud committed by an employee acting alone. One employee may not have the ability to engage in wrongdoing or may be subject to detection by other employees in the course of performing their assigned duties. However, collusion may circumvent controls. For example, comparison of recorded accountability with assets may fail to detect fraud if persons having custody of assets collude with record keepers.
Answer (A) is incorrect. A group has a better chance of successfully perpetrating a fraud than does an individual employee. Answer (C) is incorrect. Management can override controls. Answer (D) is incorrect. Even a single manager may be able to override controls.

24. Internal control cannot be designed to provide reasonable assurance regarding the achievement of objectives concerning

A. Reliability of financial reporting.

B. Elimination of all fraud.

C. Compliance with applicable laws and regulations.

D. Effectiveness and efficiency of operations.

Answer (B) is correct.
REQUIRED: The objective internal control cannot achieve.
DISCUSSION: Internal control is a process designed to provide reasonable assurance regarding the achievement of organizational objectives. Because of inherent limitations, however, no system can be designed to eliminate all fraud.
Answer (A) is incorrect. Internal control can provide reasonable assurance regarding reliability of financial reporting. Answer (C) is incorrect. Internal control can provide reasonable assurance regarding compliance with applicable laws and regulations. Answer (D) is incorrect. Internal control can provide reasonable assurance regarding effectiveness and efficiency of operations.

25. Internal controls may be preventive, detective, corrective, or directive. Which of the following is preventive?

A. Requiring two persons to open mail.

B. Reconciling the accounts receivable subsidiary file with the control account.

C. Using batch totals.

D. Preparing bank reconciliations.

Answer (A) is correct.
REQUIRED: The internal control that is preventive.
DISCUSSION: Preventive controls are designed to prevent an error or an irregularity. Detective and corrective controls attempt to identify and correct errors or irregularities that have already occurred. Preventive controls are usually more cost beneficial than detective or corrective controls. Assigning two individuals to open mail is an attempt to prevent misstatement of cash receipts.
Answer (B) is incorrect. Reconciling the subsidiary file with the master file may detect and lead to the correction of errors, but the control does not prevent errors. Answer (C) is incorrect. The use of batch totals may detect a missing or lost document but will not necessarily prevent a document from becoming lost. Answer (D) is incorrect. Bank reconciliations disclose errors in the accounts but have no preventive effect.

26. Segregation of duties is a fundamental concept in an effective system of internal control. Nevertheless, the internal auditor must be aware that this safeguard can be compromised through

    A. Lack of training of employees.

    B. Collusion among employees.

    C. Irregular employee reviews.

    D. Absence of internal auditing.

Answer (B) is correct.
    REQUIRED: The act that can compromise effective segregation of duties.
    DISCUSSION: By segregating duties, organizations make it more difficult for one person to perpetrate a fraud. When custody of the asset and recordkeeping for the asset are invested in different persons, a fraud generally cannot be executed by one of the two parties. However, if they collude, the internal control aspect of the segregation is nullified.
    Answer (A) is incorrect. Lack of training by itself cannot negate effective separation of duties. Answer (C) is incorrect. Irregular employee reviews may affect employee job performance, but they alone cannot negate effective separation of duties. Answer (D) is incorrect. While the absence of an internal audit activity may lessen the chances that an organization will maintain effective internal control over the long run, by itself it cannot negate effective segregation of duties.

1.6 Risk Management

27. Organizations face several types of risk in pursuit of their strategic objectives. The risk that the treasury function will fail to adequately reconcile the organization's bank statements is an example of

    A. Hazard risk.

    B. Financial risk.

    C. Operational risk.

    D. Strategic risk.

Answer (C) is correct.
    REQUIRED: The type of risk represented by the failure to reconcile bank statements.
    DISCUSSION: Operational risks are the risks related to the enterprise's ongoing, everyday operations. Operational risk is the risk of loss from inadequate or failed internal processes, people, and systems. These failures can relate to human resources (e.g., inadequate hiring or training practices), business processes (poor internal controls), technology, product failure (customer ill will, lawsuits), occupational safety and health incidents, environmental damage, and business continuity (power outages, natural disasters).
    Answer (A) is incorrect. Hazard risks are risks that are insurable. Examples include natural disasters, the incapacity or death of senior officers, sabotage, and terrorism. Answer (B) is incorrect. Financial risks encompass interest-rate risk, exchange-rate risk, commodity risk, credit risk, liquidity risk, and market risk. Answer (D) is incorrect. Strategic risks include global economic risk, political risk, and regulatory risk, among others.

28. A landlord owns an office building in a major floodplain. The landlord has decided to sell the building to a group of investors. The landlord has adopted a risk strategy of

    A. Risk exploitation.

    B. Risk transfer.

    C. Risk avoidance.

    D. Risk reduction.

Answer (C) is correct.
    REQUIRED: The risk strategy embodied in selling a building in a major river floodplain.
    DISCUSSION: Risk avoidance is bringing to an end the activity from which the risk arises. For instance, the risk of having a pipeline sabotaged in an unstable region can be avoided by simply selling the pipeline.
    Answer (A) is incorrect. Risk exploitation is the deliberate courting of risk in order to pursue a high return on investment. The building's purchasers are engaging in risk exploitation. Answer (B) is incorrect. Risk transfer, synonymous with risk sharing, is the offloading of some loss potential to another party. Common examples are the purchase of insurance policies, engaging in hedging operations, outsourcing an activity, and entering into joint ventures. Answer (D) is incorrect. Risk reduction (mitigation) is the act of lowering the level of risk associated with an activity. For instance, the risk of systems penetration can be reduced by maintaining a robust information security function within the organization.

29. A firm can mitigate the risk of financial loss from the possible on-the-job injury of one of its employees through

    A. Hazard insurance.

    B. Workers' compensation insurance.

    C. Key employee insurance.

    D. Liability insurance.

Answer (D) is correct.
    REQUIRED: The risk mitigation technique for potential loss from employee injury.
    DISCUSSION: Liability insurance provides an organization with financial protection against damage caused to consumers by faulty products or injury to persons suffered on the organization's premises.
    Answer (A) is incorrect. Hazard insurance is the same as homeowner's or automobile driver's insurance. It protects the organization against damage caused to its facilities by accident or natural disaster. Answer (B) is incorrect. Workers' compensation insurance benefits the injured worker, not the organization. Answer (C) is incorrect. Key employee insurance benefits the organization only in case of the death of a critical member of upper management.

30. Which one of the following is **not** a key component of the COSO Framework for enterprise risk management?

    A. Information and communication.

    B. Internal environment.

    C. Risk mapping.

    D. Control activities.

Answer (C) is correct.
    REQUIRED: The item not a key component of the COSO Framework for enterprise risk management.
    DISCUSSION: Risk mapping is a visual tool for depicting relative risks. The probabilities of the identified events can be graphed on one axis and the severity of the consequences on the other. It is not a key component of the COSO framework.
    Answer (A) is incorrect. Under the information and communication component, relevant information is identified, captured, and communicated. Answer (B) is incorrect. The internal environment sets the basis for how risk and control are viewed and addressed by an entity's people. Answer (D) is incorrect. Control activities are policies and procedures are established and executed to help ensure the risk responses management selects are effectively carried out.

Access the **Gleim CMA Premium Review System** from your Gleim Personal Classroom to continue your studies with exam-emulating multiple-choice questions!

**Page
Intentionally
Left Blank**

1.7 ESSAY QUESTIONS

Scenario for Essay Questions 1, 2

ABC Corporation participates in a highly competitive industry. To meet this competition and achieve profit goals, the company has chosen the decentralized form of organization. Each manager of a decentralized profit center is measured on the basis of profit contribution, market penetration, and return on investment. Failure to meet the objectives established by corporate management for these measures usually resulted in demotion or dismissal of a profit center manager.

The company lacks a code of ethics and a formal performance evaluation system to provide feedback to managers.

An anonymous survey of managers in the company revealed that the managers felt pressured to compromise their personal ethical standards to achieve the corporate objectives. For example, at certain plant locations, there was pressure to reduce quality control to a level that could not ensure all unsafe products would be rejected. Also, sales personnel were encouraged to use questionable sales tactics to obtain orders, including gifts and other incentives for purchasing agents.

The chief executive officer is disturbed by the survey findings. In his opinion, such behavior cannot be condoned by the company. He concludes that the company should do something about this problem.

Questions

1. Discuss what might be the causes for the ethical problems described.
2. Outline a program that could be instituted by the company to help reduce the pressures on managers to compromise personal ethical standards in their work.

Essay Questions 1, 2 — Unofficial Answers

1. Corporate management has established an environment in which there is an incompatibility (lack of goal congruence) between the achievement of corporate objectives and personal ethics. Under the current situation, severe penalties have been imposed by top management whenever subordinates do not achieve the high levels of performance established by the predetermined objectives. This has caused lower level management to take unethical courses of action.

    Corporate management apparently utilizes an authoritarian, nonparticipative management style that does not consider contributions from lower level management. As a result of this type of management style, top management may have established unreasonable expectations and may not recognize the need to change the expectations in light of changing circumstances. These factors may result in subordinates choosing any means to reach the objectives.

    The penalty and reward system appears to be inappropriate. There is no positive feedback or encouragement for effective performance, and the penalties for failure to meet objectives are heavy. No code of ethics exists, and penalties are apparently nonexistent or minor for violation of acceptable business practices that are compatible with personal ethical standards.

2. A company program to reduce the pressures on lower level management who violate the personal ethical standards and acceptable business practices might include the following actions:

    a. Adopt a participative style of management. Encourage each lower level manager to contribute to the establishment of the goals by which (s)he is to be judged.

    b. Expand the feedback system to recognize and reward good performance, allow for investigation and explanation for substandard performance, and adjust for changing conditions.

    c. Adopt a corporate code of ethics or code of acceptable business practices.

    d. Display top management support for the code evidenced by words and actions.

 Access the **Gleim CMA Premium Review System** from your Gleim Personal Classroom to continue your studies with exam-emulating essay questions!

STUDY UNIT TWO
FINANCIAL MARKETS AND TYPES OF SECURITIES

(22 pages of outline)

This study unit is the **first of four** on **corporate finance**. The relative weight assigned to this major topic in Part 2 of the exam is **20%**. The four study units are

Study Unit 2: Financial Markets and Types of Securities
Study Unit 3: Valuation Methods and Cost of Capital
Study Unit 4: Managing Current Assets
Study Unit 5: Corporate Restructuring and International Finance

If you are interested in reviewing more introductory or background material, go to www.gleim.com/CMAIntroVideos for a list of suggested third-party overviews of this topic. The following Gleim outline material is more than sufficient to help you pass the CMA exam; any additional introductory or background material is for your own personal enrichment.

2.1 FINANCIAL MARKETS AND SECURITIES OFFERINGS

1. **Aspects of Financial Markets**

    a. Financial markets facilitate the creation and transfer of financial assets and obligations. They bring together entities that have funds to invest with entities that have financing needs.

       1) The resulting transactions create assets for the former entities and obligations for the latter.

       2) Transfers of funds may be either direct or through intermediate entities, such as banks.

          a) The use of intermediate entities and financial markets improves allocative efficiency because of their special expertise.

          b) The result is the availability of relatively rapid and low-cost transfers of capital, an essential feature of a modern economy.

    b. Financial markets are not particular places, but rather the totality of supply and demand for securities.

       1) Securities include a very wide variety of instruments.

       2) Some of the most basic are stocks, corporate bonds, mortgages, consumer loans, leases, commercial paper, certificates of deposit, governmental securities, and derivatives of many kinds.

          a) Moreover, new kinds of securities are continually being developed.

2. **Money Markets and Capital Markets**

    a.   Money markets trade debt securities with maturities of less than 1 year.

        1)   These are dealer-driven markets because most transactions involve dealers who buy and sell instruments at their own risk.

            a)   The dealer is a principal in most transactions, unlike a stockbroker who acts as an agent.

        2)   Money market securities are generally short-term and marketable.

            a)   They usually have low default risk.

        3)   Money market securities include

            a)   Government Treasury bills
            b)   Government Treasury notes and bonds
            c)   Federal agency securities
            d)   Short-term tax-exempt securities
            e)   Commercial paper
            f)   Certificates of deposit
            g)   Repurchase agreements
            h)   Eurodollar CDs
            i)   Bankers' acceptances

        4)   Money markets exist in New York, London, and Tokyo.

    b.   Capital markets trade long-term debt and equity securities.

        1)   The New York Stock Exchange is an example of a capital market.

3. **Primary Markets and Secondary Markets**

    a.   Primary markets are the markets in which corporations and governmental units raise new capital by making initial offerings of their securities.

        1)   The issuer receives the proceeds of sale in a primary market.

    b.   Secondary markets provide for trading of previously issued securities among investors. Examples of secondary markets include auction markets and dealer markets.

        1)   Auction markets like the New York Stock Exchange, the American Stock Exchange, and regional exchanges conduct trading at particular physical sites. Furthermore, share prices are communicated immediately to the public.

            a)   Companies that wish to have their shares traded on an exchange must apply for listing and meet certain requirements. For example, the New York Stock Exchange has established requirements relating to the amount and value of shares outstanding, the number of shareholders, earning power, and tangible assets.

                i)   Listing is beneficial because it adds to a firm's prestige and increases the liquidity of a firm's securities.

                ii)   However, increased SEC disclosure requirements and the greater risk of a hostile takeover are possible disadvantages.

            b)   Matching of buy and sell orders communicated to brokerages with seats on the exchange is the essence of exchange trading. To facilitate this process, members known as specialists undertake to make a market in particular stocks. These firms are obliged to buy and sell those stocks.

                i)   Accordingly, a specialist maintains an inventory of stocks and sets bid and asked prices (prices at which the specialist will buy or sell, respectively) to keep the inventory in balance.

                ii)   The profit margin for the specialist is the spread, or the excess of the asked over the bid price.

          c)   Stock exchanges have expanded their role to include trading in derivatives.

              i)   Moreover, commodities markets, e.g., the Chicago Board of Trade and the Chicago Mercantile Exchange also permit trading in derivatives.

              ii)   Thus, both commodity futures (e.g., in oil, livestock, metals, grains, and fibers) and financial futures (e.g., in U.S. Treasury Securities, foreign currencies, stock indexes, bonds, and certificates of deposit) are now traded on commodity exchanges.

  2)   The over-the-counter (OTC) market is a dealer market. It consists of numerous brokers and dealers who are linked by telecommunications equipment that enables them to trade throughout the country. The OTC market conducts transactions in securities not traded on the stock exchanges.

          a)   The OTC market handles transactions involving

              i)   Bonds of U.S. companies

              ii)   Bonds of federal, state, and local governments

              iii)   Open-end investment company shares of mutual funds

              iv)   New securities issues

              v)   Most secondary stock distributions, whether or not they are listed on an exchange

          b)   The governing authority for the OTC market is the National Association of Securities Dealers (NASD). Its computerized trading system is the NASD Automated Quotation (NASDAQ) system, which supplies price quotes and volume amounts during the trading day.

          c)   The majority of stocks are traded in the OTC market, but the dollar volume of trading on the exchanges is greater because they list the largest companies.

          d)   Brokers and dealers of OTC securities may also maintain inventories of securities to match buy and sell orders efficiently.

          e)   Trading in the bonds of corporations is primarily done in the OTC market by large institutional investors, such as pension funds, mutual funds, and life insurance companies. Because very large amounts are exchanged among a few investors, dealers in the bond markets can feasibly arrange these transactions. A similar arrangement for trading of stocks would be difficult because they are owned by millions of shareholders.

4.   Financial Intermediaries

  a.   Financial intermediaries are specialized firms that help create and exchange the instruments of financial markets. Financial intermediaries increase the efficiency of financial markets through better allocation of financial resources.

    1)   A financial intermediary obtains funds from savers, issues its own securities, and uses the money to purchase an enterprise's securities. Thus, financial intermediaries create new forms of capital. For example, a savings and loan association purchases a mortgage with its funds from savers and issues a savings account or a certificate of deposit.

    b.   Financial intermediaries include

      1) Commercial banks
      2) Life insurance companies
      3) Private pension funds
      4) Nonbank thrift institutions, such as savings banks and credit unions
      5) State and local pension funds
      6) Mutual funds
      7) Finance companies
      8) Casualty insurance companies
      9) Money market funds
      10) Mutual savings banks
      11) Credit unions
      12) Investment bankers

5. **Insider Trading and Efficient Markets Hypothesis**

    a.   Insider trading is the trading of securities while possessing nonpublic information about the securities.

      1) This type of trading is illegal because it undermines investor confidence in the integrity and fairness of the financial markets.

    b.   The efficient markets hypothesis states that current stock prices immediately and fully reflect all relevant information. Hence, the market is continuously adjusting to new information and acting to correct pricing errors.

      1) In other words, securities prices are always in equilibrium. The reason is that securities are subject to intense analysis by many thousands of highly trained individuals.

      2) These analysts work for well-capitalized institutions with the resources to take very rapid action when new information is available.

    c.   The efficient markets hypothesis states that it is impossible to obtain abnormal returns consistently with either fundamental or technical analysis.

      1) Fundamental analysis is the evaluation of a security's future price movement based upon sales, internal developments, industry trends, the general economy, and expected changes in each factor.

      2) Technical analysis is the evaluation of a security's future price based on the sales price and number of shares traded in a series of recent transactions.

    d.   Under the efficient markets hypothesis, the expected return of each security is equal to the return required by the marginal investor given the risk of the security. Moreover, the price equals its fair value as perceived by investors.

    e.   The efficient markets hypothesis has three forms (versions):

      1) **Strong Form**

          a) All public and private information is instantaneously reflected in securities' prices. Thus, insider trading is assumed not to result in abnormal returns.

      2) **Semistrong Form**

          a) All publicly available data are reflected in security prices, but private or insider data are not immediately reflected. Accordingly, insider trading can result in abnormal returns.

      3) **Weak Form**

          a) Current securities prices reflect all recent past price movement data, so technical analysis will not provide a basis for abnormal returns in securities trading.

      4) Empirical data have refuted the strong form of the efficient markets hypothesis but not the weak and semistrong forms.

    f.   The market efficiently incorporates public information into securities prices. However, when making investment decisions, investors should be aware of economic information about the firm's markets and the strength of the products of the firm.

        1)   Because the possibility exists that all information is not reflected in security prices, there is an opportunity for arbitrage.

6.   **Rating Agencies**

    a.   A firm must pay to have its debt rated. Standard & Poor's and Moody's are the most frequently used agencies.

        1)   Ratings are based upon the probability of default and the protection for investors in case of default.

    b.   The ratings are determined from corporate information, such as financial statements.

        1)   Important factors involved in the analysis include the ability of the issuer to service its debt with its cash flows, the amount of debt it has already issued, the type of debt issued, and the firm's cash flow stability.

        2)   A rating may change because the rating agencies periodically review outstanding securities. A decrease in the rating may increase the firm's cost of capital or reduce its ability to borrow long-term. One reason is that many institutional investors are not allowed to purchase lower-grade securities.

        3)   A rating agency review of existing securities may be triggered by a variety of factors, e.g., a new issue of debt, an intended merger involving an exchange of bonds for stock, or material changes in the economic circumstances of the firm.

    c.   The ratings are significant because higher ratings reduce interest costs to issuing firms. Lower ratings incur higher required rates of return.

        1)   The lower the risk of default, the lower the interest rate the market will demand.

    d.   Standard & Poor's rates bonds from very high quality to very poor quality.

        1)   AAA and AA are the highest, signifying little chance of default and high quality.

        2)   A- and BBB-rated bonds are of investment grade. They have strong interest- and principal-paying capabilities.

            a)   Bonds with these ratings are the lowest-rated securities that many institutional investors are permitted to hold.

        3)   Debt rated BB and below is speculative; such bonds are junk bonds.

            a)   Junk bonds are high-yield or low-grade bonds.

            b)   These high-risk bonds have received much attention in the last decade because of their use in corporate mergers and restructurings and the increase in junk-bond defaults.

        4)   CCC to D are very poor debt ratings. The likelihood of default is significant, or the debt is already in default (D rating).

        5)   Standard & Poor's adjusts its ratings with the use of a plus-minus system. A plus indicates a stronger rating in a category, and a minus indicates a weaker rating.

    e.   Moody's rates bonds in a similar manner. Its ratings vary from Aaa for very high quality debt to D for very poor debt.

7.   **Investment Banking**

    a.   Investment bankers serve as intermediaries between businesses and the providers of capital.

        1)   They not only help to sell new securities but also assist in business combinations, act as brokers in secondary markets, and trade for their own accounts.

b. In their traditional role in the sale of new securities, investment bankers help determine the method of issuing the securities and the price to be charged, distribute the securities, provide expert advice, and perform a certification function.

   1) An issuer of new securities ordinarily selects an investment banker in a negotiated deal.

      a) Only a few large issuers seek competitive bids.

      b) The reason for the predominance of negotiated deals is that the costs of learning about the issuer and setting an issue price and fees are usually prohibitive unless the investment banker has a high probability of closing the deal.

   2) An investment banker issues securities through best efforts sales and underwriting deals.

      a) Best efforts sales of securities provide no guarantee that the securities will be sold or that enough cash will be raised.

         i) The investment banker receives commissions and is obligated to provide its best efforts to sell the securities.

      b) An underwritten deal or a firm commitment provides a guarantee.

         i) The investment banker agrees to purchase the entire issue and resell it. Thus, the issuer does not bear the risk of not being able to sell the issue.

c. A prospective issuer and an investment banker conduct preunderwriting conferences to discuss such basic questions as the amount to be raised, the type of securities to issue, and the nature of their agreement.

d. The next step is the filing of a registration statement with the SEC. This process may be necessary whether the issue is an initial public offering (item 8. that follows) or a seasoned issue (one made by a company whose securities are already publicly traded).

e. Determining the offering price of the securities is crucial. For a seasoned issue, the offering price may be pegged to the price of the existing securities, such as the market price of stock or the yield on bonds. For example, an issue of common stock may be priced at a certain percentage below the closing price on the last day of the registration period.

f. A single investment banker ordinarily does not underwrite an entire issue of securities unless the amount is relatively small.

   1) To share the risk of overpricing the issue or of a market decline during the offering period, the investment banker (the lead or managing underwriter) forms an underwriting syndicate with other firms.

   2) The members of the syndicate share in the underwriting commission, but their risk is limited to the percentage of their participation.

g. **Flotation costs**, or the costs of issuing new securities, are relatively lower for large issues than those for small issues. These costs include the following:

   1) The underwriting spread is the difference between the price paid by purchasers and the net amount received by the issuer.

   2) The issuer incurs expenses for filing fees, taxes, accountants' fees, and attorneys' fees. These costs are essentially fixed.

   3) The issuer incurs indirect costs because of management time devoted to the issue.

4) Announcement of a new issue of seasoned securities usually results in a price decline. One theory is that the announcement is a negative signal to the market. Management may not want to issue new stock when it is undervalued. Moreover, existing owners do not want to share the company's growth with additional owners.

    a) A **seasoned** security is a financial instrument that has been publicly traded long enough to eliminate any short-term effects caused by its IPO. Securities on the Euromarket must have traded for at least 40 days to qualify as "seasoned."

5) An offer of unseasoned securities (an initial public offering) tends to be significantly underpriced compared with the price in the aftermarket.

h. Flotation costs tend to be greater for common stock than for preferred stock and for stocks than for bonds.

8. **Initial Public Offerings (IPOs)**

a. A firm's first issuance of securities to the public is an initial public offering.

1) The process by which a closely held corporation issues new securities to the public is called going public. When a firm goes public, it issues its stock on a new issue or initial public offering market.

2) Later issues of stock by the same company are subsequent or secondary offerings.

    a) In a **subsequent offering**, the company offers additional shares which are usually issued from the company's treasury.

    b) In a **secondary offering**, the company issues new stock for public sale.

b. Advantages of going public include

1) The ability to raise additional funds
2) The establishment of the firm's value in the market
3) An increase in the liquidity of the firm's stock

c. Disadvantages of going public include

1) Costs of the reporting requirements of the SEC and other agencies
2) Access to the company's operating data by competing firms
3) Access to net worth information of major shareholders
4) Limitations on self-dealing by corporate insiders, such as officers and major shareholders
5) Pressure from outside shareholders for earnings growth
6) Stock prices that do not accurately reflect the true net worth of the company
7) Loss of control by management as ownership is diversified
8) Need for improved management control as operations expand
9) Increased shareholder servicing costs

d. To have its stock listed (have it traded on a stock exchange), the firm must apply to a stock exchange, pay a fee, and fulfill the exchange's requirements for membership.

1) Included in the requirements for membership is disclosure of the firm's financial data.

e. Once the decision to make an initial public offering has been made, the questions are similar to those for seasoned issues: the amount to be raised, the type of securities to sell, and the method of sale. For example, the following matters should be considered in selecting the type of securities to issue:

1) Should fixed charges be avoided? The issuance of debt would create fixed charges.

2) Is a maturity date on the security preferable, or is permanent capital more attractive?

3)   Does the firm want a cushion to protect itself from losses to the firm's creditors?

4)   How quickly and easily does the firm want to raise the capital?

5)   Is the firm concerned about losing control of the company?

6)   How does the cost of underwriting differ among the types of securities?

f.   The company's next step is to prepare and file a registration statement and prospectus with the Securities and Exchange Commission (SEC).

g.   A public issue of securities may be sold through a cash offer or a rights offer.

1)   A cash offer follows the procedures previously described.

2)   A rights offer gives existing shareholders an option to purchase new shares before they are offered to the public. If the corporate charter provides for a preemptive right, a rights offer is mandatory.

a)   The rights or options are evidenced by warrants that state the terms of the arrangement, including subscription price, the number of rights required to purchase one share, and the expiration date. Shareholders may exercise the rights, sell them, or allow them to expire.

b)   Under a standby underwriting arrangement, an underwriter may agree to buy undersubscribed shares. However, granting other shareholders an oversubscription privilege reduces the probability of needing to resort to the underwriter.

c)   The **green shoe** option allows underwriters to buy additional shares to compensate for oversubscriptions. A cost is involved because the option will be exercised only when the offer price is lower than the market price. A green shoe agreement is an option that allows the underwriter of an initial public offering to issue more shares than were originally planned if there is strong demand and the stock price rises. With more shares, the underwriter collects more fees. The option gets its name from the first company to sign such an agreement in 1963, the Green Shoe Manufacturing Co.

3)   A cash offer is made to any interested party, whereas a rights offer is made to current security holders. Debt is normally sold by cash offer, but equity securities may be sold by either means.

4)   An IPO necessarily involves a cash offer because, if existing security holders desired to purchase the new issue, no public offer would be made.

5)   A seasoned equity issue may be sold in a cash offer or a rights offer.

6)   A registered offering of a large block of a previously issued security by a current shareholder is a secondary offering. The proceeds of the sale go to the holder, not the original issuer, and the number of shares outstanding does not change. A secondary offering is also called a secondary distribution.

h.   The ability of a firm to raise capital through an IPO, the issuance of bonds, or by other means significantly depends upon the quality of the information it provides to potential investors, creditors, regulators, and others.

1)   One such source of information is a set of audited financial statements accompanied by the opinion of the independent external auditor.

a)   This opinion attests to the fairness of the financial statements. The independence and professional reputation of the auditor give the opinion its value.

2)   The unmodified opinion provides the highest level of assurance.

a)   An unmodified opinion states that the financial statements present fairly, in all material respects, the financial position, results of operations, and cash flows of the entity in conformity with accounting principles generally accepted in the United States of America.

Stop and review! You have completed the outline for this subunit. Study multiple-choice questions 1 through 5 beginning on page 69.

2.2 MEASURING SECURITIES

1. **Historical Cost as a Measurement Basis**

    a. The measurement attributes for assets and liabilities in current use are as follows:

        1) Historical cost (for assets) or historical proceeds (for liabilities)
        2) Current cost
        3) Current market value
        4) Net realizable value (for assets) or net settlement value (for liabilities)
        5) Present (i.e., discounted) value of future cash flows.

    b. The appropriate measurement basis for a given asset or liability might not always be obvious because the reporting goals of reliability and relevance are sometimes in conflict.

        1) For example, the historical cost of a piece of productive equipment may not have much relevance for a financial statement user. If the machine is vital to the firm's continuing operations, replacement cost might be more meaningful.

            a) However, selecting an appropriate replacement cost is a process subject to a great degree of judgment and subjectivity, and it might vary significantly over time.

        2) In this case, the reporting goal of reliability is considered to predominate, so historical cost is required for the reporting of property, plant, and equipment.

            a) Likewise, net realizable value is considered the appropriate measurement basis for accounts receivable.

2. **Fair Value as a Measurement Basis**

    a. For investment securities, which are often sold within weeks or days of being purchased, historical cost is not considered a useful basis for measurement.

    b. Thus, a three-way classification system for individual investment securities was created. Securities can be classified as held-to-maturity, trading, or available-for-sale.

        1) **Held-to-maturity** securities are presented net of any unamortized premium or discount.

        2) **Trading** and **available-for-sale** securities must be remeasured at fair value at every reporting date.

            a) The unrealized gain or loss associated with the adjustment is a component of net income for trading securities and of other comprehensive income for available-for-sale securities.

    c. Under the **fair value option**, the firm can elect to measure a security in any of the three categories at fair value, with the unrealized holding gains and losses passing through net income.

        1) The decision to adopt the fair value option must be made on an instrument-by-instrument basis and can only be made for the entire instrument. Once elected, the fair value option is irrevocable for that instrument.

        2) It would be beneficial to elect the fair value option when the fair market value of assets is higher than historical cost.

            a) For liabilities, it is beneficial to elect the fair value option when fair market value is less than historical cost.

    d.   The fair value option has not been met with universal approval.

        1)   While some believe it is a step toward constant reporting of the most up-to-date information possible (in the spirit of mark-to-market accounting), others believe that its case-by-case nature allows firms to manipulate earnings by cherry picking which instruments to measure at fair value.

3.   **Fair Value's Effect on Financial Statement Analysis**

    a.   Although trading and available-for-sale securities must be reported on the face of the balance sheet at fair value, many firms disclose the original cost in the notes to the financial statements.

        1)   A typical reporting arrangement might look like the following:

Balance sheet

Current assets:
Trading securities (Note 1) $10,895

Noncurrent assets:
Held-to-maturity securities (at amortized cost) $5,346
Available-for-sale securities (Note 2)   2,100

Notes to the financial statements

Note 1: Trading securities are reported at fair value.

	Cost	Fair Value Adjustments	Fair Value
Debt securities	$8,100	$ 950	$ 9,050
Equity securities	2,000	(155)	1,845
Totals		$ 795	$10,895

Note 2: Available-for-sale securities consist of an equity investment with a cost of $2,600 and a credit fair value adjustment of $500.

    b.   Having access to historical cost information can supplement the process of financial statement analysis.

        1)   During a rising securities market, liquidity ratios based on fair value will report better performance than those using historical cost.

            a)   Improved-looking liquidity could make it easier for the firm to obtain credit.

        2)   During a falling securities market, liquidity ratios based on fair value will report worse performance than those using historical cost.

            a)   If the deterioration is substantial, the firm may violate certain loan covenants, making debts come due sooner than anticipated. At the same time, falling securities prices will make ready cash harder to come by, continuously worsening the firm's situation.

            b)   This kind of self-reinforcing liquidity crisis could start the firm on a "death spiral."

        3)   Also, as noted above in reference to the fair value option for reporting, the use of fair value approaches the practice of mark-to-market accounting, which some financial statement users consider the ideal.

Stop and review! You have completed the outline for this subunit. Study multiple-choice questions 6 and 7 on page 70.

2.3 RISK AND RETURN

1. **Rate of Return**

   a. A return is the amount received by an investor as compensation for taking on the risk of the investment.

   $$Return\ on\ investment\ =\ Amount\ received\ -\ Amount\ invested$$

      1) EXAMPLE: An investor paid $100,000 for an investment that returned $112,000. The investor's return is $12,000 ($112,000 − $100,000).

   b. The rate of return is the return stated as a percentage of the amount invested.

   $$Rate\ of\ return\ =\ \frac{Return\ on\ investment}{Amount\ invested}$$

      1) EXAMPLE: The investor's rate of return is 12% ($12,000 ÷ $100,000).

2. **Two Basic Types of Investment Risk**

   a. **Systematic risk**, also called **market risk**, is the risk faced by all firms. Changes in the economy as a whole, such as the business cycle, affect all players in the market.

      1) For this reason, systematic risk is sometimes referred to as undiversifiable risk. Since all investment securities are affected, this risk cannot be offset through portfolio diversification.

   b. **Unsystematic risk**, also called **nonmarket or company risk**, is the risk inherent in a particular investment security. This type of risk is determined by the issuer's industry, products, customer loyalty, degree of leverage, management competence, etc.

      1) For this reason, unsystematic risk is sometimes referred to as diversifiable risk. Since individual securities are affected differently by economic conditions, this risk can be offset through portfolio diversification.

3. **Other Types of Investment Risk**

   a. **Credit risk** is the risk that the issuer of a debt security will default. This risk can be gauged by the use of credit-rating agencies.

   b. **Foreign exchange risk** is the risk that a foreign currency transaction will be affected by fluctuations in exchange rates.

   c. **Interest rate risk** is the risk that an investment security will fluctuate in value due to changes in interest rates. In general, the longer the time until maturity, the greater the degree of interest rate risk.

   d. **Industry risk** is the risk that a change will affect securities issued by firms in a particular industry. For example, a spike in fuel prices will negatively affect the airline industry.

   e. **Political risk** is the probability of loss from actions of governments, such as from changes in tax laws or environmental regulations or from expropriation of assets.

   f. **Liquidity risk** is the risk that a security cannot be sold on short notice for its market value.

   g. **Financial risk** is the risk of an adverse outcome based on a change in the financial markets, such as changes in interest rates or changes in investors' desired rates of return.

   h. **Purchasing-power risk** is the risk that a general rise in the price level will reduce the quantity of goods that can be purchased with a fixed sum of money.

4.   **Relationship between Risk and Return**

a.   Whether the expected return on an investment is sufficient to entice an investor depends on its risk, the risks and returns of alternative investments, and the investor's attitude toward risk.

1)   Most serious investors are risk averse. They have a diminishing marginal utility for wealth. In other words, the utility of additional increments of wealth decreases. The utility of a gain for serious investors is less than the disutility of a loss of the same amount. Due to this risk aversion, risky securities must have higher expected returns.

2)   A risk neutral investor adopts an expected value approach because (s)he regards the utility of a gain as equal to the disutility of a loss of the same amount. Thus, a risk-neutral investor has a purely rational attitude toward risk.

3)   A risk-seeking investor has an optimistic attitude toward risk. (S)he regards the utility of a gain as exceeding the disutility of a loss of the same amount.

5.   **Financial Instruments**

a.   Financial managers may select from a wide range of financial instruments in which to invest and with which to raise money.

b.   The following is a short list of widely available long-term financial instruments ranked from the lowest rate of return to the highest (and thus the lowest risk to the highest):

1)   U.S. Treasury bonds
2)   First mortgage bonds
3)   Second mortgage bonds
4)   Subordinated debentures
5)   Income bonds
6)   Preferred stock
7)   Convertible preferred stock
8)   Common stock

c.   These instruments also are ranked according to the level of security backing them. An unsecured financial instrument is much riskier than an instrument that is secured. Thus, the riskier asset earns a higher rate of return.

1)   Mortgage bonds are secured by assets, but common stock is completely unsecured. Accordingly, common stock will earn a higher rate of return than mortgage bonds.

d.   Short-term financial instruments increase the liquidity of an entity.

Stop and review! You have completed the outline for this subunit. Study multiple-choice questions 8 through 14 beginning on page 70.

2.4 BONDS

1.   **Aspects of Bonds**

a.   Bonds are the principal form of long-term debt financing for corporations and governmental bodies.

1)   A bond is a formal contractual obligation to pay an amount of money (called the **par value**, **maturity amount**, or **face amount**) to the holder at a certain date, plus, in most cases, a series of cash interest payments based on a specified percentage (called the **stated rate** or **coupon rate**) of the face amount at specified intervals.

a)   The face amount (also called the maturity amount) is received on the bond's maturity date, e.g., 20 years after the initial purchase.

          b)   The annual cash interest equals the bond's face amount times the stated (or coupon) rate, e.g., $1,000 face amount × 4% stated rate = $400 annual cash interest.

      2)   All of the terms of the agreement are stated in a document called an **indenture**.

  b.   Bringing a bond issue to market requires extensive legal and accounting work. This process is rarely worthwhile for bonds with maturities of less than 10 years.

      1)   An investment banker performs an underwriting or insurance function when it purchases an issue of securities and then resells them. The risk of price fluctuations during the distribution period is borne entirely by the investment banker.

      2)   The profit earned is the underwriting spread, or the difference between the purchase and resale prices of the securities.

  c.   In general, the longer the term of a bond, the higher will be the return (yield) demanded by investors to compensate for increased risk.

  d.   **Advantages of Bonds to the Issuer**

      1)   Interest paid on debt is tax deductible.

          a)   This is by far the most significant advantage of debt. For a corporation facing a 40%-50% marginal tax rate, the tax savings produced by the deduction of interest can be substantial.

      2)   Basic control of the firm is not shared with debtholders.

  e.   **Disadvantages of Bonds to the Issuer**

      1)   Unlike returns on equity investments, the payment of interest and principal on debt is a legal obligation.

          a)   If cash flow is insufficient to service debt, the firm could become insolvent.

      2)   The legal requirement to pay debt service raises a firm's risk level.

          a)   Shareholders will demand higher capitalization rates on retained earnings, which may result in a decline in the market price of the stock.

      3)   The long-term nature of bond debt also affects risk profiles.

          a)   Debt originally appearing to be profitable may become a burden if interest rates fall and the firm is unable to refinance.

      4)   Certain managerial prerogatives are usually given up in the contractual relationship outlined in the bond's indenture contract.

          a)   For example, specific ratios must be kept above a certain level during the term of the loan.

      5)   The amount of debt financing available to the individual firm is limited.

          a)   Generally accepted standards of the investment community will usually dictate a certain debt-equity ratio for an individual firm.

          b)   Beyond this limit, the cost of debt may rise rapidly, or debt may not be available.

  f.   **Debt covenants** are restrictions or protective clauses that are imposed on a borrower by the creditor in a formal debt agreement or an indenture.

      1)   Examples of debt covenants include the following:

          a)   Limitations on issuing long-term or short-term debt
          b)   Limitations on dividend payments
          c)   Maintaining certain financial ratios
          d)   Maintaining specific collateral that backs the debt

2) The more restrictive the debt covenant, the lower the risk that the borrower will not be able to repay its debt. The less risky the investment is for creditors, the lower the interest rate on the debt (since the risk premium is lower).

3) If the debtor breaches the debt covenant, the debt becomes due immediately.

g. **Call provisions** allow the bond issuer to exercise an option to redeem the bonds earlier than the specified maturity date.

1) Since call provisions are undesirable to investors, investors usually demand a higher rate of return when call provisions are included in the bond issue.

h. A bond indenture may require the issuer to establish and maintain a bond **sinking fund**. The objective of making payments into the fund is to segregate and accumulate sufficient assets to pay the bond principal at maturity.

1) The amounts transferred plus the revenue earned on investments provide the necessary funds.

2. **Types of Bonds**

a. Maturity Pattern

1) A **term bond** has a single maturity date at the end of its term.
2) A **serial bond** matures in stated amounts at regular intervals. Investors can choose the maturity that suits their needs.

b. Valuation

1) **Variable rate bonds** pay interest that is dependent on market conditions.
2) **Zero-coupon** or **deep-discount bonds** bear no stated rate of interest and thus involve no periodic cash payments; the interest component consists entirely of the bond's discount.
3) **Commodity-backed bonds** are payable at prices related to a commodity such as gold.

c. Redemption Provisions

1) **Callable bonds** may be repurchased by the issuer at a specified price before maturity.

   a) A callable bond is not as valuable to investors as a straight bond.

2) **Convertible bonds** may be converted into equity securities of the issuer at the option of the holder under certain conditions.

d. Securitization

1) **Mortgage bonds** are backed by specific assets, usually real estate.
2) **Debentures** are backed by the issuer's full faith and credit but not by specific collateral. Thus, debentures are riskier to investors than secured bonds.
3) **Equipment trust bonds** are secured by a lien on a specific piece of equipment, such as an airplane or a railroad car. They are used mostly by companies in the transportation industry.

e. Ownership

1) **Registered bonds** are issued in the name of the holder. Only the registered holder may receive interest and principal payments.
2) **Bearer bonds** are not individually registered. Interest and principal are paid to whomever presents the bond.

     f.   Priority

          1)   **Subordinated debentures** and **second mortgage bonds** are junior securities with claims inferior to those of senior bonds.

     g.   Repayment Provisions

          1)   **Income bonds** pay interest only if the issuer earns the interest.

          2)   **Revenue bonds** are issued by governmental units and are payable from specific revenue sources.

3. **Bond Ratings**

     a.   Investors can judge the creditworthiness of a bond issue by consulting the rating assigned by a credit-rating agency. The higher the rating, the more likely the firm is to make good its commitment to pay the interest and principal.

     b.   This field is dominated by the three largest firms: Moody's, Standard & Poor's, and Fitch.

          1)   Investment-grade bonds are considered safe investments and thus are deemed to have moderate risk.

              a)   The highest rating assigned is "triple-A."

              b)   Some fiduciary organizations (such as banks and insurance companies) are only allowed to invest in investment-grade bonds.

          2)   Non-investment grade bonds, also called speculative-grade bonds, high-yield bonds, or junk bonds, carry high risk.

              a)   A **junk bond** is a bond that is rated "BB" or lower because of its high default risk.

              b)   Junk bonds are high-risk, high-reward securities rated at less than investment grade.

     c.   The following is a short list of widely available bonds ranked from the lowest rate of return to the highest rate of return (and thus the lowest risk to the highest risk):

          1)   U.S. Treasury bonds
          2)   Secured bonds (i.e., first mortgage bonds)
          3)   Second mortgage bonds
          4)   Investment grade bonds
          5)   Subordinated bonds (i.e., deep discount bonds)
          6)   Income bonds
          7)   Junk bonds

4. **Interest Rates**

     a.   The **term structure of interest rates** is the relationship between yield to maturity and time to maturity. It is important to corporate treasurers, who must decide whether to issue short- or long-term debt, and to investors, who must decide whether to buy short- or long-term debt.

          1)   Higher interest rates on bonds will lead to an increased demand for bond investments, which decreases the demand for common stock, causing the price of common stock to fall.

b.   Therefore, it is important to understand how the long- and short-term rates are related and what causes shifts in their positions. The term structure is graphically depicted by a yield curve.

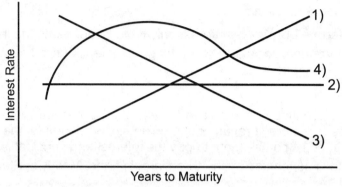

Years to Maturity

Figure 2-1

c.   The graph above illustrates four common yield curves. Since short-term interest rates are usually lower than long-term rates, the yield curve is usually upward sloping. However, other shapes do occur sometimes. The various shapes are as follows:

1)   Upward sloping
2)   Flat
3)   Downward sloping
4)   Humped

d.   Interest Rate Risk

1)   Interest rate risk is the risk that an investment security will fluctuate in value due to changes in interest rates.

a)   The duration of a bond (its term) is the best measure of interest rate risk and generally, the longer the time until maturity, the greater the degree of interest rate risk.

b)   The longer a bond's term, the more time there is for interest rate volatility to affect a bond's price, and the more sensitive its price is to interest rate changes.

2)   The interest rate is also affected by inflation expectations, among other factors. The lower (higher) the expected inflation, the lower (higher) the interest rate.

5.   **Bond Valuation**

a.   Of primary concern to a bond issuer is the amount of cash that (s)he will receive from investors on the day the bonds are sold.

1)   This amount is equal to the **present value of the cash flows** associated with the bonds discounted at the interest rate prevailing in the market at the time (called the market rate or effective rate).

a)   The cash flow associated with bonds are

i)   Face amount
ii)   Interest payments

2)   Using the effective interest rate method ensures that the bonds' **yield to maturity** (that is, their ultimate rate of return to the investor) is equal to the rate of return prevailing in the market at the time of the sale.

a)   Using the **effective rate** to determine the bonds' present value also ensures that, upon maturity, they will be valued at their face amount.

b.   This present value calculation can result in cash proceeds equal to, less than, or greater than the face amount of the bonds, depending on the relationship of the bonds' stated rate of interest to the market rate.

1)   If the bonds' **stated rate happens to be the same as the market rate** at the time of sale, the present value of the bonds will exactly equal their face amount, and the bonds are said to be sold "at par." It is rare, however, for the coupon rate to precisely match the market rate at the time the bonds are ready for sale.

2)   If the bonds' **stated rate is lower than the market rate**, investors must be offered an incentive to buy the bonds, since the bonds' periodic interest payments are lower than those currently available in the market.

   a)   In this case, the issuer receives less cash than the par value and the bonds are said to be sold at a **discount**.

EXAMPLE

An entity issues 200 6%, 5-year, $5,000 bonds when the prevailing interest rate in the market is 8%. The total face amount of bonds issued is therefore $1,000,000 ($5,000 face amount × 200 bonds). Annual cash interest payments of $60,000 ($1,000,000 face amount × 6% stated rate) will be made at the end of each year. The present value of the cash flows associated with this bond issue, discounted at the market rate of 8%, is calculated as follows:

Present value of face amount ($1,000,000 × 0.68058)	$680,580
Present value of cash interest ($60,000 × 3.99271)	239,563 (rounded)
Cash proceeds from bond issue	$920,143

Because the bonds are issued at a discount, the cash proceeds are less than the face amount. The issuer records the following entry:

Cash (present value of cash flows)	$920,143	
Discount on bonds payable (difference)	79,857	
Bonds payable (face amount)		$1,000,000

---

3)   If the bonds' **stated rate is higher than the market rate**, investors are willing to pay more for the bonds, since their periodic interest payments are higher than those currently available in the market.

   a)   In this case, the issuer receives more cash than the par value and the bonds are said to be sold at a **premium**.

EXAMPLE

An entity issues 200 8%, 5-year, $5,000 bonds when the prevailing interest rate in the market is 6%. The total face amount of bonds issued is therefore $1,000,000 ($5,000 face amount × 200 bonds). Annual cash interest payments of $80,000 ($1,000,000 face amount × 8% stated rate) will be made at the end of each year. The present value of the cash flows associated with this bond issue, discounted at the market rate of 6%, is calculated as follows:

Present value of face amount ($1,000,000 × 0.74726)	$ 747,260
Present value of cash interest ($80,000 × 4.21236)	336,989 (rounded)
Cash proceeds from bond issue	$1,084,249

Because the bonds are issued at a premium, the cash proceeds exceed the face amount. The issuer records the following entry:

Cash (present value of cash flows)	$1,084,249	
Bonds payable (face amount)		$1,000,000
Premium on bonds payable (difference)		84,249

---

4)   Sometimes the issue price is an exact percentage of the face amount. In these cases, the bonds are said to be sold at, for example, "97," "98," "101," "102," etc.

    c.   Convertible Bonds

        1)   Convertible debt may be exchanged for common stock of the issuer.

        2)   The formula for the conversion ratio is the par value of the convertible bond divided by the conversion price.

$$Conversion\ ratio = \frac{Par\ value\ of\ convertible\ bond}{Conversion\ price}$$

Stop and review! You have completed the outline for this subunit. Study multiple-choice question 15 through 20 beginning on page 72.

2.5 STOCK

1.   **Common Stock**

    a.   The common shareholders are the **owners of the corporation**, and their rights as owners, although reasonably uniform, depend on the laws of the state in which the firm is incorporated.

        1)   Equity ownership involves risk because holders of common stock are not guaranteed a return and are last in priority in a liquidation. Shareholders' capital provides the cushion for creditors if any losses occur on liquidation.

    b.   **Advantages to the Issuer**

        1)   Common stock does not require a fixed dividend; dividends are paid from profits when available.

        2)   There is no fixed maturity date for repayment of the capital.

        3)   The sale of common stock increases the creditworthiness of the firm by providing more equity.

        4)   Common stock is frequently more attractive to investors than debt because it grows in value with the success of the firm. The higher the common stock value, the more advantageous equity financing is compared with debt financing.

    c.   **Disadvantages to the Issuer**

        1)   Cash dividends on common stock are not tax-deductible by the corporation, and so must be paid out of after-tax profits.

        2)   Control (voting rights) is usually diluted as more common stock is sold. (While this aspect is disadvantageous to existing shareholders, management of the corporation may view it as an advantage.)

        3)   New common stock sales dilute earnings per share available to existing shareholders.

        4)   Underwriting costs are typically higher for common stock issues.

        5)   Too much equity may raise the average cost of capital of the firm above its optimal level.

    d.   Common shareholders ordinarily have **preemptive rights**. Preemptive rights give common shareholders the right to purchase any additional stock issuances in proportion to their current ownership percentages.

        1)   If applicable state law or the corporate charter does not provide preemptive rights, the firm may nevertheless sell to the existing common shareholders in a rights offering.

        2)   Each shareholder is issued a certificate or warrant that is an option to buy a certain number of shares at a fixed price.

    e.   As the corporation's owners, the common shareholders have voting rights, that is, they select the firm's board of directors and vote on resolutions.

    f.   A stock's **par value** represents legal capital. It is an arbitrary value assigned to stock before the stock is issued. It also represents the maximum liability of a shareholder.

2. **Preferred Stock**

   a. Preferred stock is a **hybrid of debt and equity**. It has a fixed charge and increases leverage, but payment of dividends is not a legal obligation.

      1) Also, preferred shareholders stand ahead of common shareholders in priority in the event of corporate bankruptcy.

   b. **Typical Provisions of Preferred Stock Issues**

      1) Priority in assets and earnings. If the firm goes bankrupt, the preferred shareholders have priority over common shareholders.

      2) Accumulation of dividends. If preferred dividends are cumulative, dividends in arrears must be paid before any common dividends can be paid.

      3) Participation. Preferred stock may participate with common in excess earnings of the company. For example, 8% participating preferred stock might pay a dividend each year greater than 8% when the corporation is extremely profitable, but nonparticipating preferred stock will receive no more than is stated on the face of the stock.

      4) Par value. Par value is the liquidation value, and a percentage of par equals the preferred dividend.

      5) Redeemability. Some preferred stock may be redeemed at a given time or at the option of the holder or otherwise at a time not controlled by the issuer. This feature makes preferred stock more nearly akin to debt, particularly in the case of transient preferred stock, which must be redeemed within a short time (e.g., 5 to 10 years). The SEC requires a separate presentation of redeemable preferred, nonredeemable preferred, and common stock.

      6) Voting rights. Holders of preferred stock are not ordinarily granted voting rights. However, voting rights may be conferred if preferred dividends are in arrears for a stated period.

      7) Retirement.

         a) Preferred stock issues may be **convertible** into common stock at the option of the shareholder.

         b) The issuer may have the right to repurchase the stock through a **call provision**. For example, the stock may be noncallable for a stated period, after which it may be called if the issuer pays a call premium (an amount exceeding par value).

         c) Preferred stock may have a **sinking fund** that allows for the purchase of a given annual percentage of the outstanding shares.

   c. **Advantages to the Issuer**

      1) It is a form of equity and therefore builds the creditworthiness of the firm.

      2) Control is still held by common shareholders.

      3) Superior earnings of the firm are usually still reserved for the common shareholders.

   d. **Disadvantages to the Issuer**

      1) Cash dividends on preferred stock are not deductible as a tax expense and are paid with after-tax income. The result is a substantially greater cost relative to bonds.

      2) In periods of economic difficulty, accumulated unpaid dividends (called dividends in arrears) may create major managerial and financial problems for the firm.

   e. Holding preferred stock rather than bonds provides corporations a major tax advantage. At least 70% of the dividends received from preferred stock is tax deductible, but all bond interest received is taxable. The dividends-received deduction also applies to common stock.

Stop and review! You have completed the outline for this subunit. Study multiple-choice questions 21 through 25 beginning on page 74.

2.6 STOCK DIVIDENDS

 The CMA exam tests one's understanding of what influences a company's dividends policy along with the importance of a stable policy. A candidate will need to identify the types of dividend payouts and when and how a company would use each.

1. **Dividend Policy**

   a. A dividend represents a distribution of earnings.

   b. Dividend policy determines what portion of a corporation's net income is distributed to shareholders and what portion is retained for reinvestment.

      1) A high dividend rate means a slower rate of growth. A high growth rate usually means a low dividend rate.

   c. Because both a high growth rate and a high dividend rate are desirable, the financial manager attempts to achieve the balance that maximizes the firm's share price.

      1) The most important factor to consider is the future planned uses of cash.

   d. Normally, corporations try to maintain a stable level of dividends, even though profits may fluctuate considerably, because many shareholders buy stock with the expectation of receiving a certain dividend every year. Hence, management tends not to raise dividends if the payout cannot be sustained.

      1) The desire for stability has led theorists to propound the information content or signaling hypothesis, which states that a change in dividend policy is a signal to the market regarding management's forecast of future earnings. Thus, firms generally have an active policy strategy with respect to dividends.

   e. This stability often results in a stock that sells at a higher market price because shareholders perceive less risk in receiving their dividends.

2. **Factors Influencing a Company's Dividend Policy**

   a. Legal Restrictions

      1) Dividends ordinarily cannot be paid out of paid-in capital. A corporation must have a balance in its retained earnings account before dividends can be paid.

   b. Stability of Earnings

      1) A company whose earnings fluctuate greatly from year to year will tend to pay out a smaller dividend during good years so that the same dividend can be paid even if profits are much lower.

         a) For example, a company with fluctuating earnings might pay out $1 every year whether earnings per share are $10 (10% payout rate) or $1 (100% payout rate).

   c. Rate of Growth

      1) A company with a faster growth rate will have a greater need to finance that growth with retained earnings. Thus, growth companies usually have lower dividend payout ratios. Shareholders hope to be able to obtain larger capital gains in the future.

   d. Cash Position

       1) Regardless of a firm's earnings record, cash must be available before a dividend can be paid. No dividend can be declared if all of a firm's earnings are tied up in receivables and inventories.

   e. Restrictions in Debt Agreements

       1) Restrictive covenants in bond indentures and other debt agreements often limit the dividends that a firm can declare.

   f. Tax Position of Shareholders

       1) In corporations, the shareholders may not want regular dividends because the individual owners are in such high tax brackets. They may want to forgo dividends in exchange for future capital gains or wait to receive dividends in future years when they are in lower tax brackets.

       2) However, an accumulated earnings tax is assessed on a corporation if it has accumulated retained earnings beyond its reasonably expected needs.

   g. Residual Theory of Dividends

       1) The amount (residual) of earnings paid as dividends depends on the available investment opportunities and the debt-equity ratio at which cost of capital is minimized. The rational investor should prefer reinvestment of retained earnings when the return exceeds what the investor could earn on investments of equal risk. However, the firm may prefer to pay dividends when investment opportunities are poor and the use of internal equity financing would move the firm away from its ideal capital structure.

3. **Important Dates Relative to Dividends**

   a. The **date of declaration** is the date the directors meet and formally vote to declare a dividend. On this date, the dividend becomes a **liability of the corporation**.

   b. The **date of record** is the date as of which the corporation determines the shareholders who will receive the declared dividend. Essentially, the corporation closes its shareholder records on this date.

       1) Only those shareholders who own the stock on the date of record will receive the dividend. It typically falls from 2 to 6 weeks after the declaration date.

   c. The **date of distribution** is the date on which the dividend is actually paid (when the checks are put into the mail to the investors). The payment date is usually from 2 to 4 weeks after the date of record.

   d. The **ex-dividend date** is a date established by the stock exchanges, such as 2 business days before the date of record. Unlike the other dates previously mentioned, it is not established by the corporate board of directors.

       1) The period between the ex-dividend date and the date of record gives the stock exchange members time to process any transactions so that new shareholders will receive the dividends to which they are entitled.

       2) An investor who buys a share of stock before the ex-dividend date will receive the dividend that has been previously declared. An investor who buys the stock after the ex-dividend date (but before the date of record or payment date) will not receive the declared dividend. Instead, the individual who sold the stock will receive the dividend because (s)he owned it on the ex-dividend date.

       3) Usually, a stock price will drop on the ex-dividend date by the amount of the dividend because the new investor will not receive it.

4. Stock Dividends and Stock Splits

a. Stock dividends and splits involve issuance of additional shares to existing shareholders. Shareholders are not taxed until the stock is sold.

b. A **stock dividend** is an issuance of stock and entails the transfer of a sum from the retained earnings account to a paid-in capital account.

   1) Usually, the corporation wants to give something to the shareholders but without paying out a cash dividend because the funds are needed in the business.
   2) Casual investors may believe they are receiving something of value when in essence their previous holdings are merely being divided into more pieces.
   3) Stock dividends are often used by growing companies that wish to retain earnings in the business while placating shareholders.

c. A **stock split** does not involve any accounting entries. Instead, the existing shares are divided into more shares so that the market price per share will be reduced.

   1) EXAMPLE: If a corporation has 1 million shares outstanding, each of which sells for $90, a 2-for-1 stock split will result in 2 million shares outstanding, each of which sells for about $45.
   2) **Reverse stock splits** reduce the shares outstanding, thereby increasing the market price per share.

d. Advantages of Issuing Stock Splits and Dividends

   1) Because more shares will be outstanding, the price per share will be lower. The lower price per share will induce more small investors to purchase the company's stock. Thus, because demand for the stock is greater, the price may increase.

      a) EXAMPLE: In the example above, the additional investors interested in the company at the lower price may drive the price up to $46 or $47, or slightly higher than the theoretically correct price of $45. Consequently, current shareholders will benefit from the split (or dividend) after all.

   2) A dividend or split can be a publicity gesture. Because shareholders may believe they are receiving something of value (and may be indirectly), they will have a better opinion of their company.
   3) Moreover, the more shares a corporation has outstanding, the larger the number of shareholders, who are usually good customers of their company's products.

e. On rare occasions, a firm may use a reverse stock split to raise the market price per share. For example, a 1-for-10 stock split would require shareholders to turn in 10 old shares to receive 1 new share.

5. Share Repurchases

a. A share repurchase takes place when a corporation buys its own stock back on the open market. Once in the firm's possession, these shares are called treasury shares.

b. Among the motives for a share repurchase are

   1) Mergers
   2) Share options
   3) Stock dividends
   4) Tax advantages to shareholders (e.g., favorable capital gains rates)
   5) To increase earnings per share and other ratios (e.g., increase financial leverage)
   6) To prevent a hostile takeover
   7) To eliminate a particular ownership interest

Stop and review! You have completed the outline for this subunit. Study multiple-choice questions 26 through 30 beginning on page 75.

QUESTIONS

2.1 Financial Markets and Securities Offerings

1. Which of the following financial instruments can be traded in international money markets?

   A. Mortgages.

   B. Preferred stocks.

   C. Government treasury bills.

   D. Government treasury bonds.

Answer (C) is correct.
   REQUIRED: The instruments traded in international money markets.
   DISCUSSION: Funds are borrowed or lent for short periods (less than 1 year) in money markets. Examples of instruments traded in money markets are U.S. Treasury bills, bankers' acceptances, commercial paper, negotiable certificates of deposit, money market mutual funds, Eurodollar market time deposits, and consumer credit loans. Capital markets trade stocks and long-term debt.
   Answer (A) is incorrect. Mortgages are long-term, capital market securities. Answer (B) is incorrect. Preferred stocks are long-term, capital market securities. Answer (D) is incorrect. Treasury bonds are long-term, capital market securities.

2. The strong form of the efficient markets hypothesis (EMH) states that current market prices of securities reflect

   A. All publicly available information.

   B. All information whether it is public or private.

   C. No relevant information.

   D. Only information found in past price movements.

Answer (B) is correct.
   REQUIRED: The information reflected in current market prices of securities under the strong form of the EMH.
   DISCUSSION: The EMH states that stock prices reflect all relevant information, so the market is continuously adjusting to new information. Stock prices are in equilibrium, so investors cannot earn abnormal returns. The strong form of the EMH states that all public and private information is instantaneously reflected in current market prices of securities. Thus, investors cannot earn abnormal returns.
   Answer (A) is incorrect. The semistrong form of EMH states that only publicly available information is reflected in current market prices. Answer (C) is incorrect. The EMH states that current market prices at least reflect past price movements. Answer (D) is incorrect. The weak form of the EMH states that only past price movements are reflected in current market prices.

3. The semistrong form of the efficient markets hypothesis (EMH) states that current market prices of securities reflect

   A. No pertinent information.

   B. All pertinent information.

   C. Only information contained in past price movements.

   D. Only publicly available information.

Answer (D) is correct.
   REQUIRED: The information reflected in current market prices under the semistrong form of the EMH.
   DISCUSSION: According to the EMH, stock prices are in equilibrium and investors cannot obtain abnormal returns, that is, returns in excess of the riskiness of their investments. The semistrong form of the EMH postulates that current market prices reflect all publicly available information. However, investors with inside information can still earn an abnormal return.
   Answer (A) is incorrect. The EMH states that current prices reflect at least the information contained in past price movements. Answer (B) is incorrect. The strong form of the EMH states that current market prices reflect all pertinent information, including insider information. Answer (C) is incorrect. The weak form of the EMH states that current market prices reflect only information contained in past price movements.

4. Moody's and Standard & Poor's debt ratings depend on

   A. The chances of default.

   B. The size of the company.

   C. The size and the type of issue.

   D. The firm's industry.

Answer (A) is correct.
   REQUIRED: The basis for debt ratings.
   DISCUSSION: Debt ratings are based on the probability of default and the protection for investors in case of default.
   Answer (B) is incorrect. The size of the company is relevant only insofar as it bears upon the probability of default. Answer (C) is incorrect. The size and the type of issue are relevant only insofar as they bear upon the probability of default. Answer (D) is incorrect. The firm's industry is relevant only insofar as it bears upon the probability of default.

5. If a bond is rated below BBB, it is called

    A. A zero-coupon bond.

    B. An investment grade bond.

    C. A junk bond.

    D. An income bond.

Answer (C) is correct.
    REQUIRED: The bond rated below BBB.
    DISCUSSION: AAA and AA are Standard & Poor's highest ratings. They signify the highest quality. Bonds rated A and BBB are investment grade. Bonds rated below BBB are speculative high-yield or low-grade bonds (junk bonds).
    Answer (A) is incorrect. A zero-coupon bond pays no interest and is sold at a discount. Answer (B) is incorrect. An investment grade bond is rated A or BBB. Answer (D) is incorrect. An income bond pays interest only if the issuer earns income sufficient to pay the interest.

2.2 Measuring Securities

6. An investment in trading securities is measured on the statement of financial position at the

    A. Cost to acquire the asset.

    B. Accumulated income minus accumulated dividends since acquisition.

    C. Lower of cost or market.

    D. Fair value.

Answer (D) is correct.
    REQUIRED: The means of valuing trading securities on the balance sheet.
    DISCUSSION: Under U.S. GAAP, trading securities are those held principally for sale in the near term. They are classified as current and consist of debt securities and equity securities with readily determinable fair values. Unrealized holding gains and losses on trading securities are reported in earnings. Hence, these securities are reported at fair value.
    Answer (A) is incorrect. Cost is adjusted for changes in fair value. Answer (B) is incorrect. An equity-based investment is adjusted for the investor's share of the investee's earnings, minus dividends received. Answer (C) is incorrect. Lower of cost or market is applied by U.S. GAAP to inventories, not trading securities.

7. An investment in available-for-sale securities is measured on the statement of financial position at the

    A. Cost to acquire the asset.

    B. Accumulated income less accumulated dividends since acquisition.

    C. Fair value.

    D. Par or stated value of the securities.

Answer (C) is correct.
    REQUIRED: The measurement of available-for-sale securities on the balance sheet.
    DISCUSSION: Under U.S. GAAP, available-for-sale securities are investments in debt securities that are not classified as held-to-maturity or trading securities and in equity securities with readily determinable fair values that are not classified as trading securities. They are measured at fair value in the balance sheet.
    Answer (A) is incorrect. Cost is adjusted for changes in fair value. Answer (B) is incorrect. An equity-based investment is adjusted for the investor's share of the investee's earnings, minus dividends received. Answer (D) is incorrect. The par or stated value is an arbitrary amount.

2.3 Risk and Return

8. The type of risk that is **not** diversifiable and affects the value of a portfolio is

    A. Purchasing-power risk.

    B. Market risk.

    C. Nonmarket risk.

    D. Interest-rate risk.

Answer (B) is correct.
    REQUIRED: The term for the type of risk that is not diversifiable.
    DISCUSSION: Prices of all stocks, even the value of portfolios, are correlated to some degree with broad swings in the stock market. Market risk is the risk that changes in a stock's price will result from changes in the stock market as a whole. Market risk is commonly referred to as nondiversifiable risk.
    Answer (A) is incorrect. Purchasing-power risk is the risk that a general rise in the price level will reduce the quantity of goods that can be purchased with a fixed sum of money. Answer (C) is incorrect. Nonmarket risk is the risk that is influenced by an individual firm's policies and decisions. Nonmarket risk is diversifiable since it is specific to each firm. Answer (D) is incorrect. Interest-rate risk is the risk that the value of an asset will fluctuate due to changes in the interest rate.

9. When purchasing temporary investments, which one of the following **best** describes the risk associated with the ability to sell the investment in a short period of time without significant price concessions?

    A. Interest-rate risk.

    B. Purchasing-power risk.

    C. Financial risk.

    D. Liquidity risk.

Answer (D) is correct.

    REQUIRED: The risk associated with the ability to sell investments in a short period of time without significant price concessions.

    DISCUSSION: Liquidity risk is the possibility that an asset cannot be sold on short notice for its market value. If an asset must be sold at a high discount, it is said to have a substantial amount of liquidity risk.

    Answer (A) is incorrect. Interest-rate risk is caused by fluctuations in the value of an asset as interest rates change. Its components are price risk and reinvestment-rate risk. Answer (B) is incorrect. Purchasing-power risk is the risk that a general rise in the price level (inflation) will reduce what can be purchased with a fixed sum of money. Answer (C) is incorrect. Financial risk is the risk borne by shareholders, in excess of basic business risk that arises from use of financial leverage (issuance of fixed income securities, i.e., debt and preferred stock).

10. Political risk may be reduced by

    A. Entering into a joint venture with another foreign company.

    B. Making foreign operations dependent on the domestic parent for technology, markets, and supplies.

    C. Refusing to pay higher wages and higher taxes.

    D. Financing with capital from a foreign country.

Answer (B) is correct.

    REQUIRED: The way to reduce political risk.

    DISCUSSION: Political risk is the risk that a foreign government may act in a way that will reduce the value of the company's investment. Political risk may be reduced by making foreign operations dependent on the domestic parent for technology, markets, and supplies. If the foreign operations depend on the domestic parent for technology, markets, and supplies, the foreign government is less likely to have negative effects on foreign operations.

    Answer (A) is incorrect. Political risk may be reduced by entering into a joint venture with a company from the host country rather than from a foreign country. Answer (C) is incorrect. Failure to comply with a foreign country's laws and regulations increases adverse effects against the foreign operations. Answer (D) is incorrect. Financing with capital from a foreign country is subject to more laws and regulations that can be changed by the foreign government.

11. Which of the following classes of securities are listed in order from lowest risk/opportunity for return to highest risk/opportunity for return?

    A. U.S. Treasury bonds; corporate first mortgage bonds; corporate income bonds; preferred stock.

    B. Corporate income bonds; corporate mortgage bonds; convertible preferred stock; subordinated debentures.

    C. Common stock; corporate first mortgage bonds; corporate second mortgage bonds; corporate income bonds.

    D. Preferred stock; common stock; corporate mortgage bonds; corporate debentures.

Answer (A) is correct.

    REQUIRED: The correct listing of classes of securities from lowest to highest risk/opportunity for return.

    DISCUSSION: The general principle is that risk and return are directly correlated. U.S. Treasury securities are backed by the full faith and credit of the federal government and are therefore the least risky form of investment. However, their return is correspondingly lower. Corporate first mortgage bonds are less risky than income bonds or stock because they are secured by specific property. In the event of default, the bondholders can have the property sold to satisfy their claims. Holders of first mortgages have rights paramount to those of any other parties, such as holders of second mortgages. Income bonds pay interest only in the event the corporation earns income. Thus, holders of income bonds have less risk than shareholders because meeting the condition makes payment of interest mandatory. Preferred shareholders receive dividends only if they are declared, and the directors usually have complete discretion in this matter. Also, shareholders have claims junior to those of debtholders if the enterprise is liquidated.

    Answer (B) is incorrect. The proper listing is mortgage bonds, subordinated debentures, income bonds, and preferred stock. Debentures are unsecured debt instruments. Their holders have enforceable claims against the issuer even if no income is earned or dividends declared. Answer (C) is incorrect. The proper listing is first mortgage bonds, second mortgage bonds, income bonds, and common stock. The second mortgage bonds are secured, albeit junior, claims. Answer (D) is incorrect. The proper listing is mortgage bonds, debentures, preferred stock, and common stock. Holders of common stock cannot receive dividends unless the holders of preferred stock receive the stipulated periodic percentage return, in addition to any averages if the preferred stock is cumulative.

12. The risk of loss because of fluctuations in the relative value of foreign currencies is called

    A. Expropriation risk.

    B. Multinational beta.

    C. Exchange rate risk.

    D. Undiversifiable risk.

Answer (C) is correct.
    REQUIRED: The risk of loss because of fluctuations in the relative value of foreign currencies.
    DISCUSSION: When amounts to be paid or received are denominated in a foreign currency, exchange rate fluctuations may result in exchange gains or losses. For example, if a U.S. firm has a receivable fixed in terms of units of a foreign currency, a decline in the value of that currency relative to the U.S. dollar results in a foreign exchange loss.
    Answer (A) is incorrect. Expropriation risk is the risk that the sovereign country in which the assets backing an investment are located will seize the assets without adequate compensation. Answer (B) is incorrect. The beta value in the capital asset pricing model for a multinational firm is the systematic risk of a given multinational firm relative to that of the market as a whole. Answer (D) is incorrect. The beta value in the capital asset pricing model for a multinational firm is the systematic risk of a given multinational firm relative to that of the market as a whole. It is an undiversifiable risk.

13. The marketable securities with the **least** amount of default risk are

    A. Federal government agency securities.

    B. U.S. Treasury securities.

    C. Repurchase agreements.

    D. Commercial paper.

Answer (B) is correct.
    REQUIRED: The marketable securities with the least default risk.
    DISCUSSION: The marketable securities with the lowest default risk are those issued by the federal government because they are backed by the full faith and credit of the U.S. government and are therefore the least risky form of investment.
    Answer (A) is incorrect. Securities issued by a federal agency are first backed by that agency and secondarily by the U.S. government. Agency securities are issued by agencies and corporations created by the federal government, such as the Federal Housing Administration. Answer (C) is incorrect. Repurchase agreements could become worthless if the organization agreeing to make the repurchase goes bankrupt. Answer (D) is incorrect. Commercial paper is unsecured.

14. The **best** example of a marketable security with minimal risk would be

    A. Municipal bonds.

    B. The common stock of a AAA-rated company.

    C. The commercial paper of a AAA-rated company.

    D. Stock options of a AAA-rated company.

Answer (C) is correct.
    REQUIRED: The best example of a marketable security with minimal risk.
    DISCUSSION: Of the choices given, the commercial paper of a top-rated (most creditworthy) company has the least risk. Commercial paper is preferable to stock or stock options because the latter represent only a residual equity in a corporation. Commercial paper is debt and thus has priority over stockholders' claims. Also, commercial paper is a very short-term investment. The maximum maturity allowed without SEC registration is 270 days. However, it can be sold only to sophisticated investors without registration.
    Answer (A) is incorrect. Municipal bonds are rarely considered marketable securities in that they constitute long-term debt. Answer (B) is incorrect. Common stock does not have as high a priority in company assets as commercial paper or other debt. Answer (D) is incorrect. Common stock does not have as high a priority in company assets as commercial paper or other debt.

2.4 Bonds

15. Serial bonds are attractive to investors because

    A. All bonds in the issue mature on the same date.

    B. The yield to maturity is the same for all bonds in the issue.

    C. Investors can choose the maturity that suits their financial needs.

    D. The coupon rate on these bonds is adjusted to the maturity date.

Answer (C) is correct.
    REQUIRED: The reason serial bonds are attractive to investors.
    DISCUSSION: Serial bonds have staggered maturities; that is, they mature over a period (series) of years. Thus, investors can choose the maturity date that meets their investment needs. For example, an investor who will have a child starting college in 16 years can choose bonds that mature in 16 years.
    Answer (A) is incorrect. Serial bonds mature on different dates. Answer (B) is incorrect. Bonds maturing on different dates may have different yields, or they may be the same. Usually, the earlier date maturities carry slightly lower yields than the later maturities. Answer (D) is incorrect. The coupon rate is the same for all bonds; only the selling price and yield differ.

16. All of the following may reduce the coupon rate on a bond issued at par **except** a

   A. Sinking fund.

   B. Call provision.

   C. Change in rating from AA to AAA.

   D. Conversion option.

Answer (B) is correct.

   REQUIRED: The item that will not reduce the coupon rate on a bond issued at par.

   DISCUSSION: A bond issued at par may carry a lower coupon rate than other similar bonds in the market if it has some feature that makes it more attractive to investors. For example, a sinking fund reduces default risk. Hence, investors may require a lower risk premium and be willing to accept a lower coupon rate. Other features attractive to investors include covenants in the bond indenture that restrict risky undertakings by the issuer and an option to convert the debt instruments to equity securities. The opportunity to profit from appreciation of the firm's stock justifies a lower coupon rate. An improvement in a bond's rating from AA to AAA (the highest possible) also justifies reduction in the risk premium and a lower coupon rate. However, a call provision is usually undesirable to investors. The issuer may take advantage of a decline in interest rates to recall the bond and stop paying interest before maturity.

17. Which one of the following characteristics distinguishes income bonds from other bonds?

   A. The bondholder is guaranteed an income over the life of the security.

   B. By promising a return to the bondholder, an income bond is junior to preferred and common stock.

   C. Income bonds are junior to subordinated debt but senior to preferred and common stock.

   D. Income bonds pay interest only if the issuing company has earned the interest.

Answer (D) is correct.

   REQUIRED: The characteristic of income bonds.

   DISCUSSION: An income bond is one that pays interest only if the issuing company has earned the interest, although the principal must still be paid on the due date. Such bonds are riskier than normal bonds.

   Answer (A) is incorrect. Bondholders will receive an income only if the issuing company earns sufficient income to pay the interest. Answer (B) is incorrect. All bonds have priority over preferred and common stock. Answer (C) is incorrect. Subordinated debt is junior to nonsubordinated debt.

18. If a corporation's bonds are currently yielding 8% in the marketplace, why is the firm's cost of debt lower?

   A. Market interest rates have increased.

   B. Additional debt can be issued more cheaply than the original debt.

   C. There should be no difference; cost of debt is the same as the bonds' market yield.

   D. Interest is deductible for tax purposes.

Answer (D) is correct.

   REQUIRED: The reason a firm's cost of debt is lower than its current market yield.

   DISCUSSION: Because interest is deductible for tax purposes, the actual cost of debt capital is the net effect of the interest payment and the offsetting tax deduction. The actual cost of debt equals the interest rate times (1 – the marginal tax rate). Thus, if a firm with an 8% market rate is in a 40% tax bracket, the net cost of the debt capital is 4.8% [8% × (1.0 – .40)].

   Answer (A) is incorrect. The tax deduction always causes the market yield rate to be higher than the cost of debt capital. Answer (B) is incorrect. Additional debt may or may not be issued more cheaply than earlier debt, depending upon the interest rates in the market place. Answer (C) is incorrect. The cost of debt is less than the yield rate given that bond interest is tax deductible.

19. Debentures are

   A. Income bonds that require interest payments only when earnings permit.

   B. Subordinated debt and rank behind convertible bonds.

   C. Bonds secured by the full faith and credit of the issuing firm.

   D. A form of lease financing similar to equipment trust certificates.

Answer (C) is correct.

   REQUIRED: The true statement about debentures.

   DISCUSSION: Debentures are unsecured bonds. Although no assets are mortgaged as security for the bonds, debentures are secured by the full faith and credit of the issuing firm. Debentures are a general obligation of the borrower. Only companies with the best credit ratings can issue debentures because only the company's credit rating and reputation secure the bonds.

   Answer (A) is incorrect. Debentures must pay interest regardless of earnings levels. Answer (B) is incorrect. Debentures are not subordinated except to the extent of assets mortgaged against other bond issues. Debentures are a general obligation of the borrower and rank equally with convertible bonds. Answer (D) is incorrect. Debentures have nothing to do with lease financing. Debentures are not secured by assets.

20. Short-term interest rates are

A. Usually lower than long-term rates.

B. Usually higher than long-term rates.

C. Lower than long-term rates during periods of high inflation only.

D. Not significantly related to long-term rates.

Answer (A) is correct.
REQUIRED: The true statement about short-term interest rates.
DISCUSSION: Historically, one facet of the term structure of interest rates (the relationship of yield and time to maturity) is that short-term interest rates have ordinarily been lower than long-term rates. One reason is that less risk is involved in the short run. Moreover, future expectations concerning interest rates affect the term structure. Most economists believe that a long-term interest rate is an average of future expected short-term interest rates. For this reason, the yield curve will slope upward if future rates are expected to rise, downward if interest rates are anticipated to fall, and remain flat if investors think the rate is stable. Future inflation is incorporated into this relationship. Another consideration is liquidity preference: Investors in an uncertain world will accept lower rates on short-term investments because of their greater liquidity, whereas business debtors often prefer to pay higher rates on long-term debt to avoid the hazards of short-term maturities.
Answer (B) is incorrect. Short-term rates are usually lower than long-term rates. Answer (C) is incorrect. Short-term rates are more likely to be greater than long-term rates if current levels of inflation are high. Answer (D) is incorrect. Long-term rates may be viewed as short-term rates adjusted by a risk factor.

2.5 Stock

21. The following excerpt was taken from a company's financial statements: " . . . 10% convertible participating . . . $10,000,000." What is **most** likely being referred to?

A. Bonds.

B. Common stock.

C. Stock options.

D. Preferred stock.

Answer (D) is correct.
REQUIRED: The securities most likely referred to as convertible participating.
DISCUSSION: Preferred shareholders have priority over common shareholders in the assets and earnings of the enterprise. If preferred dividends are cumulative, any past preferred dividends must be paid before any common dividends. Preferred stock may also be convertible into common stock, and it may be participating. For example, 10% fully participating preferred stock will receive additional distributions at the same rates as other shareholders if dividends paid to all shareholders exceed 10%.
Answer (A) is incorrect. Bonds normally have a coupon yield stated in percentage and may be convertible but are not participating. Answer (B) is incorrect. Common stock is not described as convertible or participating on the financial statements. Answer (C) is incorrect. Common stock options are not participating and do not have a stated yield rate.

22. In general, it is more expensive for a company to finance with equity capital than with debt capital because

A. Long-term bonds have a maturity date and must therefore be repaid in the future.

B. Investors are exposed to greater risk with equity capital.

C. Equity capital is in greater demand than debt capital.

D. Dividends fluctuate to a greater extent than interest rates.

Answer (B) is correct.
REQUIRED: The reason equity financing is more expensive than debt financing.
DISCUSSION: Providers of equity capital are exposed to more risk than are lenders because the firm is not obligated to pay them a return. Also, in case of liquidation, creditors are paid before equity investors. Thus, equity financing is more expensive than debt because equity investors require a higher return to compensate for the greater risk assumed.
Answer (A) is incorrect. The obligation to repay at a specific maturity date reduces the risk to investors and thus the required return. Answer (C) is incorrect. The demand for equity capital is directly related to its greater cost to the issuer. Answer (D) is incorrect. Dividends are based on managerial discretion and may rarely change; interest rates, however, fluctuate daily based upon market conditions.

23. The par value of a common stock represents

A. The estimated market value of the stock when it was issued.

B. The liability ceiling of a shareholder when a company undergoes bankruptcy proceedings.

C. The total value of the stock that must be entered in the issuing corporation's records.

D. A theoretical value of $100 per share of stock with any differences entered in the issuing corporation's records as discount or premium on common stock.

Answer (B) is correct.

    REQUIRED: The amount represented by the par value of common stock.

    DISCUSSION: Par value represents a stock's legal capital. It is an arbitrary value assigned to stock before it is issued. Par value represents a shareholder's liability ceiling because, as long as the par value has been paid in to the corporation, the shareholders obtain the benefits of limited liability.

    Answer (A) is incorrect. Par value is rarely the same as market value. Normally, market value will be equal to or greater than par value, but there is no relationship between the two. Answer (C) is incorrect. All assets received for stock must be entered into a corporation's records. The amount received is very rarely the par value. Answer (D) is incorrect. Par value can be any amount more or less than $100.

24. A financial manager usually prefers to issue preferred stock rather than debt because

A. Payments to preferred stockholders are not considered fixed payments.

B. The cost of fixed debt is less expensive since it is tax deductible even if a sinking fund is required to retire the debt.

C. The preferred dividend is often cumulative, whereas interest payments are not.

D. In a legal sense, preferred stock is equity; therefore, dividend payments are not legal obligations.

Answer (D) is correct.

    REQUIRED: The reason a financial manager usually would rather issue preferred stock instead of debt.

    DISCUSSION: For a financial manager, preferred stock is preferable to debt because dividends do not have to be paid on preferred stock, but failure to pay interest on debt could lead to bankruptcy. Thus, preferred stock is less risky than debt. However, debt has some advantages over preferred stock, the most notable of which is that interest payments are tax deductible. Preferred stock dividends are not.

    Answer (A) is incorrect. Preferred dividends are viewed as fixed payments since they must be made before any dividends or distributions in liquidation can be made to common shareholders. Answer (B) is incorrect. It states a reason to issue debt, not preferred stock. Answer (C) is incorrect. In the sense that they cannot be avoided, interest payments are cumulative.

25. Which one of the following rights is ordinarily sacrificed by the holders of preferred stock in exchange for other preferences received over common shareholders?

A. The right to vote for members of the board of directors and in other matters requiring a vote.

B. The right to share in the residual assets of the company upon liquidation.

C. The right to share in the periodic earnings of the company through the receipt of dividends.

D. The right to accrue dividend payments in arrears when payments are not made for a period of time.

Answer (A) is correct.

    DISCUSSION: Unlike common stockholders, preferred stockholders are not usually entitled to voting rights. Preferred stockholders sacrifices voting rights in exchange for other preferences over common stockholders.

    Answer (B) is incorrect. Preferred stock holders have priority in assets and earnings. If the firm goes bankrupt, the preferred shareholders have priority over common shareholders. Answer (C) is incorrect. Preferred stockholders receive their dividends before the common stockholders receive theirs. Answer (D) is incorrect. Forgone dividends accumulate and must eventually be paid to preferred shareholders.

2.6 Stock Dividends

26. The purchase of treasury stock with a firm's surplus cash

A. Increases a firm's assets.

B. Increases a firm's financial leverage.

C. Increases a firm's interest coverage ratio.

D. Dilutes a firm's earnings per share.

Answer (B) is correct.

    REQUIRED: The true statement about a purchase of treasury stock.

    DISCUSSION: A purchase of treasury stock involves a decrease in assets (usually cash) and a corresponding decrease in equity. Thus, equity is reduced and the debt-to-equity ratio and financial leverage increase.

    Answer (A) is incorrect. Assets decrease when treasury stock is purchased. Answer (C) is incorrect. A firm's interest coverage ratio is unaffected. Earnings, interest expense, and taxes will all be the same regardless of the transaction. Answer (D) is incorrect. The purchase of treasury stock is antidilutive; the same earnings will be spread over fewer shares. Some firms purchase treasury stock for this reason.

27. A corporation has 6,000 shares of 5% cumulative, $100 par value preferred stock outstanding and 200,000 shares of common stock outstanding. The corporation's board of directors last declared dividends for the year ended May 31, Year 1, and there were no dividends in arrears. For the year ended May 31, Year 3, the corporation had net income of $1,750,000. The board of directors is declaring a dividend for common shareholders equivalent to 20% of net income. The total amount of dividends to be paid at May 31, Year 3, is

A. $350,000

B. $380,000

C. $206,000

D. $410,000

Answer (D) is correct.
REQUIRED: The total amount of dividends to be paid given cumulative preferred stock.
DISCUSSION: If a company has cumulative preferred stock, all preferred dividends for the current and any unpaid prior years must be paid before any dividends can be paid on common stock. The total preferred dividends that must be paid equal $60,000 (6,000 shares × $100 par × 5% × 2 years), and the common dividend is $350,000 ($1,750,000 × 20%), for a total of $410,000.
Answer (A) is incorrect. The amount of $350,000 is the common stock dividend. Answer (B) is incorrect. The amount of $380,000 omits the $30,000 of cumulative dividends for the year ended May 31, Year 2. Answer (C) is incorrect. The amount of $206,000 is based on a flat rate of $1 per share of stock.

28. A 10% stock dividend **most** likely

A. Increases the size of the firm.

B. Increases shareholders' wealth.

C. Decreases future earnings per share.

D. Decreases net income.

Answer (C) is correct.
REQUIRED: The most likely effect of a stock dividend.
DISCUSSION: A stock dividend is a transfer of equity from retained earnings to paid-in capital. The debit is to retained earnings, and the credits are to common stock and additional paid-in capital. Additional shares are outstanding following the stock dividend, but every shareholder maintains the same percentage of ownership. In effect, a stock dividend divides the pie (the corporation) into more pieces, but the pie is still the same size. Hence, a corporation will have a lower EPS and a lower book value per share following a stock dividend, but every shareholder will be just as well off as previously. A stock dividend has no effect except on the composition of the shareholders' equity section of the balance sheet.

29. In practice, dividends

A. Usually exhibit greater stability than earnings.

B. Fluctuate more widely than earnings.

C. Tend to be a lower percentage of earnings for mature firms.

D. Are usually changed every year to reflect earnings changes.

Answer (A) is correct.
REQUIRED: The true statement about dividends and their relation to earnings.
DISCUSSION: Dividend policy determines the portion of net income distributed to stockholders. Corporations normally try to maintain a stable level of dividends, even though profits may fluctuate considerably, because many stockholders buy stock with the expectation of receiving a certain dividend every year. Thus, management tends not to raise dividends if the payout cannot be sustained. The desire for stability has led theorists to propound the information content or signaling hypothesis: A change in dividend policy is a signal to the market regarding management's forecast of future earnings. This stability often results in a stock that sells at a higher market price because stockholders perceive less risk in receiving their dividends.
Answer (B) is incorrect. Most companies try to maintain stable dividends. Answer (C) is incorrect. Mature firms have less need of earnings to reinvest for expansion; thus, they tend to pay a higher percentage of earnings as dividends. Answer (D) is incorrect. Most companies try to maintain stable dividends.

30. When a company desires to increase the market value per share of common stock, the company will implement

A. The sale of treasury stock.

B. A reverse stock split.

C. The sale of preferred stock.

D. A stock split.

Answer (B) is correct.
REQUIRED: The transaction that increases the market value per share of common stock.
DISCUSSION: A reverse stock split decreases the number of shares outstanding, thereby increasing the market price per share. A reverse stock split may be desirable when a stock is selling at such a low price that management is concerned that investors will avoid the stock because it has an undesirable image.
Answer (A) is incorrect. A sale of treasury stock increases the supply of shares and could lead to a decline in market price. Answer (C) is incorrect. A sale of preferred stock will take dollars out of investors' hands, thereby reducing funds available to invest in common stock; therefore, market price per share of common stock will not increase. Answer (D) is incorrect. A stock split increases the shares issued and outstanding. The market price per share is likely to decline as a result.

2.7 ESSAY QUESTIONS

Scenario for Essay Questions 1, 2

Venture Corporation is planning a large capital expenditure program to add plant capacity and to modernize manufacturing equipment. The company's projections of fund flows reveal that available internal sources of funds will not be adequate to finance the capital investment program.

A preferred stock issue has been suggested because the capital requirement is long-term and Venture has never had a preferred stock issue in its capital structure. Top management has asked the treasurer to investigate thoroughly the general attributes of preferred stock. Major points to consider that came immediately to the mind of the treasurer included cost, financial risk, and capital structure flexibility. The treasurer plans to address these points as well as any other important issues in his analysis.

Questions

1. Identify and explain the principal provisions or features usually associated with preferred stock.

2. From the viewpoint of a prospective industrial issuer, explain the advantages and disadvantages of preferred stock with respect to the financing alternatives of common stock and long-term debt.

Essay Questions 1, 2 — Unofficial Answers

1.   The principal provisions or features usually associated with preferred stock include

  - Priority dividends over common stock -- preferred dividends must be paid before common stock dividends are paid; in liquidation, preferred stock has priority equal to par value plus dividends in arrears.
  - Accumulation of dividends.
  - Limited voting privileges that usually are allowed only when dividends are in arrears.

2.   Preferred stock should be recognized as a hybrid form of financing, combining provisions from both debt and equity financing. The principal advantage of the financing with preferred stock is the flexibility provided through

  - The ability to defer dividends in time of financial hardship.
  - The fact that there is no specific maturity date and a fixed capital outlay is not required unless there is a sinking fund provision.

Other advantages of preferred stock include the fact that

  - The earnings per share are not diluted unless there is a participating provision.
  - The equity base is expanded with no, or only minimal, loss of control.
  - Due to the fixed dividend payment, the potential of financial leverage exists, although not to the same degree as debt financing.

The major disadvantages of preferred stock are the cost and restrictions that any special provisions provide. The cost disadvantage is twofold:

  - The dividend rate normally exceeds the debt interest rate.
  - The dividends paid are not tax deductible.

The special restrictions that may apply include

  - Voting rights that may restrict management control.
  - Redemption and/or sinking fund provisions that may reduce management control over liquidity or capital structure or earnings to common stockholders.

 Access the **Gleim CMA Premium Review System** from your Gleim Personal Classroom to continue your studies with exam-emulating essay questions!

STUDY UNIT THREE
VALUATION METHODS AND COST OF CAPITAL

(19 pages of outline)

This study unit is the **second of four** on **corporate finance**. The relative weight assigned to this major topic in Part 2 of the exam is **20%**. The four study units are

Study Unit 2: Financial Markets and Types of Securities
Study Unit 3: Valuation Methods and Cost of Capital
Study Unit 4: Managing Current Assets
Study Unit 5: Corporate Restructuring and International Finance

If you are interested in reviewing more introductory or background material, go to www.gleim.com/CMAIntroVideos for a list of suggested third-party overviews of this topic. The following Gleim outline material is more than sufficient to help you pass the CMA exam; any additional introductory or background material is for your own personal enrichment.

3.1 STOCK VALUATION METHODS

1. **Stock Valuation**

    a. The method of valuing a bond shown in item 5. in Study Unit 2, Subunit 4, can also be used for preferred stock.

       1) If the preferred dividend rate is less than what is prevalent in the market, then the preferred stock will sell at less than its par value.

       2) A dividend rate higher than the market average (based on a similar risk level) will result in the preferred stock selling at a premium.

       3) The discount rate used would normally be higher than that used for a bond valuation because a preferred stock is slightly more risky than a bond but has few additional advantages (other than the aforementioned advantage that preferred dividends are sometimes taxed at lower tax rates than bond interest).

    b. Common stocks can be valued in the same way, but the return is based on earnings per share rather than dividend level. Also, with common stocks, the future returns are pure estimates, so there is usually a heavy risk premium incorporated into the calculation.

       1) For example, if a bond could be sold at its face value based on an 8% interest rate, a similar preferred stock might necessitate a 10% return because of the increased risk.

       2) At the same time, a common stock might have to be valued on an assumed return of 20%. Because investors in common stock fear the risk of never getting future returns, a high risk premium must be used to calculate the common stock's value.

2.   **The Constant Growth Dividend Discount Model**

   a.   The constant growth dividend discount model (also known as the dividend growth model) is a method of arriving at the value of a stock by using expected dividends per share and discounting them back to present value. The formula is as follows:

$$\frac{Dividend\ per\ share}{Discount\ rate\ -\ Dividend\ growth\ rate}$$

   1)   This method is used when dividends are expected to grow at a constant rate. If the value obtained using this formula is greater than the stock's current fair market value, then the stock is considered to be undervalued (meaning it is worth more than its fair market value).

   b.   EXAMPLE: A company recently paid an annual dividend of $10. Dividends have grown steadily at a rate of 5% and are expected to continue indefinitely. Investors require a 12% rate of return (cost of capital) for similar investments. The value of this stock can be calculated as

$$\frac{\$10 \times (1 + .05)}{.12 - .05} = \$150$$

   c.   In order to calculate the correct dividend per share amount when given only the amount of the last annual dividend paid or the current-year earnings, it is necessary to calculate the expected dividend using the growth rate of the company.

$$Expected\ dividend = Last\ annual\ dividend\ paid \times (1 + Growth\ rate)^t$$

   t = time (years, months, periods, etc.)

3.   **Common Stock with Variable Dividend Growth**

   a.   Dividends do not always grow at a constant rate. This can make stock valuation more difficult. Many companies experience a two-stage growth. In the initial phase, growth can be very rapid and unstable. In the second phase, growth slows down and stabilizes. In these situations, the **two-stage dividend discount model** can be used to effectively calculate the stock value. This calculation requires three steps:

   1)   Calculate and sum the present value of dividends in the period of high growth.
   2)   Calculate the present value of the stock based on the period of steady growth, discounting the value back to Year 1.
   3)   Sum the totals calculated in Step 1 and Step 2.

   b.   EXAMPLE: Rapido Company expects to pay an annual dividend of $5 at the end of this year. Annual growth is expected to be at 20% for the next 2 years, after which growth is expected to stabilize at 8%. Investors require a 12% rate of return (cost of capital) for similar stock.

   Step 1: Calculate and sum the present value of dividends in the period of high growth.

End of Year	Dividend	PV Factor at 12%	PV of Dividend
1	$5.00	.893	$ 4.47
2	$5 × (1 + .20) = $6.00	.797	4.78
3	$6 × (1+.20) = $7.20	.712	5.13
		Total PV of Dividends	$14.38

   Step 2: Calculate the present value of the stock based on the period of steady growth and discount it back to Year 1. This is done using the constant growth dividend discount model. The end of Year 4 dividend is $7.78, calculated by taking the end of Year 3 dividend and multiplying it by 1 plus the Year 4 rate [$7.20 × (1 + .08)].

$$\frac{Dividend\ per\ share}{Discount\ rate\ -\ Dividend\ growth\ rate}$$

$$\frac{\$ 7.78}{.12 - .08} = \$194.50$$

Then discount the value back to Year 1, using the present value factor from the Year 3 column in the Present Value table.

$$\$194.50 \times .712 = \$138.48$$

Step 3: Sum the totals calculated in Step 1 and Step 2.

$$\$14.38 + \$138.48 = \$152.86$$

Based on the two-stage dividend discount model, $152.86 is an appropriate value for this stock, given the projected dividends per share and cost of capital.

4. **Preferred Stock Valuation**

    a. Preferred stock usually pays a fixed dividend. When this is the case, the value of the stock can be calculated as follows:

$$\frac{Dividend\ per\ share}{Cost\ of\ capital}$$

This formula also can be used when dividends on common stock are not expected to grow.

        1) EXAMPLE: Several years ago, a company issued preferred stock that pays a fixed dividend each year of $12. Investors require a 15% rate of return (cost of capital) for similar preferred stock. The value of this stock can be calculated as

$$\frac{\$12}{.15} = \$80$$

5. **Per-Share Ratios**

    a. A high price/EBITDA ratio reflects the stock market's positive assessment of the firm's generation of profits through ongoing operations. It measures how much an investor must spend to "buy" a dollar of EBITDA.

Price/EBITDA Ratio

$$\frac{Market\ price\ per\ share}{EBITDA\ per\ share}$$

        1) The origin of the EBITDA measure can be traced back to the technology boom of the 1990s. High tech companies were producing very little income, so investment bankers became creative in how they defined profits.

            a) Under the guise of comparability, the argument was that a company with debt that was paying interest expense should not be compared on a profit basis with a closely related company that operated without debt.

                i) In other words, two companies could be selling the same product at the same prices and have the same cost structure and operating income, but the company with debt would have a lower net income.

            b) The investment bankers' answer to this problem was to simply compare the operating earnings before deducting non-cash expenses.

        2) There are numerous benefits to using EBITDA, including operational comparability and as a proxy for cash flows. For example, because depreciation and amortization require cash outlays, their exclusion results in a number approximating current cash flows. However, the disadvantages of EBITDA outweigh the advantages.

        3) Disadvantages of EBITDA

            a) Overstates income: EBITDA distorts reality. From a stockholder's standpoint, investors are most concerned with the level of income and cash flow available after all expenses, including interest expense, depreciation expense, and income tax expense.

        b)   Neglects working capital requirements: EBITDA may actually be a decent proxy for cash flows for many companies; however, this profit measure does not account for the working capital needs of a business. For example, companies reporting high EBITDA figures may actually have dramatically lower cash flows once working capital requirements (i.e., inventories, receivables, payables) are tabulated.

        c)   Is not effective for valuation: Investment bankers push for more generous EBITDA valuation multiples because it serves the bankers' and clients' best interests. However, companies with debt deserve lower valuations compared to their debt-free counterparts.

    4)   Despite EBITDA's comparability benefits, and as much as investment bankers would like to use this metric, beware of EBITDA's shortcomings. Although most analysts are looking for the one-size-fits-all number, the reality of the situation is that a variety of methods need to be used to gain a more accurate financial picture of a company.

b.   **Book value per share** equals the amount of net assets available to the common shareholders divided by the number of common shares outstanding.

$$\frac{\textit{Total stockholders' equity} - \textit{Preferred equity}}{\textit{Number of common shares outstanding}}$$

    1)   When a company has preferred as well as common stock outstanding, the computation of book value per common share must consider potential claims by preferred shareholders, such as whether the preferred stock is cumulative and in arrears, or participating. It must also take into account whether the call price (or possibly the liquidation value) exceeds the carrying amount of the preferred stock.

    2)   The limitation of book value per share is that it is a valuation based solely on the amounts recorded in the books.

        a)   Unlike market value, book value does not consider future earnings potential in determining a company's valuation.

        b)   The recorded values of assets on the books are subject to accounting estimates (e.g., choice of depreciation method) that may vary across companies within the same industry. Consequently, net assets may be overstated if estimates are inaccurate.

        c)   Additionally, those same assets may be pledged as collateral on a loan. However, a pledge of collateral is not recorded as a liability on the books. Thus, book value will not account for this potential liability.

c.   The **price-earnings (P/E) ratio** equals the market price per share of common stock divided by EPS.

$$\frac{\textit{Market price}}{\textit{EPS}}$$

    1)   Growth companies are likely to have high P/E ratios. A high P/E ratio reflects the stock market's positive assessment of the firm's earnings quality and prospects.

    2)   Because of the widespread use of the P/E ratio and other measures, the relationship between accounting data and stock prices is crucial. Thus, managers have an incentive to "manage earnings," sometimes by fraudulent means.

        a)   A decrease in investors' required rate of return will cause share prices to go up, which will result in a higher P/E ratio.

        b)   A decline in the rate of dividend growth will cause the share price to decline, which will result in a lower P/E ratio.

          c)   An increasing dividend yield indicates that share price is declining, which will result in a lower P/E ratio.

    d.   **Market-to-book ratio** (also called the price-book ratio).

$$\frac{Market\ price\ per\ share}{Book\ value\ per\ share}$$

       1)   Well-managed firms should sell at high multiples of their book value, which reflects historical cost.

    e.   **Price-sales ratio** is preferred by some analysts over profit ratios.

$$\frac{Market\ price\ per\ share}{Sales\ per\ share}$$

       1)   Analysts who use the price-sales ratio believe that strong sales are the basic ingredient of profits and that sales are the item on the financial statements least subject to manipulation.

6.   **Earnings per Share (EPS)**

    a.   EPS is probably the most heavily relied-upon performance measure used by investors. EPS states the amount of current-period earnings that can be associated with a single share of a corporation's common stock.

       1)   EPS is only calculated for common stock because common shareholders are the residual owners of a corporation. Since preferred shareholders have superior claim to the firm's earnings, amounts associated with preferred stock must be removed during the calculation of EPS.

    b.   A corporation is said to have a simple capital structure if the following two conditions apply:

       1)   The firm has only common stock; i.e., there are no preferred shareholders with a superior claim to earnings in the form of dividends; and

       2)   The firm has no dilutive potential common stock.

           a)   Potential common stock (PCS) is a security or other contract that may entitle the holder to obtain common stock. Examples include convertible securities, stock options and warrants, and contingently issuable common stock.

           b)   Potential common stock is said to be dilutive if its inclusion in the calculation of EPS results in a reduction of EPS.

    c.   A firm with a simple capital structure only has to report a single category of EPS, called basic earnings per share (BEPS).

       1)   A firm with preferred stock or dilutive potential common stock must report two categories of EPS, BEPS and diluted earnings per share (DEPS).

    d.   **Earnings per share (EPS)** equals net income available to common shareholders divided by the average number of shares outstanding for the period.

$$\frac{Net\ income\ available\ to\ common\ shareholders}{Weighted\ average\ common\ shares\ outstanding}$$

       1)   Net income available to common shareholders is net income minus preferred dividends.

       2)   Both basic and diluted EPS must be presented.

       3)   Stock dividends and stock splits are deemed to have occurred at the beginning of the period.

e.   **Diluted Earnings Per Share (DEPS)**

1)   The numerator is increased by the amounts that would not have had to be paid if dilutive potential common stock had been converted, namely, dividends on convertible preferred stock and after-tax interest on convertible debt.

2)   The denominator is increased by the weighted-average number of additional shares of common stock that would have been outstanding if dilutive potential common stock had been converted.

7.   **Other Market-Based Measures**

a.   Increasing shareholder wealth is the fundamental goal of any corporation. Four common ratios measure the degree of success toward this goal.

b.   Earnings yield is the rate of return on the purchase price of a share of common stock. It is the reciprocal of the P/E ratio and thus measures the amount of earnings an investor expects to receive per dollar invested.

Earnings Yield

$$\frac{Earnings\ per\ share}{Market\ price\ per\ share}$$

1)   The earnings yield can be compared by investors to other types of investments to determine whether a given stock is comparable to other stocks in the industry or to alternative uses of the investment money.

c.   The dividend payout ratio measures what portion of accrual-basis earnings was actually paid out to common shareholders in the form of dividends.

Dividend Payout Ratio

$$\frac{Dividends\ to\ common\ shareholders}{IACS}$$

1)   Growth companies tend to have a low payout, preferring to use earnings to continue growing the firm.

d.   A related ratio is the dividend yield.

Dividend Yield

$$\frac{Dividend\ per\ share}{Market\ price\ per\ share}$$

1)   Various investors have different desires with respect to dividend yield. Historically, many long-term investors wanted a low dividend yield because capital gains were taxed at a lower tax rate than dividends; thus, letting the earnings accumulate within the company resulted in a lower overall tax expense.

a)   However, in recent years, the tax rate on dividends has been as low or lower than that on capital gains; thus, a high dividend yield has come into vogue.

2)   Also, investors in different circumstances have different perspectives on dividend yield. For example, a retiree wants regular income and therefore wants to see a high dividend yield. A person who is years away from retirement would prefer a lower dividend yield with the earnings reinvested in the business.

e.   Shareholder return measures the return on a purchase of stock.

Shareholder Return

$$\frac{Ending\ stock\ price\ -\ Beginning\ stock\ price\ +\ Annual\ dividends\ per\ share}{Beginning\ stock\ price}$$

Stop and review! You have completed the outline for this subunit. Study multiple-choice questions 1 through 9 beginning on page 97.

3.2 OPTIONS AND DERIVATIVES

1. **Overview**

    a. A **derivative instrument** is an investment transaction in which the parties' gain or loss is derived from some other economic event, for example, the price of a given stock, a foreign currency exchange rate, or the price of a certain commodity.

        1) One party enters into the transaction to speculate (incur risk), and the other enters into it to hedge (avoid risk).

    b. Derivatives are a type of financial instrument, along with cash, accounts receivable, notes receivable, bonds, preferred shares, common shares, etc. Derivatives are not, however, claims on business assets, such as those represented by equity securities.

2. **Hedging**

    a. Hedging is the process of using offsetting commitments to minimize or avoid the impact of adverse price movements.

    b. A person who would like to sell an asset in the future has a **long position** in the asset because (s)he benefits from a rise in value of the asset.

        1) To protect against a decline in value, the owner can enter into a short hedge, i.e., obtain an instrument whose value will rise if the asset's value falls.

        2) EXAMPLE: A soybean farmer hopes that the price of soybeans will rise by the time his crop is ready to go to market. The farmer is thus long in soybeans. To protect against the possibility that the price will fall in the meantime, he can obtain a short hedge.

    c. A person who would like to buy an asset in the future has a **short position** in the asset because (s)he benefits from a fall in value of the asset.

        1) To protect against a rise in value, the party can enter into a long hedge, i.e., obtain an instrument whose value will rise if the asset's value rises.

        2) EXAMPLE: An agricultural wholesaler hopes that the price of soybeans will fall by the time farmers are bringing their harvests to the warehouse. The wholesaler is thus short in soybeans. To protect against the possibility that the price will rise in the meantime, the wholesaler can obtain a long hedge.

3. **Options**

    a. Options are the most common form of derivative.

        1) A party who buys an option has bought the right to demand that the counterparty (the seller or "writer" of the option) perform some action on or before a specified future date.

        2) The exercise of an option is always at the discretion of the option holder (the buyer) who has, in effect, bought the right to exercise the option or not. The seller of an option has no choice; (s)he must perform if the holder chooses to exercise.

    b. An option has an expiration date after which it can no longer be exercised.

        1) An option that can be exercised only on its expiration date is referred to as a European option.

        2) An option that grants the buyer the right to exercise anytime on or before expiration is an American option.

    c. Determining the correct price for an option is a complex calculation, discussed in item 7. in this subunit.

        1) The **exercise price** (or strike price) is the price at which the owner can purchase or sell the asset underlying the option contract.

        2) The **option price**, also called **option premium**, is the amount the buyer pays to the seller to acquire an option.

    d.   An option can be covered or uncovered.

        1)   A covered option is one in which the seller (writer) already has possession of the underlying.

        2)   A naked (uncovered) option is a speculative instrument; since the writer does not hold the underlying, (s)he may have to acquire it at an unknown price in the future to satisfy his or her obligations under the option contract.

    e.   Options can be classified by their underlying assets.

        1)   A stock option is an option whose underlying asset is a traded stock.

        2)   An index option is an option whose underlying asset is a market index. If exercised, settlement is made by cash since delivery of the underlying is impossible.

        3)   Long-term equity anticipation securities (LEAPS) are examples of long-term stock options or index options, with expiration dates up to 3 years away.

        4)   Foreign currency options give the holder the right to buy a specific foreign currency at a designated exchange rate.

  4. **Call Options**

    a.   A call option gives the buyer (holder) the **right to purchase** (i.e., the right to "call" for) the underlying asset (stock, currency, commodity, etc.) at a fixed price.

        1)   If the price of the underlying rises above the exercise price, the option is said to be "in-the-money." The holder can exercise his or her option and buy the underlying at a bargain price.

            a)   The **intrinsic value** of a call option is the price of the underlying asset less the exercise price. Intrinsic value cannot be less than zero.

        2)   If the value of the underlying is less than the exercise price of the option, the option is "out-of-the-money," or not worth exercising.

        3)   If the value of the underlying is equal to the exercise price of the option, the option is said to be "at-the-money."

    b.   Thus, a call option represents a long position to the holder because the holder benefits from a price increase.

        1)   The seller (writer) of a call option hopes the price of the underlying will remain below the exercise price because (s)he must make the underlying available to the holder at the strike price, regardless of how much the seller must pay to obtain it. The seller of a call option is thus taking a short position.

    c.   The buyer's gain (loss) necessarily mirrors the seller's loss (gain). The amount of gain and loss on a call option can be calculated as follows:

        1)   Buyer/holder (long position):

Units of underlying × (Excess of market price over exercise price − Option price)

        2)   Seller/writer (short position):

Units of underlying × (Option price − Excess of market price over exercise price)

    d.   EXAMPLE of an in-the-money call option: Tapworth Co. bought call options giving it the right to buy 100 shares of PanGlobal Corp. stock in 30 days at $100 per share. Smith Co. sold these options to Tapworth for $3 per share. On Day 30, PanGlobal stock is trading at $105 and Tapworth exercises all of its options (since the options give Tapworth the right to buy PanGlobal stock at a better-than-market price). Tapworth's and Smith's respective gains and losses on the transaction can be calculated as follows:

Buyer's gain (loss) = 100 call options × [($105 − $100) − $3] = $200 gain
Seller's gain (loss) = 100 call options × [$3 − ($105 − $100)] = $(200) loss

e. EXAMPLE of an out-of-the-money call option: On Day 30, PanGlobal stock is trading at $97 and Tapworth's options are worthless (since having the right to buy PanGlobal at $100 gives Tapworth no advantage over buying on the open market). Tapworth's and Smith's respective gains and losses on the transaction can be calculated as follows:

> Buyer's gain (loss) = 100 call options × ($0 – $3) = $(300) loss
> Seller's gain (loss) = 100 call options × ($3 – $0) = $300 gain

f. The relationship between the buyer and seller of a call option can be depicted in the following diagram:

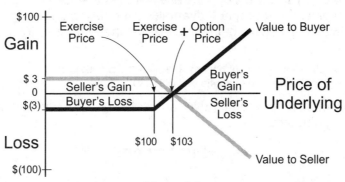

Call Options

Figure 3-1

Clearly, the accurate valuation of options is crucial.

5. **Put Options**

a. A put option gives the buyer (holder) the **right to sell** (i.e., the right to "put" onto the market) the underlying asset (stock, currency, commodity, etc.) at a fixed price.

1) If the price of the underlying falls below the exercise price, the option is said to be "in-the-money." The holder can exercise his or her option and compel the counterparty to buy the underlying at a price higher than that prevailing in the market.

a) The **intrinsic value** of a put option is the exercise price less the price of the underlying asset. Intrinsic value cannot be less than zero.

2) If the value of the underlying is higher than the exercise price of the option, the option is "out-of-the-money," or not worth exercising.

3) If the value of the underlying is equal to the exercise price of the option, the option is said to be "at-the-money."

b. Thus, a put option represents a short position to the holder because the holder benefits from a price decrease.

1) The seller (writer) of a put option hopes the price of the underlying investment will remain above the exercise price, since (s)he must buy from the holder at the strike price, regardless of the fact that the same underlying can be obtained for less in the open market. The seller of a put option is thus taking a long position.

c. The buyer's gain (loss) necessarily mirrors the seller's loss (gain). The amount of gain and loss on a put option can be calculated as follows:

1) Buyer/holder (short position):

Units of underlying × (Excess of exercise price over market price – Option price)

2) Seller/writer (long position):

Units of underlying × (Option price – Excess of exercise price over market price)

d.   EXAMPLE of an in-the-money put option: Tapworth Co. bought put options giving it the right to sell 100 shares of PanGlobal Corp. stock in 30 days at $100 per share. Smith Co. sold these options to Tapworth for $3 per share. On Day 30, PanGlobal stock is trading at $92 and Tapworth exercises all of its options (since the options give Tapworth the right to sell PanGlobal stock at a price higher than the one prevailing in the market). Tapworth's and Smith's respective gains and losses on the transaction can be calculated as follows:

Buyer's gain (loss) = 100 put options × [($100 − $92) − $3] = $500 gain
Seller's gain (loss) = 100 put options × [$3 − ($100 − $92)] = $(500) loss

e.   EXAMPLE of an out-of-the-money put option: On Day 30, PanGlobal stock is trading at $104 and Tapworth's options are worthless (since having options to sell PanGlobal at $100 gives Tapworth no advantage over selling on the open market). Tapworth's and Smith's respective gains and losses on the transaction can be calculated as follows:

Buyer's gain (loss) = 100 put options × ($0 − $3) = $(300) loss
Seller's gain (loss) = 100 put options × ($3 − $0) = $300 gain

f.   The relationship between a buyer and seller of a put option can be depicted in the following diagram:

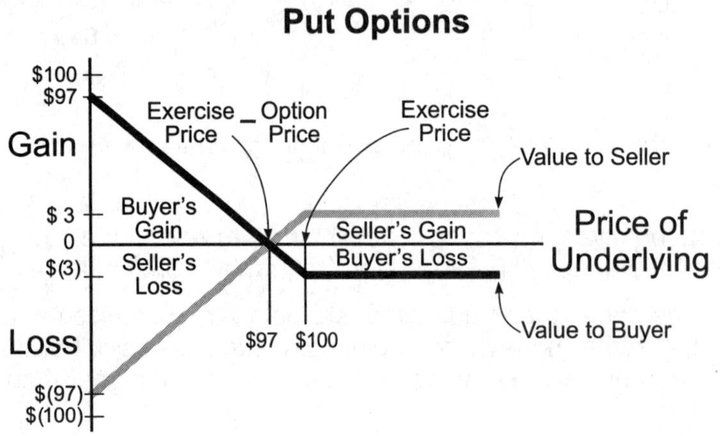

Put Options

Figure 3-2

6.   **Put-Call Parity**

a.   The put-call parity theorem mathematically depicts the combinations of investment strategies that can be devised using European options (i.e., those with a single exercise date). The two sides of this equation represent combinations with identical outcomes (given identical exercise prices for the put and the call and identical expiration dates):

Value of call + PV of exercise price* = Value of put + Value of underlying

* Discounted at the risk-free rate

1)   Look first at the left side of the equation. The buyer of a call may wish to hedge against the loss that (s)he will incur if the market price of the underlying fails to rise sufficiently. The buyer can do this by investing the present value of the exercise price in a safe investment. If the option is out-of-the-money on the expiration date, the option holder has the return from this safe investment to make up for the loss.

2) Look next at the right side of the equation. The buyer of a put may wish to hedge against the loss that (s)he will incur if the market price of the underlying fails to fall sufficiently. The buyer can do this by buying the underlying at the same time as the option. If the option is out-of-the-money on the expiration date, the option holder can simply sell the underlying at the going market price to make up for the loss.

b. The basic formula can be restated to depict the investment strategy that provides a **risk-free return**:

$$PV \text{ of exercise price} = Value \text{ of put} + Value \text{ of underlying} - Value \text{ of call}$$

1) In other words, the combination of buying a put option, buying the underlying, and selling a call option provides the same return as investing the present value of the exercise price at the risk-free rate. Knowledge of these relationships can help investors devise appropriate option strategies.

7. **Valuing an Option**

a. The two most well-known models for valuing options are the Black-Scholes formula for call options and the binomial method. The equations themselves are extremely complex and beyond the scope of an accounting text, but some general statements can be made about the factors that affect the outcomes.

1) **Exercise price.** In general, the buyer of a call option benefits from a low exercise price. Likewise, the buyer of a put option generally benefits from a high exercise price.

a) Thus, an increase in the exercise price of an option results in a decrease in the value of a call option and an increase in the value of a put option.

2) **Price of underlying.** As the price of the underlying increases, the value of a call option also will increase; the exercise price is more and more of a bargain with each additional dollar in the price of the underlying.

a) By the same token, the value of a put option will decrease as the price of the underlying increases since there is no advantage in selling at a lower-than-market price.

3) **Interest rates.** Buying a call option is like buying the underlying on credit. The purchase of the option is a form of down payment. If the option is exercised in a period of rising interest rates, the exercise price is paid in inflated dollars, making it more attractive for the option holder.

a) A rise in interest rates will therefore result in a rise in the value of a call option and a fall in the value of a put option.

4) **Time until expiration.** The more time that passes, the riskier any investment is.

a) Thus, an increase in the term of an option (both calls and puts) will result in an increase in the value of the option.

5) **Volatility of price of underlying.** The price of an asset can drop no lower than zero. Thus, there is a natural limit to the potential downside loss for either party to an option transaction. On the upside, however, there is much greater flexibility. Thus, parties to an option transaction will prefer volatility.

a) An increase in the volatility of the price of the underlying will result in an increase in the value of the option (both calls and puts).

b.   These factors and their effects can be summarized as follows:

Increase in	Value of call option will	Value of put option will
Exercise price of option	Decrease	Increase
Price of underlying	Increase	Decrease
Interest rates	Increase	Decrease
Time until expiration	Increase	Increase
Volatility of price of underlying	Increase	Increase

8.   **Forward Contracts**

a.   One method of mitigating risk is the simple forward contract. The two parties agree that, at a set future date, one of them will perform and the other will pay a specified amount for the performance.

   1)   A common example is that of a retailer and a wholesaler who agree in September on the prices and quantities of merchandise that will be shipped to the retailer's stores in time for the winter holiday season. The retailer has locked in a price and a source of supply, and the wholesaler has locked in a price and a customer.

b.   The party that has contracted to buy the underlying at a future date has taken a long position, and the party that has contracted to deliver the underlying has taken a short position. The payoff structure is similar to that for options:

   1)   If the market price of the underlying on the delivery date is higher than the contractual price, the party that has taken the long position benefits, since (s)he has locked in a lower price.

   2)   If the market price of the underlying on the delivery date is lower than the contractual price, the party that has taken the short position benefits, since (s)he is entitled to receive higher payment for the underlying than the amount currently prevailing in the market.

c.   Note the significant difference between a forward contract and an option: In a contract, both parties must meet their contractual obligations, i.e., to deliver merchandise and to pay. Neither has the option of nonperformance.

9.   **Futures Contracts**

a.   A forward contract like the one described above is appropriate for a retailer and a wholesaler, who are exchanging very specific merchandise and can take the time to address all the facets of the contract.

   1)   Traders in undifferentiated commodities, such as grains, metals, fossil fuels, and foreign currencies, often do not have this luxury. The trading process of these products is eased by the use of futures contracts.

   2)   A futures contract is a commitment to buy or sell an asset at a fixed price during a specific future month; unlike with a forward contract, the counterparty is unknown.

b.   Futures contracts are actively traded on futures exchanges.

   1)   Because futures contracts are for delivery during a given month, not a specific day, they are more flexible arrangements than forward contracts.

   2)   The clearinghouse randomly matches sellers who will deliver during a given month with buyers who are seeking delivery during the same month.

    c.   Because futures contracts are actively traded, the result is a liquid market in futures that permits buyers and sellers to net out their positions.

        1)   For example, a party who has sold a contract can net out his or her position by buying a futures contract. In contrast, a person holding a forward contract does not enjoy this liquidity.

    d.   Another distinguishing feature of futures contracts is that their prices are marked to market every day at the close of the day to each person's account. Thus, the market price is posted at the close of business each day.

        1)   A mark-to-market provision minimizes a futures contract's chance of default because profits and losses on the contracts must be received or paid each day through a clearinghouse.

        2)   This requirement of daily settlement minimizes default and is necessary because futures contracts are sold on margin (i.e., they are highly leveraged).

    e.   Another difference is that a party to a forward contract typically expects actual delivery; futures contracts are generally used as financial tools to offset the risks of changing economic conditions. Thus, the two parties simply exchange the difference between the contracted price and the market price prior to the expiration date.

        1)   This is why a trader who does not want to accidentally have to settle in a certain month buys a future for the following month.

10. Swaps

    a.   Swaps are contracts by which the parties exchange cash flows. Three types are common:

        1)   **Interest rate swaps** are agreements to exchange interest payments based on one interest structure for payments based on another structure.

            a)   For example, a firm that has fixed debt service charges may enter into a swap with a counterparty that agrees to supply the first party with interest payments based on a floating rate that more closely tracks the first party's revenues.

            b)   These agreements are highly customized.

        2)   **Currency swaps** are agreements to exchange cash flows denominated in one currency for cash flows denominated in another.

            a)   For example, a U.S. firm with revenues in euros has to pay suppliers and workers in dollars, not euros. To minimize exchange-rate risk, it might agree to exchange euros for dollars held by a firm that needs euros.

            b)   The exchange rate will be an average of the rates expected over the life of the agreement.

        3)   **Credit default swaps** are agreements whereby one of the parties indemnifies the other against default by a third party.

            a)   For example, a large bank may agree to pay a constant stream of cash to another bank as long as one of the first bank's major debtors remains current on its loans. If the customer defaults, the second bank covers the first bank's loss. One of the parties is, in effect, providing loan default insurance to the other party.

            b)   Unlike interest rate swaps, these agreements are usually bundled into large portfolios.

    b.   The swap spread is the market-determined additional yield that compensates counterparties who receive fixed payments in a swap for the credit risk involved in the swap. The swap spread will differ with the creditworthiness of the counterparty.

    c.   Most swaps are priced to be at-the-money at inception, meaning that the value of the two sets of cash flows being exchanged is the same. Naturally, as interest rates, currency exchange rates, and credit risks change, the values of the swaps will change.

11. Options can be invested in as a speculative form of investment. Alternatively, if they are combined with other positions, they can also be used in hedging.

Stop and review! You have completed the outline for this subunit. Study multiple-choice questions 10 through 16 beginning on page 100.

3.3 COST OF CAPITAL -- CURRENT

1. **Overview**

    a. Investors provide funds to corporations with the understanding that management will deploy those funds in such a way that the investor will ultimately receive a return.

        1) If management does not generate the **investors' required rate of return**, the investors will take their funds out of the corporation and redirect them to more profitable ventures.

        2) For this reason, the investors' required rate of return (also called their opportunity cost of capital) in turn becomes the firm's cost of capital.

    b. A firm's cost of capital is typically used to discount the future cash flows of long-term projects, since investments with a return higher than the cost of capital will increase the value of the firm, i.e., shareholders' wealth. (The cost of capital is not used in connection with working capital because short-term needs are met with short-term funds.)

2. **Component Costs of Capital**

    a. As described in Study Unit 2, Subunits 4 and 5, a firm's financing structure consists of three components: long-term debt, preferred equity, and common equity (retained earnings are treated as part of common equity in this analysis for reasons given below). The rate of return demanded by holders of each is the component cost for that form of capital.

        1) The component cost of **debt** is the after-tax interest rate on the debt (interest payments are tax-deductible by the firm):

            Effective rate × (1.0 − Marginal tax rate)

        2) The component cost of **preferred stock** is computed using the dividend yield ratio:

            Cash dividend on preferred stock ÷ Market price of preferred stock

        3) The component cost of **common stock** is also computed using the dividend yield ratio:

            Cash dividend on common stock ÷ Market price of common stock

        4) Generally, the component cost of **retained earnings** is considered to be the same as that for common stock (if the firm cannot find a profitable use for retained earnings, it should be distributed to the common shareholders in the form of dividends so that they can find their own alternative investments).

    b. Providers of equity capital are exposed to more risk than are lenders because (1) the firm is not legally obligated to pay them a return and (2) in case of liquidation, equity investors trail creditors in priority. To compensate for this higher level of risk, equity investors demand a higher return, making equity financing more expensive than debt.

CMA candidates will need to be able to determine the weighted-average cost of capital (WACC) and how it is applied in capital structure decisions. On the CMA exam, you will be expected to calculate WALL and the marginal cost of capital and demonstrate that you understand how they will affect investment decisions for a business.

3. **Weighted-Average Cost of Capital**

    a. Corporate management usually designates a **target capital structure** for the firm, i.e., the proportions that each component of capital should comprise in the overall combination. An example might be 10% debt, 20% preferred stock, and 70% common stock.

        1) EXAMPLE: The following excerpt is from a firm's most recent balance sheet:

Component	Carrying Amount	Proportions
11.4% Bonds Payable	$ 2,200,000	10.00%
11.5% Preferred Stock	4,600,000	20.91%
Common Stock	14,000,000	63.64%
Retained Earnings	1,200,000	5.45%
Totals	**$22,000,000**	**100.00%**

    b. A firm's **weighted-average cost of capital (WACC)** is a single, composite rate of return on its combined components of capital. The weights are based on the components' respective market values, not book values, because market value provides the best information about investors' expectations.

        1) EXAMPLE: In order to calculate its WACC, the firm must first determine the component costs of long-term debt and preferred equity. The company has historically provided a 16% return on common equity. The firm is in a 35% marginal tax bracket. Assume that the market price of the preferred stock is the same as the book value.

$$\text{Component cost of long-term debt} = \text{Effective rate} \times (1.0 - \text{Marginal tax rate})$$
$$= 11.4\% \times (1.0 - .35)$$
$$= 7.41\%$$

$$\text{Component cost of preferred equity} = \text{Cash dividend} \div \text{Market price of stock}$$
$$= (\$4,600,000 \times 11.5\%) \div \$4,600,000$$
$$= 11.5\%$$

The firm can now determine its WACC by multiplying the cost of each component of capital by the proportion of total market value represented by that component.

Component	(1) Market Value	(2) Weight		(3) Component Cost		(2) × (3) Weighted Cost
11.4% Bonds Payable	$ 2,200,000	10.00%	×	7.41%	=	0.7410%
11.5% Preferred Stock	4,600,000	20.91%	×	11.5%	=	2.4047%
Common Stock	14,000,000	63.64%	×	16.0%	=	10.1824%
Retained Earnings	1,200,000	5.45%	×	16.0%	=	0.8727%
Totals	**$22,000,000**	**100.00%**				**14.2008%**

Generally, the component cost of retained earnings is considered to be the same as that for common stock.

The firm will invest in projects that have an expected return that is greater than 14.2008% (firm's WACC). These projects will generate additional free cash flow and will create positive net present value for the shareholders.

c.   A formula to calculate the after-tax WACC where there is no preferred stock is

$$WACC = \frac{E}{V} \times R_e + \frac{D}{V} \times R_d \times (1 - T)$$

R_e	= Cost of equity
R_d	= Cost of debt
E	= Market value of the firm's equity
D	= Market value of the firm's debt
T	= Corporate tax rate
V = D + E	= Capital used to generate profits

EXAMPLE

The firm provides the following information:

Capital used to generate profits	
50% debt, 50% equity	$1,200
Cost of equity	15%
Cost of debt	5%
Corporate tax rate	40%

$$WACC = \frac{(1,200 \times 50\%)}{1,200} \times 15\% + \frac{(1,200 \times 50\%)}{1,200} \times 5\% \times (1 - 40\%) = 0.09 = 9\%$$

---

d.   Standard financial theory provides a model for the **optimal capital structure** of every firm. This model holds that shareholder wealth-maximization results from **minimizing the weighted-average cost of capital**. Thus, the focus of management should not be on maximizing earnings per share (EPS can be increased by taking on more debt, but debt increases risk).

1)   The relevant relationships are depicted below:

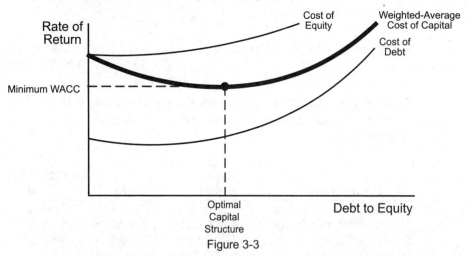

Figure 3-3

Ordinarily, firms cannot identify this optimal point precisely. Thus, they should attempt to find an optimal range for the capital structure.

4.   **Impact of Income Taxes on Capital Structure and Capital Decisions**

a.   Taxes are an important consideration because they can be anywhere from 25% to 50% of all costs.

b.   Corporate capital gains are taxed at a regular rate, and the capital gains of individuals are currently 16% or less.

c.   A dividends-received deduction renders free from taxation anywhere from 70% to 100% of dividends received by one company from investments in the stock of another company. This deduction prevents or reduces double taxation. It also encourages one company to invest in the stock of another company. However, a conflict may arise between the desires of corporate owners and individual owners in that individuals may sometimes prefer capital gains, while corporate owners would prefer dividends.

d.   Interest is a tax-deductible expense of the debtor company, but dividends are not deductible. Thus, a company needing capital would prefer to issue bonds rather than stock because the interest would be deductible. As a result, the issuer would prefer to issue debt because the interest is deductible, but the investor would prefer stock because interest on debt is fully taxable while the return on stock is only partially taxable or taxable at special low rates. Similarly, a corporation may be reluctant to issue common stock because it does not want to share control of the company, but the investor may prefer stock because of the favorable tax treatment.

e.   Multinational corporations frequently derive income from several countries. The government of each country in which a corporation does business may enact statutes imposing one or more types of tax on the corporation, so any capital decision affecting multiple countries must consider the tax provisions of each nation.

Stop and review! You have completed the outline for this subunit. Study multiple-choice questions 17 through 21 beginning on page 102.

3.4 COST OF CAPITAL -- NEW

1.   **Marginal Cost of Capital**

a.   While internally generated capital is the least expensive form of capital, a firm cannot rely solely on retained earnings to fund new projects.

1)   Retained earnings alone are rarely sufficient to fund all of a corporation's long-term needs.

2)   Also, maintaining the firm's optimal capital structure may require the issuance of new securities at some point.

b.   The marginal cost of capital is the cost to the firm of the next dollar of new capital raised after existing internal sources are exhausted.

1)   Each additional dollar raised becomes increasingly expensive as investors demand higher returns to compensate for increased risk.

2)   EXAMPLE: The company has determined that it requires $4,000,000 of new funding to fulfill its plans. Retained earnings are insufficient, and the firm wants to maintain its capital structure of 10% long-term debt, 20% preferred stock, 70% common stock. The cost of raising the $2,800,000 shortfall between retained earnings and funding needs will be at some rate above the current WACC.

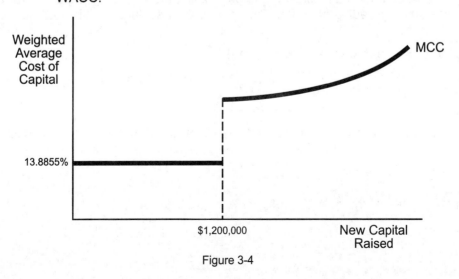

Figure 3-4

2.   **Cost of New Capital**

   a.   The cost of new capital (also called external capital) is the ratio of what the firm must pay to what the firm gets.

   1)   Because of interest rate fluctuations, the **cost of new debt** will rarely be the historical, or embedded, rate. Also, if the firm's debt load is already considerable, new debtholders will demand a higher interest rate to compensate for the increased risk.

   Annual interest ÷ Net issue proceeds

   a)   As tax rates rise, the deductibility of interest makes debt a more attractive financing option.

   2)   All new issues of equity securities involve the payment of flotation costs, which reduce the proceeds received, thereby raising the cost of capital. The **cost of new preferred stock** is thus calculated:

   Next dividend ÷ Net issue proceeds

   3)   The **cost of new common stock** is commonly calculated using the dividend growth model (also known as the discounted cash flow method), which anticipates that common shareholders will demand steadily increasing dividends over time (while assuming that the dividend payout ratio will remain constant).

   (Next dividend ÷ Net issue proceeds) + Dividend growth rate

   a)   An issue of new common stock is used mostly by young, growing companies. Mature firms rarely issue new common stock to the general public because of the issue costs involved and the depressing influence a new issue can have on the stock's price.

   b.   EXAMPLE: Retained earnings are sufficient to cover 30% of the firm's new capital needs ($1,200,000 ÷ $4,000,000). The rest must come from the other three components of capital.

   The company can issue new debt at a cost of 12.6%. The firm can also sell $100 par value preferred stock that pays a 14% dividend and has $5-per-share flotation costs. The $1,200,000 balance of retained earnings will be used, and the remainder will come from an issue of common stock. The new common stock will pay an $8 dividend that is expected to grow 2% annually. The company's common stock is currently trading at $55 per share, and the new issue will have $3-per-share flotation costs.

Cost of new long-term debt = 12.6% (given)

Cost of new preferred stock = Next dividend ÷ Net issue proceeds
                            = $14 ÷ ($100 – $5)
                            = 14.7%

Cost of new common stock = (Next dividend ÷ Net issue proceeds) + Dividend growth rate
                         = [$8 ÷ ($55 – $3)] + 2%
                         = 15.4% + 2%
                         = 17.4%

   Cost of retained earnings = (8 ÷ 55) + 2% = 16.55%

If the company maintains its current capital structure, the weighed-average cost of capital for this round of capital formation is calculated as follows:

Component	Weight		Cost of Capital		Weighted Cost
New long-term debt	10%	×	12.6%	=	1.26%
New preferred stock	20%	×	14.7%	=	2.94%
New common stock	40%	×	17.4%	=	6.96%
Retained earnings	30%	×	16.6%	=	4.98%
Total					**16.14%**

Stop and review! You have completed the outline for this subunit. Study multiple-choice questions 22 through 30 beginning on page 103.

QUESTIONS

3.1 Stock Valuation Methods

1. A company had 150,000 shares outstanding on January 1. On March 1, 75,000 additional shares were issued through a stock dividend. Then on November 1, the company issued 60,000 shares for cash. The number of shares to be used in the denominator of the EPS calculation for the year is

A. 222,500 shares.

B. 225,000 shares.

C. 235,000 shares.

D. 285,000 shares.

Answer (C) is correct.
    REQUIRED: The number of shares to be used in the denominator of the EPS calculation.
    DISCUSSION: The weighted average number of common shares outstanding during the year is the EPS denominator. Shares issued in a stock dividend are assumed to have been outstanding as of the beginning of the earliest accounting period presented. Thus, the 75,000 shares issued on March 1 are deemed to have been outstanding on January 1. The EPS denominator equals 235,000 shares {[150,000 × (12 months ÷ 12 months)] + [75,000 × (12 months ÷ 12 months)] + [60,000 × (2 months ÷ 12 months)]}.
    Answer (A) is incorrect. The weighted-average number of shares is 222,500 if the stock dividend is not treated as retroactive. Answer (B) is incorrect. The 225,000 number of shares ignores the November 1 issuance. Answer (D) is incorrect. The year-end number of outstanding shares is 285,000.

2. The equity section of a Statement of Financial Position is presented below.

Preferred stock, $100 par	$12,000,000
Common stock, $5 par	10,000,000
Paid-in capital in excess of par	18,000,000
Retained earnings	9,000,000
Net worth	$49,000,000

The book value per share of common stock is

A. $18.50

B. $5.00

C. $14.00

D. $100

Answer (A) is correct.
    REQUIRED: The book value per share of common stock.
    DISCUSSION: The book value per common share equals the net assets (equity) attributable to common shareholders divided by the common shares outstanding, or $18.50 [($10,000,000 common stock + $18,000,000 additional paid-in capital + $9,000,000 RE) ÷ ($10,000,000 ÷ $5 par)].
    Answer (B) is incorrect. The amount of $5.00 is the par value per share. Answer (C) is incorrect. The amount of $14.00 fails to include retained earnings in the portion of equity attributable to common shareholders. Answer (D) is incorrect. The amount of $100 is the par value of a preferred share.

Questions 3 and 4 are based on the following information. The Dawson Corporation projects the following for the year:

Earnings before interest and taxes	$35 million
Interest expense	$5 million
Preferred stock dividends	$4 million
Common stock dividend-payout ratio	30%
Common shares outstanding	2 million
Effective corporate income tax rate	40%

3. The expected common stock dividend per share for Dawson Corporation is

- A. $2.34
- B. $2.70
- C. $1.80
- D. $2.10

Answer (D) is correct.
REQUIRED: The expected common stock dividend per share.
DISCUSSION: The company's net income is $18,000,000 [($35,000,000 EBIT – $5,000,000 interest) × (1.0 – .4 tax rate)]. Thus, the earnings available to common shareholders equal $14,000,000 ($18,000,000 – $4,000,000 preferred dividends), and EPS is $7 ($14,000,000 ÷ 2,000,000 common shares). Given a dividend-payout ratio of 30%, the dividend to common shareholders is expected to be $2.10 per share ($7 × 30%).
Answer (A) is incorrect. The amount of $2.34 results from treating preferred dividends as tax deductible. Answer (B) is incorrect. The amount of $2.70 ignores the effect of preferred dividends. Answer (C) is incorrect. The amount of $1.80 is based on a 60% effective tax rate and ignores the effect of preferred dividends.

4. If Dawson Corporation's common stock is expected to trade at a price-earnings ratio of 8, the market price per share (to the nearest dollar) would be

- A. $104
- B. $56
- C. $72
- D. $68

Answer (B) is correct.
REQUIRED: The market price per share given the P/E ratio.
DISCUSSION: Net income is $18,000,000 [($35,000,000 EBIT – $5,000,000 interest) × (1.0 – .4 tax rate)], and EPS is $7 [($18,000,000 NI – $4,000,000 preferred dividends) ÷ 2,000,000 common shares]. Consequently, the market price is $56 ($7 EPS × 8 P/E ratio).
Answer (A) is incorrect. The amount of $104 ignores income taxes. Answer (C) is incorrect. The amount of $72 ignores the effect of preferred dividends. Answer (D) is incorrect. The amount of $68 ignores the deductibility of interest.

5. A company paid out one-half of last year's earnings in dividends. Earnings increased by 20%, and the amount of its dividends increased by 15% in the current year. The company's dividend payout ratio for the current year was

- A. 50%
- B. 57.5%
- C. 47.9%
- D. 78%

Answer (C) is correct.
REQUIRED: The dividend payout ratio given earnings and dividend increases.
DISCUSSION: The prior-year dividend payout ratio was 50%. Hence, if prior-year net income was X, the total dividend payout would have been 50%X. If earnings increase by 20%, current-year income will be 120%X. If dividends increase by 15%, the total dividends paid out will be 57.5%X (115% × 50%X), and the new dividend payout ratio will be 47.9% (57.5%X ÷ 120%X).
Answer (A) is incorrect. The prior-year payout ratio is 50%. Answer (B) is incorrect. The figure of 57.5% is 115% of the prior-year payout ratio. Answer (D) is incorrect. The figure of 78% equals 65% of 120%.

6. In calculating diluted earnings per share when a company has convertible bonds outstanding, the number of common shares outstanding must be <List A> to adjust for the conversion feature of the bonds, and the net income must be <List B> by the amount of interest expense on the bonds, net of tax.

	List A	List B
A.	Increased	Increased
B.	Increased	Decreased
C.	Decreased	Increased
D.	Decreased	Decreased

Answer (A) is correct.
REQUIRED: The appropriate calculation of diluted EPS.
DISCUSSION: The weighted-average number of shares outstanding must be increased to reflect the shares into which the bonds could be converted. Also, the effect of the bond interest on net income must be eliminated. In this way, earnings per share is calculated as if the bonds had been converted into common shares as of the start of the year.

7. A company has 100,000 outstanding common shares with a market value of $20 per share. Dividends of $2 per share were paid in the current year and the company has a dividend payout ratio of 40%. The price-earnings ratio of the company is

A. 2.5

B. 4

C. 10

D. 50

Answer (B) is correct.
REQUIRED: The P-E ratio.
DISCUSSION: The P/E ratio equals the share price divided by EPS. If the dividends per share equaled $2 and the dividend-payout ratio was 40%, EPS must have been $5 ($2 ÷ .4). Accordingly, the P/E ratio is 4 ($20 share price ÷ $5 EPS).
Answer (A) is incorrect. EPS divided by dividends per share equals 2.5. Answer (C) is incorrect. Share price divided by dividends per share equals 10. Answer (D) is incorrect. Price per share divided by the dividend-payout percentage equals 50.

8. A corporation had 40,000 shares of common stock outstanding on November 30, Year 1. On May 20, Year 2, a 10% stock dividend was declared and distributed. On June 1, Year 2, options were issued to its existing stockholders giving them the immediate right to acquire one additional share of stock for each share of stock held. The option price of the additional share was $6 per share, and no options have been exercised as of year end. The average price of common stock for the year was $20 per share. The price of the stock as of November 30, Year 2, the end of the fiscal year, was $30 per share, and the corporation's net income for the fiscal year was $229,680. The corporation had no outstanding debt during the year, and its tax rate was 30%. The basic earnings per share (rounded to the nearest cent) of common stock for the fiscal year ended November 30, Year 2, was

A. $5.22 per share.

B. $3.82 per share.

C. $5.74 per share.

D. $3.38 per share.

Answer (A) is correct.
REQUIRED: The basic earnings per share (BEPS).
DISCUSSION: BEPS is net income available to common shareholders divided by the weighted average number of common shares outstanding during the year. The denominator will include the 40,000 shares already outstanding plus the 4,000-share stock dividend (stock dividends and stock splits are deemed to have occurred at the beginning of the earliest period presented). Thus, 44,000 shares are considered to have been outstanding throughout the year. The stock options have no effect on the weighted-average shares outstanding because they were not exercised in the current period. BEPS is $5.22 ($229,680 ÷ 44,000).

9. A corporation computed the following items from its financial records for the year:

Price-earnings ratio	12
Payout ratio	.6
Asset turnover ratio	.9

The dividend yield on common stock is

- A. 5.0%
- B. 7.2%
- C. 7.5%
- D. 10.8%

Answer (A) is correct.
REQUIRED: The dividend yield given the P/E ratio, payout ratio, and asset turnover ratio.
DISCUSSION: Dividend yield is computed by dividing the dividend per share by the market price per share. The payout ratio (.6) is computed by dividing dividends by net income per share (EPS). The P/E ratio (12) is computed by dividing the market price per share by net income per share. Thus, assuming that net income per share (EPS) is $X, the market price must be $12X and the dividends per share $.6X (.6 × $X net income per share). Consequently, the dividend yield is 5.0% ($.6X dividend ÷ $12X market price per share).
Answer (B) is incorrect. The figure of 7.2% equals 12% times the payout ratio. Answer (C) is incorrect. The figure of 7.5% equals asset turnover divided by the P/E ratio. Answer (D) is incorrect. The figure of 10.8% equals 12% times the asset turnover ratio.

3.2 Options and Derivatives

10. Buying a wheat futures contract to protect against price fluctuation of wheat would be classified as a

- A. Fair value hedge.
- B. Cash flow hedge.
- C. Foreign currency hedge.
- D. Swap.

Answer (B) is correct.
REQUIRED: The correct type of hedge.
DISCUSSION: A cash flow hedge is an instrument designated as hedging the exposure to variability in expected future cash flows attributed to a particular risk.
Answer (A) is incorrect. A fair value hedge is an instrument designed as hedging the exposure to changes in fair value of an asset or liability or an identified portion thereof that is attributed to a particular risk. Answer (C) is incorrect. A foreign currency hedge is an instrument designated as hedging the exposure to variability in foreign currency. Answer (D) is incorrect. A swap is a contract between two parties in which the parties promise to make payments to one another on scheduled dates in the future and use different criteria or formulas to determine their respective payments.

11. If a corporation holds a forward contract for the delivery of U.S. Treasury bonds in 6 months and, during those 6 months, interest rates decline, at the end of the 6 months the value of the forward contract will have

- A. Decreased.
- B. Increased.
- C. Remained constant.
- D. Any of the answers may be correct, depending on the extent of the decline in interest rates.

Answer (B) is correct.
REQUIRED: The impact of an interest rate decline on the value of a forward contract.
DISCUSSION: Interest rate futures contracts involve risk-free bonds, such as U.S. Treasury bonds. When interest rates decrease over the period of a forward contract, the value of the bonds and the forward contract increase.
Answer (A) is incorrect. The value of the forward contract will increase when interest rates decrease. Answer (C) is incorrect. The value of the forward contract will increase when interest rates decrease. Answer (D) is incorrect. Any decline in interest rates increases the value of the bonds.

12. The use of derivatives to either hedge or speculate results in

- A. Increased risk regardless of motive.
- B. Decreased risk regardless of motive.
- C. Offsetting risk when hedging and increased risk when speculating.
- D. Offsetting risk when speculating and increased risk when hedging.

Answer (C) is correct.
REQUIRED: The effects on risk of hedging and speculating.
DISCUSSION: Derivatives, including options and futures, are contracts between the parties who contract. Unlike stocks and bonds, they are not claims on business assets. A futures contract is entered into as either a speculation or a hedge. Speculation involves the assumption of risk in the hope of gaining from price movements. Hedging is the process of using offsetting commitments to minimize or avoid the impact of adverse price movements.
Answer (A) is incorrect. Hedging decreases risk by using offsetting commitments that avoid the impact of adverse price movements. Answer (B) is incorrect. Speculation involves the assumption of risk in the hope of gaining from price movements. Answer (D) is incorrect. Speculating increases risk while hedging offsets risk.

13. A forward contract involves a commitment today to purchase a product

    A. On a specific future date at a price to be determined some time in the future.

    B. At some time during the current day at its present price.

    C. On a specific future date at a price determined today.

    D. Only when its price increases above its current exercise price.

Answer (C) is correct.
    REQUIRED: The terms of a forward contract.
    DISCUSSION: A forward contract is an executory contract in which the parties involved agree to the terms of a purchase and a sale, but performance is deferred. Accordingly, a forward contract involves a commitment today to purchase a product on a specific future date at a price determined today.
    Answer (A) is incorrect. The price of a future contract is determined on the day of commitment, not some time in the future. Answer (B) is incorrect. Performance is deferred in a future contract, and the price of the product is not necessarily its present price. The price can be any price determined on the day of commitment. Answer (D) is incorrect. A forward contract is a firm commitment to purchase a product. It is not based on a contingency. Also, a forward contract does not involve an exercise price (exercise price is in an option contract).

14. When a firm finances each asset with a financial instrument of the same approximate maturity as the life of the asset, it is applying

    A. Working capital management.

    B. Return maximization.

    C. Financial leverage.

    D. A hedging approach.

Answer (D) is correct.
    REQUIRED: The technique used when a firm finances a specific asset with a financial instrument having the same approximate maturity as the life of the asset.
    DISCUSSION: Maturity matching, or equalizing the life of an asset and the debt instrument used to finance that asset, is a hedging approach. The basic concept is that the company has the entire life of the asset to recover the amount invested before having to pay the lender.
    Answer (A) is incorrect. Working capital management is short-term asset management. Answer (B) is incorrect. Return maximization is more aggressive than maturity matching. It entails using the lowest cost forms of financing. Answer (C) is incorrect. Financial leverage is the relationship between debt and equity financing.

15. A distinguishing feature of a futures contract is that

    A. Performance is delayed.

    B. It is a hedge, not a speculation.

    C. Delivery is to be on a specific day.

    D. The price is marked to market each day.

Answer (D) is correct.
    REQUIRED: The distinguishing feature of a futures contract.
    DISCUSSION: A distinguishing feature of futures contracts is that their prices are marked to market every day at the close of the day. Thus, the market price is posted at the close of business each day. A mark-to-market provision minimizes a futures contract's chance of default because profits and losses on the contracts must be received or paid each day through a clearinghouse.
    Answer (A) is incorrect. Both a forward contract and a futures contract are executory. Answer (B) is incorrect. A futures contract may be speculative. Answer (C) is incorrect. A futures contract is for delivery during a given month.

16. The theory underlying the cost of capital is primarily concerned with the cost of

    A. Long-term funds and old funds.

    B. Short-term funds and new funds.

    C. Long-term funds and new funds.

    D. Short-term funds and old funds.

Answer (C) is correct.
    REQUIRED: The true statement about the theory underlying the cost of capital.
    DISCUSSION: The theory underlying the cost of capital is based primarily on the cost of long-term funds and the acquisition of new funds. The reason is that long-term funds are used to finance long-term investments. For an investment alternative to be viable, the return on the investment must be greater than the cost of the funds used. The objective in short-term borrowing is different. Short-term loans are used to meet working capital needs and not to finance long-term investments.
    Answer (A) is incorrect. The concern is with the cost of new funds; the cost of old funds is a sunk cost and of no relevance for decision-making purposes. Answer (B) is incorrect. The cost of short-term funds is not usually a concern for investment purposes. Answer (D) is incorrect. The cost of old funds is a sunk cost and of no relevance for decision-making purposes. Similarly, short-term funds are used for working capital or other temporary purposes, and there is less concern with the cost of capital and the way it compares with the return earned on the assets borrowed.

3.3 Cost of Capital -- Current

17. A firm has determined that it can minimize its weighted average cost of capital (WACC) by using a debt-equity ratio of 2/3. If the firm's cost of debt is 9% before taxes, the cost of equity is estimated to be 12% before taxes, and the tax rate is 40%, what is the firm's WACC?

A. 6.48%

B. 7.92%

C. 9.36%

D. 10.80%

Answer (C) is correct.

REQUIRED: The firm's weighted-average cost of capital.

DISCUSSION: A firm's weighted-average cost of capital (WACC) is derived by weighting the (after-tax) cost of each component of the financing structure by its proportion of the financing structure as a whole. The firm's WACC can be calculated as follows:

Component	Weight		Component Cost		Totals
Debt	40%	×	5.4%	=	2.16%
Equity	60%	×	12.0%	=	7.20%
					9.36%

$$\text{WACC} = 9.36\% = \left(\tfrac{3}{5} \times 12\%\right) + \left\{\tfrac{2}{5} \times [9\% \times (1 - 0.4)]\right\}$$

Answer (A) is incorrect. Improperly subtracting the effect of taxes from the cost of equity results in 6.48%. Answer (B) is incorrect. Improperly subtracting the effect of taxes from equity, but not from debt, results in 7.92%. Answer (D) is incorrect. Improperly using the before-tax cost of debt results in 10.80%.

18. A firm's $1,000 par value preferred stock paid its $100 per share annual dividend on April 4 of the current year. The preferred stock's current market price is $960 a share on the date of the dividend distribution. The firm's marginal tax rate (combined federal and state) is 40%, and the firm plans to maintain its current capital structure relationship. The component cost of preferred stock to the firm would be closest to

A. 6%

B. 6.25%

C. 10%

D. 10.4%

Answer (D) is correct.

REQUIRED: The component cost of preferred stock in the firm's capital structure.

DISCUSSION: The component cost of preferred stock is equal to the dividend yield, i.e., the cash dividend divided by the market price of the stock. (Dividends on preferred stock are not deductible for tax purposes; therefore, there is no adjustment for tax savings.) The annual dividend on preferred stock is $100 when the price of the stock is $960. This results in a cost of capital of about 10.4% ($100 ÷ $960).

Answer (A) is incorrect. There is no tax deductibility of preferred dividends and the denominator is the current market price, not the par value. Answer (B) is incorrect. There is no tax deductibility of preferred dividends. Answer (C) is incorrect. The denominator is the current market price, not the par value.

19. A firm has announced that it plans to finance future investments so that the firm will achieve an optimum capital structure. Which one of the following corporate objectives is consistent with this announcement?

A. Maximize earnings per share.

B. Minimize the cost of debt.

C. Maximize the net worth of the firm.

D. Minimize the cost of equity.

Answer (C) is correct.

REQUIRED: The consistent corporate objective.

DISCUSSION: Financial structure is the composition of the financing sources of the assets of a firm. Traditionally, the financial structure consists of current liabilities, long-term debt, retained earnings, and stock. For most firms, the optimum structure includes a combination of debt and equity. Debt is cheaper than equity, but excessive use of debt increases the firm's risk and drives up the weighted-average cost of capital.

Answer (A) is incorrect. The maximization of EPS may not always suggest the best capital structure. Answer (B) is incorrect. The minimization of debt cost may not be optimal; as long as the firm can earn more on debt capital than it pays in interest, debt financing may be indicated. Answer (D) is incorrect. Minimizing the cost of equity may signify overly conservative management.

20. What is the weighted average cost of capital for a firm using 65% common equity with a return of 15%, 25% debt with a return of 6%, 10% preferred stock with a return of 10%, and a tax rate of 35%?

   A. 10.333%

   B. 11.275%

   C. 11.725%

   D. 12.250%

Answer (C) is correct.

    REQUIRED: The weighted average cost of capital.

    DISCUSSION: The cost for equity capital is given as 15%, and preferred stock is 10%. The before-tax rate for debt is given as 6%, which translates to an after-tax cost of 3.9% [6% × (1.0 − .35)]. The rates are weighted as follows:

Component	Weight		Component Cost		Weighted Cost
Long-term debt	25%	×	3.9%	=	.975%
Preferred stock	10%	×	10.0%	=	1.000%
Common stock	65%	×	15.0%	=	9.750%
					11.725%

    Answer (A) is incorrect. The amount of 10.333% is an unweighted average of the three costs and ignores the tax shield. Answer (B) is incorrect. Using the complement of the tax rate instead of the tax rate to calculate the tax shield results in 11.275%. Answer (D) is incorrect. The amount of 12.250% ignores the tax savings on debt capital.

21. If k is the cost of debt and t is the marginal tax rate, the after-tax cost of debt, k_i, is **best** represented by the formula

   A. $k_i = k ÷ t$

   B. $k_i = k ÷ (1 − t)$

   C. $k_i = k(t)$

   D. $k_i = k(1 − t)$

Answer (D) is correct.

    REQUIRED: The formula representing the after-tax cost of debt.

    DISCUSSION: The after-tax cost of debt is the cost of debt times the quantity one minus the tax rate. For example, the after-tax cost of a 10% bond is 7% [10% × (1 − 30%)] if the tax rate is 30%.

    Answer (A) is incorrect. The after-tax cost of debt is the cost of debt times the quantity one minus the tax rate. Answer (B) is incorrect. The after-tax cost of debt is the cost of debt times the quantity one minus the tax rate. Answer (C) is incorrect. The cost of debt times the marginal tax rate equals the tax savings from issuing debt.

3.4 Cost of Capital -- New

22. A firm's new financing will be in proportion to the market value of its current financing shown below.

	Carrying Amount ($000 Omitted)
Long-term debt	$7,000
Preferred stock (100,000 shares)	1,000
Common stock (200,000 shares)	7,000

The firm's bonds are currently selling at 80% of par, generating a current market yield of 9%, and the corporation has a 40% tax rate. The preferred stock is selling at its par value and pays a 6% dividend. The common stock has a current market value of $40 and is expected to pay a $1.20 per share dividend this fiscal year. Dividend growth is expected to be 10% per year, and flotation costs are negligible. The firm's weighted-average cost of capital is (round calculations to tenths of a percent)

   A. 13.0%

   B. 8.13%

   C. 9.6%

   D. 9.0%

Answer (C) is correct.

    REQUIRED: The weighted-average cost of capital.

    DISCUSSION: The first step is to determine the component costs of each form of capital. Multiplying the current yield of 9% times one minus the tax rate (1.0 − .40 = .60) results in an after-tax cost of debt of 5.4% (9% × .60). Since the preferred stock is trading at par, the component cost is 6% (the annual dividend rate). The component cost of common equity is calculated using the dividend growth model, which combines the dividend yield with the growth rate. Dividing the $1.20 dividend by the $40 market price produces a dividend yield of 3%. Adding the 3% dividend yield and the 10% growth rate gives a 13% component cost of common equity.

    Once the costs of the three types of capital have been computed, the next step is to weight them according to their current market values. The market value of the long-term debt is 80% of its carrying amount, or $5,600,000 ($7,000,000 × 80%). The $1,000,000 of preferred stock is selling at par. The common stock has a current market value of $8,000,000 (200,000 shares × $40).

Long-term debt	$ 5,600,000 × 5.4% =	$ 302,400
Preferred stock	1,000,000 × 6.0% =	60,000
Common stock	8,000,000 × 13.0% =	1,040,000
Totals	$14,600,000	$1,402,400

    Thus, the weighted-average cost of capital is 9.6% ($1,402,000 ÷ $14,600,000).

    Answer (A) is incorrect. The figure of 13.0% is the cost of equity. Answer (B) is incorrect. The figure of 8.13% is the simple average. Answer (D) is incorrect. The figure of 9.0% is based on carrying amounts.

23. A preferred stock is sold for $101 per share, has a face value of $100 per share, underwriting fees of $5 per share, and annual dividends of $10 per share. If the tax rate is 40%, the cost of funds (capital) for the preferred stock is

A. 4.2%

B. 6.25%

C. 10.0%

D. 10.4%

Answer (D) is correct.
    REQUIRED: The cost of capital for a preferred stock issue.
    DISCUSSION: The cost of capital for new preferred stock is equal to the dividend on the stock divided by the net issue proceeds [$10 ÷ ($101 – $5) = 10.4%]. Because dividends on preferred stock are not deductible for tax purposes, the income tax rate is irrelevant.
    Answer (A) is incorrect. The figure of 4.2% results from improperly multiplying the dividends by the tax rate. Answer (B) is incorrect. The figure of 6.25% results from improperly multiplying the dividends by the tax rate. Answer (C) is incorrect. The figure of 10.0% results from improperly basing the calculation on par value funds received.

24. The common stock of a company is currently selling at $80 per share. The leadership of the company intends to pay a $4 per share dividend next year. With the expectation that the dividend will grow at 5% perpetually, what will the market's required return on investment be for the common stock?

A. 5%

B. 5.25%

C. 7.5%

D. 10%

Answer (D) is correct.
    REQUIRED: The market's required return.
    DISCUSSION: The dividend growth model estimates the cost of retained earnings using the dividends per share, the market price, and the expected growth rate. The current dividend yield is 5% ($4 ÷ $80). Adding the growth rate of 5% to the yield of 5% results in a required return of 10%.
    Answer (A) is incorrect. The amount of 5% represents only half of the return elements (either yield or growth). Answer (B) is incorrect. The growth rate is based on market value, not yield. Answer (C) is incorrect. The yield and growth rate are 5% each, a total of 10%.

25. A company's current capital structure is optimal, and the company wishes to maintain it.

Debt	25%
Preferred equity	5
Common equity	70

Management is planning to build a $75 million facility that will be financed according to this desired capital structure. Currently, $15 million of cash is available for capital expansion. The percentage of the $75 million that will come from a new issue of common stock is

A. 52.50%

B. 50.00%

C. 70.00%

D. 56.00%

Answer (D) is correct.
    REQUIRED: The percentage of the new financing needed that will come from a new issue of common stock.
    DISCUSSION: Because $15 million is already available, the company must finance $60 million ($75 million – $15 million). Of this amount, 70%, or $42 million, should come from the issuance of common stock to maintain the current capital structure. The $42 million represents 56% of the total $75 million.
    Answer (A) is incorrect. The 70% desired common stock percentage multiplied by the original $75 million is $52.5 million. Answer (B) is incorrect. This is a nonsense percentage in this context. Answer (C) is incorrect. The new issue of common stock will fund 70% of the financed amount, not 70% of the total project cost. The financed amount is $60 million ($75 million – $15 million cash).

Questions 26 and 27 are based on the following information. DQZ Telecom is considering a project for the coming year that will cost $50 million. DQZ plans to use the following combination of debt and equity to finance the investment.

- Issue $15 million of 20-year bonds at a price of $101, with a coupon rate of 8%, and flotation costs of 2% of par.
- Use $35 million of funds generated from earnings.
- The equity market is expected to earn 12%. U.S. Treasury bonds are currently yielding 5%. The beta coefficient for DQZ is estimated to be .60. DQZ is subject to an effective corporate income tax rate of 40%.

26. The before-tax cost of DQZ's planned debt financing, net of flotation costs, in the first year is

- A. 11.80%
- B. 8.08%
- C. 10.00%
- D. 7.92%

Answer (B) is correct.
   REQUIRED: The before-tax cost of the planned debt financing, net of flotation costs.
   DISCUSSION: The cost of new debt equals the annual interest divided by the net issue proceeds. The annual interest is $1.2 million ($15,000,000 × .08 coupon rate). The proceeds amount to $14,850,000 [($15,000,000 × 1.01) market price – ($15,000,000 × .02) flotation costs]. Thus, the company is paying $1.2 million annually for the use of $14,850,000, a cost of 8.08% ($1,200,000 ÷ $14,850,000).
   Answer (A) is incorrect. The coupon rate is 8% annually. Answer (C) is incorrect. The figure of 10.0% is the sum of the coupon rate and the flotation rate. Answer (D) is incorrect. The figure of 7.92% ignores the 2% flotation costs.

27. Assume that the after-tax cost of debt is 7% and the cost of equity is 12%. Determine the weighted-average cost of capital to DQZ.

- A. 10.50%
- B. 8.50%
- C. 9.50%
- D. 6.30%

Answer (A) is correct.
   REQUIRED: The weighted-average cost of capital given the costs of debt and equity.
   DISCUSSION: The 7% debt cost and the 12% equity cost should be weighted by the proportions of the total investment represented by each source of capital. The total project costs $50 million, of which debt is $15 million, or 30% of the total. Equity capital is the other 70%. Consequently, the weighted-average cost of capital is 10.5% [(30% × 7%) + (70% × 12%)].
   Answer (B) is incorrect. The figure of 8.50% reverses the weights. Answer (C) is incorrect. The figure of 9.50% assumes debt and equity are equally weighted. Answer (D) is incorrect. The figure of 6.30% assumes that 7% is the before-tax cost of debt and that equity is tax deductible.

28. Which one of a firm's sources of new capital usually has the lowest after-tax cost?

- A. Retained earnings.
- B. Bonds.
- C. Preferred stock.
- D. Common stock.

Answer (B) is correct.
   REQUIRED: The source of new capital that normally has the lowest after-tax cost.
   DISCUSSION: Debt financing, such as bonds, normally has a lower after-tax cost than does equity financing. The interest on debt is tax deductible, whereas the dividends on equity are not. Also, bonds are slightly less risky than stock because the bond holders have a first right to assets at liquidation.
   Answer (A) is incorrect. The cost to the company of equity instruments is in the form of dividends. Because dividends are not deductible for tax purposes, equity sources of capital have a higher after-tax cost than debt sources. Answer (C) is incorrect. Preferred stock has a higher after-tax cost than debt. Answer (D) is incorrect. Common stock has a higher after-tax cost than debt.

29. A corporation has sold $50 million of $1,000 par value, 12% coupon bonds. The bonds were sold at a discount and the corporation received $985 per bond. If the corporate tax rate is 40%, the after-tax cost of these bonds for the first year (rounded to the nearest hundredth percent) is

A. 7.31%

B. 4.87%

C. 12.00%

D. 7.09%

Answer (A) is correct.
    REQUIRED: The after-tax cost of bonds for the first year.
    DISCUSSION: Interest is 12%, and the annual interest payment on one bond is $120. Thus, the effective rate is 12.18% ($120 ÷ $985). Reducing this rate by the 40% tax savings lowers the cost to 7.31%.
    Answer (B) is incorrect. Multiplying the pretax effective rate 12.18% ($120 ÷ $985) by the tax rate of .40 instead of by (1 − .40) results in 4.87%. Answer (C) is incorrect. The nominal interest rate is 12%. Answer (D) is incorrect. The after-tax cost of the bonds equals the effective rate times the tax effect.

30. A corporation is selling $25 million of cumulative, non-participating preferred stock. The issue will have a par value of $65 per share with a dividend rate of 6%. The issue will be sold to investors for $68 per share, and issuance costs will be $4 per share. The cost of preferred stock to the corporation is

A. 5.42%

B. 5.74%

C. 6.00%

D. 6.09%

Answer (D) is correct.
    REQUIRED: The cost of financing by issuing preferred stock.
    DISCUSSION: Cost of capital for its new preferred stock is calculated as follows:

$$\begin{aligned} \text{Cost of new preferred stock} &= \text{Dividend} \div \text{Net issue proceeds} \\ &= (\$65 \times 6\%) \div (\$68 - \$4) \\ &= \$3.90 \div \$64 \\ &= 6.09\% \end{aligned}$$

    Answer (A) is incorrect. Improperly dividing the annual dividend by the sum of the issue price and the issue costs results in 5.42%. Answer (B) is incorrect. Improperly dividing the annual dividend by the issue price results in 5.74%. Answer (C) is incorrect. Improperly dividing the annual dividend by the par value results in 6.00%.

Access the **Gleim CMA Premium Review System** from your Gleim Personal Classroom to continue your studies with exam-emulating multiple-choice questions!

3.5 ESSAY QUESTIONS

Scenario for Essay Questions 1, 2, 3

Safe-T-Systems (STS) has developed safety devices marketed to manufacturing facilities in the Midwest. STS's limited product line has been well accepted, and the company is experiencing favorable profits and cash flow. The research staff is developing four new products that it believes will gain market acceptance. The marketing staff advised that there is good revenue potential for each proposed product where anticipated revenues and profits are equal relative to the level of investment. These products are independent of each other so that STS can invest in any combination of the four products or only in a single product. The investment required for each project is as follows:

Product	Investment (in millions)
Foot pedal release	$ 2.4
Power tool safety lock	1.7
Stationary machine retraction	4.6
Overhead machine retraction	3.3
Total	$12.0

STS's capital structure is currently composed of 60% long-term debt and 40% common equity (common stock and retained earnings), and management believes these contemplated transactions will maintain these capital ratios in the future. The weighted average cost of capital in this capital structure is 13.2%. The annual cost of internally generated funds from operations is 12%.

STS's cash flow in the current year will generate an estimated $2 million of funds that will be used first for product investment. STS can raise $3 million through privately placed short-term notes at a constant interest rate of 9%. Any product investments beyond $5 million ($2 million of current year cash flow and $3 million of privately placed notes) would have to be financed by a combination of long-term bonds and issuance of additional common stock. STS's effective tax rate is 40%.

	Proportion	Cost
Long-term debt	60	10%
Common stock	40	13

Questions

1. a. Explain the difference between weighted-average cost of capital and weighted marginal cost of capital.

   b. Explain why the weighted marginal cost of capital should be used instead of the weighted-average cost of capital when evaluating product investment opportunities in discounted cash flow analyses.

2. If Safe-T-Systems plans to invest up to $5 million in the development of new products during the current year, calculate the weighted marginal cost of capital for this transaction.

3. Assume Safe-T-Systems (STS) already invested $5 million in power tool safety locks and overhead machine retraction devices this year. STS is now considering investing additional funds at the same debt to equity proportions in foot pedal releases and stationary machine retraction devices. Calculate the cost of capital STS should use in its analysis.

Essay Questions 1, 2, 3 — Unofficial Answers

1.   a.   The weighted-average cost of capital is based on historical costs and thus reflects a composite rate of past financing decisions. The marginal cost of capital measures the cost of new, additional capital at current rates.

    b.   When evaluating product investment opportunities in discounted cash flow analyses, the marginal cost of capital should be used where the concern is what rates are presently available and can be used for future new investments rather than how the capital was raised in the past. The weighted-average cost of capital reflects historical rates from past decisions as well as present rates, whereas the marginal cost of capital reflects current market conditions in obtaining incremental financing and allows an evaluation of capital structure based on future events and opportunity costs.

2.   The marginal cost of capital for the first $5 million of new funds is 8.04%, calculated as follows:

Component	Weight		Component Cost		Weighted Cost
Long-term debt [9% × (1.0 – .40)]	60	×	5.4%	=	3.24%
Retained earnings	40	×	12.0%	=	4.80%
Marginal cost of capital					8.04%

3.   The marginal cost of capital that STS should use in evaluating foot pedal releases and stationary machine retraction devices is 8.80%, calculated as follows:

Component	Weight		Component Cost		Weighted Cost
Long-term debt [10% × (1.0 – .40)]	60	×	6.0%	=	3.60%
Common stock	40	×	13.0%	=	5.20%
Marginal cost of capital					8.80%

The marginal cost of capital for an investment in excess of the first $5 million has increased because of the higher market cost of new equity capital and additional long-term bonds. In order to increase the firm's value, foot pedal releases and stationary machine retraction devices would have to earn a return that exceeds 8.80%, the incremental marginal cost of capital.

 Access the **Gleim CMA Premium Review System** from your Gleim Personal Classroom to continue your studies with exam-emulating essay questions!

STUDY UNIT FOUR
MANAGING CURRENT ASSETS

(19 pages of outline)

This study unit is the **third of four** on **corporate finance**. The relative weight assigned to this major topic in Part 2 of the exam is **20%**. The four study units are

Study Unit 2: Financial Markets and Types of Securities
Study Unit 3: Valuation Methods and Cost of Capital
Study Unit 4: Managing Current Assets
Study Unit 5: Corporate Restructuring and International Finance

If you are interested in reviewing more introductory or background material, go to www.gleim.com/CMAIntroVideos for a list of suggested third-party overviews of this topic. The following Gleim outline material is more than sufficient to help you pass the CMA exam; any additional introductory or background material is for your own personal enrichment.

4.1 WORKING CAPITAL

1. **Definitions**

    a. Working capital finance concerns the optimal level, mix, and use of **current assets** and the means used to acquire them, notably **current liabilities**.

       1) The objective is to minimize the cost of maintaining liquidity (quick convertibility to cash) while guarding against the risk of insolvency.

       2) Working capital policy applies to short-term decisions, and capital structure finance applies to long-term decisions.

       3) Net working capital equals current assets minus current liabilities.

       Net working capital = Current assets – Current liabilities

    b. Permanent working capital is the minimum level of current assets maintained by a firm.

       1) Permanent working capital should increase as the firm grows.

       2) Permanent working capital generally is financed with long-term debt. Financing with short-term debt is risky because assets may not be liquidated in time to pay the debt, interest rates may rise, and loans may not be renewed.

    c. Temporary working capital fluctuates seasonally.

2.   **Working Capital Policy**

a.   A firm that adopts a **conservative** working capital policy seeks to minimize liquidity risk by increasing working capital.

1)   The firm seeks to ensure that adequate cash, inventory, and supplies are available and payables are minimized.

2)   The firm forgoes the potentially higher returns from investing in long-term assets and instead keeps that additional working capital available.

3)   This policy is reflected in a higher current ratio (current assets ÷ current liabilities) and acid-test ratio (quick assets ÷ current liabilities). Liquidity ratios are presented in Study Unit 6, Subunit 2.

b.   A firm that adopts an **aggressive** working capital policy seeks to increase profitability while accepting reduced liquidity and a higher risk of short-term cash flow problems.

1)   This policy is reflected in a lower current ratio and acid-test ratio.

c.   Carrying excessive current assets, such as inventories, increases costs.

1)   The carrying costs of inventory usually increase in proportion to the quantity of inventory. Thus, the firm with excess inventory incurs not only the opportunity costs of funds invested in inventory but also the costs of storage and insurance.

2)   Also, spoilage and obsolescence costs increase as inventories increase.

d.   The optimal level of current assets varies with the industry in which a firm operates.

1)   For example, a grocery store has spoilable inventory and cannot carry more than a few days of sales. In contrast, a uranium mine must have a high level of cash to meet ongoing expenses because its sales may be irregular.

Stop and review! You have completed the outline for this subunit. Study multiple-choice questions 1 through 4 on page 128.

4.2 CASH MANAGEMENT

CMA candidates must demonstrate an understanding of effective cash management and its value. You should (1) understand how to analyze the cost or benefit of holding cash for the organization and (2) know the motives for holding cash and be able to weigh those against the opportunity cost. CMAs will also be expected to evaluate cash budgeting by forecasting cash collection and payments. You should be able to (1) evaluate whether an organization should change the way it collects payments and (2) provide an analysis of how this should be done and the associated costs.

1.   **Managing the Level of Cash**

a.   The following are the three motives for holding cash:

1)   Transactional (as a medium of exchange)
2)   Precautionary (to provide a reserve for contingencies)
3)   Speculative (to take advantage of unexpected opportunities)

b.   The firm's optimal level of cash should be determined by a cost-benefit analysis.

1)   Because cash does not earn a return, only the amount needed to satisfy current obligations as they come due should be kept.

2)   The motives for holding cash must be balanced against the opportunity cost of missed investments in marketable securities.

a) One approach is the economic order quantity (EOQ) model originally developed for inventory management.

EOQ Model Applied to Cash Management

$$Q = \sqrt{\frac{2bT}{i}}$$

If: Q = optimal cash balance
b = fixed cost per transaction
T = total demand for cash for the period
i = interest rate on marketable securities

3) EXAMPLE: A firm projects that it needs $20,000 to pay its obligations during the upcoming month. Every marketable security transaction costs $5, and securities are currently paying 6% annual interest. The optimal cash balance can be determined by applying the EOQ model:

$$Q = \sqrt{\frac{2bT}{i}} = \sqrt{\frac{2 \times \$5 \times \$20,000}{6\% \div 12 \text{ months}}} = \sqrt{\frac{\$200,000}{.005}} = \$6,324$$

The firm's optimal cash balance for the upcoming month is $6,324, and its average balance will be $3,162 ($6,324 ÷ 2).

2. **Forecasting Future Cash Flows**

a. Managing cash flows begins with the cash budget. It states projected receipts and payments for the purpose of matching inflows and outflows.

1) The budget is for a specific period, but cash budgeting is an ongoing, cumulative activity. It is re-evaluated constantly to ensure all objectives are met.

b. Cash receipts are based on projected sales, credit terms, and estimated collection rates.

1) EXAMPLE: A firm forecasts the following cash collections for the next 4 months:

	Cash Sales	Credit Sales
July	$40,000	$160,000
August	60,000	220,000
September	80,000	340,000
October	70,000	300,000

On average, 50% of credit sales are paid for in the month of sale, 30% in the month after sale, and 15% in the second month after sale (5% are expected to be uncollectible). The firm's projected cash collections for October can be calculated as follows:

October cash sales			$ 70,000
October credit sales:	$300,000 × 50%	=	150,000
September credit sales:	$340,000 × 30%	=	102,000
August credit sales:	$220,000 × 15%	=	33,000
Total October collections			$355,000

c.   Cash payments are based on budgeted purchases and total sales.

1)   EXAMPLE: The firm forecasts the following cash payments for the next 4 months:

	Purchases	Total Sales
July	$200,000	$200,000
August	250,000	280,000
September	300,000	420,000
October	350,000	370,000

On average, the firm pays for 50% of purchases in the month of purchase and 25% in each of the 2 following months. Payroll is projected as 10% of that month's sales and operating expenses are 20% of the following month's sales (November's sales are projected to be $280,000). Interest of $5,000 is paid every month. The firm's projected cash payments for October can be calculated as follows:

October purchases:	$350,000 × 50%	=	$175,000
September purchases:	$300,000 × 25%	=	75,000
August purchases:	$250,000 × 25%	=	62,500
October payroll:	$370,000 × 10%	=	37,000
October op. expenses	$280,000 × 20%	=	56,000
Interest			5,000
Total October disbursements			$410,500

3.   **Speeding Up Cash Collections**

a.   The period from when a payor mails a check until the funds are available in the payee's bank is float. Firms use various strategies to decrease the float time for receipts.

b.   The product of the daily amount of receipts and the number of days of reduced float is the increase in the average cash balance. This amount is multiplied by an annual rate of return on short-term investments, which is the opportunity cost of the funds, to arrive at the **annual benefit**.

(Daily cash receipts × Days of reduced float) × Opportunity cost of funds

1)   EXAMPLE: A firm has $22,000 in daily cash receipts. It is considering a plan that costs $0 and speeds up collections by 2 days. The result is an additional $44,000 in the firm's average cash balance ($22,000 × 2 days). Marketable securities currently pay 6% annually.

Benefit = $44,000 × 6% = $2,640 annually

c.   The benefit of any plan to speed up cash collections must exceed the cost.

1)   EXAMPLE: A firm has daily cash receipts of $150,000. A bank has offered to reduce the collection time by 2 days, increasing the firm's average cash balance by $300,000 ($150,000 × 2 days). The bank will charge a monthly fee of $1,250. Money market funds are expected to average 8% during the year.

Benefit (loss) = Interest earned − Cost
= ($300,000 × 8%) − ($1,250 × 12 months)
= $24,000 − $15,000
= $9,000 annually

    d.   A **lockbox system** is a popular means of speeding up cash receipts.

        1)   Customers submit their payments to a mailbox rather than to the firm's offices.

            a)   Bank personnel remove the envelopes from the mailbox and deposit the checks to the firm's account immediately.

        2)   The bank generally charges a flat monthly fee for this service.

        3)   For firms doing business nationwide, a lockbox network is appropriate.

            a)   The country is divided into regions according to customer population patterns.

            b)   A lockbox arrangement is then established with a bank in each region.

        4)   Refer to the example presented in item 3.c.1) on the previous page to calculate the net benefit of a lockbox system.

    e.   **Concentration banking** is another means of speeding up cash receipts.

        1)   Customers submit their payments to a local branch office. Subsequently, the branch office deposits the checks into a local bank account. The local bank then transfers the funds to a concentration account at one of the firm's principal banks.

    f.   Transfer of funds by wire speeds up cash management. A wire transfer is any electronic funds transfer (EFT) by means of a two-way system.

4.   **Slowing Cash Payments**

    a.   Payment (disbursement) **float** is the period from when the payor mails a check until the funds are subtracted from the payor's account. To increase payment float, a firm may send checks to its vendors without being certain that it has sufficient funds to cover them all.

        1)   For these situations, some banks offer **overdraft protection**. The bank guarantees (for a fee) to cover any shortage with a transfer from the firm's master account.

    b.   Other methods for increasing payment float include

        1)   Zero balance accounts (ZBAs). ZBAs are checking accounts in which a balance of $0 is maintained by automatically transferring funds from a master account in an amount only large enough to cover checks presented for payment.

        2)   Centralizing accounts payable.

        3)   Controlled disbursement accounts.

5.   **Compensating Balance**

    a.   A compensating balance is the minimum amount that a bank requires a firm to keep frozen in its account. Compensating balances are noninterest-bearing and are meant to compensate the bank for various services rendered, such as unlimited check writing. These balances incur opportunity costs because they are unavailable for investment purposes.

Stop and review! You have completed the outline for this subunit. Study multiple-choice questions 5 through 11 beginning on page 129.

4.3 MARKETABLE SECURITIES MANAGEMENT

1. **Managing Marketable Securities**

    a.   Idle cash incurs an opportunity cost, i.e., the return that could be earned if the cash was invested. To offset this cost, firms invest their idle cash balances in marketable securities.

       1)   An entity also must consider whether the maturities of marketable securities match the needs for the cash.

    b.   Beyond achieving an optimal risk and after-tax return trade-off, the most important aspects of marketable securities management are liquidity and safety.

       1)   Liquidity is the ability to convert an investment into cash quickly and without a loss of principal.

       2)   Marketable securities management thus concerns low-yield, low-risk instruments that are traded on highly active markets (money market instruments).

2. **Types of Marketable Securities**

    a.   The money market is the market for short-term investments where firms invest their temporary surpluses of cash.

       1)   The money market is not formally organized. It consists of many financial institutions, firms, and government agencies offering instruments of various risk levels and short- to medium-range maturities.

    b.   U.S. Treasury obligations are (1) the safest investment, (2) exempt from state and local taxation, and (3) highly liquid.

       1)   Treasury bills (T-bills) have maturities of 1 year or less. They have no coupon rate and are sold at a discount.

          a)   T-bills are often held as a substitute for cash since they have no default risk.

       2)   Treasury notes (T-notes) have maturities of 1 to 10 years. They provide the lender with an interest payment every 6 months.

       3)   Treasury bonds (T-bonds) have maturities of 10 years or longer. They provide the lender with an interest payment every 6 months.

    c.   Federal agency securities are backed by either (1) the full faith and credit of the U.S. government or (2) only by the issuing agency.

       1)   State and local governments issue short-term securities exempt from taxation.

    d.   Repurchase agreements (repos) are a means for dealers in government securities to finance their portfolios.

       1)   When a firm buys a repo, it is temporarily purchasing some of the dealer's government securities. The dealer agrees to repurchase them at a later time for a specific (higher) price.

       2)   In essence, the firm gives the securities dealer a secured, short-term loan.

       3)   Maturities vary from overnight to a few days.

    e.   Bankers' acceptances are drafts drawn by a nonfinancial firm on deposits at a bank.

       1)   The drawer (firm) then sells the draft to an investor (holder).

       2)   One advantage is that the acceptance by the bank is a guarantee of payment at maturity.

          a)   The payee can rely on the creditworthiness of the bank rather than on that of the (presumably riskier) drawer.

       3)   A second advantage is that, because they are backed by the prestige of a large bank, these instruments are highly marketable once they have been accepted.

    f.   Commercial paper consists of unsecured, short-term notes issued by large companies that are very good credit risks.

    g.   Certificates of deposit (CDs) are a form of savings deposit that cannot be withdrawn before maturity without a high penalty.

        1)   CDs often yield a lower return than commercial paper and bankers' acceptances because they are less risky.

        2)   Negotiable CDs are CDs that can be sold in the secondary market.

    h.   Eurodollars are time deposits of U.S. dollars in banks located abroad.

    i.   Money-market mutual funds invest in short-term, low-risk securities.

        1)   In addition to paying interest, these funds allow investors to write checks on their balances.

Stop and review! You have completed the outline for this subunit. Study multiple-choice questions 12 through 16 beginning on page 131.

4.4 PORTFOLIO MANAGEMENT

1.   **Efficient Portfolios**

    a.   An investor wants to maximize return and minimize risk when choosing a portfolio of investments. A feasible portfolio that offers the highest expected return for a given risk or the least risk for a given expected return is an efficient portfolio.

    b.   An **indifference curve** represents combinations of portfolios having equal utility to the investor. Given that risk and returns are plotted on the horizontal and vertical axes, respectively, and that the investor is risk averse, the curve has an increasingly positive slope. As risk increases, the additional required return per unit of additional risk also increases.

        1)   The steeper the slope of an indifference curve, the more risk averse an investor is.

        2)   The higher the curve, the greater is the investor's level of utility.

        3)   In the diagram below, A, B, C, D, and E are indifference curves. A represents the highest level of utility and E the lowest. On a given curve, each point represents the same total utility to a risk-averse investor. For example, points 1, 2, and 3 are different combinations of risk and return that yield the same utility. The investor is indifferent as to which combination is chosen.

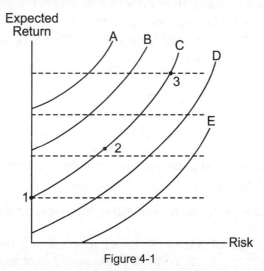

Figure 4-1

    c.   Two important decisions are involved in managing a company's portfolio:

        1)   The amount of money to invest

        2)   The securities in which to invest

    d.   The investment in securities should be based on expected net cash flows and cash flow uncertainty evaluations.

        1)   Arranging a portfolio so that the maturity of funds will coincide with the need for funds will maximize the average return on the portfolio and provide increased flexibility.

            a)   **Maturity matching** ensures that securities will not have to be sold unexpectedly.

        2)   If its cash flows are relatively uncertain, a security's marketability and market risk are important factors to be considered. Transaction costs are also a consideration.

            a)   Higher-yield long-term securities provide less certainty.

        3)   When cash flows are relatively certain, the maturity date becomes the most important concern.

2.   **Hedging**

    a.   Hedging is the process of using offsetting commitments to minimize or avoid the impact of adverse price movements. Hedging transactions are often used to protect positions in (1) securities, (2) commodity buying, and (3) foreign currency.

        1)   Thus, the purchase or sale of a derivative or other instrument is a hedge if it is expected to reduce the risk of adverse price movements in an asset.

            a)   For example, if a flour company buys and uses 1 million bushels of wheat each month, it may wish to guard against increases in wheat costs when it has committed to sell at a price related to the current cost of wheat. The company will purchase wheat futures contracts that will result in gains if the price of wheat increases (offsetting the actual increased costs).

        2)   A natural hedge is a method of reducing financial risk by investing in two different items whose performance tends to cancel each other. However, natural hedges are not perfect in that they do not eliminate all risk.

            a)   Buying insurance is a natural hedge.

            b)   Pair trading, or buying long and short positions in highly correlated stocks, can be an effective method of hedging securities.

            c)   Investing in both stocks and bonds is sometimes viewed as a natural hedge, since the performance of one offsets the other.

        3)   Futures contracts are used to hedge commodities. They are agreements to buy or sell assets at a fixed price that are to be delivered and paid for later.

            a)   Long hedges are futures contracts that are purchased to protect against price increases.

            b)   Short hedges are futures contracts that are sold to protect against price declines.

            c)   Because commodities can be bought and sold **on margin**, considerable leverage is involved. Leverage is most beneficial to the speculator who is seeking large returns and is willing to bear proportionate risk.

3.   **Measures of Risk**

    a.   Risk is the chance that the actual return on an investment will differ from the expected return.

    b.   The **expected rate of return ($\overline{R}$)** on an investment is determined using an expected value calculation. It is an average of the possible outcomes weighted according to their probabilities.

Expected rate of return ($\overline{R}$) = $\sum$ (Possible rate of return × Probability)

EXAMPLE

A company is considering investing in the common stock of one of two firms, Xatalan Corp. and Yarmouth Co. The expected rates of return on the two securities based on the weighted-averages of their probable outcomes are calculated as follows:

Xatalan Corporation Stock						Yarmouth Company Stock					
Rate of Return %		Probability %		Weighted Average		Rate of Return %		Probability %		Weighted Average	
80 %	×	60%	=	48 %		30 %	×	70%	=	21 %	
(50)%	×	40%	=	(20)%		(10)%	×	30%	=	(3)%	
Expected rate of return (R̄)				**28 %**		**Expected rate of return (R̄)**				**18 %**	

The expected rate of return on Xatalan Corporation stock is higher, but the risk of each investment also should be measured.

---

    c.   One way to measure risk is with the **standard deviation (variance)** of the distribution of an investment's return. The standard deviation measures the tightness of the distribution and the riskiness of the investment.

        1)   A large standard deviation reflects a broadly dispersed probability distribution, meaning the range of possible returns is wide. Conversely, the smaller the standard deviation, the tighter the probability distribution and the lower the risk.

            a)   Thus, the following general statement can be made: the greater the standard deviation, the riskier the investment.

4. **Security Risk vs. Portfolio Risk**

    a.   These calculations apply to investments in individual securities. When a portfolio is held, however, additional considerations apply. Risk and return should be evaluated for the entire portfolio, not for individual assets.

    b.   The expected return on a portfolio is the weighted average of the returns on the individual securities.

    c.   However, the risk of the portfolio is usually not an average of the standard deviations of the particular securities. Thanks to the diversification effect, combining securities results in a portfolio risk that is less than the average of the standard deviations because the returns are imperfectly correlated.

5. **Correlation**

    a.   The **correlation coefficient (*r*)** measures the degree to which any two variables, e.g., two stocks in a portfolio, are related. It has a range from 1.0 to −1.0.

        1)   Perfect positive correlation (1.0) means the two variables always move together.
        2)   Perfect negative correlation (−1.0) means the two variables always move in the opposite direction.
        3)   Given perfect negative correlation, risk would, in theory, be eliminated.

            a)   This method is used to hedge risk when investing in stocks.

        4)   In practice, the existence of market risk makes perfect correlation nearly impossible.

            a)   The normal range for the correlation of two randomly selected stocks is .50 to .70. The result is a reduction in, but not elimination of, risk.

6. **Covariance**

    a.   The correlation coefficient of two securities can be combined with their standard deviations to arrive at their covariance, a measure of their mutual volatility.

Covariance of a Two-Stock Portfolio

Correlation coefficient × *Standard deviation₁* × *Standard deviation₂*

EXAMPLE

The coefficient of correlation of Xatalan Corporation stock and Yarmouth Company stock is 0.6, meaning they move in the same direction 60% of the time. Additionally, Xatalan Corporation's stock has a standard deviation of 63.37% and Yarmouth Company's stock has a standard deviation of 88.31%. The covariance of a portfolio consisting entirely of these two stocks is calculated as follows:

$$\text{Covariance of two-stock portfolio} = 0.6 \times .6337 \times .8831$$
$$= .3358$$

---

7. **Risk and Diversification**

    a. **Specific risk**, also called diversifiable risk, unsystematic risk, residual risk, or unique risk, is the risk associated with a specific investee's operations: new products, patents, acquisitions, competitors' activities, etc.

        1) Specific risk is the risk that can be potentially eliminated by diversification.

            a) **Diversification** is a hedging technique that makes a wide variety of investments within a portfolio so that the positive performance of some investments cancels out the negative performance of other investments.

        2) In principle, diversifiable risk should continue to decrease as the number of different securities held increases.

            a) In practice, however, the benefits of diversification become extremely small when more than about 20 to 30 different securities are held. Moreover, commissions and other transaction costs increase with greater diversification.

            b) Thus, the benefits of diversification can decline to near zero when the number of securities held increases beyond 40.

    b. **Market risk**, also called undiversifiable risk or systematic risk, is the risk of the stock market as a whole. Some conditions in the national economy affect all businesses, which is why equity prices so often move together.

8. **Beta**

    a. The effect of an individual security on the volatility of a portfolio is measured by its sensitivity to movements by the overall market. This sensitivity is stated in terms of a stock's **beta coefficient (β)**.

        1) Beta is the best measure of the risk of an individual security held in a diversified portfolio because it determines how the security affects the risk of the portfolio.

        2) An average-risk stock has a beta of 1.0 because its returns are perfectly positively correlated with those on the market portfolio. For example, if the market return increases by 20%, the return on the security increases by 20%.

        3) A beta of less than 1.0 means that the security is less volatile than the market; e.g., if the market return increases by 20% and the security's return increases only 10%, the security has a beta of .5.

        4) A beta of more than 1.0 indicates a volatile security; e.g., if the return increases 30% when the market return increases by 15%, the security has a beta of 2.0.

    b. The beta coefficient is the slope of the regression line for the returns of an individual security (the dependent variable) and the overall market return (the independent variable).

        1) The beta for a security may also be calculated by dividing the covariance of the return on the market and the return on the security by the variance of the return on the market.

    c. The beta of a portfolio is the weighted average of the betas of the individual securities.

9. **Capital Asset Pricing Model (CAPM)**

   a.   Investors want to reduce their risk, and therefore take advantage of diversification, by holding a portfolio of securities. In order to measure how a particular security contributes to the risk and return of a diversified portfolio, investors can use the capital asset pricing model (CAPM).

   b.   The CAPM quantifies the required return on an equity security by relating the security's level of risk to the average return available in the market (portfolio).

   c.   The CAPM formula is based on the idea that the investor must be compensated for his or her investment in two ways: time value of money and risk.

      1)   The time value component is the risk-free rate (denoted R_F in the formula). It is the return provided by the safest investments, e.g., U.S. Treasury securities.

      2)   The risk component consists of

         a)   The market risk premium (denoted $R_M - R_F$), which is the return provided by the market over and above the risk-free rate, weighted by

         b)   A measure of the security's risk, called beta (β).

CAPM Formula

$$Required\ rate\ of\ return = R_F + \beta(R_M - R_F)$$

If: R_F = Risk-free return
        R_M = Market return
        β = Measure of the systematic risk or volatility of the individual security in comparison to the market (diversified portfolio)

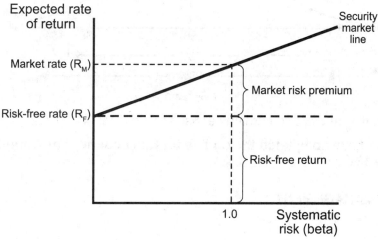

Figure 4-2

EXAMPLE

An investor is considering the purchase of a stock with a beta value of 1.2. Treasury bills are currently paying 8.6%, and the expected average return on the market is 10.1%. (Remember, U.S. Treasuries are considered as close to a risk-free investment as there can be.) To be induced to buy this stock, the return that the investor must receive is calculated as follows:

$$Required\ rate\ of\ return = R_F + \beta(R_M - R_F)$$
$$= 8.6\% + 1.2(10.1\% - 8.6\%)$$
$$= 8.6\% + 1.8\%$$
$$= 10.4\%$$

    d.   There are two practical problems with the use of CAPM:

        1)   It is hard to estimate the risk-free rate of return on projects under different economic environments.

        2)   The CAPM is a single-period model. It should not be used for projects lasting more than 1 year.

10. **Quantitative Risk Assessment Tools**

    a.   **Value at risk (VaR)** is a technique that employs a normal distribution (bell curve) to determine the maximum potential gain or loss within a certain period at a given level of confidence.

        1)   The highest point in the curve represents the most probable event with all other possible situations equally distributed around the most probable event.

        2)   Within 1.96 standard deviations from the most probable event, the potential gain or loss can be calculated with 95% confidence.

        3)   Within 2.57 standard deviations from the most probable event, the potential gain or loss can be calculated with 99% confidence.

        4)   For example, management can state with 95% confidence that the potential loss associated with a given risk is $3.7 billion.

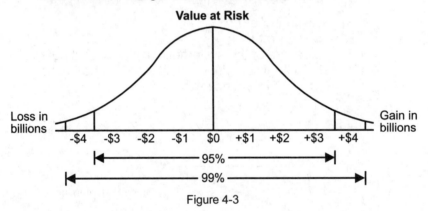

Figure 4-3

    b.   Cash flow at risk and earnings at risk are identical in application to VaR.

Stop and review! You have completed the outline for this subunit. Study multiple-choice question 17 on page 132.

4.5 RECEIVABLES MANAGEMENT

1. **Overview**

    a.   Accounts receivable are carried for competitive and investment purposes.

        1)   A firm almost always must offer credit if its competitors do.

        2)   Customers who choose to pay beyond the stated time limit can be charged financing fees (interest income to the firm).

        3)   Due to the interaction of these two factors, managing accounts receivable must involve the sales, finance, and accounting functions.

    b.   Factors influencing the level of receivables include the soundness of the

        1)   Procedures for evaluating customer creditworthiness,
        2)   Formula for establishing standard credit terms,
        3)   System for tracking accounts receivable and billing customers, and
        4)   Procedures for following up on overdue accounts.

   c.   The optimal credit policy does not seek merely to maximize sales.

      1)   This result could be accomplished by increasing discounts, offering longer payment periods, or accepting riskier customers.

         a)   But the firm cannot ignore the increase in bad debts and its negative effect on cash inflows.

         b)   Thus, the firm must balance default risk (bad debt experience) and sales maximization.

   d.   **Default risk** is the probability that a particular customer will be unwilling or unable to pay a debt.

      1)   To manage (not necessarily minimize) default risk, firms often require written agreements to be signed by the customer, outlining the terms of credit and the consequences for nonpayment.

      2)   Firms often use credit scoring to determine whether to extend credit to a specific customer. Credit scoring assigns numerical values to the elements of credit worthiness.

   e.   The **cash conversion cycle** is the time that passes, on average, between the firm's payment for a purchase of inventory and the collection of cash from a customer on the sale of that inventory.

      1)   The operating cycle is the cash cycle plus the time between purchases and payment.

2.   **Aging Accounts Receivable**

   a.   A common analytical tool is an aging schedule of accounts receivable. It stratifies the accounts depending on time outstanding.

   b.   Since accounts that have been outstanding longest are also the least likely to be collected, an aging of accounts receivable provides useful information on collectability.

EXAMPLE

Midburg prepares the following aging schedule of its accounts receivable:

Balance Range	Less than 30 Days	31-60 Days	61-90 Days	Over 90 Days	Total Balances
$0 - $100	$ 5,000	$ 200	$ 100	$ 100	$ 5,400
$100 - $1,000	8,000	3,800			11,800
$1,000 - $5,000	20,000	2,000	1,900		23,900
$5,000 - $10,000	38,000		8,000	900	46,900
Over $10,000		12,000			12,000
Totals	$71,000	$18,000	$10,000	$1,000	$100,000

Midburg then applies an appropriate percentage to each stratum based on experience.

Aging Intervals	Balance	Estimated Uncollectible	Ending Allowance
Less than 30 days	$ 71,000	2%	$1,420
30-60 days	18,000	12%	2,160
61-90 days	10,000	15%	1,500
Over 90 days	1,000	20%	200
Total	$100,000		$5,280

3.   **Basic Receivables Terms**

   a.   The most common credit terms offered are 2/10, net 30. This convention means that the customer may either deduct 2% of the invoice amount if the invoice is paid within 10 days, or must pay the entire balance by the 30th day.

      1)   Credit terms do not include quantity discounts, which affect the prices of purchases, not financing.

   b.   The **average collection period** (also called the days sales outstanding in receivables) is the average number of days that pass between the time of a sale and payment of the invoice.

4.   **Assessing the Impact of a Change in Credit Terms**

   a.   Amounts of receivables are an opportunity cost, i.e., the return that could be earned if those amounts were invested elsewhere. A key aspect of any change in credit terms is balancing the competitive need to offer credit with the opportunity cost incurred.

   b.   The increased investment in receivables is calculated with this formula:

$$\text{Incremental variable costs} \times \frac{\text{Incremental average collection period}}{\text{Days in year}}$$

      1)   EXAMPLE: The firm is evaluating a proposal to relax its credit standards. Under the new plan, credit sales are expected to increase by $600,000. The new customers attracted by this plan are expected to have a 40-day average collection period. Variable costs are 80% of sales.

Increase in sales	$600,000
Times: Variable cost ratio	× 80%
Increase in variable costs	$480,000

Increased investment in receivables = $480,000 × (40 days ÷ 360 days)
= $53,333

   c.   The cost of a change in credit terms is calculated with this formula:

Increased investment in receivables × Opportunity cost of funds

      1)   Opportunity cost is the maximum benefit forgone by choosing an investment.
      2)   EXAMPLE: Money market instruments are currently paying 12%.

Increased investment in receivables	$53,333
Times: Opportunity cost of funds	× 12%
Cost of new credit plan	$ 6,400

   d.   The **benefit or loss** resulting from a change in credit terms is calculated with this formula:

Incremental contribution margin − Cost of change

      1)   EXAMPLE: The firm can now calculate the net benefit from the proposed change in credit policy:

Increase in sales	$600,000
Times: Contribution margin ratio	× 20%
Increase in contribution margin	$120,000
Less: Cost of new credit plan	(6,400)
Benefit of new credit plan	$113,600

5.   **Factoring**

   a.   Factoring is a transfer of receivables to a third party (a factor) who assumes the responsibility of collection.

    b.   A factor usually receives a high financing fee plus a fee for collection. Furthermore, the factor often operates more efficiently than its clients because of the specialized nature of its services.

EXAMPLE

A factor charges a 2% fee plus an interest rate of 18% on all cash advanced to a transferor of accounts receivable. Monthly sales are $100,000, and the factor advances 90% of the receivables submitted after deducting the 2% fee and the interest. Credit terms are net 60 days. What is the cost to the transferor of this arrangement?

Amount of receivables submitted	$100,000	
Minus: 10% reserve	(10,000)	
Minus: 2% factor's fee	(2,000)	
Amount accruing to the transferor	$ 88,000	
Minus: 18% interest for 60 days	(2,640)	[$88,000 × 18% × (60 ÷ 360)]
Amount to be received immediately	$ 85,360	

The transferor also will receive the $10,000 reserve at the end of the 60-day period if it has not been absorbed by sales returns and allowances. Thus, the total cost to the transferor to factor the receivables for the month is $4,640 ($2,000 factor fee + interest of $2,640). Assuming that the factor has approved the customers' credit in advance (the sale is without recourse), the transferor will not absorb any bad debts.

---

    c.   **Credit card sales** are a common form of factoring. The retailer benefits by prompt receipt of cash and avoidance of bad debts and other costs. In return, the credit card company charges a fee.

6. **Pledging**

    a.   A pledge (a general assignment) is the use of receivables as collateral (security) for a loan. The borrower agrees to use collections of receivables to repay the loan.

        1)   Upon default, the lender can sell the receivables to recover the loan proceeds.

        2)   Because a pledge is a relatively informal arrangement, it is not reflected in the accounts.

Stop and review! You have completed the outline for this subunit. Study multiple-choice questions 18 through 25 beginning on page 132.

4.6 INVENTORY MANAGEMENT

1. **Overview**

    a.   Inventory is primarily held for sale to customers. Additional reasons for carrying inventory include:

        1)   Protecting against supply uncertainty (vendors may have financial difficulties or shipments may be delayed).

        2)   Protecting against fluctuations in demand (in order to capitalize on unexpected spikes in demand, extra inventory must be carried).

            a)   These considerations are balances to ensure that operations are not interrupted by inventory shortages.

    b.   **Costs related to inventory.** Minimizing total inventory cost involves constant evaluation of the tradeoffs among the four components:

        1)   **Purchase costs** are the actual invoice amounts charged by suppliers and include shipping costs. This is also referred to as investment in inventory.

        2)   **Carrying costs** are associated with holding inventory: (a) storage, (b) insurance, (c) security, (d) inventory taxes, (e) depreciation or rent of facilities, (f) interest, (g) obsolescence and spoilage, and (h) the opportunity cost of funds invested in inventory.

        3)   **Ordering costs** are the costs of placing an order with a vendor. They are independent of the number of units ordered. For internally manufactured units, they are the costs of setting up a production line.

4) **Stockout costs** are the opportunity cost of missing a customer order. These can also include the costs of expediting a special shipment necessitated by insufficient inventory on hand.

5) EXAMPLE: The following cost data are available for an item of inventory:

Invoice price	$300.00 per unit
Shipping costs	$ 15.00 per unit
Inventory insurance	$ 5.00 per unit
Handling	80.00 per order
Order cost	15.00 per order
Cost of capital	20%

The per-unit purchase cost and the cost of carrying a unit of inventory can be calculated as follows:

Invoice price	$300
Shipping costs	15
Per-unit purchase cost	$315
Times: Cost of capital	× 20%
Opportunity cost	$ 63
Insurance on inventory	5
Per-unit carrying cost	$ 68

c. The optimal level of inventory is the one that (1) considers the reasons for carrying inventory and (2) minimizes total inventory cost.

d. To protect against the risk of stockouts, a level of extra stock, **safety stock**, is held.

1) Maintaining safety stock increases carrying costs.

2) Determining the appropriate level of safety stock involves balancing the variability of demand, variability in lead time, and level of risk of stockout the firm is willing to accept.

3) The cost of safety stock is the carrying cost of the safety stock plus the expected stockout cost.

e. The challenge inherent in minimizing total inventory cost is illustrated in the following diagram:

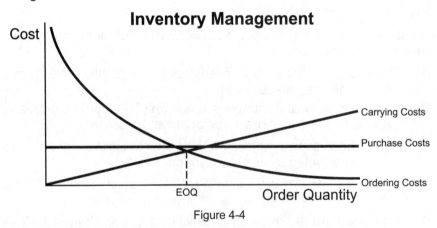

Figure 4-4

f. The following relationships exist:

1) Stockout costs can be minimized only by incurring high carrying costs.

2) Carrying costs can be minimized only by incurring the high fixed costs of placing many small orders.

3) Ordering costs can be minimized but only at the cost of storing large quantities.

2. **Just-in-Time and Kanban Inventory Systems**

    a. In a just-in-time (JIT) inventory system, the storage of inventory is treated as a nonvalue-adding activity.

        1) All materials inventories (and their associated carrying costs) are reduced or eliminated entirely. Binding agreements with suppliers ensure that materials arrive exactly when they are needed and not before.

        2) JIT is a pull or demand-driven system. Production of goods does not begin until an order has been received. In this way, finished goods inventories also are eliminated.

    b. Another method of improving inventory flow is the kanban system, developed by the Toyota Motor Corporation (kanban is not characteristic of Japanese industry as a whole).

        1) Kanban means ticket. Tickets (also described as cards or markers) control the flow of production or parts so that they are produced or obtained in the needed amounts at the needed times.

        2) A basic kanban system includes a withdrawal kanban that states the quantity that a later process should withdraw from its predecessor, a production kanban that states the output of the preceding process, and a vendor kanban that tells a vendor what, how much, where, and when to deliver.

3. **Inventory Replenishment Models**

    a. **Lead time** is the time between placing an order with a supplier and receipt of the goods.

        1) When lead time is known and demand is uniform, goods can be timed to arrive just as inventory on hand is exhausted.

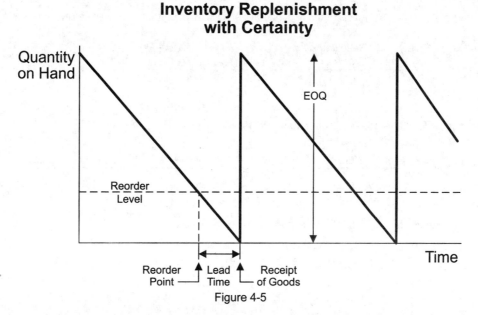

Inventory Replenishment with Certainty

Figure 4-5

    b. The **reorder point** can be calculated as follows:

(Average demand × Lead time) + Safety stock

    c. The certainty depicted in the graph above is rare outside of just-in-time systems. Accordingly, safety stock is held as a hedge against contingencies.

        1) Determining the appropriate level of safety stock involves a probabilistic calculation.

        2) It balances the variability of demand with the acceptable risk of stockout costs.

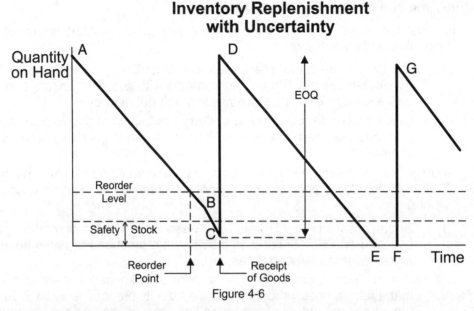

Inventory Replenishment with Uncertainty

Figure 4-6

d.   The diagram above assumes uncertainty. At point B, during the lead time of an order, demand increased, and the safety stock was used. Receipt of the order restored quantities to point D. During EF, a stockout occurred because of a delay in receipt of the order. Receipt of the order restored quantities to point G.

e.   The total cost of carrying safety stock consists of two components:

Cost of carrying safety stock = Expected stockout cost + Carrying cost

---

EXAMPLE of the Cost of Safety Stock

A firm has prepared the following schedule of the likelihood of stockouts at various levels of safety stock for the upcoming year:

Safety Stock Level	Resulting Stockout		Probability		Expected Stockout
200	0	×	10%	=	0
100	100	×	20%	=	20
0	100	×	15%	=	15

Expected stockout costs for the year are calculated as follows:

Safety Stock Level	Expected Stockout		Unit Cost of Stockout		Orders per Year		Expected Stockout Costs
200	0	×	$3.50	×	18	=	$0
100	20	×	$3.50	×	18	=	$1,260
0	15	×	$3.50	×	18	=	$945

Carrying costs for the various levels of safety stock are calculated as follows:

Safety Stock Level		Unit Carrying Costs		Total Carrying Costs
200	×	$4.00	=	$800
100	×	$4.00	=	$400
0	×	$4.00	=	$0

The annual cost of safety stock for each level can now be calculated. In this case, the cost of safety stock is minimized by holding 200 units.

Safety Stock Level	Expected Stockout Costs		Total Carrying Costs		Total Costs of Safety Stock
200	$0	+	$800	=	$800
100	$1,260	+	$400	=	$1,660
0	$945	+	$0	=	$945

4. **Determining the Order Quantity**

    a.   Refer to the graph "Inventory Replenishment with Uncertainty" on the previous page. Peak inventory is at different levels at points D and G.

        1)   By contrast, the order quantities (lines CD and FG) are the same length. This indicates that effective inventory management is concerned not with the peak level of inventory but with the size of each order.

    b.   The **economic order quantity (EOQ)** model is a mathematical means of determining the order quantity. It minimizes the sum of ordering costs and carrying costs.

$$Economic\ order\ quantity\ (EOQ)\ =\ \sqrt{\frac{2aD}{k}}$$

        If: a = fixed cost per purchase order (i.e., ordering costs)
             D = periodic demand in units
             k = carrying costs per unit

        NOTE: This concept is depicted in the graph "Inventory Management" on page 124.

    c.   The following are the assumptions of the EOQ model:

        1)   Demand is uniform.
        2)   Carrying costs are constant.
        3)   The same quantity is ordered at each reorder point.
        4)   No quantity discounts are allowed.
        5)   Sales are perfectly predictable.
        6)   Lead time is known with certainty.
        7)   Deliveries are consistent.
        8)   Adequate inventory is maintained to avoid stockouts.

    d.   A change in any of the variables changes the EOQ solution. If demand or order costs rise, each order must contain more units. If carrying costs rise, each order must contain fewer units.

Stop and review! You have completed the outline for this subunit. Study multiple-choice questions 26 through 30 beginning on page 135.

QUESTIONS

4.1 Working Capital

1. Net working capital is the difference between

    A. Current assets and current liabilities.

    B. Fixed assets and fixed liabilities.

    C. Total assets and total liabilities.

    D. Shareholders' investment and cash.

Answer (A) is correct.
  REQUIRED: The definition of net working capital.
  DISCUSSION: Net working capital is defined by accountants as the difference between current assets and current liabilities. Working capital is a measure of short-term solvency.
  Answer (B) is incorrect. Working capital refers to the difference between current assets and current liabilities; fixed assets are not a component. Answer (C) is incorrect. Total assets and total liabilities are not components of working capital; only current items are included. Answer (D) is incorrect. Shareholders' equity is not a component of working capital; only current items are included in the concept of working capital.

2. Determining the appropriate level of working capital for a firm requires

    A. Changing the capital structure and dividend policy of the firm.

    B. Maintaining short-term debt at the lowest possible level because it is generally more expensive than long-term debt.

    C. Offsetting the benefit of current assets and current liabilities against the probability of technical insolvency.

    D. Maintaining a high proportion of liquid assets to total assets in order to maximize the return on total investments.

Answer (C) is correct.
  REQUIRED: The requirement for determining the appropriate level of working capital.
  DISCUSSION: Working capital finance concerns the determination of the optimal level, mix, and use of current assets and current liabilities. The objective is to minimize the cost of maintaining liquidity while guarding against the possibility of technical insolvency. Technical insolvency is defined as the inability to pay debts as they come due.
  Answer (A) is incorrect. Capital structure and dividends relate to capital structure finance, not working capital finance. Answer (B) is incorrect. Short-term debt is usually less expensive than long-term debt. Answer (D) is incorrect. Liquid assets do not ordinarily earn high returns relative to long-term assets, so holding the former will not maximize the return on total assets.

3. Which one of the following would increase the net working capital of a firm?

    A. Cash payment of payroll taxes payable.

    B. Purchase of a new plant financed by a 20-year mortgage.

    C. Cash collection of accounts receivable.

    D. Refinancing a short-term note payable with a 2-year note payable.

Answer (D) is correct.
  REQUIRED: The transaction that increases working capital.
  DISCUSSION: Net working capital equals current assets minus current liabilities. Refinancing a short-term note with a 2-year note payable decreases current liabilities, thus increasing working capital.
  Answer (A) is incorrect. A cash payment of payroll taxes decreases current assets and current liabilities by equal amounts. Answer (B) is incorrect. Buying a new plant with a 20-year mortgage has no effect on current assets or current liabilities. Answer (C) is incorrect. Cash collection of an account receivable increases one current asset and decreases another by the same amount.

4. A company is experiencing a sharp increase in sales activity and a steady increase in production, so management has adopted an aggressive working capital policy. Therefore, the company's current level of net working capital

    A. Would most likely be the same as in any other type of business condition as business cycles tend to balance out over time.

    B. Would most likely be lower than under other business conditions in order that the company can maximize profits while minimizing working capital investment.

    C. Would most likely be higher than under other business conditions so that there will be sufficient funds to replenish assets.

    D. Would most likely be higher than under other business conditions as the company's profits are increasing.

Answer (B) is correct.
  REQUIRED: The effect of an aggressive working capital policy.
  DISCUSSION: When a firm has an aggressive working capital policy, management keeps the investment in working capital at a minimum. Thus, a growing company would want to invest its funds in capital goods and not in idle assets. This policy maximizes return on investment at the price of the risk of minimal liquidity.
  Answer (A) is incorrect. The growing company is more apt to emphasize production rather than protecting against technical insolvency by maintaining a high level of working capital. Answer (C) is incorrect. The company will prefer to expend funds on capital goods. Answer (D) is incorrect. The company needs its profits to invest in new production equipment in order to grow.

4.2 Cash Management

5. What is the benefit for a firm with daily cash receipts of $15,000 to be able to speed up collections by 2 days, assuming an 8% annual return on short-term investments and no cost to the company to speed up collections?

A. $2,400 daily benefit.

B. $2,400 annual benefit.

C. $15,000 annual benefit.

D. $30,000 annual benefit.

Answer (B) is correct.
    REQUIRED: The amount of benefit.
    DISCUSSION: Speeding up collections by 2 days will raise the firm's average cash balance by $30,000. At 8% interest, the benefit will be $2,400 annually [($15,000 × 2 days) × .08].
    Answer (A) is incorrect. This figure is the annual, not the daily, benefit. Answer (C) is incorrect. This figure is the amount of daily cash receipts. Answer (D) is incorrect. This figure is the reduction in receivables.

6. A consultant recommends that a company hold funds for the following two reasons:

    Reason #1: Cash needs can fluctuate substantially throughout the year.

    Reason #2: Opportunities for buying at a discount may appear during the year.

The cash balances used to address the reasons given above are correctly classified as

	Reason #1	Reason #2
A.	Speculative balances	Speculative balances
B.	Speculative balances	Precautionary balances
C.	Precautionary balances	Speculative balances
D.	Precautionary balances	Precautionary balances

Answer (C) is correct.
    REQUIRED: The correct classifications for the reasons for a firm to hold cash.
    DISCUSSION: The three motives for holding cash are as a medium of exchange, as a precautionary measure, and for speculation. Reason #1 can be classified as a precautionary measure, and Reason #2 can be classified as holding cash for speculation.
    Answer (A) is incorrect. Reason #1 is fulfilled by precautionary balances. Answer (B) is incorrect. This combination results from reversing the correct balances. Answer (D) is incorrect. Reason #2 is fulfilled by speculative balances.

7. An entity has received proposals from several banks to establish a lockbox system to speed up receipts. The entity receives an average of 700 checks per day averaging $1,800 each, and its cost of short-term funds is 7% per year. Assuming that all proposals will produce equivalent processing results and using a 360-day year, which one of the following proposals is optimal for the entity?

A. A $0.50 fee per check.

B. A flat fee of $125,000 per year.

C. A fee of 0.03% of the amount collected.

D. A compensating balance of $1,750,000.

Answer (D) is correct.
    REQUIRED: The optimal fee structure for a lockbox system.
    DISCUSSION: Multiplying 700 checks times 360 days results in a total of 252,000 checks per year. Accordingly, using a $0.50 fee per check, total annual cost is $126,000 (252,000 × $.50), which is less desirable than a $125,000 flat fee. Given that the annual collections equal $453,600,000 (700 checks × $1,800 × 360 days), a fee of 0.03% of the amount collected is also less desirable because the annual fee would be $136,080 ($453,600,000 × .03%). The best option is therefore to maintain a compensating balance of $1,750,000 when the cost of funds is 7%, resulting in a total cost of $122,500 ($1,750,000 × 7%).
    Answer (A) is incorrect. A $0.50 fee per check will result in an annual cost of $126,000. Answer (B) is incorrect. An annual cost of $125,000 is not optimal. Answer (C) is incorrect. A fee of 0.03% of the amount collected will result in an annual cost of $136,080.

8. The **most** direct way to prepare a cash budget for a manufacturing firm is to include

A. Projected sales, credit terms, and net income.

B. Projected net income, depreciation, and goodwill impairment.

C. Projected purchases, percentages of purchases paid, and net income.

D. Projected sales and purchases, percentages of collections, and terms of payments.

Answer (D) is correct.
    REQUIRED: The most direct way of preparing a cash budget for a manufacturing firm.
    DISCUSSION: The most direct way of preparing a cash budget requires incorporation of sales projections and credit terms, collection percentages, estimated purchases and payment terms, and other cash receipts and disbursements. In other words, preparation of the cash budget requires consideration of both inflows and outflows.
    Answer (A) is incorrect. Net income is an accrual-basis number. Answer (B) is incorrect. Net income, goodwill impairment, and depreciation are accrual-basis amounts. Answer (C) is incorrect. Collection percentages must be considered, and net income includes noncash elements.

9. A compensating balance

    A. Compensates a financial institution for services rendered by providing it with deposits of funds.

    B. Is used to compensate for possible losses on a marketable securities portfolio.

    C. Is a level of inventory held to compensate for variations in usage rate and lead time.

    D. Is the amount of prepaid interest on a loan.

Answer (A) is correct.
    REQUIRED: The true statement about compensating balances.
    DISCUSSION: A compensating balance is a minimum amount that the bank requires the firm to keep in its demand account. Compensating balances are noninterest-bearing and are meant to compensate the bank for various services rendered, such as unlimited check writing. These funds are unavailable for investment purposes and thus incur an opportunity cost.
    Answer (B) is incorrect. In financial accounting, a valuation allowance is used to reflect losses on marketable securities. Answer (C) is incorrect. Safety stock is held for such purposes. Answer (D) is incorrect. Interest deducted in advance is discount interest.

10. Shown below is a forecast of sales for the first 4 months of the year (all amounts are in thousands of dollars).

	January	February	March	April
Cash sales	$ 15	$ 24	$18	$14
Sales on credit	100	120	90	70

On average, 50% of credit sales are paid for in the month of sale, 30% in the month following the sale, and the remainder is paid 2 months after the month of sale. Assuming there are no bad debts, the expected cash inflow for March is

    A. $138,000

    B. $122,000

    C. $119,000

    D. $108,000

Answer (C) is correct.
    REQUIRED: The expected cash inflows for March.
    DISCUSSION: Cash inflows for March would consist of 50% of March credit sales ($90 × 50% = $45), plus 30% of February credit sales ($120 × 30% = $36), plus 20% of January credit sales ($100 × 20% = $20), plus cash sales for March of $18. Consequently, total collections equal $119,000.
    Answer (A) is incorrect. The amount of $138,000 equals the sum of February credit sales and March cash sales. Answer (B) is incorrect. The amount of $122,000 equals 50% of January credit sales, 30% of February credit sales, 20% of March credit sales, and 100% of March cash sales. Answer (D) is incorrect. The amount of $108,000 is the total sales for March, not the total cash collections for March.

11.

	Purchases	Sales
January	$150,000	$100,000
February	150,000	200,000
March	150,000	250,000
April	130,000	250,000
May	130,000	300,000
June	100,000	230,000

A cash payment equal to 50% of purchases is made at the time of purchase, and 25% is paid in each of the next 2 months. Purchases for the previous November and December were $140,000 per month. Payroll for a month is 10% of that month's sales, and other operating expenses are 15% of the following month's sales (July sales were $210,000). Interest payments were $25,000 paid quarterly in January and April. Cash disbursements for the month of April were

    A. $130,000

    B. $140,000

    C. $210,000

    D. $235,000

Answer (D) is correct.
    REQUIRED: The cash disbursements for April.
    DISCUSSION: Cash disbursements for the month of April are calculated as follows:

April purchases:	$130,000 × 50%	=	$ 65,000
March purchases:	150,000 × 25%	=	37,500
February purchases:	150,000 × 25%	=	37,500
April payroll:	250,000 × 10%	=	25,000
April op. expenses:	300,000 × 15%	=	45,000
Interest		=	25,000
Total April disbursements		=	$235,000

    Answer (A) is incorrect. The purchases for the month equal $130,000. Answer (B) is incorrect. The amount of $140,000 excludes other operating expenses, payroll, and interest. Answer (C) is incorrect. The amount of $210,000 excludes the $25,000 interest payment.

4.3 Marketable Securities Management

12. In smaller businesses in which the management of cash is but one of numerous functions performed by the treasurer, various cost incentives and diversification arguments suggest that surplus cash should be invested in

- A. Commercial paper.
- B. Bankers' acceptances.
- C. Money market mutual funds.
- D. Corporate bonds.

Answer (C) is correct.

REQUIRED: The most efficient manner in which a small firm could invest short-term surpluses of cash.

DISCUSSION: A small firm with surplus cash should invest for the highest return and lowest risk. The ability to convert the investment into cash without a loss of principal is also important. Money market mutual funds invest in money market certificates such as treasury bills, negotiable CDs, and commercial paper. Because of diversification, these mutual funds are superior to any single instrument.

Answer (A) is incorrect. A small firm may not have enough surplus cash to invest in commercial paper, which usually consists of secured or unsecured promissory notes of large corporations. Answer (B) is incorrect. Bankers' acceptances do not provide the diversification of a mutual fund. Answer (D) is incorrect. An increase in interest rates could cause a substantial loss in principal.

13. When managing cash and short-term investments, a corporate treasurer is primarily concerned with

- A. Maximizing rate of return.
- B. Minimizing taxes.
- C. Investing in Treasury bonds since they have no default risk.
- D. Liquidity and safety.

Answer (D) is correct.

REQUIRED: The primary concern when managing cash and short-term investments.

DISCUSSION: Cash and short-term investments are crucial to a firm's continuing success. Sufficient liquidity must be available to meet payments as they come due. At the same time, liquid assets are subject to significant control risk. Therefore, liquidity and safety are the primary concerns of the treasurer when dealing with highly liquid assets. Cash and short-term investments are held because of their ability to facilitate routine operations of the company. These assets are not held for purposes of achieving investment returns.

Answer (A) is incorrect. Most companies are not in business to earn high returns on liquid assets (i.e., they are held to facilitate operations). Answer (B) is incorrect. The holding of cash and cash-like assets is not a major factor in controlling taxes. Answer (C) is incorrect. Investments in Treasury bonds do not have sufficient liquidity to serve as short-term assets.

14. All of the following are alternative marketable securities suitable for investment **except**

- A. U.S. Treasury bills.
- B. Eurodollars.
- C. Commercial paper.
- D. Convertible bonds.

Answer (D) is correct.

REQUIRED: The item that is not a marketable security.

DISCUSSION: Marketable securities are near-cash items used primarily for short-term investment. Examples include U.S. Treasury bills, Eurodollars, commercial paper, money-market mutual funds with portfolios of short-term securities, bankers' acceptances, floating rate preferred stock, and negotiable CDs of U.S. banks. A convertible bond is not a short-term investment because its maturity date is usually more than 1 year in the future and its price can be influenced substantially by changes in interest rates or by changes in the investee's stock price.

Answer (A) is incorrect. U.S. Treasury bills are short-term marketable securities. Answer (B) is incorrect. Eurodollars are short-term marketable securities. Answer (C) is incorrect. Commercial paper is a short-term marketable security.

15. Which security is **most** often held as a substitute for cash?

- A. Treasury bills.
- B. Common stock.
- C. Gold.
- D. Aaa corporate bonds.

Answer (A) is correct.

REQUIRED: The security most often held as a substitute for cash.

DISCUSSION: A Treasury bill is a short-term U.S. government obligation that is sold at a discount from its face value. A Treasury bill is highly liquid and nearly risk-free, and it is often held as a substitute for cash.

16. The **best** example of a marketable security with minimal risk would be

    A. Municipal bonds.

    B. The common stock of an AAA-rated company.

    C. Gold.

    D. The commercial paper of an AAA-rated company.

Answer (D) is correct.
    REQUIRED: The best example of a marketable security with minimal risk.
    DISCUSSION: Of the choices given, the commercial paper of a top-rated (most creditworthy) company has the least risk. Commercial paper is preferable to stock or stock options because the latter represent only a residual equity in a corporation. Commercial paper is debt and thus has priority over shareholders' claims. Also, commercial paper is a very short-term investment. The maximum maturity allowed without SEC registration is 270 days. However, it can be sold only to sophisticated investors without registration.
    Answer (A) is incorrect. Municipal bonds are rarely considered marketable securities in the accounting sense. They constitute long-term debt. Answer (B) is incorrect. Common stock does not have as high a priority in company assets as commercial paper or other debt. Answer (C) is incorrect. Gold is a commodity, not a security. Also, its price fluctuates for many reasons that do not affect the value of commercial paper.

4.4 Portfolio Management

17. The state of the economy has a strong effect on expected returns as shown below:

State of the Economy	Probability	Stock Returns
Recession	.35	–10%
Stable	.40	10%
Expansion	.25	30%

What is the expected rate of return?

    A. 8%

    B. 10%

    C. 15%

    D. 30%

Answer (A) is correct.
    REQUIRED: The expected rate of return on a stock given probabilities for different situations and corresponding returns.
    DISCUSSION: The expected rate of return on an investment is the sum of the weighted averages of the possible outcomes weighted by their probabilities. The computation is performed as follows:

State of the Economy	Possible Rate of Return		Probability		Weighted Averages
Recession	(10)%	×	35%	=	(3.5)%
Stable	10%	×	40%	=	4.0%
Expansion	30%	×	25%	=	7.5%
Expected rate of return					8.0%

    Answer (B) is incorrect. The figure of 10% is a simple average of the returns. Answer (C) is incorrect. The figure of 15% results from adding, rather than subtracting, the average for the recession state. Answer (D) is incorrect. The figure of 30% results from failing to weight the rates of return by their probabilities.

4.5 Receivables Management

18. The average collection period for a firm measures the number of days

    A. After a typical credit sale is made until the firm receives the payment.

    B. For a typical check to "clear" through the banking system.

    C. Beyond the end of the credit period before a typical customer payment is received.

    D. Before a typical account becomes delinquent.

Answer (A) is correct.
    REQUIRED: The meaning of a firm's average collection period.
    DISCUSSION: The average collection period measures the number of days between the date of sale and the date of collection. It should be related to a firm's credit terms. For example, a firm that allows terms of 2/15, net 30, should have an average collection period of somewhere between 15 and 30 days.
    Answer (B) is incorrect. It describes the concept of float. Answer (C) is incorrect. The average collection period includes the total time before a payment is received, including the periods both before and after the end of the normal credit period. Answer (D) is incorrect. It describes the normal credit period.

19. Which of the following represents a firm's average gross receivables balance?

  I.   Days' sales in receivables × accounts receivable turnover.

  II. Average daily sales × average collection period.

  III. Net sales ÷ average gross receivables.

    A. I only.

    B. I and II only.

    C. II only.

    D. II and III only.

Answer (C) is correct.
    REQUIRED: The calculation of the average gross receivables balance.
    DISCUSSION: A firm's average gross receivables balance can be calculated by multiplying average daily sales by the average collection period (days' sales outstanding). Alternatively, annual credit sales can be divided by the accounts-receivable turnover (net credit sales ÷ average accounts receivable) to obtain the average balance in receivables.
    Answer (A) is incorrect. Alternative I cannot be correct. Neither of the multiplicands is a dollar figure, so the product could not be the dollar balance of receivables. Answer (B) is incorrect. Alternative I cannot be correct. Neither of the multiplicands is a dollar figure, so the product could not be the dollar balance of receivables. Answer (D) is incorrect. Alternative III cannot be correct. It contains average gross receivables, the amount being calculated.

20. An aging of accounts receivable measures the

    A. Ability of the firm to meet short-term obligations.

    B. Average length of time that receivables have been outstanding.

    C. Percentage of sales that have been collected after a given time period.

    D. Amount of receivables that have been outstanding for given lengths of time.

Answer (D) is correct.
    REQUIRED: The item measured by an aging of accounts receivable.
    DISCUSSION: The purpose of an aging of receivables is to classify receivables by due date. Those that are current (not past due) are listed in one column, those less than 30 days past due in another column, etc. The amount in each category can then be multiplied by an estimated bad debt percentage that is based on a company's credit experience and other factors. The theory is that the oldest receivables are the least likely to be collectible. Aging the receivables and estimating the uncollectible amounts is one method of arriving at the appropriate balance sheet valuation of the accounts receivable account.
    Answer (A) is incorrect. An aging schedule is used for receivables, not liabilities. Answer (B) is incorrect. An aging schedule concerns specific accounts, not averages. Answer (C) is incorrect. An aging schedule focuses on uncollected receivables.

21. When a company analyzes credit applicants and increases the quality of the accounts rejected, the company is attempting to

    A. Maximize sales.

    B. Increase bad-debt losses.

    C. Increase the average collection period.

    D. Maximize profits.

Answer (D) is correct.
    REQUIRED: The purpose of increasing the quality of accounts rejected.
    DISCUSSION: Increasing the quality of the accounts rejected means that fewer sales will be made. The company is therefore not trying to maximize its sales or increase its bad debt losses. The objective is to reduce bad debt losses and thereby maximize profits.
    Answer (A) is incorrect. Tightening credit will reduce sales. Answer (B) is incorrect. Tightening credit will reduce bad debt losses. Answer (C) is incorrect. Most likely, higher quality accounts will mean a shorter average collection period.

22. An organization would usually offer credit terms of 2/10, net 30 when

    A. The organization can borrow funds at a rate exceeding the annual interest cost.

    B. The organization can borrow funds at a rate less than the annual interest cost.

    C. The cost of capital approaches the prime rate.

    D. Most competitors are offering the same terms, and the organization has a shortage of cash.

Answer (D) is correct.
    REQUIRED: The reason for offering credit terms of 2/10, net 30.
    DISCUSSION: Because these terms involve an annual interest cost of over 36%, a company would not offer them unless it desperately needed cash. Also, credit terms are typically somewhat standardized within an industry. Thus, if most companies in the industry offer similar terms, a firm will likely be forced to match the competition or lose market share.
    Answer (A) is incorrect. If the company does not need cash, it would not offer cash discounts, regardless of its cost of capital, unless required to match competition. Answer (B) is incorrect. The ability to borrow at a lower rate is a reason for not offering cash discounts. Answer (C) is incorrect. The relationship between the cost of capital and the prime rate may not be relevant if the firm cannot borrow at the prime rate.

23. Which one of the following statements is most likely to be **true** if a seller extends credit to a purchaser for a period of time longer than the purchaser's operating cycle? The seller

A. Will have a lower level of accounts receivable than those companies whose credit period is shorter than the purchaser's operating cycle.

B. Is, in effect, financing more than just the purchaser's inventory needs.

C. Can be certain that the purchaser will be able to convert the inventory into cash before payment is due.

D. Has no need for a stated discount rate or credit period.

Answer (B) is correct.
   REQUIRED: The true statement about extending credit for a period longer than the purchaser's operating cycle.
   DISCUSSION: The normal operating cycle is the period from the acquisition of inventory to the collection of the account receivable. If trade credit is for a period longer than the normal operating cycle, the seller must be financing more than just the purchase of inventory.
   Answer (A) is incorrect. A seller who extends long-term credit will have a higher level of receivables than a firm with a shorter credit period. Answer (C) is incorrect. The seller is not guaranteed that a purchaser will resell the merchandise. Answer (D) is incorrect. Offering a discount may accelerate payment.

24. A company believes that its collection costs could be reduced through modification of collection procedures. This action is expected to result in a lengthening of the average collection period from 28 days to 34 days; however, there will be no change in uncollectible accounts. The company's budgeted credit sales for the coming year are $27,000,000, and short-term interest rates are expected to average 8%. To make the changes in collection procedures cost beneficial, the minimum savings in collection costs (using a 360-day year) for the coming year would have to be

A. $30,000

B. $36,000

C. $180,000

D. $360,000

Answer (B) is correct.
   REQUIRED: The minimum savings in collection costs that would be necessary to make the lengthened credit period beneficial.
   DISCUSSION: If the change is adopted, the company's average balance in receivables will increase by $450,000 {$27,000,000 × [(34 days – 28 days) ÷ 360 days]}. The minimum savings that the company must experience to justify the change is therefore $36,000 ($450,000 × 8%).

25. A company had total sales of $500,000 in the first quarter of the year, which was the same amount as it recorded in the first quarter of the prior year. However, its accounts receivable balance increased from $230,000 last year to $300,000 this year. Which one of the following is the **most** likely explanation for the increase in the accounts receivable balance?

A. The company initiated the use of factoring in the current year.

B. The company shortened its payment terms in the current year from 60 days to 30 days.

C. The company discontinued the use of factoring in the current year.

D. The company hired more people in its credit and collections department.

Answer (C) is correct.
   REQUIRED: The most likely explanation for the increase in the accounts receivable balance.
   DISCUSSION: Factoring is a transfer of receivables to a third party (a factor) who assumes the responsibility of collection. The factor often operates more efficiently than its clients because of the specialized nature of its services. If the company stopped selling accounts receivable to the factor, there would be more accounts receivable in the current year.
   Answer (A) is incorrect. If the company started to use factoring, the current year's accounts receivable would be less than the prior year's. Answer (B) is incorrect. Changes in payment terms do not affect accounts receivable balance. Answer (D) is incorrect. Hiring more people in the credit and collections department would not reduce the accounts receivable balance.

4.6 Inventory Management

26. The optimal level of inventory is affected by all of the following **except** the

    A. Usage rate of inventory per time period.

    B. Cost per unit of inventory.

    C. Current level of inventory.

    D. Cost of placing an order for merchandise.

Answer (C) is correct.
    REQUIRED: The item that does not affect the optimal level of inventory.
    DISCUSSION: The optimal level of inventory is affected by the factors in the economic order quantity (EOQ) model and delivery or production lead times. These factors are the annual demand for inventory, the carrying cost, which includes the interest on funds invested in inventory, the usage rate, and the cost of placing an order or making a production run. The current level of inventory has nothing to do with the optimal inventory level.
    Answer (A) is incorrect. The usage rate of inventory is a factor in determining how much inventory to carry. Answer (B) is incorrect. The cost of inventory affects carrying costs and a firm wants to minimize its inventory carrying costs. Answer (D) is incorrect. The cost of placing an order affects how often orders are placed. A firm wants to minimize its ordering costs.

27. An example of a carrying cost is

    A. Disruption of production schedules.

    B. Quantity discounts lost.

    C. Handling costs.

    D. Spoilage.

Answer (D) is correct.
    REQUIRED: The inventory carrying cost.
    DISCUSSION: Inventory costs consist of four categories: purchase costs, order or set-up costs, carrying (holding) costs, and stockout costs. Carrying costs include storage costs for inventory items plus opportunity cost (i.e., the cost incurred by investing in inventory rather than making an income-earning investment). Examples are insurance, spoilage, interest on invested capital, obsolescence, and warehousing costs.
    Answer (A) is incorrect. Disruption of production schedules may result from a stockout. Answer (B) is incorrect. Quantity discounts lost are related to ordering costs or inventory acquisition costs. Answer (C) is incorrect. Shipping and handling costs are included in acquisition costs.

28. A major supplier has offered a corporation a year-end special purchase whereby it could purchase 180,000 cases of sport drink at $10 per case. The corporation normally orders 30,000 cases per month at $12 per case. The corporation's cost of capital is 9%. In calculating the overall opportunity cost of this offer, the cost of carrying the increased inventory would be

    A. $32,400

    B. $40,500

    C. $64,800

    D. $81,000

Answer (A) is correct.
    REQUIRED: The cost of carrying the increased inventory.
    DISCUSSION: If the corporation makes the special purchase of 6 months of inventory (180,000 cases ÷ 30,000 cases per month), the average inventory for the 6-month period will be $900,000 [(180,000 × $10) ÷ 2]. If the special purchase is not made, the average inventory for the same period will be the average monthly inventory of $180,000 [(30,000 × $12) ÷ 2]. Accordingly, the incremental average inventory is $720,000 ($900,000 − $180,000), and the interest cost of the incremental 6-month investment is $32,400 [($720,000 × 9%) ÷ 2].
    Answer (B) is incorrect. The amount of $40,500 is the result of assuming an incremental average inventory of $900,000. Answer (C) is incorrect. The interest cost for 12 months is $64,800. Answer (D) is incorrect. The amount of $81,000 is the result of assuming an incremental average inventory of $900,000 and a 12-month period.

29. The following information regarding inventory policy was assembled. The company uses a 50-week year in all calculations.

Sales	12,000 units per year
Order quantity	4,000 units
Safety stock	1,500 units
Lead time	5 weeks

The reorder point is

    A. 5,500 units.

    B. 2,700 units.

    C. 1,200 units.

    D. 240 units.

Answer (B) is correct.
    REQUIRED: The level of inventory at which an order should be placed.
    DISCUSSION: The reorder point is the inventory level at which an order should be placed. It can be quantified using the following equation:

Reorder point = (Average weekly demand × Lead time) +
               Safety stock
        = [(12,000 units ÷ 50 weeks) × 5 weeks] +
          1,500 units
        = 1,200 units + 1,500 units
        = 2,700 units

    Answer (A) is incorrect. This number of units equals the order size plus the safety stock. Answer (C) is incorrect. This number of units omits safety stock. Answer (D) is incorrect. This number of units is the average weekly usage.

30. In inventory management, the safety stock will tend to increase if the

    A. Carrying cost increases.

    B. Cost of running out of stock decreases.

    C. Variability of the lead time increases.

    D. Variability of the usage rate decreases.

Answer (C) is correct.
    REQUIRED: The factor that will cause safety stocks to increase.
    DISCUSSION: A company maintains safety stocks to protect itself against the losses caused by stockouts. These can take the form of lost sales or lost production time. Safety stock is necessary because of the variability in lead time and usage rates. As the variability in lead time increases, a company will tend to carry larger safety stocks.
    Answer (A) is incorrect. An increase in inventory carrying costs makes it less economical to carry safety stocks. Answer (B) is incorrect. If the cost of stockouts declines, the incentive to carry large safety stocks is reduced. Answer (D) is incorrect. A decline in the variability of usage makes it easier to plan orders, and safety stocks will be less necessary.

Access the **Gleim CMA Premium Review System** from your Gleim Personal Classroom to continue your studies with exam-emulating multiple-choice questions!

4.7 ESSAY QUESTIONS

Scenario for Essay Questions 1, 2, 3, 4

Attract-One, Inc. (AOI), a moderately profitable producer of fragrances, has been in business for a number of years and sells its products through its U.S. retailer network. In the last year, AOI has developed and introduced a line of fragrances that has had wide public acceptance. Retailer remittances have grown to an average of $200,000 each business day, with additional collections of $1,250,000 a day for each 4-day period following the special occasions of Valentine's Day, Mother's Day, June graduations, and Christmas.

AOI is continuing to expand its network of retail outlets and introduce new lines of consumer products, fully expecting continued growth of the company. As a result, Steve Louhan, treasurer, has been hired to direct AOI's cash management function. After reviewing the company's centralized operations, Louhan found that retailer remittances take an average of 5 mail days to reach AOI. An additional 2 days are needed for in-house processing before bank deposits are made.

Louhan has investigated various regional lockbox arrangements as a means to accelerate this cash collection process. Louhan determined that with a three-bank system, one each in the eastern, central, and western regions of the U.S., mail times could be reduced by 2 days. In addition, the in-house check processing would be eliminated. The banks would provide AOI with a listing of daily transactions and any supporting documents that retailers submit with payments. The lockbox service charges would be $1,000 per month for each bank, and Louhan estimates that 6% interest could be earned on short-term investments.

Louhan is also considering various ways of investing available funds, including the use of marketable securities. He believes this is particularly important during the peak periods when cash inflows are large.

Questions

1. Briefly describe the responsibilities of the cash management function.

2. Identify and describe at least two motives for a company to hold cash.

3. a. Identify and explain at least three characteristics of marketable securities that a company should consider when investing.

    b. Identify at least three types of financial instruments that would meet Attract-One, Inc.'s cash and investing needs.

4. Recommend whether or not Attract-One, Inc., should implement a lockbox system by preparing an analysis using a 360-day year.

Essay Questions 1, 2, 3, 4 — Unofficial Answers

1.   The responsibilities of the cash management function include planning and controlling cash collections, disbursements, and cash balances in order to maintain liquidity, as well as develop banking relationships.

2.   At least two motives for a company to hold cash include using cash for

   a.   Transactions, since cash is necessary to conduct business, such as purchases, paying wages, taxes, or dividends

   b.   Precautions against unexpected needs, as cash inflows and outflows are unpredictable

3.   a.   At least three characteristics that a firm should consider when investing in marketable securities include

      1)   Default risk, as safety of principal is an important concern for investments that are to be included in the short-term portfolio

      2)   Marketability, as the securities should be easy to sell for cash liquidity needs

      3)   Maturity, as yields are generally higher, but riskier for longer-term investment

   b.   At least three types of financial instruments that would meet Attract-One, Inc.'s cash and investing needs include

      1)   U.S. Treasury bills
      2)   Negotiable certificates of deposit
      3)   Prime commercial paper

4.   The benefit or loss on a proposed cash management system is found by determining whether the incremental interest income earned will exceed the cost of the new system. If implemented, the new system would accelerate the company's collections by 4 days (2 days mail time + 2 days processing time).

Interest income from average daily balances:	
($200,000 × 4 days saved × .06)	$48,000
Interest income from additional holiday volume:	
[($1,250,000 × 4 days saved × 4 holidays) ÷ 360 days] × .06	3,333
Total incremental interest income	$51,333
Less: Cost of lockbox system:	
(3 banks × $1,000 per month × 12 months)	(36,000)
Net benefit from implementing lockbox system	$15,333

NOTE: Interest income from time savings of daily average collections alone exceeds cost of implementation. Interest income associated with holiday savings is an additional benefit. Since the incremental interest income that can be earned from implementing the lockbox system exceeds its cost, the system should be adopted.

 Access the **Gleim CMA Premium Review System** from your Gleim Personal Classroom to continue your studies with exam-emulating essay questions!

STUDY UNIT FIVE
CORPORATE RESTRUCTURING
AND INTERNATIONAL FINANCE

(25 pages of outline)

This study unit is the **fourth of four** on **corporate finance**. The relative weight assigned to this major topic in Part 2 of the exam is **20%**. The four study units are

Study Unit 2: Financial Markets and Types of Securities
Study Unit 3: Valuation Methods and Cost of Capital
Study Unit 4: Managing Current Assets
Study Unit 5: Corporate Restructuring and International Finance

If you are interested in reviewing more introductory or background material, go to www.gleim.com/CMAIntroVideos for a list of suggested third-party overviews of this topic. The following Gleim outline material is more than sufficient to help you pass the CMA exam; any additional introductory or background material is for your own personal enrichment.

5.1 MERGERS AND ACQUISITIONS (M&As) AND BANKRUPTCY

1. **Mergers**

    a. A merger is a business transaction in which an acquiring firm absorbs a second firm, and the acquiring firm remains in business as a combination of the two merged firms. A merger is legally straightforward; however, approval of the shareholders of each firm is required.

    1) A **consolidation** is similar to a merger, but a new entity is formed and neither of the merging entities survives.

    b. Three common types of mergers are as follows:

    1) A **horizontal merger** occurs when two firms in the same line of business combine.

    2) A **vertical merger** (vertical integration) combines a firm with one of its suppliers or customers.

    3) A **conglomerate merger** involves two unrelated firms in different industries.

    c. A merger is usually a negotiated arrangement between a single bidder and the acquired firm.

    1) Payment is most frequently in stock.

    2) The bidder is often a cash-rich firm in a mature industry and is seeking growth possibilities.

    3) The acquired firm is usually growing and in need of cash.

2. **Acquisitions**

    a. An acquisition is the purchase of all of another firm's assets or a controlling interest in its stock.

        1) For purpose of the CMA exam, acquisitions are valued using the **discounted cash flow method** (this method is presented in detail in Subunit 8.3).

    b. An acquisition of all of a firm's assets requires a vote of that firm's shareholders. It also entails the costly transfer of legal title, but it avoids the minority interest that may arise if the acquisition is by purchase of stock.

    c. An acquisition by stock purchase is advantageous because it can be effected when management and the board of directors are hostile to the combination, and it does not require a formal vote of the firm's shareholders.

        1) If the acquiring firm's offer is rejected by the acquiree's management, a tender offer may be made directly to the acquiree's shareholders to obtain a controlling interest.

        2) A tender offer is a general invitation by an individual or a corporation to all shareholders of another corporation to tender their shares for a specified price.

    d. Takeovers effected through tender offers may be friendly or hostile.

        1) When the takeover is friendly, the target is usually a successful firm in a growth industry, payment may be in cash or stock, and management of the target often has a high percentage of ownership.

        2) When the takeover is hostile, the target is usually in a mature industry and is underperforming, more than one bidder may emerge, management ownership is likely to be low, payment is more likely to be in cash, and the initial bidder is probably a corporate raider.

3. **Motivation for M&As**

    a. Different stakeholders within an entity will have different reasons for seeking or avoiding M&As.

        1) Managerial motivation is an issue because not all business decisions are based purely on economic considerations. Thus, the increased salary, fringe benefits, power, and prestige that often results from managing a larger enterprise may affect a manager's decision to consummate an M&A that is not favorable to the shareholders.

        2) Fear of negative personal consequences, i.e., being fired or replaced, may also cause a manager to resist a favorable combination, perhaps by entering into another combination that preserves the manager's position.

    b. There are also benefits to the entity as a whole.

        1) Diversification stabilizes earnings and reduces the risks to employees and creditors.

        2) A combination may provide not only specific new investment opportunities but also a strategic position that will allow the combined entity to exploit conditions that may arise in the future. For example, the acquisition of a firm in a different industry may lead to the development of a broad product line if circumstances are favorable.

        3) Greater market power because of reduced competition. However, antitrust restrictions, the globalization of markets, and the emergence of new forms of competition work against concentration of market power.

        4) A firm may be a target if its breakup value exceeds the cost of its acquisition. Thus, the acquirer may earn a profit by selling the assets piecemeal.

5) Synergy exists if the value of the combined firm exceeds the sum of the values of the separate firms.

    a) Operational synergy arises because the combined firm may be able to operate more efficiently and reduce costs. The new firm may also gain a new product line and a stronger distribution system, potentially increasing revenues.

    b) Financial synergy may reduce the cost of capital for both firms because the cost of issuing both debt and equity securities is lower for larger firms. Another benefit is the availability of additional internal capital.

    c) The synergy of a business combination can be determined by using the risk adjusted discount rate to discount the incremental cash flows of the newly formed entity.

6) Inefficient management may be replaced in a merger or acquisition by the management of the acquiring or merging firm, or the competency of existing management may be improved.

7) Another advantage is that the combined firm's optimal capital structure may allow for increased use of debt financing, with attendant tax savings from greater interest deductions.

4. **Defenses against Takeovers**

  a. **Greenmail**

    1) A targeted repurchase (greenmail) is a defensive tactic used to protect against takeover after a bidder buys a large number of shares on the open market and then makes (or threatens to make) a tender offer.

      a) If management and the board are opposed to the takeover (a hostile tender offer), the potential acquirer is offered the opportunity to sell his or her already acquired shares back to the corporation at an amount substantially above market value (i.e., paying greenmail).

    2) In conjunction with greenmail, management may reach a standstill agreement in which the bidder agrees not to acquire additional shares.

  b. **Staggered Election of Directors**

    1) Staggered terms for directors requires new shareholders to wait several years before being able to place their own people on the board.

    2) Another antitakeover amendment to the corporate charter may require a supermajority (e.g., 80%) for approval of a combination.

  c. **Golden Parachutes**

    1) So-called golden parachutes are provisions passed by a board of directors requiring large payments to specified executives if the executives are fired.

    2) Shareholders have often been unhappy with golden parachute payoffs and have filed suit to stop such payments.

  d. **Fair Price Provisions**

    1) Warrants are issued to shareholders that permit purchase of stock at a small percentage (often half) of market price in the event of a takeover attempt.

      a) The plan is intended to protect shareholder interests if the corporation is confronted by a coercive or unfair takeover attempt.

    2) The objective is not to deter takeovers but to ensure that all shareholders are treated equally.

      a) In the event of a friendly tender offer, the outstanding stock rights (warrants) may be repurchased by the corporation for a few cents per share, thus paving the way for the takeover.

e. **Voting-Rights Plans**

1) Voting-rights plans contain provisions that prevent shareholders who hold a certain ownership percentage from voting on takeover issues.

f. **Leveraged Recapitalization**

1) Leveraged recapitalization, or restructuring, occurs when a company obtains a substantial amount of new debt and uses the funds to pay a cash dividend.

    a) This results in a significant decrease in equity relative to debt, even to the point where net assets could be a negative amount. Such a debt load would discourage a potential acquirer.

g. **LBOs and Going Private**

1) A leveraged buyout (LBO) is a financing technique by which a company is purchased using very little equity. The cash-offer price is financed with large amounts of debt. An LBO is often used when a company is sold to management or some other group of employees, but it is also used in hostile takeovers.

    a) The company's assets serve as collateral for a loan to finance the purchase.

    b) In addition to greater financial leverage, the firm may benefit from an LBO because of savings in administrative costs from no longer being publicly traded. Furthermore, if the managers become owners, they have greater incentives and greater operational flexibility.

    c) The high degree of risk in LBOs results from the fixed charges for interest on the loan and the lack of cash for expansion.

2) Going private entails the purchase of the publicly owned stock of a corporation by a small group of private investors, usually including senior managers. Accordingly, the stock is delisted (if it is traded on an exchange) because it will no longer be traded. Such a transaction is usually structured as a leveraged buyout.

h. **Poison Pill**

1) A target corporation's charter, bylaws, or contracts may include a wide variety of provisions that reduce the value of the target to potential tender offerors. For example, a valuable contract may terminate by its terms upon a specified form of change of ownership of the target. Two types of poison pills are flip-over rights and flip-in rights.

    a) **Flip-over rights.** The charter of a target corporation may provide for its shareholders to acquire in exchange for their stock (in the target) a relatively greater interest (e.g., twice the shares of stock of equivalent value) in an acquiring entity.

    b) **Flip-in rights.** Acquisition of more than a specified ownership interest (e.g., 25%) in the target corporation permits shareholders, except for the acquirer, to purchase additional shares at a reduced price.

i. **Issuing Stock**

1) The target corporation significantly increases the amount of outstanding stock.

j. **Reverse Tender**

1) The target corporation may respond with a tender offer to acquire control of the tender offeror.

k. **ESOP**

   1) The trustees of an employee stock ownership plan are usually favorable to current management. Thus, they are likely to vote the shares allocated to the ESOP against a raider, who will probably destabilize the target corporation's current structure.

l. **White Knight Merger**

   1) Target management arranges an alternative tender offer with a different acquirer that will be more favorable to incumbent management and shareholders.

m. **Crown Jewel Transfer**

   1) The target corporation sells or otherwise disposes of one or more assets that made it a desirable target.

n. **Legal Action**

   1) A target corporation may challenge one or more aspects of a tender offer. A resulting delay increases costs to the raider and enables further defensive action.

5. **Other Restructurings**

a. A **spin-off** is the creation of a new separate entity from another entity, with the new entity's shares being distributed on a pro rata basis to existing shareholders of the parent entity.

   1) Existing shareholders will have the same proportion of ownership in the new entity that they had in the parent.

   2) A spin-off is a type of dividend to existing shareholders.

b. A divestiture involves the sale of an operating unit of a firm to a third party.

c. Reasons for spin-offs and divestitures include governmental antitrust litigation, refocusing of a firm's operations, and raising capital for the core business operation.

d. An **equity carve-out** involves the sale of a portion of the firm through a public offering.

   1) They provide a way to quickly raise capital and bring in new management while still maintaining control.

e. A **split-up** is when an entity splits into two or more entities. Shares in the original entity are exchanged for shares in the new entities.

f. **Tracking stock** is stock issued in a division or segment of a parent entity. This provides investors with the opportunity to invest in only a portion of the entity. However, they have no claims on the assets of the division or segment. Rather, the parent entity maintains control over the division or segment.

g. Tax benefits may arise from a combination.

6. **Conditions for Bankruptcy**

a. A firm may be either insolvent when its debts exceed its assets or illiquid when cash flows are insufficient to meet maturing obligations.

   1) The early signals of financial distress include late payments, plant closings, negative earnings, employee layoffs, falling stock prices, and dividend reductions.

b. A firm may respond to insolvency by combining with another firm, selling assets, reducing costs, issuing new debt or equity securities, or negotiating with creditors to restructure its obligations. However, these private workouts may be unlikely to succeed or may already have failed.

c. Consequently, a formal bankruptcy may be declared either voluntarily by the debtor or involuntarily due to a petition brought by creditors. The two major options are bankruptcy reorganization and liquidation.

7. **The Bankruptcy Code**

    a.   Bankruptcy is a formal way of resolving the conflict between creditor rights and debtor relief. The objectives are to ensure that (1) debtor assets are fairly distributed to creditors, and (2) the debtor is given a fresh start.

    b.   The main chapters of the Bankruptcy Code include

        1)   Chapter 7: Liquidation

        2)   Chapter 9: Adjustment of Debts of a Municipality

        3)   Chapter 11: Reorganization

        4)   Chapter 12: Adjustment of Debts of a Family Farmer or Fisherman with Regular Annual Income

        5)   Chapter 13: Adjustment of Debts of an Individual with Regular Income

    c.   The following summarizes the eligibility for filing under Chapters 7, 11, and 13:

TYPES OF BANKRUPTCY	ELIGIBLE	INELIGIBLE
Chapter 7 Liquidation (voluntary or involuntary)	Individuals (subject to disqualification by the means test) Partnerships Corporations	Municipalities (eligible under Ch. 9) Railroads Insurers Banks Credit unions S&Ls
Chapter 11 Reorganization (voluntary or involuntary)	Railroads Most persons that may be debtors under Chapter 7	Shareholders Commodities brokers Insurers Banks Credit unions S&Ls
Chapter 13 Adjustment of debts of an individual (voluntary only)	Individuals	Nonindividuals Individuals without regular income

---

Background

The largest corporate bankruptcy in U.S. history was that of Lehman Brothers Holdings, Inc., a distinguished investment banking firm founded in the town of Montgomery, Alabama. When it filed for Chapter 11 reorganization in September 2008 after 158 years of operation, Lehman Brothers reported a capital structure of 3% equity and 97% debt. The firm's collapse wiped out over $40 billion of equity.

---

8. **Chapter 7 Liquidation**

    a.   A voluntary or an involuntary petition for liquidation may be filed in federal bankruptcy court.

    b.   Individual debtors may receive a discharge under Chapter 7 from most debts that remain unpaid after distribution of the debtor's estate. A corporation or a partnership does not receive a discharge in bankruptcy.

    c.   When the court issues an order for relief, creditors' collection activities must cease immediately. Moreover, the court usually appoints an interim trustee to take control of the debtor's estate.

    d.   Secured creditors are entitled to the proceeds of the sale of specific property pledged for a lien or a mortgage.

        1)   If the proceeds do not fully satisfy the secured creditors' claims, the balances are treated as claims of general or unsecured creditors.

e.   The other assets of the bankruptcy estate are distributed according to the absolute priority rule.

    1)   A claim with a higher priority (senior unsecured creditor) is fully satisfied before claims with a lower priority (junior unsecured creditor) are paid.

f.   The following are the classes of priority claims listed in order of rank:

    1)   Claims for administrative expenses and claims for expenses incurred in preserving and collecting the estate

    2)   Claims of suppliers who extended unsecured credit after an involuntary case has begun but before a trustee is appointed

    3)   Wages up to a certain limit owed to employees earned within the 180 days preceding the earlier of the filing of the petition or the cessation of business

    4)   Certain contributions owed to employee benefit plans that were to have been paid within 180 days prior to filing

    5)   Claims of grain or fish producers up to a certain amount each for grain or fish deposited with the debtor but not paid for or returned

    6)   Claims of consumers for the return of up to a certain amount each in deposits

    7)   Certain income and other taxes owed to governmental entities

    8)   Death and injury claims arising from operation of a motor vehicle or vessel by a legally intoxicated person

    9)   Claims of general or unsecured creditors

    10)   Claims of preferred shareholders, who may receive an amount up to the par value of the issue

    11)   Claims of common shareholders

EXAMPLE

A firm is being liquidated several months after its Chapter 7 bankruptcy filing. The receiver has compiled the following information.

Assets	$100,000
Common shares (at par)	21,000
Preferred shares (at par)	4,000
Secured bonds	45,000
Senior unsecured debt	30,000
Junior unsecured debt	20,000
Wage payable	6,000
Taxes owed	4,000
Credit from suppliers since filing	2,000
Court/trustee costs	1,500

Before the junior creditors are paid, all claims with a higher priority must be satisfied. Thus, before the junior creditors are paid, the secured bonds, court/trustee costs, credit from suppliers since filing, wages payable, taxes owed, and senior unsecured debt creditors must all be paid (in that order). After all of these debts are completely paid off, the firm is left with $11,500 ($100,000 – $45,000 – $1,500 – $2,000 – $6,000 – $4,000 – $30,000) to pay the junior unsecured creditors. The junior unsecured creditors will receive 57.5% ($11,500 ÷ $20,000) of their claims.

---

9.   **Chapter 11 Reorganization**

a.   Reorganization allows a distressed business enterprise to restructure its finances. The primary purpose of the restructuring is usually the continuation of the business.

    1)   Reorganization is a process of negotiation whereby the debtor firm and its creditors develop a plan for the adjustment and discharge of debts. Partnerships, corporations, and any person who may be a debtor under Chapter 7 (except stock and commodity brokers) are eligible debtors under Chapter 11.

    2)   Such a plan may provide for a change of management or liquidation.

3)   A plan of reorganization must divide creditors' claims and shareholders' interests into classes, and claims in each class must be treated equally.

   a)   The plan must specify which classes of creditors are impaired creditors and how they will be treated. A class is impaired if its rights are altered under the plan.

4)   Junior creditors likely favor reorganization in hopes of recovering a larger portion of debt than they would receive after higher ranked creditors' claims are satisfied through liquidation. They hope that the firm's financial condition can improve.

Stop and review! You have completed the outline for this subunit. Study multiple-choice questions 1 through 8 beginning on page 164.

5.2 FOREIGN EXCHANGE RATES -- SYSTEMS AND CALCULATIONS

 Questions pertaining to currency exchange rates on the CMA exam will require the candidate to calculate forward and spot rates. In addition, a candidate should be able to understand how to determine if a currency has appreciated or depreciated and how that will influence purchasing power.

1.   **The Market for Foreign Currency**

   a.   For international exchanges to occur, the two currencies involved must be easily convertible at some prevailing exchange rate. The exchange rate is the price of one country's currency in terms of another country's currency.

   b.   Four systems for setting exchange rates are in use. Each is described in items 2. through 5. beginning below.

   1)   Fixed rates
   2)   Freely floating rates
   3)   Managed floating rates
   4)   Pegged rates

BACKGROUND to Currency Exchange Rates

The gold standard prevailed from 1876 to 1913, i.e., countries pegged one unit of their currencies to a specified amount of gold. The gold standard was suspended during World War I. Following the war and during the Great Depression, the gold standard's reimplementation did not achieve universal success.

In 1944, during World War II, the United States convened a meeting of delegates from all 45 allied nations in Bretton Woods, New Hampshire. The convention's purpose was to establish a monetary system for the postwar world that would encourage rebuilding and prosperity while avoiding a disastrous repeat of the Great Depression. Under the resulting Bretton Woods Agreement, the U.S. guaranteed convertibility of the dollar into a certain quantity of gold, and all other nations in turn pegged their currencies to the dollar. To ensure stability, governments agreed that they would prevent exchange rates from fluctuating more than 1% plus or minus from their original rates.

This system could not be sustained after about 25 years. It was generally agreed that the U.S. currency was pegged too high, and in August 1971, President Richard Nixon ended direct convertibility of paper dollars into gold. By 1973, it was clear that any governmental intervention in currency markets was unworkable and a floating exchange rate system was established.

---

2.   **Fixed Exchange Rate System**

   a.   In a fixed exchange rate system, the value of a country's currency in relation to another country's currency is either fixed or allowed to fluctuate only within a very narrow range.

   b.   The one very significant advantage to a fixed exchange rate is that it makes for a high degree of predictability in international trade because the element of uncertainty about gains and losses on exchange rate fluctuations is eliminated.

   c.   A disadvantage is that a government can manipulate the value of its currency.

3. **Freely Floating Exchange Rate System**

   a. In a freely floating exchange rate system, the government steps aside and allows exchange rates to be determined entirely by the market forces of supply and demand.

   b. The disadvantage is that a freely floating system makes a country vulnerable to economic conditions in other countries.

4. **Managed Float Exchange Rate System**

   a. In a managed float exchange rate system, the government allows market forces to determine exchange rates until they move too far in one direction or another. The government will then intervene to maintain the currency within the broad range considered appropriate.

      1) This system is the one currently in use by the major trading nations.

   b. The advantage of managed float is that it has the market-response nature of a freely floating system while still allowing for government intervention when necessary.

   c. The criticism of managed float is that it makes exporting countries vulnerable to sudden changes in exchange rates and lacks the self-correcting mechanism of a freely floating system.

5. **Pegged Exchange Rate System**

   a. In a pegged exchange rate system, a government fixes the rate of exchange for its currency with respect to another country's currency (or to a "basket" of several currencies).

   b. The pegging country then calculates its currency's movement with respect to the currencies of third countries based on the movements of the currency to which it has been pegged.

6. **Exchange Rate Basics**

   a. The **spot rate** is the number of units of a foreign currency that can be received today in exchange for a single unit of the domestic currency.

EXAMPLE

A currency trader is willing to give 1.652 Swiss francs today in exchange for a single British pound. Today's spot rate for the pound is therefore 1.652 Swiss francs, and today's spot rate for the franc is £0.6053 (1 ÷ ₣1.652).

---

   b. The **forward rate** is the number of units of a foreign currency that can be received in exchange for a single unit of the domestic currency at some definite date in the future.

EXAMPLE

The currency trader contracts to provide 1.654 Swiss francs in exchange for a single British pound 30 days from now. Today's 30-day forward rate for the pound is therefore 1.654 Swiss francs, and the 30-day forward rate for the franc is £0.6046 (1 ÷ ₣1.654).

---

   c. If the domestic currency exchanges for more units of a foreign currency in the forward market than in the spot market, the domestic currency is said to be trading at a **forward premium** with respect to the foreign currency.

EXAMPLE

Since the pound exchanges for more francs in the forward market than in the spot market (₣1.654 > ₣1.652), the pound is currently trading at a forward premium with respect to the franc. This reflects the market's belief that the pound is going to increase in value in relation to the franc.

---

d. If the domestic currency exchanges for fewer units of a foreign currency in the forward market than in the spot market, the domestic currency is said to be trading at a **forward discount** with respect to the foreign currency.

EXAMPLE

Since the franc exchanges for fewer pounds in the forward market than in the spot market (£0.6046 < £0.6053), the franc is currently trading at a forward discount with respect to the pound. This reflects the market's belief that the franc is going to lose value in relation to the pound.

---

e. The forward premium or discount on one currency with respect to another currency can be calculated by multiplying the percentage spread by the number of forward periods in a year:

Calculation of Forward Premium or Discount

$$\frac{Forward\ rate - Spot\ rate}{Spot\ rate} \times \frac{Days\ in\ year}{Days\ in\ forward\ period}$$

EXAMPLE

Using the information above:

Pound forward premium = [(₣1.654 − ₣1.652) ÷ ₣1.652] × (360 days ÷ 30 days)
= (₣0.002 ÷ ₣1.652) × 12
= 0.00121 × 12
= 1.45%

Franc forward discount = [(£0.6046 − £0.6053) ÷ £0.6053] × (360 days ÷ 30 days)
= (−£0.0007 ÷ £0.6053) × 12
= −0.00120 × 12
= −1.45%

---

f. The implications of these relationships can be generalized as follows:

If the domestic currency is trading at a forward	Then it is expected to
Premium	Gain purchasing power
Discount	Lose purchasing power

g. A **cross rate** is used when the two currencies involved are not stated in terms of each other. The exchange must be valued in terms of a third currency, very often the U.S. dollar.

$$Cross\ rate = \frac{Domestic\ currency\ per\ U.S.\ dollar}{Foreign\ currency\ per\ U.S.\ dollar}$$

EXAMPLE

A firm in Sweden needs to make a payment of 100,000 yen today. However, the krona is not stated in terms of yen, so a cross rate must be calculated.

The spot rate for a single U.S. dollar at the time of the transaction is 6.8395 kronor and 79.8455 yen.

Cross rate = kr6.8395 ÷ ¥79.8455
= 0.0857 kronor per yen

The company needs kr8,570 to settle its debt (¥100,000 × 0.0857).

---

7. **Exchange Rates and Purchasing Power**

   a. The graph below depicts the relationship between the supply of and demand for a foreign currency by consumers and investors who use a given domestic currency:

Exchange Rate Equilibrium

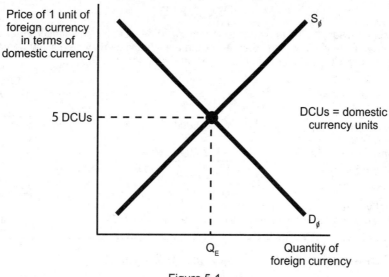

Figure 5-1

   1) The demand curve for the foreign currency is downward sloping because, when that currency becomes cheaper, goods and services denominated in that currency become more affordable to domestic consumers, leading them to demand more of that currency.

   2) The supply curve for the foreign currency is upward sloping because, when that currency becomes more expensive, goods and services become more affordable to users of the foreign currency, leading them to inject more of their currency into the domestic market.

8. **Appreciation and Depreciation Against Another Currency**

   a. When one currency gains purchasing power with respect to another currency, the first currency is said to have appreciated against the second currency.

   1) By the same token, the second currency is said to have depreciated (lost purchasing power) against the first.

   b. This phenomenon has definite implications for international trade.

EXAMPLE

A U.S. company buys merchandise from an EU company for €1,000,000, due in 60 days. On the day of the sale, $0.795 is required to buy a single euro. By the 60th day, $0.812 is required to buy a euro.

The dollar has thus weakened against the euro, and the euro has strengthened against the dollar; i.e., the dollar has lost purchasing power with respect to the euro.

The U.S. firm only needed $795,000 to pay off a €1,000,000 debt on the date of sale but must now use $812,000 to pay off the €1,000,000 debt.

9.   **Effective Interest Rate on a Foreign Currency Loan**

  a.   When loans are taken out in foreign currencies, appreciation and depreciation of the two currencies can affect the value of interest and principal paid.

    1)   This in turn can affect the effective interest rate.

EXAMPLE

A U.S. company takes out a 1-year, 12,000,000 peso loan at 6.5% to pay a Mexican supplier. After a year, the U.S. company repays the loan with interest, but in the meantime, the peso has experienced a slight appreciation. Thus, the company's effective rate on the loan is higher than the stated rate, calculated as follows:

		Times: Conversion Rate	Equals: Equivalent USD
Amount borrowed	12,000,000 Pesos	0.0921496	$1,105,795
Times: Stated rate	6.5%		
Equals: Interest charged	780,000 Pesos		
Total repayment	12,780,000 Pesos	0.0940000	1,201,320
Difference			$ 95,525

Effective rate:
Difference ÷ Amount borrowed = ($95,525 ÷ $1,105,795)   **8.64%**

---

10.   **Foreign Trade and a Country's Balance of Payments**

  a.   A country's balance of payments is the net of all transactions between domestic parties and parties in a particular foreign country.

    1)   If a country's currency is weak, its goods and services are more affordable to foreign consumers. These countries tend to have a positive balance of trade.

    2)   By the same token, if a country's currency is strong, its goods and services are more expensive to foreign consumers. These countries tend to have a negative balance of trade.

  b.   As a short-term measure, a government can attempt to correct a deficit balance of payments by deliberately devaluing its currency. This makes the country's goods more affordable, causing exports to rise.

    1)   However, this approach has its own disadvantages. By making imports more expensive, consumers complain because they have fewer choices.

    2)   Also, over the long run, domestic producers can raise their own prices to match those of the more expensive imported goods.

Stop and review! You have completed the outline for this subunit. Study multiple-choice questions 9 through 14 beginning on page 166.

5.3 FOREIGN EXCHANGE RATES -- FACTORS AFFECTING RATES AND RISK MITIGATION TECHNIQUES

1. **Factors Affecting Exchange Rates**

    a. The five factors that affect currency exchange rates can be classified as three trade-related factors and two financial factors. Each is discussed in detail in items 2. and 3. beginning below and on the following page.

        1) Trade-related factors

            a) Relative inflation rates
            b) Relative income levels
            c) Government intervention

        2) Financial factors

            a) Relative interest rates
            b) Ease of capital flow

2. **Trade-Related Factors That Affect Exchange Rates**

    a. **Relative Inflation Rates**

        1) When the rate of inflation in a given country rises relative to the rates of other countries, the demand for that country's currency falls.

            a) This inward shift of the demand curve results from the lowered desirability of that currency, a result of its falling purchasing power.

        2) As investors unload this currency, there is more of it available, reflected in an outward shift of the supply curve.

        3) A new equilibrium point will be reached at a lower price in terms of investors' domestic currencies.

            a) An investor's domestic currency has gained purchasing power in the country where inflation is worse.

Changes in Supply and Demand for the Currency of a Foreign Country Experiencing Higher Relative Inflation

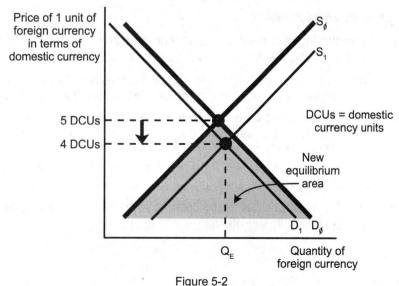

Figure 5-2

b.   **Relative Income Levels**

1)   Citizens with higher incomes look for new consumption opportunities in other countries, driving up the demand for those currencies and shifting the demand curve to the right.

a)   Thus, as incomes rise in one country, the prices of foreign currencies rise as well, and the local currency will depreciate.

Changes in Supply and Demand for the Currency of a Foreign Country When Domestic Incomes Rise

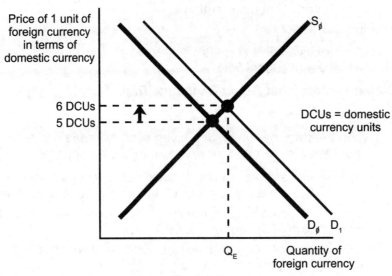

Figure 5-3

c.   **Government Intervention**

1)   Actions by national governments, such as trade barriers and currency restrictions, complicate the process of exchange rate determination.

3.   **Financial Factors That Affect Exchange Rates**

a.   **Relative Interest Rates**

1)   When the interest rates in a given country rise relative to those of other countries, the demand for that country's currency rises.

a)   This outward shift of the demand curve results from the influx of other currencies seeking the higher returns available in that country.

2)   As more and more investors buy up the high-interest country's currency with which to make investments, there is less of it available, reflected in an inward shift of the supply curve.

3)   A new equilibrium point will be reached at a higher price in terms of investors' domestic currencies.

a)   An investor's domestic currency has lost purchasing power in the country paying higher returns.

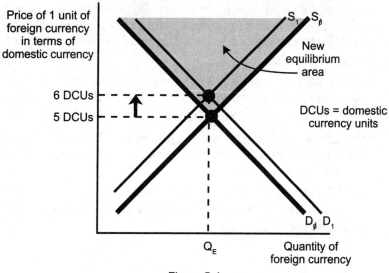

Figure 5-4

b. **Ease of Capital Flow**

1) If a country with high real interest rates loosens restrictions against the cross-border movement of capital, the demand for the currency will rise as investors seek higher returns.

2) This factor has become by far the most important of the five factors listed.

a) The speed with which capital can be moved electronically and the huge amounts involved in the "wired" global economy easily dominate the effects of the trade-related factors.

4. **Graphical Depiction**

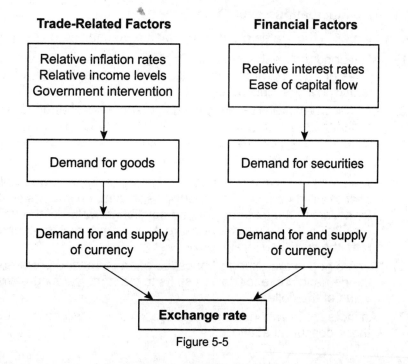

Figure 5-5

5.   **Calculating Simultaneous Effects on Exchange Rates**

    a.   Differential Interest Rates

        1)   Interest rate parity (IRP) theory holds that exchange rates will settle at an equilibrium point where the difference between the forward rate and the spot rate (i.e., the forward premium or discount) equals the exact amount necessary to offset the difference in interest rates between the two countries.

    b.   Differential Inflation Rates

        1)   Purchasing power parity (PPP) theory explains differences in exchange rates as the result of the differing inflation rates in the two countries.

    c.   International Fisher Effect (IFE) Theory

        1)   International Fisher Effect (IFE) theory also focuses on how the spot rate will change over time, but it uses the interplay between real and nominal interest rates to explain the change.

            a)   If all investors require a given real rate of return, then differences between currencies can be explained by each country's expected inflation rate.

    d.   Aspects of the Three Theories

        1)   The three theories can be summarized as follows:

Theory	Deals with	Explanatory Variable
Interest rate parity (IRP)	Forward rate	Interest rates
Purchasing power parity (PPP)	Percentage change in spot rate	Inflation rates
International Fisher Effect (IFE)	Percentage change in spot rate	Interest rates

        2)   Each of the three theories isolates a single factor as the principal cause of exchange rate differences. However, as depicted in Figure 5-5 on the previous page, multiple factors are actually at work in the determination of exchange rates.

        3)   With regard to high-inflation currencies,

            a)   IRP theory suggests that they usually trade at large forward discounts.
            b)   PPP and IFE theory suggest that they will weaken over time.
            c)   IFE theory suggests that their economies will have high interest rates.

6.   **Exchange Rate Fluctuations over Time**

    a.   Long-term exchange rates are dictated by the purchasing-power parity theorem.

        1)   In the long run, real prices should be the same worldwide (net of government taxes or trade barriers and transportation costs) for a given good. Exchange rates will adjust until purchasing-power parity is achieved.

        2)   In other words, relative price levels determine exchange rates. In the real world, exchange rates do not perfectly reflect purchasing-power parity, but relative price levels are clearly important determinants of those rates.

    b.   Medium-term exchange rates are dictated by the economic activity in a country.

        1)   When the U.S. is in a recession, spending on imports (as well as domestic goods) will decrease. This reduced spending on imports shifts the supply curve for dollars to the left, causing the equilibrium value of the dollar to increase (assuming the demand for dollars is constant); that is, at any given exchange rate, the supply to foreigners is less.

        2)   If more goods are exported because of an increased preference for U.S. goods, the demand curve for dollars shifts to the right, causing upward pressure on the value of the dollar.

        3)   An increase in imports or a decrease in exports will have effects opposite to those described above.

   c.   Short-term exchange rates are dictated by interest rates.

       1)   Big corporations and banks invest their large reserves of cash where the real interest rate is highest. A rise in the real interest rate in a country will lead to an appreciation of the currency because it will be demanded for investment at the higher real interest rate, thereby shifting the demand curve to the right (outward).

       2)   The reverse holds true for a decline in real interest rates because that currency will be sold as investors move their money out of the country.

       3)   However, the interplay of interest rates and inflation must also be considered. Inflation of a currency relative to a second currency causes the first currency to depreciate relative to the second. Moreover, nominal interest rates increase when inflation rates are expected to increase.

Due to exchange rate fluctuations, there are risks involved with international trade. As a CMA candidate, you will need to be able to identify and be prepared to explain the methods used to mitigate the risks. Additionally, you should be able to analyze the best method to manage this risk with supporting calculations.

7. Risks of Exchange Rate Fluctuation

   a.   When a firm sells merchandise to a foreign customer, the firm's receivable might be denominated in the customer's currency.

       1)   The downside risk to a foreign-denominated receivable is that the foreign currency might depreciate against the firm's domestic currency.

       2)   If the foreign currency has depreciated by the settlement date, the firm will receive fewer units of its domestic currency than it would have if the transaction had been settled at the time of the sale.

   b.   Likewise, when a firm buys merchandise from a foreign supplier, the firm's payable might be denominated in the supplier's currency.

       1)   The downside risk to a foreign-denominated payable is that the foreign currency might appreciate against the firm's domestic currency.

       2)   If the foreign currency has appreciated by the settlement date, the firm will be forced to buy more units of the foreign currency to settle the payable than it would have if the transaction had been settled at the time of the purchase.

Summary of Exchange Rate Risk

Foreign-Denominated Transaction	Results in a Foreign-Denominated	Downside Risk is that Foreign Currency
Sale	Receivable	Depreciates
Purchase	Payable	Appreciates

8. Hedging in Response to Exchange Rate Risk

   a.   Hedging as a Tool against Uncertainty

       1)   When hedging, some amount of possible upside is forgone in order to protect against the potential downside.

   b.   Hedging a Foreign-Denominated Receivable

       1)   When the downside risk is that the foreign currency will depreciate by the settlement date, the hedge is to sell the foreign currency forward to lock in a definite price.

EXAMPLE

A U.S. company knows that it will be receiving 5,000,000 pesos in 30 days from the sale of some equipment at one of its facilities in Mexico. The spot rate for a peso is $0.77, and the 30-day forward rate is $0.80. The firm wants to be sure that it will be able to sell the pesos it will be receiving in 30 days for $0.80 each. The firm thus hedges by selling 5,000,000 pesos 30 days forward. The company is buying a guarantee that it will be able to sell 5,000,000 pesos in 30 days and receive $4,000,000 (5,000,000 × $0.80) in return.

The spot rate on day 30 turns out to be $0.82. Thus, the U.S. company could have made more money by forgoing the hedge and simply waiting to convert the pesos on day 30. However, this possibility was not worth the risk that the peso might have fallen below $0.80.

The counterparty to the hedge just described (i.e., the buyer of pesos) might also be hedging but could be speculating or simply making a market in the instrument. The two parties are indifferent to each other's goals.

    c.   Hedging a Foreign-Denominated Payable

        1) When the downside risk is that the foreign currency will appreciate by the settlement date, the hedge is to purchase the foreign currency forward to lock in a definite price.

EXAMPLE

A U.S. company knows that it will need 100,000 Canadian dollars in 60 days to pay an invoice. The firm thus hedges by purchasing 100,000 Canadian dollars 60 days forward. The company is essentially buying a guarantee that it will have C$100,000 available for use in 60 days. The 60-day forward rate for a Canadian dollar is US $0.99. Thus, for the privilege of having a guaranteed receipt of 100,000 Canadian dollars, the company will commit now to paying $99,000 in 60 days.

The counterparty to the hedge just described (i.e., the seller of Canadian dollars) might also be hedging, but could be speculating or simply making a market in the instrument. The two parties are indifferent to each other's goals.

    d.   Managing Net Receivables and Payables Positions

        1) A firm can reduce its exchange rate risk by maintaining a position in each foreign currency of receivables and payables that net to near zero.

        2) Large multinational corporations often establish multinational netting centers as special departments to execute whichever strategy is selected.

            a) They enter into foreign currency futures contracts when necessary to achieve balance.

9. **Tools for Mitigating Exchange Rate Risk -- Short-Term**

    a. **Money Market Hedges**

        1) The least complex tool for hedging exchange rate risk is the money market hedge.

        2) A firm with a receivable denominated in a foreign currency can borrow the amount and convert it to its domestic currency now, then pay off the foreign loan when the receivable is collected.

        3) A firm with a payable denominated in a foreign currency can buy a money market instrument denominated in that currency that is timed to mature when the payable is due. Exchange rate fluctuations between the transaction date and the settlement date are avoided.

    b. **Futures Contracts**

        1) Futures contracts are essentially commodities that are traded on an exchange, making them available to more parties.

        2) Futures contracts are only available for generic amounts (e.g, 62,500 British pounds, 100,000 Brazilian reals, 12,500,000 Japanese yen) and with specific settlement dates (typically the third Wednesday in March, June, September, and December).

        3) Because futures contracts are impersonal, the two parties need never know each other's identity.

c. **Currency Options**

1) Two types of options are available:

a) A call option gives the holder the right to buy (i.e., call for) a specified amount of currency in a future month at a specified price. Call options are among the many tools available to hedge payables.

b) A put option gives the holder the right to sell (i.e., put onto the market) a specified amount of currency in a future month at a specified price. Put options are among the many tools available to hedge receivables.

2) Currency options are available from two sources: options exchanges (similar to those for futures contracts) and the over-the-counter market.

a) Exchange-traded options are only available for predefined quantities of currency.

b) Options available in over-the-counter markets are provided by commercial banks and brokerage houses.

3) An option is exercised only if the party purchasing the option chooses to.

10. **Tools for Mitigating Exchange Rate Risk -- Long-Term**

a. **Forward Contracts**

1) Large corporations that have close relationships with major banks are able to enter into contracts for individual transactions concerning large amounts. These contracts are unavailable to smaller firms or firms without a history with a particular bank.

2) The bank guarantees that it will make available to the firm a given quantity of a certain currency at a definite rate at some point in the future. The price charged by the bank for this guarantee is called the premium.

EXAMPLE

A large U.S. firm purchases equipment from a Korean manufacturer for 222,000,000 won, due in 90 days. The exchange rate on the date of sale is $1 to 1,110 won. The U.S. firm suspects that the won may appreciate over the next 90 days and wants to lock in a forward rate of 1-to-1,110. The firm negotiates a contract whereby its bank promises to deliver 222,000,000 won to the firm in 90 days for $200,000. In return for this guarantee, the firm will pay the bank a 2% premium ($200,000 × 2% = $4,000).

---

b. **Currency Swaps**

1) A broker brings together two parties who would like to hedge exchange rate risk by swapping cash flows in each other's currency.

EXAMPLE

The Australian owner of a new office building in Shanghai is currently signing 20-year lease agreements with tenants. At the same time, a Shanghai-based consultant has just signed a 20-year outsourcing contract in Melbourne. The Australian landlord is going to have cash flows denominated in yuan, and the Chinese consultant is going to have cash flows denominated in Australian dollars.

A broker working for a large investment bank engineers an agreement whereby the two will exchange cash flows each month for the next 20 years. A mechanism is agreed upon to determine the appropriate exchange rate.

Stop and review! You have completed the outline for this subunit. Study multiple-choice questions 15 through 20 beginning on page 167.

5.4 EFFECTS OF FOREIGN EXCHANGE FLUCTUATIONS

1. **Definitions**

    a. The **functional currency** is the currency of the primary economic environment in which the entity operates. Normally, that environment is the one in which it primarily generates and expends cash.

    b. A **foreign currency** is any currency other than the entity's functional currency.

    c. The **reporting currency** is the currency in which an entity prepares its financial statements.

    d. **Foreign currency transactions** are fixed in a currency other than the functional currency. They result when an entity

        1) Buys or sells on credit;
        2) Borrows or lends;
        3) Is a party to a derivative instrument; or,
        4) For other reasons, acquires or disposes of assets, or incurs or settles liabilities, fixed in a foreign currency.

    e. A company has **transaction exposure** if its payables or receivables are denominated in a foreign currency.

2. **Aspects of Cross-Border Transactions**

    a. Transactions are recorded at the spot rate in effect at the transaction date.

    b. Transaction gains and losses are recorded at each balance sheet date and at the date the receivable or payable is settled. The gains or losses ordinarily are included in the determination of net income.

    c. When the amount of the functional currency exchangeable for a unit of the currency in which the transaction is fixed increases, a transaction gain or loss is recognized on a receivable or payable, respectively. The opposite occurs when the exchange rate (functional currency to foreign currency) decreases.

3. **Exchange Rate Exposure**

    a. When a U.S. firm purchases from, or sells to, an entity in a foreign country, the transaction is recorded in U.S. dollars (the firm's domestic currency).

        Foreign sale:
        Accounts receivable $100,000
            Sales $100,000

        Foreign purchase:
        Inventory $100,000
            Accounts payable $100,000

        1) The dollar, however, might not be the currency in which the transaction will have to be settled (typically 30 days later).
        2) If the exchange rate of the two currencies (i.e., the units of one currency required to purchase a single unit of the other) is fixed, the existence of a foreign-denominated receivable or payable raises no measurement issue.

    b. If the exchange rate is not fixed, however, as is the case with most pairs of currencies in today's managed float exchange rate environment (item 4. in Subunit 5.2), it is extremely rare for the two currencies to still have the same exchange rate at the end of the deferral period as they had at the beginning.

        1) It is highly likely, then, that the firm will incur a gain or loss on this transaction arising from a change in the exchange rates.

    c.   The gains and losses arising from exchange rate fluctuations are of two types:

        1)   The gain or loss incurred at the settlement date, which affects the firm's cash flows, is termed a **transaction gain or loss**.

            a)   Transaction gains and losses, and their associated risk-mitigation techniques, are the subject of Subunit 5.3.

        2)   The other type of gain or loss, which does not affect cash flows, is termed a **translation gain or loss**.

            a)   Translation gains and losses arise from the use of accrual-basis accounting and must be calculated whenever financial statements are prepared during the payment deferral period.

4.   **Two-Transaction Perspective on Exchange Rate Fluctuations**

    a.   Two-transaction treatment is in accordance with U.S. GAAP.

        1)   The rationale underlying the two-transaction perspective is that the purchase or sale of merchandise is one transaction, and the future acquisition of foreign currency (either to pay a liability or as proceeds from a sale) is a separate transaction.

        2)   By not settling immediately, the importer or exporter has assumed some degree of exchange rate risk, which is a financing decision, not a merchandising decision. These exchange gains or losses could have been avoided if full settlement had been made on the date of the purchase or sale.

    b.   One-transaction treatment is impermissible under U.S. GAAP.

        1)   The one-transaction perspective views all aspects of an exchange as a single transaction. Accordingly, for foreign trade activities, the original amount recorded is considered an estimate, subject to adjustment when the exact cash outlay required for the purchase or the exact cash received from the sale is known.

        2)   The one-transaction perspective emphasizes the cash-payment aspect of the exchange and views the transaction as incomplete until it is finally settled.

5.   **Accounting for Transaction Gains and Losses**

    a.   A **transaction gain (loss)** results from a change in exchange rates between the functional currency and the currency in which the transaction is denominated. It is the change in functional currency cash flows

        1)   Actually realized on settlement and
        2)   Expected on unsettled transactions.

    b.   Transactions are recorded at the spot rate in effect at the transaction date.

    c.   Transaction gains and losses are recorded at each balance sheet date and at the date the receivable or payable is settled. The gains or losses ordinarily are included in earnings.

    d.   When the amount of the functional currency exchangeable for a unit of the currency in which the transaction is fixed increases, a transaction gain or loss is recognized on a receivable or payable, respectively. The opposite occurs when the exchange rate (functional currency to foreign currency) decreases.

EXAMPLE of Transaction Gains and Losses

On December 15, Year 1, Boise Co. purchased electronic components from Kinugasa Corporation. Boise must pay Kinugasa ¥15,000,000 on January 15, Year 2. The exchange rate in effect on December 15, Year 1, was $.01015 per yen, giving the transaction a value on Boise's books of $152,250 (¥15,000,000 × $.01015).

Transaction Date:		
Inventory	$152,250	
Accounts payable		$152,250

The exchange rate on December 31, Year 1, Boise's reporting date, has fallen to $.01010 per yen. The balance of the payable must be adjusted in the amount of $750 [(¥15,000,000 × ($.01015 – $.01010)].

Reporting Date:		
Accounts payable	$750	
Transaction gain		$750

The exchange rate on January 15, Year 2, has risen to $.01020 per yen. To settle the payable, the balance must be adjusted in the amount of $1,500 [¥15,000,000 × ($.01010 – $.01020)].

Settlement Date:		
Accounts payable ($152,250 – $750)	$151,500	
Transaction loss	1,500	
Cash		$153,000

---

    e.   The occurrence of transaction gains and losses can be summarized as follows:

Effects of Exchange Rate Fluctuations

Transaction That Will Be Settled in a Foreign Currency	Results in a Foreign-Denominated	Foreign Currency Appreciates	Foreign Currency Depreciates
Sale	Receivable	Transaction gain	Transaction loss
Purchase	Payable	Transaction loss	Transaction gain

6. **Remeasurement**

    a.   Remeasurement is necessary when the currency of the accounting records differs from the functional currency.

    b.   Remeasurement attempts to make the financial statement items look as if the underlying transactions previously had been recorded in the functional currency.

        1)   Balance sheet items carried at historical cost are remeasured at the **historical rate**, i.e., the exchange rate in effect on the day of the transaction that gave rise to them.

            a)   Balance sheet items carried at their current or future values (e.g., present value or net realizable value) are remeasured using the **current rate** on the reporting date.

        2)   Revenues, expenses, gains, and losses are restated using **historical rates**.

    c.   Any net remeasurement gain or loss arising from application of the temporal method is recognized on the income statement as a component of income from continuing operations.

        1)   As a result, maintaining the books of a subsidiary in a local currency other than the functional currency increases earnings volatility.

        2)   Thus, all ratios that use current earnings or components thereof are affected by exchange rate fluctuations arising during the remeasurement process.

7. **Translation**

   a. Translation is necessary when the functional currency differs from the reporting currency.

      1) Assets and liabilities are restated using the **current exchange rate** on the reporting date.

         a) Stockholders' equity items are restated at their **historical rates**.

      2) Revenues, expenses, gains, and losses are restated using the historical rates in effect at the time they were recognized. If this is impracticable, however, a weighted-average rate for the period may be used.

   b. A gain or loss on foreign currency translation is a component of **other comprehensive income**, not earnings.

      1) Thus, even large exchange rate fluctuations between the functional and reporting currencies will have little effect on income statement ratios.

EXAMPLE of Differing Currencies

A U.S.-based conglomerate has a subsidiary in Poland that keeps its books using the zloty (Ż), its local currency. However, since its primary operations involve Eurozone activities, its functional currency is the euro (€). To prepare the consolidated financial statements, the parent first must remeasure all unsettled transactions of the subsidiary from zloties to euros. These remeasured amounts are then translated into dollars ($).

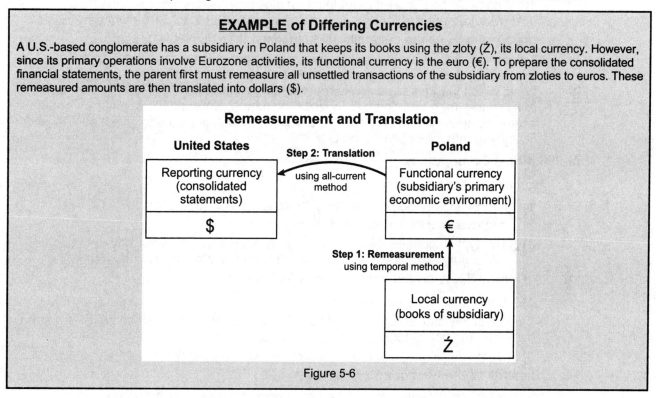

Figure 5-6

Stop and review! You have completed the outline for this subunit. Study multiple-choice questions 21 through 23 beginning on page 169.

5.5 INTERNATIONAL TRADE

1. **Analysis of Foreign Investments**

   a. Valid reasons for expansion of international business include

      1) Securing a new source of raw materials
      2) Expanding into new markets
      3) Seeking lower costs of production
      4) Avoiding trade restrictions

b.   A company planning a foreign investment can either purchase the stock of a foreign corporation or make a **direct foreign investment**. A direct foreign investment involves buying equipment and buildings for a new company. The advantages of a direct foreign investment include

      1)   Lower taxes in the foreign nation

      2)   Annual depreciation allowances for the amount invested

      3)   Access to foreign capital sources

      4)   Avoiding trade restrictions imposed on foreign companies in the customers' market

c.   Cost of capital for foreign projects is higher because of the increased

      1)   Exchange-rate risk and the purchasing power parity

      2)   Sovereignty (or political) risk arising from possible expropriation (or other restrictions), with net losses to the parent company

      3)   The likelihood of laws requiring financing from certain sources, such as a requirement that foreign subsidiaries must be at least 51% owned by locals

d.   Foreign operations are more difficult to manage than domestic operations.

e.   Ownership rights in foreign corporations are sometimes evidenced by American Depository Receipts (ADRs). The foreign stocks are deposited with a large U.S. bank, which in turn issues ADRs representing ownership in the foreign shares. The ADR shares then trade on a U.S. stock exchange, whereas the company's original shares trade in foreign stock markets. ADRs allow Americans to invest abroad and foreigners to raise capital in the U.S.

2.   **Multinational Corporations**

    a.   **Benefits to the home country** include

      1)   Improved earnings and exports of products to foreign subsidiaries

      2)   Improved ability to obtain scarce resources

      3)   The typical benefits of free trade, i.e., greater product availability, a better international monetary system, and improved international understanding

    b.   **Adverse effects on the home country** include

      1)   Loss of jobs and tax revenues

      2)   Instability caused by reduced flexibility of operation in a foreign political system and the risk of expropriation

      3)   Competitive advantage of multinationals over domestic rivals

    c.   **Benefits to the host country** include

      1)   New investment of capital, technology, and management abilities

      2)   Improvements in output and efficiency along with the resulting stronger balance of payments

      3)   Stimulation of competition, increased tax revenues, and higher standard of living

    d.   **Adverse effects on the host country** include

      1)   Remittance of royalties, dividends, and profits that can result in a net capital outflow

      2)   Setting of transfer prices among subsidiaries so that profits will be earned where taxes are lowest or restrictions on the export of profits are least stringent

      3)   Multinationals engaging in anticompetitive activities, such as the formation of cartels

3.   **Methods of Financing International Trade**

    a.   **Cross-Border Factoring**

      1)   A factor purchases receivables and assumes the risk of collection.

2) Cross-border factoring is a method of consummating a transaction by a network of factors across borders. The exporter's factor contacts correspondent factors in other countries to assist in the collection of accounts receivable.

b. **Letters of Credit**

1) Under a letter of credit, an issuer (usually a bank) undertakes with the account party (an importer-buyer that obtains the letter of credit) to verify that the beneficiary (seller-exporter) has performed under the contract, e.g., by shipping goods.

2) Thus, the issuer pays the beneficiary when it presents documents (such as bills of lading) that provide evidence of performance. The issuer then is reimbursed by the account party.

c. **Banker's Acceptances**

1) Banker's acceptances are time drafts drawn on deposits in a bank. They are short-term credit investments created by a nonfinancial firm and guaranteed (accepted) by a bank as to payment.

2) Acceptances are traded at discounts in secondary markets. These instruments have been a popular investment for money market funds.

d. **Forfaiting**

1) Forfaiting is a form of factoring that involves the sale by exporters of large, medium- to long-term receivables to buyers (forfaiters) who are willing and able to bear the costs and risks of credit and collections.

e. **Countertrade**

1) Countertrade at its simplest is barter -- the exchange of goods or services for other goods or services rather than merely for cash.

4. **International Tax Considerations**

a. Multinational corporations frequently derive income from several countries. The government of each country in which a corporation does business may enact statutes imposing one or more types of tax on the corporation.

1) To avoid double taxation, two or more countries may adopt treaties to coordinate or synchronize the effects of their taxing statutes.

2) Most countries tax only the income sourced to that country.

3) The U.S. taxes worldwide income (from whatever source derived) of a domestic corporation. Double taxation is avoided by allowing a credit for income tax paid to foreign countries or by treaty provisions.

4) In the case of foreign corporations, the U.S. taxes only income sourced to the U.S. Ordinarily, such income is effectively connected with engaging in a trade or business of the U.S. Certain U.S. source income, e.g., gain on the sale of most stock, is not taxed by the U.S.

b. **Transfer pricing** is an important aspect of the tax calculation for multinational corporations that transfer inventories between branches in different countries.

1) The U.S. tax laws have limits on the amount of profit that can be transferred from a U.S. parent to a foreign subsidiary or branch.

2) Thus, transfer prices charged to foreign subsidiaries may differ substantially from those charged to domestic subsidiaries.

3) The existence of tariffs in the foreign country may necessitate a lower transfer price to reduce a tariff based on the inventory value.

Stop and review! You have completed the outline for this subunit. Study multiple-choice questions 24 through 30 beginning on page 170.

QUESTIONS

5.1 Mergers and Acquisitions (M&As) and Bankruptcy

1. A horizontal merger is a merger between

   A. Two or more firms from different and unrelated markets.

   B. Two or more firms at different stages of the production process.

   C. A producer and its supplier.

   D. Two or more firms in the same market.

Answer (D) is correct.
   REQUIRED: The example of a horizontal merger.
   DISCUSSION: A horizontal merger is one between competitors in the same market. From the viewpoint of the Justice Department, it is the most closely scrutinized type of merger because it has the greatest tendency to reduce competition.
   Answer (A) is incorrect. A merger between firms in different and unrelated markets is a conglomerate merger. Answer (B) is incorrect. A merger between two or more firms at different stages of the production process is a vertical merger. Answer (C) is incorrect. A merger between a producer and a supplier is a vertical merger.

2. The acquisition of a retail shoe store by a shoe manufacturer is an example of

   A. Vertical integration.

   B. A conglomerate.

   C. Market extension.

   D. Horizontal integration.

Answer (A) is correct.
   REQUIRED: The type of transaction represented.
   DISCUSSION: The acquisition of a shoe retailer by a shoe manufacturer is an example of vertical integration. Vertical integration is typified by a merger or acquisition involving companies that are in the same industry but at different levels in the supply chain. In other words, one of the companies supplies inputs for the other.
   Answer (B) is incorrect. A conglomerate is a company made up of subsidiaries in unrelated industries. Answer (C) is incorrect. Market extension involves expanding into new market areas. Answer (D) is incorrect. Horizontal integration involves a merger between competing firms in the same industry.

3. A business combination may be legally structured as a merger, a consolidation, or an acquisition. Which of the following describes a business combination that is legally structured as a merger?

   A. The surviving company is one of the two combining companies.

   B. The surviving company is neither of the two combining companies.

   C. An investor-investee relationship is established.

   D. A parent-subsidiary relationship is established.

Answer (A) is correct.
   REQUIRED: The characteristic of a business combination legally structured as a merger.
   DISCUSSION: In a business combination legally structured as a merger, the assets and liabilities of one of the combining companies are transferred to the books of the other combining company (the surviving company). The surviving company continues to exist as a separate legal entity. The nonsurviving company ceases to exist as a separate entity. Its stock is canceled, and its books are closed.
   Answer (B) is incorrect. It describes a consolidation in which a new firm is formed to account for the assets and liabilities of the combining companies. Answer (C) is incorrect. It describes an acquisition. A parent-subsidiary relationship exists when the investor holds more than 50% of the outstanding stock of the investee. Answer (D) is incorrect. It describes an acquisition. A parent-subsidiary relationship exists when the investor holds more than 50% of the outstanding stock of the investee.

4. When firm B merges with firm C to create firm BC, what has occurred?

   A. A tender offer.

   B. An acquisition of assets.

   C. An acquisition of stock.

   D. A consolidation.

Answer (D) is correct.
   REQUIRED: The occurrence when firm B merges with firm C to create firm BC.
   DISCUSSION: A consolidation is a business transaction in which a new company is organized to take over the combining companies. An entirely new company is formed, and neither of the merging companies survives. Firm B merges with firm C to form an entirely new company called BC, and neither B nor C survives. Therefore, this is a consolidation.
   Answer (A) is incorrect. A tender offer is used in an acquisition by a firm to the shareholders of another firm to tender their shares for a specified price. Answer (B) is incorrect. In an acquisition of assets, both companies continue to operate separately. Answer (C) is incorrect. In an acquisition of assets or stock, both companies continue to operate separately.

5. Chapter 7 of the Federal Bankruptcy Code will grant a debtor a discharge when the debtor

   A. Is a corporation or a partnership.

   B. Is an entity, other than a partnership or corporation, that could successfully reorganize under Chapter 11 of the Federal Bankruptcy Code.

   C. Is an insurance company.

   D. Unjustifiably destroyed information relevant to the bankruptcy proceeding.

Answer (B) is correct.
   REQUIRED: The basis for granting a discharge to a debtor under Chapter 7 of the Bankruptcy Code.
   DISCUSSION: A general discharge of most debts is provided a person (but not a partnership or corporation) under Chapter 7. Certain entities are not eligible, including railroads, insurance companies, banks, credit unions, and savings and loan associations. Liquidation and discharge under Chapter 7 are not restricted to cases in which Chapter 11 reorganization would not be successful.
   Answer (A) is incorrect. Partnerships and corporations do not receive a general discharge under Chapter 7. They are simply liquidated. Answer (C) is incorrect. Insurance companies are ineligible to file under Chapter 7. Answer (D) is incorrect. Destroying information can result in denial of general discharge. Only if it is justified, e.g., accidental destruction not intended to defraud creditors, might it not result in denial of discharge.

6. Which of the following is indicative of insolvency?

   A. Payments to creditors are late.

   B. The market value of the firm's stock has declined substantially.

   C. Operating cash flows of the firm cannot meet current obligations.

   D. Dividends are not declared because of inadequate retained earnings.

Answer (C) is correct.
   REQUIRED: The indicator of insolvency.
   DISCUSSION: A firm is insolvent when its debts exceed its assets (stock-based insolvency) or when its cash flows are inadequate to meet maturing obligations (flow-based insolvency).
   Answer (A) is incorrect. Late payments are an early signal of potential insolvency. Answer (B) is incorrect. A declining share price is an early signal of potential insolvency. Answer (D) is incorrect. Elimination of dividends is an early signal of potential insolvency.

7. Which of the following is **not** an early signal of potential financial distress?

   A. Negative earnings.

   B. Employee layoffs.

   C. Rapidly falling stock prices.

   D. Stagnant cash flows.

Answer (D) is correct.
   REQUIRED: The item not an early signal of financial distress.
   DISCUSSION: Mere stagnation of cash flows does not indicate potential insolvency. Flow-based insolvency occurs when cash flows are inadequate, not when they are simply not growing at the desired rate.
   Answer (A) is incorrect. Negative earnings are an early signal of potential insolvency. Answer (B) is incorrect. Layoffs are an early signal of potential insolvency. Answer (C) is incorrect. A declining share price is an early signal of potential insolvency.

8. A plan of reorganization under Chapter 11

   A. May be filed by any party in interest for 120 days after entry of the order for relief.

   B. Must be filed by the trustee and approved by the creditors within 180 days after entry of the order for relief.

   C. Must treat all classes of claims and ownership interests equally.

   D. Must treat all claims or interests in the same class equally.

Answer (D) is correct.
   REQUIRED: The correct statement about a plan of reorganization.
   DISCUSSION: A Chapter 11 plan must designate classes of creditors' claims and owners' interests; state the treatment to be given each class; indicate which classes will or will not be impaired; allow for equal treatment of the members within a class unless they agree otherwise; and provide for an adequate method of payment. If the debtor is a corporation, the plan must also protect voting rights, state that no nonvoting stock will be issued, and require that selection of officers and directors be effected in a manner to protect the parties in interest.
   Answer (A) is incorrect. Only the debtor may file a plan within 120 days after entry of the order for relief. If the debtor fails to file or if the creditors do not approve of the plan within 180 days of the entry of the order for relief, any party in interest (including the trustee) may file a plan. Answer (B) is incorrect. Only the debtor may file a plan within 120 days after entry of the order for relief. If the debtor fails to file or if the creditors do not approve of the plan within 180 days of the entry of the order for relief, any party in interest (including the trustee) may file a plan. Answer (C) is incorrect. The plan must be fair and equitable but all classes need not be treated the same. However, no party may receive less than the amount that would have been distributed in a liquidation.

5.2 Foreign Exchange Rates -- Systems and Calculations

9. What is the role of gold in the present international monetary system?

A. Gold is quoted in United States dollars only.

B. All of the major currencies of the world, except the United States dollar, have a fixed value in terms of gold.

C. Gold is like any other asset whose value depends upon supply and demand.

D. Gold is the reserve asset of the International Monetary Fund.

Answer (C) is correct.
REQUIRED: The role of gold in the present international monetary system.
DISCUSSION: Gold has no special role in the modern international monetary system. The present system is based upon managed floating currency exchange rates. Consequently, gold is treated as a commodity, the price of which depends upon supply and demand.
Answer (A) is incorrect. Although most exchanges quote the price of gold in U.S. dollars, the dollar's value is not linked to that of gold. Answer (B) is incorrect. Floating exchange rates have existed since about 1973. Tying currency values to a gold standard, in effect, fixes exchange rates. Answer (D) is incorrect. The only reserves of the IMF are international currencies.

10. In foreign currency markets, the phrase "managed float" refers to the

A. Tendency for most currencies to depreciate in value.

B. Discretionary buying and selling of currencies by central banks.

C. Necessity of maintaining a highly liquid asset, such as gold, to conduct international trade.

D. Fact that actual exchange rates are set by private business people in trading nations.

Answer (B) is correct.
REQUIRED: The meaning of the phrase "managed float."
DISCUSSION: Exchange rates "float" when they are set by supply and demand, not by agreement among countries. In a managed float, central banks buy and sell currencies at their discretion to avoid erratic fluctuations in the foreign currency market. The objective of such transactions is to "manage" the level at which a particular currency sells in the open market. For instance, if there is an oversupply of a country's currency on the foreign currency market, the central bank will purchase that currency to support the market.
Answer (A) is incorrect. Currencies do not have an inherent tendency to depreciate or appreciate. Answer (C) is incorrect. Currencies no longer have to be supported by gold. Answer (D) is incorrect. Central banks, not private business people, manage the quantity of currency on the market.

11. An overvalued foreign currency exchange rate

A. Represents a tax on exports and a subsidy to imports.

B. Represents a subsidy to exports and a tax on imports.

C. Has an effect on capital flows but no effect on trade flows.

D. Has no effect on capital flows but does affect trade flows.

Answer (A) is correct.
REQUIRED: The effect of an overvalued exchange rate.
DISCUSSION: If a country's currency is strong, its goods and services are more expensive to foreign consumers. At the same time, foreign goods become relatively more affordable to domestic consumers.
Answer (B) is incorrect. An overvalued domestic currency will have the opposite effect. Answer (C) is incorrect. Both will be affected. Answer (D) is incorrect. Both will be affected.

12. If the value of the U.S. dollar in foreign currency markets changes from $1 = .75 euros to $1 = .70 euros,

A. The euro has depreciated against the dollar.

B. Products imported from Europe to the U.S. will become more expensive.

C. U.S. tourists in Europe will find their dollars will buy more European products.

D. U.S. exports to Europe should decrease.

Answer (B) is correct.
REQUIRED: The effect of a depreciation in the value of the dollar.
DISCUSSION: Since it now takes fewer euros to buy a single dollar, the dollar has declined in value relative to the euro; i.e., the euro has gained purchasing power. As a result, imports from Europe will become more expensive and will tend to decrease.
Answer (A) is incorrect. Since it now takes fewer euros to buy a single dollar, the euro has appreciated (gained purchasing power) relative to the dollar. Answer (C) is incorrect. Since a dollar will now fetch fewer euros than before, U.S. tourists will find European goods more expensive. Answer (D) is incorrect. Since the euro has gained purchasing power against the dollar, U.S. exports should increase.

13. One U.S. dollar is being quoted at 100 Japanese yen on the spot market and at 102.5 Japanese yen on the 90-day forward market; hence, the annual effect in the forward market is that the U.S. dollar is at a

A. Premium of 10%.

B. Premium of 2.5%.

C. Discount of 10%.

D. Discount of 0.025%.

Answer (A) is correct.
 REQUIRED: The annual effect in the forward market of the difference between the current (spot) rate and the 90-day rate.
 DISCUSSION: A forward currency premium or discount is calculated by multiplying the percentage spread by the number of forward periods in a year:

$$\frac{Forward\ rate\ -\ Spot\ rate}{Spot\ rate} \times \frac{Days\ in\ year}{Days\ in\ forward\ period}$$

In this case, the calculation is as follows:

Forward premium = [(¥102.5 – ¥100) ÷ ¥100] × (360 ÷ 90)
    = 0.025 × 4
    = 10%

 Answer (B) is incorrect. This percentage is the premium for 90 days. Answer (C) is incorrect. The effect is a 10% premium, not discount. Answer (D) is incorrect. The 90-day effect is a 2.5% or 0.025 premium.

14. Of the following transactions, the one that would result in worsening the U.S. balance of payments account is the

A. Receipt of dividends by an American corporation from its German subsidiary.

B. Buying of IBM shares by a Kuwaiti investor.

C. U.S. export of military equipment to Saudi Arabia.

D. Expenditure of a U.S. resident vacationing in France.

Answer (D) is correct.
 REQUIRED: The transaction requiring a debit in the U.S. balance of payments account.
 DISCUSSION: A U.S. resident vacationing abroad transfers money to the foreign country, worsening the U.S. balance of payments and improving that of the other country.
 Answer (A) is incorrect. A transfer of dividends into the U.S. improves the balance of payments. Answer (B) is incorrect. The purchase of a U.S. financial instrument by a foreigner improves the balance of payments. Answer (C) is incorrect. The purchase of U.S. goods by a foreign country improves the balance of payments.

5.3 Foreign Exchange Rates -- Factors Affecting Rates and Risk Mitigation Techniques

15. Assuming exchange rates are allowed to fluctuate freely, which one of the following factors would likely cause a nation's currency to appreciate on the foreign exchange market?

A. A relatively rapid rate of growth in income that stimulates imports.

B. A high rate of inflation relative to other countries.

C. A slower rate of growth in income than in other countries, which causes imports to lag behind exports.

D. Domestic real interest rates that are lower than real interest rates abroad.

Answer (C) is correct.
 REQUIRED: The factor causing a currency to appreciate given freely fluctuating exchange rates.
 DISCUSSION: Assuming that exchange rates are allowed to fluctuate freely, a nation's currency will appreciate if the demand for it is constant or increasing while supply is decreasing. For example, if the nation decreases its imports relative to exports, less of its currency will be used to buy foreign currencies for import transactions and more of its currency will be demanded for export transactions. Thus, the supply of the nation's currency available in foreign currency markets decreases. If the demand for the currency increases or does not change, the result is an increase in (appreciation of) the value of the currency.
 Answer (A) is incorrect. An increase in imports drives down the value of the nation's currency. Answer (B) is incorrect. A high rate of inflation devalues a nation's currency. Answer (D) is incorrect. Lower interest rates relative to those in other countries discourage foreign investment, decreases demand for the nation's currency, and reduces its value.

16. Two countries have flexible exchange rate systems and an active trading relationship. If incomes <List A> in Country 1, everything else being equal, then the currency of Country 1 will tend to <List B> relative to the currency of Country 2.

	List A	List B
A.	Rise	Remain constant
B.	Fall	Depreciate
C.	Rise	Depreciate
D.	Remain constant	Appreciate

Answer (C) is correct.
REQUIRED: The effect of a change in incomes in one nation on its currency.
DISCUSSION: Citizens with higher incomes look for new consumption opportunities in other countries, driving up the demand for those currencies and shifting the demand curve to the right. Thus, as incomes rise in one country, the prices of foreign currencies rise as well, and the local currency will depreciate.
Answer (A) is incorrect. If incomes in Country 1 rise, its currency will tend to depreciate relative to the currencies of other countries. Answer (B) is incorrect. If incomes in Country 1 fall, its currency will tend to appreciate relative to the currencies of other countries. Answer (D) is incorrect. If incomes in Country 1 remain constant, its currency will not tend to appreciate or depreciate relative to the currencies of other countries.

17. If the central bank of a country raises interest rates sharply, the country's currency will likely

A. Increase in relative value.

B. Remain unchanged in value.

C. Decrease in relative value.

D. Decrease sharply in value at first and then return to its initial value.

Answer (A) is correct.
REQUIRED: The effect on a country's currency if its central bank raises interest rates sharply.
DISCUSSION: If the interest rates in a given country rise, money will pour in from all over the world in pursuit of that country's higher returns. This increase in demand for the country's currency will boost its purchasing power.
Answer (B) is incorrect. A currency tends to increase relative to other currencies when interest rates in the country rise sharply. More investors will want to earn the higher rates of return available in that country. Answer (C) is incorrect. A currency tends to increase relative to other currencies when interest rates in the country rise sharply. More investors will want to earn the higher rates of return available in that country. Answer (D) is incorrect. A currency tends to increase relative to other currencies when interest rates in the country rise sharply. More investors will want to earn the higher rates of return available in that country.

18. If the annual U.S. inflation rate is expected to be 5% while the euro is expected to depreciate against the U.S. dollar by 10%, an Italian firm importing from its U.S. parent can expect its euro costs for these imports to

A. Decrease by about 10%.

B. Decrease by about 5%.

C. Increase by about 5%.

D. Increase by about 16.7%.

Answer (D) is correct.
REQUIRED: The combined effect of inflation and currency depreciation.
DISCUSSION: Inflation in the U.S. means that $1.05 now has the purchasing power formerly enjoyed by $1.00. The 10% depreciation of the euro means that its purchasing power in dollars has declined to 90%. Dividing the U.S. inflation factor of 1.05 by the new euro value of .90 and subtracting 1 results in a net loss of euro purchasing power against the dollar of 16.67%.
Answer (A) is incorrect. The euro's loss of purchasing power through depreciation against the dollar outweighs the dollar's loss of purchasing power against all other currencies due to inflation. Thus, euro costs will increase, not decrease. Answer (B) is incorrect. The euro's loss of purchasing power through depreciation against the dollar outweighs the dollar's loss of purchasing power against all other currencies due to inflation. Thus, euro costs will increase, not decrease. Answer (C) is incorrect. This percentage is the difference between the currency depreciation and the inflation rate.

19. Which one of the following statements supports the conclusion that the U.S. dollar has gained purchasing power against the Japanese yen?

- A. Inflation has recently been higher in the U.S. than in Japan.
- B. The dollar is currently trading at a premium in the forward market with respect to the yen.
- C. The yen's spot rate with respect to the dollar has just fallen.
- D. Studies recently published in the financial press have shed doubt on the interest rate parity (IRP) theory.

Answer (C) is correct.
　REQUIRED: The statement that supports the conclusion that the U.S. dollar has gained purchasing power against the Japanese yen.
　DISCUSSION: If the yen's spot rate has just fallen, then more yen are required to buy a single dollar. The yen has therefore depreciated, i.e., lost purchasing power. At the same time, the dollar has gained purchasing power.
　Answer (A) is incorrect. This statement reflects a loss, not a gain, of purchasing power for the dollar. Answer (B) is incorrect. No conclusion can be drawn about changes in purchasing power simply from a statement about forward rates. Answer (D) is incorrect. No conclusion can be drawn about changes in purchasing power simply from evidence for or against the interest rate parity (IRP) theory.

20. An American importer of English clothing has contracted to pay an amount fixed in British pounds 3 months from now. If the importer worries that the U.S. dollar may depreciate sharply against the British pound in the interim, it would be well advised to

- A. Buy pounds in the forward exchange market.
- B. Sell pounds in the forward exchange market.
- C. Buy dollars in the futures market.
- D. Sell dollars in the futures market.

Answer (A) is correct.
　REQUIRED: The action to hedge a liability denominated in a foreign currency.
　DISCUSSION: The American importer should buy pounds now. If the dollar depreciates against the pound in the next 90 days, the gain on the forward exchange contract would offset the loss from having to pay more dollars to satisfy the liability.
　Answer (B) is incorrect. Selling pounds would compound the risk of loss for someone who has incurred a liability. However, it would be an appropriate hedge of a receivable denominated in pounds. Answer (C) is incorrect. The importer needs pounds, not dollars. Answer (D) is incorrect. Although buying pounds might be equivalent to selling dollars for pounds, this is not the best answer. This choice does not state what is received for the dollars.

5.4 Effects of Foreign Exchange Fluctuations

21. If an entity's books of account are not maintained in its functional currency, U.S. GAAP require remeasurement into the functional currency prior to the translation process. An item that should be remeasured by use of the current exchange rate is

- A. An investment in bonds to be held until maturity.
- B. A plant asset and the associated accumulated depreciation.
- C. A patent and the associated accumulated amortization.
- D. The revenue from a long-term construction contract.

Answer (A) is correct.
　REQUIRED: The item that should be remeasured into the functional currency using the current exchange rate.
　DISCUSSION: When remeasurement is necessary, the temporal method is applied. The essence of the temporal method is to make the financial statement items look as if the underlying transactions had been recorded in the functional currency to begin with. Balance sheet items carried at their future values, such as held-to-maturity investments in bonds, are remeasured using the current rate on the reporting date.
　Answer (B) is incorrect. Property, plant, and equipment is remeasured at the historical rate. Answer (C) is incorrect. Intangible assets are remeasured at the historical rate. Answer (D) is incorrect. Revenues, expenses, gains, and losses are remeasured using historical rates.

22. The economic effects of a change in foreign exchange rates on a relatively self-contained and integrated operation within a foreign country relate to the net investment by the reporting enterprise in that operation. Consequently, translation adjustments that arise from the consolidation of that operation

    A. Directly affect cash flows but should not be reflected in income.

    B. Directly affect cash flows and should be reflected in income.

    C. Do not directly affect cash flows and should not be reflected in income.

    D. Do not directly affect cash flows but should be reflected in income.

Answer (C) is correct.
    REQUIRED: The true statement about translation adjustments arising from consolidation of a self-contained foreign operation with its U.S. parent/investor.
    DISCUSSION: When a foreign operation is relatively self-contained, the cash generated and expended by the entity is normally in the currency of the foreign country, and that currency is deemed to be the operation's functional currency. Related translation adjustments do not directly affect the parent's cash flows and are not reflected in net income.
    Answer (A) is incorrect. When an operation is relatively self-contained, the assumption is that translation adjustments do not affect cash flows. Answer (B) is incorrect. When an operation is relatively self-contained, the assumption is that translation adjustments do not affect cash flows. Additionally, translation adjustments should be included in other comprehensive income, not recognized in income. Answer (D) is incorrect. Translation adjustments should be included in other comprehensive income, not recognized in income.

23. A company owns a foreign subsidiary. Included among the subsidiary's liabilities for the year just ended are 400,000 of revenue received in advance, recorded when $.50 was the dollar equivalent per drongo, and a deferred tax liability for 187,500 drongos, recognized when $.40 was the dollar equivalent per drongo. The rate of exchange in effect at year-end was $.35 per drongo. If the U.S. dollar is the functional currency, what total should be included for these two liabilities on the company's consolidated balance sheet at year end?

    A. $205,625

    B. $215,000

    C. $265,625

    D. $275,000

Answer (D) is correct.
    REQUIRED: The total of two liability accounts of a foreign subsidiary in the consolidated statements.
    DISCUSSION: When a foreign entity's functional currency is the U.S. dollar, the financial statements of the entity recorded in a foreign currency must be remeasured in terms of the U.S. dollar. Revenue received in advance (deferred income) is considered a nonmonetary balance sheet item and is translated at the applicable historical rate (400,000 drongos × $.50 per drongo = $200,000). Deferred charges and credits (except policy acquisition costs for life insurance companies) are also remeasured at historical exchange rates. The deferred tax liability (a deferred credit) should be remeasured at the historical rate (187,500 drongos × $.40 per drongo = $75,000). The total for these liabilities is therefore $275,000 ($200,000 + $75,000).
    Answer (A) is incorrect. Applying the year-end rate to the total liabilities results in $205,625. Answer (B) is incorrect. The historical, not current, rate should be used to remeasure the deferred income. Answer (C) is incorrect. The historical rate is used to remeasure nonmonetary balance sheet items, including deferred tax assets and liabilities.

5.5 International Trade

24. Direct foreign investment allows firms to avoid

    A. Exposure to political risk.

    B. The cost of exchange rate fluctuations.

    C. Trade restrictions imposed on foreign companies in the customers' market.

    D. Domestic regulations on the use of foreign technology.

Answer (C) is correct.
    REQUIRED: The advantage of a direct foreign investment.
    DISCUSSION: Reasons for international business expansion, known as direct foreign investment, can be both revenue-oriented (seeking new markets or avoiding trade restrictions) and cost-oriented (seeking cheaper inputs or favorable exchange rates).
    Answer (A) is incorrect. Direct foreign investment increases exposure to political risk. Answer (B) is incorrect. Direct foreign investment increases exposure to exchange rate risk. Answer (D) is incorrect. A multinational company is subject to its home country's regulations on the use of foreign technology.

25. All of the following are valid reasons for expansion of international business by U.S. multinational corporations **except** to

    A. Secure new sources for raw materials.

    B. Find additional areas where their products can be successfully marketed.

    C. Minimize their costs of production.

    D. Protect their domestic market from competition from foreign manufacturers.

Answer (D) is correct.
    REQUIRED: The statement not a valid reason for a multinational corporation, known as direct foreign investment, expanding into a foreign country.
    DISCUSSION: Reasons for international business expansion, known as direct foreign investment, can be both revenue-oriented (seeking new markets or avoiding trade restrictions) and cost-oriented (seeking cheaper inputs or favorable exchange rates). An attempt to protect the firm's domestic market from foreign competition by expanding operations into foreign countries is unlikely.
    Answer (A) is incorrect. Securing new sources of raw materials is one of the sound cost-related reasons firms have for international business expansion. Answer (B) is incorrect. Seeking new markets is one of the sound revenue-related reasons firms have for international business expansion. Answer (C) is incorrect. Attempting to minimize the costs of production is one of the sound cost-related reasons firms have for international business expansion.

26. Which one of the following statements concerning American Depository Receipts (ADRs) is **false**?

    A. ADRs facilitate the banking procedures for U.S. multinational firms.

    B. ADRs allow Americans to invest abroad.

    C. ADRs allow foreigners to raise capital in the U.S.

    D. ADRs are securities issued by American banks acting as custodians of shares of foreign firms.

Answer (A) is correct.
    REQUIRED: The false statement concerning ADRs.
    DISCUSSION: Ownership rights in foreign corporations are sometimes evidenced by American Depository Receipts (ADRs). The foreign stocks are deposited with a large U.S. bank, which in turn issues ADRs representing ownership in the foreign shares. The ADR shares then trade on a U.S. stock exchange, whereas the company's original shares trade in foreign stock markets. ADRs allow foreign companies to develop a U.S. shareholder base without being subject to many SEC restrictions.
    Answer (B) is incorrect. The purpose of an ADR is to allow Americans to invest abroad. Answer (C) is incorrect. ADRs are designed to allow foreign firms to raise capital in the U.S. Answer (D) is incorrect. ADRs are securities issued by American banks acting as custodians of shares of foreign firms.

27. Which of the following is **not** a political risk of investing in a foreign country?

    A. Rebellions could result in destruction of property.

    B. Assets could be expropriated.

    C. Foreign-exchange controls could limit the repatriation of profits.

    D. A foreign customer might default on its debt.

Answer (D) is correct.
    REQUIRED: The item that is not a political risk of investing in foreign-based assets.
    DISCUSSION: Political risks include the threat of expropriation of company assets, destruction of assets in rebellions in third-world nations, and limitations on the repatriation of profits (or even initial investments). Default by a foreign customer is not a political risk, but a risk of doing business either locally or internationally.

28. A British company currently has domestic operations only. It plans to invest equal amounts of money on projects either in the U.S. or in China. The company will select the country based on risk and return for its portfolio of domestic and international projects taken together. The risk reduction benefits of investing internationally (based on 50% of British domestic operations and 50% foreign operations) will be the greatest when there is perfectly

    A. Positive correlation between the British return and the U.S. return.

    B. Negative correlation between the U.S. return and the Chinese return.

    C. Positive correlation between the U.S. return and the Chinese return.

    D. Negative correlation between the Chinese return and the British return.

Answer (D) is correct.
    REQUIRED: The correlation yielding the greatest benefits from an international business portfolio.
    DISCUSSION: Portfolio theory concerns the composition of an investment portfolio that is efficient in balancing the risk with the rate of return of the portfolio. Diversification reduces risk. This firm's goal is to balance the risk inherent in having 100% of its operations in Britain. This will be accomplished when the foreign investment moves in the opposite direction from the domestic (British) operations.
    Answer (A) is incorrect. A positive correlation between the foreign investment and domestic operations will increase risk, not reduce it. Answer (B) is incorrect. The correlation between the U.S. investment and the Chinese investment is irrelevant; the investment must be in one or the other of those two countries. Answer (C) is incorrect. The relevant correlation is one between the domestic (British) operations and one of the two alternatives.

29. A company located in Belgium currently manufactures products at its domestic plant and exports them to the U.S. since it is less expensive to produce at home. The company is considering the possibility of setting up a plant in the U.S. All of the following factors would encourage the company to consider direct foreign investment in the U.S. **except** the

A. Expectation of more stringent trade restrictions by the U.S.

B. Depreciation of the U.S. dollar against Belgium's currency.

C. Widening of the gap in production costs between the United States and Belgium locations.

D. Changing demand for the company's exports to the U.S. due to exchange rate fluctuations.

Answer (C) is correct.
   REQUIRED: The factor not an advantage of direct foreign investment.
   DISCUSSION: Production costs in the home country are already lower than those in the U.S. Widening this gap would not serve the firm's interests.
   Answer (A) is incorrect. Avoiding trade restrictions is one of the sound revenue-related reasons firms have for international business expansion. Answer (B) is incorrect. If the foreign currency depreciates against the home country's currency, operations in the foreign country are made even less expensive. Answer (D) is incorrect. Avoiding exchange rate risk is one of the sound cost-related reasons for international business expansion.

30. All of the following are concerns that are unique to foreign investments **except**

A. Exchange rate changes.

B. Purchasing power parity.

C. Changes in interest rates.

D. Expropriation.

Answer (C) is correct.
   REQUIRED: The concept not unique to foreign investments.
   DISCUSSION: Interest rates are an aspect of doing business within any modern economy. They are not unique to foreign investment.
   Answer (A) is incorrect. Changes in the exchange rates of currencies are an inherent aspect of doing business in foreign countries. Answer (B) is incorrect. The purchasing power parity theorem is an explanatory mechanism for the setting of long-term exchange rates between currencies. Answer (D) is incorrect. The risk of expropriation by a foreign government is an inherent risk of doing business internationally.

 Access the **Gleim CMA Premium Review System** from your Gleim Personal Classroom to continue your studies with exam-emulating multiple-choice questions!

5.6 ESSAY QUESTIONS

Scenario for Essay Questions 1, 2, 3

Deerfield Devices, Inc., a U.S. manufacturer of computer peripheral equipment, is considering establishing an overseas manufacturing facility. The reduced costs of this facility, particularly lower wage rates, would allow Deerfield to compete more effectively as the company has become vulnerable to lower-cost, imported peripheral equipment. Deerfield has investigated many opportunities over the past year and has now narrowed the field to the following three alternatives.

- The government of Brazil has expressed interest in having Deerfield locate its plant in Brasilia, and Deerfield is interested in increasing its presence in the South American market. However, Brazil's trade regulations regarding the type of investment being proposed by Deerfield require that Deerfield form a joint venture with a local partner. Deerfield would have a minority share in the joint venture but would maintain operating control by controlling the technology. In addition, Deerfield would have to operate under foreign exchange regulations that would restrict the amount of profits the company would be allowed to repatriate each year.

- Nigeria has made an attractive offer to Deerfield that includes support from the local government, local investment in the building of the facility, and the purchase of a portion of the plant's output. In return, Deerfield must enter into a countertrade agreement with Nigeria whereby Deerfield would accept payment in the form of goods for the peripheral equipment purchased by Nigeria.

- Deerfield is also interested in locating its plant in Mexico City as distribution throughout the United States would be less difficult than from the other locations being considered. In addition, the plant would be close to Deerfield's headquarters in Houston, Texas. Mexico has offered both tariff and tax relief as well as local equity investment to encourage Deerfield to locate there. However, Deerfield must enter into a buy-back arrangement whereby the company would agree to purchase 75% of the total output of the manufacturing plant for the next 4 years.

Questions

1. Discuss the reasons a host country would

    a. Require foreign investors to form joint ventures with local nationals
    b. Restrict the repatriation of profits

2. Explain why some host countries insist on countertrade agreements.

3. Describe several benefits investing companies expect to receive when agreeing to participate in countertrade and buy-back arrangements.

Essay Questions 1, 2, 3 — Unofficial Answers

1. a. The reasons a host country would require foreign investors to form joint ventures with local nationals include

    1) Participation in dividend policies, transfer pricing decisions, and other strategic control issues
    2) Promotion of the transfer of technology and increased employment
    3) Sharing in the profits from foreign investment
    4) Retaining control of their industries and resources

    b. The reasons a host country would restrict the repatriation of profits include

    1) Reduction of the drain on foreign reserves from the host country that are needed to buy other necessities
    2) Retention of the profits for a longer period of time to improve chances of success
    3) Protection of local investment and encouragement for foreign investors to stay longer

2. Host countries insist on countertrade agreements to

    a. Stimulate their own economies
    b. Act as a positive influence on their balance of payments transactions
    c. Gain access to new markets by using the marketing skills and outlets of the purchasing companies

3. Benefits investing companies expect to receive when agreeing to participate in countertrade and buy-back arrangements include

    a. Gaining access to new international markets
    b. Gaining new sources of supply such as natural resources
    c. Obtaining lower costs and increased profits from lower wages and other production costs
    d. Relief from local taxes
    e. Capital loans and equity investments to defray start-up costs

---

 Access the **Gleim CMA Premium Review System** from your Gleim Personal Classroom to continue your studies with exam-emulating essay questions!

STUDY UNIT SIX
RATIO ANALYSIS

(23 pages of outline)

This study unit is the **first of two** on **financial statement analysis**. The relative weight assigned to this major topic in Part 2 of the exam is **25%**. The two study units are

Study Unit 6: Ratio Analysis
Study Unit 7: Activity Measures and Financing

If you are interested in reviewing more introductory or background material, go to www.gleim.com/CMAIntroVideos for a list of suggested third-party overviews of this topic. The following Gleim outline material is more than sufficient to help you pass the CMA exam; any additional introductory or background material is for your own personal enrichment.

6.1 QUALITIES OF RATIO ANALYSIS

1. Overview

   a. Ratio analysis is an important tool for analyzing a firm's financial performance.

      1) Ratios are not useful unless they can be compared against a standard or benchmark.

      2) The following are common benchmarks to use in ratio analysis:

         a) Industry norm. This is the most common type of comparison.
         b) Aggregate economy.
         c) Firm's past performance.

   b. Ratio analysis can be used to analyze financial statements, judge efficiency, locate weakness, formulate plans, and compare performance.

      1) Different users, such as management, investors, and creditors, use ratio analysis to determine the financial health of a firm for their decision-making purposes.

      2) Ratios can provide insights into how efficiently and effectively the firm has been able to use its resources and earn profits.

         a) Ratios can be used to identify weaknesses even when the firm as a whole is operating effectively.

         b) Management then can target those weak areas for improvement.

      3) Ratios also can be used to formulate plans.

         a) Progress toward the achievement of these plans can be tracked by analyzing the changes in ratios over time.

   c. Ratio analysis provides the tools to determine how well a firm is performing over the years compared to other similar firms.

      1) Firms can also determine how well different divisions are performing among themselves in different years.

2.   Ratio analysis is subject to inherent limitations that can affect its usefulness.

   a.   Ratios are constructed from accounting data, much of which is subject to estimation. Also, **accounting profit** differs from **economic profit**. Economic profit is the excess of revenues over explicit and implicit costs. Accounting profit, however, does not account for implicit costs. This difference is covered in detail in Study Unit 10, Subunit 1.

      1)   Many studies have found a relationship between accounting data and stock prices. Thus, managers may manipulate accounting data to improve results.

      2)   One reason for manipulation is the observed tendency of the stock price of a public company to continue to move upward or downward for months after an earnings announcement, depending on whether the report was favorable or unfavorable, respectively.

   b.   A firm's management has an incentive to **window dress** financial statements to improve results.

      1)   For example, if the current or quick ratio is greater than 1.0, paying liabilities on the last day of the year will increase the ratio.

   c.   Development of ratios for comparison with **industry averages** is more useful for firms that operate within a particular industry than for conglomerates (firms that operate in a variety of industries).

      1)   For comparison purposes, industry averages can be obtained from industry journals and sources, such as Robert Morris Associates and Standard & Poor's.

      2)   Size differentials among firms affect comparability because of differences in access to and cost of capital, economies of scale, and width of markets.

      3)   Generalizations regarding which ratios are strong indicators of a firm's financial position may change from industry to industry, firm to firm, and division to division.

      4)   Industry averages may include data from capital-intensive and labor-intensive firms. They may also include data from firms with greatly divergent policies regarding leverage.

         a)   Some industry averages may be based on small samples.

   d.   **Earnings quality** is a measure of how useful reported earnings are as a performance indicator. If earnings have a high degree of variability, many ratios will become less meaningful.

      1)   Consistency of earnings is an aspect of quality. A company that has widely varying earnings levels from year to year will be said to have a low level of earnings quality because looking at a single year's earnings will not tell you anything about the long-term aspects of the company.

      2)   Earnings quality is enhanced when a firm uses certain accounting principles as opposed to others. For example, the use of declining-balance depreciation enhances earnings because assets are written down earlier than if straight-line depreciation were used. Similarly, during a period of inflation, LIFO earnings quality is higher than that of FIFO.

   e.   Variances in ratio analysis could entirely, or in part, be attributed to inflation.

      1)   For example, if LIFO is used, fixed assets and depreciation as well as inventory will be understated.

      2)   The interest rate increases that accompany inflation will decrease the value of outstanding long-term debt.

      3)   Many assets are recorded at **historical cost**, so their fair value may not be reflected on the balance sheet.

    f.   Comparability of financial statement amounts and the ratios derived from them is impaired if different firms choose different **accounting policies**. Also, changes in a firm's own accounting policies may create some distortion in the comparison of the results over a period of years.

        1)   Current performance and trends may be misinterpreted if sufficient years of historical analysis are not considered.

        2)   Some data may be presented either before or after taxes.

        3)   Comparability among firms may be impaired if they have different fiscal years.

    g.   Ratio analysis may be affected by **seasonal factors**.

        1)   For example, inventory and receivables may vary widely, and year-end balances may not reflect the averages for the period.

    h.   The geographical locations of firms may affect comparability because of differences in labor markets, price levels, governmental regulation, taxation, and other factors.

    i.   Ratio analysis may be applied ineffectively.

        1)   Ratio analysis may be distorted by failing to use an average or weighted average.

        2)   Different sources of information may compute ratios differently.

        3)   Misleading conclusions may result if improper comparisons are selected.

        4)   Whether a certain level of a ratio is favorable depends on the underlying circumstances. For example, a high quick ratio indicates high liquidity, but it may also imply that excessive cash is being held.

        5)   Different ratios may yield opposite conclusions about a firm's financial health. Thus, the net effects of a set of ratios should be analyzed.

Stop and review! You have completed the outline for this subunit. Study multiple-choice questions 1 and 2 on page 198.

6.2 LIQUIDITY RATIOS -- CALCULATIONS

    1.   **Liquidity**

        a.   Liquidity is a firm's ability to pay its **current obligations** as they come due and thus remain in business in the short run. Liquidity reflects the ease with which assets can be converted to cash.

            1)   Liquidity ratios measure this ability by relating a firm's liquid assets to its current liabilities.

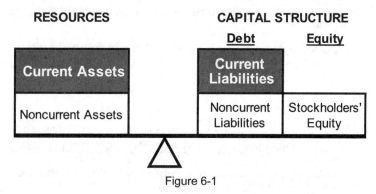

Figure 6-1

b.   EXAMPLE of a balance sheet:

RESOURCES				FINANCING		
CURRENT ASSETS:	**Current Year End**	**Prior Year End**		**CURRENT LIABILITIES:**	**Current Year End**	**Prior Year End**
Cash and equivalents	$ 325,000	$ 275,000		Accounts payable	$ 150,000	$ 75,000
Available-for-sale securities	165,000	145,000		Notes payable	50,000	50,000
Accounts receivable (net)	120,000	115,000		Accrued interest on note	5,000	5,000
Notes receivable	55,000	40,000		Current maturities of L.T. debt	100,000	100,000
Inventories	85,000	55,000		Accrued salaries and wages	15,000	10,000
Prepaid expenses	10,000	5,000		Income taxes payable	70,000	35,000
Total current assets	**$ 760,000**	**$ 635,000**		**Total current liabilities**	**$ 390,000**	**$ 275,000**
NONCURRENT ASSETS:				**NONCURRENT LIABILITIES:**		
Equity-method investments	$ 120,000	$ 115,000		Bonds payable	$ 500,000	$ 600,000
Property, plant, and equipment	1,000,000	900,000		Long-term notes payable	90,000	60,000
Less: Accum. depreciation	(85,000)	(55,000)		Employee-related obligations	15,000	10,000
Goodwill	5,000	5,000		Deferred income taxes	5,000	5,000
Total noncurrent assets	**$1,040,000**	**$ 965,000**		**Total noncurrent liabilities**	**$ 610,000**	**$ 675,000**
				Total liabilities	**$1,000,000**	**$ 950,000**
				STOCKHOLDERS' EQUITY:		
				Preferred stock, $50 par	$ 120,000	$ 0
				Common stock, $1 par	500,000	500,000
				Additional paid-in capital	110,000	100,000
				Retained earnings	70,000	50,000
				Total stockholders' equity	**$ 800,000**	**$ 650,000**
Total assets	**$1,800,000**	**$1,600,000**		**Total liabilities and stockholders' equity**	**$1,800,000**	**$1,600,000**

NOTE: This balance sheet provides input for the examples throughout this study unit.

c.   Current assets are the most liquid. They are expected to be converted to cash, sold, or consumed within 1 year or the operating cycle, whichever is longer. Ratios involving current assets thus measure a firm's ability to continue operating in the short run.

   1)   Current assets include, in descending order of liquidity, cash and equivalents; marketable securities; receivables; inventories; and prepaid items.

d.   Current liabilities, by the same token, are ones that must be settled the soonest. Specifically, they are expected to be settled or converted to other liabilities within 1 year or the operating cycle, whichever is longer.

   1)   Current liabilities include accounts payable, notes payable, current maturities of long-term debt, unearned revenues, taxes payable, wages payable, and other accruals.

e.   Net working capital reports the resources the company would have to continue operating in the short run if it had to liquidate all of its current liabilities at once.

Net Working Capital

Current assets − Current liabilities

   1)   EXAMPLE: Current Year: $760,000 − $390,000 = $370,000
                    Prior Year: $635,000 − $275,000 = $360,000

      a)   Although the company's current liabilities increased, its current assets increased by $10,000 more.

2. **Liquidity Ratios**

    a.   The **current ratio** is the most common measure of liquidity.

Current Ratio

$$\frac{Current\ assets}{Current\ liabilities}$$

    1)   EXAMPLE: Current Year: $760,000 ÷ $390,000 = 1.949
                    Prior Year: $635,000 ÷ $275,000 = 2.309

        a)   Although working capital increased in absolute terms ($10,000), current assets now provide less proportional coverage of current liabilities than in the prior year.

    2)   A low ratio indicates a possible solvency problem.

        a)   A firm with a low current ratio may become insolvent. Therefore, care should be taken when determining whether to extend credit to a firm with a low ratio.

    3)   An overly high ratio indicates that management may not be investing idle assets productively.

    4)   The quality of accounts receivable and merchandise inventory should be considered before evaluating the current ratio.

        a)   Obsolete or overvalued inventory or receivables can artificially inflate the current ratio.

    5)   The general principle is that the current ratio should be proportional to the operating cycle. Thus, a shorter cycle may justify a lower ratio.

        a)   For example, a grocery store has a short operating cycle and can survive with a lower current ratio than could a gold mining company, which has a much longer operating cycle.

    b.   The **quick (acid test) ratio** excludes inventories and prepaids from the numerator, recognizing that those assets are difficult to liquidate at their stated values. The quick ratio is thus a more conservative measure than the basic current ratio.

Quick (Acid Test) Ratio

$$\frac{Cash\ +\ Marketable\ securities\ +\ Net\ receivables}{Current\ liabilities}$$

    1)   EXAMPLE:

           Current Year: ($325,000 + $165,000 + $120,000 + $55,000) ÷ $390,000 = 1.705
           Prior Year: ($275,000 + $145,000 + $115,000 + $40,000) ÷ $275,000 = 2.091

        a)   In spite of its increase in total working capital, the company's position in its most liquid assets deteriorated significantly.

    2)   This ratio measures the firm's ability to easily pay its short-term debts and avoids the problem of inventory valuation.

    c.   The **cash ratio** is an even more conservative variation.

Cash Ratio

$$\frac{Cash\ +\ Marketable\ securities}{Current\ liabilities}$$

    1)   EXAMPLE: Current Year: ($325,000 + $165,000) ÷ $390,000 = 1.256
                    Prior Year: ($275,000 + $145,000) ÷ $275,000 = 1.527

        a)   In this working capital measure, the company's position declined, but coverage is still positive; i.e., the ratio is greater than 1.

d. The **cash flow ratio** reflects the significance of cash flow for settling obligations as they become due.

Cash Flow Ratio

$$\frac{Cash\ flow\ from\ operations}{Current\ liabilities}$$

1) EXAMPLE: The company's cash flows from operations for the two most recent years were $382,000 and $291,000, respectively.

Current Year: $382,000 ÷ $390,000 = 0.979
Prior Year: $291,000 ÷ $275,000 = 1.058

a) Unlike the prior year, the cash flows generated by the company in the most recent year were not sufficient to cover current liabilities.

e. The **net working capital ratio** is the most conservative of the working capital ratios.

Net Working Capital Ratio

$$\frac{Current\ assets\ -\ Current\ liabilities}{Total\ assets}$$

1) EXAMPLE: Current Year: ($760,000 – $390,000) ÷ $1,800,000 = 0.206
Prior Year: ($635,000 – $275,000) ÷ $1,600,000 = 0.225

a) Current liabilities are taking a bigger "bite" out of working capital than in the prior year.

3. **Liquidity of Current Liabilities**

a. The liquidity of current liabilities is the ease with which a firm can issue new debt or raise new structured (convertible, puttable, callable, etc.) funds.

1) The liquidity of current liabilities indicates the ease of funding or availability of sources of funding. A firm's ability to borrow in the financial markets is generally a function of its size, reputation, creditworthiness, and capital levels.

2) Raising liquidity during an adverse situation often requires a combination of both asset liquidity and liability liquidity.

Stop and review! You have completed the outline for this subunit. Study multiple-choice questions 3 through 9 beginning on page 199.

6.3 LIQUIDITY RATIOS -- EFFECTS OF TRANSACTIONS

Some of the questions pertaining to liquidity ratios that a candidate will encounter on the CMA exam focus on the effects that typical business transactions have on a firm's liquidity rather than on the mechanics of calculating the ratios. This subunit consists entirely of such questions. Please review Subunit 6.2 before attempting to answer the questions in this subunit.

Stop and review! You have completed the outline for this subunit. Study multiple-choice questions 10 through 18 beginning on page 201.

6.4 PROFITABILITY RATIOS -- CALCULATIONS

1. **Income Statement Percentages**

a. Gross profit margin is the percentage of gross revenues that remains with the firm after paying for merchandise. The key analysis with respect to the gross profit margin is whether it remains stable with any increase or decrease in sales.

Gross Profit Margin Ratio

$$\frac{Net\ sales\ -\ Cost\ of\ goods\ sold}{Net\ sales}$$

1) For example, a 10% increase in sales should be accompanied by at least a 10% increase in gross profit. Thus, the gross profit margin should remain relatively constant at different sales levels.

b. Operating profit margin is the percentage that remains after selling and general and administrative expenses have been paid.

Operating Profit Margin

$$\frac{Operating\ income}{Net\ sales}$$

1) The ratio of net operating income to sales may also be defined as earnings before interest and taxes (EBIT) divided by net sales.

c. **Net profit margin** is the percentage that remains after other gains and losses (including interest expense) and income taxes have been added or deducted.

Net Profit Margin Ratio

$$\frac{Net\ income}{Net\ sales}$$

1) EXAMPLE:

	Dollars	Percent
Net sales	$1,800,000	100.0%
Cost of goods sold	(1,450,000)	(80.6%)
Gross margin	**$ 350,000**	**19.4%**
SG&A expenses	(160,000)	(8.9%)
Operating income	**$ 190,000**	**10.6%**
Other income and loss	(40,000)	(2.2%)
EBIT	$ 150,000	8.3%
Interest expense	(15,000)	(0.8%)
Earnings before taxes	$ 135,000	7.5%
Income taxes (40%)	(54,000)	(3.0%)
Net income	**$ 81,000**	**4.5%** (Net profit margin)

2) The numerator may also be stated in terms of the net income available to common shareholders.

3) Another form of the ratio excludes nonrecurring items from the numerator, e.g., unusual or infrequent items, discontinued operations, extraordinary items, and effects of accounting changes. The result is sometimes called the net profit margin. This adjustment may be made for any ratio that includes net income.

a) Still other numerator refinements are to exclude equity-based earnings and items in the other income and other expense categories.

d. **Earnings before interest, taxes, depreciation, and amortization (EBITDA)** is a commonly used performance measure that approximates cash-basis profits from ongoing operations.

1) EBITDA is arrived at by adding back the two major noncash expenses to EBIT.

2) EBITDA is a controversial measure that is only used for companies that look bad under other ratios. Basically, it shows how a company is performing if fixed costs are ignored.

EBITDA Margin

$$\frac{EBITDA}{Net\ sales}$$

2.   **Profitability Ratios**

    a.   Return on assets, or ROA (also called return on total assets, or ROTA), is a straightforward measure of how well management is deploying the firm's assets in the pursuit of a profit.

Return on Assets (ROA)

$$\frac{Net\ income}{Average\ total\ assets}$$

        1)   EXAMPLE:

            Return on assets (ROA) = Net income ÷ Average total assets
                = \$81,000 ÷ [(\$1,800,000 + \$1,600,000) ÷ 2]
                = \$81,000 ÷ \$1,700,000
                = 4.76%

    b.   Return on equity (ROE) measures the return per owner dollar invested.

Return on Equity (ROE)

$$\frac{Net\ income}{Average\ total\ equity}$$

        1)   EXAMPLE:

            Return on equity (ROE) = Net income ÷ Average total equity
                = \$81,000 ÷ [(\$800,000 + \$650,000) ÷ 2]
                = \$81,000 ÷ \$725,000
                = 11.17%

    c.   The sustainable growth rate equals the return on equity times the difference of 1 and the dividend payout ratio.

Sustainable Growth Rate

$$ROE \times (1\ -\ Dividend\ payout\ ratio)$$

        1)   This ratio measures the potential growth of a firm without borrowing additional funds.

        2)   The retention ratio, or the difference of 1 and the dividend payout ratio, is the portion of the income kept to grow the firm.

    d.   The difference in the two denominators is total liabilities. ROE will therefore always be greater than ROA.

3.   **The DuPont Model -- ROA**

    a.   The DuPont model begins with the standard equation for ROA and breaks it down into two component ratios, one that focuses on the income statement and one that relates income to the balance sheet.

DuPont Model for Return on Assets

$$\frac{Net\ income}{Average\ total\ assets} = \frac{Net\ income}{Net\ sales} \times \frac{Net\ sales}{Average\ total\ assets}$$

$$= Net\ profit\ margin \times Total\ asset\ turnover$$

        1)   EXAMPLE:

Return on assets (ROA) = Net profit margin × Total asset turnover
                = (Net income ÷ Net sales) × (Net sales ÷ Average total assets)
                = (\$81,000 ÷ \$1,800,000) × {\$1,800,000 ÷ [(\$1,800,000 + \$1,600,000) ÷ 2]}
                = 4.5% × 1.06
                = 4.77%

        2)   This breakdown emphasizes that shareholder return may be explained in terms of both profit margin and the efficiency of asset management.

b.   The two components of the DuPont equation are interrelated because they both involve net sales.

1)   Profit margin on sales is another name for the net profit margin calculated in the DuPont model.

a)   If net sales increase and all other factors remain the same, the net profit margin worsens because more sales are only generating the same bottom line.

2)   Total asset turnover measures the level of capital investment relative to sales volume.

a)   If net sales increase and all other factors remain the same, the asset turnover ratio improves because more sales are being produced by the same amount of assets.

4.   **The DuPont Model -- ROE**

a.   To examine the **return on equity (ROE) ratio**, it can be subdivided by the DuPont model into three different efficiency components.

DuPont Model for Return on Equity

$$ROE = \frac{Net\ income}{Net\ sales} \times \frac{Net\ sales}{Average\ total\ assets} \times \frac{Average\ total\ assets}{Average\ total\ equity}$$

$$= Net\ profit\ margin \times Assets\ turnover \times Equity\ multiplier$$

1)   EXAMPLE:

$$ROE = \frac{\$81,000}{\$1,800,000} \times \frac{\$1,800,000}{[(\$1,800,000 + \$1,600,000) \div 2]} \times \frac{[(\$1,800,000 + \$1,600,000) \div 2]}{[(\$800,000 + \$650,000) \div 2]}$$

$$= 0.045 \times 1.06 \times 2.345$$

$$= 11.19\%$$

a)   The net profit margin component examines a company's efficiency in generating earnings from sales. It measures the amount of earnings that the company makes from every $1 of sales.

b)   The assets turnover component examines how efficiently the company is deploying the totality of its resources to generate revenues. It measures how much sales a company generates from each $1 of assets.

c)   The equity multiplier measures a company's financial leverage. High financial leverage means that the company relies more on debt to finance its assets. So, on the one hand, by raising capital with debt, the company can increase its equity multiplier and improve its return on equity. But, on the other hand, taking on additional debt may worsen the company's solvency and increase the risk of going bankrupt.

5.   **Inconsistent Definitions**

a.   Under various return ratios, the numerator ("return") may be adjusted by

1)   Subtracting preferred dividends to leave only income available to common stockholders

2)   Adding back minority interest in the income of a consolidated subsidiary (when invested capital is defined to include the minority interest)

3)   Adding back interest expense

4)   Adding back both interest expense and taxes so that the numerator is EBIT; this results in the basic earning power ratio, which enhances comparability of firms with different capital structures and tax planning strategies

b. The denominator ("equity" or "assets") may be adjusted by

1) Excluding nonoperating assets, such as investments, intangible assets, and the other asset category

2) Excluding unproductive assets, such as idle plant, intangible assets, and obsolete inventories

3) Excluding current liabilities to emphasize long-term capital

4) Excluding debt and preferred stock to arrive at equity capital

5) Stating invested capital at market value

Stop and review! You have completed the outline for this subunit. Study multiple-choice questions 19 through 23 beginning on page 203.

6.5 PROFITABILITY RATIOS -- EFFECTS OF TRANSACTIONS

Some of the questions pertaining to profitability ratios that a candidate will encounter on the CMA exam focus on the effects typical business transactions have on a firm's profitability rather than on the mechanics of calculating the ratios. This subunit consists entirely of such questions. Please review Subunit 6.4 before attempting to answer the questions in this subunit.

Stop and review! You have completed the outline for this subunit. Study multiple-choice questions 24 and 25 on page 205.

6.6 FACTORS AFFECTING REPORTED PROFITABILITY

1. **Factors Involved**

   a. Among the many factors involved in measuring profitability are the definition of income; the stability, sources, and trends of revenue; revenue relationships; and expenses, including cost of sales.

      1) This analysis attempts to answer questions about the relevant income measure, income quality, the persistence of income, and the firm's earning power.

2. **Income**

   a. Estimates are necessary to calculate income, for example, allocations of revenue and expense over accounting periods, useful lives of assets, and amounts of future liabilities.

   b. Income is measured in accordance with a selection from among generally accepted accounting principles. For example, selecting between the accrual basis and cash basis of accounting.

      1) Accrual accounting records the financial effects of transactions and other events and circumstances when they occur rather than when their associated cash is paid or received.

      2) Under the cash basis, revenues are recognized when cash is received and expenses are recognized when cash is paid.

   c. Incentives for disclosure about the income measure vary with the interest group: financial analysts, auditors, accountants, management, directors, shareholders, competitors, creditors, and regulators.

      1) The pressures from some groups may lead to suboptimal financial reporting.

   d. Users have different needs, but financial statements are general purpose.

      1) For example, investors are interested in profitability, but creditors are interested in security.

3. **Revenues**

   a. Revenues are inflows or other enhancements of assets of the firm or settlements of its liabilities from delivering or producing goods, rendering services, or other activities that constitute the firm's ongoing major or central operations.

   b. Understanding the sources of revenue is especially important in diversified firms.

      1) Common-size analysis is useful when markets and product lines have differing rates of growth, potential, and profitability.

   c. Trend percentage analysis and evaluation of management's discussion and analysis (MD&A) in the firm's annual report are useful techniques for assessing the persistence of the firm's revenues.

4. **Recognition Principles**

   a. Recognition of revenues, expenses, gains, losses, and changes in related assets and liabilities involves, among other things, the application of pervasive expense recognition principles: associating cause and effect, systematic and rational allocation, and immediate recognition.

      1) The FASB's Conceptual Framework defines matching, a term that has been given a variety of meanings in accounting literature, as essentially synonymous with associating cause and effect.

      2) Matching "is simultaneous or combined recognition of the revenues and expenses that result directly and jointly from the same transactions or other events." Such a direct relationship is found when revenue for sales of goods is recognized in the same period as the cost of the goods sold.

   b. According to the revenue recognition principle, revenue should be recognized when they are realized or realizable and when they are earned.

      1) Revenues are **realized** when goods or services have been exchanged for cash or claims to cash.

         a) For example, revenues are realized when inventory is exchanged for cash.

         b) Revenues are also realized when inventory is exchanged for claims to cash, which is recorded as a receivable by the party holing the claims.

      2) Revenues are **realizable** when goods or services have been exchanged for assets that are readily convertible into cash or claims to cash.

      3) Revenues are **earned** when the earning process has been substantially completed and the entity is entitled to the resulting benefits or revenues.

      4) The two conditions are usually met when goods are delivered or services are rendered, that is, at the time of sale, which is customarily the time of delivery.

   c. Immediate recognition is the applicable principle when costs cannot be directly or feasibly related to specific revenues and their benefits are used up in the period in which they are incurred. Utilities expense is a common example.

   d. As a reflection of the accounting profession's conservatism, expenses and losses have historically been subject to less stringent recognition criteria than revenues and gains.

      1) Expenses and losses are not subject to the realization criterion.

      2) Rather, expenses and losses are recognized when a consumption of economic benefits occurs during the entity's primary activities or when the ability of existing assets to provide future benefits has been impaired.

         a) An expense or loss may also be recognized when a liability has been incurred or increased without the receipt of corresponding benefits; a probable and reasonably estimable contingent loss is an example.

      3) Long-lived assets, such as equipment, buildings, and intangibles, are depreciated or amortized over their useful lives. Natural resources are depleted, usually on a units-of-production basis.

e.   Systematic and rational allocation procedures do not directly relate costs and revenues but are applied when a causal relationship is "generally, but not specifically, identified."

1)   This expense recognition principle is appropriate when (a) an asset provides benefits over several periods (its estimated useful life), (b) the asset is used up as a result of events affecting the entity, and (c) the expense resulting from such wastage is indirectly (not directly and traceably) related to specific revenues and particular periods.

2)   The usual example is depreciation.

f.   The following are exceptions to the basic revenue recognition rules:

1)   Revenues from long-term contracts may be recognized using the percentage-of-completion method. This method allows for revenue to be recognized at various stages of the contract although the entire job is not complete.

2)   Revenues from long-term contracts may also be recognized using the completion-of-production method. This method is an appropriate basis for recognition if products or other assets are readily realizable, e.g., precious metals and some agricultural products.

3)   If the collectibility of assets is relatively uncertain, revenues and gains may be recognized as cash is received using the installment sales method or the cost recovery method.

5.   **Cost of Goods Sold and Gross Profit**

a.   Cost of goods sold is the single largest cost element for any seller of merchandise and thus has the greatest impact on profitability. A company's gross profit margin is the percentage of its gross sales that it is able to keep after paying for merchandise.

1)   EXAMPLE:

	Current Year		Prior Year	
Gross sales	$1,827,000	100.0%	$1,418,000	100.0%
Sales discounts	(15,000)	(0.8%)	(10,000)	(0.7%)
Sales return and allowances	(12,000)	(0.7%)	(8,000)	(0.6%)
Net sales	$1,800,000	98.5%	$1,400,000	98.7%
Cost of goods sold	(1,450,000)	(79.4%)	(1,170,000)	(82.5%)
Gross profit	$ 350,000	19.1%	$ 230,000	16.2%

b.   A change in the gross profit margin can indicate that the firm has priced its products differently while maintaining the same cost structure or that it has changed the way it controls the costs of production and/or inventory management.

6.   **Major Categories of Expenses for a Company**

a.   Selling expenses are incurred in selling or marketing. Examples include sales representatives' salaries, rent for sales department, commissions, and traveling expenses; advertising; selling department salaries and expenses; samples; and credit and collection costs, including bad debt expenses. Shipping (i.e., freight-out) costs are also often classified as selling costs.

b.   General and administrative expenses are incurred for the direction of the enterprise as a whole and are not related wholly to a specific function, e.g., selling or manufacturing. They include accounting, legal, and other fees for services; officers' salaries; insurance; wages of office staff; miscellaneous supplies; and office occupancy costs.

c.   Depreciation is the allocation of the costs of equipment that benefit subsequent periods. Usually, the cost of a fixed asset minus salvage or residual value is expensed over the asset's useful life. Because of the noncash nature and relatively fixed amount of depreciation, it is not extremely meaningful except in relation to depreciable assets. This ratio may detect changes in the composite rate.

        1)   Depreciation on equipment used in the production of merchandise for sale is considered a product cost and is thus included in cost of goods sold, not administrative expenses.

   d.   Maintenance and repairs expense varies with the amount of plant and equipment and the extent of output. It also has fixed and variable components and does not vary directly with revenues. Moreover, this expense is discretionary and is therefore a means of smoothing income. Thus, it relates to earnings quality.

        1)   Maintenance is also a factor in estimating assets' useful lives and the calculation of depreciation.

   e.   Interest expense is recognized based on the passage of time. In the case of bonds, notes, and capital leases, the effective interest method is used. A typical analytical tool is the calculation of the trend of the average effective interest rate for the firm and comparison with the rates for other firms. It is generally reported on the income statement under other expenses and losses.

   f.   Amortization of special costs such as those of intangible assets is usefully analyzed by comparison of trends with respect to revenues, unamortized special costs, and net property and equipment.

   g.   Income tax expense is an important item in financial statements because of its magnitude.

        1)   Accrual accounting for income taxes is characterized by interperiod tax allocation that matches tax expense with accrual income. The analysis must be aware of both temporary and permanent tax differences between accrual accounting and tax law.

        2)   Intraperiod tax allocation allocates tax to the components of income (continuing operations, discontinued operations, extraordinary items, other comprehensive income, and items debited or credited directly to equity). The analysis should extend to comparisons of effective tax rates (expense ÷ pre-tax income) over time.

7.   Trends in Expenses

   a.   Analyzing trends in expenses is facilitated by the use of percentages, i.e., a detailed analysis of the expense line items found on the common-size income statements.

        1)   EXAMPLE:

	Current Year		Prior Year	
Net sales	$1,800,000	100.0%	$1,400,000	100.0%
Selling expenses:				
Sales salaries and commissions	$ 12,000	0.67%	$ 1,000	0.07%
Freight-out	16,000	0.89%	5,000	0.36%
Travel	10,000	0.56%	5,000	0.36%
Advertising	8,000	0.44%	3,000	0.21%
Office supplies	4,000	0.22%	1,000	0.07%
Total selling expenses	$ 50,000	2.78%	$ 15,000	1.07%
Administrative expenses:				
Executive salaries	$ 6,000	0.33%	$ 4,000	0.29%
Professional salaries	4,000	0.22%	4,000	0.29%
Wages	2,000	0.11%	1,000	0.07%
Depreciation	1,000	0.06%	500	0.04%
Office supplies	2,000	0.11%	500	0.04%
Total administrative expenses	$ 15,000	0.83%	$ 10,000	0.73%
Total operating expenses	$ 65,000	3.61%	$ 25,000	1.80%

        2)   The company's operating expenses increased overall; this would be expected during a period of rising sales. However, not every expense line item increased proportionally. The company devoted much more effort to moving product out the door by increasing the proportion of sales salaries and commissions and freight-out.

3) Also note that, while professional salaries were the same absolute amount in both years, they were a smaller proportion of all administrative expenses in the current year because of the greater amount spent overall.

8. **Effects of Accounting Changes**

   a. The types of accounting changes are changes in (1) accounting principle, (2) accounting estimates, and (3) the reporting entity. Accounting changes and error corrections affect financial ratios.

   b. A **change in accounting principle** occurs when an entity (1) adopts a generally accepted principle different from the one previously used, (2) changes the **method** of applying a generally accepted principle, or (3) changes to a generally accepted principle when the principle previously used is no longer generally accepted.

      1) **Retrospective application**, if practicable, is required for all direct effects and the related income tax effects of a change in principle.

         a) An example of a direct effect is an adjustment of an inventory balance to implement a change in the method of measurement.

      2) Retrospective application requires that carrying amounts of (a) assets, (b) liabilities, and (c) retained earnings at the beginning of the first period reported be adjusted for the cumulative effect of the new principle on all periods not reported.

         a) All periods reported must be individually adjusted for the period-specific effects of applying the new principle.

   c. A **change in accounting estimate** results from new information and a reassessment of the future benefits and obligations represented by assets and liabilities. Its effects should be accounted for only in the period of change and any future periods affected, i.e., prospectively.

      1) A change in estimate inseparable from (effected by) a change in principle is accounted for as a change in estimate. An example is a change in a method of depreciation, amortization, or depletion of long-lived, nonfinancial assets.

   d. A change in reporting entity is retrospectively applied to interim and annual statements.

      1) A change in reporting entity does not result from a business combination or consolidation of a variable interest entity.

   e. An **accounting error** results from (1) a mathematical mistake, (2) a mistake in the application of GAAP, or (3) an oversight or misuse of facts existing when the statements were prepared. A change to a generally accepted accounting principle from one that is not is an error correction, not an accounting change.

      1) An accounting error related to a prior period is reported as a prior-period adjustment by restating the prior-period statements. Restatement requires the same adjustments as retrospective application of a new principle.

      2) Error corrections related to prior periods result in restatement.

         a) After retrospective application or restatement, the comparative financial statements and ratios should be comparable and consistent.

         b) However, changing prior years' net income and related EPS figures may undermine shareholders' confidence in the accounting methods.

Stop and review! You have completed the outline for this subunit. Study multiple-choice questions 26 and 27 on page 206.

6.7 SOLVENCY

1. **Elements of Solvency**

    a. Solvency is a firm's ability to pay its **noncurrent obligations** as they come due and thus remain in business in the long run (contrast with liquidity).

    1) The key ingredients of solvency are the firm's capital structure and degree of leverage.

    b. A firm's capital structure includes its sources of financing, both long- and short-term. These sources can be in the form of debt (external sources) or equity (internal sources).

    1) Capital structure decisions affect the **risk profile** of a firm. For example, a company with a higher percent of debt capital will be riskier than a firm with a high percentage of equity capital. Thus, when there is a lot of debt, equity investors will demand a higher rate of return on their investments to compensate for the risk brought about by the high use of financial leverage.

    2) Alternatively, a company with a high level of equity capital will be able to borrow at lower rates because debt holders will accept lower interest in exchange for the lower risk indicated by the equity cushion.

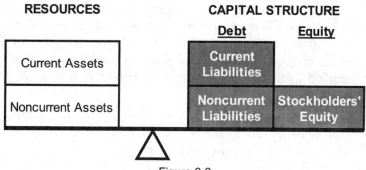

Figure 6-2

    c. Debt is the creditor interest in the firm.

    1) The firm is contractually obligated to repay debtholders. The terms of repayment (i.e., timing of interest and principal) are specified in the debt agreement.

    2) As long as the return on debt exceeds the amount of interest paid, the use of debt financing is advantageous to a firm. This is because interest payments on debt are tax-deductible.

    3) The tradeoff is that an increased debt load makes a firm riskier (since debt must be paid regardless of whether the company is profitable). At some point, either a firm will have to pay a higher interest rate than its return on debt or creditors will simply refuse to lend any more money.

    d. Equity is the ownership interest in the firm.

    1) Equity is the permanent capital of an enterprise, contributed by the firm's owners in the hopes of earning a return.

    2) However, a return on equity is uncertain because equity embodies only a residual interest in the firm's assets (residual because it is the claim left over after all debt has been satisfied).

    3) Periodic returns to owners of excess earnings are referred to as dividends. The firm may be contractually obligated to pay dividends to preferred stockholders but not to common stockholders.

e. **Capital adequacy** is a term normally used in connection with financial institutions. A bank must be able to pay those depositors that demand their money on a given day and still be able to make new loans.

   1) Capital adequacy can be discussed in terms of solvency (the ability to pay long-term obligations as they mature), liquidity (the ability to pay for day-to-day ongoing operations), reserves (the specific amount a bank must have on hand to pay depositors), or sufficient capital.

2. **Capital Structure Ratios**

   a. These ratios report the relative proportions of debt and equity in a firm's capital structure at a given reporting date.

   b. The total debt to total capital ratio measures the percentage of the firm's capital structure provided by creditors.

Total Debt to Total Capital Ratio

$$\frac{\text{Total debt}}{\text{Total capital}}$$

   1) EXAMPLE: Current Year: $\$1,000,000 \div \$1,800,000 = 0.556$
       Prior Year: $\$\ \ 950,000 \div \$1,600,000 = 0.594$

      a) The company became slightly less reliant on debt in its capital structure during the current year. Although total debt rose, equity rose by a greater percentage. The company is thus less leveraged than before.

   2) When total debt to total capital is low, it means more of the firm's capital is supplied by the stockholders. Thus, creditors prefer this ratio to be low as a cushion against losses.

   c. The debt to equity ratio is a direct comparison of the firm's debt load versus its equity stake.

Debt to Equity Ratio

$$\frac{\text{Total debt}}{\text{Stockholders' equity}}$$

   1) EXAMPLE: Current Year: $\$1,000,000 \div \$800,000 = 1.25$
       Prior Year: $\$\ \ 950,000 \div \$650,000 = 1.46$

      a) The amount by which the company's debts exceed its equity stake declined in the current year.

   2) Like the previous ratio, the debt to equity ratio reflects long-term debt-payment ability. Again, a low ratio means a lower relative debt burden and thus better chances of repayment of creditors.

   d. The long-term debt to equity ratio reports the long-term debt burden carried by a company per dollar of equity.

Long-Term Debt to Equity Ratio

$$\frac{\text{Long-term debt}}{\text{Stockholders' equity}}$$

   1) EXAMPLE: Current Year: $\$610,000 \div \$800,000 = 0.763$
       Prior Year: $\$675,000 \div \$650,000 = 1.038$

      a) The company has greatly improved its long-term debt burden. It now carries less than one dollar of long-term debt for every dollar of equity.

      b) A low ratio means a firm will have an easier time raising new debt (since its low current debt load makes it a good credit risk).

e. The debt to total assets ratio (also called the debt ratio) reports the total debt burden carried by a company per dollar of assets.

Debt to Total Assets Ratio

$$\frac{Total\ liabilities}{Total\ assets}$$

1) EXAMPLE: Current Year: $1,000,000 ÷ $1,800,000 = 0.556
Prior Year: $ 950,000 ÷ $1,600,000 = 0.594

   a) Although total liabilities increased in absolute terms, this ratio improved because total assets increased even more.

2) Numerically, this ratio is identical to the debt to total capital ratio.

3. **Earnings Coverage**

   a. These ratios are a creditor's best measure of a firm's ongoing ability to generate the earnings that will allow it to service debt out of current earnings.

   b. The times interest earned ratio is an income statement approach to evaluating a firm's ongoing ability to meet the interest payments on its debt obligations.

Times Interest Earned Ratio

$$\frac{EBIT}{Interest\ expense}$$

1) EXAMPLE: Current Year: $150,000 ÷ $15,000 = 10.00 times
Prior Year: $125,000 ÷ $10,000 = 12.50 times

   a) The company is less able to comfortably pay interest expense. In the prior year, EBIT was twelve and a half times interest expense, but in the current year, it is only ten times.

2) For the ratio to be meaningful, net income cannot be used in the numerator. Since what is being measured is the ability to pay interest, earnings before interest and taxes is appropriate.

3) The most accurate calculation of the numerator includes only earnings expected to recur. Consequently, unusual or infrequent items, extraordinary items, discontinued operations, and the effects of accounting changes should be excluded.

4) The denominator should include capitalized interest.

   c. The earnings to fixed charges ratio (also called the fixed charge coverage ratio) extends the times interest earned ratio to include the interest portion associated with long-term lease obligations.

Earnings to Fixed Charges Ratio

$$\frac{EBIT\ +\ Interest\ portion\ of\ operating\ leases}{Interest\ expense\ +\ Interest\ portion\ of\ operating\ leases\ +\ Dividends\ on\ preferred\ stock}$$

1) This is a more conservative ratio since it measures the coverage of earnings over all fixed charges, not just interest expense.

   d. The cash flow to fixed charges ratio removes the difficulties of comparing amounts prepared on an accrual basis.

Cash Flow to Fixed Charges Ratio

$$\frac{Pre\text{-}tax\ operating\ cash\ flow}{Interest\ expense\ +\ Interest\ portion\ of\ operating\ leases\ +\ Dividends\ on\ preferred\ stock}$$

Stop and review! You have completed the outline for this subunit. Study multiple-choice questions 28 through 33 beginning on page 206.

6.8 LEVERAGE

 For the purpose of the CMA exam, be sure that you understand and can calculate both leverage ratios. However, calculating these ratios is just one aspect of how you could be tested on this topic. Candidates should be fully prepared to apply these calculations and demonstrate an understanding through multiple-choice or essay questions of how changes in cost structure may affect these ratios. Ensure that you understand what risks and advantages are associated with high operating or financial leverage.

1. **Types of Leverage**

   a. Leverage is the relative amount of fixed cost in a firm's overall cost structure. Leverage creates risk because fixed costs must be covered, regardless of the level of sales.

      1) **Operating leverage** arises from the use of a high level of plant and machinery in the production process, revealed through charges for depreciation, property taxes, etc.

      2) **Financial leverage** arises from the use of a high level of debt in the firm's financing structure, revealed through amounts paid out for interest.

   b. Thus, although leverage arises from items on the balance sheet, it is measured by examining its effects on the income statement. A general statement of leverage is

$$\text{Degree of leverage} = \frac{\textit{Pre-fixed-cost income amount}}{\textit{Post-fixed-cost income amount}}$$

2. **Degree of Operating Leverage (DOL)**

   a. Calculation of the DOL requires financial information prepared on the variable-costing basis, since variable costing isolates the use of fixed costs in the firm's ongoing operations.

      ### Degree of Operating Leverage (DOL) -- Single-Period Version

$$\frac{\textit{Contribution margin}}{\textit{Operating income or EBIT}}$$

   b. A firm's DOL varies with the level of sales, as shown in the following example:

      1) EXAMPLE:

Degree of Operating Leverage at Various Levels of Sales

Sales volume:	100 Units	250 Units	500 Units	750 Units	1,000 Units
Net sales ($1,000 per unit)	$ 100,000	$ 250,000	$ 500,000	$ 750,000	$1,000,000
Variable costs ($800 per unit)	(80,000)	(200,000)	(400,000)	(600,000)	(800,000)
Contribution margin	$ 20,000	$ 50,000	$ 100,000	$ 150,000	$ 200,000
Fixed costs	(100,000)	(100,000)	(100,000)	(100,000)	(100,000)
Operating income (loss)	$ (80,000)	$ (50,000)	$ 0	$ 50,000	$ 100,000
Degree of operating leverage (DOL)	(0.25)	(1.00)	Undef.	3.00	2.00

      2) This firm breaks even at sales of 500 units.

      3) As the example demonstrates, DOL is not a meaningful measure when the firm incurs an operating loss.

c. Two versions of DOL are in common use.

    1) The version shown on the previous page compares contribution margin and variable-basis operating income in a single reporting period.

    2) The percentage-change version of DOL measures the changes in income statement amounts from one period to another.

Degree of Operating Leverage (DOL) -- Percentage-Change Version

$$\frac{\%\Delta \text{ in operating income or EBIT}}{\%\Delta \text{ in sales}}$$

    a) The percentage-change version is necessary when the only financial reports available are those prepared on the absorption basis.

    b) Note that, in this version, the numerator and denominator are different from those in the single-period version.

3) EXAMPLE:

Degree of Operating Leverage
Period-to-Period Percentage Change

	Current Year	Prior Year
Net sales	$1,800,000	$1,400,000
Cost of goods sold	(1,450,000)	(1,170,000)
Gross margin	$ 350,000	$ 230,000
SG&A expenses	(160,000)	(80,000)
Operating income	$ 190,000	$ 150,000
Other income and loss	(40,000)	(25,000)
EBIT	**$ 150,000**	**$ 125,000**
Interest expense	(15,000)	(10,000)
Earnings before taxes	$ 135,000	$ 115,000
Income taxes (40%)	(54,000)	(46,000)
Net income	$ 81,000	$ 69,000

Numerator: %Δ in EBIT = ($150,000 − $125,000) ÷ $125,000   = 20.00%

Denominator: %Δ in sales = ($1,800,000 − $1,400,000) ÷ $1,400,000   = 28.57%

Degree of operating leverage (DOL) = 20.00% ÷ 28.57% = 0.7

    a) Every 1% change in sales generates a 0.7% change in EBIT.

d. A firm with high operating leverage necessarily carries a greater degree of risk because fixed costs must be covered regardless of the level of sales.

    1) However, such a firm is also able to expand production rapidly in times of higher product demand. Thus, the more leveraged a firm is in its operations, the more sensitive operating income is to changes in sales volume.

3. **Degree of Financial Leverage (DFL)**

    a. The DFL also results from a pre-fixed-cost income to post-fixed-cost income comparison, this time on the firm's financing structure.

Degree of Financial Leverage (DFL) -- Single-Period Version

$$\frac{\text{Earnings before interest and taxes (EBIT)}}{\text{Earnings before taxes (EBT)}}$$

    1) This formula isolates the effects of interest as the only truly fixed financing cost.

2) EXAMPLE:

Degree of Financial Leverage
Single-Period Version

	Current Year	Prior Year
Net sales	$1,800,000	$1,400,000
Cost of goods sold	(1,450,000)	(1,170,000)
Gross margin	$ 350,000	$ 230,000
SG&A expenses	(160,000)	(80,000)
Operating income	$ 190,000	$ 150,000
Other income and loss	(40,000)	(25,000)
EBIT	**$ 150,000**	**$ 125,000**
Interest expense	(15,000)	(10,000)
Earnings before taxes	**$ 135,000**	**$ 115,000**
Income taxes (40%)	(54,000)	(46,000)
Net income	$ 81,000	$ 69,000

Degree of financial leverage

Current year: $150,000 ÷ $135,000 = $1.11   The company needs $1.11 of EBIT to
Prior year: $125,000 ÷ $115,000 = $1.09   generate $1.00 of EBT. Last year,
only $1.09 of EBIT was needed to
generate $1.00 of EBT.

b.   Two versions of DFL are in common use.

1)   The version shown on the previous page and in the example above compares EBIT and EBT from a single reporting period.

2)   The percentage-change version examines the changes in income statement amounts over two periods.

Degree of Financial Leverage (DFL) -- Percentage-Change Version

$$\frac{\%\Delta \ in \ net \ income}{\%\Delta \ in \ EBIT}$$

a)   Note that in the percentage-change version, the numerator and denominator are different from those in the single-period version.

3)   EXAMPLE:

Numerator: %Δ in net income = ($81,000 – $69,000) ÷ $69,000   = 17.39%
Denominator: %Δ in EBIT = ($150,000 – $125,000) ÷ $125,000   = 20.00%

Degree of financial leverage (DFL) = 17.39% ÷ 20.00% = 0.8696

a)   Every 1% change in EBIT generates a 0.87% change in net income.

c.   A firm with high financial leverage necessarily carries a greater degree of risk because debt must be serviced regardless of the level of earnings.

1)   However, if such a firm is profitable, there is more residual profit for the shareholders after debt service (interest on debt is tax-deductible), reflected in higher earnings per share. Furthermore, debt financing permits the current equity holders to retain control.

Stop and review! You have completed the outline for this subunit. Study multiple-choice questions 34 and 35 beginning on page 208.

6.9 COMMON-SIZE FINANCIAL STATEMENTS

1. **Percentages and Comparability**

   a. Analyzing the financial statements of steadily growing firms and firms of different sizes within an industry presents certain difficulties.

      1) To overcome this obstacle, common-size statements restate financial statement line items in terms of a percentage of a given amount, such as total assets for a balance sheet or net sales for an income statement.

   b. Items on common-size financial statements are expressed as percentages of sales (on the income statement) or total assets (on the balance sheet). The base amount is assigned the value of 100%.

      1) Thus, on an income statement, sales is valued at 100%, while all other amounts are a percentage of sales. On the balance sheet, total assets are 100%, as is the total of liabilities and stockholders' equity. Each line item can be interpreted in terms of its proportion of the baseline figure.

   c. EXAMPLES:

Income statement External reporting format	Current Year	Prior Year	Income statement Common-size format	Current Year	Prior Year
Net sales	$1,800,000	$1,400,000	Net sales	100.0%	100.0%
Cost of goods sold	(1,650,000)	(1,330,000)	Cost of goods sold	(91.7%)	(95.0%)
Gross profit	150,000	70,000	Gross profit	8.3%	5.0%
Selling expenses	(50,000)	(15,000)	Selling expenses	(2.8%)	(1.1%)
General and admin. expenses	(15,000)	(10,000)	General and admin. expenses	(0.8%)	(0.7%)
Operating income	85,000	45,000	Operating income	4.7%	3.2%
Other revenues and gains	20,000	0	Other revenues and gains	1.1%	0.0%
Other expenses and losses	(35,000)	(10,000)	Other expenses and losses	(1.9%)	(0.7%)
Income before taxes	70,000	35,000	Income before taxes	3.9%	2.5%
Income taxes (40%)	(28,000)	(14,000)	Income taxes (40%)	(1.6%)	(1.0%)
Net income	$ 42,000	$ 21,000	Net income	2.3%	1.5%

Balance sheet External reporting format	Current Year End	Prior Year End	Balance sheet Common-size format	Current Year End	Prior Year End
Assets:			Assets:		
Current assets	$ 760,000	$ 635,000	Current assets	42.2%	39.7%
Noncurrent assets	1,040,000	965,000	Noncurrent assets	57.8%	60.3%
Total assets	$1,800,000	$1,600,000	Total assets	100.0%	100.0%
Liabilities and stockholders' equity:			Liabilities and stockholders' equity:		
Current liabilities	$ 390,000	$ 275,000	Current liabilities	21.7%	17.2%
Noncurrent liabilities	610,000	675,000	Noncurrent liabilities	33.9%	42.2%
Total liabilities	$1,000,000	$ 950,000	Total liabilities	55.6%	59.4%
Stockholders' equity	800,000	650,000	Stockholders' equity	44.4%	40.6%
Total liabilities and stockholders' equity	$1,800,000	$1,600,000	Total liabilities and stockholders' equity	100.0%	100.0%

   d. Preparing common-size statements makes it easier to analyze differences among companies of various sizes or comparisons between a similar company and an industry average.

      1) For example, comparing the efficiency of a company with $1,800,000 of revenues to a company with $44 billion in revenues is difficult unless the numbers are reduced to a common denominator.

2. **Vertical and Horizontal Analysis**

    a. The common-size statements on the previous page are an example of vertical analysis (i.e., the percentages are based on numbers above or below in the same column).

        1) Alternatively, there is a concept known as horizontal analysis wherein the amounts for several periods are stated in percentages of a base-year amount. These are often called trend percentages.

    b. One period is designated the base period, to which the other periods are compared. Each line item of the base period is thus 100%.

        1) EXAMPLE:

Income statement
External reporting format

	Current Year	Prior Year	2nd Prior Year
Net sales	$1,800,000	$1,400,000	$1,500,000
Cost of goods sold	(1,650,000)	(1,330,000)	(1,390,000)
Gross profit	**$ 150,000**	**$ 70,000**	**$ 110,000**

Income statement
Trend analysis

	Current Year	Prior Year	2nd Prior Year
Net sales	120.0%	93.3%	100.0%
Cost of goods sold	118.7%	95.7%	100.0%
Gross profit	**136.4%**	**63.6%**	**100.0%**

Even though sales and cost of goods sold declined only slightly from the base year to the next year, gross profit plunged (on a percentage basis). By the same token, when sales recovered in the current year, the gain in gross profit was (proportionally) greater than the increases in its two components.

    c. There is also a form of horizontal analysis that does not use common sizes. This method is used to calculate the growth (or decline) of key financial line items.

        1) For example, if a company's sales increased from $100,000 to $120,000, there would be a third column showing the percentage increase, which was 20% in this case.

        2) This is another form of management by exception. Managers can look at the third column (the percentage change column) and see which accounts have experienced the most change since the previous period.

Stop and review! You have completed the outline for this subunit. Study multiple-choice questions 36 and 37 on page 209.

6.10 EFFECTS OF OFF-BALANCE-SHEET FINANCING

1. **Purposes**

    a. Reducing a company's debt load improves its ratios, making its securities more attractive investments. Also, many loan covenants contain restrictions on the total debt load that a company is permitted to carry.

        1) However, reducing debt and hiding it are two very different things. Firms that carry extensive debt financing but attempt to disguise the fact are engaging in off-balance-sheet financing.

        2) Eliminating debt from the balance sheet through off-balance-sheet financing will improve a company's debt to equity ratio because there will be less debt reported.

      b.   Off-balance-sheet financing takes four principal forms, which are outlined below.

2.   **Investments in Unconsolidated Subsidiaries**

      a.   Any equity ownership of less than 50% in a subsidiary results in the parent firm reporting the equity investment as an asset.

      b.   The result is that the subsidiary's debts, for which the parent could be substantially responsible, are not reflected as liabilities of the parent.

      c.   Establishing a **joint venture** will accomplish the same purpose as an unconsolidated subsidiary because joint ventures are usually accounted for on the equity basis since none of the ventures are typically considered to hold control.

3.   **Special Purpose Entities**

      a.   A firm may create another firm for the sole purpose of keeping the liabilities associated with a specific project off the parent firm's books.

      b.   For example, when a company wishes to construct a factory, large amounts of new debt must be taken on. A special purpose entity (SPE) can be established solely to build and operate the new plant while absorbing the debt incurred during construction.

          1)   Once the plant is complete, the parent firm will often establish a take-or-pay contract with the SPE. Under a take-or-pay arrangement, the company agrees to either buy all the output of the factory or to make guaranteed payments.

          2)   This way, the financial solvency of the SPE is ensured and the company has acquired a steady source of supply without taking on a large debt burden.

      c.   In late 2001, the national media revealed that Enron Corporation had hidden a huge amount of debt for which it was responsible by "off-loading" it onto the balance sheets of SPEs. These SPEs had been deliberately structured so that Enron would not have to consolidate them.

          1)   In 2003, the FASB responded to these abuses by issuing pronouncements on variable interest entities (VIEs). Any arrangement that meets the criteria of a VIE must be reported on a consolidated basis with another entity.

4.   **Operating Leases**

      a.   A long-term contract to acquire property or equipment may be structured in such a way that the full amount of the debt does not appear on the firm's balance sheet (although this will become more difficult when new lease accounting standards take effect in 2019).

      b.   Leases are covered in further detail in Study Unit 7, Subunit 3.

5.   **Factoring Receivables with Recourse**

      a.   Factoring (selling) accounts receivable to a finance company is a strategy used by firms who need to accelerate their cash flows or who simply do not wish to maintain a collection operation.

          1)   If the factoring transaction is "with recourse," the firm remains contingently liable to the finance company in the case of debtor default. This contingent liability does not have to be reported on the company's balance sheet.

Stop and review! You have completed the outline for this subunit. Study multiple-choice question 38 on page 210.

QUESTIONS

6.1 Qualities of Ratio Analysis

1. A chief financial officer has been tracking the activities of the company's nearest competitor for several years. Among other trends, the CFO has noticed that this competitor is able to take advantage of new technology and bring new products to market more quickly than the CFO's company. In order to determine the reason for this, the CFO has been reviewing the following data regarding the two companies:

	Company	Competitor
Accounts receivable turnover	6.85	7.35
Return on assets	15.34	14.74
Times interest earned	15.65	12.45
Current ratio	2.11	1.23
Debt/equity ratio	42.16	55.83
Degree of financial leverage	1.06	1.81
Price/earnings ratio	26.56	26.15

On the basis of this information, which one of the following is the **best** initial strategy for the CFO to follow in attempting to improve the flexibility of the company?

  A. Seek cost cutting measures that would increase the company's profitability.

  B. Investigate ways to improve asset efficiency and turnover times to improve liquidity.

  C. Seek additional sources of outside financing for new product introductions.

  D. Increase the company's investment in short-term securities to increase the current ratio.

Answer (C) is correct.
    REQUIRED: The best initial strategy to improve flexibility.
    DISCUSSION: The company's times interest earned, debt/equity ratio, and degree of financial leverage all reveal that the company is less leveraged than its competitor. The two firms' price-earnings ratios are comparable, so the company should be able to raise new capital fairly easily, either debt or equity. Thus, the company should seek additional sources of outside financing for new product introductions.
    Answer (A) is incorrect. Cutting costs makes it harder to take advantage of new opportunities or to innovate. Cost cutting is a last resort and the company's return on assets is already better than its competitor's. Answer (B) is incorrect. The receivables turnover is not much different than that of the competitor. Answer (D) is incorrect. Increasing investment in short-term securities would not change the current ratio.

2. A bank has received loan applications from three companies in the plastics manufacturing business and currently has the funds to grant only one of these requests. Specific data shown below has been selected from these applications for review and comparison with industry averages.

	S	R	H	Industry
Total sales (millions)	$4.27	$3.91	$4.86	$4.30
Net profit margin	9.55%	9.85%	10.05%	9.65%
Current ratio	1.82	2.02	1.96	1.95
Return on assets	12.0%	12.6%	11.4%	12.4%
Debt/equity ratio	52.5%	44.6%	49.6%	48.3%
Financial leverage	1.30	1.02	1.56	1.33

Based on the information above, select the strategy that should be the **most** beneficial to the bank.

  A. The bank should not grant any loans, as none of these companies represents a good credit risk.

  B. Grant the loan to S, as all the company's data approximate the industry average.

  C. Grant the loan to R, as both the debt/equity ratio and degree of financial leverage are below the industry average.

  D. Grant the loan to H, as the company has the highest net profit margin and degree of financial leverage.

Answer (C) is correct.
    REQUIRED: The most beneficial strategy.
    DISCUSSION: The bank's primary concern is the customer's ability to pay back a loan. Crucial in deciding the likelihood of payback is how much of the customer's capital structure is made up of debt currently, that is, before the loan is made. R's is well below the industry average (a few percentage points can mean the difference between a good credit risk and a poor one) and is the lowest of the three potential customers. Also, R is clearly the least leveraged of the three by far, as revealed by its low degree of financial leverage.
    Answer (A) is incorrect. R is a good credit risk. Answer (B) is incorrect. Debt makes up more than half of S's capital structure; "approximating industry averages" is meaningless when just a few percentage points can mean the difference between a good credit risk and a poor one. Answer (D) is incorrect. While a high profit margin may be indicative of the ability to pay back a loan, a high degree of financial leverage indicates the opposite, and H's is well above the industry average.

6.2 Liquidity Ratios -- Calculations

Questions 3 through 5 are based on the following information.

Tosh Enterprises reported the following account information:

Accounts receivable	$400,000	Inventory	$800,000
Accounts payable	260,000	Land	500,000
Bonds payable, due in 10 years	600,000	Short-term prepaid expense	80,000
Cash	200,000		
Interest payable, due in 3 months	20,000		

3. The current ratio for Tosh Enterprises is

A. 1.68

B. 2.14

C. 5.00

D. 5.29

Answer (D) is correct.
REQUIRED: The current ratio.
DISCUSSION: The current ratio equals current assets divided by current liabilities. Current assets consist of cash, accounts receivable, inventory, and prepaid expenses, a total of $1,480,000 ($400,000 + $200,000 + $800,000 + $80,000). Current liabilities consist of accounts payable and interest payable, a total of $280,000 ($260,000 + $20,000). Hence, the current ratio is 5.29 ($1,480,000 ÷ $280,000).
Answer (A) is incorrect. The figure of 1.68 includes long-term bonds payable among the current liabilities. Answer (B) is incorrect. The figure of 2.14 is the quick ratio. Answer (C) is incorrect. The figure of 5.00 excludes prepaid expenses from current assets.

4. What is Tosh Enterprises' quick (acid test) ratio?

A. 0.68

B. 1.68

C. 2.14

D. 2.31

Answer (C) is correct.
REQUIRED: The quick ratio.
DISCUSSION: The quick (acid test) ratio equals the quick assets divided by current liabilities. For Tosh, quick assets consist of cash ($200,000) and accounts receivable ($400,000), a total of $600,000. Current liabilities consist of accounts payable ($260,000) and interest payable ($20,000) for a total of $280,000. Hence, the quick ratio is 2.14 ($600,000 ÷ $280,000).
Answer (A) is incorrect. This ratio includes long-term bonds payable among the current liabilities. Answer (B) is incorrect. This ratio includes long-term bonds payable among the current liabilities and inventory and prepaid expenses among the quick assets. Answer (D) is incorrect. This ratio excludes interest payable from the current liabilities.

5. Tosh Enterprises' amount of working capital is

A. $600,000

B. $1,120,000

C. $1,200,000

D. $1,220,000

Answer (C) is correct.
REQUIRED: The amount of working capital.
DISCUSSION: Working capital equals current assets minus current liabilities. For Tosh Enterprises, current assets consist of cash, accounts receivable, inventory, and prepaid expenses, a total of $1,480,000 ($400,000 + $200,000 + $800,000 + $80,000). Current liabilities consist of accounts payable and interest payable for a total of $280,000 ($260,000 + $20,000). Accordingly, working capital is $1,200,000 ($1,480,000 – $280,000).
Answer (A) is incorrect. The amount of $600,000 includes long-term bonds payable among the current liabilities. Answer (B) is incorrect. The amount of $1,120,000 excludes prepaid expenses from current assets. Answer (D) is incorrect. The amount of $1,220,000 excludes interest payable from current liabilities.

6. A financial analyst has obtained the following data from financial statements:

Cash	$ 200,000
Marketable securities	100,000
Accounts receivable, net	300,000
Inventories, net	480,000
Prepaid expenses	120,000
Total current assets	$1,200,000
Accounts payable	$250,000
Income taxes	50,000
Accrued liabilities	100,000
Current portion of long-term debt	200,000
Total current liabilities	$600,000

In order to determine ability to pay current obligations, the financial analyst would calculate the cash ratio as

A. .50

B. .80

C. 1.00

D. 1.20

Answer (A) is correct.
REQUIRED: The cash ratio given relevant information.
DISCUSSION: The cash ratio, a more conservative measure of liquidity than the quick ratio, is calculated as follows:

Cash ratio = (Cash + Marketable securities) ÷ Current liabilities
= ($200,000 + $100,000) ÷ $600,000
= 0.5

Answer (B) is incorrect. Improperly including only inventories in the numerator results in a ratio of .80. Answer (C) is incorrect. Improperly including accounts receivable in the numerator results in a ratio of 1.00. Answer (D) is incorrect. Improperly including accounts receivable and prepaid expenses in the numerator results in a ratio of 1.20.

7. Given an acid test ratio of 2.0, current assets of $5,000, and inventory of $2,000, the value of current liabilities is

A. $1,500

B. $2,500

C. $3,500

D. $6,000

Answer (A) is correct.
REQUIRED: The value of current liabilities given the acid test ratio, current assets, and inventory.
DISCUSSION: The acid test, or quick, ratio equals the quick assets (cash, marketable securities, and accounts receivable) divided by current liabilities. Current assets equal the quick assets plus inventory and prepaid expenses. (This question assumes that the entity has no prepaid expenses.) Given current assets of $5,000, inventory of $2,000, and no prepaid expenses, the quick assets must be $3,000. Because the acid test ratio is 2.0, the quick assets are double the current liabilities. Current liabilities therefore are equal to $1,500 ($3,000 quick assets ÷ 2.0).

Answer (B) is incorrect. Dividing the current assets by 2.0 results in $2,500. Current assets includes inventory, which should not be included in the calculation of the acid test ratio. Answer (C) is incorrect. Adding inventory to current assets rather than subtracting it results in $3,500. Answer (D) is incorrect. Multiplying the quick assets by 2 instead of dividing by 2 results in $6,000.

8. What is the acid test (or quick) ratio?

Cash	$ 10,000
Marketable securities	18,000
Accounts receivable	120,000
Inventories	375,000
Prepaid expenses	12,000
Accounts payable	75,000
Long-term debt -- current portion	20,000
Long-term debt	400,000
Sales	1,650,000

A. 1.56

B. 1.97

C. 2.13

D. 5.63

Answer (A) is correct.
REQUIRED: The acid test ratio given relevant information.
DISCUSSION: The acid test (quick) ratio equals the quick assets (cash, marketable securities, and accounts receivable) divided by current liabilities. The acid test ratio is thus 1.558 [($10,000 + $18,000 + $120,000) ÷ ($75,000 + $20,000)].

Answer (B) is incorrect. Improperly leaving the current portion of long-term debt from the denominator results in 1.9. Answer (C) is incorrect. Improperly including prepaid expenses in the numerator and leaving the current portion of long-term debt out of the denominator results in 2.13. Answer (D) is incorrect. Improperly including inventories and prepaid expenses in the numerator results in 5.63.

Question 9 is based on the following information.
A company has a current ratio of 1.4, a quick,
or acid test, ratio of 1.2, and the following partial
summary balance sheet:

Cash	$ 10
Accounts receivable	___
Inventory	___
Fixed assets	___
Total assets	$100
Current liabilities	$___
Long-term liabilities	40
Stockholders' equity	30
Total liabilities and equity	$___

9. The company has an accounts receivable balance
of

A. $26

B. $36

C. $66

D. $100

Answer (A) is correct.
   REQUIRED: The accounts receivable balance.
   DISCUSSION: Total assets equal total liabilities and equity.
Hence, if total assets equal $100, total liabilities and equity must
equal $100, and current liabilities must equal $30 ($100 – $40
– $30). Because the quick ratio equals the quick assets (cash
+ accounts receivable) divided by current liabilities, the quick
assets must equal $36 ($30 × 1.2 quick ratio), and the accounts
receivable balance is $26 ($36 – $10 cash).
   Answer (B) is incorrect. The quick assets equal $36.
Answer (C) is incorrect. The sum of the quick assets and current
liabilities equals $66. Answer (D) is incorrect. Total assets equal
$100.

6.3 Liquidity Ratios -- Effects of Transactions

10. A company has current assets of $400,000 and
current liabilities of $500,000. The company's current
ratio will be increased by

A. The purchase of $100,000 of inventory on
   account.

B. The payment of $100,000 of accounts payable.

C. The collection of $100,000 of accounts
   receivable.

D. Refinancing a $100,000 long-term loan with
   short-term debt.

Answer (A) is correct.
   REQUIRED: The transaction that will increase a current ratio
of less than 1.0.
   DISCUSSION: The current ratio equals current assets
divided by current liabilities. An equal increase in both the
numerator and denominator of a current ratio less than 1.0
causes the ratio to increase. The company's current ratio is .8
($400,000 ÷ $500,000). The purchase of $100,000 of inventory
on account would increase the current assets to $500,000 and
the current liabilities to $600,000, resulting in a new current ratio
of .833.
   Answer (B) is incorrect. This transaction decreases the
current ratio. Answer (C) is incorrect. The current ratio would be
unchanged. Answer (D) is incorrect. This transaction decreases
the current ratio.

11. A corporation has a current ratio of 2 to 1 and
a quick ratio (acid test) of 1 to 1. A transaction that
would change the quick ratio but **not** the current ratio
is the

A. Sale of inventory on account at cost.

B. Collection of accounts receivable.

C. Payment of accounts payable.

D. Purchase of a patent for cash.

Answer (A) is correct.
   REQUIRED: The transaction that would affect the quick ratio
but not the current ratio.
   DISCUSSION: The quick (acid test) ratio equals the quick
assets (cash, marketable securities, and accounts receivable)
divided by current liabilities. The current ratio is equal to current
assets divided by current liabilities. The sale of inventory (not a
quick current asset) on account increases accounts receivable
(a quick asset), thereby changing the quick ratio. The sale of
inventory on account, however, replaces one current asset with
another, and the current ratio is unaffected.
   Answer (B) is incorrect. Neither ratio is changed. Answer (C)
is incorrect. The current, not the quick, ratio changes. Answer (D)
is incorrect. Both decrease.

Questions 12 through 17 are based on the following information. Depoole Company is a manufacturer of industrial products that uses a calendar year for financial reporting purposes. Assume that total quick assets exceeded total current liabilities both before and after the transaction described. Further assume that Depoole has positive profits during the year and a credit balance throughout the year in its retained earnings account.

12. Depoole's payment of a trade account payable of $64,500 will

   A. Increase the current ratio, but the quick ratio would not be affected.

   B. Increase the quick ratio, but the current ratio would not be affected.

   C. Increase both the current and quick ratios.

   D. Decrease both the current and quick ratios.

Answer (C) is correct.
   REQUIRED: The effect of paying a trade account payable on the current and quick ratios.
   DISCUSSION: Current assets consist of more assets than quick assets; thus, if quick assets exceed current liabilities, then current assets do also. It can also be concluded that both ratios are greater than 1. An equal reduction in the numerator and the denominator, such as a payment of a trade payable, will cause each ratio to increase.

13. Depoole's purchase of raw materials for $85,000 on open account will

   A. Increase the current ratio.

   B. Decrease the current ratio.

   C. Increase net working capital.

   D. Decrease net working capital.

Answer (B) is correct.
   REQUIRED: The effect of a credit purchase of raw materials on the current ratio or working capital.
   DISCUSSION: The purchase increases both the numerator and denominator of the current ratio by adding inventory to the numerator and payables to the denominator. Because the ratio before the purchase was greater than 1, the ratio is decreased.
   Answer (A) is incorrect. The current ratio is decreased. Answer (C) is incorrect. The purchase of raw materials on account has no effect on working capital (current assets and current liabilities change by the same amount). Answer (D) is incorrect. The purchase of raw materials on account has no effect on working capital (current assets and current liabilities change by the same amount).

14. Depoole's collection of a current accounts receivable of $29,000 will

   A. Increase the current ratio.

   B. Decrease the current ratio and the quick ratio.

   C. Increase the quick ratio.

   D. Not affect the current or quick ratios.

Answer (D) is correct.
   REQUIRED: The effect of collection of a current account receivable on the current and quick ratios.
   DISCUSSION: Collecting current accounts receivable has no effect on either the current ratio or the quick ratio because assets (both current and quick) are reduced for the collection of receivables and increased by the same amount for the receipt of cash. Current liabilities are unchanged by the transaction.

15. Obsolete inventory of $125,000 was written off by Depoole during the year. This transaction

   A. Decreased the quick ratio.

   B. Increased the quick ratio.

   C. Increased net working capital.

   D. Decreased the current ratio.

Answer (D) is correct.
   REQUIRED: The effect of writing off obsolete inventory.
   DISCUSSION: Writing off obsolete inventory reduces current assets, but not quick assets (cash, marketable securities, and accounts receivable). Thus, the current ratio was reduced and the quick ratio was unaffected.
   Answer (A) is incorrect. The quick ratio was not affected. Answer (B) is incorrect. The quick ratio was not affected. Answer (C) is incorrect. Working capital was decreased.

16. Depoole's issuance of serial bonds in exchange for an office building, with the first installment of the bonds due late this year,

    A. Decreases net working capital.

    B. Decreases the current ratio.

    C. Decreases the quick ratio.

    D. Affects all of the answers as indicated.

Answer (D) is correct.
    REQUIRED: The effect of issuing serial bonds with the first installment due late this year.
    DISCUSSION: The first installment is a current liability; thus the amount of current liabilities increases with no corresponding increase in current assets. The effect is to decrease working capital, the current ratio, and the quick ratio.
    Answer (A) is incorrect. The bond issuance would also decrease the current ratio and the quick ratio. Answer (B) is incorrect. The bond issuance would also decrease net working capital and the quick ratio. Answer (C) is incorrect. The bond issuance would also decrease net working capital and the current ratio.

17. Depoole's early liquidation of a long-term note with cash affects the

    A. Current ratio to a greater degree than the quick ratio.

    B. Quick ratio to a greater degree than the current ratio.

    C. Current and quick ratio to the same degree.

    D. Current ratio but not the quick ratio.

Answer (B) is correct.
    REQUIRED: The effect of an early liquidation of a long-term note with cash.
    DISCUSSION: The numerators of the quick and current ratios are decreased when cash is expended. Early payment of a long-term liability has no effect on the denominator (current liabilities). Since the numerator of the quick ratio, which includes cash, net receivables, and marketable securities, is less than the numerator of the current ratio, which includes all current assets, the quick ratio is affected to a greater degree.

18. A company has a 2-to-1 current ratio. This ratio would increase to more than 2 to 1 if

    A. A previously declared stock dividend were distributed.

    B. The company wrote off an uncollectible receivable.

    C. The company sold merchandise on open account that earned a normal gross margin.

    D. The company purchased inventory on open account.

Answer (C) is correct.
    REQUIRED: The transaction that would increase a current ratio that is greater than 1.
    DISCUSSION: The current ratio equals current assets divided by current liabilities. Thus, an increase in current assets or a decrease in current liabilities, by itself, increases the current ratio. The sale of inventory at a profit increases current assets without changing liabilities. Inventory decreases, and receivables increase by a greater amount. Thus, total current assets and the current ratio increase.
    Answer (A) is incorrect. The distribution of a stock dividend affects only stockholders' equity accounts (debit common stock dividend distributable and credit common stock). Answer (B) is incorrect. Writing off an uncollectible receivable does not affect total current assets. The allowance account absorbs the bad debt. Thus, the balance of net receivables is unchanged. Answer (D) is incorrect. The purchase of inventory increases current assets and current liabilities by the same amount. The transaction reduces a current ratio in excess of 1.0 since the numerator and denominator of the ratio increase by the same amount.

6.4 Profitability Ratios -- Calculations

19. A firm is experiencing a growth rate of 9% with a return on assets of 12%. If the debt ratio is 36% and the market price of the stock is $38 per share, what is the return on equity?

    A. 7.68%

    B. 9.0%

    C. 12.0%

    D. 18.75%

Answer (D) is correct.
    REQUIRED: The return on equity.
    DISCUSSION: Assume that the firm has $100 in assets, with debt of $36 and equity of $64. Income (return) is $12. The $12 return on assets equates to an 18.75% return on equity ($12 ÷ $64).
    Answer (A) is incorrect. The figure of 7.68% is based on 64% of the ROA. Answer (B) is incorrect. The figure of 9.0% is the growth rate, not a return. Answer (C) is incorrect. The figure of 12.0% is the return on assets, not return on equity.

Questions 20 and 21 are based on the following information. The financial statements for Dividendosaurus, Inc., for the current year are as follows:

Balance Sheet		Statement of Income and Retained Earnings	
Cash	$100	Sales	$ 3,000
Accounts receivable	200	Cost of goods sold	(1,600)
Inventory	50	Gross profit	$ 1,400
Net fixed assets	600	Operations expenses	(970)
Total	$950	Operating income	$ 430
		Interest expense	(30)
Accounts payable	$140	Income before tax	$ 400
Long-term debt	300	Income tax	(200)
Capital stock	260	Net income	$ 200
Retained earnings	250	Add: Jan. 1 retained earnings	150
Total	$950	Less: Dividends	(100)
		Dec. 31 retained earnings	$ 250

20. Dividendosaurus has return on assets of

A. 21.1%

B. 39.2%

C. 42.1%

D. 45.3%

Answer (A) is correct.
REQUIRED: The return on assets.
DISCUSSION: The return on assets is the ratio of net income to total assets. For Dividendosaurus, it equals 21.1% ($200 net income ÷ $950 total assets).
Answer (B) is incorrect. The ratio of net income to common equity is 39.2%. Answer (C) is incorrect. The ratio of income before tax to total assets is 42.1%. Answer (D) is incorrect. The ratio of income before interest and tax to total assets is 45.3%.

21. Dividendosaurus has a profit margin of

A. 6.67%

B. 13.33%

C. 14.33%

D. 46.67%

Answer (A) is correct.
REQUIRED: The profit margin.
DISCUSSION: The profit margin is the ratio of net income to sales. For Dividendosaurus, it equals 6.67% ($200 net income ÷ $3,000 sales).
Answer (B) is incorrect. The ratio of income before tax to sales is 13.33%. Answer (C) is incorrect. The ratio of income before interest and taxes to sales is 14.33%. Answer (D) is incorrect. The ratio of gross profit to sales is 46.67%.

22. The following information pertains to the year ended December 31:

Sales	$720,000
Net income	120,000
Average total assets	480,000

Which one of the following formulas depicts the use of the DuPont model to calculate return on assets?

A. (720,000 ÷ 480,000) × (720,000 ÷ 120,000)

B. (480,000 ÷ 720,000) × (720,000 ÷ 120,000)

C. (720,000 ÷ 480,000) × (120,000 ÷ 720,000)

D. (480,000 ÷ 720,000) × (120,000 ÷ 720,000)

Answer (C) is correct.
REQUIRED: The formula used to compute ROA.
DISCUSSION: The DuPont model depicts return on assets as total asset turnover (sales divided by average total assets) times the profit margin (net income divided by sales). Therefore, the ROA calculation uses the formula [($720,000 ÷ $480,000) × ($120,000 ÷ $720,000)].

23. In Year 3, gross profit margin remained unchanged from Year 2. But, in Year 3, the company's net profit margin declined from the level reached in Year 2. This could have happened because, in Year 3,

A. Corporate tax rates increased.

B. Cost of goods sold increased relative to sales.

C. Sales increased at a faster rate than operating expenses.

D. Common share dividends increased.

Answer (A) is correct.
    REQUIRED: The factor that could bring about a reduction in net profit margin with no change in gross profit margin.
    DISCUSSION: Gross profit margin is net sales minus cost of goods sold. Net profit margin is gross profit margin minus all remaining expenses and losses, one of which is income taxes. If corporate tax rates increased, net profit margin would decrease, leaving gross profit margin unchanged.
    Answer (B) is incorrect. A change in cost of goods sold would have affected gross profit margin. Answer (C) is incorrect. Sales increasing faster than operating expenses would have resulted in an increase, not a decrease, to net profit margin. Answer (D) is incorrect. Any impact on dividends cannot be determined from the information given.

6.5 Profitability Ratios -- Effects of Transactions

24. A corporation experienced the following year-over-year changes:

Net profit margin	Increased	25%
Total asset turnover	Increased	40%
Total assets	Decreased	10%
Total equity	Increased	40%

Using DuPont analysis, what is the year-over-year change in return on equity (ROE)?

A. Increased 95.0%.

B. Increased 63.0%.

C. Increased 12.5%.

D. Increased 10.0%.

Answer (C) is correct.
    REQUIRED: The calculation of return on equity using the DuPont method.
    DISCUSSION: The ROE using the DuPont analysis is calculated as follows:

> *Net profit margin × Total asset turnover × Equity multiplier (Total assets ÷ Total equity)*

    The best way to solve this problem is to use actual numbers for the return on equity comparison of this year to last year. Assuming that last year the corporation had a net profit margin of .025, total asset turnover of 1.05, total assets of $500,000, and total equity of $200,000, last year's ROE is equal to 6.56% [.025 × 1.05 × ($500,000 ÷ $200,000)].
    By using the information given in the problem, the current-year amounts can be calculated, resulting in a net profit margin of .03125 (increased by 25%), total asset turnover of 1.47 (increased by 40%), total assets of $450,000 (decreased by 10%), and total equity of $280,000 (increased by 40%). Therefore, this year's ROE is equal to 7.38% [.03125 × 1.47 × (450,000 ÷ 280,000)].
    The increase in ROE from last year to this year can now be calculated as 12.5% [(7.38 – 6.56) ÷ 6.56].
    Answer (A) is incorrect. The DuPont Model for ROE is as follows: Net profit margin × Total asset turnover × Equity multiplier (Total assets ÷ Total equity). The year-over-year change is not calculated by simply adding and subtracting the increases and decreases from last year to this year. The incorrect amount of 95% results from adding and subtracting the year-over-year changes (25% + 40% – 10% + 40%). Answer (B) is incorrect. The year-over-year change is not calculated by simply dividing the increase in the net profit margin by the increase in the total asset turnover. Answer (D) is incorrect. This answer choice incorrectly multiplies the year-over-year change for the net profit margin by the year-over-year change for the total asset turnover to get an increase in ROE of 10.0%.

25. According to the DuPont formula, which one of the following will **not** increase a profitable firm's return on equity?

A. Increasing total asset turnover.

B. Increasing net profit margin.

C. Lowering corporate income taxes.

D. Lowering equity multiplier.

Answer (D) is correct.
    REQUIRED: The item that would not increase a profitable firm's ROE.
    DISCUSSION: Lowering the equity multiplier would not increase a profitable firm's return on equity. The DuPont model depicts return on assets as total asset turnover (sales divided by average total assets) times the profit margin (net income divided by sales).
    Answer (A) is incorrect. Increasing total asset turnover would increase a profitable firm's return on equity. Answer (B) is incorrect. Increasing net profit margin would increase a profitable firm's return on equity. Answer (C) is incorrect. Lowering corporate income taxes would increase a profitable firm's return on equity.

6.6 Factors Affecting Reported Profitability

26. Which one of the following ratios would be **most** affected by miscellaneous or non-recurring income?

- A. Net profit margin.
- B. Operating profit margin.
- C. Gross profit margin.
- D. Debt-to-equity ratio.

Answer (A) is correct.
    REQUIRED: The factors affecting reported profitability ratios.
    DISCUSSION: Net profit margin is expressed as net income over sales. Net income would include miscellaneous or non-recurring income. This ratio would be the most affected because the amounts for miscellaneous or non-recurring income would be included in the numerator of the ratio.
    Answer (B) is incorrect. Operating profit margin is equal to operating income divided by net sales. Neither sales nor operating income would include miscellaneous or non-recurring income. Therefore, this ratio would not be affected by those amounts. Answer (C) is incorrect. Gross profit margin is expressed as gross profit divided by net sales. Gross profit is equal to revenues less the cost of goods sold, not including miscellaneous or non-recurring income. Therefore, this ratio would not be affected by those amounts. Answer (D) is incorrect. The debt-to-equity ratio is expressed as total debt divided by stockholders' equity. Neither debt nor stockholders' equity would include miscellaneous or non-recurring income. Therefore, this ratio would not be affected by those amounts.

27. A company bought a new machine and estimated that the machine will have a useful life of 10 years and a salvage value of $5,000. After the machine has been put in service for 2 years, the company has decided to change the estimate of the useful life to 7 years. Which one of the following statements describes the proper way to revise a useful life estimate?

- A. Revisions in useful life are permitted only if approved by the SEC.
- B. Retroactive changes must be made to correct previously recorded depreciation.
- C. Only future years will be affected by the revision.
- D. Both current and future years will be affected by the revision.

Answer (D) is correct.
    REQUIRED: The proper treatment of a change in an asset's useful life.
    DISCUSSION: A change in useful life is accounted for in the current year by taking the current book value and dividing it by the new remaining useful life. This will change depreciation in the current and future years.
    Answer (A) is incorrect. A change in the useful life is considered a change in accounting estimates. A change in accounting estimate is not required to be submitted to the SEC. Answer (B) is incorrect. Previous depreciation is kept as is. Only the depreciation going forward will be adjusted to account for the new useful life. Answer (C) is incorrect. Current-year depreciation will also be affected.

6.7 Solvency

28. The relationship of the total debt to the total equity of a corporation is a measure of

- A. Liquidity.
- B. Profitability.
- C. Creditor risk.
- D. Solvency.

Answer (C) is correct.
    REQUIRED: The characteristic measured by the relationship of total debt to total equity.
    DISCUSSION: The debt to equity ratio is a measure of risk to creditors. It indicates how much equity cushion is available to absorb losses before the interests of debt holders would be impaired. The less leveraged the company, the safer the creditors' interests.
    Answer (A) is incorrect. Liquidity concerns how quickly cash can be made available to pay debts as they come due. Answer (B) is incorrect. The debt to equity ratio evaluates a company's capital structure and is thus oriented toward the balance sheet. It does not measure the use (profits) made of assets. Answer (D) is incorrect. Solvency is the availability of assets to service debt. Technically, whenever the debt to equity ratio can be computed with a meaningful answer, it can be said that the firm is solvent because assets, by definition, have to exceed debts.

Questions 29 and 30 are based on the following information.

Selected data from Ostrander Corporation's financial statements for the years indicated are presented in thousands.

Year 2 Operations			December 31	
			Year 2	Year 1
Net credit sales	$4,175			
Cost of goods sold	2,880	Cash	$ 32	$ 28
Interest expense	50	Trading securities	169	172
Income tax	120	Accounts receivable (net)	210	204
Gain on disposal of a segment		Merchandise inventory	440	420
(net of tax)	210	Tangible fixed assets	480	440
Administrative expense	950	Total assets	1,397	1,320
Net income	385	Current liabilities	370	368
		Total liabilities	790	750
		Common stock outstanding	226	210
		Retained earnings	381	360

29. The times interest earned ratio for Ostrander Corporation for Year 2 is

A. .57 times.

B. 7.70 times.

C. 3.50 times.

D. 6.90 times.

Answer (D) is correct.
REQUIRED: The times interest earned ratio for Year 2.
DISCUSSION: The interest coverage ratio is computed by dividing earnings before interest and taxes by interest expense. Net income of $385, minus the disposal gain of $210, is added to income taxes of $120 and interest expense of $50 to produce a ratio numerator of $345. Dividing $345 by $50 results in an interest coverage of 6.90 times.
Answer (A) is incorrect. This figure is the debt ratio. Answer (B) is incorrect. This figure is based on net income from operations after taxes and interest. Answer (C) is incorrect. This figure results from not adding interest and taxes to net income after the gain on disposal is subtracted.

30. The total debt to equity ratio for Ostrander Corporation in Year 2 is

A. 3.49

B. 0.77

C. 2.07

D. 1.30

Answer (D) is correct.
REQUIRED: The total debt to equity ratio for Year 2.
DISCUSSION: Total equity consists of the $226 of capital stock and $381 of retained earnings, or $607. Debt is given as the $790 of total liabilities. Thus, the ratio is 1.30 ($790 ÷ $607).
Answer (A) is incorrect. Total liabilities divided by common stock outstanding equals 3.49. Answer (B) is incorrect. Equity divided by debt equals 0.77. Answer (C) is incorrect. Total liabilities divided by retained earnings equals 2.07.

31. A debt to equity ratio is

A. About the same as the debt to assets ratio.

B. Higher than the debt to assets ratio.

C. Lower than the debt to assets ratio.

D. Not correlated with the debt to assets ratio.

Answer (B) is correct.
REQUIRED: The true statement comparing the debt to equity and debt to assets ratios.
DISCUSSION: Because debt plus equity equals assets, a debt to equity ratio would have a lower denominator than a debt to assets ratio. Thus, the debt to equity ratio would be higher than the debt to assets ratio.
Answer (A) is incorrect. The ratios would always be different unless either debt or equity equaled zero. Answer (C) is incorrect. The lower denominator in the debt to equity ratio means that it would always be higher than the debt to assets ratio. Answer (D) is incorrect. The two ratios are related in that they always move in the same direction.

Questions 32 and 33 are based on the following information. Assume the following information pertains to Ramer Company, Matson Company, and for their common industry for a recent year.

	Ramer	Matson	Industry Average
Current ratio	3.50	2.80	3.00
Accounts receivable turnover	5.00	8.10	6.00
Inventory turnover	6.20	8.00	6.10
Times interest earned	9.00	12.30	10.40
Debt to equity ratio	0.70	0.40	0.55
Return on investment	0.15	0.12	0.15
Dividend payout ratio	0.80	0.60	0.55
Earnings per share	$3.00	$2.00	--

32. The attitudes of both Ramer and Matson concerning risk are **best** explained by the

A. Current ratio, accounts receivable turnover, and inventory turnover.

B. Dividend payout ratio and earnings per share.

C. Current ratio and earnings per share.

D. Debt to equity ratio and times interest earned.

Answer (D) is correct.
   REQUIRED: The statement that best explains the companies' attitudes toward risk.
   DISCUSSION: Matson is the more conservative company because it is less highly leveraged (lower debt to equity ratio and a higher interest coverage). Moreover, it also pays out a smaller portion of its earnings in the form of dividends (lower dividend payout ratio). These ratios reflect management intent.
   Answer (A) is incorrect. These are liquidity ratios that do not concern risk incurrence. Answer (B) is incorrect. EPS does not indicate management's intent with respect to risk. Answer (C) is incorrect. The current ratio and EPS are not indicators of the level of risk accepted.

33. Some of the ratios and data for Ramer and Matson are affected by income taxes. Assuming no interperiod income tax allocation, which of the following items would be directly affected by income taxes for the period?

A. Current ratio and debt to equity ratio.

B. Accounts receivable turnover and inventory turnover.

C. Return on investment and earnings per share.

D. Debt to equity ratio and dividend payout ratio.

Answer (C) is correct.
   REQUIRED: The ratios directly affected by income taxes.
   DISCUSSION: Income taxes are an expense of the business and affect rates of return and earnings per share. Any ratio that uses net income as a part of the calculation is affected, e.g., return on investment, EPS, and dividend payout.
   Answer (A) is incorrect. Neither ratio is based on net income. Answer (B) is incorrect. These turnover ratios are based on asset accounts and figures at the top of the income statement, not net income. Answer (D) is incorrect. The debt to equity ratio is not affected by taxes.

6.8 Leverage

34. This year, an entity increased earnings before interest and taxes (EBIT) by 17%. During the same period, net income after tax increased by 42%. The degree of financial leverage that existed during the year is

A. 1.70

B. 4.20

C. 2.47

D. 5.90

Answer (C) is correct.
   REQUIRED: The degree of financial leverage.
   DISCUSSION: The percentage-change version of the degree of financial leverage equals the percentage change in net income over the percentage change in EBIT. Accordingly, the entity's degree of financial leverage is 2.47 (42% ÷ 17%).

35. A firm with a higher degree of operating leverage when compared to the industry average implies that the

   A. Firm has higher variable costs.

   B. Firm's profits are more sensitive to changes in sales volume.

   C. Firm is more profitable.

   D. Firm is less risky.

Answer (B) is correct.
    REQUIRED: The effect of a higher degree of operating leverage (DOL).
    DISCUSSION: Operating leverage is a measure of the degree to which fixed costs are used in the production process. A company with a higher percentage of fixed costs (higher operating leverage) has greater risk than one in the same industry that relies more heavily on variable costs. However, such a firm is also able to expand production rapidly in times of higher product demand. Thus, the more leveraged a firm is in its operations, the more sensitive operating income is to changes in sales volume.
    Answer (A) is incorrect. A firm with higher operating leverage has higher fixed costs and lower variable costs. Answer (C) is incorrect. A firm with higher leverage will be relatively more profitable than a firm with lower leverage when sales are high. The opposite is true when sales are low. Answer (D) is incorrect. A firm with higher leverage is more risky. Its reliance on fixed costs is greater.

6.9 Common-Size Financial Statements

36. In financial statement analysis, expressing all financial statement items as a percentage of base-year amounts is called

   A. Horizontal common-size analysis.

   B. Vertical common-size analysis.

   C. Trend analysis.

   D. Ratio analysis.

Answer (A) is correct.
    REQUIRED: The term for expressing all financial statement items as a percentage of base-year amounts.
    DISCUSSION: Expressing financial statement items as percentages of corresponding base-year figures is a horizontal form of common-size (percentage) analysis that is useful for evaluating trends. The base amount is assigned the value of 100%, and the amounts for other years are denominated in percentages compared to the base year.
    Answer (B) is incorrect. Vertical common-size (percentage) analysis presents figures for a single year expressed as percentages of a base amount on the balance sheet (e.g., total assets) and on the income statement (e.g., sales). Answer (C) is incorrect. The term "trend analysis" is most often applied to the quantitative techniques used in forecasting to fit a curve to given data. Answer (D) is incorrect. It is a general term.

37. In assessing the financial prospects for a firm, financial analysts use various techniques. An example of vertical, common-size analysis is

   A. An assessment of the relative stability of a firm's level of vertical integration.

   B. A comparison in financial ratio form between two or more firms in the same industry.

   C. Advertising expense is 2% greater compared with the previous year.

   D. Advertising expense for the current year is 2% of sales.

Answer (D) is correct.
    REQUIRED: The example of vertical, common-size analysis.
    DISCUSSION: Vertical, common-size analysis compares the components within a set of financial statements. A base amount is assigned a value of 100%. For example, total assets on a common-size balance sheet and net sales on a common-size income statement are valued at 100%. Common-size statements permit evaluation of the efficiency of various aspects of operations. An analyst who states that advertising expense is 2% of sales is using vertical, common-size analysis.
    Answer (A) is incorrect. Vertical integration occurs when a corporation owns one or more of its suppliers or customers. Answer (B) is incorrect. Vertical, common-size analysis restates financial statements amounts as percentages. Answer (C) is incorrect. A statement that advertising expense is 2% greater than in the previous year results from horizontal analysis.

6.10 Effects of Off-Balance-Sheet Financing

38. Careful reading of an annual report will reveal that off-balance-sheet debt includes

- A. Amounts due in future years under operating leases.
- B. Transfers of accounts receivable without recourse.
- C. Current portion of long-term debt.
- D. Amounts due in future years under capital leases.

Answer (A) is correct.

REQUIRED: The off-balance-sheet debt.

DISCUSSION: Off-balance-sheet debt includes any type of liability for which the company is responsible but that does not appear on the balance sheet. The most common example is the amount due in future years on operating leases. Under U.S. GAAP, operating leases are not capitalized; instead, only the periodic payments of rent are reported when actually paid. Capital leases (those similar to a purchase) must be capitalized and reported as liabilities.

Answer (B) is incorrect. Transfers of accounts receivable without recourse do not create a liability for the company. This transaction is simply a transfer of receivables for cash. Answer (C) is incorrect. The current portion of long-term debt is shown on the balance sheet as a current liability. Answer (D) is incorrect. Amounts due in future years under capital leases are required to be recognized under U.S. GAAP.

Access the **Gleim CMA Premium Review System** from your Gleim Personal Classroom to continue your studies with exam-emulating multiple-choice questions!

6.11 ESSAY QUESTIONS

Scenario for Essay Questions 1, 2, 3

Foyle, Inc., prepared the comparative income statements for the three most recent fiscal years that are shown below. While profitable, Foyle has been losing market share and is concerned about future performance. Also presented are data about Foyle's largest competitor and the industry average.

	Year 1	Year 2	Year 3	Competitor	Ind. Avg.
Revenue	$20,000	$24,000	$30,000	$45,000	$28,000
Cost of goods sold	12,000	12,000	18,000	21,600	14,000
Gross profit	8,000	12,000	12,000	23,400	14,000
Sales and marketing	2,000	2,000	2,000	5,000	3,000
General and administrative	1,500	2,000	3,000	3,150	2,500
Research and development	1,500	2,000	1,000	4,000	1,500
Operating income	$ 3,000	$ 6,000	$ 6,000	$11,250	$ 7,000

Questions

1. Using the three Foyle, Inc., statements,

    a.   Prepare a comparative common-size statement using revenue as the base measure.

    b.   Prepare a common base-year income statement using Year 1 as the base year. Show your calculations.

2. Calculate Foyle's growth rate of both revenue and operating income for Year 2 and Year 3. Show your calculations.

3. By evaluating Foyle's performance against the performance of Foyle's largest competitor and the industry average, identify and discuss three areas Foyle should target for further investigation and performance improvement. Support your discussion with data.

Essay Questions 1, 2, 3 — Unofficial Answers

1. a.

	Year 1	Year 2	Year 3
Revenue	100%	100%	100%
Cost of goods sold	60%	50%	60%
Gross profit	40%	50%	40%
Sales & marketing	10%	8.3%	6.7%
General & admin.	7.5%	8.3%	10%
Research & dev.	7.5%	8.3%	3.3%
Operating income	15%	25%	20%

   b.

	Year 1	Year 2	Year 3
Revenue	100%	120%	150%
Cost of goods sold	100%	100%	150%
Gross profit	100%	150%	150%
Sales & marketing	100%	100%	100%
General & admin.	100%	133%	200%
Research & dev.	100%	133%	66.7%
Operating income	100%	200%	200%

2. Revenue

   Year 2: ($24,000 − $20,000) ÷ $20,000 = 20%

   Year 3: ($30,000 − $24,000) ÷ $24,000 = 25%

   Operating Income

   Year 2: ($6,000 − $3,000) ÷ $3,000 = 100%

   Year 3: ($6,000 − $6,000) ÷ $6,000 = 0%

3. Foyle's gross profit margin of 50% was comparable in Year 2 to the competitor's 52% and the industry average's 50%, but Foyle has fallen to 40% in Year 3. Foyle's operating income percentage of 25% was the same in Year 2 as the competitor and industry average, but Foyle has fallen to 20% in Year 3.

   Foyle in Year 3 has lower sales and marketing costs than the competitor and industry average (6.7% vs. 11.1% and 10.7%) but higher general and administrative costs (10% vs. 7% and 8.9%). Foyle's research and development costs are substantially below both the competitor and industry average (3.3% vs. 8.9% and 5.4%).

Access the **Gleim CMA Premium Review System** from your Gleim Personal Classroom to continue your studies with exam-emulating essay questions!

STUDY UNIT SEVEN
ACTIVITY MEASURES AND FINANCING

(13 pages of outline)

This study unit is the **second of two** on **financial statement analysis**. The relative weight assigned to this major topic in Part 2 of the exam is **25%**. The two study units are

Study Unit 6: Ratio Analysis
Study Unit 7: Activity Measures and Financing

If you are interested in reviewing more introductory or background material, go to www.gleim.com/CMAIntroVideos for a list of suggested third-party overviews of this topic. The following Gleim outline material is more than sufficient to help you pass the CMA exam; any additional introductory or background material is for your own personal enrichment.

7.1 ACTIVITY MEASURES

1. **Income Statement to Balance Sheet**

   a. Activity ratios measure how quickly the two major noncash assets are converted to cash.

      1) Activity ratios measure results over a period of time and thus draw information from the firm's income statement as well as from the balance sheet.

   b. EXAMPLE of a balance sheet:

RESOURCES			FINANCING		
CURRENT ASSETS:	Current Year End	Prior Year End	**CURRENT LIABILITIES:**	Current Year End	Prior Year End
Cash and equivalents	$ 325,000	$ 275,000	Accounts payable	$ 150,000	$ 75,000
Available-for-sale securities	165,000	145,000	Notes payable	50,000	50,000
Accounts receivable (net)	120,000	115,000	Accrued interest on note	5,000	5,000
Notes receivable	55,000	40,000	Current maturities of L.T. debt	100,000	100,000
Inventories	85,000	55,000	Accrued salaries and wages	15,000	10,000
Prepaid expenses	10,000	5,000	Income taxes payable	70,000	35,000
Total current assets	**$ 760,000**	**$ 635,000**	**Total current liabilities**	**$ 390,000**	**$ 275,000**
NONCURRENT ASSETS:			**NONCURRENT LIABILITIES:**		
Equity-method investments	$ 120,000	$ 115,000	Bonds payable	$ 500,000	$ 600,000
Property, plant, and equipment	1,000,000	900,000	Long-term notes payable	90,000	60,000
Less: Accum. depreciation	(85,000)	(55,000)	Employee-related obligations	15,000	10,000
Goodwill	5,000	5,000	Deferred income taxes	5,000	5,000
Total noncurrent assets	**$1,040,000**	**$ 965,000**	**Total noncurrent liabilities**	**$ 610,000**	**$ 675,000**
			Total liabilities	**$1,000,000**	**$ 950,000**
			STOCKHOLDERS' EQUITY:		
			Preferred stock, $50 par	$ 120,000	$ 0
			Common stock, $1 par	500,000	500,000
			Additional paid-in capital	110,000	100,000
			Retained earnings	70,000	50,000
			Total stockholders' equity	**$ 800,000**	**$ 650,000**
Total assets	**$1,800,000**	**$1,600,000**	**Total liabilities and stockholders' equity**	**$1,800,000**	**$1,600,000**

c.   EXAMPLE of an income statement:

	Current Year	Prior Year
Net sales	$1,800,000	$1,400,000
Cost of goods sold	(1,450,000)	(1,170,000)
Gross profit	$ 350,000	$ 230,000
SG&A expenses	(160,000)	(80,000)
Operating income	$ 190,000	$ 150,000
Other revenues and losses	(40,000)	(25,000)
Earnings before interest and taxes	$ 150,000	$ 125,000
Interest expense	(15,000)	(10,000)
Earnings before taxes	$ 135,000	$ 115,000
Income taxes (40%)	(54,000)	(46,000)
Net income	$ 81,000	$ 69,000

NOTE: This balance sheet and income statement provide inputs for the examples throughout this subunit.

2.   **Receivables**

a.   Accounts receivable turnover measures the efficiency of accounts receivable collection.

Accounts Receivable Turnover

$$\frac{Net\ credit\ sales}{Average\ accounts\ receivable}$$

1)   Average accounts receivable equals beginning accounts receivable plus ending accounts receivable, divided by 2.

a)   If a business is highly seasonal, a simple average of beginning and ending balances is inadequate. The monthly balances should be averaged instead.

2)   EXAMPLE: All of the company's sales are on credit. Accounts receivable at the balance sheet date of the second prior year were $105,000.

Current Year: $1,800,000 ÷ [($120,000 + $115,000) ÷ 2] = 15.3 times
Prior Year: $1,400,000 ÷ [($115,000 + $105,000) ÷ 2] = 12.7 times

a)   The company turned over its accounts receivable balance 2.6 more times during the current year, even as receivables were growing in absolute terms. Thus, the company's effectiveness at collecting accounts receivable has improved noticeably.

3)   A higher turnover implies that customers may be paying their accounts promptly.

a)   Because sales are the numerator, higher sales without an increase in receivables will result in a higher turnover. Because receivables are the denominator, encouraging customers to pay quickly (thereby lowering the balance in receivables) also results in a higher turnover ratio.

4)   A lower turnover implies that customers are taking longer to pay.

a)   If the discount period is extended, customers will be able to wait longer to pay while still getting the discount.

b. Days' sales outstanding in receivables (also called the average collection period) measures the average number of days it takes to collect a receivable.

Days' Sales Outstanding in Receivables

$$\frac{Days\ in\ year}{Accounts\ receivable\ turnover}$$

1) EXAMPLE: Current Year: 365 days ÷ 15.3 times = 23.9 days*
   Prior Year: 365 days ÷ 12.7 times = 28.7 days

   *Uses rounded number (15.3 times). The result, 23.9 days, will be used in later figures.

   a) Because the denominator [calculated in item 2.a.2)] increased and the numerator is a constant, days' sales will necessarily decrease. In addition to improving its collection practices, the company also may have become better at assessing the creditworthiness of its customers.

   2) Besides 365, other possible numerators are 360 (for simplicity) and 300 (the number of business days in a year).

   3) Days' sales outstanding in receivables can be compared with the firm's credit terms to determine whether the average customer is paying within the credit period.

3. **Inventory**

   a. Inventory turnover measures the efficiency of inventory management. In general, the higher the turnover, the better inventory is being managed.

Inventory Turnover

$$\frac{Cost\ of\ goods\ sold}{Average\ inventory}$$

1) Average inventory equals beginning inventory plus ending inventory, divided by 2.

   a) If a business is highly seasonal, a simple average of beginning and ending balances is inadequate. The monthly balances should be averaged instead.

2) EXAMPLE: The balance in inventories at the balance sheet date of the second prior year was $45,000.

   Current Year: $1,450,000 ÷ [($85,000 + $55,000) ÷ 2] = 20.7 times
   Prior Year: $1,170,000 ÷ [($55,000 + $45,000) ÷ 2] = 23.4 times

   a) The company did not turn over its inventories as many times during the current year. This is to be expected during a period of growing sales (and building inventory level) and so is not necessarily a sign of poor inventory management.

3) A higher turnover implies strong sales or that the firm may be carrying low levels of inventory.

4) A lower turnover implies that the firm may be carrying excess levels of inventory or inventory that is obsolete.

   a) Because cost of goods sold is the numerator, higher sales without an increase in inventory balances result in a higher turnover.

   b) Because inventory is the denominator, reducing inventory levels also results in a higher turnover ratio.

5) The ideal level for inventory turnover is industry specific, with the nature of the inventory items impacting the ideal ratio. For example, spoilable items such as meat and dairy products will mandate a higher turnover ratio than would natural resources such as gold, silver, and coal. Thus, a grocery store should have a much higher inventory turnover ratio than a uranium mine or a jewelry store.

b. Days' sales in inventory measures the efficiency of the company's inventory management practices.

Days' Sales in Inventory

$$\frac{Days\ in\ year}{Inventory\ turnover}$$

1) EXAMPLE: Current Year: 365 days ÷ 20.7 times = 17.6 days
Prior Year: 365 days ÷ 23.4 times = 15.6 days

    a) Because the numerator is a constant, the decreased inventory turnover calculated meant that days' sales tied up in inventory would increase. This is a common phenomenon during a period of increasing sales. However, it can also occur during periods of declining sales.

4. **Payables**

a. Accounts payable turnover measures the efficiency with which a firm manages the payment of vendors' invoices.

Accounts Payable Turnover

$$\frac{Purchases}{Average\ accounts\ payable}$$

1) Average accounts payable equals beginning accounts payable plus ending accounts payable, divided by 2.

    a) If a business is highly seasonal, a simple average of beginning and ending balances is inadequate. The monthly balances should be averaged instead.

2) EXAMPLE: The company had current- and prior-year purchases of $1,480,000 and $1,220,000, respectively. Net accounts payable and inventory at the balance sheet date of the 2nd prior year were $65,000 and $5,000, respectively.

Current Year: $1,480,000 ÷ [($150,000 + $75,000) ÷ 2] = 13.2 times
Prior Year: $1,220,000 ÷ [($75,000 + $65,000) ÷ 2] = 17.4 times

    a) The company is now carrying a much higher balance in payables, so it is not surprising that the balance is turning over less often. It also may be the case that the company was paying invoices too soon in the prior year.

3) A higher turnover implies that the firm is taking less time to pay off suppliers and may indicate that the firm is taking advantage of discounts.

4) A lower turnover implies that the firm is taking more time to pay off suppliers and forgoing discounts.

b. Days' purchases in accounts payable measures the average number of days it takes to settle a payable.

Days' Purchases in Accounts Payable

$$\frac{Days\ in\ year}{Accounts\ payable\ turnover}$$

1) EXAMPLE: Current Year: 365 days ÷ 13.2 times = 27.7 days*
Prior Year: 365 days ÷ 17.4 times = 21.0 days

*The rounded number, 13.2, yields 27.7 days, which will be used in later calculations.

    a) The slower turnover lowers the denominator, thereby increasing the days' purchases in payables. This substantially extended period reflects mostly the fact that the balance in payables has doubled. It also may imply that the company was paying its suppliers too quickly in the prior year.

2) The days' purchases in accounts payable can be compared with the average credit terms offered by a company's suppliers to determine whether the firm is paying its invoices on a timely basis (or too soon).

5. **Operating Cycle**

    a. A firm's operating cycle is the amount of time that passes between the acquisition of inventory and the collection of cash on the sale of that inventory.

Operating Cycle

Days' sales outstanding in receivables + Days' sales in inventory

        1) EXAMPLE: Current Year: 23.9 days + 17.6 days = 41.5 days
                       Prior Year: 28.7 days + 15.6 days = 44.3 days

            a) The company has managed to slightly reduce its operating cycle, even while increasing sales and building inventories.

**Operating Cycle
41.5 Days**

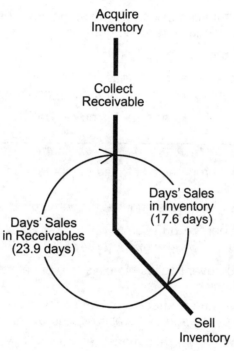

Figure 7-1

        2) For example, the operating cycle for a grocery store may be as short as 2 or 3 weeks, and the operating cycle for a jewelry store may be over a year.

6. **Cash Cycle**

    a. The cash cycle is that portion of the operating cycle that is not accounted for by days' purchases in accounts payable.

        1) This is somewhat counterintuitive because the cash cycle is the portion of the operating cycle when the company does **not** have cash, i.e., when cash is tied up in the form of inventory or accounts receivable.

Operating cycle – Days' purchases in accounts payable

        2) EXAMPLE: Current Year: 41.5 days – 27.7 days = 13.8 days
                       Prior Year: 44.3 days – 21.0 days = 23.3 days

            a) Of the company's total operating cycle of 41.5 days, cash is held for the 27.7 days that payables are outstanding. The 13.8 days of the cash cycle represent the period when cash is tied up as other forms of current assets.

7.   **Working Capital**

    a.   The working capital turnover ratio measures how effectively a company is using working capital to generate sales.

Working Capital Turnover

$$\frac{Sales}{Working\ Capital}$$

        1)   Working capital equals current assets minus current liabilities.

        2)   EXAMPLE: Current Year: \$1,800,000 ÷ (\$760,000 − \$390,000) = 4.86 times
                           Prior Year: \$1,400,000 ÷ (\$635,000 − \$275,000) = 3.89 times

             a)   The company turned over its working capital balance .97 more times during the current year, even as working capital was growing in absolute terms. Thus, the company's effectiveness at producing sales with working capital has improved.

        3)   A higher turnover implies that the company is generating a lot of sales for the amount of money it takes to generate those sales.

8.   **Other Activity Concepts**

    a.   The fixed assets turnover ratio measures how efficiently the company is deploying its investment in net property, plant, and equipment (PPE) to generate revenues.

Fixed Assets Turnover Ratio

$$\frac{Net\ sales}{Average\ net\ property,\ plant,\ and\ equipment}$$

        1)   Average net property, plant, and equipment equals beginning PPE plus ending PPE, divided by 2.

        2)   EXAMPLE: Two years ago, net property, plant, and equipment was \$860,000.

            Current Year: \$1,800,000 ÷ [(\$915,000 + \$845,000) ÷ 2] = 2.05 times
            Prior Year: \$1,400,000 ÷ [(\$845,000 + \$860,000) ÷ 2] = 1.64 times

        3)   A higher turnover implies effective use of net property, plant, and equipment to generate sales.

        4)   This ratio is largely affected by the capital intensiveness of the company and its industry, by the age of the assets, and by the depreciation method used.

    b.   The total assets turnover ratio measures how efficiently the company is deploying the totality of its resources to generate revenues.

Total Assets Turnover Ratio

$$\frac{Net\ sales}{Average\ total\ assets}$$

        1)   Average total assets equals beginning total assets plus ending total assets, divided by 2.

        2)   EXAMPLE: Total assets 2 years ago were \$1,520,000.

            Current Year: \$1,800,000 ÷ [(\$1,800,000 + \$1,600,000) ÷ 2] = 1.06 times
            Prior Year: \$1,400,000 ÷ [(\$1,600,000 + \$1,520,000) ÷ 2] = .897 times

        3)   A higher turnover implies effective use of net assets to generate sales.

        4)   Certain assets, for example, investments, do not relate to net sales. Their inclusion decreases the ratio.

Stop and review! You have completed the outline for this subunit. Study multiple-choice questions 1 through 14 beginning on page 225.

7.2 SHORT-TERM FINANCING

1. **Basics**

    a. Companies will often procure short-term financing to obtain funds for short-term objectives.

    b. Some loan terms describe discount rates using **basis points**. A basis point is one-hundredth of 1%.

    1) EXAMPLE: 300 basis points equals 3%.

    c. Sources of short-term financing include the following:

    1) Market-based instruments,

    2) Spontaneous sources (those that arise in the normal course of business, such as accounts payable), and

    3) Commercial banks.

2. **Spontaneous Forms of Financing**

    a. Trade credit resulting in accounts payable is the largest source of credit for small firms. It is created when a firm is offered credit terms by its suppliers.

    1) Trade credit results from a situation where a customer can purchase goods on account (not using cash), receive the goods, and pay the supplier at a later date. Trade credit is usually given for a specific number of days (i.e., 30, 60, or 90).

       a) Trade credit terms are usually given as 2/10, net 30. This means that the firm will receive a 2% discount if the entire balance is paid within 10 days and that the entire balance, whether or not the discount is taken, is due within 30 days.

       b) When the discount is taken, the amount of usable funds required can be calculated as follows:

       Usable funds = Invoice amount × (1.0 − Discount %)

       c) EXAMPLE: A firm received an invoice for $120,000 with terms of 2/10, net 30, and the firm wishes to pay within the discount window.

       $$\text{Amount needed} = \text{Invoice amount} \times (1.0 - \text{Discount \%})$$
       $$= \$120,000 \times (100\% - 2\%)$$
       $$= \$120,000 \times 98\%$$
       $$= \$117,600$$

    2) EXAMPLE: Vendor A delivers goods to Firm B at a price of $160,000 with the balance due in 30 days. Firm B has effectively received a 30-day, interest-free loan.

    3) The advantages of trade credit are that it is widely available and is free during the discount period.

    b. Accrued expenses, such as salaries, wages, interest, dividends, and taxes payable, are other sources of (interest-free) spontaneous financing.

    1) For instance, employees work 5, 6, or 7 days a week but are paid only every 2 weeks.

    2) Accruals have the additional advantage of fluctuating directly with operating activity, satisfying the matching principle.

3. **Cost of Not Taking a Discount**

   a. If an early payment discount is offered, the firm ordinarily should take the discount.

      1) In order to take the discount, the firm must either have enough funds on hand or use an alternative source of financing to acquire the funds early enough to pay within the discount window.

         a) This means that a firm must decide, given their financial capabilities, whether taking the discount is the best course of action.

         b) In some cases, the costs of **not** taking the discount are less than the costs of the alternative sources of financing that would be necessary if the firm were to take the discount. In situations like this, the firm should not take the discount.

      2) The annualized cost of not taking a discount can be calculated with the following formula:

$$\frac{Discount\ \%}{100\%\ -\ Discount\ \%} \times \frac{Days\ in\ year}{Total\ payment\ period\ -\ Discount\ period}$$

      3) EXAMPLE: A vendor has delivered goods on terms of 2/10, net 30. The firm has chosen to pay on day 30. The effective rate paid by not taking the discount is calculated as follows (using a 360-day year):

$$\begin{aligned}
\text{Cost of not taking discount} &= [2\% \div (100\% - 2\%)] \times [360 \text{ days} \div (30 \text{ days} - 10 \text{ days})] \\
&= (2\% \div 98\%) \times (360 \text{ days} \div 20 \text{ days}) \\
&= 2.0408\% \times 18 \\
&= 36.73\%
\end{aligned}$$

      The firm chose to finance $160,000 for 30 days rather than $156,800 ($160,000 × 98%) for 10 days. In effect, the cost is $3,200 ($160,000 – $156,800) to finance the last 20 days. Only companies in dire cash flow situations would incur a 36.73% cost of funds.

4. **Short-Term Bank Loans**

   a. Commercial banks offer term loans and lines of credit. These loans are second only to spontaneous credit as a source of short-term financing.

      1) The advantage is that bank loans provide financing not available from trade credit, etc. Thus, a firm can benefit from growth opportunities. The disadvantages are (a) the increased risk of insolvency, (b) the risk that short-term loans may not be renewed, and (c) the imposition of contractual restrictions, such as a compensating balance requirement.

      2) A term loan, such as a note, must be repaid by a certain date.

      3) A line of credit is an informal borrowing arrangement, generally for a 1-year period. It allows the debtor to reborrow amounts up to a maximum, as long as certain minimum payments are made each month (similar to a consumer's credit card).

         a) An advantage of a line of credit is that it is often an unsecured loan that is self-liquidating; that is, the assets acquired (e.g., inventory) provide the cash to pay the loan.

         b) A major disadvantage of a line of credit is that it is not a legal commitment to give credit, thus, it might not be renewed. A second is that a bank might require the borrower to "clean up" its debt for a certain period during the year, e.g., for 1 or 2 months.

5. **Effective Interest Rate on a Loan**

   a. The effective rate on any financing arrangement is the ratio of the amount the firm must pay to the amount the firm can use. The most basic statement of this ratio uses the dollar amounts generated by the equations illustrated on the previous pages.

   $$\textit{Effective interest rate} = \frac{\textit{Net interest expense}}{\textit{Usable funds}}$$

   b. As with all financing arrangements, the effective rate can be calculated without reference to dollar amounts:

   $$\textit{Effective rate on discounted loan} = \frac{\textit{Stated rate}}{\textit{(1.0 - Stated rate)}}$$

      1) EXAMPLE: The firm calculates the effective rate on this loan without using dollar amounts.

      Effective rate = Stated rate ÷ (1.0 − Stated rate)
      = 8% ÷ (100% − 8%)
      = 8% ÷ 92%
      = 8.696%

6. **Simple Interest Loans**

   a. A simple interest loan is one in which the interest is paid at the end of the loan term.
   b. With simple interest loans, the loan amount is equal to the amount of usable funds actually received by the borrower.
   c. The total amount of interest is the loan amount times the stated rate.

   $$\textit{Interest expense} = \textit{Loan amount} \times \textit{Stated rate}$$

      1) EXAMPLE: A firm's bank will lend the firm $120,000 for 1 year at a nominal annual rate of 6%, due at the end of the loan term.

      Interest expense = Loan amount × Stated rate
      = $120,000 × 6%
      = $7,200

   d. The effective rate and the nominal rate on a simple interest loan are the same.

      1) EXAMPLE: The firm calculates the effective rate on this loan as follows:

      Effective rate = Net interest expense ÷ Usable funds
      = $7,200 ÷ $120,000
      = 6.0%

7. **Discounted Loans**

   a. A discounted loan requires the interest to be paid at the beginning of the loan term.
   b. Since interest must be paid at the beginning of the loan term, the amount of usable funds actually received by the borrower is the loan amount minus any interest that must be paid. Once the amount of usable funds is known, the loan amount can be calculated as follows:

   $$\textit{Loan amount} = \frac{\textit{Usable funds}}{\textit{(1.0 - Stated rate)}}$$

      1) EXAMPLE: A firm needs $90,000 of usable funds. Its bank has offered to make a loan at an 8% nominal rate on a discounted basis.

      Loan amount = Usable funds ÷ (1.0 − Stated rate)
      = $90,000 ÷ (100% − 8%)
      = $90,000 ÷ 92%
      = $97,826

c.   The total amount of interest in the loan amount times the stated rate.

$$Interest\ expense\ =\ Loan\ amount\ \times\ Stated\ rate$$

d.   Because the borrower has the use of a smaller amount, the effective rate on a discounted loan is higher than its nominal rate:

Effective rate = Net interest expense ÷ Usable funds
= ($97,826 × 8%) ÷ $90,000
= $7,826 ÷ $90,000
= 8.696%

8.   **Loans with Compensating Balances**

a.   Rather than charge cash interest, banks sometimes require borrowers to maintain a compensating balance during the term of a financing arrangement.

$$Loan\ amount\ =\ \frac{Usable\ funds}{(1.0\ -\ Compensating\ balance\ \%)}$$

1)   EXAMPLE: A firm has received an invoice for $120,000 with terms of 2/10, net 30. The firm's bank will lend it the necessary amount for 30 days at a nominal annual rate of 6% with a compensating balance of 10%.

Loan amount = Usable funds ÷ (1.0 − Compensated balance %)
= ($120,000 × 98%) ÷ (100% − 10%)
= $117,600 ÷ 90%
= $130,667

b.   As with a discounted loan, the borrower has access to a smaller amount than the face amount of the loan and so pays an effective rate higher than the nominal rate.

Effective rate = Net interest expense ÷ Usable funds
= ($130,667 × 6%) ÷ $117,600
= $7,840 ÷ $117,600
= 6.667%

c.   Once again, the dollar amounts involved are not needed to determine the effective rate.

$$Effective\ rate\ with\ comp.\ balance\ =\ \frac{Stated\ rate}{(1.0\ -\ Compensating\ balance\ \%)}$$

Effective rate = Stated rate ÷ (1.0 − Compensating balance %)
= 6% ÷ (100% − 10%)
= 6% ÷ 90%
= 6.667%

d.   If the loan is offered on a discounted basis with a compensating balance requirement, the formula for the effective rate is

$$Effective\ rate\ =\ \frac{Stated\ rate}{(1.0\ -\ Stated\ rate\ -\ Compensating\ balance\ \%)}$$

9.   **Lines of Credit with Commitment Fees**

a.   A line of credit is the right to draw cash at any time up to a specified maximum. A line of credit may have a definite term, or it may be revolving; that is, the borrower can continuously pay off and reborrow from it.

1)   Sometimes a bank charges a borrower a commitment fee on the unused portion.

2)   EXAMPLE: A firm's bank extended a $1,000,000 line of credit at a nominal rate of 8% with a 0.5% commitment fee on the unused portion. The average loan balance during the year was $400,000.

Annual cost = Interest expense on average balance + Commitment fee on unused portion
  = (Average balance × Stated rate) + [(Credit limit − Average balance) × Commitment fee %]
  = ($400,000 × 8%) + [($1,000,000 − $400,000) × 0.5%]
  = $32,000 + $3,000
  = $35,000

10. **Market-Based Instruments**

  a. **Bankers' acceptances** can be sources of short-term financing.

    1) After acceptance, the drawer is no longer the primary responsible party and can sell the instrument to an investor at a discount.

    2) Once the instrument's term is reached after, for example, 90 days, the investor presents it to the accepting bank and demands payment.

    3) At that time, the drawer must have sufficient funds to cover it on deposit at the bank.

      a) In this way, the drawer obtained financing for 90 days.

    4) Bankers' acceptances are sold on a discount basis, which is the difference between the face amount and the proceeds received from the investor is interest expense to the drawer.

  b. **Commercial paper** consists of short-term, unsecured notes payable issued in large denominations ($100,000 or more) by large corporations with high credit ratings to other corporations and institutional investors, such as pension funds, banks, and insurance companies. Maturities of commercial paper are at most 270 days.

    1) The annualized rate of commercial paper can be calculated as follows:

$$Annualized\ rate = \frac{Face\ value - Net\ proceeds}{Net\ proceeds} \times Number\ of\ terms\ per\ year$$

    2) Commercial paper is a lower-cost source of funds than bank loans. It is usually issued at below the prime rate.

    3) No general secondary market exists for commercial paper.

    4) The advantages of commercial paper are that it (a) provides broad and efficient distribution, (b) provides a great amount of funds (at a given cost), and (c) avoids costly financing arrangements.

    5) The disadvantages are that (a) it is an impersonal market and (b) the total amount of funds available is limited to the excess liquidity of big corporations.

11. **Secured Financing**

  a. Loans can be secured by pledging receivables, i.e., committing the proceeds of the receivables to paying off the loan.

    1) A bank often lends up to 80% of outstanding receivables, depending upon the average age of the accounts and the probability of collection.

  b. A trust receipt is an instrument issued by a borrower that provides inventory as collateral. It is signed by the borrower and acknowledges that

    1) The inventory is held in trust for the lender, and
    2) Any proceeds of sale are to be paid to the lender.

  c. A chattel mortgage is a loan secured by personal property (movable property such as equipment or livestock). A floating lien is a loan secured by property, such as inventory, the composition of which may be constantly changing.

12. **Hedging**

    a. **Maturity matching** equalizes the life of an acquired asset with the debt instrument used to finance it. Because it mitigates financial risk, maturity matching is a hedging approach to financing.

        1) For instance, a debt due in 30 days should be paid with funds currently invested in a 30-day marketable security, not with proceeds from a 10-year bond issue.

        2) Moreover, long-term debt should not be paid with funds needed for day-to-day operations. Careful planning is needed to ensure that dedicated funds are available to retire long-term debt as it matures.

Stop and review! You have completed the outline for this subunit. Study multiple-choice questions 15 through 29 beginning on page 230.

7.3 LONG-TERM FINANCING

1. **Leases**

    a. A lease is a long-term, contractual agreement in which the owner of property (the lessor) allows another party (the lessee) the right to use the property for a stated period in exchange for a stated payment.

        1) Leases are a well-structured and widely used tool for obtaining the use of long-lived assets without tying up the large amounts of capital that would be needed for an outright purchase (U.S. airlines routinely lease anywhere from one-quarter to one-half of their passenger jets).

    b. The fundamental issue is whether the lease is a purchase-and-financing arrangement (a **capital lease**) or merely a long-term rental contract (an **operating lease**).

        1) Lessees have a strong incentive not to treat leases as purchase-and-financing arrangements because such contracts require the reporting of large amounts of debt on the balance sheet.

        2) Lessors, on the other hand, would prefer that a lease be treated as a purchase-and-financing arrangement because that allows them to report the long-term receivable.

    c. Another issue is deciding whether to finance an asset purchase using lease financing or debt financing.

        1) Management should select the financing option that results in the lowest present value of **after-tax outflows**.

            a) After-tax outflows consider the effect of interest expense and depreciation expense on cash outflows. These expenses create tax-shield benefits that offset lease, or loan, payments (i.e., cash outflows) in an amount equal to the firm's tax rate multiplied by the expense.

        2) The difference between the present value of the lease financing option and the present value of the debt financing option is the **net advantage**.

2. **Convertible Securities**

    a. Convertible securities are debt or preferred stock securities that contain a provision allowing the holder to convert the securities into some specified number of common shares after a specified time has elapsed.

        1) The conversion feature is an enticement to potential investors that allows the corporation to raise capital at a cost lower than a straight new common equity issue.

3. **Stock Purchase Warrants**

   a. A stock purchase warrant is, in effect, a call option on the corporation's common stock. After a specified time has elapsed, the holder of the warrant can exchange the warrant plus a specified amount of cash for some number of shares of common stock.

      1) Warrants are used to lower the cost of debt.

4. **Retained Earnings**

   a. Retained earnings are the cumulative accrual-basis income of the corporation minus amounts paid out in cash dividends minus amounts reclassified as additional paid-in capital from stock dividends.

      1) Retained earnings are the lowest-cost form of capital (all internally generated, no issue costs).

Stop and review! You have completed the outline for this subunit. Study multiple-choice question 30 on page 235.

QUESTIONS

7.1 Activity Measures

1. Based on the data presented below, what is the cost of sales for the year?

Current ratio	3.5
Acid test ratio	3.0
Year-end current liabilities	$600,000
Beginning inventory	$500,000
Inventory turnover	8.0

A. $1,600,000

B. $2,400,000

C. $3,200,000

D. $6,400,000

Answer (C) is correct.

   REQUIRED: The cost of sales given various ratios, ending liabilities, and beginning inventory.

   DISCUSSION: The current ratio is the ratio of current assets to current liabilities. Since the current ratio and current liabilities are known, current assets can be determined as follows:

Current assets ÷ Current liabilities = Current ratio
Current assets ÷ $600,000 = 3.5
Current assets = $600,000 × 3.5
= $2,100,000

Quick assets can be determined similarly:

Quick assets ÷ Current liabilities = Acid test ratio
Quick assets ÷ $600,000 = 3.0
Quick assets = $600,000 × 3.0
= $1,800,000

Assuming the company had no prepaid expenses, the difference between current assets and quick assets is inventory.

Ending inventory = Current assets – quick assets
= $2,100,000 – $1,800,000
= $300,000

Once ending inventory is known, average inventory can be determined [($500,000 + $300,000) ÷ 2 = $400,000], and, finally, cost of sales can be calculated:

Cost of sales ÷ Average inventory = Inventory turnover
Cost of sales ÷ $400,000 = 8.0
Cost of sales = $400,000 × 8.0
= $3,200,000

   Answer (A) is incorrect. Doubling, rather than averaging, beginning and ending inventory results in $1,600,000. Answer (B) is incorrect. Using ending, rather than average, inventory results in $2,400,000. Answer (D) is incorrect. Summing, rather than averaging, beginning and ending inventory results in $6,400,000.

2. A company has $3 million per year in credit sales. The company's average day's sales outstanding is 40 days. Assuming a 360-day year, what is the company's average amount of accounts receivable outstanding?

A. $500,000

B. $333,333

C. $250,000

D. $75,000

Answer (B) is correct.
REQUIRED: Average accounts receivable outstanding.
DISCUSSION: Dividing $3 million of sales by 360 days results in an average of $8,333.33 per day. Multiplying the average daily sales by the 40 days outstanding results in $333,333.
Answer (A) is incorrect. Using 60 days outstanding results in $500,000. Answer (C) is incorrect. Using 30 days outstanding results in $250,000. Answer (D) is incorrect. Dividing sales by 40 days results in $75,000, which is a meaningless solution.

3. The difference between average and ending inventory is immaterial.

Current ratio	2.0
Quick ratio	1.5
Current liabilities	$120,000
Inventory turnover (based on cost of goods sold)	8 times
Gross profit margin	40%

Net sales for the year were

A. $800,000

B. $480,000

C. $1,200,000

D. $240,000

Answer (A) is correct.
REQUIRED: The net sales for the year.
DISCUSSION: Net sales can be calculated indirectly from the inventory turnover ratio and the other ratios given. If the current ratio is 2.0, and current liabilities are $120,000, current assets must be $240,000 (2.0 × $120,000). Similarly, if the quick ratio is 1.5, the total quick assets must be $180,000 (1.5 × $120,000). The only major difference between quick assets and current assets is that inventory is not included in the definition of quick assets. Consequently, ending inventory must be $60,000 ($240,000 – $180,000). The inventory turnover ratio (COGS ÷ average inventory) is 8. Thus, cost of goods sold must be 8 times average inventory, or $480,000, given no material difference between average and ending inventory. If the gross profit margin is 40%, the cost of goods sold percentage is 60%, cost of goods sold equals 60% of sales, and net sales must be $800,000 ($480,000 ÷ 60%).
Answer (B) is incorrect. Cost of goods sold is $480,000. Answer (C) is incorrect. The amount of $1,200,000 is based on a 60% gross profit margin. Answer (D) is incorrect. Current assets equal $240,000.

4. A change in credit policy has caused an increase in sales, an increase in discounts taken, a decrease in the amount of bad debts, and a decrease in the investment in accounts receivable. Based upon this information, the company's

A. Average collection period has decreased.

B. Percentage discount offered has decreased.

C. Accounts receivable turnover has decreased.

D. Working capital has increased.

Answer (A) is correct.
REQUIRED: The true statement about a change in credit policy that has resulted in greater sales and a reduction in accounts receivable.
DISCUSSION: An increase in discounts taken accompanied by declines in receivables balances and doubtful accounts all indicate that collections on the increased sales have been accelerated. Accordingly, the average collection period must have declined. The average collection period is a ratio calculated by dividing the number of days in a year (365) by the receivable turnover. Thus, the higher the turnover, the shorter the average collection period. The turnover increases when either sales (the numerator) increase, or receivables (the denominator) decrease. Accomplishing both higher sales and a lower receivables increases the turnover and results in a shorter collection period.
Answer (B) is incorrect. A decrease in the percentage discount offered provides no incentive for early payment. Answer (C) is incorrect. Accounts receivable turnover (sales ÷ average receivables) has increased. Answer (D) is incorrect. No information is given relative to working capital elements other than receivables. Both receivables and cash are elements of working capital, so an acceleration of customer payments will have no effect on working capital.

Questions 5 and 6 are based on the following information. The year-end financial statements for Queen Bikes reflect the data presented as follows. Ten percent of Queen's net sales are in cash.

	Year 1	Year 2	Year 3
Net sales	1,500 units at $100	1,200 units at $100	1,200 units at $125
Ending inventory	100 units at $50	100 units at $50	100 units at $50
Average receivables	$12,500	$12,000	$14,400
Net income	$18,750	$ 9,400	$26,350

5. Queen's inventory turnover ratios for Year 2 and Year 3 are

A. 24 and 24, respectively.

B. 12 and 18, respectively.

C. 12 and 12, respectively.

D. 18 and 18, respectively.

Answer (C) is correct.
   REQUIRED: The inventory turnover for Year 2 and Year 3 using cost of sales as the basis.
   DISCUSSION: The cost of the 1,200 units sold in Year 2 at $50 each would have been $60,000. Dividing the $60,000 cost of sales by the $5,000 average inventory results in a turnover of 12. The 1,200 units sold in Year 3 also would have cost $60,000 and the turnover would again be 12.
   Answer (A) is incorrect. Using sales dollars as the basis, turnover was 24 in Year 2. Answer (B) is incorrect. Turnover for Year 2 and Year 3 was 12 ($60,000 COGS ÷ $5,000 average inventory). Answer (D) is incorrect. Turnover for Year 2 and Year 3 was 12 ($60,000 COGS ÷ $5,000 average inventory).

6. Queen's receivables turnover ratios for Year 2 and Year 3 are

A. 10.8 and 9.0, respectively.

B. 9.0 and 9.375, respectively.

C. 10.00 and 10.42, respectively.

D. 1.00 and 1.04, respectively.

Answer (B) is correct.
   REQUIRED: The receivables turnover ratios for Year 2 and Year 3.
   DISCUSSION: The receivables turnover ratio equals net credit sales divided by average accounts receivables. For Year 2 the calculation is [($120,000 × .9) ÷ $12,000] = 9.0, and for Year 3 it is [($150,000 × .9) ÷ $14,400] = 9.375.
   Answer (A) is incorrect. The ratios for Years 1 and 2 are 10.8 and 9.0. Answer (C) is incorrect. The ratios 10.00 and 10.42 are derived by incorrectly using 100% of net sales as the denominator instead of 90%. Answer (D) is incorrect. The ratios 1.00 and 1.04 are derived by incorrectly using 10% of net sales as the denominator instead of 90%.

7. A C corporation computed the following items from its financial records for the current year:

Current ratio	2 to 1
Inventory turnover	54 days
Accounts receivable turnover	24 days
Current liabilities turnover	36 days

The number of days in the operating cycle for the current year was

A. 60

B. 90

C. 78

D. 42

Answer (C) is correct.
   REQUIRED: The number of days in the operating cycle.
   DISCUSSION: The operating cycle is the time needed to turn cash into inventory, inventory into receivables, and receivables back into cash. It is equal to the sum of the number of days' sales in inventory and the number of days' sales in receivables. The number of days' sales in inventory is given as 54 days. The number of days' sales in receivables is given as 24. Therefore, the number of days in the operating cycle is 78 (54 + 24).
   Answer (A) is incorrect. The sum of the number of days' sales in receivables and the number of days' purchases in accounts payable is 60. Answer (B) is incorrect. The sum of the number of days' sales in inventory and the number of days' purchases in payables is 90. Answer (D) is incorrect. The sum of the number of days' sales in inventory and the number of days' sales in receivables minus the number of days' purchases in payables is 42.

8. Accounts receivable turnover ratio will normally decrease as a result of

- A. The write-off of an uncollectible account (assume the use of the allowance for doubtful accounts method).
- B. A significant sales volume decrease near the end of the accounting period.
- C. An increase in cash sales in proportion to credit sales.
- D. A change in credit policy to lengthen the period for cash discounts.

Answer (D) is correct.
  REQUIRED: The event that will cause the accounts receivable turnover ratio to decrease.
  DISCUSSION: The accounts receivable turnover ratio equals net credit sales divided by average receivables. Hence, it will decrease if a company lengthens the credit period or the discount period because the denominator will increase as receivables are held for longer times.
  Answer (A) is incorrect. Write-offs do not reduce net receivables (gross receivables – the allowance) and will not affect the receivables balance and therefore the turnover ratio if an allowance system is used. Answer (B) is incorrect. A decline in sales near the end of the period signifies fewer credit sales and receivables, and the effect of reducing the numerator and denominator by equal amounts is to increase the ratio if the fraction is greater than 1.0. Answer (C) is incorrect. An increase in cash sales with no decrease in credit sales will not affect receivables.

9. The days' sales in receivables ratio will be understated if the company

- A. Uses a natural business year for its accounting period.
- B. Uses a calendar year for its accounting period.
- C. Uses average receivables in the ratio calculation.
- D. Does not use average receivables in the ratio calculation.

Answer (A) is correct.
  REQUIRED: The reason the days' sales in receivables ratio will be understated.
  DISCUSSION: The days' sales in receivables ratio equals the days in the year divided by the receivables turnover ratio (sales ÷ average receivables). Days' sales may also be computed based only on ending receivables. In either case, use of the natural business year tends to understate the ratio because receivables will usually be at a low point at the beginning and end of the natural year. For example, a ski resort may close its books on May 31, a low point in its operating cycle.
  Answer (B) is incorrect. Using a calendar year will not necessarily affect the usefulness of the days' sales ratio. Answer (C) is incorrect. Using average receivables would not always understate the ratio. The ratio could be higher or lower depending on changes in sales volume or the percentage of credit to cash sales, or other factors. Answer (D) is incorrect. The ratio could be higher or lower depending on changes in sales volume or the percentage of credit to cash sales, or other factors.

10. A firm has a current ratio of 2.5 and a quick ratio of 2.0. If the firm experienced $2 million in cost of sales and sustains an inventory turnover of 8.0, what are the firm's current assets?

- A. $1,000,000
- B. $500,000
- C. $1,500,000
- D. $1,250,000

Answer (D) is correct.
  REQUIRED: The total of current assets.
  DISCUSSION: The only major difference between the current ratio and the quick ratio is the inclusion of inventory in the numerator. If cost of sales is $2 million and inventory turns over 8 times per year, then average inventory is $250,000 ($2,000,000 ÷ 8). Since the only difference between the two ratios is inventory, inventory must equal .5 (2.5 – 2.0) times current liabilities; therefore, current liabilities are $500,000. Thus, current assets divided by $500,000 equals 2.5. Therefore, current assets must equal $1,250,000 (2.5 × $500,000).
  Answer (A) is incorrect. The amount of quick assets is $1,000,000. Answer (B) is incorrect. The amount of current liabilities is $500,000. Answer (C) is incorrect. Adding inventory to current assets results in $1,500,000.

11. The selected data pertain to a company at December 31:

Quick assets	$ 208,000
Acid test ratio	2.6 to 1
Current ratio	3.5 to 1
Net sales for the year	$1,800,000
Cost of sales for the year	$ 990,000
Average total assets for the year	$1,200,000

The company's asset turnover ratio for the year is

A. .675

B. .825

C. 1.21

D. 1.50

Answer (D) is correct.
   REQUIRED: The asset turnover ratio for the year.
   DISCUSSION: The asset turnover ratio equals $1,800,000 of net sales divided by $1,200,000 of average total assets. The asset turnover ratio is therefore equal to 1.5.

Question 12 is based on the following information.
A company sells 10,000 skateboards a year at $66 each. All sales are on credit, with terms of 3/10, net 30, that is, a 3% discount if payment is made within 10 days; otherwise full payment is due at the end of 30 days. One half of the customers are expected to take advantage of the discount and pay on day 10. The other half are expected to pay on day 30. Sales are expected to be uniform throughout the year for both types of customers.

---

12. What is the expected average collection period for the company?

A. 5 days.

B. 10 days.

C. 15 days.

D. 20 days.

Answer (D) is correct.
   REQUIRED: The average collection period.
   DISCUSSION: The average collection period is the average time it takes to receive payment from customers. Because one-half of the customers will pay on day 10 and half will pay on day 30, the average collection period is 20 days [0.5(10 days) + 0.5(30 days)].
   Answer (A) is incorrect. Assuming half of the customers pay on day 10 but ignoring the remaining customers results in 5 days. Answer (B) is incorrect. Assuming all customers take the discount results in 10 days. Answer (C) is incorrect. The amount of 15 days assumes half of the customers pay on day 30 but ignores the remaining half of the customers who pay on day 10.

13. A high sales-to-working-capital ratio could indicate

A. Unprofitable use of working capital.

B. Sales are not adequate relative to available working capital.

C. The firm is undercapitalized.

D. The firm is not susceptible to liquidity problems.

Answer (C) is correct.
   REQUIRED: The meaning of a high sales-to-working-capital ratio.
   DISCUSSION: A high sales-to-working-capital ratio is usually favorable because working capital, by itself, is an unprofitable use of resources. A firm does not earn money by holding cash, inventory, or receivables. Such assets should be minimized. However, a high ratio of sales to working capital may indicate either very high sales (a good situation) or a low supply of working capital (a potentially bad situation). Thus, a high ratio could indicate that a firm is undercapitalized and does not have the resources to invest in working capital.
   Answer (A) is incorrect. A high ratio means low levels of working capital compared to sales. The firm may be using its current assets effectively. Answer (B) is incorrect. A high ratio means low levels of working capital compared to sales. The firm may be using its current assets effectively. Answer (D) is incorrect. A high ratio may indicate insufficient working capital to support the company's sales level, with resulting liquidity problems.

14. To determine the operating cycle for a retail department store, which one of the following pairs of items is needed?

A. Days' sales in accounts receivable and average merchandise inventory.

B. Cash turnover and net sales.

C. Accounts receivable turnover and inventory turnover.

D. Asset turnover and return on sales.

Answer (C) is correct.
   REQUIRED: The pair of items needed to determine the operating cycle for a retailer.
   DISCUSSION: The operating cycle is the time needed to turn cash into inventory, inventory into receivables, and receivables back into cash. For a retailer, it is the time from purchase of inventory to collection of cash. Thus, the operating cycle of a retailer is equal to the sum of the number of days' sales in inventory and the number of days' sales in receivables. Inventory turnover equals cost of goods sold divided by average inventory. The days' sales in inventory equals 365 (or another period chosen by the analyst) divided by the inventory turnover. Accounts receivable turnover equals net credit sales divided by average receivables. The days' sales in receivables equals 365 (or other number) divided by the accounts receivable turnover.
   Answer (A) is incorrect. Cost of sales must be known to calculate days' sales in inventory. Answer (B) is incorrect. These items are insufficient to permit determination of the operating cycle. Answer (D) is incorrect. These items are insufficient to permit determination of the operating cycle.

7.2 Short-Term Financing

15. Which one of the following provides a spontaneous source of financing for a firm?

A. Accounts payable.

B. Mortgage bonds.

C. Accounts receivable.

D. Debentures.

Answer (A) is correct.
   REQUIRED: The item that provides a spontaneous source of financing.
   DISCUSSION: Trade credit is a spontaneous source of financing because it arises automatically as part of a purchase transaction. Because of its ease in use, trade credit is the largest source of short-term financing for many firms both large and small.
   Answer (B) is incorrect. Mortgage bonds and debentures do not arise automatically as a result of a purchase transaction. Answer (C) is incorrect. The use of receivables as a financing source requires an extensive factoring arrangement and often involves the creditor's evaluation of the credit ratings of the borrower's customers. Answer (D) is incorrect. Mortgage bonds and debentures do not arise automatically as a result of a purchase transaction.

16. If a firm purchases materials from its supplier on a 2/10, net 40, cash discount basis, the equivalent annual interest rate (using a 360-day year) of forgoing the cash discount and making payment on the 40th day is

A. 2%

B. 18.36%

C. 24.49%

D. 36.72%

Answer (C) is correct.
   REQUIRED: The equivalent annual interest charge for not taking the discount.
   DISCUSSION: The buyer could satisfy the $100 obligation by paying $98 on the 10th day. By choosing to wait until the 40th day, the buyer is effectively paying a $2 interest charge for the use of $98 for 30 days (40-day credit period – 10-day discount period). The annualized cost of not taking this discount can be calculated as follows:

$$\frac{Discount\ \%}{100\% - Discount\ \%} \times \frac{Days\ in\ year}{Total\ payment\ period - Discount\ period}$$

Cost of not taking discount = [2% ÷ (100% – 2%)] ×
          [360 days ÷ (40 days – 10 days)]
    = (2% ÷ 98%) × (360 days ÷ 30 days)
    = 2.0408% × 12
    = 24.49%

   Answer (A) is incorrect. The figure of 2% is the discount rate. Answer (B) is incorrect. The figure of 18.36% is based on the 40-day credit period. Answer (D) is incorrect. The figure of 36.72% is based on a 20-day credit period.

17. If a retailer's terms of trade are 3/10, net 45 with a particular supplier, what is the cost on an annual basis of **not** taking the discount? Assume a 360-day year.

A. 24.00%

B. 37.11%

C. 36.00%

D. 31.81%

Answer (D) is correct.

   REQUIRED: The cost of not taking a discount when the terms are 3/10, net 45.

   DISCUSSION: If the gross amount of the invoice is $1,000, the buyer will pay $970 [$1,000 × (1.0 – .03)] if (s)he takes the discount. If (s)he does not, (s)he will pay $30 for the use of $970 for up to an additional 35 days. The percentage cost of not taking the discount is the annualized interest rate, that is, the $30 cost divided by the $970 effectively borrowed for 35 days, multiplied by the number of 35-day periods in a 360-day year. Thus, the cost of forgoing the discount is 31.81% [($30 ÷ $970) × (360 ÷ 35)]. The annualized cost of not taking a discount is calculated with this formula:

$$\frac{Discount\ \%}{100\% - Discount\ \%} \times \frac{Days\ in\ year}{Total\ payment\ period - Discount\ period}$$

Cost of not taking discount = [3% ÷ (100% – 3%)] × [360 days ÷ (45 days – 10 days)]
= (3% ÷ 97%) × (360 days ÷ 35 days)
= 3.0928% × 10.29
= 31.81%

   Answer (A) is incorrect. The figure of 24.00% assumes payment of $20 to borrow $1,000 for 30 days. Answer (B) is incorrect. The figure of 37.11% assumes terms of 3/10, net 40. Answer (C) is incorrect. The figure of 36.00% assumes payment of $30 to borrow $1,000 for 30 days.

18. Which one of the following financial instruments generally provides the largest source of short-term credit for small firms?

A. Installment loans.

B. Commercial paper.

C. Trade credit.

D. Bankers' acceptances.

Answer (C) is correct.

   REQUIRED: The largest source of short-term credit for small firms.

   DISCUSSION: Trade credit is a spontaneous source of financing because it arises automatically as part of a purchase transaction. Because of its ease in use, trade credit is the largest source of short-term financing for many firms both large and small.

   Answer (A) is incorrect. Installment loans are usually a longer-term source of financing and are more difficult to acquire than trade credit. Answer (B) is incorrect. Commercial paper is normally used only by large companies with high credit ratings. Answer (D) is incorrect. Bankers' acceptances are drafts drawn on bank deposits; the acceptance is a guarantee of payment at maturity, not a source of credit.

19. Which one of the following statements concerning cash discounts is **correct**?

A. The cost of not taking a 2/10, net 30 cash discount is usually less than the prime rate.

B. With trade terms of 2/15, net 60, if the discount is not taken, the buyer receives 45 days of free credit.

C. The cost of not taking the discount is higher for terms of 2/10, net 60 than for 2/10, net 30.

D. The cost of not taking a cash discount is generally higher than the cost of a bank loan.

Answer (D) is correct.

   REQUIRED: The true statement about cash discounts.

   DISCUSSION: Payments should be made within the discount periods if the cost of not taking discounts exceeds the firm's cost of capital. For example, failing to take a discount when terms are 2/10, net 30 means that the firm is paying an effective annual interest rate exceeding 36%. Thus, the cost of not taking a discount is usually higher than the cost of a bank loan.

   Answer (A) is incorrect. The cost of not taking a discount when terms are 2/10, net 30 exceeds 36% annually, which is higher than the prime rate has ever been. Answer (B) is incorrect. The buyer is paying the amount of discount not taken in exchange for the extra 45 days of credit. Answer (C) is incorrect. Paying 2% for 20 days of credit is more expensive than paying 2% for 50 days of the same amount of credit.

20. Which one of the following responses is **not** an advantage to a corporation that uses the commercial paper market for short-term financing?

- A. This market provides more funds at lower rates than other methods provide.

- B. The borrower avoids the expense of maintaining a compensating balance with a commercial bank.

- C. There are no restrictions as to the type of corporation that can enter into this market.

- D. This market provides a broad distribution for borrowing.

Answer (C) is correct.
REQUIRED: The item not an advantage of using commercial paper for short-term financing.
DISCUSSION: Commercial paper is a short-term, unsecured note payable issued in large denominations by major companies with excellent credit ratings. Maturities usually do not exceed 270 days. Commercial paper is a lower cost source of funds than bank loans, and no compensating balances are required. Commercial paper provides a broad and efficient distribution of debt, and costly financing arrangements are avoided. But the market is not open to all companies because only major corporations with high credit ratings can participate.
Answer (A) is incorrect. Lower rates are an advantage of commercial paper. Answer (B) is incorrect. Avoidance of compensating balance requirements is an advantage of commercial paper. Answer (D) is incorrect. Broad debt distribution is an advantage of commercial paper.

21. Commercial paper

- A. Has a maturity date greater than 1 year.

- B. Is usually sold only through investment banking dealers.

- C. Ordinarily does not have an active secondary market.

- D. Has an interest rate lower than Treasury bills.

Answer (C) is correct.
REQUIRED: The true statement about commercial paper.
DISCUSSION: Commercial paper is an unsecured note that is sold by only the most creditworthy firms. It is issued at a discount from its face amount and has a term of 270 days or less. Commercial paper usually has a lower interest rate than other means of financing. No general (active) secondary market exists for commercial paper, but most dealers will repurchase an issue that they have sold.
Answer (A) is incorrect. Commercial paper usually has a maturity date of 270 days or less to avoid securities registration requirements. Answer (B) is incorrect. Commercial paper is often issued directly by the borrowing firm. Answer (D) is incorrect. Interest rates must be higher than those of Treasury bills to entice investors. Commercial paper is more risky than Treasury bills.

22. The following forms of short-term borrowing are available to a firm:

- Floating lien
- Factoring
- Revolving credit
- Chattel mortgages
- Bankers' acceptances
- Lines of credit
- Commercial paper

The forms of short-term borrowing that are unsecured credit are

- A. Floating lien, revolving credit, chattel mortgage, and commercial paper.

- B. Factoring, chattel mortgage, bankers' acceptances, and line of credit.

- C. Floating lien, chattel mortgage, bankers' acceptances, and line of credit.

- D. Revolving credit, bankers' acceptances, line of credit, and commercial paper.

Answer (D) is correct.
REQUIRED: The forms of short-term borrowing that are unsecured credit.
DISCUSSION: An unsecured loan is a loan made by a bank based on credit information about the borrower and the ability of the borrower to repay the obligation. The loan is not secured by collateral but is made on the signature of the borrower. Revolving credit, bankers' acceptances, lines of credit, and commercial paper are all unsecured means of borrowing.
Answer (A) is incorrect. A chattel mortgage is a loan secured by personal property (movable property such as equipment or livestock). Also, a floating lien is secured by property, such as inventory, the composition of which may be constantly changing. Answer (B) is incorrect. A chattel mortgage is a loan secured by personal property (movable property such as equipment or livestock). Also, factoring is a form of financing in which receivables serve as security. Answer (C) is incorrect. A chattel mortgage is a loan secured by personal property (movable property such as equipment or livestock). Also, a floating lien is secured by property, such as inventory, the composition of which may be constantly changing.

Questions 23 and 24 are based on the following information. Morton Company needs to pay a supplier's invoice of $50,000 and wants to take a cash discount of 2/10, net 40. The firm can borrow the money for 30 days at 12% per annum plus a 10% compensating balance.

23. The amount Morton Company must borrow to pay the supplier within the discount period and cover the compensating balance is

A. $55,000

B. $55,056

C. $55,556

D. $54,444

Answer (D) is correct.
REQUIRED: The amount to borrow to pay the supplier within the discount period and cover the compensating balance requirement.
DISCUSSION: Morton's total borrowings can be calculated as follows:

Total borrowings = Amount needed ÷
(1.0 – Compensating balance %)
= ($50,000 × 98%) ÷ (100% – 10%)
= $49,000 ÷ 90%
= $54,444

Answer (A) is incorrect. The amount of $55,000 is 110% of the invoice. Answer (B) is incorrect. This amount is a nonsense answer. Answer (C) is incorrect. The amount of $55,556 assumes no cash discount.

24. Assuming Morton Company borrows the money on the last day of the discount period and repays it 30 days later, the effective interest rate on the loan is

A. 12.00%

B. 13.33%

C. 13.20%

D. 13.48%

Answer (B) is correct.
REQUIRED: The effective interest rate on the loan.
DISCUSSION: Morton's effective rate on this loan can be calculated as follows:

Effective rate = Stated rate ÷ (1.0 – Compensating balance %)
= 12% ÷ (100% – 10%)
= 12% ÷ 90%
= 13.33%

Answer (A) is incorrect. This percentage is the contract rate. Answer (C) is incorrect. This percentage assumes that the company has access to loan funds of $50,000 and is calculated by determining interest based on a loan total of $55,000. Answer (D) is incorrect. This percentage is calculated by determining interest on a loan amount of $55,056.

25. On January 1, a C corporation received a $300,000 line of credit at an interest rate of 12% from a bank and drew down the entire amount on February 1. The line of credit agreement requires that an amount equal to 15% of the loan be deposited into a compensating balance account. What is the effective annual cost of credit for this loan arrangement?

A. 11.00%

B. 12.00%

C. 12.94%

D. 14.12%

Answer (D) is correct.
REQUIRED: The effective annual cost of credit.
DISCUSSION: The effective interest rate on this financing arrangement can be calculated as follows:

Effective rate = Stated rate ÷ (1.0 – Compensating balance %)
= 12% ÷ (100% – 15%)
= 12% ÷ 85%
= 14.12%

The amount of the loan is not needed to calculate the effective rate.

Answer (A) is incorrect. The nominal rate for 11 months is 11.00%. Answer (B) is incorrect. The nominal rate of interest is 12.00%. Answer (C) is incorrect. This percentage equals $33,000 (11 months of interest) divided by $255,000.

Questions 26 and 27 are based on the following information. Skilantic Company needs to pay a supplier's invoice of $60,000 and wants to take a cash discount of 2/10, net 40. The firm can borrow the money for 30 days at 11% per annum plus a 9% compensating balance.

26. The amount Skilantic must borrow to pay the supplier within the discount period and cover the compensating balance is

A. $60,000

B. $65,934

C. $64,615

D. $58,800

Answer (C) is correct.

REQUIRED: The amount the company must borrow to pay the supplier within the discount period and cover the compensating balance requirement.

DISCUSSION: Skilantic's total borrowings on this loan can be calculated as follows:

$$
\begin{aligned}
\text{Total borrowings} &= \text{Amount needed} \div \\
&\quad (1.0 - \text{Compensating balance \%}) \\
&= (\$60{,}000 \times 98\%) \div (100\% - 9\%) \\
&= \$58{,}800 \div 91\% \\
&= \$64{,}615
\end{aligned}
$$

Answer (A) is incorrect. The amount of $60,000 is the invoice amount. Answer (B) is incorrect. The amount of $65,934 assumes the amount paid to the supplier is $60,000. Answer (D) is incorrect. The amount of $58,800 is the amount to be paid to the supplier.

27. Assuming Skilantic borrows the money on the last day of the discount period and repays it 30 days later, the effective interest rate on the loan is

A. 11%

B. 10%

C. 12.09%

D. 9.90%

Answer (C) is correct.

REQUIRED: The effective interest rate when a company borrows to take a discount when the terms are 2/10, net 40.

DISCUSSION: Skilantic's effective rate on this loan can be calculated as follows:

$$
\begin{aligned}
\text{Effective rate} &= \text{Stated rate} \div (1.0 - \text{Compensating balance \%}) \\
&= 11\% \div (100\% - 9\%) \\
&= 11\% \div 91\% \\
&= 12.09\%
\end{aligned}
$$

Answer (A) is incorrect. This percentage is the contract rate. Answer (B) is incorrect. The effective rate is greater than the contract rate. The usable funds are less than the face amount of the note. Answer (D) is incorrect. The effective rate is greater than the contract rate. The usable funds are less than the face amount of the note.

28. With respect to the use of commercial paper by an industrial firm, which one of the following statements is most likely to be **true**?

A. The commercial paper is issued through a bank.

B. The commercial paper has a maturity of 60-270 days.

C. The commercial paper is secured by the issuer's assets.

D. The commercial paper issuer is a small company.

Answer (B) is correct.

REQUIRED: The statement most likely to be true with respect to the use of commercial paper.

DISCUSSION: Most commercial paper has a maturity of between 60 and 270 days.

Answer (A) is incorrect. Large corporations with high credit ratings, not banks, issue commercial paper. Answer (C) is incorrect. Commercial paper consists of unsecured notes payable issued in large denominations ($100,000 or more). Answer (D) is incorrect. Commercial paper is issued by large companies with high credit ratings to other companies and institutional investors.

29. Which one of the following statements about trade credit is **correct**? Trade credit is

A. Not an important source of financing for small firms.

B. A source of long-term financing to the seller.

C. Subject to risk of buyer default.

D. Usually an inexpensive source of external financing.

Answer (C) is correct.
    REQUIRED: The true statement about trade credit.
    DISCUSSION: Trade credit is a spontaneous source of financing because it arises automatically as part of a purchase transaction. The terms of payment are set by the supplier, but trade credit usually requires payment within a short period of time. Trade credit is an important source of credit for all businesses but especially for buyers, such as small businesses, that might not have access to other credit markets. Like all forms of financing, trade credit is subject to the risk of buyer default.
    Answer (A) is incorrect. Trade credit is an important source of financing for small firms. Answer (B) is incorrect. Trade credit is ordinarily a short-term source of financing. Answer (D) is incorrect. The cost of trade credit depends on the credit terms and the price paid. A seller with generous payment terms may charge a higher price for its merchandise.

7.3 Long-Term Financing

30. A major use of warrants in financing is to

A. Lower the cost of debt.

B. Avoid dilution of earnings per share.

C. Maintain managerial control.

D. Permit the buy-back of bonds before maturity.

Answer (A) is correct.
    REQUIRED: The major use of warrants in financing.
    DISCUSSION: Warrants are long-term options that give holders the right to buy common stock in the future at a specific price. If the market price goes up, the holders of warrants will exercise their rights to buy stock at the special price. If the market price does not exceed the exercise price, the warrants will lapse. Issuers of debt sometimes attach stock purchase warrants to debt instruments as an inducement to investors. The investor then has the security of fixed-return debt plus the possibility for large gains if stock prices increase significantly. If warrants are attached, debt can sell at an interest rate slightly lower than the market rate.
    Answer (B) is incorrect. Outstanding warrants dilute earnings per share. They are included in the denominator of the EPS calculation even if they have not been exercised. Answer (C) is incorrect. Warrants can, if exercised, result in a dilution of management's holdings. Answer (D) is incorrect. A call provision in a bond indenture, not the use of warrants, permits the buyback of bonds.

Access the **Gleim CMA Premium Review System** from your Gleim Personal Classroom to continue your studies with exam-emulating multiple-choice questions!

7.4 ESSAY QUESTIONS

Scenario for Essay Questions 1, 2

The accounting staff of CCB Enterprises has completed the preparation of financial statements for Fiscal Year 5. The Statement of Income for the current year and the Comparative Statement of Financial Position for Year 5 and Year 4 are reproduced below and on the next page.

The accounting staff calculates selected financial ratios after the financial statements are prepared. Average balance sheet account balances are used in computing ratios involving income statement accounts. Ending balance sheet account balances are used in computing ratios involving only balance sheet items. The ratios have not been calculated for Year 5. Financial ratios that were calculated for Year 4 and their respective values are as follows:

• Times interest earned	5.16 times
• Return on total assets	12.5%
• Return on operating assets	20.2%
• Return on common stockholders' equity	29.1%

CCB Enterprises
Statement of Income
Year Ended December 31, Year 5
($000 omitted)

Revenue:		
Net sales	$800,000	
Other	60,000	
Total revenue		$860,000
Expenses:		
Cost of goods sold	$540,000	
Research and development	25,000	
Selling and administrative	155,000	
Interest	20,000	
Total expenses		(740,000)
Income before income taxes		$120,000
Income taxes		(48,000)
Net income		$ 72,000

```
                              CCB Enterprises
                   Comparative Statement of Financial Position
                         December 31, Year 5 and Year 4
                                ($000 omitted)
```

Assets	Year 5	Year 4
Current assets:		
Cash and short-term investments	$ 26,000	$ 21,000
Receivables, less allowance for doubtful accounts		
($1,100 in Year 5 and $1,400 in Year 4)	48,000	50,000
Inventories, at lower of FIFO cost or market	65,000	62,000
Prepaid items and other current assets	5,000	3,000
Total current assets	$144,000	$136,000
Other assets:		
Investments, at cost	$106,000	$106,000
Deposits	10,000	8,000
Total other assets	$116,000	$114,000
Property, plant, and equipment:		
Land	$ 12,000	$ 12,000
Buildings and equipment, less accumulated		
depreciation ($126,000 in Year 5 and $122,000 in Year 4)	268,000	248,000
Total property, plant, and equipment	$280,000	$260,000
Total assets	$540,000	$510,000
Liabilities and Stockholders' Equity		
Current liabilities:		
Short-term loans	$ 22,000	$ 24,000
Accounts payable	72,000	71,000
Salaries, wages, and other	26,000	27,000
Total current liabilities	$120,000	$122,000
Long-term debt:	160,000	171,000
Total liabilities	$280,000	$293,000
Stockholders' equity:		
Common stock, at par	$ 44,000	$ 42,000
Paid-in capital in excess of par	64,000	61,000
Total paid-in capital	$108,000	$103,000
Retained earnings	152,000	114,000
Total stockholders' equity	$260,000	$217,000
Total liabilities and stockholders' equity	$540,000	$510,000

Questions

1. Explain how the use of financial ratios can be advantageous to management.

2. Calculate the following financial ratios for Year 5 for CCB Enterprises (round your answer to three decimal places):

    a. Times interest earned
    b. Receivables turnover ratio
    c. Inventory turnover
    d. Days' sales in inventory
    e. Total debt ratio
    f. Total debt/equity ratio
    g. Current ratio
    h. Quick (acid test) ratio

Essay Questions 1, 2 — Unofficial Answers

1. Financial ratios relate financial statement line items to each other. By calculating standardized ratios, management can assess the firm's liquidity, financial activity, solvency, and profitability. Management can also compare the firm's performance to that of others in its industry.

2. Year 5 financial ratios:

   a. Times interest earned = Earnings before interest and taxes (EBIT) ÷ Interest expense
      = ($120,000 + $20,000) ÷ $20,000
      = 7 times

   b. Receivables turnover ratio = Net credit sales ÷ Average receivables
      = $800,000 ÷ [($48,000 + $50,000) ÷ 2]
      = $800,000 ÷ $49,000
      = 16.327 times

   c. Inventory turnover ratio = Cost of goods sold ÷ Average inventory
      = $540,000 ÷ [($65,000 + $62,000) ÷ 2]
      = $540,000 ÷ $63,500
      = 8.504 times

   d. Days' sales in inventory = Days in year ÷ Inventory turnover ratio
      = 365 days ÷ 8.504
      = 42.921 days

   e. Total debt ratio = Total liabilities ÷ Total assets
      = $280,000 ÷ $540,000
      = 0.519
      = 51.9%

   f. Total debt to equity ratio = Total liabilities ÷ Total stockholders' equity
      = $280,000 ÷ $260,000
      = 1.08

   g. Current ratio = Current assets ÷ Current liabilities
      = $144,000 ÷ $120,000
      = 1.2

   h. Quick (acid test) ratio = (Cash + Marketable securities + Net receivables) ÷ Current liabilities
      = ($26,000 + $48,000) ÷ $120,000
      = 0.617

 Access the **Gleim CMA Premium Review System** from your Gleim Personal Classroom to continue your studies with exam-emulating essay questions!

STUDY UNIT EIGHT
INVESTMENT DECISIONS

(19 pages of outline)

Investment Decisions

Management accountants must be able to help management analyze decisions. This involves making cash flow estimates, calculating the time value of money, and being able to apply discounted cash flow concepts, such as net present value and internal rate of return. Non-discounting analysis techniques are also covered on the CMA exam, as are the income tax implications for investment decision analysis. Candidates will also be tested on such things as ranking investment projects, performing risk analysis, and evaluating real options.

This study unit is on **investment decisions**. The relative weight assigned to this major topic in Part 2 of the exam is **15%**.

If you are interested in reviewing more introductory or background material, go to www.gleim.com/CMAIntroVideos for a list of suggested third-party overviews of this topic. The following Gleim outline material is more than sufficient to help you pass the CMA exam; any additional introductory or background material is for your own personal enrichment.

8.1 THE CAPITAL BUDGETING PROCESS

1. **Capital Budgeting**

    a. Capital budgeting is the process of identifying, analyzing, and selecting investments in long-term projects. It is this long-term aspect of capital budgeting that presents the management accountant with specific challenges.

       1) By their nature, capital projects affect multiple accounting periods and will constrain the organization's financial planning well into the future. Once made, capital budgeting decisions tend to be relatively inflexible, unless real options exist (real options are covered in Subunit 8.2).

       2) An **opportunity cost** is the maximum benefit forgone by using a scarce resource for a given purpose and not for the next-best alternative.

          a) In capital budgeting, the most basic application of this concept is the desire to invest the company's limited funds in the most promising capital project(s).

    b. Capital budgeting applications include

       1) Buying equipment
       2) Building facilities
       3) Acquiring a business
       4) Developing a product or product line
       5) Expanding into new markets

    c.   A firm must accurately forecast future changes in demand in order to have the necessary production capacity when demand for its product is strong, without having excess idle capacity when demand slackens.

    d.   Planning is crucial because of possible changes in capital markets, inflation, interest rates, and the money supply.

    e.   As with every other business decision, the tax consequences of a new investment (and possible disinvestment of a replaced asset) must be considered.

        1)   All capital budgeting decisions need to be evaluated on an after-tax basis because taxes may affect decisions differently. Companies that operate in multiple tax jurisdictions may find the decision process more complex. Another possibility is that special tax concessions may be negotiated for locating an investment in a given locale.

2.   **Types of Costs Considered in Capital Budgeting Analysis**

NOTE: These costs are also covered in Study Unit 10, Subunit 1.

    a.   **Relevant** costs differ among alternatives.

        1)   Relevant costs are **avoidable** and may be eliminated by ceasing an activity or by improving efficiency.

        2)   An **incremental** cost is the increase in total cost resulting from selecting one option instead of another.

    b.   **Irrelevant costs** do not vary between different alternatives and therefore do not affect the decision.

        1)   A **sunk cost** cannot be avoided because it occurred in the past.

            a)   A sunk cost is irrelevant because it has already been incurred and cannot be changed.

            b)   An example is the amount of money already spent on manufacturing equipment.

        2)   A **committed cost** is a cost that will be incurred in the future due to previously made decisions.

            a)   An example is a future lease payment in a long-term lease.

3.   **The Stages in Capital Budgeting**

    a.   Identification and definition. Those projects and programs that are needed to attain the entity's objectives are identified and defined.

        1)   For example, a firm that wishes to be the low-cost producer in its industry will be interested in investing in more efficient manufacturing machinery. A company that wishes to quickly expand into new markets will look at acquiring another established firm.

        2)   Defining the projects and programs determines their extent and facilitates cost, revenue, and cash flow estimation.

            a)   This stage is the most difficult.

    b.   Search. Potential investments are subjected to a preliminary evaluation by representatives from each function in the entity's value chain.

        1)   Dismal projects are dismissed at this point, while others are passed on for further evaluation.

    c.   Information-acquisition. The costs and benefits of the projects that passed the search phase are enumerated.

        1)   Quantitative financial factors are given the most scrutiny at this point.

            a)   These include initial investment and periodic cash inflow.

2) Nonfinancial measures, both quantitative and qualitative, are also identified and addressed.

a) Examples include the need for additional training on new equipment and higher customer satisfaction based on improved product quality.

b) Also, uncertainty about technological developments, demand, competitors' actions, governmental regulation, and economic conditions should be considered.

d. Selection. Employing one of the selection models (net present value, internal rate of return, etc.) and relevant nonfinancial measures, the project(s) that will increase shareholder value by the greatest margin is (are) chosen for implementation.

e. Financing. Sources of funds for selected projects are identified. These can come from the company's operations, the issuance of debt, or the sale of the company's stock.

f. Implementation and monitoring. Once projects are underway, they must be kept on schedule and within budgetary constraints.

1) This step also involves determining whether previously unforeseen problems or opportunities have arisen and what changes in plans are appropriate.

4. **Steps in Ranking Potential Investments**

a. Capital budgeting requires choosing among investment proposals. Thus, a ranking procedure for such decisions is needed. The following are steps in the ranking procedure:

1) **Determine the asset cost or net investment.**

a) The net investment is the net outlay, or gross cash requirement, minus cash recovered from the trade or sale of existing assets, with any necessary adjustments for applicable tax consequences. Cash outflows in subsequent periods also must be considered.

b) Moreover, the investment required includes funds to provide for increases in net working capital, for example, the additional receivables and inventories resulting from the acquisition of a new manufacturing plant. This change in net working capital is treated as an initial cost of the investment (a cash outflow) that will be recovered at the end of the project (i.e., the salvage value is equal to the initial cost).

2) **Calculate estimated cash flows**, period by period, using the acquired assets.

a) Reliable estimates of cost savings or revenues are necessary.

b) Net cash flow is the economic benefit or cost, period by period, resulting from the investment.

c) Economic life is the time period over which the benefits of the investment proposal are expected to be obtained, as distinguished from the physical or technical life of the asset involved.

d) Depreciable life is the period used for accounting and tax purposes over which cost is to be systematically and rationally allocated. It is based upon permissible or standard guidelines and may have no particular relevance to economic life. Because depreciation is deductible for income tax purposes, thereby shielding some revenue from taxation, depreciation gives rise to a depreciation tax shield.

3) **Relate the cash-flow benefits to their cost** by using one of several methods to evaluate the advantage of purchasing the asset.

4) **Rank the investments.**

    a) A firm's **hurdle rate** is the minimum rate of return on a project or investment that an investor is willing to accept.

        i) The riskier the project, the higher the hurdle rate.

        ii) The lower the firm's discount rate, the lower the acceptable hurdle rate.

        iii) A common pitfall in capital budgeting is the tendency to use the company's current rate of return as the hurdle rate. This can lead to rejecting projects that should be accepted.

5. **Cash Flows**

    a. Relevant cash flows are a much more reliable guide when judging capital projects because only they provide a true measure of a project's potential to affect shareholder value.

        1) The relevant cash flows can be divided into the following three categories:

            a) **Net initial investment**

                i) Cost of new equipment
                ii) Initial working capital requirements
                iii) After-tax proceeds from disposal of old equipment

            b) **Annual net cash flows**

                i) After-tax cash collections from operations (excluding depreciation effect)
                ii) Tax savings from depreciation deductions (depreciation tax shield)

            c) **Project termination cash flows**

                i) After-tax proceeds from disposal of new equipment
                ii) Recovery of working capital (untaxed)

EXAMPLE

A company is determining the relevant cash flows for a potential capital project. The company has a 40% tax rate.

1) **Net initial investment:**

    a) The project will require an initial outlay of $500,000 for new equipment.

    b) The company expects to commit $12,000 of working capital for the duration of the project in the form of increased accounts receivable and inventories.

    c) Calculating the after-tax proceeds from disposal of the existing equipment is a two-step process.

        i) First, the tax gain or loss is determined.

Disposal value	$ 5,000
Less: Tax basis	(20,000)
Tax-basis loss on disposal	**$(15,000)**

        ii) The after-tax effect on cash can then be calculated.

Disposal value	$ 5,000
Add: Tax savings on loss ($15,000 × .40)	6,000
After-tax cash inflow from disposal	**$11,000**

    d) The cash outflow required for this project's net initial investment is therefore $(501,000) [$(500,000) + $(12,000) + $11,000].

-- Continued on next page --

EXAMPLE -- Continued

2) **Annual net cash flows:**

    a) The project is expected to generate $100,000 annually from ongoing operations.

        i) However, 40% of this will have to be paid out in the form of income taxes.

Annual cash collections	$100,000
Less: Income tax expense ($100,000 × .40)	(40,000)
After-tax cash inflow from operations	**$ 60,000**

    b) The project is slated to last 8 years.

        i) The new equipment is projected to have a salvage value of $50,000 and will generate $62,500 per year in depreciation charges ($500,000 ÷ 8). The annual savings is $25,000 [($62,500 – $0) × .40].

        NOTE: On the CMA exam, salvage value is never subtracted when calculating the depreciable base for tax purposes because this is a provision allowed by U.S. tax laws.

        ii) Unlike the income from operations, the depreciation charges will generate a tax savings. This is referred to as the **depreciation tax shield**.

    c) The annual net cash inflow from the project is thus $85,000 ($60,000 + $25,000) for the last 8 years.

3) **Project termination cash flows:**

    a) Proceeds of $50,000 are expected from disposal of the new equipment at the end of the project.

        i) First, the tax gain or loss is determined.

Disposal value	$50,000
Less: Tax basis	0
Tax-basis gain on disposal	**$50,000**

        ii) The after-tax effect on cash can then be calculated.

Tax basis gain on disposal	$50,000
Less: Tax liability on gain ($50,000 × .40)	(20,000)
After-tax cash inflow from disposal	**$30,000**

    b) Once the project is over, the company will recover the $12,000 of working capital it committed to the project.

    c) The net cash inflow upon project termination is therefore $42,000 ($30,000 + $12,000).

---

    b. As the example above indicates, tax considerations are essential when considering capital projects.

6. **Other Considerations**

    a. Effects of inflation on capital budgeting.

        1) In an inflationary environment, future dollars are worth less than today's dollars. Thus, the firm will require a higher rate of return to compensate.

    b. Post-audits should be conducted to serve as a control mechanism and to deter managers from proposing unprofitable investments.

        1) Actual-to-expected cash flow comparisons should be made, and unfavorable variances should be explained. The reason may be an inaccurate forecast or implementation problems.

        2) Individuals who supplied unrealistic estimates should have to explain differences. Knowing that a post-audit will be conducted may cause managers to provide more realistic forecasts in the future.

        3) The temptation to evaluate the outcome of a project too early must be overcome. Until all cash flows are known, the results can be misleading.

        4) Assessing the receipt of expected nonquantitative benefits is inherently difficult.

Stop and review! You have completed the outline for this subunit. Study multiple-choice questions 1 through 6 beginning on page 258.

8.2 RISK ANALYSIS AND REAL OPTIONS

1. **Risk analysis** attempts to measure the likelihood of the variability of future returns from the proposed capital investment. The following techniques are frequently used to analyze or account for risk:

   a. **Informal method.** NPVs are calculated at the firm's desired rate of return, and the possible projects are individually reviewed. If the NPVs are relatively close for two mutually exclusive projects, the apparently less risky project is chosen.

   b. **Risk-adjusted discount rates.** The discount rate of a capital investment is generally the company's cost of capital. However, when a capital investment is **more or less risky** than is normal for a company, its discount rate is adjusted accordingly. The discount rate is increased (above the company's cost of capital) for riskier projects, and decreased (below the company's cost of capital) for less risky projects. Thus, discounts rates may vary among capital investments depending on the company's cost of capital and the type of investment. Additionally, some investments may be accepted (rejected) with internal rates of return (IRR) that are less than (greater than) the company's cost of capital (IRR is covered in detail in Subunit 8.3).

   c. **Certainty equivalent adjustments.** This technique is directly drawn from the concept of utility theory. It forces the decision maker to specify at what point the firm is indifferent to the choice between a certain sum of money and the expected value of a risky sum. The technique is not frequently used because decision makers are not familiar with the concept.

   d. **Simulation analysis.** This method represents a refinement of standard profitability theory. The computer is used to generate many examples of results based upon various assumptions. Project simulation is frequently expensive. Unless a project is exceptionally large and expensive, full-scale simulation is usually not worthwhile.

   e. **Sensitivity analysis.** Forecasts of many calculated NPVs under various assumptions are compared to see how sensitive NPV is to changing conditions. Changing the assumptions about a certain variable or group of variables may drastically alter the NPV. Thus, the asset may appear to be much riskier than was originally predicted. In summary, sensitivity analysis is simply an iterative process of recalculated returns based on changing assumptions.

   f. **Scenario analysis.** The profitability of a capital investment is analysed under various economic scenarios.

   g. The **Monte Carlo Simulation** is used to generate the probability distribution of all possible outcomes from a capital investment.

      1) The performance of a quantitative model under uncertainty may be investigated by randomly selecting values for each of the variables in the model (based on the probability distribution of each variable) and then calculating the value of the solution. This process is performed a large number of times.

2. **Real options** are options to modify the capital investment.

   a. Real options are not measurable with the same accuracy as financial options because the formulas applicable to the latter may not be appropriate for the former. Thus, other methods, e.g., decision-tree analysis with recognition of probabilities and outcomes and simulations, are used in conjunction with discounted cash flow methods.

   b. Management accountants should be able to determine what real options are embedded in a project, to measure their value, and to offer advice about structuring a project to include such options. The following are among the types of real options:

      1) **Abandonment** of a project entails selling its assets or employing them in an alternative project. Abandonment should occur when, as a result of an ongoing evaluation process, the entity determines that the abandonment value of a new or existing project exceeds the NPV of the project's future cash flows.

2) The option to **delay** allows the option holder to postpone implementation of the project without losing the opportunity.

   a) The option holder should pay attention to costs and benefits as they change.

3) The option to **expand** allows the option holder to move forward with or expand a project after the initial stage has been implemented.

   a) This allows a firm to expand its operation in the future at little or no cost.

4) The option to **scale back** allows the option holder to shrink a project after the initial stage has been implemented.

5) The flexibility option to vary inputs, for example, by switching fuels.

6) The capacity option to vary output, for example, to respond to economic conditions by raising or lowering output or by temporarily shutting down.

7) The option to enter a new geographical market, for example, in a market where NPV is apparently negative but the follow-up investment option is promising.

8) The new product option, for example, the opportunity to sell a complementary or a next-generation product even though the initial product is unprofitable.

c. Qualitative considerations. Although real options may often not be readily quantifiable, adding them to a project is always a consideration because doing so is frequently inexpensive and the potential risk reduction is great.

   1) The option is usually more valuable the later it is exercised, the more variable the underlying risk, or the higher the level of interest rates.

3. **Risk Tolerance and the Certainty Equivalent**

   a. Risk tolerance is the acceptable degree of variability in returns.

      1) A company with a high risk tolerance is willing to risk big losses for the chance at big gains.

      2) A company with a low risk tolerance will avoid seeking big gains in order to avoid the possibility of big losses.

   b. The certainty equivalent is the guaranteed return that a company would accept over taking a risk on a higher, but uncertain return.

      1) The certainty equivalent specifies at what point the company is indifferent to the choice between a certain sum of money and the expected value of a risky investment.

Stop and review! You have completed the outline for this subunit. Study multiple-choice question 7 on page 260.

8.3 DISCOUNTED CASH FLOW ANALYSIS

CMA candidates can expect a variety of questions that will require the use of either Present Value or Future Value tables. The CMA exam will provide the necessary data to answer the question either within the given information of the question itself or through the Time Value tables. The Gleim online courses will familiarize you with how to use these tables on the actual exam by providing the necessary data within the question and by providing an emulation of how to access the Present/Future Value tables.

1. **Time Value of Money**

   a. A dollar received in the future is worth less than a dollar received today. Thus, when analyzing capital projects, the management accountant must discount the relevant cash flows using the time value of money.

   b. A quantity of money to be received or paid in the future is worth less than the same amount now. The difference is measured in terms of interest calculated using the appropriate discount rate.

2.   **Present and Future Value**

    a.   Standard tables have been developed to facilitate the calculation of present and future values. Each entry in one of these tables represents the factor by which any monetary amount can be modified to obtain its present or future value.

    b.   The **present value (PV) of a single amount** is the value today of some future payment.

        1)   It equals the future payment times the present value of 1 (a factor found in a standard table) for the given number of periods and interest rate.

EXAMPLE

Present Value

No. of Periods	6%	8%	10%
1	0.943	0.926	0.909
2	0.890	0.857	0.826
3	0.840	0.794	0.751
4	0.792	0.735	0.683
5	0.747	0.681	0.621

The present value of $1,000, to be received in 3 years and discounted at 8%, is $794 ($1,000 × 0.794).

---

    c.   The **future value (FV) of a single amount** is the amount available at a specified time in the future based on a single investment (deposit) today. The FV is the amount to be computed if one knows the present value and the appropriate discount rate.

        1)   It equals the current payment times the future value of 1 (a factor found in a standard table) for the given number of periods and interest rate.

EXAMPLE

Future Value

No. of Periods	6%	8%	10%
1	1.0600	1.0800	1.1000
2	1.1236	1.1664	1.2100
3	1.1910	1.2597	1.3310
4	1.2625	1.3605	1.4641
5	1.3382	1.4693	1.6105

The future value of $1,000 invested today for 4 years at 10% interest will be $1,464 ($1,000 × 1.464).

---

    d.   **Annuities**

        1)   An annuity is usually a series of equal payments at equal intervals of time, e.g., $1,000 at the end of every year for 10 years.

            a)   An **ordinary annuity (annuity in arrears)** is a series of payments occurring at the end of each period.

                i)   The first payment of an ordinary annuity is discounted.
                ii)   Interest is not earned for the first period of an ordinary annuity.

            b)   An **annuity due (annuity in advance)** is a series of payments at the beginning of each period.

                i)   The first payment of an annuity due is not discounted.
                ii)   Interest is earned on the first payment of an annuity due.

EXAMPLE

No. of Periods	Present Value		
	6%	8%	10%
1	0.943	0.926	0.909
2	1.833	1.783	1.736
3	2.673	2.577	2.487
4	3.465	3.312	3.170
5	4.212	3.993	3.791

To calculate the present value of an **ordinary annuity** of four payments of $1,000 each discounted at 10%, multiply $1,000 by the appropriate factor ($1,000 × 3.170 = $3,170).

Using the same table, the present value of an **annuity due** of four payments of $1,000 each also may be calculated. This value equals $1,000 times the factor for one less period (4 − 1 = 3), increased by 1.0. Thus, the present value of the annuity due for four periods at 10% is $3,487 [$1,000 × (2.487 + 1.0)].

The present value of the annuity due ($3,487) is greater than the present value of the ordinary annuity ($3,170) because the payments occur 1 year sooner.

c) The FV of an annuity is the value that a series of equal payments will have at a certain moment in the future if interest is earned at a given rate.

EXAMPLE

No. of Periods	Future Value		
	6%	8%	10%
1	1.0000	1.0000	1.0000
2	2.0600	2.0800	2.1000
3	3.1836	3.2464	3.3100
4	4.3746	4.5061	4.6410
5	5.6371	5.8667	6.1051

To calculate the FV of a 3-year **ordinary annuity** with payments of $1,000 each at 6% interest, multiply $1,000 by the appropriate factor ($1,000 × 3.184 = $3,184).

The FV of an **annuity due** also may be determined from the same table. Multiply the $1,000 payment by the factor for one additional period (3 + 1 = 4) decreased by 1.0 (4.375 − 1.0 = 3.375) to arrive at a FV of $3,375 ($1,000 × 3.375).

The future value of the annuity due ($3,375) is greater than the future value of an ordinary annuity ($3,184). The deposits are made earlier.

3. **Net Present Value**

   a. The net present value (NPV) method expresses a project's return in **dollar terms**.

      1) NPV nets the expected cash flows (inflows and outflows) related to a project, then discounts them at the hurdle rate, also called the desired rate of return.

         a) If the NPV of a project is positive, the project is desirable because it has a higher rate of return than the company's desired rate.

2)   EXAMPLE:

a)   The company discounts the relevant net cash flows using a hurdle rate of 6% (its desired rate of return).

Period	Net Cash Flow	6% PV Factor	Discounted Cash Flows
Initial Investment	$(501,000)	1.00000	$(501,000)
Year 1	77,000	0.94340	72,642
Year 2	77,000	0.89000	68,530
Year 3	77,000	0.83962	64,651
Year 4	77,000	0.79209	60,991
Year 5	85,000	0.74726	63,517
Year 6	85,000	0.70496	59,922
Year 7	85,000	0.66506	56,530
Year 8	101,800	0.62741	63,870
Net Present Value			**$ 9,653**

b)   Because the project has net present value > $0, it is profitable given the company's hurdle rate.

4.   **Internal Rate of Return**

a.   The internal rate of return (IRR) expresses project's return in **percentage terms**.

1)   The IRR of an investment is the discount rate at which the investment's NPV equals zero. In other words, it is the rate that makes the present value of the expected cash inflows equal the present value of the expected cash outflows.

a)   If the IRR is higher than the company's desired rate of return, then the investment is desirable.

2)   EXAMPLE:

a)   Using the same relevant cash flows as above, the NPV using a 7% discount rate is as follows:

Period	Net Cash Flow	7% PV Factor	Discounted Cash Flows
Initial Investment	$(501,000)	1.00000	$(501,000)
Year 1	77,000	0.93458	71,963
Year 2	77,000	0.87344	67,255
Year 3	77,000	0.81630	62,855
Year 4	77,000	0.76290	58,743
Year 5	85,000	0.71299	60,604
Year 6	85,000	0.66634	56,639
Year 7	85,000	0.62275	52,934
Year 8	101,800	0.58201	59,249
Net Present Value			**$ (10,758)**

b)   The higher discount rate (6% to 7%) causes the NPV to become negative. Thus, the IRR of this project is somewhere around 6.5%.

i)   Because the company's desired rate of return is 6%, the project should be accepted, the same decision that was arrived at using the net present value method.

5. **Pitfalls of IRR**

a. IRR used in isolation is seldom the best route to a sound capital budgeting decision. The following factors reduce the usefulness of IRR:

1) **Direction of cash flows.** When the direction of the cash flows changes, focusing simply on IRR can be misleading.

a) EXAMPLE: Below are the net cash flows for two potential capital projects.

	Initial	**Period 1**
Project X	$(222,240)	$240,000
Project Y	222,240	(240,000)

i) The cash flow amounts are the same in absolute value, but the directions differ. In choosing between the two, a decision maker might be tempted to select the project that has a cash inflow earlier and a cash outflow later.

b) The IRR for both projects is 8%, which can be proved as follows:

Project X	Project Y
$(222,240) × 1.000 = $(222,240)	$222,240 × 1.000 = $ 222,240
240,000 × 0.926 = 222,240	(240,000) × 0.926 = $(222,240)
$ 0	$ 0

c) Discounting the cash flows at the company's hurdle rate of 6% reveals a different picture.

Project X	Project Y
$(222,240) × 1.000 = $(222,240)	$222,240 × 1.000 = $ 222,240
240,000 × 0.943 = 226,320	(240,000) × 0.943 = (226,320)
$ 4,080	$ (4,080)

i) It turns out that, given a hurdle rate lower than the rate at which the two projects have the same return, the project with the positive cash flow earlier is by far the less desirable of the two.

ii) Clearly, a decision maker can be seriously misled if (s)he uses the simple direction of the cash flows as the tiebreaker when two projects have the same IRR.

d) An investment will have multiple IRRs if there are changes in the direction of net cash flows.

i) This effect is known as the multiple IRR problem.

2) **Mutually exclusive projects.** As with changing cash flow directions, focusing only on IRR when capital is limited can lead to unsound decisions.

a) EXAMPLE: Below are the cash flows for two potential capital projects.

	Initial	**Period 1**	**IRR**
Project S	$(178,571)	$200,000	12%
Project T	(300,000)	330,000	10%

b) If capital is available for only one project, using IRR alone would suggest that Project S be selected.

c)   Once again, however, discounting both projects' net cash flows at the company's hurdle rate suggests a different decision.

Project S	Project T
$(178,571) × 1.000 = $(178,571)	$(300,000) × 1.000 = $(300,000)
200,000 × 0.943 = 188,600	330,000 × 0.943 = 311,190
$ 10,029	**$ 11,190**

  i)   While Project S has the distinction of giving the company a higher IRR, Project T is in fact preferable because it adds more to shareholder value.

3)   **Varying rates of return.** A project's NPV can easily be determined using different desired rates of return for different periods. The IRR is limited to a single summary rate for the entire project.

4)   **Multiple investments.** NPV amounts from different projects can be added, but IRR rates cannot. The IRR for the whole is not the sum of the IRRs for the parts.

6.   **Comparing Cash Flow Patterns**

a.   Often a decision maker must choose between two mutually exclusive projects, one whose inflows are higher in the early years but fall off drastically later and one whose inflows are steady throughout the project's life.

  1)   The higher a firm's hurdle rate, the more quickly a project must pay off.
  2)   Firms with low hurdle rates prefer a slow and steady payback.

b.   EXAMPLE: Consider the net cash flows of the following two projects:

	Initial	Year 1	Year 2	Year 3	Year 4
Project K	$(200,000)	$140,000	$100,000	–	–
Project L	(200,000)	65,000	65,000	$65,000	$65,000

  1)   A graphical representation of the two projects at various discount rates helps to illustrate the factors a decision maker must consider in such a situation.

NPV Profiles

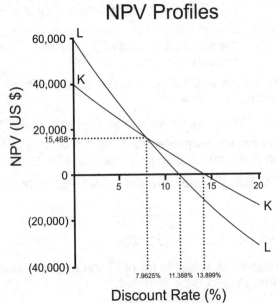

Discount Rate (%)

Figure 8-1

c.   The NPV profile can be of great practical use to managers trying to make investment decisions. It gives the manager a clear insight into the following questions:

1)   How sensitive is a project's profitability to changes in the discount rate?

a)   At a hurdle rate of exactly 7.9625%, a decision maker is indifferent between the two projects. The net present value of both is $15,468 at that discount rate.

b)   At hurdle rates below 7.9625%, the project whose inflows last longer into the future is the better investment (L).

c)   At hurdle rates above 7.9625%, the project whose inflows are "front-loaded" is the better choice (K).

2)   At what discount rates is an investment project still a profitable opportunity?

a)   At any hurdle rate above 13.899%, Project K loses money. This is its IRR, i.e., the rate at which its NPV = $0 (Project L's is 11.388%).

7.   **Comparing NPV and IRR**

a.   The reinvestment rate becomes critical when choosing between the NPV and IRR methods. NPV assumes the cash flows from the investment can be reinvested at the project's discount rate, that is, the desired rate of return.

b.   The NPV and IRR methods give the same accept/reject decision if projects are independent. Independent projects have unrelated cash flows. Hence, all acceptable independent projects can be undertaken.

c.   If one of two or more mutually exclusive projects is accepted, the others must be rejected.

1)   The NPV and IRR methods may rank mutually exclusive projects differently if

a)   The cost of one project is greater than the cost of another.

b)   The timing, amounts, and directions of cash flows differ among projects.

c)   The projects have different useful lives.

d)   The cost of capital or desired rate of return varies over the life of a project. The NPV can easily be determined using different desired rates of return for different periods. The IRR determines one rate for the project.

e)   Multiple investments are involved in a project. NPV amounts are addable, but IRR rates are not. The IRR for the whole is not the sum of the IRRs for the parts.

2)   The IRR method assumes that the cash flows will be reinvested at the internal rate of return.

a)   If the project's funds are not reinvested at the IRR, the ranking calculations obtained may be in error.

b)   The NPV method gives a better grasp of the problem in many decision situations because the reinvestment is assumed to be in the desired rate of return.

EXAMPLE

Project	Initial Cost	Year-End Cash Flow	IRR	NPV (k = 10%)
A	$1,000	$1,200	20%	$91
B	$ 50	$ 100	100%	$41

- IRR preference ordering: B, A
- NPV preference ordering: A, B
- When choosing between mutually exclusive projects, the ranking differences between NPV and IRR become very important. In the example, a firm using IRR would accept B and reject A. A firm using NPV would make exactly the opposite choice.

d. NPV and IRR are the soundest investment rules from a shareholder wealth maximization perspective.

e. The problem can be seen more clearly using a net present value profile. The NPV profile is a plot of a project's NPV at different discount rates. The NPV is plotted on the vertical axis and the rate of return (k) on the horizontal axis.

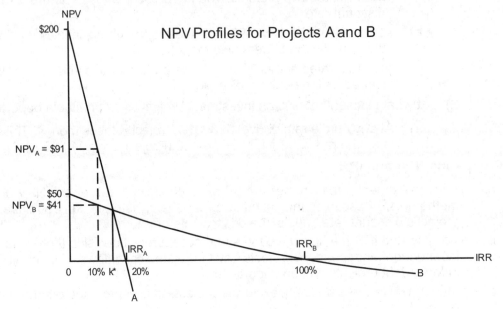

Figure 8-2

f. The manager concerned with shareholder wealth maximization should choose the project with the greatest NPV, not the largest IRR.

1) IRR is a percentage measure of wealth, but NPV is an absolute measure.

Stop and review! You have completed the outline for this subunit. Study multiple-choice questions 8 through 14 beginning on page 260.

8.4 PAYBACK AND DISCOUNTED PAYBACK

1. The traditional **payback period** is the number of years required to return the original investment, that is, the time necessary for a new asset to pay for itself. Note that no accounting is made for the time value of money under this method.

a. Companies using the payback method set a maximum length of time within which projects must pay for themselves to be considered acceptable.

b. **If the cash flows are constant**, the formula is

$$Payback\ period = \frac{Initial\ net\ investment}{Annual\ expected\ cash\ flow}$$

1) EXAMPLE: A project is being considered that will require an outlay of $200,000 immediately and will return a steady cash flow of $52,000 for the next 4 years. The company requires a 4-year payback period on all capital projects.

a) Payback period = $200,000 ÷ $52,000 = 3.846 years

b) The project's payback period is less than the company's maximum, and the project is thus acceptable.

c. **If the cash flows are not constant**, the calculation must be in cumulative form.

1) EXAMPLE: Instead of the smooth inflows predicted on the previous page, the project's cash stream is expected to vary. The payback period is calculated as follows:

End of Year	Cash Inflow	Remaining Initial Investment
Year 0	$ 0	$200,000
Year 1	48,000	152,000
Year 2	54,000	98,000
Year 3	54,000	44,000
Year 4	42,000	2,000

a) At the end of 4 years, the original investment has still not been recovered, so the project is rejected.

d. The advantage of the payback method is its simplicity.

1) To some extent, the payback period measures risk. The longer the period, the more risky the investment.

2) The payback method provides a rough indication of a project's liquidity. The longer the period, the less liquid the investment.

e. The disadvantages of the payback method include

1) Disregarding all cash inflows after the payback cutoff date.

2) Disregarding the time value of money. Weighting all cash inflows equally ignores the fact that money has a cost.

2. The **discounted payback method**, also called breakeven time, is sometimes used to overcome the second disadvantage (above) of the basic payback method.

a. The net cash flows in the denominator are discounted to calculate the period required to recover the initial investment.

Period	Cash Inflow	6% PV Factor	Discounted Cash Flow	Remaining Initial Investment
Initial Investment	$ 0	1.00000	$ 0	$200,000
Year 1	48,000	0.94340	45,283	154,717
Year 2	54,000	0.89000	48,060	106,657
Year 3	54,000	0.83962	45,339	61,318
Year 4	42,000	0.79209	33,268	28,050

1) After 4 years, the project is much further from paying off than under the basic method.

2) Clearly then, this is a **more conservative** technique than the traditional payback method.

b. The discounted payback method's advantage is that it acknowledges the time value of money.

1) Its disadvantages are that it loses the simplicity of the basic payback method and still ignores cash flows after the arbitrary cutoff date.

c. The discounted payback method can also be used to calculate the **breakeven time**, which is the period required for the discounted cumulative cash inflows on a project to equal the discounted cumulative cash outflows (usually but not always the initial cost).

1) Thus, it is the time necessary for the present value of the discounted cash flows to equal zero. This period begins at the outset of a project, not when the initial cash outflow occurs.

3. **Other Payback Methods**

    a. The **bailout payback method** incorporates the salvage value of the asset into the calculation. It measures the length of the payback period when the periodic cash inflows are combined with the salvage value.

    b. The **payback reciprocal** (1 ÷ payback) is sometimes used as an estimate of the internal rate of return.

Stop and review! You have completed the outline for this subunit. Study multiple-choice questions 15 through 20 beginning on page 262.

8.5 RANKING INVESTMENT PROJECTS

1. **Capital rationing** exists when a firm sets a limit on the amount of funds to be invested during a given period. In such situations, a firm cannot afford to undertake all profitable projects.

    a. Another way of stating this is that the firm cannot invest the entire amount needed to fund its theoretically optimal capital budget.

        1) Only those projects that will return the greatest NPV for the limited capital available in the internal capital market can be undertaken.

    b. Reasons for capital rationing include

        1) A lack of nonmonetary resources (e.g., managerial or technical personnel)

        2) A desire to control estimation bias (overly favorable projections of a project's cash flows)

        3) An unwillingness to issue new equity (e.g., because of its cost or a reluctance to reveal data in regulatory filings)

2. The **profitability index** (or excess present value index) is a method for ranking projects to ensure that limited resources are placed with the investments that will return the highest NPV.

$$\text{Profitability index} = \frac{\text{PV of future cash flows}}{\text{Net investment}}$$

    a. If the profitability index is **greater than 1**, the project should be accepted.

        1) If the profitability index is greater than 1, the required rate of return must be less than the IRR.

    b. If the profitability index is **less than 1**, the project should be rejected.

        1) If the profitability index is less than 1, the required rate of return must be higher than the IRR.

    c. EXAMPLE: A company has $200,000 to invest. It can therefore either invest in Project F or in Projects G and H.

	Initial	Year 1	Year 2	Year 3	Year 4
Project F	$(200,000)	$140,000	$100,000	-	-
Project G	(88,950)	30,000	30,000	$30,000	$30,000
Project H	(88,440)	30,000	28,000	28,000	34,000

1) Discounting each project at 6% results in the following:

	NPV	Divided by: Initial Investment	Equals: Profitability Index
Project F	$21,020	$200,000	0.105
Project G	15,000	88,950	0.169
Project H	15,218	88,440	0.172

2) In an environment of capital rationing, the company can see that it should invest first in Project H, then in Project G, and, if new funding is found, last in Project F.

NOTE: On the CMA exam, the numerator of the profitability index may be calculated in one of two ways: (1) as the net present value of all cash flows or (2) as the present value only of cash inflows. If the net of all cash flows is used, the profitability index will be less than 1. If only the future net cash inflows are used, that is, if the initial investment is excluded, the profitability index will be greater than 1. The calculation of the numerator does not affect the choice of the most profitable project.

d. The NPV method and profitability index result in the same project selection.

3. **Internal capital market** is a way of referring to the provision of funds by one division of a firm to another division. A division operating in a mature industry that generates a lot of cash can provide funding to another division that is in the cash-hungry development stage.

a. An advantage is the avoidance of stock issue costs or interest costs on new debt.

b. A disadvantage is that calling it a "market" is somewhat misleading. The dynamics of the process are more akin to centralized planning and budgeting than to the workings of a free marketplace.

4. **Linear programming** is a technique (now usually computerized) for optimizing resource allocations so as to select the most profitable or least costly way to use available resources.

a. It involves optimizing an objective function subject to the net of constraint equations.

b. For example, a linear programming application can maximize NPV for a group of projects in a capital rationing situation (expenditure constraint).

Stop and review! You have completed the outline for this subunit. Study multiple-choice questions 21 through 26 beginning on page 264.

8.6 COMPREHENSIVE EXAMPLES OF INVESTMENT DECISIONS

CMA candidates will be expected to have an understanding of how to calculate net present value (NPV) and internal rate of return (IRR) as well as be able to identify the criteria used to compare, evaluate, and recommend capital projects. You should also have an understanding of how these methods are affected by independent versus mutually exclusive projects. Pay close attention to the requirements to recognize whether the projects are independent.

The two comprehensive examples in this subunit demonstrate the calculations for NPV, IRR, payback period, and the profitability index. Review these examples and then practice answering questions and test yourself on how these problems will be presented on the exam in both multiple-choice and essay questions. If you receive an essay question with a scenario requiring you to provide any or all of these calculations, be prepared to show your work in the answer box utilizing the word processing tools.

1. EXAMPLE: Hazman Company plans to replace an old piece of equipment that is obsolete and expected to be unreliable under the stress of daily operations. The equipment is fully depreciated, and no salvage value can be realized upon its disposal. One piece of equipment being considered as a replacement will provide an annual cash savings of $7,000 before income taxes and without regard to the effect of depreciation. The equipment costs $18,000 and has an estimated useful life of 5 years. No salvage value will be used for depreciation purposes because the equipment is expected to have no value at the end of 5 years.

    Hazman uses the straight-line depreciation method on all equipment for both book and tax purposes. Hence, annual depreciation is $3,600. The company is subject to a 40% tax rate. Hazman's desired rate of return is 14%, so it will use the 14% column from a present value table.

    Analysis of cash flows:

Annual cash savings	$ 7,000	
Less: Income taxes (40%)	(2,800)	
After-tax cash savings		$4,200
Historical cost of equipment	$18,000	
Divided by: Useful life	÷ 5	
Annual depreciation	$ 3,600	
Times: Tax rate	× 40%	
Depreciation tax shield		1,440
Annual after-tax cash inflows		$5,640

    a. **Net present value** = (After-tax cash flows × Present value of an annuity)
          − Net investment
        = ($5,640 × 3.43) − $18,000
        = $19,345 − $18,000
        = $1,345

    b. **Internal rate of return.** The goal is to find the discount rate that most nearly equals the net investment.

Net present value at 16% ($5,640 × 3.27)	$ 18,443
Net present value at 18% ($5,640 × 3.13)	(17,653)
Difference	$ 790
Net present value at 16%:	$ 18,443
Initial investment	(18,000)
Difference	$ 443
Estimated increment [($443 ÷ $790) × 2%]	1.1%
Rate used	+ 16.0%
Internal rate of return	17.1%

    c. **Payback period** = Net investment ÷ After-tax cash flow
        = $18,000 ÷ $5,640
        = 3.19 years

    d. **Profitability index** = PV of future cash flows ÷ Net investment
        = ($5,640 × 3.43) ÷ $18,000
        = $19,345 ÷ $18,000
        = 1.07

2.   EXAMPLE: The management of Flesher Farms is trying to decide whether to buy a new team of mules at a cost of $1,000 or a new tractor at a cost of $10,000. They will perform the same job. But because the mules require more laborers, the annual return is only $250 of net cash inflows. The tractor will return $2,000 of net cash inflows per year. The mules have a working life of 8 years, and the tractor has a working life of 10 years. Neither investment is expected to have a salvage value at the end of its useful life. Flesher Farms' desired rate of return is 6%.

a.   **Net Present Value**

	Mules	Tractor
Net cash inflows	$ 250	$ 2,000
Times: Present value factor	6.210	7.360
Present value	$1,553	$14,720
Minus: Initial investment	(1,000)	(10,000)
Net present value	$ 553	$ 4,720

b.   **Internal Rate of Return**

   1)   Mules: Initial investment ÷ Net cash inflows = $1,000 ÷ $250 = 4

      a)   On the 8-year line, a factor of 4 indicates a rate of return of approximately 18.7%.

   2)   Tractor: Initial investment ÷ Net cash inflows = $10,000 ÷ $2,000 = 5

      a)   On the 10-year line, a factor of 5 indicates a rate of return of approximately 15.2%.

c.   **Payback Period**

   1)   Mules: Initial investment ÷ Net cash inflows = $1,000 ÷ $250 = 4 years
   2)   Tractor: Initial investment ÷ Net cash inflows = $10,000 ÷ $2,000 = 5 years

d.   **Profitability Index**

   1)   Mules: Present value of cash inflows ÷ Initial investment = $1,553 ÷ $1,000
                                                                     = 1.553

   2)   Tractor: Present value of cash inflows ÷ Initial investment = $14,720 ÷ $10,000
                                                                       = 1.472

e.   The mule investment has the higher IRR, the quicker payback, and the better profitability index.

   1)   However, the tractor has the better net present value. The various methods thus give different answers to the investment question.

   2)   Either investment will be profitable. Management may decide to let noneconomic factors influence the decision.

      a)   For example, the mules will require the use of more laborers. If unemployment in the community is high, management might wish to achieve a social goal of providing more jobs.

      b)   Alternatively, a labor shortage might convince management to buy the tractor to reduce labor worries.

Stop and review! You have completed the outline for this subunit. Study multiple-choice questions 27 through 30 beginning on page 267.

QUESTIONS

8.1 The Capital Budgeting Process

1. In equipment-replacement decisions, which one of the following does **not** affect the decision-making process?

    A. Current disposal price of the old equipment.

    B. Operating costs of the old equipment.

    C. Original fair market value of the old equipment.

    D. Cost of the new equipment.

Answer (C) is correct.

    REQUIRED: The irrelevant factor when making an equipment replacement decision.

    DISCUSSION: All relevant costs should be considered when evaluating an equipment-replacement decision. These include the cost of the new equipment, the disposal price of the old equipment, and the operating costs of the old equipment versus the operating costs of the new equipment. The original cost or fair market value of the old equipment is a sunk cost and is irrelevant to future decisions.

2. The term that refers to costs incurred in the past that are **not** relevant to a future decision is

    A. Discretionary cost.

    B. Full absorption cost.

    C. Underallocated indirect cost.

    D. Sunk cost.

Answer (D) is correct.

    REQUIRED: The past costs not relevant to a future decision.

    DISCUSSION: A sunk cost cannot be avoided because it represents an expenditure that has already been made or an irrevocable decision to incur the cost.

    Answer (A) is incorrect. A discretionary cost is characterized by uncertainty about the input-output relationship; advertising and research are examples. Answer (B) is incorrect. Full absorption costing includes in production costs materials, labor, and both fixed and variable overhead. Answer (C) is incorrect. Underallocated indirect cost is a cost that has not yet been charged to production.

3. Of the following decisions, capital budgeting techniques would **least** likely be used in evaluating the

    A. Acquisition of new aircraft by a cargo company.

    B. Design and implementation of a major advertising program.

    C. Trade for a star quarterback by a football team.

    D. Adoption of a new method of allocating nontraceable costs to product lines.

Answer (D) is correct.

    REQUIRED: The decision least likely to be evaluated using capital budgeting techniques.

    DISCUSSION: Capital budgeting is the process of identifying, analyzing, and selecting projects on which the returns are expected to occur over a period of more than 1 year. Thus, capital budgeting concerns the acquisition or disposal of long-term assets and the financing ramifications of such decisions. The adoption of a new method of allocating nontraceable costs to product lines has no effect on a company's cash flows, does not concern the acquisition of long-term assets, and is not concerned with financing. Hence, capital budgeting is irrelevant to such a decision.

    Answer (A) is incorrect. A new aircraft represents a long-term investment in a capital good. Answer (B) is incorrect. A major advertising program is a high cost investment with long-term effects. Answer (C) is incorrect. A star quarterback is a costly asset who is expected to have a substantial effect on the team's long-term profitability.

Questions 4 through 6 are based on the following information. The Moore Corporation is considering the acquisition of a new machine. The machine can be purchased for $90,000; it will cost $6,000 to transport to Moore's plant and $9,000 to install. It is estimated that the machine will last 10 years, and it is expected to have an estimated salvage value of $5,000. Over its 10-year life, the machine is expected to produce 2,000 units per year, each with a selling price of $500 and combined material and labor costs of $450 per unit. Federal tax regulations permit machines of this type to be depreciated using the straight-line method over 5 years with no estimated salvage value. Moore has a marginal tax rate of 40%.

4. What is the net cash outflow at the beginning of the first year that Moore Corporation should use in a capital budgeting analysis?

A. $(85,000)

B. $(90,000)

C. $(96,000)

D. $(105,000)

Answer (D) is correct.
REQUIRED: The initial net cash outflow that should be used in a capital budgeting analysis.
DISCUSSION: Initially, the company must invest $105,000 in the machine, consisting of the invoice price of $90,000, the delivery costs of $6,000, and the installation costs of $9,000.
Answer (A) is incorrect. The amount of $(85,000) erroneously includes salvage value but ignores delivery and installation costs. Answer (B) is incorrect. The amount of $(90,000) ignores the outlays needed for delivery and installation costs, both of which are an integral part of preparing the new asset for use. Answer (C) is incorrect. The amount of $(96,000) fails to include installation costs in the total.

5. What is the net cash flow for the third year that Moore Corporation should use in a capital budgeting analysis?

A. $68,400

B. $68,000

C. $64,200

D. $79,000

Answer (A) is correct.
REQUIRED: The net cash flows for the third year that would be used in a capital budgeting analysis.
DISCUSSION: The company will receive net cash inflows of $50 per unit ($500 selling price – $450 of variable costs), or a total of $100,000 per year. This amount will be subject to taxation, but, for the first 5 years, there will be a depreciation deduction of $21,000 per year ($105,000 cost divided by 5 years). Therefore, deducting the $21,000 of depreciation expense from the $100,000 of contribution margin will result in taxable income of $79,000. After income taxes of $31,600 ($79,000 × 40%), the net cash flow in the third year is $68,400 ($100,000 – $31,600).
Answer (B) is incorrect. The amount of $68,000 deducts salvage value when calculating depreciation expense, which is not required by the tax law. Answer (C) is incorrect. The amount of $64,200 assumes depreciation is deducted for tax purposes over 10 years rather than 5 years. Answer (D) is incorrect. The amount of $79,000 is taxable income.

6. What is the net cash flow for the tenth year of the project that Moore Corporation should use in a capital budgeting analysis?

A. $100,000

B. $81,000

C. $68,400

D. $63,000

Answer (D) is correct.
REQUIRED: The net cash flow for the tenth year of the project that would be used in a capital budgeting analysis.
DISCUSSION: The company will receive net cash inflows of $50 per unit ($500 selling price – $450 of variable costs), or a total of $100,000 per year. This amount will be subject to taxation, as will the $5,000 gain on sale of the investment, bringing taxable income to $105,000. No depreciation will be deducted in the tenth year because the asset was fully depreciated after 5 years. Because the asset was fully depreciated (book value was zero), the $5,000 salvage value received would be fully taxable. After income taxes of $42,000 ($105,000 × 40%), the net cash flow in the tenth year is $63,000 ($105,000 – $42,000).
Answer (A) is incorrect. The amount of $100,000 overlooks the salvage proceeds and the taxes to be paid. Answer (B) is incorrect. The amount of $81,000 miscalculates income taxes. Answer (C) is incorrect. The amount of $68,400 assumes that depreciation is deducted; it also overlooks the receipt of the salvage proceeds.

8.2 Risk Analysis and Real Options

7. A large conglomerate with operating divisions in many industries uses risk-adjusted discount rates in evaluating capital investment decisions. Consider the following statements concerning the use of risk-adjusted discount rates.

I.   The conglomerate may accept some investments with internal rates of return less than the conglomerate's overall average cost of capital.

II. Discount rates vary depending on the type of investment.

III. The conglomerate may reject some investments with internal rates of return greater than the cost of capital.

IV. Discount rates may vary depending on the division.

Which of the above statements are **correct**?

   A. I and III only.

   B. II and IV only.

   C. II, III, and IV only.

   D. I, II, III, and IV.

Answer (D) is correct.
   REQUIRED: The true statement about use of risk-adjusted discount rates.
   DISCUSSION: Risk analysis attempts to measure the likelihood of the variability of future returns from the proposed capital investment. Risk can be incorporated into capital budgeting decisions in a number of ways, one of which is to use a risk-adjusted discount rate. A risk-adjusted discount rate is used when the capital investment is more or less risky than is normal for the company. This technique adjusts the interest rate used for discounting upward as an investment becomes riskier. The expected flow from the investment must be relatively larger, or the increased discount rate will generate a negative net present value, and the proposed acquisition will be rejected. Accordingly, the IRR (the rate at which the NPV is zero) for a rejected investment may exceed the cost of capital when the risk-adjusted rate is higher than the IRR. Conversely, the IRR for an accepted investment may be less than the cost of capital when the risk-adjusted rate is less than the IRR. In this case, the investment presumably has very little risk. Furthermore, risk-adjusted rates may also reflect the differing degrees of risk, not only among investments, but by the same investments undertaken by different organizational subunits.
   Answer (A) is incorrect. Discount rates may vary with the project or with the subunit of the organization. Answer (B) is incorrect. The company may accept some projects with IRRs less than the cost of capital or reject some project with IRRs greater than the cost of capital. Answer (C) is incorrect. The company may accept some projects with IRRs less than the cost of capital or reject some project with IRRs greater than the cost of capital.

8.3 Discounted Cash Flow Analysis

8. The net present value (NPV) method of investment project analysis assumes that the project's cash flows are reinvested at the

   A. Computed internal rate of return.

   B. Risk-free interest rate.

   C. Discount rate used in the NPV calculation.

   D. Firm's accounting rate of return.

Answer (C) is correct.
   REQUIRED: The rate at which the NPV method assumes early cash inflows are reinvested.
   DISCUSSION: The NPV method is used when the discount rate is specified. It assumes that cash flows from the investment can be reinvested at the particular project's discount rate.
   Answer (A) is incorrect. The internal rate of return method assumes that cash flows are reinvested at the internal rate of return. Answer (B) is incorrect. The NPV method assumes that cash flows are reinvested at the NPV discount rate. Answer (D) is incorrect. The NPV method assumes that cash flows are reinvested at the NPV discount rate.

Questions 9 through 12 are based on the following information.

The following data pertain to a 4-year project being considered by Metro Industries:

- A depreciable asset that costs $1,200,000 will be acquired on January 1. The asset, which is expected to have a $200,000 salvage value at the end of 4 years, qualifies as 3-year property under the Modified Accelerated Cost Recovery System (MACRS).

- The new asset will replace an existing asset that has a tax basis of $150,000 and can be sold on the same January 1 for $180,000.

- The project is expected to provide added annual sales of 30,000 units at $20. Additional cash operating costs are: variable, $12 per unit; fixed, $90,000 per year.

- A $50,000 working capital investment that is fully recoverable at the end of the fourth year is required.

Metro is subject to a 40% income tax rate and rounds all computations to the nearest dollar. Assume that any gain or loss affects the taxes paid at the end of the year in which it occurred. The company uses the net present value method to analyze investments and will employ the following factors and rates.

Period	Present Value of $1 at 12%	Present Value of $1 Annuity at 12%	MACRS
1	0.89	0.89	33%
2	0.80	1.69	45
3	0.71	2.40	15
4	0.64	3.04	7

9. The discounted cash flow for the fourth year MACRS depreciation on the new asset is

A. $0

B. $17,920

C. $21,504

D. $26,880

Answer (C) is correct.
   REQUIRED: The discounted cash flow for the fourth year MACRS depreciation deduction on the new asset.
   DISCUSSION: Tax law allows taxpayers to ignore salvage value when calculating depreciation under MACRS. Thus, the depreciation deduction is 7% of the initial $1,200,000 cost, or $84,000. At a 40% tax rate, the deduction will save the company $33,600 in taxes in the fourth year. The present value of this savings is $21,504 ($33,600 × 0.64 present value of $1 at 12% for four periods).
   Answer (A) is incorrect. A tax savings will result in the fourth year from the MACRS deduction. Answer (B) is incorrect. The amount of $17,920 is based on a depreciation calculation in which salvage value is subtracted from the initial cost. Answer (D) is incorrect. The appropriate discount factor for the fourth period is 0.64, not 0.80.

10. The discounted, net-of-tax amount that relates to disposal of the existing asset is

A. $150,000

B. $169,320

C. $180,000

D. $190,680

Answer (B) is correct.
   REQUIRED: The discounted, net-of-tax amount relating to the disposal of the existing asset.
   DISCUSSION: The cash inflow from the existing asset is $180,000, but that amount is subject to tax on the $30,000 gain ($180,000 – $150,000 tax basis). The tax on the gain is $12,000 ($30,000 × 40%). Because the tax will not be paid until year end, the discounted value is $10,680 ($12,000 × .89 PV of $1 at 12% for one period). Thus, the net-of-tax inflow is $169,320 ($180,000 – $10,680). NOTE: This asset was probably a Section 1231 asset, and any gain on sale qualifies for the special capital gain tax rates. Had the problem not stipulated a 40% tax rate, the capital gains rate would be used. An answer based on that rate is not among the options.
   Answer (A) is incorrect. The amount of $150,000 is the tax basis of the asset. Answer (C) is incorrect. The amount of $180,000 ignores the impact of income taxes. Answer (D) is incorrect. The discounted present value of the income taxes is an outflow and is deducted from the inflow from the sale of the asset.

11. The expected incremental sales will provide a discounted, net-of-tax contribution margin over 4 years of

A. $57,600

B. $92,160

C. $273,600

D. $437,760

Answer (D) is correct.
   REQUIRED: The expected net-of-tax contribution margin over 4 years.
   DISCUSSION: Additional annual sales are 30,000 units at $20 per unit. If variable costs are expected to be $12 per unit, the unit contribution margin is $8, and the total before-tax annual contribution margin is $240,000 (30,000 units × $8). The after-tax total annual contribution margin is $144,000 [$240,000 × (1.0 – .4)]. This annual increase in the contribution margin should be treated as an annuity. Thus, its present value is $437,760 ($144,000 × 3.04 PV of an annuity of $1 at 12% for four periods).
   Answer (A) is incorrect. The amount of $57,600 multiplies the annual increase in contribution margin by the tax rate instead of the PV factor. Answer (B) is incorrect. The amount of $92,160 is based on only 1 year's results, not 4. Answer (C) is incorrect. The amount of $273,600 improperly includes fixed costs in the calculation of the contribution margin.

12. Refer to the information on the preceding page(s). The overall discounted-cash-flow impact of the working capital investment on Metro's project is

A. $(2,800)

B. $(18,000)

C. $(50,000)

D. $(59,200)

Answer (B) is correct.
 REQUIRED: The overall discounted-cash-flow impact of the working capital investment.
 DISCUSSION: The working capital investment is treated as a $50,000 outflow at the beginning of the project and a $50,000 inflow at the end of 4 years. Accordingly, the present value of the inflow after 4 years should be subtracted from the initial $50,000 outlay. The overall discounted-cash-flow impact of the working capital investment is $18,000 [$50,000 – ($50,000 × .64 PV of $1 at 12% for four periods)].
 Answer (A) is incorrect. The firm will have its working capital tied up for 4 years, which results in a cost of $18,000 at 12% interest. Answer (C) is incorrect. The working capital investment is recovered at the end of the fourth year. Hence, the working capital cost of the project is the difference between $50,000 and the present value of $50,000 in 4 years. Answer (D) is incorrect. The answer cannot exceed $50,000, which is the amount of the cash outflow.

13. The rankings of mutually exclusive investments determined using the internal rate of return method (IRR) and the net present value method (NPV) may be different when

A. The lives of the multiple projects are equal and the size of the required investments are equal.

B. The required rate of return equals the IRR of each project.

C. The required rate of return is higher than the IRR of each project.

D. Multiple projects have unequal lives and the size of the investment for each project is different.

Answer (D) is correct.
 REQUIRED: The circumstances in which IRR and NPV rankings of mutually exclusive projects may differ.
 DISCUSSION: The two methods ordinarily yield the same results, but differences can occur when the duration of the projects and the initial investments differ. The reason is that the IRR method assumes cash inflows from the early years will be reinvested at the internal rate of return. The NPV method assumes that early cash inflows are reinvested at the NPV discount rate.
 Answer (A) is incorrect. The two methods will give the same results if the lives and required investments are the same. Answer (B) is incorrect. If the required rate of return equals the IRR, the two methods will yield the same decision. Answer (C) is incorrect. If the required rate of return is higher than the IRR, both methods will yield a decision not to acquire the investment.

14. A corporation has not yet decided on its hurdle rate for use in the evaluation of capital budgeting projects. This lack of information will prohibit the corporation from calculating a project's

	Accounting Rate of Return	Net Present Value	Internal Rate of Return
A.	No	No	No
B.	Yes	Yes	Yes
C.	No	Yes	Yes
D.	No	Yes	No

Answer (D) is correct.
 REQUIRED: The capital budgeting technique(s), if any, that require determination of a hurdle rate.
 DISCUSSION: A hurdle rate is not necessary in calculating the accounting rate of return. That return is calculated by dividing the net income from a project by the investment in the project. Similarly, a company can calculate the internal rate of return (IRR) without knowing its hurdle rate. The IRR is the discount rate at which the net present value is $0. However, the NPV cannot be calculated without knowing the company's hurdle rate. The NPV method requires that future cash flows be discounted using the hurdle rate.
 Answer (A) is incorrect. The accounting rate of return and the IRR, but not the NPV, can be calculated without knowing the hurdle rate. Answer (B) is incorrect. The accounting rate of return and the IRR, but not the NPV, can be calculated without knowing the hurdle rate. Answer (C) is incorrect. The accounting rate of return and the IRR, but not the NPV, can be calculated without knowing the hurdle rate.

8.4 Payback and Discounted Payback

15. The capital budgeting model that is generally considered the **best** model for long-range decision making is the

A. Payback model.

B. Accounting rate of return model.

C. Unadjusted rate of return model.

D. Discounted cash flow model.

Answer (D) is correct.
 REQUIRED: The best capital budgeting model for long-range decision making.
 DISCUSSION: The capital budgeting methods that are generally considered the best for long-range decision making are the internal rate of return and net present value methods. These are both discounted cash flow methods.
 Answer (A) is incorrect. The payback method gives no consideration to the time value of money or to returns after the payback period. Answer (B) is incorrect. The accounting rate of return does not consider the time value of money. Answer (C) is incorrect. The unadjusted rate of return does not consider the time value of money.

16. A company has a payback goal of 3 years on new equipment acquisitions. A new sorter is being evaluated that costs $450,000 and has a 5-year life. Straight-line depreciation will be used; no salvage is anticipated. The company is subject to a 40% income tax rate. To meet the company's payback goal, the sorter must generate reductions in annual cash operating costs of

A. $60,000

B. $100,000

C. $150,000

D. $190,000

Answer (D) is correct.
REQUIRED: The cash savings that must be generated to achieve a targeted payback period.
DISCUSSION: Given a periodic constant cash flow, the payback period is calculated by dividing cost by the annual cash inflows, or cash savings. To achieve a payback period of 3 years, the annual increment in net cash inflow generated by the investment must be $150,000 ($450,000 ÷ 3-year targeted payback period). This amount equals the total reduction in cash operating costs minus related taxes. Depreciation is $90,000 ($450,000 ÷ 5 years). Because depreciation is a noncash deductible expense, it shields $90,000 of the cash savings from taxation. Accordingly, $60,000 ($150,000 – $90,000) of the additional net cash inflow must come from after-tax net income. At a 40% tax rate, $60,000 of after-tax income equals $100,000 ($60,000 ÷ 60%) of pre-tax income from cost savings, and the outflow for taxes is $40,000. Thus, the annual reduction in cash operating costs required is $190,000 ($150,000 additional net cash inflow required + $40,000 tax outflow).
Answer (A) is incorrect. The amount of $60,000 is after-tax net income from the cost savings. Answer (B) is incorrect. The amount of $100,000 is the pre-tax income from the cost savings. Answer (C) is incorrect. The amount of $150,000 ignores the impact of depreciation and income taxes.

17. A characteristic of the payback method (before taxes) is that it

A. Incorporates the time value of money.

B. Neglects total project profitability.

C. Uses accrual accounting inflows in the numerator of the calculation.

D. Uses the estimated expected life of the asset in the denominator of the calculation.

Answer (B) is correct.
REQUIRED: The characteristic of the payback method.
DISCUSSION: The payback method calculates the number of years required to complete the return of the original investment. This measure is computed by dividing the net investment required by the average expected cash flow to be generated, resulting in the number of years required to recover the original investment. Payback is easy to calculate but has two principal disadvantages: It ignores the time value of money, and it gives no consideration to returns after the payback period. Thus, it ignores total project profitability.
Answer (A) is incorrect. The payback method does not incorporate the time value of money. Answer (C) is incorrect. The payback method uses the net investment in the numerator of the calculation. Answer (D) is incorrect. Payback uses the net annual cash inflows in the denominator of the calculation.

18. The length of time required to recover the initial cash outlay of a capital project is determined by using the

A. Discounted cash flow method.

B. Payback method.

C. Weighted net present value method.

D. Net present value method.

Answer (B) is correct.
REQUIRED: The method of determining the time required to recover the initial cash outlay of a capital project.
DISCUSSION: The payback method measures the number of years required to complete the return of the original investment. This measure is computed by dividing the net investment by the average expected cash inflows to be generated, resulting in the number of years required to recover the original investment. The payback method gives no consideration to the time value of money, and there is no consideration of returns after the payback period.
Answer (A) is incorrect. The discounted cash flow method computes a rate of return. Answer (C) is incorrect. The net present value method is based on discounted cash flows; the length of time to recover an investment is not the result. Answer (D) is incorrect. The net present value method is based on discounted cash flows; the length of time to recover an investment is not the result.

19. Which one of the following statements about the payback method of investment analysis is **correct**? The payback method

A. Does not consider the time value of money.

B. Considers cash flows after the payback has been reached.

C. Uses discounted cash flow techniques.

D. Generally leads to the same decision as other methods for long-term projects.

Answer (A) is correct.
   REQUIRED: The true statement about the payback method of investment analysis.
   DISCUSSION: The payback method calculates the amount of time required to complete the return of the original investment, i.e., the time it takes for a new asset to pay for itself. Although the payback method is easy to calculate, it has disadvantages. The time value of money and returns after the payback period are not considered.
   Answer (B) is incorrect. The payback method ignores cash flows after payback. Answer (C) is incorrect. The payback method does not use discounted cash flow techniques. Answer (D) is incorrect. The payback method may lead to different decisions.

20. The payback reciprocal can be used to approximate a project's

A. Profitability index.

B. Net present value.

C. Accounting rate of return if the cash flow pattern is relatively stable.

D. Internal rate of return if the cash flow pattern is relatively stable.

Answer (D) is correct.
   REQUIRED: The item that can be approximated by a project's payback reciprocal.
   DISCUSSION: The payback reciprocal (1 ÷ payback) has been shown to approximate the internal rate of return (IRR) when the periodic cash flows are equal and the life of the project is at least twice the payback period.
   Answer (A) is incorrect. The payback reciprocal is not related to the profitability index. Answer (B) is incorrect. The payback reciprocal approximates the IRR, which is the rate at which the NPV is $0. Answer (C) is incorrect. The accounting rate of return is based on accrual-income based figures, not on discounted cash flows.

8.5 Ranking Investment Projects

21. The profitability index (excess present value index)

A. Represents the ratio of the discounted net cash outflows to cash inflows.

B. Is the relationship between the net discounted cash inflows less the discounted cash outflows divided by the discounted cash outflows.

C. Is calculated by dividing the discounted profits by the cash outflows.

D. Is the ratio of the discounted net cash inflows to discounted cash outflows.

Answer (D) is correct.
   REQUIRED: The true statement about the profitability index.
   DISCUSSION: The profitability index (excess present value index) of an investment is the ratio of the present value of the future net cash flows (or only cash inflows) to the net initial investment. This tool is a variation of the NPV method that facilitates comparison of different-sized investments.
   Answer (A) is incorrect. The cash inflows are also discounted in the profitability index. Answer (B) is incorrect. The numerator is the discounted net cash inflows. Answer (C) is incorrect. The profitability index is based on cash flows, not profits.

22. The recommended technique for evaluating projects when capital is rationed and there are no mutually exclusive projects from which to choose is to rank the projects by

A. Accounting rate of return.

B. Payback.

C. Internal rate of return.

D. Profitability index.

Answer (D) is correct.
   REQUIRED: The best ranking method when capital is rationed and projects are not mutually exclusive.
   DISCUSSION: The profitability index (excess present value index) is often used to decide among investment alternatives when more than one is acceptable. The profitability index of an investment is the ratio of the present value of the future net cash flows (or only cash inflows) to the net initial investment. The profitability index is a variation of the net present value method and facilitates comparison of different-sized investments.
   Answer (A) is incorrect. The accounting rate of return is a poor technique. It ignores the time value of money. Answer (B) is incorrect. The payback method ignores the time value of money and long-term profitability. Answer (C) is incorrect. The internal rate of return is not effective when alternative investments have different lives.

Questions 23 and 24 are based on the following information. Mercken Industries is contemplating four projects, Project P, Project Q, Project R, and Project S. The capital costs and estimated after-tax net cash flows of each independent project are listed below. Mercken's desired after-tax opportunity cost is 12%, and the company has a capital budget for the year of $450,000. Idle funds cannot be reinvested at greater than 12%.

	Project P	Project Q	Project R	Project S
Initial cost	$200,000	$235,000	$190,000	$210,000
Annual cash flows				
Year 1	$ 93,000	$ 90,000	$ 45,000	$ 40,000
Year 2	93,000	85,000	55,000	50,000
Year 3	93,000	75,000	65,000	60,000
Year 4	0	55,000	70,000	65,000
Year 5	0	50,000	75,000	75,000
Net present value	$ 23,370	$ 29,827	$ 27,333	$ (7,854)
Internal rate of return	18.7%	17.6%	17.2%	10.6%
Excess present value index	1.12	1.13	1.14	0.96

23. During this year, Mercken will choose

A. Projects P, Q, and R.

B. Projects P, Q, R, and S.

C. Projects Q and R.

D. Projects P and Q.

Answer (C) is correct.

REQUIRED: The investments that will be chosen given capital rationing.

DISCUSSION: Only two of the projects can be selected because three would require more than $450,000 of capital. Project S can immediately be dismissed because it has a negative net present value (NPV). Using the NPV and the profitability index methods, the best investments appear to be Q and R. The internal rate of return (IRR) method indicates that P is preferable to R. However, it assumes reinvestment of funds during Years 4 and 5 at the IRR (18.7%). Given that reinvestment will be at a rate of at most 12%, the IRR decision criterion appears to be unsound in this situation.

Answer (A) is incorrect. The amount of capital available limits the company to two projects. Answer (B) is incorrect. The amount of capital available limits the company to two projects. Answer (D) is incorrect. The profitability index and NPV are higher for R than P.

24. If Mercken is able to accept only one project, the company would choose

A. Project P.

B. Project Q because it has the highest net present value.

C. Project P because it has the highest internal rate of return.

D. Project P because it has the shortest payback period.

Answer (B) is correct.

REQUIRED: The project chosen if only one can be undertaken.

DISCUSSION: Because unused funds cannot be invested at a rate greater than 12%, the company should select the investment with the highest net present value. Project Q is preferable to R because its return on the incremental $45,000 invested ($235,000 cost of Q – $190,000 cost of R) is greater than 12%.

Answer (A) is incorrect. Project P has a life of only 3 years, and the high IRR would be earned only for that period and could not be reinvested at that rate in Years 4 and 5. Also, P's NPV is lower than that of Q. Answer (C) is incorrect. Although P's IRR of 18.7% for 3 years exceeds Q's (17.6% for 5 years), the funds from P cannot be invested in Years 4 and 5 at greater than 12%. Answer (D) is incorrect. The payback period is a poor means of ranking projects. It ignores both reinvestment rates and the time value of money.

25. The technique that reflects the time value of money and is calculated by dividing the present value of the future net after-tax cash inflows that have been discounted at the desired cost of capital by the initial cash outlay for the investment is called the

A. Capital rationing method.

B. Average rate of return method.

C. Profitability index method.

D. Accounting rate of return method.

Answer (C) is correct.

REQUIRED: The technique that divides the present value of future net cash inflows by the initial cash outlay.

DISCUSSION: The profitability index (excess present value index) of an investment is the ratio of the present value of the future net cash flows (or only cash inflows) to the net initial investment. In organizations with unlimited capital funds, this index is unnecessary. If capital rationing is in place, the index is used to rank projects by their return per dollar invested.

Answer (A) is incorrect. Capital rationing is not a technique but rather a condition that characterizes capital budgeting when insufficient capital is available to finance all profitable investment opportunities. Answer (B) is incorrect. The average rate of return method does not divide the future cash flows by the cost of the investment. Answer (D) is incorrect. The accounting rate of return does not recognize the time value of money.

26. Capital budgeting methods are often divided into two classifications: project screening and project ranking. Which one of the following is considered a ranking method rather than a screening method?

A. Net present value.

B. Time-adjusted rate of return.

C. Profitability index.

D. Accounting rate of return.

Answer (C) is correct.

REQUIRED: The method considered a project ranking rather than a screening method.

DISCUSSION: The profitability index is the ratio of the present value of future net cash inflows to the initial cash investment. This variation of the net present value method facilitates comparison of different-sized investments. Were it not for this comparison feature, the profitability index would be no better than the net present value method. Thus, it is the comparison, or ranking, advantage that makes the profitability index different from the other capital budgeting tools.

Answer (A) is incorrect. The net present value (NPV > 0) is a capital budgeting tool that screens investments; i.e., the investment must meet a certain standard to be acceptable. Answer (B) is incorrect. The time-adjusted rate of return is a capital budgeting tool that screens investments; i.e., the investment must meet a certain standard (rate of return) to be acceptable. Answer (D) is incorrect. The accounting rate of return is a capital budgeting tool that screens investments; i.e., the investment must meet a certain standard (rate of return) to be acceptable.

8.6 Comprehensive Examples of Investment Decisions

Questions 27 and 28 are based on the following information. Don Adams Breweries is considering an expansion project with an investment of $1,500,000. The equipment will be depreciated to zero salvage value on a straight-line basis over 5 years. The expansion will produce incremental operating revenue of $400,000 annually for 5 years. The company's opportunity cost of capital is 12%. Ignore taxes.

27. What is the NPV of the investment?

A. $0

B. $(58,000)

C. $(116,000)

D. $1,442,000

Answer (B) is correct.
REQUIRED: The NPV of the investment.
DISCUSSION: First, calculate the annual earnings and cash flows:

Operating revenues	$400,000
Less: depreciation	(300,000)
Book income	$100,000
Cash flow	$400,000

The cash flows associated with the investment are then discounted accordingly:

	Amount	Discount Factor	Present Value
Year 0 initial investment	$(1,500,000)	1	$(1,500,000)
Years 1 through 5 cash flow	400,000	3.605	1,442,000
Net Present Value			$ (58,000)

Answer (A) is incorrect. There is a negative NPV. Answer (C) is incorrect. The amount of $(116,000) overstates the negative NPV. Answer (D) is incorrect. The amount of $1,442,000 is the present value of the future cash flows, not the NPV.

28. What is the IRR of the investment?

A. 10.43%

B. 12.68%

C. 16.32%

D. 19.17%

Answer (A) is correct.
REQUIRED: The IRR of the investment.
DISCUSSION: First, calculate the annual earnings and cash flows:

Operating revenues	$400,000
Less depreciation	300,000
Book income	100,000
Cash flow	400,000

IRR is calculated by trial and error. Calculate the NPV at different discount rates.

NPV at 10% = ($400,000 × discount factor for 10%, 5 years) – $1,500,000 = $400,000 × 3.791 – $1,500,000 = $16,400
NPV at 11% = $400,000 × 3.696 – $1,500,000 = $(21,600)

Thus, IRR lies between 10% and 11%. By interpolation, the actual IRR appears to be 10.43% {10 + [16,400 ÷ (16,400 + 21,600)]}.

NOTE: The NPV tables do not contain the factor for 11%. You can deduce the answer using the factor for 12%, but you can't interpolate.

Questions 29 and 30 are based on the following information. McLean, Inc., is considering the purchase of a new machine that will cost $150,000. The machine has an estimated useful life of 3 years. Assume that 30% of the depreciable base will be depreciated in the first year, 40% in the second year, and 30% in the third year. The new machine will have a $10,000 resale value at the end of its estimated useful life. The machine is expected to save the company $85,000 per year in operating expenses. McLean uses a 40% estimated income tax rate and a 16% hurdle rate to evaluate capital projects.

Discount rates for a 16% rate are as follows:

	Present Value of $1	Present Value of an Ordinary Annuity of $1
Year 1	.862	.862
Year 2	.743	1.605
Year 3	.641	2.246

29. What is the net present value of this project?

A. $15,842

B. $13,278

C. $40,910

D. $9,432

Answer (B) is correct.
    REQUIRED: The NPV of the new machine.
    DISCUSSION: The NPV method discounts the expected cash flows from a project using the required rate of return. A project is acceptable if its NPV is positive. The future cash inflows consist of $85,000 of saved expenses per year minus income taxes after deducting depreciation. In the first year, the after-tax cash inflow is $85,000 minus taxes of $16,000 {[$85,000 − ($150,000 × 30%) depreciation] × 40%}, or $69,000. In the second year, the after-tax cash inflow is $85,000 minus taxes of $10,000 {[$85,000 − ($150,000 × 40%) depreciation] × 40%}, or $75,000. In the third year, the after-tax cash inflow (excluding salvage value) is again $69,000. Also in the third year, the after-tax cash inflow from the salvage value is $6,000 [$10,000 × (1 − 40%)]. Accordingly, the total for the third year is $75,000 ($69,000 + $6,000). The sum of these cash flows discounted using the factors for the present value of $1 at a rate of 16% is calculated as follows:

$69,000 × .862	=	$ 59,478
$75,000 × .743	=	55,725
$75,000 × .641	=	48,075
Discounted cash inflows		$163,278

Thus, the NPV is $13,278 ($163,278 − $150,000 initial outflow).
    Answer (A) is incorrect. Ignoring tax on the cash proceeds received from salvage value results in an NPV of $15,842. Answer (C) is incorrect. The amount of $40,910 equals the present value of a 3-year annuity of $85,000 discounted at 16%, minus $150,000. Answer (D) is incorrect. Failing to include the cash proceeds from salvage value results in an NPV of $9,432.

30. The payback period for this investment would be

A. 2.94 years.

B. 1.76 years.

C. 2.09 years.

D. 1.14 years.

Answer (C) is correct.
    REQUIRED: The payback period for an investment.
    DISCUSSION: The payback period is the number of years required for the cumulative undiscounted net cash inflows to equal the original investment. The future net cash inflows consist of $69,000 in Years 1 and 3, and $75,000 in Year 2. After 2 years, the cumulative undiscounted net cash inflow equals $144,000. Thus, $6,000 ($150,000 − $144,000) is to be recovered in Year 3, and payback should be complete in approximately 2.09 years [2 years + ($6,000 ÷ $69,000 net cash inflow in third year)].
    Answer (A) is incorrect. This number of years does not consider depreciation. Answer (B) is incorrect. This number of years ignores the tax effects. Answer (D) is incorrect. This number of years results from considering the depreciation as a cash inflow and failing to account for the income tax.

Access the Gleim CMA Premium Review System from your Gleim Personal Classroom to continue your studies with exam-emulating multiple-choice questions!

8.7 ESSAY QUESTIONS

Scenario for Essay Questions 1, 2

Kravel Corporation is a diversified company with several manufacturing plants. Kravel's Dayton Plant has been supplying parts to truck manufacturers for over 30 years. The last shipment of truck parts from the Dayton Plant will be made December 31, Year 6. Kravel's management is currently studying three alternatives relating to its soon-to-be-idle plant and equipment in Dayton.

1. Wasson Industries has offered to buy the Dayton Plant for $3,000,000 cash on January 1, Year 7.

2. Harr Enterprises has offered to lease the Dayton facilities for 4 years beginning on January 1, Year 7. Harr's annual lease payments would be $500,000 plus 10% of the gross dollar sales of all items produced in the Dayton Plant. Probabilities of Harr's annual gross dollar sales from the Dayton Plant are estimated as follows:

Annual Gross Dollar Sales	Estimated Probability
$2,000,000	.1
4,000,000	.4
6,000,000	.3
8,000,000	.2

3. Kravel is considering the production of souvenir items to be sold in connection with upcoming sporting events. The Dayton Plant would be used to produce 70,000 items per month at an annual cash outlay of $2,250,000 during Year 7, Year 8, and Year 9. Linda Yetter, Vice President of Marketing, has recommended a selling price of $5 per item and believes the items will sell uniformly throughout Year 8, Year 9, and Year 10.

The adjusted basis of the Dayton Plant as of the close of business on December 31, Year 6, will be $4,200,000. Kravel has used straight-line depreciation for all capital assets at the Dayton Plant. If the Dayton Plant is not sold, the annual straight-line depreciation charge for the plant and equipment will be $900,000 each year for the next 4 years. The market value of the plant and equipment on December 31, Year 10, is estimated to be $600,000.

Kravel requires an after-tax rate of return of 16% for capital investment decisions and is subject to a corporate tax rate of 40% on all income.

Questions

1. Calculate the present value (at December 31, Year 6) of the expected after-tax cash flows for each of the three alternatives available to Kravel Corporation regarding the Dayton Plant. Assume all recurring cash flows take place at the end of the year.

2. Discuss the additional factors, both quantitative and qualitative, Kravel Corporation should consider before a decision is made regarding the disposition or use of the idle plant and equipment at the Dayton Plant.

Essay Questions 1, 2 — Unofficial Answers

1. The present values of the expected after-tax cash flows of the three alternatives available to Kravel Corporation can be calculated as follows:

Alternative 1 – Sell plant to Wasson Industries:

Proceeds from sale of plant		$3,000,000
Salvage value	$ 3,000,000	
Less: Adjusted basis	(4,200,000)	
Accrual-basis loss on sale	$(1,200,000)	
Times: Tax rate	× 40%	
Tax benefit from loss on sale		480,000
After-tax cash inflow from sale		$3,480,000

Alternative 2 – Lease plant to Harr Enterprises:

	Annual Gross Dollar Sales		Estimated Probability		Expected Value of Sales
	$2,000,000	×	0.1	=	$ 200,000
	4,000,000	×	0.4	=	1,600,000
	6,000,000	×	0.3	=	1,800,000
	8,000,000	×	0.2	=	1,600,000
Expected annual gross sales					$5,200,000
Times: Portion for lease payment					× 10%
Variable portion of lease payment					$ 520,000
Add: Fixed portion of lease payment					500,000
Before-tax cash flow from lease					$1,020,000
Less: Income taxes (40%)					(408,000)
After-tax cash flow from lease					$ 612,000
Times: PV factor					× 2.798
Present value of lease payments					$1,712,376

Annual depreciation expense		$ 900,000
Times: Tax rate		× 40%
Annual depreciation tax shield		$ 360,000
Times: PV factor		× 2.798
PV of depreciation tax shield		$1,007,280

Proceeds from sale of plant		$ 600,000
Salvage value	$ 600,000	
Less: Book value at 12/31/Yr 10	(600,000)	
Accrual-basis gain (loss) on disposal	$ 0	
Times: Tax rate	× 40%	
Tax effect from gain (loss) on sale		0
After-tax cash inflow from sale		$ 600,000
Times: PV factor		× .552
PV of proceeds from sale of plant		$ 331,200
Present value of after-tax cash flows		$3,050,856

Alternative 3 – Keep plant and produce souvenir items:

Income taxes should be recognized in the years in which the revenues are earned. Tax expense for Years 8, 9, and 10 is therefore $780,000 [($4,200,000 – $2,250,000) × .40].

Since depreciation expense is included in cost of goods sold, the depreciation tax shield only arises in years when product is sold. The shield for Years 8 and 9 is $360,000 ($900,000 × .40). The depreciation recognized for income tax purposes in Year 10 would be $1,800,000, which consists of the Year 9 depreciation charge included in the Year 10 cost of goods sold and the Year 10 depreciation charge recognized in Year 10 when the plant is presumably being used as a warehouse. Thus, the depreciation tax shield in Year 10 is $720,000 ($1,800,000 × .40).

Since the book value of the plant is expected to equal its salvage value at the end of Year 10, there will be no tax effect from an accrual-basis gain or loss, and thus the relevant cash flow is the entire proceeds.

	Year 7	Year 8	Year 9	Year 10
Sales revenue (70,000 × $5 × 12 months)	$ 0	$ 4,200,000	$ 4,200,000	$ 4,200,000
Less: Annual cash outlays	(2,250,000)	(2,250,000)	(2,250,000)	0
Expected annual cash flows	$(2,250,000)	$ 1,950,000	$ 1,950,000	$ 4,200,000
Less: Income taxes	0	(780,000)	(780,000)	(780,000)
After-tax cash flows	$(2,250,000)	$ 1,170,000	$ 1,170,000	$ 3,420,000
Add: Depreciation tax shield	0	360,000	360,000	720,000
Add: Termination salvage value	--	--	--	600,000
Net after-tax cash flows	$(2,250,000)	$ 1,530,000	$ 1,530,000	$ 4,740,000
Times: PV factor	× 0.862	× 0.743	× 0.641	× 0.552
Present value of after-tax cash flows	$(1,939,500)	$ 1,136,790	$ 980,730	$ 2,616,480
Net present value of after-tax cash flows				$ 2,794,500

2. While considering its decision regarding the Dayton Plant, Kravel must consider

- That all of Alternative 1's cash flows take place immediately, making it the least risky of the three.

- The adequacy of the cash flows estimates and the appropriateness of the hurdle rate used.

- The timing of cash flows of each of the alternatives in light of the firm's overall cash budget.

- The possibility that the manufacture of truck parts will once again be a profitable use of the plant. Alternative 1 precludes this option permanently, and, under Alternative 2, it will not be available until Year 11.

 Access the **Gleim CMA Premium Review System** from your Gleim Personal Classroom to continue your studies with exam-emulating essay questions!

STUDY UNIT NINE
CVP ANALYSIS

(12 pages of outline)

This study unit is the **first of two** on **decision analysis**. The relative weight assigned to this major topic in Part 2 of the exam is **20%**. The two study units are

Study Unit 9: CVP Analysis
Study Unit 10: Marginal Analysis and Pricing

If you are interested in reviewing more introductory or background material, go to www.gleim.com/CMAIntroVideos for a list of suggested third-party overviews of this topic. The following Gleim outline material is more than sufficient to help you pass the CMA exam; any additional introductory or background material is for your own personal enrichment.

9.1 SHORT-RUN PROFIT MAXIMIZATION

1. **Marginal Revenue and Marginal Cost**

   a. Marginal revenue is the additional (also called incremental) revenue produced by generating one additional unit of output. Mathematically, it is the difference in total revenue at each level of output.

      1) While total revenue keeps increasing with the sale of additional units, it increases by ever smaller amounts. This is reflected in a constantly decreasing marginal revenue.

      2) EXAMPLE: A company has the following revenue data for one of its products:

Units of Output		Unit Price		Total Revenue	Marginal Revenue
1	×	$580	=	$ 580	$580
2	×	575	=	1,150	570
3	×	570	=	1,710	560
4	×	565	=	2,260	550
5	×	560	=	2,800	540
6	×	555	=	3,330	530
7	×	550	=	3,850	520
8	×	545	=	4,360	510
9	×	540	=	4,860	500
10	×	535	=	5,350	490
11	×	530	=	5,830	480
12	×	525	=	6,300	470

   a) Revenue by itself cannot determine the proper level of output. Cost data must also be considered.

b. Marginal cost is the additional (also called incremental) cost incurred by generating one additional unit of output. Mathematically, it is the difference in total cost at each level of output.

   1) Typically, unit cost decreases for a while as the process becomes more efficient. Past a certain point, however, the process becomes less efficient and unit cost increases.

      a) Thus, while total cost increases gradually for a while, at some point it begins to increase sharply. This is reflected in a decreasing, then increasing, marginal cost.

   2) EXAMPLE: A company has the following cost data for the product (for simplicity, each unit of output requires exactly one unit of input):

Units of Output	Unit Cost	Total Cost	Marginal Cost
1	$570	$ 570	$570
2	405	810	240
3	340	1,020	210
4	305	1,220	200
5	287	1,435	215
6	279	1,675	240
7	279	1,955	280
8	284	2,275	320
9	295	2,655	380
10	310	3,095	440
11	327	3,595	500
12	347	4,165	570

2. Profit Maximization

a. The firm's goal is to maximize profits, not revenues. Thus, marginal revenue data must be compared with marginal cost data to determine the point of profit maximization.

   1) Profit is maximized at the output level where marginal revenue equals marginal cost.

Profit Maximization

Marginal revenue = Marginal cost

      a) Beyond this point, increasing production results in a level of costs so high that the total profit is diminished.

   2) EXAMPLE: Comparing its marginal revenue and marginal cost data allows the company to determine the point of profit maximization.

Units of Output	Marginal Revenue	Cost	Profit	Total Revenue	Cost	Profit
1	$580 −	$570 =	$ 10	$ 580 −	$ 570 =	$ 10
2	570 −	240 =	330	1,150 −	810 =	340
3	560 −	210 =	350	1,710 −	1,020 =	690
4	550 −	200 =	350	2,260 −	1,220 =	1,040
5	540 −	215 =	325	2,800 −	1,435 =	1,365
6	530 −	240 =	290	3,330 −	1,675 =	1,655
7	520 −	280 =	240	3,850 −	1,955 =	1,895
8	510 −	320 =	190	4,360 −	2,275 =	2,085
9	500 −	380 =	120	4,860 −	2,655 =	2,205
10	**490 −**	**440 =**	**50**	**5,350 −**	**3,095 =**	**2,255**
11	480 −	500 =	(20)	5,830 −	3,595 =	2,235
12	470 −	570 =	(100)	6,300 −	4,165 =	2,135

      a) Beyond the output level of 10 units, marginal profit turns negative. Note that this is, by definition, the point of highest total profit.

3.   **Short-Run Cost Relationships**

    a.   To make marginal analysis meaningful, total cost must be broken down into its fixed and variable components.

        1)   EXAMPLE: Cost analysis reveals that the inputs to the company's process have the following cost structure:

Units of Output	Total Costs		Fixed Costs		Variable Costs	
	In Total	Average	In Total	Average	In Total	Average
1	$ 570	$570	$300	$300	$ 270	$270
2	810	405	300	150	510	255
3	1,020	340	300	100	720	240
4	1,220	305	300	75	920	230
5	1,435	287	300	60	1,135	227
6	1,675	279	300	50	1,375	229
7	1,955	279	300	43	1,655	236
8	2,275	284	300	38	1,975	247
9	2,655	295	300	33	2,355	262
10	3,095	310	300	30	2,795	280
11	3,595	327	300	27	3,295	300
12	4,165	347	300	25	3,865	322

    b.   These relationships can be depicted graphically as follows:

        Legend
         MC = marginal cost
        ATC = average total cost
        AVC = average variable cost
        AFC = average fixed cost

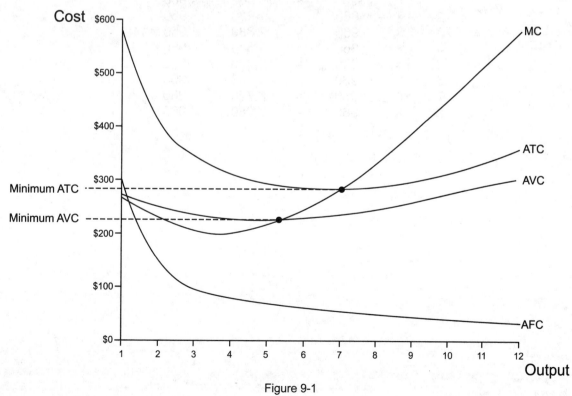

Cost Relationships in the Short Run

Figure 9-1

1) Average fixed cost (AFC) declines for as long as production increases. This is because the fixed amount of cost is being spread over more and more units.

   a) AFC is thus an asymptotic function, always approaching the x axis without ever intersecting with it.

2) Average variable cost (AVC) declines quickly and then gradually begins increasing.

   a) AVC is at its lowest where MC crosses it, between 5 and 6 units. This is confirmed by reference to the data in the tables (MC: $215-$240, AVC: $227-$229).

3) Average total cost (ATC) behaves similarly. It declines rapidly and then begins a gradual increase.

   a) ATC also reaches its minimum at the point where MC crosses it, just after 7 units (MC: $280, AVC: $279).

4) As a general statement, ATC = AFC + AVC.

   a) Thus, the distance between the ATC and AVC curves is always the same as the distance between the AFC curve and the x axis.

4. Pure Competition

a. A purely competitive market is characterized by a large number of buyers and sellers acting independently and a homogeneous or standardized product (e.g., agricultural commodities).

1) Marginal revenue equals price.
2) EXAMPLE: A firm in pure competition has the following revenue data:

Units of Output		Unit Price (Average Revenue)		Total Revenue	Marginal Revenue
1	×	$960	=	$ 960	$960
2	×	960	=	1,920	960
3	×	960	=	2,880	960
4	×	960	=	3,840	960
5	×	960	=	4,800	960
6	×	960	=	5,760	960
7	×	960	=	6,720	960
8	×	960	=	7,680	960

b. The following graph depicts the relationships among total revenue (TR), average revenue (AR), and marginal revenue (MR) for a firm in pure competition.

**Revenue Relationships for
a Purely Competitive Firm**

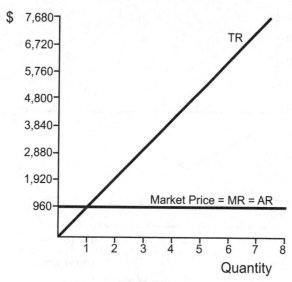

Figure 9-2

1) TR is a straight line with a constant positive slope. The price, MR, and AR curves are identical.

c. As noted in 2.a.1), short-run profit maximization is achieved when marginal revenue equals marginal cost. As long as the next unit of output adds more in revenue (MR) than in cost (MC), the firm will increase total profit or decrease total losses.

1) For a purely competitive firm, price = MC is the same as MR = MC.

2) EXAMPLE: The firm has performed the following marginal analysis:

Units of Output	Revenue		Cost		Profit	
	Total	Marginal	Total	Marginal	Total	Marginal
1	$ 960	$960	$1,800	$1,800	$(840)	$(840)
2	1,920	960	2,500	700	(580)	260
3	2,880	960	3,100	600	(220)	360
4	3,840	960	3,600	500	240	460
5	4,800	960	4,200	600	600	360
6	5,760	960	5,080	880	680	80
7	**6,720**	**960**	**6,040**	**960**	**680**	**0**
8	7,680	960	7,160	1,120	520	(160)

3)   The following graph depicts the short-run profit-maximizing quantity for a firm in pure competition (a "price taker"):

Price Taking for a Purely Competitive Firm

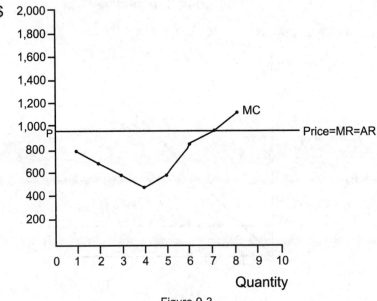

Figure 9-3

a)   Being in a purely competitive industry, the firm has no choice but to find its price along the horizontal MR curve.

b)   The profit-maximizing quantity to produce is found at the point where the MC curve crosses MR.

c)   Point A reveals a quantity of 7 units. This is confirmed by consulting the table and verifying that at an output of 7, MR = MC.

5.   Monopoly

a.   In a monopoly market, the industry consists of one firm and the product has no close substitutes.

1)   To increase sales of its product, a monopolist may lower its price.

2)   Thus, a monopolist's marginal revenue continuously decreases as it raises output. Past the point where MR = $0, the monopolist's total revenue begins to decrease.

Units of Output		Unit Price (Average Revenue)		Total Revenue	Marginal Revenue
1	×	$960	=	$ 960	$960
2	×	910	=	1,820	860
3	×	860	=	2,580	760
4	×	810	=	3,240	660
5	×	760	=	3,800	560
6	×	710	=	4,260	460
7	×	660	=	4,620	360
8	×	610	=	4,880	260

3) The monopolist has the power to set output at the level where profits are maximized, that is, where **MR = MC**. This is called "price searching."

Price Searching for a Monopolist

Units of Output	Revenue		Cost		Profit	
	Total	Marginal	Total	Marginal	Total	Marginal
1	$ 960	$960	$ 800	$ 800	$ 160	$ 160
2	1,820	860	1,480	680	340	180
3	2,580	760	1,980	500	600	260
4	3,240	660	2,320	340	920	320
5	**3,800**	**560**	**2,800**	**480**	**1,000**	**80**
6	4,260	460	3,480	680	780	(220)
7	4,620	360	4,620	1,140	0	(780)
8	4,880	260	5,920	1,300	(1,040)	(1,040)

    a) Profit is maximized at an output of 5 units.

6. **Monopolistic Competition**

    a. An industry in monopolistic competition has a large number of firms. The number is fewer than in pure competition, but it is great enough that firms cannot collude. That is, they cannot act together to restrict output and fix the price.

        1) To maximize profits (or minimize losses) in the short run or long run, a firm in monopolistic competition produces at the level of output at which MR = MC.

7. **Oligopoly**

    a. An oligopoly is an industry with a few large firms. Firms operating in an oligopoly are mutually aware and mutually interdependent. Their decisions as to price, advertising, etc., are to a very large extent dependent on the actions of the other firms.

        1) Prices tend to be rigid (sticky) because of the interdependence among firms.

Stop and review! You have completed the outline for this subunit. Study multiple-choice questions 1 through 5 beginning on page 285.

9.2 COST-VOLUME-PROFIT (CVP) ANALYSIS -- THEORY

1. **Purpose**

    a. Also called **breakeven analysis**, CVP analysis is a tool for understanding the interaction of revenues with fixed and variable costs.

        1) It illuminates how changes in assumptions about cost behavior and the relevant ranges in which those assumptions are valid may affect the relationships among revenues, variable costs, and fixed costs at various production levels.

        2) Thus, CVP analysis allows management to discern the probable effects of changes in sales volume, sales price, product mix, etc.

    b. The **breakeven point** is the level of output at which total revenues equal total expenses.

        1) It is the point at which all fixed costs have been covered and operating income is zero.

2. **Assumptions of CVP**

   a. Cost and revenue relationships are predictable and linear. These relationships are true over the relevant range of activity and specified time span.

   b. Unit selling prices do not change.

   c. Inventory levels do not change; i.e., production equals sales.

   d. Total **variable costs** change proportionally with volume, but unit variable costs do not change.

   e. **Fixed costs** remain constant over the relevant range of volume, but unit fixed costs vary indirectly with volume.

   f. The relevant range of volume may vary based on the time frame (e.g., operating period) being considered. Therefore, the classification of fixed and variable costs may vary each time frame.

   g. The revenue (sales) mix does not change.

   h. The time value of money is ignored.

3. **Breakeven Point for a Single Product**

   a. The breakeven point can be calculated in units and in sales dollars.

      1) The simplest calculation for breakeven **in units** is to divide fixed costs by the unit contribution margin (UCM).

$$UCM = Unit\ sales\ price - Unit\ variable\ cost$$

$$Breakeven\ point\ in\ units = \frac{Fixed\ costs}{UCM}$$

      2) The breakeven point **in sales dollars** equals fixed costs divided by the contribution margin ratio (CMR).

$$CMR = \frac{UCM}{Unit\ selling\ price}$$

$$Breakeven\ point\ in\ dollars = \frac{Fixed\ costs}{CMR}$$

EXAMPLE

A manufacturer's product has a unit sales price of $0.60 and a unit variable cost of $0.20. Fixed costs are $10,000.

Unit selling price	$0.60
Minus: Unit variable costs	(0.20)
Unit contribution margin (UCM)	$0.40

Breakeven point in units = Fixed costs ÷ UCM
= $10,000 ÷ $0.40
= 25,000 units

The manufacturer's contribution margin ratio is 66.667% ($0.40 ÷ $0.60).

Breakeven point in dollars = Fixed costs ÷ CMR
= $10,000 ÷ .66667
= $15,000

4. **Margin of Safety**

    a. The margin of safety is the excess of budgeted sales over breakeven sales.

        1) It is the amount by which sales can decline before losses occur.

$$Margin\ of\ safety = Planned\ sales - Breakeven\ sales$$

        2) The **margin of safety ratio** shows the percent by which sales can decline before the breakeven point is reached.

$$Margin\ of\ safety\ ratio = \frac{Margin\ of\ safety}{Planned\ sales}$$

EXAMPLE

In units:

Margin of safety   = Planned sales – Breakeven sales
               = 35,000 – 25,000
               = 10,000 units

Margin of safety ratio $= \dfrac{Margin\ of\ safety}{Planned\ sales}$

                   $= \dfrac{10,000}{35,000}$

                   = 28.6%

In dollars:

Margin of safety   = Planned sales – Breakeven sales
               = (35,000 units × $0.60) – $15,000
               = $21,000 – $15,000
               = $6,000

Margin of safety ratio $= \dfrac{Margin\ of\ safety}{Planned\ sales}$

                   $= \dfrac{\$6,000}{\$21,000}$

                   = 28.6%

Stop and review! You have completed the outline for this subunit. Study multiple-choice questions 6 through 9 beginning on page 286.

9.3 CVP ANALYSIS -- BASIC CALCULATIONS

The ability to apply the mathematical principles of breakeven analysis quickly is a crucial skill on Part 2 of the CMA exam. This subunit consists entirely of questions that "drill" the candidate on this ability. Please review Subunit 9.2 before attempting to answer the questions in this subunit.

Stop and review! You have completed the outline for this subunit. Study multiple-choice questions 10 through 16 beginning on page 287.

9.4 CVP ANALYSIS -- TARGET INCOME CALCULATIONS

1. **Target Operating Income**

    a. An amount of operating income, either in dollars or as a percentage of sales, is frequently required.

        1) By treating target income as an additional fixed cost, CVP analysis can be applied.

$$Target\ income\ in\ units = \frac{Fixed\ costs + Target\ operating\ income}{UCM}$$

EXAMPLE

The manufacturer from the previous example with the $0.40 contribution margin per unit wants to find out how many units must be sold to generate $25,000 of operating income.

    Target unit volume   = (Fixed costs + Target operating income) ÷ UCM
                      = ($10,000 + $25,000) ÷ $0.40
                      = $35,000 ÷ $0.40
                      = 87,500 units

2.   Target Net Income

a.   A variation of this problem asks for net income (an after-tax amount) instead of operating income (a pretax amount).

$$Target\ income\ in\ units = \frac{Fixed\ costs + [Target\ net\ income \div (1.0 - tax\ rate)]}{UCM}$$

1)   EXAMPLE: The manufacturer wants to generate $30,000 of net income. The effective tax rate is 40%.

Target unit volume = {Fixed costs + [Target net income ÷ (1.0 − .40)]} ÷ UCM
= [$10,000 + ($30,000 ÷ .60)] ÷ $.40
= 150,000 units

3.   Other Target Income Situations

a.   Other target income situations call for the application of the standard formula for operating income.

$$Operating\ income = Sales - Variable\ costs - Fixed\ costs$$

EXAMPLE

If units are sold at $6.00 and variable costs are $2.00, how many units must be sold to realize operating income of 15% ($6.00 × .15 = $.90 per unit) before taxes, given fixed costs of $37,500?

Operating income = Sales − Variable costs − Fixed costs
$0.90 × Q = ($6.00 × Q) − ($2.00 × Q) − $37,500
$3.10 × Q = $37,500
Q = 12,097 units

Selling 12,097 units results in $72,582 of revenues. Variable costs are $24,194, and operating income is $10,888 ($72,582 × 15%). The proof is that variable costs of $24,194, plus fixed costs of $37,500, plus operating income of $10,888, equals $72,582 of sales.

---

b.   The operating income formula can also be used in this situation.

EXAMPLE

If variable costs are $1.20, fixed costs are $10,000, and selling price is $2, and the company targets a $5,000 after-tax profit when the tax rate is 30%, the calculation is as follows:

$ 2Q = [$5,000 ÷ (1.0 − 0.3)] + $1.20Q + $10,000
$.8Q = $7,142.86 + $10,000
$.8Q = $17,142.86
Q = $17,142.86 ÷ .8
Q = 21,428.575 units

If the company plans to sell 21,429 units at $2 each, revenue will be $42,858. The following is the pro forma income statement for the target net income:

Sales (21,429 × $2)	$ 42,858
Less: Variable costs (21,429 × $1.20)	(25,715)
Contribution margin	$ 17,143
Less: Fixed costs	(10,000)
Operating income	$ 7,143
Income taxes (30%)	(2,143)
Net income	$ 5,000

Stop and review! You have completed the outline for this subunit. Study multiple-choice questions 17 through 23 beginning on page 290.

9.5 CVP ANALYSIS -- MULTI-PRODUCT CALCULATIONS

1. **Multiple Products (or Services)**

   a. A multi-product breakeven point in units can be calculated as follows:

   $$\text{Multi-product breakeven point} = \frac{\text{Total fixed costs}}{\text{Weighted-average selling price} - \text{Weighted-average variable cost}}$$

   $$\text{Multi-product breakeven point} = \frac{\text{Total fixed expenses}}{\text{Weighted-average UCM}}$$

   1) The weighted-average selling price and weighted-average variable costs are calculated using the sales percentage of the individual products in the total sales mix.

   2) The multi-product breakeven point provides the breakeven point of composite units, which is a mixture of all the different products.

      a) From this, individual breakeven points can be calculated.

   b. A multi-product breakeven point in sales dollars can be calculated as follows:

   $$\text{Weighted-average contribution margin ratio (CMR)} = \frac{\text{Weighted-average UCM}}{\text{Weighted-average unit selling price}}$$

   $$\text{Multi-product breakeven point} = \frac{\text{Total fixed costs}}{\text{Weighted-average CMR}}$$

EXAMPLE

A manufacturer produces two products, Product V and Product W. Total fixed costs are $75,000. Variable cost and sales data for these products are as follows:

	Product V	Product W
Selling price per unit	$10	$18
Variable cost per unit	$7	$14
Budget sales (units)	6,000	18,000

The multi-product breakeven point in units can be calculated as follows:

$$\begin{aligned}
\text{Weighted-average UCM} &= \left[(\$10 - \$7) \times \frac{6,000}{6,000 + 18,000} \right] + \left[(\$18 - \$14) \times \frac{18,000}{6,000 + 18,000} \right] \\
&= (\$3 \times 25\%) + (\$4 \times 75\%) \\
&= \$3.75
\end{aligned}$$

$$\begin{aligned}
\text{Multi-product breakeven point} &= \frac{\text{Total fixed costs}}{\text{Weighted-average UCM}} \\
&= \frac{\$75,000}{\$3.75} \\
&= 20,000 \text{ composite units}
\end{aligned}$$

Therefore, the breakeven point in Product V

$$\begin{aligned}
&= 20,000 \text{ composite units} \times \left(\frac{6,000}{6,000 + 18,000} \right) \\
&= 5,000 \text{ units}
\end{aligned}$$

-- Continued on next page --

EXAMPLE -- Continued

Therefore, the breakeven point for Product W

$$= 20{,}000 \text{ composite units} \times \left(\frac{18{,}000}{6{,}000 + 18{,}000} \right)$$

$$= 15{,}000 \text{ units}$$

The multi-product breakeven point in sales dollars can be calculated as follows:

Weighted-average CMR $= \dfrac{\text{Weighted-average UCM}}{\text{Weighted-average unit selling price}}$

Weighted-average CMR $= \dfrac{\$3.75}{\left(\$10 \times \dfrac{6{,}000}{6{,}000 + 18{,}000} \right) + \left(\$18 \times \dfrac{18{,}000}{6{,}000 + 18{,}000} \right)}$

$$= \frac{\$3.75}{(\$10 \times 25\%) + (\$18 \times 75\%)}$$

$$= \frac{\$3.75}{\$16}$$

$$= 0.234375$$

Multi-product breakeven point $= \dfrac{\text{Total fixed costs}}{\text{Weighted-average CMR}}$

$$= \frac{\$75{,}000}{0.234375}$$

$$= \$320{,}000$$

---

2. **Choice of Product**

    a. When resources are limited, a company may produce only a single product.

        1) A breakeven analysis of the point where the same operating income or loss will result, regardless of the product selected, is calculated by setting the breakeven formulas of the individual products equal to each other.

        2) EXAMPLE: Assume a lessor can rent property to either of two lessees. One lessee offers a rental fee of $100,000 per year plus 2% of revenues. The other lessee offers $20,000 per year plus 5% of revenues. The optimal solution depends on the level of revenues. A typical CMA question asks at what level the lessor will be indifferent. The solution is to equate the two formulas as follows:

            $$\$100{,}000 + .02 R = \$20{,}000 + .05 R$$
            $$.03 R = \$80{,}000$$
            $$R = \$80{,}000 \div .03$$
            $$R = \$2{,}666{,}667$$

            Where: R = revenues

            Thus, if revenues are expected to be less than $2,666,667, the lessor would prefer the larger fixed rental of $100,000 and the smaller variable rental.

Stop and review! You have completed the outline for this subunit. Study multiple-choice questions 24 through 30 beginning on page 294.

QUESTIONS

9.1 Short-Run Profit Maximization

1. In the short run in perfect competition, a firm maximizes profit by producing the rate of output at which the price is equal to

A. Total cost.

B. Total variable cost.

C. Average fixed costs.

D. Marginal cost.

Answer (D) is correct.
    REQUIRED: The profit-maximizing price in the short run in perfect competition.
    DISCUSSION: A firm should increase production until marginal revenue equals marginal cost. In the short run, this is the same as saying a firm in perfect competition will increase production until marginal cost equals price. The result is the short-run maximization of profits. As long as selling price exceeds marginal cost, a firm should continue producing. In the short run in perfect competition, the market price equals marginal revenue because no firm can affect price by its production decisions.
    Answer (A) is incorrect. There would be no profit when selling price and total costs are the same. Answer (B) is incorrect. Equating selling price to total variable costs leaves nothing to cover fixed costs. Answer (C) is incorrect. Using only average fixed costs ignores variable costs, which increase in total with every unit produced.

2. A characteristic of a monopoly is that

A. A monopoly will produce when marginal revenue is equal to marginal cost.

B. There is a unique relationship between the market price and the quantity supplied.

C. In optimizing profits, a monopoly will increase its supply curve to where the demand curve becomes inelastic.

D. There are multiple prices for the product to the consumer.

Answer (A) is correct.
    REQUIRED: The characteristic of a monopoly.
    DISCUSSION: A monopoly consists of a single firm with a unique product. Such a firm has significant price control. For profit maximization, it increases production until its marginal revenue equals its marginal cost (unless marginal revenue is less than average variable cost, which will cause the firm to shut down). When a monopoly exists, consumers will face higher prices and lower output than in perfect competition.
    Answer (B) is incorrect. The monopolist is in control of the quantity supplied. Thus, the supply can be limited to produce the profit-maximizing price. Answer (C) is incorrect. A monopolist will increase supply as long as the demand curve is inelastic. Inelasticity means that an increase in price will cause a less-than-proportionate decline in demand. Answer (D) is incorrect. There is only one price when a monopoly exists.

3. The distinguishing characteristic of oligopolistic markets is

A. A single seller of a homogeneous product with no close substitute.

B. A single seller of a heterogeneous product with no close substitute.

C. Lack of entry and exit barriers in the industry.

D. Mutual interdependence of firm pricing and output decisions.

Answer (D) is correct.
    REQUIRED: The distinguishing characteristic of oligopolistic markets.
    DISCUSSION: The oligopoly model is much less specific than the other market structures, but there are typically few firms in the industry. Thus, the decisions of rival firms do not go unnoticed. Products can be either differentiated or standardized. Prices tend to be rigid (sticky) because of the interdependence among firms. Entry is difficult because of either natural or created barriers. Price leadership is typical in oligopolistic industries. Under price leadership, price changes are announced first by a major firm. Once the industry leader has spoken, other firms in the industry match the price charged by the leader. The mutual interdependence of the firms influences both pricing and output decisions.
    Answer (A) is incorrect. Oligopolies contain several firms; a single seller is characteristic of a monopoly. Answer (B) is incorrect. Oligopolies contain several firms; a single seller is characteristic of a monopoly. Answer (C) is incorrect. Oligopolies are typified by barriers to entry; that is the reason the industry has only a few firms.

4. Monopolistic competition is characterized by a

  A. Relatively large group of sellers who produce differentiated products.

  B. Relatively small group of sellers who produce differentiated products.

  C. Monopolistic market where the consumer is persuaded that there is perfect competition.

  D. Relatively large group of sellers who produce a homogeneous product.

Answer (A) is correct.
    REQUIRED: The true statement about monopolistic competition.
    DISCUSSION: Monopolistic competition is characterized by a large number of firms offering differentiated products. Entry into the market is relatively easy, firms have some price control, and substantial nonprice competition exists, such as advertising.
    Answer (B) is incorrect. Monopolistic competition is characterized by a relatively large group of sellers. Answer (C) is incorrect. The market is not monopolistic. There are many sellers. Answer (D) is incorrect. Products are not homogeneous in monopolistic competition; although products may appear to be similar, they have differences in service, quality, or other attributes.

5. At the current output level the price is $10, the average variable cost is $6, the average total cost is $10, and marginal cost is $8. To maximize profits, a consultant would recommend that the firm should

  A. Decrease production.

  B. Increase production.

  C. Shut down.

  D. Not change production.

Answer (B) is correct.
    REQUIRED: The action a firm should take when marginal cost is less than selling price.
    DISCUSSION: A firm should continue increasing production as long as marginal cost is less than selling price. Profit is maximized when marginal cost equals selling price. (In pure competition, selling price is the same as marginal revenue.)
    Answer (A) is incorrect. A firm in pure competition should increase production as long as the marginal cost is less than selling price. Answer (C) is incorrect. A firm should not shut down as long as selling price exceeds variable cost. Answer (D) is incorrect. A firm in pure competition should continue increasing production as long as the marginal cost is less than selling price.

9.2 Cost-Volume-Profit (CVP) Analysis -- Theory

6. One of the major assumptions limiting the reliability of breakeven analysis is that

  A. Efficiency and productivity will continually increase.

  B. Total variable costs will remain unchanged over the relevant range.

  C. Total fixed costs will remain unchanged over the relevant range.

  D. The cost of production factors varies with changes in technology.

Answer (C) is correct.
    REQUIRED: The major assumption limiting the use of breakeven analysis.
    DISCUSSION: One of the inherent simplifying assumptions used in CVP analysis is that fixed costs remain constant over the relevant range of activity.
    Answer (A) is incorrect. Breakeven analysis assumes no changes in efficiency and productivity. Answer (B) is incorrect. Total variable costs, by definition, change across the relevant range. Answer (D) is incorrect. The cost of production factors is assumed to be stable; this is what is meant by relevant range.

7. Which one of the following is **true** regarding a relevant range?

  A. Total variable costs will not change.

  B. Total fixed costs will not change.

  C. Actual fixed costs usually fall outside the relevant range.

  D. The relevant range cannot be changed after being established.

Answer (B) is correct.
    REQUIRED: The true statement about a relevant range.
    DISCUSSION: The relevant range is the range of activity over which unit variable costs and total fixed costs are constant.
    Answer (A) is incorrect. Variable costs will change in total, but unit variable costs will be constant across the relevant range. Answer (C) is incorrect. Actual fixed costs should not vary greatly from budgeted fixed costs for the relevant range. Answer (D) is incorrect. The relevant range can change whenever production activity changes; the relevant range is merely an assumption used for budgeting and control purposes.

8. The breakeven point in units increases when unit costs

A. Increase and sales price remains unchanged.

B. Decrease and sales price remains unchanged.

C. Remain unchanged and sales price increases.

D. Decrease and sales price increases.

Answer (A) is correct.
    REQUIRED: The event that causes the breakeven point in units to increase.
    DISCUSSION: The breakeven point in units is calculated by dividing total fixed costs by the unit contribution margin. If selling price is constant and costs increase, the unit contribution margin will decline, resulting in an increase of the breakeven point.
    Answer (B) is incorrect. A decrease in costs will cause the unit contribution margin to increase, lowering the breakeven point. Answer (C) is incorrect. An increase in the selling price will increase the unit contribution margin, resulting in a lower breakeven point. Answer (D) is incorrect. Both a cost decrease and a sales price increase will increase the unit contribution margin, resulting in a lower breakeven point.

9. Cost-volume-profit (CVP) analysis is a key factor in many decisions, including choice of product lines, pricing of products, marketing strategy, and use of productive facilities. A calculation used in a CVP analysis is the breakeven point. Once the breakeven point has been reached, operating income will increase by the

A. Gross margin per unit for each additional unit sold.

B. Contribution margin per unit for each additional unit sold.

C. Fixed costs per unit for each additional unit sold.

D. Variable costs per unit for each additional unit sold.

Answer (B) is correct.
    REQUIRED: The amount by which operating income will increase once the breakeven point has been reached.
    DISCUSSION: At the breakeven point, total revenue equals total fixed costs plus the variable costs incurred at that level of production. Beyond the breakeven point, each unit sale will increase operating income by the unit contribution margin (unit sales price – unit variable cost) because fixed cost will already have been recovered.
    Answer (A) is incorrect. The gross margin equals sales price minus cost of goods sold, including fixed cost. Answer (C) is incorrect. All fixed costs have been covered at the breakeven point. Answer (D) is incorrect. Operating income will increase by the unit contribution margin, not the unit variable cost.

9.3 CVP Analysis -- Basic Calculations

10. Which of the following would decrease unit contribution margin the **most**?

A. A 15% decrease in selling price.

B. A 15% increase in variable expenses.

C. A 15% decrease in variable expenses.

D. A 15% decrease in fixed expenses.

Answer (A) is correct.
    REQUIRED: The change in a CVP variable causing the greatest decrease in UCM.
    DISCUSSION: Unit contribution margin (UCM) equals unit selling price minus unit variable costs. It can be decreased by either lowering the price or raising the variable costs. As long as UCM is positive, a given percentage change in selling price must have a greater effect than an equal but opposite percentage change in variable cost. The example below demonstrates this point.

Original:	$\begin{aligned} \text{UCM} &= \text{SP} - \text{UVC} \\ &= \$100 - \$50 \\ &= \$50 \end{aligned}$
Lower Selling Price:	$\begin{aligned} \text{UCM} &= (\text{SP} \times .85) - \text{UVC} \\ &= \$85 - \$50 \\ &= \$35 \end{aligned}$
Higher Variable Cost:	$\begin{aligned} \text{UCM} &= \text{SP} - (\text{UVC} \times 1.15) \\ &= \$100 - \$57.50 \\ &= \$42.50 \end{aligned}$

Since $35 < $42.50, the lower selling price has the greater effect.
    Answer (B) is incorrect. A 15% increase in variable expenses will not decrease the CM as much as a 15% decrease in sales price. Answer (C) is incorrect. A decrease in variable expenses would increase UCM. Answer (D) is incorrect. Fixed expenses have no effect on the contribution margin.

Question 11 is based on the following information.

Delphi Company has developed a new product that will be marketed for the first time during the next fiscal year. Although the Marketing Department estimates that 35,000 units could be sold at $36 per unit, Delphi's management has allocated only enough manufacturing capacity to produce a maximum of 25,000 units of the new product annually. The fixed costs associated with the new product are budgeted at $450,000 for the year, which includes $60,000 for depreciation on new manufacturing equipment.

Data associated with each unit of product are presented as follows. Delphi is subject to a 40% income tax rate.

Direct material	$ 7.00
Direct labor	3.50
Manufacturing overhead	4.00
Variable manufacturing cost	$14.50
Selling expenses	1.50
Total variable cost	$16.00

11. The number of units of the new product that Delphi Company must sell during the next fiscal year in order to break even is

A. 20,930

B. 18,140

C. 22,500

D. 25,500

Answer (C) is correct.
REQUIRED: The breakeven point in units.
DISCUSSION: The breakeven point in units equals total fixed costs divided by the unit contribution margin. The unit contribution margin is $20 ($36 selling price – $16 unit variable cost). Hence, the breakeven point is 22,500 units ($450,000 ÷ $20).
Answer (A) is incorrect. The figure of 20,930 units excludes the $1.50 of variable selling expenses from the unit contribution margin. Answer (B) is incorrect. The figure of 18,140 units excludes the $1.50 of variable selling expenses from the unit contribution margin and the depreciation from the fixed costs. Answer (D) is incorrect. The figure of 25,500 units adds the $60,000 of depreciation to the fixed costs.

Question 12 is based on the following information. Bruell Electronics Co. is developing a new product, surge protectors for high-voltage electrical flows. The cost information below relates to the product:

	Unit Costs
Direct materials	$3.25
Direct labor	4.00
Distribution	.75

The company will also be absorbing $120,000 of additional fixed costs associated with this new product. A corporate fixed charge of $20,000 currently absorbed by other products will be allocated to this new product.

12. If the selling price is $14 per unit, the breakeven point in units (rounded to the nearest hundred) for surge protectors is

A. 8,500 units.

B. 10,000 units.

C. 15,000 units.

D. 20,000 units.

Answer (D) is correct.
REQUIRED: The breakeven point in units.
DISCUSSION: The breakeven point in units for a new product equals total additional fixed costs divided by the unit contribution margin. Unit variable costs total $8 ($3.25 + $4.00 + $.75). Thus, UCM is $6 ($14 unit selling price – $8 unit variable cost), and the breakeven point is 20,000 units ($120,000 ÷ $6).
Answer (A) is incorrect. A breakeven point of 8,500 units ignores variable costs. Answer (B) is incorrect. The breakeven point is 20,000 units when the contribution margin is $6 per unit. Answer (C) is incorrect. This number of units equals fixed costs divided by unit variable cost.

Questions 13 and 14 are based on the following information. Barnes Corporation manufactures skateboards and is in the process of preparing next year's budget. The pro forma income statement for the current year is presented below.

Sales		$1,500,000
Cost of sales:		
Direct materials	$250,000	
Direct labor	150,000	
Variable overhead	75,000	
Fixed overhead	100,000	(575,000)
Gross profit		$ 925,000
Selling and G&A:		
Variable	$200,000	
Fixed	250,000	(450,000)
Operating income		$ 475,000

13. The breakeven point (rounded to the nearest dollar) for Barnes Corporation for the current year is

A. $146,341

B. $636,364

C. $729,730

D. $181,818

Answer (B) is correct.

REQUIRED: The breakeven point in dollars.

DISCUSSION: Fixed costs total $350,000 ($100,000 overhead + $250,000 SG&A). Variable costs total $675,000. Given sales of $1,500,000, the contribution margin is $825,000 ($1,500,000 − $675,000). Thus, the contribution margin percentage is 55% ($825,000 ÷ $1,500,000). Dividing the $350,000 of fixed costs by 55% produces a breakeven point of $636,363.64.

Answer (A) is incorrect. The amount of $146,341 does not even cover fixed costs. Answer (C) is incorrect. The amount of $729,730 in sales results in a small profit. Answer (D) is incorrect. The amount of $181,818 does not cover the $350,000 of fixed costs.

14. For the coming year, the management of Barnes Corporation anticipates a 10% increase in sales, a 12% increase in variable costs, and a $45,000 increase in fixed expenses. The breakeven point for next year will be

A. $729,027

B. $862,103

C. $214,018

D. $474,000

Answer (A) is correct.

REQUIRED: The breakeven point following an increase in sales, variable costs, and fixed expenses.

DISCUSSION: Sales are expected to be $1,650,000 ($1,500,000 × 1.10), variable costs $756,000 ($675,000 × 1.12), and fixed expenses $395,000 ($350,000 + $45,000). Thus, the contribution margin will be $894,000 ($1,650,000 − $756,000), and the contribution margin percentage is 54.1818%. The breakeven point is therefore $729,027 ($395,000 fixed expenses ÷ .541818).

Answer (B) is incorrect. The contribution margin percentage is computed by dividing the contribution margin (total sales − total variable costs) by total sales, not by dividing the total variable costs by total sales. Answer (C) is incorrect. The amount of $214,018 does not cover fixed costs. Answer (D) is incorrect. The amount of $474,000 barely covers fixed costs.

15. The breakeven point in units sold is 44,000. If fixed costs are equal to $880,000 annually and variable costs are $10 per unit, what is the contribution margin per unit?

    A. $0.05

    B. $20.00

    C. $44.00

    D. $88.00

Answer (B) is correct.
    REQUIRED: The contribution margin per unit.
    DISCUSSION: The breakeven point in units is equal to the fixed costs divided by the contribution margin per unit. Thus, the UCM is $20.00 ($880,000 ÷ 44,000 units).
    Answer (A) is incorrect. The amount of $0.05 results from inverting the numerator and denominator in the calculation. Answer (C) is incorrect. The amount of $44.00 results from using variable cost as part of the calculation. Answer (D) is incorrect. The amount of $88.00 results from dividing by an erroneous denominator.

16. A manufacturer contemplates a change in technology that would reduce fixed costs from $800,000 to $700,000. However, the ratio of variable costs to sales will increase from 68% to 80%. What will happen to the breakeven level of revenues?

    A. Decrease by $301,470.50.

    B. Decrease by $500,000.

    C. Decrease by $1,812,500.

    D. Increase by $1,000,000.

Answer (D) is correct.
    REQUIRED: The change in breakeven level.
    DISCUSSION: The original breakeven level was:

Breakeven point = Fixed costs ÷ Contribution margin ratio
              = $800,000 ÷ (1.0 − .68)
              = $2,500,000

The new level is:

Breakeven point = Fixed costs ÷ Contribution margin ratio
              = $700,000 ÷ (1.0 − .80)
              = $3,500,000

    Thus, there is an increase of $1,000,000 ($3,500,000 − $2,500,000).
    Answer (A) is incorrect. The amount of a $301,470.50 decrease uses the variable cost percentage in the denominator instead of the contribution margin percentage. Answer (B) is incorrect. The amount of a $500,000 decrease uses the same contribution margin percentage (20%) in both calculations. Answer (C) is incorrect. The amount of a $1,812,500 decrease reverses the two contribution margin percentages.

9.4 CVP Analysis -- Target Income Calculations

17. A manufacturer is considering introducing a new product that will require a $250,000 investment of capital. The necessary funds would be raised through a bank loan at an interest rate of 8%. The fixed operating costs associated with the product would be $122,500, while the contribution margin percentage would be 42%. Assuming a selling price of $15 per unit, determine the number of units (rounded to the nearest whole unit) the manufacturer would have to sell to generate earnings before interest and taxes (EBIT) of 32% of the amount of capital invested in the new product.

    A. 35,318 units.

    B. 32,143 units.

    C. 25,575 units.

    D. 23,276 units.

Answer (B) is correct.
    REQUIRED: The level of sales required to achieve a targeted EBIT given relevant data.
    DISCUSSION: The manufacturer has determined it must generate EBIT equal to 32% of the capital invested in this project, or $80,000 ($250,000 × 32%). The number of units it must produce to achieve this level of EBIT can be derived as follows:

Breakeven point = (Fixed costs + EBIT) ÷ Unit contribution margin
              = ($122,500 + $80,000) ÷ ($15 × 42%)
              = $202,500 ÷ $6.30
              = 32,142.86 units

    Answer (A) is incorrect. Improperly including interest as a fixed cost results in 35,318. Answer (C) is incorrect. Improperly including interest as a fixed cost and using the cost percentage in the calculation instead of the contribution margin percentage results in 25,575. Answer (D) is incorrect. Improperly using the complement of the contribution margin percentage instead of the contribution margin percentage results in 23,276.

Questions 18 and 19 are based on the following information.

Delphi Company has developed a new product that will be marketed for the first time during the next fiscal year. Although the Marketing Department estimates that 35,000 units could be sold at $36 per unit, Delphi's management has allocated only enough manufacturing capacity to produce a maximum of 25,000 units of the new product annually. The fixed costs associated with the new product are budgeted at $450,000 for the year, which includes $60,000 for depreciation on new manufacturing equipment.

Data associated with each unit of product are presented as follows. Delphi is subject to a 40% income tax rate.

Direct material	$ 7.00
Direct labor	3.50
Manufacturing overhead	4.00
Variable manufacturing cost	$14.50
Selling expenses	1.50
Total variable cost	$16.00

18. The maximum after-tax profit that can be earned by Delphi Company from sales of the new product during the next fiscal year is

A. $30,000

B. $50,000

C. $110,000

D. $66,000

Answer (A) is correct.
   REQUIRED: The maximum after-tax profit.
   DISCUSSION: Delphi's breakeven point is 22,500 units ($450,000 fixed costs ÷ $20 UCM). The unit contribution margin (UCM) is $20 ($36 selling price – $16 unit variable costs). At the breakeven point, all fixed costs have been recovered. Hence, pretax profit equals the unit contribution margin times unit sales in excess of the breakeven point, or $50,000 [(25,000 unit sales – 22,500 BEP) × $20 UCM]. After-tax profit is $30,000 [$50,000 × (1.0 – .40)].
   Answer (B) is incorrect. The amount of $50,000 is the pre-tax profit. Answer (C) is incorrect. The amount of $110,000 fails to include depreciation as a fixed cost and ignores income taxes. Answer (D) is incorrect. The amount of $66,000 fails to include depreciation as a fixed cost.

19. Delphi Company's management has stipulated that it will not approve the continued manufacture of the new product after the next fiscal year unless the after-tax profit is at least $75,000 the first year. The unit selling price to achieve this target profit must be at least

A. $37.00

B. $36.60

C. $34.60

D. $39.00

Answer (D) is correct.
   REQUIRED: The unit selling price to achieve a targeted after-tax profit.
   DISCUSSION: If X represents the necessary selling price, 25,000 equals maximum sales volume, $16 is the variable cost per unit, $450,000 is the total fixed cost, and $125,000 [$75,000 target after-tax profit ÷ (1.0 – .40)] is the desired pre-tax profit, the following formula may be solved to determine the requisite unit price:

$$25,000 (X - \$16) - \$450,000 = \$125,000$$
$$25,000X - \$400,000 - \$450,000 = \$125,000$$
$$25,000X = \$975,000$$
$$X = \$39$$

   Answer (A) is incorrect. The amount of $37.00 does not consider income taxes. Answer (B) is incorrect. The amount of $36.60 excludes depreciation. Answer (C) is incorrect. The amount of $34.60 does not include depreciation or taxes.

Questions 20 and 21 are based on the following information. Bruell Electronics Co. is developing a new product, surge protectors for high-voltage electrical flows. The cost information below relates to the product:

	Unit Costs
Direct materials	$3.25
Direct labor	4.00
Distribution	.75

The company will also be absorbing $120,000 of additional fixed costs associated with this new product. A corporate fixed charge of $20,000 currently absorbed by other products will be allocated to this new product.

20. How many surge protectors (rounded to the nearest hundred) must Bruell Electronics sell at a selling price of $14 per unit to gain $30,000 additional income before taxes?

A. 10,700 units.

B. 12,100 units.

C. 20,000 units.

D. 25,000 units.

Answer (D) is correct.
 REQUIRED: The number of units to be sold to generate a targeted pre-tax income.
 DISCUSSION: The number of units to be sold to generate a specified pre-tax income equals the sum of total fixed costs and the targeted pre-tax income, divided by the unit contribution margin. Unit variable costs total $8 ($3.25 + $4.00 + $.75), and UCM is $6 ($14 unit selling price – $8). Thus, the desired unit sales level equals 25,000 units [($120,000 + $30,000) ÷ $6].
 Answer (A) is incorrect. The number of 10,700 units is based on a UCM equal to selling price. Answer (B) is incorrect. A contribution margin of $6 per unit necessitates sales of 25,000 units to produce a $30,000 before-tax profit. Answer (C) is incorrect. The number of 20,000 units is the breakeven point.

21. How many surge protectors (rounded to the nearest hundred) must Bruell Electronics sell at a selling price of $14 per unit to increase after-tax income by $30,000? Bruell Electronics' effective income tax rate is 40%.

A. 10,700 units.

B. 12,100 units.

C. 20,000 units.

D. 28,300 units.

Answer (D) is correct.
 REQUIRED: The number of units to be sold to generate a specified after-tax income.
 DISCUSSION: The number of units to be sold to generate a specified pre-tax income equals the sum of total fixed costs and the targeted pre-tax income, divided by the unit contribution margin. Given a desired after-tax income of $30,000 and a tax rate of 40%, the targeted pre-tax income must be $50,000 [$30,000 ÷ (1.0 – .40)]. Unit variable costs total $8 ($3.25 + $4.00 + $.75), and UCM is $6 ($14 unit selling price – $8). Hence, the desired unit sales level is 28,333 [($120,000 + $50,000) ÷ $6]. Rounded to the nearest hundred, the answer is 28,300 units.
 Answer (A) is incorrect. The number of 10,700 units is based on a UCM equal to the selling price and $30,000 of pretax income. Answer (B) is incorrect. A $6 UCM necessitates sales of 28,300 units to produce a $30,000 after-tax profit. Answer (C) is incorrect. The number of 20,000 units is the breakeven point.

22. A company, which is subject to a 40% income tax rate, had the following operating data for the period just ended:

Selling price per unit	$60
Variable cost per unit	$22
Fixed costs	$504,000

Management plans to improve the quality of its sole product by (1) replacing a component that costs $3.50 with a higher-grade unit that costs $5.50 and (2) acquiring a $180,000 packing machine. The company will depreciate the machine over a 10-year life with no estimated salvage value by the straight-line method of depreciation. If the company wants to earn after-tax income of $172,800 in the upcoming period, it must sell

   A. 19,300 units.

   B. 21,316 units.

   C. 22,500 units.

   D. 23,800 units.

23. A manufacturer is considering dropping a product line. It currently produces a multi-purpose woodworking clamp in a simple manufacturing process that uses special equipment. Variable costs amount to $6.00 per unit. Fixed overhead costs, exclusive of depreciation, have been allocated to this product at a rate of $3.50 a unit and will continue whether or not production ceases. Depreciation on the special equipment amounts to $20,000 a year. Fixed costs are $18,000. The clamp has a selling price of $10 a unit. Ignoring tax effects, the minimum number of units that would have to be sold in the current year to break even on a cash flow basis is

   A. 4,500 units.

   B. 5,000 units.

   C. 20,000 units.

   D. 36,000 units.

Answer (C) is correct.
   REQUIRED: The number of units to be sold to generate a targeted after-tax profit given that variable costs and fixed costs increase.
   DISCUSSION: The units to be sold equal fixed costs plus the desired pretax profit, divided by the unit contribution margin. In the preceding year, the unit contribution margin is $38 ($60 selling price – $22 unit variable cost). That amount will decrease by $2 to $36 in the upcoming year because of use of a higher-grade component. Fixed costs will increase from $504,000 to $522,000 as a result of the $18,000 ($180,000 ÷ 10 years) increase in fixed costs attributable to depreciation on the new machine. Dividing the $172,800 of desired after-tax income by 60% (the complement of the tax rate) produces a desired before-tax income of $288,000. Hence, the breakeven point in units is 22,500 [($522,000 + $288,000) ÷ $36].
   Answer (A) is incorrect. The number of 19,300 units does not take income taxes into consideration. Answer (B) is incorrect. The number of 21,316 units fails to consider the increased variable costs from the introduction of the higher-priced component. Answer (D) is incorrect. The number of 23,800 units does not take income taxes into consideration, and it includes the entire cost of the new machine as a fixed cost.

Answer (A) is correct.
   REQUIRED: The breakeven point in units on a cash flow basis.
   DISCUSSION: The BEP in units is equal to fixed costs divided by the unit contribution margin ($10 unit selling price – $6 unit variable cost). Hence, the number of units that must be sold to break even on continuation of the product line is 4,500 [$18,000 fixed costs ÷ ($10 – $6)]. Fixed overhead allocated is not considered in this calculation because it is not a cash flow element, and will continue regardless of the decision.
   Answer (B) is incorrect. The BEP is equal to the salvage value (not depreciation) divided by the UCM of $4 ($10 – $6). Depreciation is a non-cash flow element, and therefore should not be considered in the cash flow breakeven point calculation. Answer (C) is incorrect. The BEP is equal to the salvage value (not depreciation) divided by the UCM of $4 ($10 – $6). Depreciation is a non-cash flow element, and therefore should not be considered in the cash flow breakeven point calculation. Answer (D) is incorrect. Unit fixed costs should not be subtracted in determining the unit contribution margin. The fixed costs will continue regardless so they are not included in the calculation. Therefore, the $18,000 salvage value will be divided by the $4 unit contribution margin in determining the cash flow breakeven point in units.

9.5 CVP Analysis -- Multi-Product Calculations

Question 24 is based on the following information.

Moorehead Manufacturing Company produces two products for which the data presented to the right have been tabulated. Fixed manufacturing cost is applied at a rate of $1.00 per machine hour. The sales manager has had a $160,000 increase in the budget allotment for advertising and wants to apply the money to the most profitable product. The products are not substitutes for one another in the eyes of the company's customers.

Per Unit	XY-7	BD-4
Selling price	$4.00	$3.00
Variable manufacturing cost	2.00	1.50
Fixed manufacturing cost	.75	.20
Variable selling cost	1.00	1.00

24. Suppose Moorehead has only 100,000 machine hours that can be made available to produce additional units of XY-7 and BD-4. If the potential increase in sales units for either product resulting from advertising is far in excess of this production capacity, which product should be advertised and what is the estimated increase in contribution margin earned?

A. Product XY-7 should be produced, yielding a contribution margin of $75,000.

B. Product XY-7 should be produced, yielding a contribution margin of $133,333.

C. Product BD-4 should be produced, yielding a contribution margin of $187,500.

D. Product BD-4 should be produced, yielding a contribution margin of $250,000.

Answer (D) is correct.

REQUIRED: The more profitable product and the estimated increase in contribution margin.

DISCUSSION: The machine hours are a scarce resource that must be allocated to the product(s) in a proportion that maximizes the total CM. Given that potential additional sales of either product are in excess of production capacity, only the product with the greater CM per unit of scarce resource should be produced. XY-7 requires .75 hours; BD-4 requires .2 hours of machine time (given fixed manufacturing cost applied at $1 per machine hour of $.75 for XY-7 and $.20 for BD-4).

XY-7 has a CM of $1.33 per machine hour ($1 UCM ÷ .75 hours), and BD-4 has a CM of $2.50 per machine hour ($.50 ÷ .2 hours). Thus, only BD-4 should be produced, yielding a CM of $250,000 (100,000 × $2.50). The key to the analysis is CM per unit of scarce resource.

Answer (A) is incorrect. Product XY-7 actually has a CM of $133,333, which is lower than the $250,000 CM for product BD-4. Answer (B) is incorrect. Product BD-4 has a higher CM at $250,000. Answer (C) is incorrect. Product BD-4 has a CM of $250,000.

Questions 25 through 27 are based on the following information. Siberian Ski Company recently expanded its manufacturing capacity to allow it to produce up to 15,000 pairs of cross-country skis of the mountaineering model or the touring model. The sales department assures management that it can sell between 9,000 pairs and 13,000 pairs (units) of either product this year. Because the models are very similar, Siberian Ski will produce only one of the two models. The information below was compiled by the accounting department.

	Model	
	Mountaineering	Touring
Selling price per unit	$88.00	$80.00
Variable costs per unit	52.80	52.80

Fixed costs will total $369,600 if the mountaineering model is produced but will be only $316,800 if the touring model is produced. Siberian Ski is subject to a 40% income tax rate.

25. The total sales revenue at which Siberian Ski Company would make the same profit or loss regardless of the ski model it decided to produce is

A. $880,000

B. $422,400

C. $924,000

D. $686,400

Answer (A) is correct.
   REQUIRED: The sales revenue resulting in the same profit or loss regardless of which model is produced.
   DISCUSSION: The sales revenue at which the same profit or loss will be made equals the unit price times the units sold for each kind of skis. Accordingly, if M is the number of units sold of mountaineering skis and T is the number of units sold of touring skis, this level of sales revenue may be stated as $88M or $80T, and M is therefore equal to ($80 ÷ $88)T. Moreover, given the same profit or loss, the difference between sales revenue and total costs (variable + fixed) will also be the same for the two kinds of skis. Solving the equation below by substituting for M yields sales revenue of $880,000 [(11,000 × $80) or (10,000 × $88)].

$$Sales_M - VC_M - FC_M = Sales_T - VC_T - FC_T$$
$$\$88M - \$52.80M - \$369,600 = \$80T - \$52.80T - \$316,800$$
$$\$35.2M - \$52,800 = \$27.2T$$
$$\$35.2(\$80 ÷ \$88)T = \$27.2T + \$52,800$$
$$T = 11,000 \text{ units}$$
$$M = 10,000 \text{ units}$$

26. If the Siberian Ski Company Sales Department could guarantee the annual sale of 12,000 pairs of either model, Siberian Ski would

A. Produce 12,000 pairs of touring skis because they have a lower fixed cost.

B. Be indifferent as to which model is sold because each model has the same variable cost per unit.

C. Produce 12,000 pairs of mountaineering skis because they have a lower breakeven point.

D. Produce 12,000 pairs of mountaineering skis because they are more profitable.

Answer (D) is correct.
   REQUIRED: The model that should be produced if sales are exactly 12,000 pairs.
   DISCUSSION: Preparing income statements determines which model will produce the greater profit at a sales level of 12,000 pairs. Thus, as indicated below, the mountaineering skis should be produced.

	Mountain	Touring
Sales	$1,056,000	$960,000
Variable costs	(633,600)	(633,600)
Fixed costs	(369,600)	(316,800)
Operating Income	$ 52,800	$ 9,600

   Answer (A) is incorrect. At a sales volume of 12,000 pairs, the higher contribution margin of the mountaineering skis results in a greater profit. Answer (B) is incorrect. The lower selling price of the touring skis results in a lower contribution margin per unit sold. Answer (C) is incorrect. Breakeven point is not a consideration. A sales volume of 12,000 units is above the breakeven point for both models.

27. If Siberian Ski Company desires an after-tax net income of $24,000, how many pairs of touring model skis will the company have to sell?

A. 13,118 pairs.

B. 12,529 pairs.

C. 13,853 pairs.

D. 4,460 pairs.

Answer (A) is correct.
   REQUIRED: The units of touring model skis the company will have to sell to produce a given after-tax profit.
   DISCUSSION: The breakeven sales volume equals total fixed costs divided by the unit contribution margin (UCM). In the breakeven formula, the desired profit should be treated as a fixed cost. Because the UCM is stated in pretax dollars, the targeted profit must be adjusted for taxes. Hence, the targeted after-tax net income of $24,000 is equivalent to a pretax profit of $40,000 [$24,000 ÷ (1.0 – .40)]. The sum of the pretax profit and the fixed costs is $356,800 ($316,800 + $40,000). Consequently, the desired sales volume is 13,118 pairs of touring skis [$356,800 ÷ ($80 selling price – $52.80 unit variable cost)].

Questions 28 through 30 are based on the following information. MultiFrame Company has the following revenue and cost budgets for the two products it sells:

	Plastic Frames	Glass Frames
Sales price	$10.00	$15.00
Direct materials	(2.00)	(3.00)
Direct labor	(3.00)	(5.00)
Fixed overhead	(3.00)	(4.00)
Net income per unit	$ 2.00	$ 3.00
Budgeted unit sales	100,000	300,000

The budgeted unit sales equal the current unit demand, and total fixed overhead for the year is budgeted at $975,000. Assume that the company plans to maintain the same proportional mix. In numerical calculations, MultiFrame rounds to the nearest cent and unit.

28. The total number of units MultiFrame needs to produce and sell to break even is

A. 150,000 units.

B. 354,545 units.

C. 177,273 units.

D. 300,000 units.

Answer (A) is correct.
REQUIRED: The total units sold at the breakeven point.
DISCUSSION: The calculation of the breakeven point is to divide the fixed costs by the contribution margin per unit. This determination is more complicated for a multi-product firm. If the same proportional product mix is maintained, one unit of plastic frames is sold for every three units of glass frames. Accordingly, a composite unit consists of four frames: one plastic and three glass. For plastic frames, the unit contribution margin is $5 ($10 − $2 − $3). For glass frames, the unit contribution margin is $7 ($15 − $3 − $5). Thus, the composite unit contribution margin is $26 ($5 + $7 + $7 + $7), and the breakeven point is 37,500 packages ($975,000 FC ÷ $26). Because each composite unit contains four frames, the total units sold equal 150,000.

29. The total number of units needed to break even if the budgeted direct labor costs were $2 for plastic frames instead of $3 is

A. 154,028 units.

B. 144,444 units.

C. 156,000 units.

D. 146,177 units.

Answer (B) is correct.
REQUIRED: The breakeven point in units if labor costs for the plastic frames are reduced.
DISCUSSION: If the labor costs for the plastic frames are reduced by $1, the composite unit contribution margin will be $27 {($10 − $2 − $2) + [($15 − $3 − $5) × 3]}. Hence, the new breakeven point is 144,444 units [4 units × ($975,000 FC ÷ $27)].

30. The total number of units needed to break even if sales were budgeted at 150,000 units of plastic frames and 300,000 units of glass frames with all other costs remaining constant is

A. 171,958 units.

B. 418,455 units.

C. 153,947 units.

D. 365,168 units.

Answer (C) is correct.
REQUIRED: The total number of units needed to break even if the product mix is changed.
DISCUSSION: The unit contribution margins for plastic frames and glass frames are $5 ($10 − $2 − $3) and $7 ($15 − $3 − $5), respectively. If the number of plastic frames sold is 50% of the number of glass frames sold, a composite unit will contain one plastic frame and two glass frames. Thus, the composite unit contribution margin will be $19 ($5 + $7 + $7), and the breakeven point in units will be 153,947 [3 units × ($975,000 ÷ $19)].

Access the **Gleim CMA Premium Review System** from your Gleim Personal Classroom to continue your studies with exam-emulating multiple-choice questions!

9.6 ESSAY QUESTIONS

Scenario for Essay Questions 1, 2

Don Masters and two of his colleagues are considering opening a law office in a large metropolitan area that would make inexpensive legal services available to those who could not otherwise afford these services. The intent is to provide easy access for their clients by having the office open 360 days per year, 16 hours each day from 7:00 a.m. to 11:00 p.m. The office would be staffed by a lawyer, paralegal, legal secretary, and clerk-receptionist for each of the two 8-hour shifts.

To determine the feasibility of the project, Masters hired a marketing consultant to assist with market projections. The results of this study show that, if the firm spends $500,000 on advertising the first year, the number of new clients expected each day would have the following probability distribution.

Number of New Clients per Day	Probability
20	.10
30	.30
55	.40
85	.20

Masters and his associates believe these numbers are reasonable and are prepared to spend the $500,000 on advertising. Other pertinent information about the operation of the office is given below.

- The only charge to each new client would be $30 for the initial consultation. All cases that warranted further legal work would be accepted on a contingency basis with the firm earning 30% of any favorable settlements or judgments. Masters estimates that 20% of new client consultations will result in favorable settlements or judgments averaging $2,000 each. It is not expected that there will be repeat clients during the first year of operations.

- The hourly wages of the staff are projected to be $25 for the lawyer, $20 for the paralegal, $15 for the legal secretary, and $10 for the clerk-receptionist. Fringe benefit expense will be 40% of the wages paid. A total of 400 hours of overtime is expected for the year; this will be divided equally between the legal secretary and the clerk-receptionist positions. Overtime will be paid at one and one-half times the regular wage, and the fringe benefit expense will apply to the full wage.

- Masters has located 6,000 square feet of suitable office space that rents for $28 per square foot annually. Associated expenses will be $22,000 for property insurance and $32,000 for utilities.

- It will be necessary for the group to purchase malpractice insurance, which is expected to cost $180,000 annually.

- The initial investment in office equipment will be $60,000; this equipment has an estimated useful life of 4 years.

- The cost of office supplies has been estimated to be $4 per expected new client.

Questions

1. Determine how many new clients must visit the law office being considered by Don Masters and his colleagues for the venture to break even during its first year of operations.

2. Using the information provided by the marketing consultant, determine if it is feasible for the law office to achieve breakeven operations.

Essay Questions 1, 2 — Unofficial Answers

1. In order to break even during the first year of operations, 10,220 clients must visit the law office being considered by Don Masters and his colleagues, as calculated below.

Breakeven Calculations for First Year of Operations

Fixed expenses:

Advertising		$ 500,000
Rent (6,000 × $28)		168,000
Property insurance		22,000
Utilities		32,000
Malpractice insurance		180,000
Depreciation ($60,000 ÷ 4)		15,000
Wages and fringe benefits		
Regular wages:		
($25 + $20 + $15 + $10) × 16 hours × 360 days	$403,200	
Overtime wages:		
(200 × $15 × 1.5) + (200 × $10 × 1.5)	7,500	
Total wages	$410,700	
Fringe benefits at 40%	164,280	574,980
Total fixed expenses		$1,491,980

Unit contribution margin = Unit revenue – Unit variable cost
= [$30 + ($2,000 × .2 × .3)] – $4
= ($30 + $120) – $4
= $146

Breakeven point = Fixed costs ÷ UCM
= $1,491,980 ÷ $146
= 10,219.04 clients

2. Based on the report of the marketing consultant, the expected number of new clients during the first year is 18,000, as calculated below. Therefore, it is feasible for the law office to break even during the first year of operations as the breakeven point is 10,220 clients.

Expected value = (20 × .10) + (30 × .30) + (55 × .40) + (85 × .20)
= 50 clients per day

Annual clients = 50 × 360 days
= 18,000 clients per year

 Access the **Gleim CMA Premium Review System** from your Gleim Personal Classroom to continue your studies with exam-emulating essay questions!

STUDY UNIT TEN
MARGINAL ANALYSIS AND PRICING

(20 pages of outline)

This study unit is the **second of two** on **decision analysis**. The relative weight assigned to this major topic in Part 2 of the exam is **20%**. The two study units are

Study Unit 9: CVP Analysis
Study Unit 10: Marginal Analysis and Pricing

Marginal analysis allows economic decisions to be made based on projecting the results of varying the levels of resource consumption and output production. Thus, marginal revenue data must be compared with marginal cost data to determine the point of profit maximization. Additionally, the impact of income tax on each level of production must be considered in order to determine the profitability at each level and whether the company will meet its required rate of return.

If you are interested in reviewing more introductory or background material, go to www.gleim.com/CMAIntroVideos for a list of suggested third-party overviews of this topic. The following Gleim outline material is more than sufficient to help you pass the CMA exam; any additional introductory or background material is for your own personal enrichment.

10.1 DECISION MAKING -- APPLYING MARGINAL ANALYSIS

When applying marginal analysis to decision making, a CMA candidate must be able to easily identify avoidable and unavoidable costs. Unavoidable costs have no relevance to the decision-making process to drop or add a segment. This may seem simple, but a typical CMA exam question will not include whether the costs are relevant or irrelevant, and you must be able to readily identify them as such, calculate the cost, and recommend a course of action. Incorrectly identifying a cost for whatever reason could easily lead to an incorrect calculation and evaluation of the situation.

1. **Accounting Costs vs. Economic Costs**

   a. The accounting concept of costs includes only explicit costs, i.e., those that represent actual outlays of cash, the allocation of outlays of cash, or commitments to pay cash. Examples include the incurrence of payables, the satisfaction of payables, and the recognition of depreciation.

   b. The economic concept of costs includes both explicit and implicit costs.

      1) Implicit in any business decision is opportunity cost, defined as "the contribution to income that is forgone by not using a limited resource in its best alternative use."

   c. EXAMPLE: A manufacturer's accounting cost for a new product line consists only of the costs associated with the new machinery and personnel, but the economic cost includes the 4.75% return the company could make by simply investing the money in certificates of deposit.

2.   **Explicit vs. Implicit Costs**

    a.   Explicit costs are those requiring actual cash disbursements. For this reason, they are sometimes called out-of-pocket or outlay costs.

        1)   Explicit costs are accounting costs, that is, they are recognized in a concern's formal accounting records.

        2)   For example, an entrepreneur opening a gift shop has to make certain cash disbursements to get the business up and running.

Inventory	$50,000
Display cases	9,000
Rent	4,000
Utilities	1,000
Total explicit costs	**$64,000**

    b.   Implicit costs are **opportunity costs**, i.e., the maximum benefit forgone by using a scarce resource for a given purpose and not for the next-best alternative.

        1)   To measure the true economic success or failure of the venture, the entrepreneur in the example above must account for more than just the explicit costs that can easily be found in the accounting records.

            a)   The entrepreneur's opportunity costs are the most important implicit costs. (S)he could have simply gone to work for another company rather than open the gift shop.

            b)   The money put into startup costs could have been invested in financial instruments.

            c)   A normal profit is a crucial implicit cost. In this example, the normal profit is the income that the entrepreneur could have earned applying his or her skill to another venture.

Salary forgone	$35,000
Investment income forgone	3,600
Total implicit costs	**$38,600**

    c.   Economic costs are total costs.

        1)   The true hurdle for an economic decision is whether the revenues from the venture will cover all costs, both explicit and implicit.

$$\begin{aligned}\textbf{Economic costs} &= \text{Total costs} \\ &= \text{Explicit costs} + \text{Implicit costs} \\ &= \$64,000 + \$38,600 \\ &= \mathbf{\$102,600}\end{aligned}$$

3.   **Accounting vs. Economic Profit**

    a.   Accounting profits are earned when the (book) income of an organization exceeds the (book) expenses.

        1)   After the first year of operation, the gift shop owner made a tidy accounting profit.

Sales revenue	$100,000
Explicit costs	(64,000)
Accounting profit	**$ 36,000**

b. Economic profits are a significantly higher hurdle. They are not earned until the organization's income exceeds not only costs as recorded in the accounting records, but the firm's implicit costs as well. Economic profit is also called pure profit.

1) Once total costs are taken into account, a different picture emerges.

Accounting profit	$ 36,000
Implicit costs	(38,600)
Economic loss	**$ (2,600)**

4. **Relevant vs. Irrelevant Factors**

a. In decision making, an organization must focus on only relevant revenues and costs. To be relevant, the revenues and costs must

1) Be made in the future

a) Costs that have already been incurred or to which the organization is committed, called **sunk costs**, have no bearing on any future decisions.

b) EXAMPLE: A manufacturer is considering upgrading its production equipment due to the obsolescence of its current machinery. The amounts paid for the existing equipment are sunk costs; they make no difference in the decision to modernize.

2) Differ among the possible alternative courses of action

a) EXAMPLE: A manufacturer is considering purchasing production equipment from Meen Co. costing $400,000 with an estimated operating life of 5 years, or from Neem Equipment Ltd. costing $600,000 with an estimated operating life of 8 years.

b. Only avoidable costs are relevant. Unavoidable costs are irrelevant.

1) An **avoidable cost** may be saved by not adopting a particular option. Avoidable costs might include variable raw material costs and direct labor costs.

2) An **unavoidable cost** is one that cannot be avoided if a particular action is taken.

a) For example, if a company has a long-term lease on a building, closing out the business in that building will not eliminate the need to pay rent. Thus, the rent is an unavoidable cost.

c. **Incremental (marginal or differential) costs** are inherent in the concept of relevance.

1) Throughout the relevant range, the incremental cost of an additional unit of output is the same.

a) Once a certain level of output is reached, however, the current production capacity is insufficient and another increment of fixed costs must be incurred.

d. Another pitfall in relevant cost determination is the use of unit revenues and costs.

1) The emphasis should be on total relevant revenues and costs because unit data may include irrelevant amounts or may have been computed for an output level different from the one for which the analysis is being made.

5. **Marginal, Differential, or Incremental Analysis**

   a. The typical problem for which marginal (differential or incremental) analysis can be used involves choices among courses of action.

EXAMPLE

Sam is driving a 20-year-old automobile that gets poor fuel mileage and is subject to recurring repair bills.

1. The car is fully paid for, but a major engine overhaul may or may not be required within the next 12 months. The new car he is considering is a high-performance model and will not get noticeably higher fuel mileage than his current car.

2. Sam must decide between continuing to drive his current car or purchasing the new one, and he now must separate the costs that are relevant to the decision from those that are irrelevant.

Variable costs:	Relevant	Irrelevant
Repairs	✓	
Overhaul	✓	
Fixed costs, recurring:		
Loan	✓	
Insurance	✓	
License Plates		✓
Fixed costs, one-time:		
Trade-in value	✓	

3. Each item designated as relevant will both occur in the future and be different depending on which car Sam chooses.

---

   b. **Quantitative analysis** emphasizes the ways in which revenues and costs vary with the option chosen. Thus, the focus is on incremental revenues and costs, not the totals of all revenues and costs for the given option.

   1) A useful measurement of the quantitative effects of different options is to measure each option's contribution margin per unit of constraint.

      a) **Contribution margin** is a product's price minus all associated variable costs.

      b) The **constraint** is any measure of activity, such as direct labor hours, machine hours, beds occupied, computer time used, flight hours, miles driven, or contracts, that drives an entity's costs.

      c) When a constraint is limited or unavailable, the manager should direct limited resources toward those products and services that produce the most contribution margin per unit of constraint.

      d) An **optimum strategy** uses as much of the constraint as necessary to fill demand for the product or service with the highest contribution margin per unit of constraint. The remaining units of constraint are used on the product or service with the next highest contribution margin per unit until there is no available constraint..

EXAMPLE

A manufacturer assembled the following data regarding their two product lines.

	Product A	Product B
Annual unit demand	10,000	20,000
Selling Price	$100	$ 80
Variable manufacturing cost	(55)	(42)
Fixed manufacturing cost	(10)	(10)
Variable selling and administrative	(10)	(12)
Fixed selling and administrative	(7)	(4)
Unit operating profit	$ 18	$ 12
Machine hours per unit	2.5	2.0

The manufacturer has 55,000 machine hours available.

Filling all demand would require 25,000 (10,000 units × 2.5 machine hours per unit) machine hours for Product A and 40,000 (20,000 units × 2 machine hours per unit) machine hours for Product B. The total time required is therefore 65,000 machine hours, but since there are only 55,000 available, the manufacturer must determine the contribution margin per machine hour for the two products to determine what to produce.

The contribution per machine hour can be calculated as follows:

	Product A	Product B
Sales price	$100	$ 80
Variable manufacturing cost	(55)	(42)
Variable S & A	(10)	(12)
Contribution margin	$ 35	$ 26
Divided by: machine hours per unit	÷ 2.5	÷ 2.0
Contribution margin per machine hour	$ 14	$ 13

The manufacturer will produce as much as it can with the higher contribution margin per hour, then use any time left over to produce the other. Therefore, 10,000 units of Product A will be produced and the remaining 30,000 [55,000 – (10,000 units × 2.5 machine hours per unit)] hours will be used to produce 15,000 units (30,000 remaining hours ÷ 2.0 machine hours per unit) of Product B. This is the optimum strategy.

6. **Qualitative Factors**

   a. Caution always must be used in applying marginal analysis. Many qualitative factors, including those listed below, should be considered.

      1) Special price concessions place the firm in violation of the price discrimination provisions of the Robinson-Patman Act of 1936.
      2) Government contract pricing regulations apply.
      3) Sales to a special customer affect sales in the firm's regular market.
      4) Regular customers learn of a special price and demand equal terms.
      5) Disinvestment, such as by dropping a product line, will hurt sales in the other product lines (e.g., the dropped product may have been an unintended loss leader).
      6) An outsourced product's quality is acceptable and the supplier is reliable.
      7) Employee morale may be affected. If employees are laid off or asked to work too few or too many hours, morale may be affected favorably or unfavorably.

Stop and review! You have completed the outline for this subunit. Study multiple-choice questions 1 through 4 beginning on page 319.

10.2 DECISION MAKING -- SPECIAL ORDERS

1.   **Submitting Bids for the Lowest Selling Price**

   a.   Bids should be made at prices that meet or exceed incremental cost depending on how competitive the bid needs to be.

      1)   A bid lower than incremental cost can result in lower profit for the company.

         a)   However, lower bids are more competitive and are therefore closer to incremental cost.

      2)   The company must weigh quantitative and qualitative factors when deciding on a final bid.

         a)   Whether available capacity exists affects whether fixed costs will be included in the lowest possible bid price.

2.   **Special Orders When Available Capacity Exists**

   a.   When a manufacturer has available production capacity, there is no opportunity cost involved when accepting a special order. This occurs because fixed costs are already committed and there is still available capacity.

      1)   When there is available capacity, fixed costs are **irrelevant**.

      2)   The company should accept the order if the minimum price for the product is equal to the variable costs.

EXAMPLE

Normal unit pricing for a manufacture's product is as follows:

Direct materials and labor	$15.00
Variable overhead	3.00
Fixed overhead	5.00
Variable selling	1.50
Fixed selling and administrative	12.00
Total cost	$36.50

If the manufacturer receives a special order for which capacity exists, the lowest bid the company could offer is $19.50 ($15.00 + $3.00 + $1.50).

---

3.   **Special Orders in the Absence of Available Capacity**

   a.   When a manufacturer lacks available production capacity, the differential (marginal or incremental) costs of accepting the order must be considered.

      1)   Although fixed costs are committed, since there is no available capacity, the manufacturer will have to reduce production of existing product lines to fill the special order.

      2)   This means that the revenue, variable costs, and fixed costs related to reduced production of existing product lines are **relevant**.

EXAMPLE

Using the information from above, if the manufacturer receives a special order for which capacity does not exist, the lowest bid the company could offer is $36.50.

In addition to fixed costs, any revenue lost from reducing or stopping production on other product lines would be relevant when determining the lowest acceptable bid price.

Stop and review! You have completed the outline for this subunit. Study multiple-choice questions 5 through 9 beginning on page 320.

10.3 DECISION MAKING -- MAKE OR BUY

1. **Make-or-Buy Decisions (Insourcing vs. Outsourcing)**

    a. The firm should use available resources as efficiently as possible before outsourcing.

        1) If the total relevant costs of production are **less** than the cost to buy the item, it should be made in-house.

        2) If the total relevant costs of production are **more** than the costs to buy the item, it should be bought (outsourced).

    b. As with a special order, the manager considers only the costs relevant to the investment decision. The key variable is total relevant costs, not all total costs.

        1) Sunk costs are irrelevant.

        2) Costs that do not differ between two alternatives should be ignored because they are not relevant to the decision being made.

        3) Opportunity costs must be considered when idle capacity is not available. They are of primary importance because they represent the forgone opportunities of the firm.

            a) In some situations, a firm may decide to stop processing one product in order to free up capacity for another product, reducing relevant costs and affecting the decision to make or buy.

    c. The firm also should consider the **qualitative factors** of the decision.

        1) Will the product quality be as high if a component is outsourced rather than produced internally?

        2) How reliable are the suppliers?

2. **Make-or-Buy Decisions When Available Capacity Exists**

    a. When there is available capacity, fixed costs are **irrelevant** in deciding whether to make or buy the product.

EXAMPLE

Lawton must determine whether to make or buy an order of 1,000 frames. Lawton can purchase the frames for $13 or make them in-house. Lawton currently has adequate available capacity. Cost information for the frames is as follows:

Total variable costs	$10
Allocable fixed costs	5
Total unit costs	$15

Since there is available capacity, the allocable fixed costs are not relevant. The total relevant costs of $10 are less than the $13 cost to purchase, therefore, Lawton should make the frames.

---

3. **Make-or-Buy Decisions in the Absence of Available Capacity**

    a. When there is no available capacity, the differential (marginal or incremental) costs of accepting the order must be considered.

        1) This means that the revenue, variable costs, and fixed costs related to reduced production of existing product lines are **relevant** in deciding whether to make or buy the product.

EXAMPLE

Lawton has received another special order for 1,000 frames, but this month there is no available capacity.

Since there is no available capacity, the allocable fixed costs are relevant. The total relevant costs of $15 are more than the $13 cost to purchase, therefore, Lawton should purchase the frames.

Stop and review! You have completed the outline for this subunit. Study multiple-choice questions 10 through 13 beginning on page 323.

10.4 DECISION MAKING -- OTHER SITUATIONS

1. **Sell-or-Process-Further Decisions**

    a. In determining whether to sell a product at the **split-off point** or process the item further at additional cost, the joint cost of the product is irrelevant because it is a sunk cost.

        1) **Joint (common) costs** are those costs incurred up to the point where the products become separately identifiable, called the split-off point.

            a) Joint costs include direct materials, direct labor, and manufacturing overhead. Because they are not separately identifiable, they must be allocated to the individual joint products.

    b. At the split-off point, the joint products acquire separate identities, and costs incurred after the split-off point are separable costs.

        1) Separable costs can be identified with a particular joint product and are allocated to a specific unit of output.

        2) Separable costs are relevant when determining whether to sell or process further.

    c. Since joint costs cannot be traced to individual products, they must be allocated. The methods available for this allocation include

        1) The **physical-measure-based approach** employs a physical measure, such as volume, weight, or a linear measure.

        2) **Market-based approaches** assign a proportionate amount of the total cost to each product on a monetary basis.

            a) Sales-value at split-off method
            b) Estimated net realizable value (NRV) method
            c) Constant-gross-margin percentage NRV method

    d. The **physical-unit method** allocates joint production costs to each product based on their relative proportions of the measure selected.

        1) EXAMPLE: A refinery processes 1,000 barrels of crude oil and incurs $100,000 of processing costs. The process results in the following outputs. Under the physical unit method, the joint costs up to split-off are allocated as follows:

Asphalt	$100,000 × (300 barrels ÷ 1,000 barrels) =	$ 30,000
Fuel oil	$100,000 × (300 barrels ÷ 1,000 barrels) =	30,000
Diesel fuel	$100,000 × (200 barrels ÷ 1,000 barrels) =	20,000
Kerosene	$100,000 × (100 barrels ÷ 1,000 barrels) =	10,000
Gasoline	$100,000 × (100 barrels ÷ 1,000 barrels) =	10,000
Joint costs allocated		$100,000

        2) The physical-unit method's simplicity makes it appealing, but it does not match costs with the individual products' revenue-generating potential.

        3) However, its limitations are that it treats low-value products that are large in size as if they were valuable. As a result, a large, low-value product might always show a loss, whereas a small, high-value product will always show a profit.

    e. The **sales-value at split-off method** is based on the relative sales values of the separate products at split-off.

1) EXAMPLE: The refinery estimates that the five outputs can sell for the following prices at split-off:

Asphalt	300 barrels at $ 60/barrel =	$ 18,000
Fuel oil	300 barrels at $180/barrel =	54,000
Diesel fuel	200 barrels at $160/barrel =	32,000
Kerosene	100 barrels at $ 80/barrel =	8,000
Gasoline	100 barrels at $180/barrel =	18,000
Total sales value at split-off		$130,000

The total expected sales value for the entire production run at split-off is thus $130,000. Multiply the total joint costs to be allocated by the proportion of the total expected sales of each product:

Asphalt	$100,000 × ($18,000 ÷ $130,000) =	$ 13,846
Fuel oil	$100,000 × ($54,000 ÷ $130,000) =	41,539
Diesel fuel	$100,000 × ($32,000 ÷ $130,000) =	24,615
Kerosene	$100,000 × ($ 8,000 ÷ $130,000) =	6,154
Gasoline	$100,000 × ($18,000 ÷ $130,000) =	13,846
Joint costs allocated		$100,000

f. The **estimated net realizable value (NRV)** method also allocates joint costs based on the relative market values of the products.

1) The significant difference is that, under the estimated NRV method, all separable costs necessary to make the product salable are subtracted before the allocation is made.

2) EXAMPLE: The refinery estimates final sales prices as follows:

Asphalt	300 barrels at $ 70/barrel =	$21,000
Fuel oil	300 barrels at $200/barrel =	60,000
Diesel fuel	200 barrels at $180/barrel =	36,000
Kerosene	100 barrels at $ 90/barrel =	9,000
Gasoline	100 barrels at $190/barrel =	19,000

From these amounts, separable costs are subtracted (these costs are given):

Asphalt	$21,000 – $1,000 =	$ 20,000
Fuel oil	$60,000 – $1,000 =	59,000
Diesel fuel	$36,000 – $1,000 =	35,000
Kerosene	$ 9,000 – $2,000 =	7,000
Gasoline	$19,000 – $2,000 =	17,000
Total net realizable value		$138,000

Multiply the total joint costs to be allocated by the proportion of the final expected sales of each product:

Asphalt	$100,000 × ($20,000 ÷ $138,000) =	$ 14,493
Fuel oil	$100,000 × ($59,000 ÷ $138,000) =	42,754
Diesel fuel	$100,000 × ($35,000 ÷ $138,000) =	25,362
Kerosene	$100,000 × ($ 7,000 ÷ $138,000) =	5,072
Gasoline	$100,000 × ($17,000 ÷ $138,000) =	12,319
Joint costs allocated		$100,000

g. The **constant-gross-margin percentage NRV** method is based on allocating joint costs so that the gross-margin percentage is the same for every product.

1) The three steps under this method are

a) Determine the overall gross-margin percentage.

b) Subtract the appropriate gross margin from the final sales value of each product to calculate total costs for that product.

c) Subtract the separable costs to arrive at the joint cost amount.

2)   EXAMPLE: The refinery uses the same calculation of expected final sales price as under the estimated NRV method:

Asphalt	300 barrels at $ 70/barrel	=	$ 21,000
Fuel oil	300 barrels at $200/barrel	=	60,000
Diesel fuel	200 barrels at $180/barrel	=	36,000
Kerosene	100 barrels at $ 90/barrel	=	9,000
Gasoline	100 barrels at $190/barrel	=	19,000
	Total of final sales prices		$145,000

The final sales value for the entire production run is thus $145,000. From this total, the joint costs and total separable costs are deducted to arrive at a total gross margin for all products:

$145,000 – $100,000 – $7,000 = $38,000

The gross margin percentage can then be derived:

$38,000 ÷ $145,000 = 26.21% (rounded)

Deduct gross margin from each product to arrive at actual cost of goods sold:

Asphalt	$21,000 – ($21,000 × 26.21%) =	$15,497
Fuel oil	$60,000 – ($60,000 × 26.21%) =	44,276
Diesel fuel	$36,000 – ($36,000 × 26.21%) =	26,565
Kerosene	$ 9,000 – ($ 9,000 × 26.21%) =	6,641
Gasoline	$19,000 – ($19,000 × 26.21%) =	14,021

Deduct the separable costs from each product to arrive at the allocated joint costs:

Asphalt	$15,497 – $1,000 =	$ 14,497
Fuel oil	$44,276 – $1,000 =	43,276
Diesel fuel	$26,565 – $1,000 =	25,565
Kerosene	$ 6,641 – $2,000 =	4,641
Gasoline	$14,021 – $2,000 =	12,021
	Joint costs allocated	$100,000

EXAMPLE

Chief uses a joint process that yields two products, X and Y. Each product can be sold at its split-off point or processed further. All the additional processing costs are variable and can be traced to each product. Joint production costs are $25,000. Other sales and cost data are as follows:

	Product X	Product Y
Sales value at split-off point	$55,000	$30,000
Final sales value if processed further	75,000	45,000
Additional costs beyond split-off	12,000	17,000

Chief must evaluate whether the profit would be higher to sell at the split-off point or to process further:

	Product X	Product Y
Sales value	$ 75,000	$ 45,000
Allocated joint costs	(16,176)*	(8,824)**
Further processing costs	(12,000)	(17,000)
Profit	$ 46,824	$ 19,176

	Split Off X	Split Off Y
Sales value	$55,000	$30,000
Allocated joint costs	(16,176)*	(8,824)**
Profit	$38,824	$21,176

$$* \left[\left(\frac{\$55,000}{\$55,000 + \$30,000} \right) \times \$25,000 \right]$$

$$** \left[\left(\frac{\$30,000}{\$55,000 + \$30,000} \right) \times \$25,000 \right]$$

The profit is higher for Product X after further processing and higher for Y at the split-off point. Accordingly, Chief should process Product X further and sell Product Y at the split-off point.

2. Add-or-Drop-a-Segment Decisions

a. Disinvestment decisions are the opposite of capital budgeting decisions. They are decisions to terminate, rather than start, an operation, product or product line, business segment, branch, or major customer.

   1) In general, if the marginal cost of a project exceeds the marginal revenue, the firm should disinvest.

b. Four steps should be taken in making a disinvestment decision:

   1) Identify fixed costs that will be eliminated by the disinvestment decision (e.g., insurance on equipment used).

   2) Determine the revenue needed to justify continuing operations. In the short run, this amount should at least equal the variable cost of production or continued service.

   3) Establish the opportunity cost of funds that will be received upon disinvestment (e.g., salvage value).

   4) Determine whether the carrying amount of the assets is equal to their economic value. If not, reevaluate the decision using current fair value rather than the carrying amount.

c. When a firm disinvests, excess capacity exists unless another project uses this capacity immediately. The cost of idle capacity should be treated as a relevant cost.

EXAMPLE

A company needs to decide whether to discontinue unprofitable segments. Abbreviated income statements of the two possible unprofitable segments are shown below. The other segments, not shown, are profitable with income over $200,000.

	Department A	Department B
Sales	$275,000	$115,000
Cost of goods sold	160,000	55,000
Other variable costs	130,000	50,000
Allocated corporate costs	75,000	30,000
Income (loss)	$(90,000)	$(20,000)

Only relevant costs should be considered in making this decision. Since the allocated corporate costs are still going to be incurred if the segment is discontinued, these costs should be ignored. Therefore, the income (loss) for each segment is calculated as follows:

	Department A	Department B
Sales	$ 275,000	$115,000
Cost of goods sold	(160,000)	(55,000)
Other variable costs	(130,000)	(50,000)
Income (loss)	$ (15,000)	$ 10,000

Since $15,000 will be saved if Department A is discontinued, it should be discontinued. However, discontinuing Department B will negate $10,000 of profit, so it should continue.

Stop and review! You have completed the outline for this subunit. Study multiple-choice questions 14 through 16 beginning on page 325.

10.5 PRICE ELASTICITY OF DEMAND

1.   **Demand -- the Buyer's Side of the Market**

   a.   Demand is a schedule of the amounts of a good or service that consumers are willing and able to purchase at various prices during a period of time.

   1)   Quantity demanded is the amount that will be purchased at a specific price during a period of time.

Demand Schedule

Price per Unit	Quantity Demanded
$10	0
9	1
8	2
7	3
6	4
5	5
4	6
3	7
2	8
1	9
0	10

2.   **Changes in Quantity Demanded**

   a.   The law of demand states that if all other factors are held constant (ceteris paribus), the price of a product and the quantity demanded are inversely (negatively) related. The higher the price, the lower the quantity demanded.

   1)   A demand schedule can be graphically depicted as a relationship between the prices of a commodity (on the vertical axis) and the quantity demanded at the various prices (horizontal axis), holding other determinants of demand constant.

Law of Demand

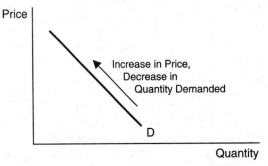

Figure 10-1

   a)   As the price of a good falls, consumers have more buying power (also called higher real income). They can buy more of the good with the same amount of money. This is termed the income effect.

   b)   As the price of one good falls, it becomes cheaper relative to other goods. Consumers will thus have a tendency to spend money on the cheaper good in preference to the more expensive one. This is termed the substitution effect.

3. **Changes in Demand**

   a. Whereas a change in price results in a change in quantity demanded, i.e., movement along a demand curve (depicted in the preceding graph), a change in one of the determinants of demand results in a change in demand, i.e., a shift of the curve itself.

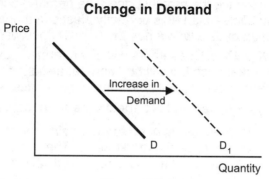

Change in Demand

Figure 10-2

4. **Price Elasticity of Demand**

   a. The price elasticity of demand (E_d) measures the sensitivity of the quantity demanded of a product to a change in its price.

$$E_d = \frac{Percentage\ change\ in\ quantity\ demanded}{Percentage\ change\ in\ price}$$

   1) Elasticity describes the reaction to a change in price from one level to another. Thus, the most accurate way of calculating elasticity is the **midpoint formula**, which measures elasticity across a range.

$$E_d = \frac{\%\ \Delta\ Q}{\%\ \Delta\ P} = \frac{|Q_1 - Q_2| \div |Q_1 + Q_2|}{|P_1 - P_2| \div |P_1 + P_2|}$$

   2) Note that, because elasticity is always measured with a positive number, absolute value is used in the formula.

EXAMPLE

As the price for a particular product changes, the quantity of the product demanded changes according to the following schedule:

Total Quantity Demanded	Price per Unit
100	$45
150	40
200	35
225	30
230	25
232	20

The product's elasticity of demand (E_d) when price falls from $30 to $25 is 0.1210.

$$E_d = [(230 - 225) \div (230 + 225)] \div [(\$30 - \$25) \div (\$30 + \$25)]$$
$$= (5 \div 455) \div (\$5 \div \$55)$$
$$= 0.0110 \div 0.0909$$
$$= 0.1210$$

---

   b. When the demand elasticity coefficient is

   1) **Greater than one**, demand is in a relatively elastic range. A small change in price results in a significant change in quantity demanded.

   2) **Equal to one**, demand has unitary elasticity (usually a very limited range). A single-unit change in price brings about a single-unit change in quantity demanded.

3) **Less than one**, demand is in a relatively inelastic range. A large change in price results in an insignificant change in quantity demanded.

4) **Infinite**, demand is perfectly elastic (depicted as a horizontal line).

   a) In pure competition, the number of firms is so great that one firm cannot influence the market price. The demand curve faced by a single seller in such a market is perfectly elastic (although the demand curve for the market as a whole has the normal downward slope).

   b) EXAMPLE: Consumers will buy a farmer's total output of soybeans at the market price but will buy none at a slightly higher price. Moreover, the farmer cannot sell below the market price without incurring losses.

5) **Equal to zero**, demand is perfectly inelastic (depicted as a vertical line).

   a) Some consumers' need for a certain product is so high that they will pay whatever price the market sets. The number of these consumers is limited and the amount they desire is relatively fixed.

   b) EXAMPLE: Addiction to illegal drugs tends to result in demand that is unresponsive to price changes. In this example, existing buyers (addicts) will not be driven out of the market by a rise in price, and no new buyers will be induced to enter the market by a reduction in price.

c. Price elasticity of demand is useful for a firm wondering how a change in the price of a product will affect total revenue from that product.

Effect on Total Revenue

	Elastic Range	Unitary Elasticity	Inelastic Range
Price increase	Decrease	No change	Increase
Price decrease	Increase	No change	Decrease

Stop and review! You have completed the outline for this subunit. Study multiple-choice questions 17 through 23 beginning on page 326.

10.6 PRICING

1. **Pricing Objectives**

   a. Profit maximization is assumed in classical economic theory to be the overriding goal of all firms.

   b. Target margin maximization is the process of setting prices to reach a specified percentage ratio of profits to sales.

   c. Volume-oriented objectives set prices to meet target sales volumes or market shares.

   d. Image-oriented objectives set prices to enhance the consumer's perception of the firm's merchandise mix.

   e. Stabilization objectives set prices to maintain a stable relationship between the firm's prices and the industry leader's prices.

2. **Price-Setting Factors**

   a. Supply of and demand for products and services are determined by customers' demand, the actions of competitors, and costs.

   b. Internal Factors

      1) Marketing objectives may include survival, current profit maximization, market-share leadership, or product-quality leadership.

      2) Marketing-mix strategy.

3) All relevant costs (variable, fixed, and total costs) in the value chain from R&D to customer service affect the amount of a product that the company is willing to supply. Thus, the lower costs are in relation to a given price, the greater the amount supplied.

4) Organizational locus of pricing decisions.

5) Capacity.

  a) For example, under peak-load pricing, prices vary directly with capacity usage. Thus, when idle capacity is available, that is, when demand falls, the price of a product or service tends to be lower given a peak-load pricing approach. When demand is high, the price charged will be higher. Peak-load pricing is often used by public utilities.

c. External Factors

1) The type of market (pure competition, monopolistic competition, oligopolistic competition, or monopoly) affects the price. For example, a monopolist is usually able to charge a higher price because it has no competitors. However, a company selling a relatively undifferentiated product in a highly competitive market may have no control over price. Market structures are discussed in detail in item 4., beginning on the next page.

2) Customer perception of value and price is the value that the customer thinks (s)he is deriving from consuming a product or a service and the price the customer is willing to pay. In other words, the higher (lower) the price, the higher (lower) the perceived value.

3) The price-demand relationship.

  a) The demand curve for normal goods is ordinarily downward sloping to the right (quantity demanded increases as the price decreases).

  b) However, over some intermediate range of prices, the reaction to a price increase for prestige goods is an increase, not a decrease, in the quantity demanded. Within this range, the demand curve is upward sloping. The reason is that consumers interpret the higher price to indicate a better or more desirable product. Above some price level, the relationship between price and quantity demanded will again become negatively sloped.

  c) If demand is price elastic (inelastic), the ratio of the percentage change in quantity demanded to the percentage change in price is greater (less) than 1.0. For example, if customer demand is price elastic, a price increase will result in the reduction of the seller's total revenue.

4) Competitors' products, costs, prices, and amounts supplied.

d. The time horizon for price setting is important. Whether the decision is for the short-term (generally, less than 1 year) or the long-term determines which costs are relevant and whether prices are set to achieve tactical goals or earn a targeted return on investment. For example, short-term fixed costs may be variable in the long-term, and short-term prices may be raised (lowered) when customer demand is strong (weak).

1) From the long-term perspective, maintaining price stability may be preferable to responding to short-term fluctuations in demand. A policy of predictable prices is desirable when the company wishes to cultivate long-term customer relationships. This policy is only feasible, however, when the company can predict its long-term costs.

3.   **Price Setting by Cartels**

    a.   A cartel arises when a group of firms joins together for price-fixing purposes. This practice is illegal except in international markets.

        1)   For example, the international diamond cartel DeBeers has successfully maintained the market price of diamonds for many years by incorporating into the cartel almost all major diamond-producing sources.

    b.   A cartel is a collusive oligopoly. Its effects are similar to those of a monopoly. Each firm will restrict output, charge a higher (collusive or agreed-to) price, and earn the maximum profit.

        1)   Thus, each firm in effect becomes a monopolist, but only because it is colluding with other members of the cartel.

4.   **General Pricing Approaches**

    a.   **Market-Based Pricing**

        1)   Pricing under this approach starts with a target price (item 6., beginning on page 316, has a detailed discussion) and involves basing prices on the product's perceived value and competitors' actions rather than on the seller's cost. Nonprice variables in the marketing mix augment the perceived value. Market comparables, which are assets with similar characteristics, are used to estimate the price of a product.

            a)   For example, a cup of coffee may have a higher price at an expensive restaurant than at a fast-food outlet.

        2)   Market-based pricing is typical when there are many competitors and the product is undifferentiated, as in many commodities markets, e.g., agricultural products or natural gas.

    b.   **Competition-Based Pricing**

        1)   Going-rate pricing bases price largely on competitors' prices.

        2)   Sealed-bid pricing bases price on a company's perception of its competitors' prices.

    c.   **New Product Pricing**

        1)   Price skimming is the practice of setting an introductory price relatively high to attract buyers who are not concerned about price and to recover research and development costs.

        2)   Penetration pricing is the practice of setting an introductory price relatively low to gain deep market penetration quickly.

    d.   **Pricing by Intermediaries**

        1)   Using markups tied closely to the price paid for a product

        2)   Using markdowns, a reduction in the original price set on a product

    e.   **Price Adjustments**

        1)   Geographical Pricing

            a)   FOB-origin pricing charges each customer its actual freight costs.

            b)   A seller that uses uniform delivered pricing charges the same price, inclusive of shipping, to all customers regardless of their location.

                i)   This policy is easy to administer, permits the company to advertise one price nationwide, and facilitates marketing to faraway customers.

            c)   Zone pricing sets differential freight charges for customers on the basis of their location. Customers are not charged actual average freight costs.

    d) Basing-point pricing charges each customer the freight costs incurred from a specified city to the destination regardless of the actual point of origin of the shipment.

    e) A seller that uses freight-absorption pricing absorbs all or part of the actual freight charges. Customers are not charged actual delivery costs.

2) Discounts and Allowances

    a) Cash discounts encourage prompt payment, improve cash flows, and avoid bad debts.

    b) Quantity discounts encourage large volume purchases.

    c) Trade (functional) discounts are offered to other members of the marketing channel for performing certain services, such as selling.

    d) Seasonal discounts are offered for sales out of season. They help smooth production.

    e) Allowances (e.g., trade-in and promotional allowances) reduce list prices.

3) Discriminatory pricing adjusts for differences among customers, the forms of a product, or locations.

4) Psychological pricing is based on consumer psychology. For example, consumers who cannot judge quality may assume higher prices correlate with higher quality.

5) Promotional pricing temporarily reduces prices below list or even cost to stimulate sales.

6) Value pricing entails redesigning products to improve quality without raising prices or offering the same quality at lower prices.

7) International pricing adjusts prices to local conditions.

f. **Product-Mix Pricing**

1) Product-line pricing sets price steps among the products in the line based on costs, consumer perceptions, and competitors' prices.

2) Optional-product pricing requires the firm to choose which products to offer as accessories and which as standard features of a main product.

3) Captive-product pricing involves products that must be used with a main product, such as razor blades with a razor. Often the main product is relatively cheap, but the captive products have high markups.

4) By-product pricing usually sets prices at any amount in excess of storing and delivering by-products. Such prices allow the seller to reduce the costs and therefore the prices of the main products.

5) Product-bundle pricing entails selling combinations of products at a price lower than the combined prices of the individual items. This strategy promotes sales of items consumers might not otherwise buy if the price is low enough. An example is season tickets for sports events.

g. **Illegal Pricing**

1) Certain pricing tactics are illegal. For example, pricing products below cost to destroy competitors (predatory pricing) is illegal.

    a) The U.S. Supreme Court has held that a price is predatory if it is below an appropriate measure of costs and the seller has a reasonable prospect of recovering its losses in the future through higher prices or greater market share.

2) Also illegal is price discrimination among customers. The Robinson-Patman Act of 1936 makes such pricing illegal if it has the effect of lessening competition, although price discrimination may be permissible if the competitive situation requires it and if costs of serving some customers are lower. The Robinson-Patman Act applies to manufacturers, not service entities.

      3)   Another improper form of pricing is collusive pricing. Companies may not conspire to restrict output and set artificially high prices. Such behavior violates antitrust laws.

      4)   Still another inappropriate pricing tactic is selling below cost in other countries (dumping), which may trigger retaliatory tariffs and other sanctions.

5.   **Cost-Based Pricing**

   a.   This process begins with a cost determination followed by setting a price that will recover the value chain costs and provide the desired return on investment (i.e., the cost plus target rate of return).

      1)   When an industry is characterized by significant product differentiation, e.g., the automobile industry, cost-based and market-based pricing approaches are combined.

      2)   Basing prices on cost assumes that costs can be correctly determined. Thus, cost-behavior patterns, cost traceability, and cost drivers become important determinants of profitability.

   b.   In markup pricing, also called cost-plus pricing, the cost of the product is calculated, and then a percentage of those costs is added to determine price.

      1)   A cost-plus price equals the cost plus a markup, which is usually determined at the discretion of the company. Cost may be defined in many ways. Most companies use either absorption manufacturing cost or total cost when calculating the price. Variable costs may be used as the basis for cost, but then fixed costs must be covered by the markup.

Four Common Cost-Plus Pricing Formulas

```
Price = Total cost + (Total cost × Markup percentage)
Price = Abs. mfg. cost + (Abs. mfg. cost × Markup percentage)
Price = Var. mfg. cost + (Var. mfg. cost × Markup percentage)
Price = Tot. var. cost + (Tot. var. cost × Markup percentage)
```

   c.   The costs of unused capacity in production facilities, distribution channels, marketing organizations, etc., are ordinarily not assignable to products or services on a cause-and-effect basis, so their inclusion in overhead rates may distort pricing decisions.

      1)   Including the fixed costs of unused capacity in a cost-based price results in higher prices and in what is known as the downward (black hole) demand spiral.

      2)   As higher prices depress demand, unused capacity costs and the fixed costs included in prices will increase. As a result of still higher prices, demand will continue to spiral downward.

         a)   One way to avoid this problem is not to assign unused capacity costs to products or services. The result should be better operating decisions and better evaluation of managerial performance.

6.   **Target Pricing**

   a.   A target price is the expected market price for a product or service, given the company's knowledge of its consumers' perceptions of value and competitors' responses.

      1)   The company's contacts with its customers and its market research studies provide information about consumers' perceptions of value.

      2)   The company must also gain information about competitors' potential responses by learning about their technological expertise, products, costs, and financial positions. This information may be obtained from competitors' customers, suppliers, employees, and financial reports. Reverse engineering of their products is also possible.

b. Target operating income per unit is the sales amount needed to cover the variable costs, fixed costs, and the net income the company wants to achieve during the period divided by the number of units forecast to be sold. Subtracting the net income from target operating income determines the target cost per unit. Relevant costs are all future value-chain costs whether variable or fixed.

   1) Because it may be lower than the full cost of the product, the target cost may not be achievable unless the company adopts comprehensive cost-reduction measures.

c. Target pricing takes a product's entire life cycle into consideration. **Product life cycle** is the cycle through which every product goes from introduction to withdrawal or eventual demise.

d. **Value engineering** is a means of reaching targeted cost levels. It is a systematic approach to assessing all aspects of the value chain cost buildup for a product: R&D, design of products, design of processes, production, marketing, distribution, and customer service. The purpose is to minimize costs without sacrificing customer satisfaction.

   1) Value engineering requires identifying value-added and nonvalue-added costs. **Value-added costs** are costs of activities that cannot be eliminated without reducing the quality, responsiveness, or quantity of the output required by a customer or the organization.

   2) Value engineering also requires distinguishing between cost incurrence and locked-in costs. Cost incurrence is the actual use of resources, whereas **locked-in (designed-in) costs** will result in use of resources in the future as a result of past decisions. Traditional cost accounting focuses on budget comparisons, but value engineering emphasizes controlling costs at the design stage before they are locked in.

7. **Product Life Cycle and Pricing Decisions**

   a. The strategy in the **precommercialization** (product development) stage is to innovate by conducting R&D, marketing research, and production tests. During product development, the entity has no sales, but it has high investment costs.

   b. The **introduction stage** is characterized by slow sales growth and lack of profits because of the high expenses of promotion and selective distribution to generate awareness of the product and encourage customers to try it. Thus, the per-customer cost is high.

      1) Competitors are few, basic versions of the product are produced, and higher-income customers (innovators) are usually targeted. Cost-plus prices are charged. They may initially be high to permit cost recovery when unit sales are low.

      2) The strategy is to infiltrate the market, plan for financing to cope with losses, build supplier relations, increase production and marketing efforts, and plan for competition.

   c. In the **growth stage**, sales and profits increase rapidly, cost per customer decreases, customers are early adopters, new competitors enter an expanding market, new product models and features are introduced, and promotion spending declines or remains stable.

      1) The entity enters new market segments and distribution channels and attempts to build brand loyalty and achieve the maximum share of the market. Thus, prices are set to penetrate the market, distribution channels are extended, and the mass market is targeted through advertising.

         a) Competition increases and prices fall.

d. In the **maturity stage**, sales peak but growth declines, competitors are most
    numerous but may begin to decline in number, and per-customer cost is low.

    1) Profits are high for large market-share entities. For others, profits may fall
        because of competitive price-cutting and increased R&D spending to develop
        improved versions of the product.

    2) The strategy is to defend market share and maximize profits through
        diversification of brands and models to enter new market segments; still more
        intensive distribution, cost cutting, advertising and promotions to encourage
        brand switching; and emphasizing customer service.

e. During the **decline stage**, sales and profits drop as prices are cut, and some entities
    leave the market. Customers include late adopters (laggards), and per-customer cost
    is low.

    1) Weak products and unprofitable distribution media are eliminated, and advertising
        budgets are pared to the level needed to retain the most loyal customers. The
        strategy is to withdraw by reducing production, promotion, and inventory.

f. **Graphical Depiction**

Product Life Cycle

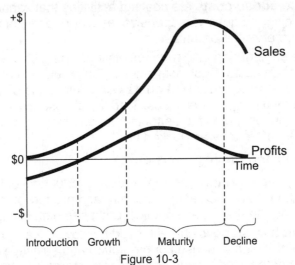

Figure 10-3

8. **Life-Cycle Costing**

a. The product life cycle begins with R&D, proceeds through the introduction and growth
    stages, continues into the product's mature stage, and finally ends with the harvest
    or decline stage and the final provision of customer support. Life-cycle costing is
    sometimes used as a basis for cost planning and product pricing.

    1) Life-cycle costing estimates a product's revenues and expenses over its
        expected life cycle. The result is to highlight upstream (e.g., raw materials,
        research and development) and downstream (e.g., distribution, marketing)
        costs in the cost planning process that often receive insufficient attention.
        Emphasis is on the need to price products to cover all costs, not just production
        costs.

b. A concept related to life-cycle cost that is relevant to pricing is whole-life cost, which
    equals life-cycle costs plus after-purchase costs (operating, support, repair, and
    disposal) incurred by customers. Reduction of whole-life costs is a strong competitive
    weapon. Customers may pay a premium for a product with low after-purchase costs.

**Stop and review! You have completed the outline for this subunit. Study multiple-choice
questions 24 through 29 beginning on page 329.**

QUESTIONS

10.1 Decision Making -- Applying Marginal Analysis

Questions 1 and 2 are based on the following information. Gleason Co. has two products, a frozen dessert and ready-to-bake breakfast rolls, ready for introduction. However, plant capacity is limited, and only one product can be introduced at present. Therefore, Gleason has conducted a market study at a cost of $26,000, to determine which product will be more profitable. The results of the study follow.

Sales of Desserts at $1.80/unit		Sales of Rolls at $1.20/unit	
Volume	Probability	Volume	Probability
250,000	.30	200,000	.20
300,000	.40	250,000	.50
350,000	.20	300,000	.20
400,000	.10	350,000	.10

The costs associated with the two products have been estimated by Gleason's cost accounting department and are as follows:

	Dessert	Rolls
Ingredients per unit	$ .40	$ .25
Direct labor per unit	.35	.30
Variable overhead per unit	.40	.20
Production tooling*	48,000	25,000
Advertising	30,000	20,000

*Gleason treats production tooling as a current operating expense rather than capitalizing it as a fixed asset.

1. The cost incurred by Gleason for the market study is a(n)

A. Incremental cost.

B. Prime cost.

C. Opportunity cost.

D. Sunk cost.

Answer (D) is correct.

REQUIRED: The term referring to the cost of the market study.

DISCUSSION: A sunk cost is a previously incurred cost that is the result of a past irrevocable management decision. Nothing can be done in the future about sunk costs. The market study cost is an example.

Answer (A) is incorrect. An incremental cost is the additional cost of a new strategy or increased production. It is also called a differential cost. Answer (B) is incorrect. Prime costs are variable costs of direct material and direct labor. Answer (C) is incorrect. An opportunity cost is the revenue obtainable from an alternative use of a resource.

2. Assuming that Gleason elects to produce the frozen dessert, the profit that would have been earned on the breakfast rolls is a(n)

A. Deferrable cost.

B. Sunk cost.

C. Avoidable cost.

D. Opportunity cost.

Answer (D) is correct.

REQUIRED: The term referring to the profit lost by not choosing the alternative.

DISCUSSION: An opportunity cost is the maximum return that could have been earned on the next best alternative use of a resource. In this case, the lost profit on the rolls is an opportunity cost.

Answer (A) is incorrect. A deferrable cost is one that can be deferred to a future period. Answer (B) is incorrect. A sunk cost is one that cannot be reversed since it is the result of a past irrevocable decision. Answer (C) is incorrect. An avoidable cost is an ongoing cost that may be eliminated by ceasing to perform some economic activity or segment thereof or by improving the efficiency by which such activity is accomplished.

3. What is the opportunity cost of making a component part in a factory given no alternative use of the capacity?

A. The variable manufacturing cost of the component.

B. The total manufacturing cost of the component.

C. The total variable cost of the component.

D. Zero.

Answer (D) is correct.
    REQUIRED: The opportunity cost of making a component if there is no alternative use for the factory.
    DISCUSSION: Opportunity cost is the benefit forgone by not selecting the best alternative use of scarce resources. The opportunity cost is zero when no alternative use for the production facility is available.

4. The opportunity cost of making a component part in a factory with no excess capacity is the

A. Variable manufacturing cost of the component.

B. Fixed manufacturing cost of the component.

C. Cost of the production given up in order to manufacture the component.

D. Net benefit given up from the best alternative use of the capacity.

Answer (D) is correct.
    REQUIRED: The opportunity cost of making a component in a factory with no excess capacity.
    DISCUSSION: An opportunity cost is the maximum benefit forgone by using a scarce resource for a given purpose. It is the benefit provided by the next best use of that resource. Thus, in a factory operating at full capacity, the opportunity cost of making a component is the benefit given up by not selecting an alternative use of the plant capacity.
    Answers (A) and (B) are incorrect. An opportunity cost is the benefit derived from the next best use of the resource, not an out-of-pocket cost. Answer (C) is incorrect. An opportunity cost is the benefit forgone, not the cost.

10.2   Decision Making -- Special Orders

Questions 5 through 7 are based on the following information. The Sommers Company manufactures a variety of industrial valves. Currently, the company is operating at about 70% capacity and is earning a satisfactory return on investment. Management has been approached by Glascow Industries Ltd. of Scotland with an offer to buy 120,000 units of a pressure valve. Glascow manufactures a valve that is almost identical to Sommers' pressure valve; however, a fire in Glascow Industries' valve plant has shut down its manufacturing operations. Glascow needs the 120,000 valves over the next 4 months to meet commitments to its regular customers; the company is prepared to pay $19 each for the valves, FOB shipping point. Sommers' product cost, based on current attainable standards, for the pressure valve is as follows:

Direct materials	$ 5.00
Direct labor	6.00
Manufacturing overhead	9.00
Total cost	$20.00

Manufacturing overhead is applied to production at the rate of $18 per standard direct labor hour. This overhead rate is made up of the following components:

Variable factory overhead	$ 6.00
Fixed factory overhead-direct	8.00
Fixed factory overhead-allocated	4.00
Applied manufacturing overhead rate	$18.00

In determining selling prices, Sommers adds a 40% markup to product cost. This provides a $28 suggested selling price for the pressure valve. The Marketing Department, however, has set the current selling price at $27 to maintain market share. Production management believes that it can handle the Glascow Industries order without disrupting its scheduled production. The order would, however, require additional fixed factory overhead of $12,000 per month in the form of supervision and clerical costs. If management accepts the order, 30,000 pressure valves will be manufactured and shipped to Glascow Industries each month for the next 4 months. Shipments will be made in weekly consignments, FOB shipping point.

5. What is the incremental profit (loss) before tax associated with the Glascow order?

A. ($168,000)

B. ($120,000)

C. $552,000

D. $600,000

Answer (C) is correct.

REQUIRED: The incremental profit (loss) before tax in a special order.

DISCUSSION: The incremental revenue is found by taking the $19 per unit price and multiplying it by the 120,000 units ordered. Then, the variable costs per unit are multiplied by 120,000 to get a $600,000 cost for materials ($5 × 120,000), a $720,000 cost for labor ($6 × 120,000), and a $360,000 cost for overhead ($3 × 120,000). The variable costs are added to the additional fixed overhead cost of $48,000 (4 months × $12,000) to get a total incremental cost of $1,728,000. Then, the total cost is subtracted from the revenue to get an incremental profit before tax of $552,000 ($2,280,000 − $1,728,000).

Answer (A) is incorrect. A $168,000 loss is found by using a variable overhead rate of $9 per unit. Answer (B) is incorrect. A $120,000 loss is found by using a variable overhead rate of $9 per unit. Answer (D) is incorrect. A $600,000 profit is found by not subtracting the fixed overhead.

6. How many additional direct labor hours would be required each month to fill the Glascow order?

A. 10,000

B. 15,000

C. 30,000

D. 120,000

Answer (B) is correct.

REQUIRED: The number of additional direct labor hours required to fill an order.

DISCUSSION: The manufacturing overhead rate is $18 per standard direct labor hour and the standard product cost includes $9 of manufacturing overhead per pressure valve. Accordingly, the standard direct labor hour per finished valve is 1/2 hour ($9 ÷ $18). Therefore, 30,000 units per month would require 15,000 direct labor hours.

Answer (A) is incorrect. This number of hours is found by dividing the direct labor per pressure valve by the manufacturing overhead rate to find the standard direct labor hour per finished valve. Answer (C) is incorrect. The number of pressure valves produced in a month is 30,000. Answer (D) is incorrect. The total number of valves ordered is 120,000.

7. What is the minimum unit price that Sommers could accept without reducing net income?

A. $14

B. $14.40

C. $20

D. $20.40

Answer (B) is correct.

REQUIRED: The minimum unit price without reducing net income.

DISCUSSION: The minimum unit price without reducing net income must cover variable costs plus the additional fixed cost. Therefore, the three variable costs of $5.00 for direct materials, $6.00 for direct labor, and $3.00 for variable overhead are added to the additional fixed cost per unit $.40 ($48,000 ÷ 120,000). The total is $14.40.

Answer (A) is incorrect. Not adding the fixed cost results in $14. Answer (C) is incorrect. Using a variable overhead rate of $9 and ignoring fixed overhead results in $20. Answer (D) is incorrect. Using a variable overhead rate of $9 results in $20.40.

Questions 8 and 9 are based on the following information. Kator Co. is a manufacturer of industrial components. One of their products that is used as a subcomponent in auto manufacturing is KB-96. This product has the following financial structure per unit:

Selling price	$150
Direct materials	$ 20
Direct labor	15
Variable manufacturing overhead	12
Fixed manufacturing overhead	30
Shipping and handling	3
Fixed selling and administrative	10
Total costs	$ 90

8. Kator Co. has received a special, one-time order for 1,000 KB-96 parts. Assume that Kator is operating at full capacity and that the contribution margin of the output that would be displaced by the special order is $10,000. Using the original data, the minimum price that is acceptable for this one-time special order is in excess of

A. $60

B. $70

C. $87

D. $100

Answer (A) is correct.
    REQUIRED: The minimum acceptable price.
    DISCUSSION: Given no excess capacity, the price must cover the incremental costs. The incremental costs for KB-96 equal $50 ($20 direct materials + $15 direct labor + $12 variable overhead + $3 shipping and handling). Opportunity cost is the benefit of the next best alternative use of scarce resources. Because acceptance of the special order would cause the company to forgo a contribution margin of $10,000, that amount must be reflected in the price. Hence, the minimum unit price is $60 [$50 unit incremental cost + ($10,000 lost CM ÷ 1,000 units)].
    Answer (B) is incorrect. The amount of $70 includes fixed selling and administrative costs. Answer (C) is incorrect. The amount of $87 includes fixed manufacturing overhead but omits shipping and handling costs. Answer (D) is incorrect. The amount of $100 is based on full absorption cost.

9. Kator Co. has received a special, one-time order for 1,000 KB-96 parts. Assuming Kator has excess capacity, the minimum price that is acceptable for this one-time special order is in excess of

A. $47

B. $50

C. $60

D. $77

Answer (B) is correct.
    REQUIRED: The minimum acceptable price.
    DISCUSSION: A company must cover the incremental costs of a special order when it has excess capacity. The incremental costs for product KB-96 are $50 ($20 direct materials + $15 direct labor + $12 variable overhead + $3 shipping and handling). The fixed costs will not change as a result of the special order, so they are not relevant. Thus, any price in excess of $50 per unit is acceptable.
    Answer (A) is incorrect. The amount of $47 ignores the shipping and handling costs. Answer (C) is incorrect. The amount of $60 includes fixed selling and administrative costs. Answer (D) is incorrect. The amount of $77 includes fixed manufacturing overhead but omits shipping and handling costs.

10.3 Decision Making -- Make or Buy

10. Listed below are a company's monthly unit costs to manufacture and market a particular product.

Manufacturing costs:
Direct materials	$2.00
Direct labor	2.40
Variable indirect	1.60
Fixed indirect	1.00

Marketing costs:
Variable	2.50
Fixed	1.50

The company must decide to continue making the product or buy it from an outside supplier. The supplier has offered to make the product at the same level of quality that the company can make it. Fixed marketing costs would be unaffected, but variable marketing costs would be reduced by 30% if the company were to accept the proposal. What is the maximum amount per unit that the company can pay the supplier without decreasing operating income?

A. $8.50

B. $6.75

C. $7.75

D. $5.25

Answer (B) is correct.
  REQUIRED: The maximum amount paid to an outside supplier without decreasing operating income.
  DISCUSSION: The key to this question is, what costs will the company avoid if it buys from the outside supplier? It will no longer incur the $2.00 of direct materials, nor the $2.40 of direct labor, nor the $1.60 of variable overhead, nor $0.75 ($2.50 × 30%) of the variable marketing costs. (Regardless of whether the company makes or buys, it will still incur 70% of the variable marketing costs.) The firm will therefore avoid costs of $6.75 ($2.00 + $2.40 + $1.60 + $0.75). Hence, it will at least break even by paying no more than $6.75.
  Answer (A) is incorrect. The amount of $8.50 assumes that all variable marketing costs are avoidable. Answer (C) is incorrect. The amount of $7.75 assumes that fixed manufacturing costs of $1 are avoidable. Answer (D) is incorrect. The amount of $5.25 results from subtracting the savings in marketing costs from the manufacturing savings.

11. In a make-versus-buy decision, the relevant costs include variable manufacturing costs as well as

A. Factory management costs.

B. General office costs.

C. Avoidable fixed costs.

D. Depreciation costs.

Answer (C) is correct.
  REQUIRED: The relevant costs in a make-versus-buy decision.
  DISCUSSION: The relevant costs in a make-versus-buy decision are those that differ between the two decision choices. These costs include any variable costs plus any avoidable fixed costs. Avoidable fixed costs will not be incurred if the "buy" decision is selected.
  Answer (A) is incorrect. Factory management costs are unlikely to differ regardless of which decision is selected. Answer (B) is incorrect. General office costs are unlikely to differ regardless of which decision is selected. Answer (D) is incorrect. Depreciation costs are unlikely to differ regardless of which decision is selected.

Questions 12 and 13 are based on the following information. Stewart Industries has been producing two bearings, components B12 and B18, for use in production.

	B12	B18
Machine hours required per unit	2.5	3.0
Standard cost per unit:		
Direct material	$ 2.25	$ 3.75
Direct labor	4.00	4.50
Manufacturing overhead:		
Variable (See Note 1)	2.00	2.25
Fixed (See Note 2)	3.75	4.50
	$12.00	$15.00

Stewart's annual requirement for these components is 8,000 units of B12 and 11,000 units of B18. Recently, Stewart's management decided to devote additional machine time to other product lines resulting in only 41,000 machine hours per year that can be dedicated to the production of the bearings. An outside company has offered to sell Stewart the annual supply of the bearings at prices of $11.25 for B12 and $13.50 for B18. Stewart wants to schedule the otherwise idle 41,000 machine hours to produce bearings so that the company can minimize its costs (maximize its net benefits).

Note 1: Variable manufacturing overhead is applied on the basis of direct labor hours.
Note 2: Fixed manufacturing overhead is applied on the basis of machine hours.

12. Stewart will maximize its net benefits by

A. Purchasing 4,800 units of B12 and manufacturing the remaining bearings.

B. Purchasing 8,000 units of B12 and manufacturing 11,000 units of B18.

C. Purchasing 11,000 units of B18 and manufacturing 8,000 units of B12.

D. Purchasing 4,000 units of B18 and manufacturing the remaining bearings.

Answer (D) is correct.
REQUIRED: The combination of purchasing and manufacturing that will maximize net benefits.
DISCUSSION: Purchasing will increase the company's costs by $3 ($11.25 – $2.25 – $4 – $2) for each B12 bearing, or $1.20 per hour ($3 ÷ 2.5 hrs). Buying B18 will only cost the company an additional $1 per machine hour [($13.50 – $3.75 – $4.50 – $2.25) ÷ 3 machine hours]. Thus, the company should make all the needed B12s and compensate for the machine hours constraint by purchasing B18s. Given that each unit of B12 requires 2.5 hours of machine time, the company can produce the needed 8,000 units in 20,000 hours (2.5 × 8,000). The remaining 21,000 hours (41,000 – 20,000) can then be used for the production of 7,000 B18s (21,000 ÷ 3 hrs.). Because the annual requirement of B18s is 11,000 units, the other 4,000 units will have to be purchased.
Answer (A) is incorrect. Purchasing 4,800 units of B12 will increase the company's costs by $3 per B12 bearing. Purchasing B18s costs less. The company should not purchase any B12 bearings. Answer (B) is incorrect. Purchasing B12 bearings is not cost effective. By manufacturing all the B12 units needed, the company can also produce 7,000 units of B18. Answer (C) is incorrect. After manufacturing 8,000 units of B12, there are enough hours left to produce 7,000 units of B18, so only 4,000 units of B18 need to be purchased.

13. The net benefit (loss) per machine hour that would result if Stewart accepts the supplier's offer of $13.50 per unit for Component B18 is

A. $.50
B. $(1.00)
C. $(1.75)
D. Some amount other than those given.

Answer (B) is correct.
REQUIRED: The net benefit (loss) per machine hour that would result from buying a component.
DISCUSSION: The variable costs of producing B18 total $10.50 ($3.75 + $4.50 + $2.25). Thus, purchasing at $13.50 would result in a loss of $3 per bearing. Given that each bearing requires 3 hours of machine time, the loss is $1 per machine hour.
Answer (A) is incorrect. Subtracting $13.50 from $15.00 and dividing by 3 machine hours results in $.50. Answer (C) is incorrect. Not including variable manufacturing overhead when calculating the costs of producing B18 results in $(1.75) [($8.25 – $13.50) ÷ 3 machine hours]. Answer (D) is incorrect. The loss per machine hour that results from buying a component is $(1.00) [($10.50 – $13.50) ÷ 3].

10.4 Decision Making -- Other Situations

Questions 14 and 15 are based on the following information. Whitehall Corporation produces chemicals used in the cleaning industry. During the previous month, Whitehall incurred $300,000 of joint costs in producing 60,000 units of AM-12 and 40,000 units of BM-36. Whitehall uses the units-of-production method to allocate joint costs. Currently, AM-12 is sold at split-off for $3.50 per unit. Flank Corporation has approached Whitehall to purchase all of the production of AM-12 after further processing. The further processing will cost Whitehall $90,000.

14. Concerning AM-12, which one of the following alternatives is **most** advantageous?

A. Whitehall should process further and sell to Flank if the total selling price per unit after further processing is greater than $3.00, which covers the joint costs.

B. Whitehall should continue to sell at split-off unless Flank offers at least $4.50 per unit after further processing, which covers Whitehall's total costs.

C. Whitehall should process further and sell to Flank if the total selling price per unit after further processing is greater than $5.00.

D. Whitehall should process further and sell to Flank if the total selling price per unit after further processing is greater than $5.25, which maintains the same gross profit percentage.

Answer (C) is correct.
  REQUIRED: The most advantageous processing and selling alternative.
  DISCUSSION: The unit price of the product at the split-off point is known to be $3.50, so the joint costs are irrelevant. The additional unit cost of further processing is $1.50 ($90,000 ÷ 60,000 units). Consequently, the unit price must be at least $5.00 ($3.50 opportunity cost + $1.50).
  Answer (A) is incorrect. The joint costs are irrelevant. Answer (B) is incorrect. The unit price must cover the $3.50 opportunity cost plus the $1.50 of additional costs. Answer (D) is incorrect. Any price greater than $5 will provide greater profits, in absolute dollars, even though the gross profit percentage declines.

15. Assume that Whitehall Corporation agreed to sell AM-12 to Flank Corporation for $5.50 per unit after further processing. During the first month of production, Whitehall sold 50,000 units with 10,000 units remaining in inventory at the end of the month. With respect to AM-12, which one of the following statements is **true**?

A. The operating profit last month was $50,000, and the inventory value is $15,000.

B. The operating profit last month was $50,000, and the inventory value is $45,000.

C. The operating profit last month was $125,000, and the inventory value is $30,000.

D. The operating profit last month was $200,000, and the inventory value is $30,000.

Answer (B) is correct.
  REQUIRED: The operating profit and inventory value after specified sales of a product.
  DISCUSSION: Joint costs are allocated based on units of production. Accordingly, the unit joint cost allocated to AM-12 is $3.00 [$300,000 ÷ (60,000 units of AM-12 + 40,000 units of BM-36)]. The unit cost of AM-12 is therefore $4.50 [$3.00 joint cost + ($90,000 additional cost ÷ 60,000 units)]. Total inventory value is $45,000 (10,000 units × $4.50), and total operating profit is $50,000 [50,000 units sold × ($5.50 unit price – $4.50 unit cost)].
  Answer (A) is incorrect. The $3 unit joint cost should be included in the inventory value. Answer (C) is incorrect. The $1.50 unit additional cost should be included in total unit cost. Answer (D) is incorrect. The $3 unit joint cost should be included in the cost of goods sold, and inventory should include the $1.50 unit additional cost.

16. A company manufactures jet engines on a cost-plus basis. The cost of a particular jet engine the company manufactures is shown as follows:

Direct materials	$200,000
Direct labor	150,000
Overhead:	
Supervisor's salary	20,000
Fringe benefits on direct labor	15,000
Depreciation	12,000
Rent	11,000
Total cost	$408,000

If production of this engine were discontinued, the production capacity would be idle, and the supervisor would be laid off. When asked to bid on the next contract for this engine, the minimum unit price that the company should bid is

A. $408,000

B. $365,000

C. $397,000

D. $385,000

Answer (D) is correct.

REQUIRED: The minimum unit price that should be bid.

DISCUSSION: The company will need to cover its variable costs and any other incremental costs. Thus, direct materials ($200,000), direct labor ($150,000), the supervisor's salary ($20,000), and fringe benefits on direct labor ($15,000) are the incremental unit costs of manufacturing the engines. The breakeven price is therefore $385,000 ($200,000 + $150,000 + $20,000 + $15,000).

Answer (A) is incorrect. Depreciation and rent are allocated costs that will be incurred even if the contract is lost. Answer (B) is incorrect. The supervisor's salary will have to be covered. The $20,000 salary is an avoidable cost. Answer (C) is incorrect. Depreciation is a cost that cannot be avoided.

10.5 Price Elasticity of Demand

Questions 17 through 19 are based on the following information. Condensed monthly operating income data for Korbin, Inc., for May follows:

	Urban Store	Suburban Store	Total
Sales	$80,000	$120,000	$200,000
Variable costs	32,000	84,000	116,000
Contribution margin	$48,000	$ 36,000	$ 84,000
Direct fixed costs	20,000	40,000	60,000
Store segment margin	$28,000	$ (4,000)	$ 24,000
Common fixed cost	4,000	6,000	10,000
Operating income	$24,000	$ (10,000)	$ 14,000

Additional information regarding Korbin's operations follows:

- One-fourth of each store's direct fixed costs would continue if either store is closed.
- Korbin allocates common fixed costs to each store on the basis of sales dollars.
- Management estimates that closing the Suburban Store would result in a 10% decrease in the Urban Store's sales, while closing the Urban Store would not affect the Suburban Store's sales.
- The operating results for May are representative of all months.

17. A decision by Korbin to close the Suburban Store would result in a monthly increase (decrease) in Korbin's operating income of

A. $(10,800)

B. $(6,000)

C. $(1,200)

D. $4,000

Answer (A) is correct.

REQUIRED: The effect on operating income of closing the Suburban Store.

DISCUSSION: If the Suburban Store is closed, one-fourth of its direct fixed costs will continue. Thus, the segment margin that should be used to calculate the effect of its closing on Korbin's operating income is $6,000 {$36,000 contribution margin – [$40,000 direct fixed costs × (1.0 – .25)]}. In addition, the sales (and contribution margin) of the Urban Store will decline by 10% if the Suburban store closes. A 10% reduction in Urban's $48,000 contribution margin will reduce income by $4,800. Accordingly, the effect of closing the Suburban Store is to decrease operating income by $10,800 ($6,000 + $4,800).

Answer (B) is incorrect. The amount of $(6,000) overlooks the decline in profitability at the Urban Store. Answer (C) is incorrect. The amount of $(1,200) assumes that the effect on the Urban Store is a $4,800 increase in contribution margin. Answer (D) is incorrect. Profits will decline.

18. Korbin is considering a promotional campaign at the Suburban Store that would not affect the Urban Store. Increasing annual promotional expense at the Suburban Store by $60,000 in order to increase this store's sales by 10% would result in a monthly increase (decrease) in Korbin's operating income during the year (rounded) of

A. $(5,000)

B. $(1,400)

C. $487

D. $7,000

Answer (B) is correct.

REQUIRED: The effect on monthly income of an advertising campaign.

DISCUSSION: The $60,000 advertising campaign will increase direct fixed costs by $5,000 per month ($60,000 ÷ 12). Sales and contribution margin will also increase by 10%. Hence, the contribution margin for the Suburban Store will increase by $3,600 ($36,000 × 10%), and income will decline by $1,400 ($5,000 – $3,600).

Answer (A) is incorrect. The amount of $(5,000) is the monthly advertising cost. Answer (C) is incorrect. The contribution margin of the Suburban Store will increase by $3,600, which is $1,400 less than the increased advertising cost. Answer (D) is incorrect. The amount of $7,000 omits the 10% increase in variable costs from the calculation.

19. One-half of the Suburban Store's dollar sales are from items sold at variable cost to attract customers to the store. Korbin is considering the deletion of these items, a move that would reduce the Suburban Store's direct fixed expenses by 15% and result in a 20% loss of Suburban Store's remaining sales volume. This change would not affect the Urban Store. A decision by Korbin to eliminate the items sold at cost would result in a monthly increase (decrease) in Korbin's operating income of

A. $(5,200)

B. $(1,200)

C. $(7,200)

D. $2,000

Answer (B) is correct.

REQUIRED: The effect on monthly income of eliminating sales made at variable cost.

DISCUSSION: If 50% of the Suburban Store's sales are at variable cost, its contribution margin (sales – variable costs) must derive wholly from sales of other items. However, eliminating sales at variable cost reduces other sales by 20%. Thus, the effect is to reduce the contribution margin to $28,800 ($36,000 × .8). Moreover, fixed costs will be reduced by 15% to $34,000 ($40,000 × .85). Consequently, the new segment margin is $(5,200) ($34,000 direct fixed costs – $28,800 contribution margin), a decrease of $1,200 [$(5,200) – $(4,000)].

Answer (A) is incorrect. The amount of $(5,200) is the new segment margin. Answer (C) is incorrect. The amount of $(7,200) is the reduction in the Suburban Store's contribution margin. Answer (D) is incorrect. Operating income must decrease.

20. Long Lake Golf Course has raised greens fees for a nine-hole game due to an increase in demand.

	Previous Rate	New Rate	Average Games Played at Previous Rate	Average Games Played at New Rate
Regular weekday	$10	$11	80	70
Senior citizen	6	8	150	82
Weekend	15	20	221	223

Which one of the following is **true**?

A. The regular weekday and weekend demand is inelastic.

B. The regular weekday and weekend demand is elastic.

C. The senior citizen demand is elastic, and weekend demand is inelastic.

D. The regular weekday demand is inelastic, and weekend demand is elastic.

Answer (C) is correct.

REQUIRED: The true statement about the elasticity of greens fees as indicated by changes in demand related to higher rates.

DISCUSSION: The price elasticity of demand is the percentage change in quantity demanded divided by the percentage change in price. If the elasticity coefficient is greater than one, demand is elastic. If the coefficient is less than one, demand is inelastic. When the percentage changes are calculated as the change over the range (the arc method), the coefficient for senior citizens indicates that demand is elastic:

E_d = [(150 − 82) ÷ (150 + 82)] ÷ [($8 − $6) ÷ ($8 + $6)]
= (68 ÷ 232) ÷ ($2 ÷ $14)
= 29.3% ÷ 14.3%
= 2.05

The coefficient for weekends indicates that demand is inelastic:

E_d = [(223 − 221) ÷ (223 + 221)] ÷ [($20 − $15) ÷ ($20 + $15)]
= (2 ÷ 444) ÷ ($5 ÷ $35)
= 0.45% ÷ 14.3%
= 0.0315

Answer (A) is incorrect. Weekday demand is elastic. Answer (B) is incorrect. Weekend demand is inelastic. Answer (D) is incorrect. Weekday demand is elastic, and weekend demand is inelastic.

21. If the coefficient of elasticity is zero, then the consumer demand for the product is said to be

   A. Perfectly inelastic.

   B. Perfectly elastic.

   C. Unit inelastic.

   D. Unit elastic.

Answer (A) is correct.
   REQUIRED: The applicable term when the coefficient of elasticity is zero.
   DISCUSSION: When the coefficient of elasticity (percentage change in demand/change in price) is less than one, demand is inelastic. When the coefficient is zero, the demand is perfectly inelastic.
   Answer (B) is incorrect. Demand is perfectly elastic when the coefficient is infinite. Answer (C) is incorrect. Unitary inelasticity is a meaningless term. Answer (D) is incorrect. Unitary elasticity exists when the coefficient is exactly one.

22. As the price for a particular product changes, the quantity of the product demanded changes according to the following schedule:

Total Quantity Demanded	Price per Unit
100	$50
150	45
200	40
225	35
230	30
232	25

The price elasticity of demand for this product when the price decreases from $50 to $45 is

   A. 0.20

   B. 10.00

   C. 0.10

   D. 3.80

Answer (D) is correct.
   REQUIRED: The price elasticity of demand using the arc method.
   DISCUSSION: A product's price elasticity of demand is measured as the percentage change in quantity demanded divided by the percentage change in price. When price falls from $50 to $45, the coefficient is 3.8, calculated as follows:

$$E_d = [(150 - 100) \div (150 + 100)] \div [(\$50 - \$45) \div (\$50 + \$45)]$$
$$= (50 \div 250) \div (\$5 \div \$95)$$
$$= 20.0\% \div 5.26\%$$
$$= 3.8$$

   Answer (A) is incorrect. The 10% decline in price divided by the 50% change in quantity demanded equals 0.20. Answer (B) is incorrect. This figure assumes a 5% change in price. It also does not calculate the change over the sum of the endpoints of the range. Answer (C) is incorrect. The percentage change in price is 0.10.

23. A company noticed that they were losing business to other firms. In view of this, the company decided to change its monthly charges for its various telephone services as follows:

	Previous Rate	New Rate
Call waiting	$ 8	$ 4
Caller ID	6	4
International calling	3	1
Internet access	15	13

In response to these price changes, the demand for the above services changed as follows:

	Previous Demand	New Demand
Call waiting	100	150
Caller ID	50	70
International calling	30	40
Internet access	150	160

Using the midpoint method, the price elasticity of demand is the highest for

   A. Call waiting.

   B. Caller ID.

   C. International calling.

   D. Internet access.

Answer (B) is correct.
   REQUIRED: The product with the highest price elasticity of demand using the point method.
   DISCUSSION: Price elasticity of demand measures the responsiveness of demand for a product to a change in price. The coefficient is calculated by dividing the percentage change in quantity demanded by the percentage change in price. The point method uses this formula:

$$E_d = \frac{|Q_1 - Q_2|}{|P_1 - P_2|} \div \frac{|Q_1 + Q_2|}{|P_1 + P_2|}$$

By convention, elasticity of demand is reported as a positive number. Thus, the calculation for caller ID is as follows:

$$E_d = \frac{|70 - 50|}{|\$4 - \$6|} \div \frac{|70 + 50|}{|\$4 + \$6|} = \frac{|20 \div 120|}{|\$2 \div \$10|} = \frac{0.167}{0.200} = 0.833$$

   Answer (A) is incorrect. The price elasticity of demand for call waiting is only 0.6. Answer (C) is incorrect. The price elasticity of demand for international calling is only 0.286. Answer (D) is incorrect. The price elasticity of demand for Internet access is only 0.452.

10.6 Pricing

24. Which of the following price adjustment strategies is designed to stabilize production for the selling firm?

A. Cash discounts.

B. Quantity discounts.

C. Functional discounts.

D. Seasonal discounts.

Answer (D) is correct.
REQUIRED: The price adjustment strategy intended to stabilize production.
DISCUSSION: Seasonal discounts are designed to smooth production by the selling firm. For example, a ski manufacturer offers seasonal discounts to retailers in the spring and summer to encourage early ordering.
Answer (A) is incorrect. Cash discounts encourage prompt payment. Answer (B) is incorrect. Quantity discounts encourage large volume purchases. Answer (C) is incorrect. Functional or trade discounts are provided to channel members in return for the performance of certain functions, such as selling, storing, and recordkeeping.

25. Several surveys point out that most managers use full product costs, including unit fixed costs and unit variable costs, in developing cost-based pricing. Which one of the following is **least** associated with cost-based pricing?

A. Price stability.

B. Price justification.

C. Target pricing.

D. Fixed-cost recovery.

Answer (C) is correct.
REQUIRED: The concept least associated with cost-based pricing.
DISCUSSION: A target price is the expected market price of a product, given the company's knowledge of its customers and competitors. Hence, under target pricing, the sales price is known before the product is developed. Subtracting the unit target profit margin determines the long-term unit target cost. If cost-cutting measures do not permit the product to be made at or below the target cost, it will be abandoned.
Answer (A) is incorrect. Full-cost pricing promotes price stability. It limits the ability to cut prices. Answer (B) is incorrect. Full-cost pricing provides evidence that the company is not violating antitrust laws against predatory pricing. Answer (D) is incorrect. Full-cost pricing has the advantage of recovering the full long-term costs of the product. In the long term, all costs are relevant.

26. The **most** fundamental responsibility center affected by the use of market-based transfer prices is a(n)

A. Production center.

B. Investment center.

C. Cost center.

D. Profit center.

Answer (D) is correct.
REQUIRED: The most fundamental responsibility center affected by the use of market-based transfer prices.
DISCUSSION: Transfer prices are often used by profit centers and investment centers. Profit centers are the more fundamental of these two centers because investment centers are responsible not only for revenues and costs but also for invested capital.
Answer (A) is incorrect. A production center may be a cost center, a profit center, or even an investment center. Transfer prices are not used in a cost center. Transfer prices are used to compute profitability, but a cost center is responsible only for cost control. Answer (B) is incorrect. An investment center is not as fundamental as a profit center. Answer (C) is incorrect. Transfer prices are not used in a cost center.

27. A manufacturer produces portable televisions. The manufacturer's product manager proposes to increase the cost structure by adding voice-activated volume/channel controls to the television, and also adding three additional repair personnel to deal with products returned due to defects. Are these costs value-added or nonvalue-added?

	Cost of Voice-Activated Controls	Cost of Additional Repair Personnel
A.	Value-added	Value-added
B.	Value-added	Nonvalue-added
C.	Nonvalue-added	Value-added
D.	Nonvalue-added	Nonvalue-added

Answer (B) is correct.
REQUIRED: The correct classification of costs as value-added or nonvalue-added.
DISCUSSION: The additional cost of the voice-activated controls is a value-added cost because it provides new functionality for the consumer. The cost of additional repair personnel, on the other hand, is nonvalue-added since it is incurred to address deficiencies in quality.
Answer (A) is incorrect. Costs incurred to compensate for poor quality are nonvalue-added costs. Answer (C) is incorrect. Costs that provide additional functionality for the customer are considered value-added. Answer (D) is incorrect. Costs that provide additional functionality for the customer are considered value-added.

28. A start-up company wants to use cost-based pricing for its only product, a unique new video game. The company expects to sell 10,000 units in the upcoming year. Variable costs will be $65 per unit and annual fixed operating costs (including depreciation) amount to $80,000. The company's balance sheet is as follows:

Assets	
Current assets	$100,000
Plant & equipment	425,000

Liabilities & Equity	
Accounts payable	$ 25,000
Debt	200,000
Equity	300,000

If the company wants to earn a 20% return on equity, at what price should it sell the new product?

A. $75.00

B. $78.60

C. $79.00

D. $81.00

Answer (C) is correct.
 REQUIRED: The target price for a new product given relevant data.
 DISCUSSION: The net income the company will require is calculated as follows:

$$\text{Return on equity} = \text{Net income} \div \text{Equity}$$
$$\text{Net income} = \text{Equity} \times \text{Return on equity}$$
$$= \$300,000 \times 20\%$$
$$= \$60,000$$

The necessary selling price can then be derived:

$$\text{Net income} = [(\text{Selling price} - \text{Variable costs}) \times \text{Units sold}] - \text{Fixed costs}$$
$$\text{Selling price} = (\text{Net income} + \text{Fixed costs} + \text{Variable costs}) \div \text{Units sold}$$
$$= (\$60,000 + \$80,000 + \$650,000) \div 10,000$$
$$= \$790,000 \div 10,000$$
$$= \$79 \text{ per unit}$$

Answer (A) is incorrect. Improperly applying the return on equity percentage only to current assets results in $75.00. Answer (B) is incorrect. The price would have to be $79. Answer (D) is incorrect. Basing the rate of return on fixed assets rather than equity results in $81.00.

29. An entity has just developed a new product with a manufacturing cost of $30. The Marketing Director has identified three marketing approaches for this new product.

Approach X   Set a selling price of $36 and have the firm's sales staff sell the product at a 10% commission with no advertising program. Estimated annual sales would be 10,000 units.

Approach Y   Set a selling price of $38, have the firm's sales staff sell the product at a 10% commission, and back them up with a $30,000 advertising program. Estimated annual sales would be 12,000 units.

Approach Z   Rely on wholesalers to handle the product. The entity would sell the new product to the wholesalers at $32 per unit and incur no selling expenses. Estimated annual sales would be 14,000 units.

Rank the three alternatives in order of net profit, from highest net profit to lowest.

A. X, Y, Z.

B. Y, Z, X.

C. Z, X, Y.

D. Z, Y, X.

Answer (C) is correct.
 REQUIRED: Calculation of the profit of various new products.
 DISCUSSION: The estimated net profit of the entity's three alternatives can be calculated as follows:

	X	Y	Z
Selling price	$ 36	$ 38	$ 32
Times: sales units	× 10,000	× 12,000	× 14,000
Estimated sales	$360,000	$456,000	$448,000
Less: commissions	(36,000)	(45,600)	0
Gross sales	$324,000	$410,400	$448,000
Less: advertising	0	(30,000)	0
Net sales	$324,000	$380,400	$448,000
Less: manufacturing cost	(300,000)	(360,000)	(420,000)
Net profit	$ 24,000	$ 20,400	$ 28,000

Answer (A) is incorrect. Approach Z is more profitable than Approach X. Answer (B) is incorrect. Approach Y is the least profitable alternative. Answer (D) is incorrect. Approach X is more profitable than Approach Y.

10.7 ESSAY QUESTIONS

Scenario for Essay Questions 1, 2

Sonimad Mining Company produces and sells bulk raw coal to other coal companies. Sonimad mines and stockpiles the coal; it is then passed through a one-step crushing process before being loaded onto river barges for shipment to customers. The annual output of 10 million tons, which is expected to remain stable, has an average cost of $20 per ton with an average selling price of $27 per ton.

Management is evaluating the possibility of further processing the coal by sizing and cleaning to expand markets and enhance product revenue. Management has rejected the possibility of constructing a sizing and cleaning plant, which would require a significant long-term capital investment.

Bill Rolland, controller of Sonimad, has asked Amy Kimbell, mining engineer, to develop cost and revenue projections for further processing the coal through a variety of contractual arrangements. After extensive discussions with vendors and contractors, Kimbell has prepared the following projections of incremental costs of sizing and cleaning Sonimad's annual output:

Direct labor (employee leasing)	$600,000 per year
Supervisory personnel (employee leasing)	100,000 per year
Heavy equipment rental, operating, and maintenance costs	25,000 per month
Contract sizing and cleaning	3.50 per ton
Outbound rail freight (per 60-ton rail car)	240 per car

In addition to the preceding cost information, market samples obtained by Kimbell have shown that electrical utilities enter into contracts for sized and cleaned coal similar to that mined by Sonimad at an expected average price of $36 per ton.

Kimbell has learned that 5% of the raw bulk output that enters the sizing and cleaning process will be lost as a primary product. Normally, 75% of this product loss can be salvaged as coal fines. These are small pieces ranging from dust-like particles up to pieces 2 inches in diameter. Coal fines are too small for use by electrical utilities but are frequently sold to steel manufacturers for use in blast furnaces.

Unfortunately, the price for coal fines frequently fluctuates between $14 and $24 per ton (FOB shipping point), and the timing of market volume is erratic. While companies generally sell all their coal fines during a year, it is not unusual to stockpile this product for several months before making any sales.

Questions

1. Prepare an analysis to show whether it would be more profitable for Sonimad Mining Company to continue to sell the raw bulk coal or to process it further through sizing and cleaning. (Note: Ignore any value related to the coal fines in your analysis.)

2. a. Taking into consideration any potential value to the coal fines, prepare an analysis to show if the fines would affect the results of your analysis prepared in Question 1.

    b. What other factors should be considered in evaluating a sell-or-process-further decision?

Essay Questions 1, 2 — Unofficial Answers

1. The analysis shown below indicates that it would be more profitable for Sonimad Mining company to continue to sell raw bulk coal without further processing. (This analysis ignores any value related to coal fines.)

Incremental Sales Revenue:

Sales revenue after further processing (9,500,000 tons × $36)	$342,000,000
Sales revenue from bulk raw coal (10,000,000 tons × $27)	270,000,000
Incremental sales revenue	$ 72,000,000

Incremental costs:

Direct labor	$ 600,000
Supervisory personnel	100,000
Heavy equipment costs ($25,000 × 12 months)	300,000
Sizing and clearing (10,000,000 tons × $3.50)	35,000,000
Outbound rail freight (9,500,000 tons ÷ 60 tons) × $240 per car	38,000,000
Incremental costs	$ 74,000,000
Incremental gain (loss)	$ (2,000,000)

2. a. The analysis shown below indicates that the potential revenue from the coal fines by-product would result in additional revenue, ranging between $5,250,000 and $9,000,000, depending on the market price of the fines.

   1) Coal fines = 75% of 5% of raw bulk tonnage
      = .75 × (10,000,000 × .05)
      = 375,000 tons

   Potential additional revenue:

   Minimum: 375,000 tons at $14 per ton = $5,250,000
   Maximum: 375,000 tons at $24 per ton = $9,000,000

   Since the incremental loss is $2 million, as calculated in Question 1 above, including the coal fines in the analysis indicates that further processing provides a positive result and is, therefore, favorable.

   b. Other factors that should be considered in evaluating a sell-or-process-further decision include the

   1) Stability of the current customer market and how it compares to the market for sized and cleaned coal

   2) Storage space needed for the coal fines until they are sold and the handling costs of coal fines

   3) Reliability of cost (e.g., rail freight rates) and revenue estimates, and the risk of depending on these estimates

   4) Timing of the revenue stream from coal fines and impact on the need for liquidity

   5) Possible environmental problems, i.e., dumping of waste and smoke from unprocessed coal

---

Access the **Gleim CMA Premium Review System** from your Gleim Personal Classroom to continue your studies with exam-emulating essay questions!

APPENDIX A
PV/FV TABLES

PRESENT VALUE OF ORDINARY ANNUITY

	1%	2%	3%	4%	5%	6%	7%	8%	9%	10%	12%	14%	16%	18%	20%	
1	0.990	0.980	0.971	0.962	0.952	0.943	0.935	0.926	0.917	0.909	0.893	0.877	0.862	0.847	0.833	1
2	1.970	1.942	1.913	1.886	1.859	1.833	1.808	1.783	1.759	1.736	1.690	1.647	1.605	1.566	1.528	2
3	2.941	2.884	2.829	2.775	2.723	2.673	2.624	2.577	2.531	2.487	2.402	2.322	2.246	2.174	2.106	3
4	3.902	3.808	3.717	3.630	3.546	3.465	3.387	3.312	3.240	3.170	3.037	2.914	2.798	2.690	2.589	4
5	4.853	4.713	4.580	4.452	4.329	4.212	4.100	3.993	3.890	3.791	3.605	3.433	3.274	3.127	2.991	5
6	5.795	5.601	5.417	5.242	5.076	4.917	4.767	4.623	4.486	4.355	4.111	3.889	3.685	3.498	3.326	6
7	6.728	6.472	6.230	6.002	5.786	5.582	5.389	5.206	5.033	4.868	4.564	4.288	4.039	3.812	3.605	7
8	7.652	7.325	7.020	6.733	6.463	6.210	5.971	5.747	5.535	5.335	4.968	4.639	4.344	4.078	3.837	8
9	8.566	8.162	7.786	7.435	7.108	6.802	6.515	6.247	5.995	5.759	5.328	4.946	4.607	4.303	4.031	9
10	9.471	8.983	8.530	8.111	7.722	7.360	7.024	6.710	6.418	6.145	5.650	5.216	4.833	4.494	4.192	10
11	10.368	9.787	9.253	8.760	8.306	7.887	7.499	7.139	6.805	6.495	5.938	5.453	5.029	4.656	4.327	11
12	11.255	10.575	9.954	9.385	8.863	8.384	7.943	7.536	7.161	6.814	6.194	5.660	5.197	4.793	4.439	12
13	12.134	11.348	10.635	9.986	9.394	8.853	8.358	7.904	7.487	7.103	6.424	5.842	5.342	4.910	4.533	13
14	13.004	12.106	11.296	10.563	9.899	9.295	8.745	8.244	7.786	7.367	6.628	6.002	5.468	5.008	4.611	14
15	13.865	12.849	11.938	11.118	10.380	9.712	9.108	8.559	8.061	7.606	6.811	6.142	5.575	5.092	4.675	15
16	14.718	13.578	12.561	11.652	10.838	10.106	9.447	8.851	8.313	7.824	6.974	6.265	5.668	5.162	4.730	16
18	16.398	14.992	13.754	12.659	11.690	10.828	10.059	9.372	8.756	8.201	7.250	6.467	5.818	5.273	4.812	18
20	18.046	16.351	14.877	13.590	12.462	11.470	10.594	9.818	9.129	8.514	7.469	6.623	5.929	5.353	4.870	20
22	19.660	17.658	15.937	14.451	13.163	12.042	11.061	10.201	9.442	8.772	7.645	6.743	6.011	5.410	4.909	22
24	21.243	18.914	16.936	15.247	13.799	12.550	11.469	10.529	9.707	8.985	7.784	6.835	6.073	5.451	4.937	24
26	22.795	20.121	17.877	15.983	14.375	13.003	11.826	10.810	9.929	9.161	7.896	6.906	6.118	5.480	4.956	26
28	24.316	21.281	18.764	16.663	14.898	13.406	12.137	11.051	10.116	9.307	7.984	6.961	6.152	5.502	4.970	28
30	25.808	22.396	19.600	17.292	15.372	13.765	12.409	11.258	10.274	9.427	8.055	7.003	6.177	5.517	4.979	30
32	27.270	23.468	20.389	17.874	15.803	14.084	12.647	11.435	10.406	9.526	8.112	7.035	6.196	5.528	4.985	32
34	28.703	24.499	21.132	18.411	16.193	14.368	12.854	11.587	10.518	9.609	8.157	7.060	6.210	5.536	4.990	34
36	30.108	25.489	21.832	18.908	16.547	14.621	13.035	11.717	10.612	9.677	8.192	7.079	6.220	5.541	4.993	36
38	31.485	26.441	22.492	19.368	16.868	14.846	13.193	11.829	10.691	9.733	8.221	7.094	6.228	5.545	4.995	38
40	32.835	27.355	23.115	19.793	17.159	15.046	13.332	11.925	10.757	9.779	8.244	7.105	6.233	5.548	4.997	40

PRESENT VALUE OF $1

	1%	2%	3%	4%	5%	6%	7%	8%	9%	10%	12%	14%	16%	18%	20%	
1	0.990	0.980	0.971	0.962	0.952	0.943	0.935	0.926	0.917	0.909	0.893	0.877	0.862	0.847	0.833	1
2	0.980	0.961	0.943	0.925	0.907	0.890	0.873	0.857	0.842	0.826	0.797	0.769	0.743	0.718	0.694	2
3	0.971	0.942	0.915	0.889	0.864	0.840	0.816	0.794	0.772	0.751	0.712	0.675	0.641	0.609	0.579	3
4	0.961	0.924	0.888	0.855	0.823	0.792	0.763	0.735	0.708	0.683	0.636	0.592	0.552	0.516	0.482	4
5	0.951	0.906	0.863	0.822	0.784	0.747	0.713	0.681	0.650	0.621	0.567	0.519	0.476	0.437	0.402	5
6	0.942	0.888	0.837	0.790	0.746	0.705	0.666	0.630	0.596	0.564	0.507	0.456	0.410	0.370	0.335	6
7	0.933	0.871	0.813	0.760	0.711	0.665	0.623	0.583	0.547	0.513	0.452	0.400	0.354	0.314	0.279	7
8	0.923	0.853	0.789	0.731	0.677	0.627	0.582	0.540	0.502	0.467	0.404	0.351	0.305	0.266	0.233	8
9	0.914	0.837	0.766	0.703	0.645	0.592	0.544	0.500	0.460	0.424	0.361	0.308	0.263	0.225	0.194	9
10	0.905	0.820	0.744	0.676	0.614	0.558	0.508	0.463	0.422	0.386	0.322	0.270	0.227	0.191	0.162	10
11	0.896	0.804	0.722	0.650	0.585	0.527	0.475	0.429	0.388	0.350	0.287	0.237	0.195	0.162	0.135	11
12	0.887	0.788	0.701	0.625	0.557	0.497	0.444	0.397	0.356	0.319	0.257	0.208	0.168	0.137	0.112	12
13	0.879	0.773	0.681	0.601	0.530	0.469	0.415	0.368	0.326	0.290	0.229	0.182	0.145	0.116	0.093	13
14	0.870	0.758	0.661	0.577	0.505	0.442	0.388	0.340	0.299	0.263	0.205	0.160	0.125	0.099	0.078	14
15	0.861	0.743	0.642	0.555	0.481	0.417	0.362	0.315	0.275	0.239	0.183	0.140	0.108	0.084	0.065	15
16	0.853	0.728	0.623	0.534	0.458	0.394	0.339	0.292	0.252	0.218	0.163	0.123	0.093	0.071	0.054	16
18	0.836	0.700	0.587	0.494	0.416	0.350	0.296	0.250	0.212	0.180	0.130	0.095	0.069	0.051	0.038	18
20	0.820	0.673	0.554	0.456	0.377	0.312	0.258	0.215	0.178	0.149	0.104	0.073	0.051	0.037	0.026	20
22	0.803	0.647	0.522	0.422	0.342	0.278	0.226	0.184	0.150	0.123	0.083	0.056	0.038	0.026	0.018	22
24	0.788	0.622	0.492	0.390	0.310	0.247	0.197	0.158	0.126	0.102	0.066	0.043	0.028	0.019	0.013	24
26	0.772	0.598	0.464	0.361	0.281	0.220	0.172	0.135	0.106	0.084	0.053	0.033	0.021	0.014	0.009	26
28	0.757	0.574	0.437	0.333	0.255	0.196	0.150	0.116	0.090	0.069	0.042	0.026	0.016	0.010	0.006	28
30	0.742	0.552	0.412	0.308	0.231	0.174	0.131	0.099	0.075	0.057	0.033	0.020	0.012	0.007	0.004	30
32	0.727	0.531	0.388	0.285	0.210	0.155	0.115	0.085	0.063	0.047	0.027	0.015	0.009	0.005	0.003	32
34	0.713	0.510	0.366	0.264	0.190	0.138	0.100	0.073	0.053	0.039	0.021	0.012	0.006	0.004	0.002	34
36	0.699	0.490	0.345	0.244	0.173	0.123	0.088	0.063	0.045	0.032	0.017	0.009	0.005	0.003	0.001	36
38	0.685	0.471	0.325	0.225	0.157	0.109	0.076	0.054	0.038	0.027	0.013	0.007	0.004	0.002	0.001	38
40	0.672	0.453	0.307	0.208	0.142	0.097	0.067	0.046	0.032	0.022	0.011	0.005	0.003	0.001	0.001	40

FUTURE VALUE OF ORDINARY ANNUITY

	1%	2%	3%	4%	5%	6%	7%	8%	9%	10%	12%	14%	16%	18%	20%	
1	1.000	1.000	1.000	1.000	1.000	1.000	1.000	1.000	1.000	1.000	1.000	1.000	1.000	1.000	1.000	1
2	2.010	2.020	2.030	2.040	2.050	2.060	2.070	2.080	2.090	2.100	2.120	2.140	2.160	2.180	2.200	2
3	3.030	3.060	3.091	3.122	3.153	3.184	3.215	3.246	3.278	3.310	3.374	3.440	3.506	3.572	3.640	3
4	4.060	4.122	4.184	4.246	4.310	4.375	4.440	4.506	4.573	4.641	4.779	4.921	5.066	5.215	5.368	4
5	5.101	5.204	5.309	5.416	5.526	5.637	5.751	5.867	5.985	6.105	6.353	6.610	6.877	7.154	7.442	5
6	6.152	6.308	6.468	6.633	6.802	6.975	7.153	7.336	7.523	7.716	8.115	8.536	8.977	9.442	9.930	6
7	7.214	7.434	7.662	7.898	8.142	8.394	8.654	8.923	9.200	9.487	10.089	10.730	11.414	12.142	12.916	7
8	8.286	8.583	8.892	9.214	9.549	9.897	10.260	10.637	11.028	11.436	12.300	13.233	14.240	15.327	16.499	8
9	9.369	9.755	10.159	10.583	11.027	11.491	11.978	12.488	13.021	13.579	14.776	16.085	17.519	19.086	20.799	9
10	10.462	10.950	11.464	12.006	12.578	13.181	13.816	14.487	15.193	15.937	17.549	19.337	21.321	23.521	25.959	10
11	11.567	12.169	12.808	13.486	14.207	14.972	15.784	16.645	17.560	18.531	20.655	23.045	25.733	28.755	32.150	11
12	12.683	13.412	14.192	15.026	15.917	16.870	17.888	18.977	20.141	21.384	24.133	27.271	30.850	34.931	39.581	12
13	13.809	14.680	15.618	16.627	17.713	18.882	20.141	21.495	22.953	24.523	28.029	32.089	36.786	42.219	48.497	13
14	14.947	15.974	17.086	18.292	19.599	21.015	22.550	24.215	26.019	27.975	32.393	37.581	43.672	50.818	59.196	14
15	16.097	17.293	18.599	20.024	21.579	23.276	25.129	27.152	29.361	31.772	37.280	43.842	51.660	60.965	72.035	15
16	17.258	18.639	20.157	21.825	23.657	25.673	27.888	30.324	33.003	35.950	42.753	50.980	60.925	72.939	87.442	16
18	19.615	21.412	23.414	25.645	28.132	30.906	33.999	37.450	41.301	45.599	55.750	68.394	84.141	103.740	128.117	18
20	22.019	24.297	26.870	29.778	33.066	36.786	40.995	45.762	51.160	57.275	72.052	91.025	115.380	146.628	186.688	20
22	24.472	27.299	30.537	34.248	38.505	43.392	49.006	55.457	62.873	71.403	92.503	120.436	157.415	206.345	271.031	22
24	26.973	30.422	34.426	39.083	44.502	50.816	58.177	66.765	76.790	88.497	118.155	158.659	213.978	289.494	392.484	24
26	29.526	33.671	38.553	44.312	51.113	59.156	68.676	79.954	93.324	109.182	150.334	208.333	290.088	405.272	567.377	26
28	32.129	37.051	42.931	49.968	58.403	68.528	80.698	95.339	112.968	134.210	190.699	272.889	392.503	566.481	819.223	28
30	34.785	40.568	47.575	56.085	66.439	79.058	94.461	113.283	136.308	164.494	241.333	356.787	530.312	790.948	1181.882	30
32	37.494	44.227	52.503	62.701	75.299	90.890	110.218	134.214	164.037	201.138	304.848	465.820	715.747	1103.496	1704.109	32
34	40.258	48.034	57.730	69.858	85.067	104.184	128.259	158.627	196.982	245.477	384.521	607.520	965.270	1538.688	2456.118	34
36	43.077	51.994	63.276	77.598	95.836	119.121	148.913	187.102	236.125	299.127	484.463	791.673	1301.027	2144.649	3539.009	36
38	45.953	56.115	69.159	85.970	107.710	135.904	172.561	220.316	282.630	364.043	609.831	1030.998	1752.822	2988.389	5098.373	38
40	48.886	60.402	75.401	95.026	120.800	154.762	199.635	259.057	337.882	442.593	767.091	1342.025	2360.757	4163.213	7343.858	40

FUTURE VALUE OF $1

	1%	2%	3%	4%	5%	6%	7%	8%	9%	10%	12%	14%	16%	18%	20%	
1	1.010	1.020	1.030	1.040	1.050	1.060	1.070	1.080	1.090	1.100	1.120	1.140	1.160	1.180	1.200	1
2	1.020	1.040	1.061	1.082	1.103	1.124	1.145	1.166	1.188	1.210	1.254	1.300	1.346	1.392	1.440	2
3	1.030	1.061	1.093	1.125	1.158	1.191	1.225	1.260	1.295	1.331	1.405	1.482	1.561	1.643	1.728	3
4	1.041	1.082	1.126	1.170	1.216	1.262	1.311	1.360	1.412	1.464	1.574	1.689	1.811	1.939	2.074	4
5	1.051	1.104	1.159	1.217	1.276	1.338	1.403	1.469	1.539	1.611	1.762	1.925	2.100	2.288	2.488	5
6	1.062	1.126	1.194	1.265	1.340	1.419	1.501	1.587	1.677	1.772	1.974	2.195	2.436	2.700	2.986	6
7	1.072	1.149	1.230	1.316	1.407	1.504	1.606	1.714	1.828	1.949	2.211	2.502	2.826	3.185	3.583	7
8	1.083	1.172	1.267	1.369	1.477	1.594	1.718	1.851	1.993	2.144	2.476	2.853	3.278	3.759	4.300	8
9	1.094	1.195	1.305	1.423	1.551	1.689	1.838	1.999	2.172	2.358	2.773	3.252	3.803	4.435	5.160	9
10	1.105	1.219	1.344	1.480	1.629	1.791	1.967	2.159	2.367	2.594	3.106	3.707	4.411	5.234	6.192	10
11	1.116	1.243	1.384	1.539	1.710	1.898	2.105	2.332	2.580	2.853	3.479	4.226	5.117	6.176	7.430	11
12	1.127	1.268	1.426	1.601	1.796	2.012	2.252	2.518	2.813	3.138	3.896	4.818	5.936	7.288	8.916	12
13	1.138	1.294	1.469	1.665	1.886	2.133	2.410	2.720	3.066	3.452	4.363	5.492	6.886	8.599	10.699	13
14	1.149	1.319	1.513	1.732	1.980	2.261	2.579	2.937	3.342	3.797	4.887	6.261	7.988	10.147	12.839	14
15	1.161	1.346	1.558	1.801	2.079	2.397	2.759	3.172	3.642	4.177	5.474	7.138	9.266	11.974	15.407	15
16	1.173	1.373	1.605	1.873	2.183	2.540	2.952	3.426	3.970	4.595	6.130	8.137	10.748	14.129	18.488	16
18	1.196	1.428	1.702	2.026	2.407	2.854	3.380	3.996	4.717	5.560	7.690	10.575	14.463	19.673	26.623	18
20	1.220	1.486	1.806	2.191	2.653	3.207	3.870	4.661	5.604	6.727	9.646	13.743	19.461	27.393	38.338	20
22	1.245	1.546	1.916	2.370	2.925	3.604	4.430	5.437	6.659	8.140	12.100	17.861	26.186	38.142	55.206	22
24	1.270	1.608	2.033	2.563	3.225	4.049	5.072	6.341	7.911	9.850	15.179	23.212	35.236	53.109	79.497	24
26	1.295	1.673	2.157	2.772	3.556	4.549	5.807	7.396	9.399	11.918	19.040	30.167	47.414	73.949	114.475	26
28	1.321	1.741	2.288	2.999	3.920	5.112	6.649	8.627	11.167	14.421	23.884	39.204	63.800	102.967	164.845	28
30	1.348	1.811	2.427	3.243	4.322	5.743	7.612	10.063	13.268	17.449	29.960	50.950	85.850	143.371	237.376	30
32	1.375	1.885	2.575	3.508	4.765	6.453	8.715	11.737	15.763	21.114	37.582	66.215	115.520	199.629	341.822	32
34	1.403	1.961	2.732	3.794	5.253	7.251	9.978	13.690	18.728	25.548	47.143	86.053	155.443	277.964	492.224	34
36	1.431	2.040	2.898	4.104	5.792	8.147	11.424	15.968	22.251	30.913	59.136	111.834	209.164	387.037	708.802	36
38	1.460	2.122	3.075	4.439	6.385	9.154	13.079	18.625	26.437	37.404	74.180	145.340	281.452	538.910	1020.675	38
40	1.489	2.208	3.262	4.801	7.040	10.286	14.974	21.725	31.409	45.259	93.051	188.884	378.721	750.378	1469.772	40

APPENDIX B
GLOSSARY OF ACCOUNTING TERMS
U.S. TO BRITISH VS. BRITISH TO U.S.

U.S. TO BRITISH

U.S.	British
Accounts payable	Trade creditors
Accounts receivable	Trade debtors
Accrual	Provision (for liability or charge)
Accumulated depreciation	Aggregate depreciation
Additional paid-in capital	Share premium account
Allowance	Provision (for diminution in value)
Allowance for doubtful accounts	Provision for bad debt
Annual Stockholders' Meeting	Annual General Meeting
Authorized capital stock	Authorized share capital
Bellweather stock	Barometer stock
Bylaws	Articles of Association
Bond	Loan finance
Capital lease	Finance lease
Certificate of Incorporation	Memorandum of Association
Checking account	Current account
Common stock	Ordinary shares
Consumer price index	Retail price index
Corporation	Company
Cost of goods sold	Cost of sales
Credit Memorandum	Credit note
Equity	Reserves
Equity interest	Ownership interest
Financial statements	Accounts
Income statement	Profit and loss account
Income taxes	Taxation
Inventories	Stocks
Investment bank	Merchant bank
Labor union	Trade union
Land	Freehold
Lease with bargain purchase option	Hire purchase contract
Liabilities	Creditors
Listed company	Quoted company
Long-term investments	Fixed asset investments
Long-term lease	Long leasehold
Merchandise trade	Visible trade
Mutual funds	Unit trusts
Net income	Net profit
Note payable	Bill payable
Note receivable	Bill receivable
Paid-in surplus	Share premium
Par value	Nominal value
Pooling of interests method	Merger accounting
Preferred stock	Preference share
Prime rate	Base rate
Property, plant, and equipment	Tangible fixed assets
Provision for bad debts	Charge
Purchase method	Acquisition accounting
Purchase on account	Purchase on credit
Real estate	Property
Revenue	Income
Reversal of accrual	Release of provision
Sales on account	Sales on credit
Sales/revenue	Turnover
Savings and loan association	Building society
Shareholders' equity	Shareholders' funds
Stock	Inventory
Stockholder	Shareholder
Stock dividend	Bonus share
Stockholders' equity	Share capital and reserves or Shareholders' funds
Taxable income	Taxable profit
Treasury bonds	Gilt-edged stock (gilts)

BRITISH TO U.S.

Accounts	Financial statements
Acquisition accounting	Purchase method
Aggregate depreciation	Accumulated depreciation
Annual General Meeting	Annual Stockholders' Meeting
Articles of Association	Bylaws
Authorized share capital	Authorized capital stock
Barometer stock	Bellweather stock
Base rate	Prime rate
Bill payable	Note payable
Bill receivable	Note receivable
Bonus share	Stock dividend
Building society	Savings and loan association
Charge	Provision for bad debts
Company	Corporation
Cost of sales	Cost of goods sold
Credit note	Credit Memorandum
Creditors	Liabilities
Current account	Checking account
Finance lease	Capital lease
Fixed asset investments	Long-term investments
Freehold	Land
Gilt-edged stock (gilts)	Treasury bonds
Hire purchase contract	Lease with bargain purchase option
Income	Revenue
Inventory	Stock
Loan finance	Bond
Long leasehold	Long-term lease
Memorandum of Association	Certificate of Incorporation
Merchant bank	Investment bank
Merger accounting	Pooling of interests method
Net profit	Net income
Nominal value	Par value
Ordinary shares	Common stock
Ownership interest	Equity interest
Preference share	Preferred stock
Profit and loss account	Income statement
Property	Real estate
Provision for bad debt	Allowance for doubtful accounts
Provision (for diminution in value)	Allowance
Provision (for liability or charge)	Accrual
Purchase on credit	Purchase on account
Quoted company	Listed company
Release of provision	Reversal of accrual
Reserves	Equity
Retail price index	Consumer price index
Sales on credit	Sales on account
Share capital and reserves or Shareholders' funds	Stockholders' equity
Shareholder	Stockholder
Shareholders' funds	Shareholders' equity
Share premium	Paid-in surplus
Share premium account	Additional paid-in capital
Stocks	Inventories
Tangible fixed assets	Property, plant, and equipment
Taxable profit	Taxable income
Taxation	Income taxes
Trade creditors	Accounts payable
Trade debtors	Accounts receivable
Trade union	Labor union
Turnover	Sales/revenue
Unit trusts	Mutual funds
Visible trade	Merchandise trade

APPENDIX C
ICMA CONTENT SPECIFICATION OUTLINES, LEARNING OUTCOME STATEMENTS, AND CROSS-REFERENCES

The following pages consist of a reprint of the ICMA's Content Specification Outlines (CSOs), Learning Outcome Statements (LOSs), and related information for Part 2, effective January 1, 2015. In addition, we have provided cross-references to the Gleim CMA study units. Please use these CSOs and LOSs as reference material only. The ICMA's CSOs and LOSs have been carefully analyzed and have been incorporated into Study Units 1 through 10 to provide systematic and rational coverage of exam topics.

We believe we provide comprehensive coverage of the subject matter tested on the CMA exam. If, after taking the exam, you feel that certain topics, concepts, etc., tested were not covered or were inadequately covered, please go to www.gleim.com/feedbackCMA2. We do not want information about CMA questions, only information/feedback about our CMA Review System's coverage.

Effective January 1, 2015

Content Specification Outlines
Certified Management Accountant (CMA) Examinations

The content specification outlines presented on pages 341 and 342 represent the body of knowledge that will be covered on the CMA examinations. The outlines may be changed in the future when new subject matter becomes part of the common body of knowledge.

Candidates for the CMA designation are required to take and pass Parts 1 and 2.

Candidates are responsible for being informed on the most recent developments in the areas covered in the outlines. This includes understanding of public pronouncements issued by accounting organizations as well as being up-to-date on recent developments reported in current accounting, financial and business periodicals.

The content specification outlines serve several purposes. The outlines are intended to:

- Establish the foundation from which each examination will be developed.
- Provide a basis for consistent coverage on each examination.
- Communicate to interested parties more detail as to the content of each examination part.
- Assist candidates in their preparation for each examination.
- Provide information to those who offer courses designed to aid candidates in preparing for the examinations.

Important additional information about the content specification outlines and the examinations is listed below and on the following page.

1. The coverage percentage given for each major topic within each examination part represents the relative weight given to that topic in an examination part. The number of questions presented in each major topic area approximates this percentage.

2. Each examination will sample from the subject areas contained within each major topic area to meet the relative weight specifications. No relative weights have been assigned to the subject areas within each major topic. No inference should be made from the order in which the subject areas are listed or from the number of subject areas as to the relative weight or importance of any of the subjects.

3. Each major topic within each examination part has been assigned a coverage level designating the depth and breadth of topic coverage, ranging from an introductory knowledge of a subject area (Level A) to a thorough understanding of and ability to apply the essentials of a subject area (Level C). Detailed explanations of the coverage levels and the skills expected of candidates are presented on the following page.

4. The topics for Parts 1 and 2 have been selected to minimize the overlapping of subject areas among the examination parts. The topics within an examination part and the subject areas within topics may be combined in individual questions.

5. With regard to U.S. Federal income taxation issues, candidates will be expected to understand the impact of income taxes when reporting and analyzing financial results. In addition, the tax code provisions that impact decisions (e.g., depreciation, interest, etc.) will be tested.

6.   Candidates for the CMA designation are assumed to have knowledge of the following: preparation of financial statements, business economics, time-value of money concepts, statistics and probability.

7.   Parts 1 and 2 are four-hour exams and each contains 100 multiple-choice questions and 2 essay questions. Candidates will have three hours to complete the multiple-choice questions and one hour to complete the essay section. A small number of the multiple-choice questions on each exam are being validated for future use and will not count in the final score.

8.   For the essay questions, both written and quantitative responses will be required. Candidates will be expected to present written answers that are responsive to the question asked, presented in a logical manner, and demonstrate an appropriate understanding of the subject matter. It should be noted that candidates are expected to have working knowledge in the use of word processing and electronic spreadsheets.

In order to more clearly define the topical knowledge required by a candidate, varying levels of coverage for the treatment of major topics of the content specification outlines have been identified and defined. The cognitive skills that a successful candidate should possess and that should be tested on the examinations can be defined as follows:

Knowledge: Ability to remember previously learned material such as specific facts, criteria, techniques, principles, and procedures (i.e., identify, define, list).

Comprehension: Ability to grasp and interpret the meaning of material (i.e., classify, explain, distinguish between).

Application: Ability to use learned material in new and concrete situations (i.e., demonstrate, predict, solve, modify, relate).

Analysis: Ability to break down material into its component parts so that its organizational structure can be understood; ability to recognize causal relationships, discriminate between behaviors, and identify elements that are relevant to the validation of a judgment (i.e., differentiate, estimate, order).

Synthesis: Ability to put parts together to form a new whole or proposed set of operations; ability to relate ideas and formulate hypotheses (i.e., combine, formulate, revise).

Evaluation: Ability to judge the value of material for a given purpose on the basis of consistency, logical accuracy, and comparison to standards; ability to appraise judgments involved in the selection of a course of action (i.e., criticize, justify, conclude).

The three levels of coverage can be defined as follows:

Level A: Requiring the skill levels of knowledge and comprehension.

Level B: Requiring the skill levels of knowledge, comprehension, application, and analysis.

Level C: Requiring all six skill levels, knowledge, comprehension, application, analysis, synthesis, and evaluation.

The levels of coverage as they apply to each of the major topics of the Content Specification Outlines are shown on the following pages with each topic listing. The levels represent the manner in which topic areas are to be treated and represent ceilings, i.e., a topic area designated as Level C may contain requirements at the "A," "B," or "C" level, but a topic designated as Level B will not contain requirements at the "C" level.

CMA Content Specification Overview

Part 2   **Financial Decision Making**
               (4 hours – 100 questions and 2 essay questions)

Financial Statement Analysis	25%	Level C
Corporate Finance	20%	Level C
Decision Analysis	20%	Level C
Risk Management	10%	Level C
Investment Decisions	15%	Level C
Professional Ethics	10%	Level C

Candidates for the CMA designation are assumed to have knowledge of the following: preparation of financial statements, business economics, time-value of money concepts, statistics and probability. Questions in both parts of the CMA exam will assume that the successful candidate can effectively integrate and synthesize this knowledge with the specific topics covered in the content specification outline.

On the following pages, we have reproduced verbatim the ICMA's Content Specification Outlines (CSOs) and Learning Outcome Statements (LOSs) for Part 2. We also have provided cross-references to the study units and subunits in this book that correspond to the CSOs' and LOSs' coverage. If one entry appears above a list, it applies to all items in that list.

Part 2 – Financial Decision Making

A. **Financial Statement Analysis (25% - Levels A, B, and C)**

    1.   *Basic Financial Statement Analysis* (6.9)

        a.   Common size financial statements
        b.   Common base year financial statements

    2.   *Financial Ratios*

        a.   Liquidity (6.2-6.3)
        b.   Leverage (6.7-6.8)
        c.   Activity (7.1)
        d.   Profitability (6.4-6.5)
        e.   Market (3.1)

    3.   *Profitability analysis*

        a.   Income measurement analysis (6.4, 6.6)
        b.   Revenue analysis (4.5-4.6, 6.6)
        c.   Cost of sales analysis (6.6)
        d.   Expense analysis (6.6)
        e.   Variation analysis (6.6, 6.9)

    4.   *Special Issues*

        a.   Impact of foreign operations (5.4)
        b.   Effects of changing prices and inflation (6.1)
        c.   Off-balance sheet financing (6.10)
        d.   Impact of changes in accounting treatment (6.6)
        e.   Accounting and economic concepts of value and income (10.1)
        f.   Earnings quality (6.1)

B. **Corporate Finance (20% - Levels A, B, and C)**

    1.   *Risk and return* (2.3, 4.4)

        a.   Calculating return
        b.   Types of risk
        c.   Relationship between risk and return

    2.   *Long-term financial management*

        a.   Term structure of interest rates (2.4)
        b.   Types of financial instruments (2.4-2.5)
        c.   Cost of capital (3.3-3.4)
        d.   Valuation of financial instruments (3.1-3.2)

    3.   *Raising capital*

        a.   Financial markets and regulation (2.1)
        b.   Market efficiency (2.1)
        c.   Financial institutions (2.1)
        d.   Initial and secondary public offerings (2.1)
        e.   Dividend policy and share repurchases (2.5-2.6)
        f.   Lease financing (7.3)

    4.   *Working capital management*

        a.   Working capital terminology (4.1)
        b.   Cash management (4.2)
        c.   Marketable securities management (4.3-4.4)
        d.   Accounts receivable management (4.5)
        e.   Inventory management (4.6)
        f.   Types of short-term credit (4.5, 7.2)
        g.   Short-term credit management (7.2)

    5.   *Corporate restructuring* (5.1)

        a.   Mergers and acquisitions
        b.   Bankruptcy
        c.   Other forms of restructuring

6.   *International finance*

    a.   Fixed, flexible, and floating exchange rates (5.2)
    b.   Managing transaction exposure (5.3-5.4)
    c.   Financing international trade (5.5)
    d.   Tax implications of transfer pricing (5.5)

C.   **Decision Analysis (20% - Levels A, B, and C)**

1.   *Cost/volume/profit analysis*

    a.   Breakeven analysis (9.2-9.5)
    b.   Profit performance and alternative operating levels (9.2-9.5)
    c.   Analysis of multiple products (9.5)

2.   *Marginal analysis*

    a.   Sunk costs, opportunity costs and other related concepts (10.1, 10.4)
    b.   Marginal costs and marginal revenue (9.1)
    c.   Special orders and pricing (10.2)
    d.   Make versus buy (10.3)
    e.   Sell or process further (10.4)
    f.   Add or drop a segment (10.4)
    g.   Capacity considerations (10.1-10.4)

3.   *Pricing*

    a.   Pricing methodologies (10.6)
    b.   Target costing (10.6)
    c.   Elasticity of demand (10.5)
    d.   Product life cycle considerations (10.6)
    e.   Market structure considerations (9.1, 10.6)

D.   **Risk Management (10% - Levels A, B, and C)**

1.   *Enterprise risk* (1.6)

    a.   Types of risk
    b.   Risk identification and assessment
    c.   Risk mitigation strategies
    d.   Managing risk

E.   **Investment Decisions (15% - Levels A, B, and C)**

1.   *Capital budgeting process* (8.1)

    a.   Stages of capital budgeting
    b.   Incremental cash flows
    c.   Income tax considerations

2.   *Discounted cash flow analysis* (8.3, 8.6)

    a.   Net present value
    b.   Internal rate of return
    c.   Comparison of NPV and IRR

3.   *Payback and discounted payback* (8.4, 8.6)

    a.   Uses of payback method
    b.   Limitations of payback method
    c.   Discounted payback

4.   *Risk analysis in capital investment* (8.2)

    a.   Sensitivity analysis
    b.   Real options

F.   **Professional Ethics (10% - Levels A, B, and C)**

1.   *Ethical considerations for management accounting and financial management professionals*

    a.   IMA's "Statement of Ethical Professional Practice" (1.1)
    b.   Fraud triangle (1.4)
    c.   Evaluation and resolution of ethical issues (1.1-1.3)

2.   *Ethical considerations for the organization*

    a.   IMA's Statement on Management Accounting, "Values and Ethics: From Inception to Practice" (1.3)
    b.   U.S. Foreign Corrupt Practices Act (1.2)
    c.   Corporate responsibility for ethical conduct (1.3)

Certified Management Accountant
Learning Outcome Statements
(Content Specification Outline effective January 2015)
Part 2 - Financial Decision Making

A. Financial Statement Analysis (25% - Levels A, B, and C)

Part 2 – Section A.1. Basic Financial Statement Analysis (6.9)

- a.   for the balance sheet and income statement prepare and analyze common-size financial statements; i.e., calculate percentage of assets and sales, respectively; also called vertical analysis
- b.   for the balance sheet and income statement prepare a comparative financial statement horizontal analysis; i.e., calculate trend year over year for every item on the financial statement compared to base year
- c.   calculate the growth rate of individual line items on the balance sheet and income statement

Part 2 – Section A.2. Financial Ratios

The candidate should be able to:

Liquidity (6.2-6.3)

- a.   calculate and interpret the current ratio, the quick (acid-test) ratio, the cash ratio, the cash flow ratio, and the net working capital ratio
- b.   explain how changes in one or more of the elements of current assets, current liabilities, and/or unit sales can change the liquidity ratios and calculate that impact
- c.   demonstrate an understanding of the liquidity of current liabilities

Leverage

- d.   define solvency (6.7)
- e.   define operating leverage and financial leverage (6.8)
- f.   calculate degree of operating leverage and degree of financial leverage (6.8)
- g.   demonstrate an understanding of the effect on the capital structure and solvency of a company with a change in the composition of debt vs. equity by calculating leverage ratios (6.7-6.8)
- h.   calculate and interpret the financial leverage ratio, and determine the effect of a given change in capital structure on this ratio (6.7-6.8)
- i.   calculate and interpret the following ratios: debt to equity, long-term debt to equity, and debt to total assets (6.7)
- j.   define, calculate and interpret the following ratios: fixed charge coverage (earnings to fixed charges), interest coverage (times interest earned), and cash flow to fixed charges (6.7)
- k.   discuss how capital structure decisions affect the risk profile of a firm (6.7)

Activity (7.1)

- l.   calculate and interpret accounts receivable turnover, inventory turnover and accounts payable turnover
- m.   calculate and interpret days sales outstanding in receivables, days sales in inventory, and days purchases in accounts payable
- n.   define and calculate the operating cycle and cash cycle of a firm
- o.   calculate and interpret total assets turnover and fixed asset turnover

Profitability (6.4-6.5)

- p.   calculate and interpret gross profit margin percentage, operating profit margin percentage, net profit margin percentage, and earnings before interest, taxes, depreciation, and amortization (EBITDA) margin percentage
- q.   calculate and interpret return on assets (ROA) and return on equity (ROE)

Market (3.1)

- r.   calculate and interpret the market/book ratio, the price/earnings ratio and price to EBITDA ratio
- s.   calculate and interpret book value per share
- t.   identify and explain the limitations of book value per share
- u.   calculate and interpret basic and diluted earnings per share
- v.   calculate and interpret earnings yield, dividend yield, dividend payout ratio and shareholder return

General (SU 6)

- w.   identify the limitations of ratio analysis
- x.   demonstrate a familiarity with the sources of financial information about public companies and industry ratio averages
- y.   evaluate the financial strength and performance of an entity based on multiple ratios

<u>Part 2 – Section A.3. Profitablity analysis</u>

    a.   demonstrate an understanding of the factors that contribute to inconsistent definitions of "equity," "assets" and "return" when using ROA and ROE (6.4)

    b.   determine the effect on return on total assets of a change in one or more elements of the financial statements (6.4)

    c.   identify factors to be considered in measuring income, including estimates, accounting methods, disclosure incentives, and the different needs of users (6.6)

    d.   explain the importance of the source, stability, and trend of sales and revenue (6.6)

    e.   demonstrate an understanding of the relationship between revenue and receivables and revenue and inventory (4.5-4.6, 6.6)

    f.   determine and analyze the effect on revenue of changes in revenue recognition and measurement methods (6.6)

    g.   analyze cost of sales by calculating and interpreting the gross profit margin (6.6)

    h.   distinguish between gross profit margin, operating profit margin and net profit margin and analyze the effects of changes in the components of each (6.4)

    i.   define and perform a variation analysis (percentage change over time) (6.6, 6.9)

    j.   calculate and interpret sustainable equity growth (6.4)

<u>Part 2 – Section A.4. Special issues</u>

The candidate should be able to:

    a.   demonstrate an understanding of the impact of foreign exchange fluctuations

        1.   identify and explain issues in the accounting for foreign operations (e.g., historical vs. current rate and the treatment of translation gains and losses) (5.4)

        2.   define functional currency (5.4)

        3.   calculate the financial ratio impact of a change in exchange rates (5.4)

        4.   discuss the possible impact on management and investor behavior of volatility in reported earnings (5.2-5.4)

    b.   demonstrate an understanding of the impact of inflation on financial ratios and the reliability of financial ratios (6.1)

    c.   define and explain off-balance sheet financing

        1.   identify and describe the following forms of off-balance sheet financing: (i) leases; (ii) special purpose entities; (iii) sale of receivables; and (iv) joint ventures (6.10)

        2.   explain why companies use off-balance sheet financing (6.10)

        3.   calculate the impact of off-balance sheet financing on the debt to equity ratio (6.10)

    d.   describe how to adjust financial statements for changes in accounting treatments (principles, estimates, and errors) and how these adjustments impact financial ratios (6.6)

    e.   distinguish between book value and market value; and distinguish between accounting profit and economic profit (3.1, 10.1)

    f.   identify the determinants and indicators of earnings quality, and explain why they are important (6.1)

B. Corporate Finance (20% - Levels A, B, and C)

<u>Part 2 – Section B.1. Risk and return</u>

The candidate should be able to:

    a.   calculate rates of return (2.3, 4.4)

    b.   identify and demonstrate an understanding of systematic (market) risk and unsystematic (company) risk (2.3, 4.4)

    c.   identify and demonstrate an understanding of credit risk, foreign exchange risk, interest rate risk, market risk, industry risk and political risk (2.3, 4.4)

    d.   demonstrate an understanding of the relationship between risk and return (2.3, 4.4)

    e.   distinguish between individual security risk and portfolio risk (4.4)

    f.   demonstrate an understanding of diversification (2.3, 4.4)

    g.   define beta and explain how a change in beta impacts a security's price (4.4)

    h.   demonstrate an understanding of the Capital Asset Pricing Model (CAPM) and calculate the expected risk-adjusted returns using CAPM (4.4)

<u>Part 2 – Section B.2. Long-term financial management</u>

The candidate should be able to:

    a.   describe the term structure of interest rates, and explain why it changes over time (2.4)

    b.   define and identify the characteristics of common stock and preferred stock (2.5)

    c.   identify and describe the basic features of a bond such as maturity, par value, coupon rate, provisions for redeeming, conversion provisions, covenants, options granted to the issuer or investor, indentures, and restrictions (2.4)

    d.   identify and evaluate debt issuance or refinancing strategies (2.4)

e. value bonds, common stock, and preferred stock using discounted cash flow methods (2.4, 3.1)
f. demonstrate an understanding of duration as a measure of bond interest rate sensitivity (2.4)
g. explain how income taxes impact financing decisions (2.4-2.5)
h. define and demonstrate an understanding of derivatives and their uses (3.2)
i. identify and describe the basic features of futures and forwards (3.2)
j. distinguish a long position from a short position (3.2)
k. define options and distinguish between a call and a put by identifying the characteristics of each (3.2)
l. define exercise price, strike price, option premium and intrinsic value (3.2)
m. demonstrate an understanding of the interrelationship of the variables that comprise the value of an option; e.g., relationship between exercise price and strike price, and value of a call (3.2)
n. define swaps for interest rate and foreign currency (3.2)
o. define and identify characteristics of other sources of long-term financing, such as leases, convertible securities, and warrants (7.2)
p. demonstrate an understanding of the relationship among inflation, interest rates, and the prices of financial instruments (2.4, 3.2)
q. define the cost of capital and demonstrate an understanding of its applications in capital structure decisions (3.3-3.4)
r. determine the weighted average cost of capital and the cost of its individual components (3.3-3.4)
s. calculate the marginal cost of capital (3.4)
t. explain the importance of using marginal cost as opposed to historical cost (3.4)
u. demonstrate an understanding of the use of the cost of capital in capital investment decisions (3.3-3.4)
v. demonstrate an understanding of how income taxes impact capital structure and capital investment decisions (3.3-3.4)
w. use the constant growth dividend discount model to value stock and demonstrate an understanding of the two-stage dividend discount model (3.1)
x. demonstrate an understanding of relative or comparable valuation methods, such as price/earnings (P/E) ratios, market/book ratios, and price/sales ratios (3.1)

Part 2 – Section B.3. Raising capital

The candidate should be able to:

a. identify the characteristics of the different types of financial markets and exchanges (2.1)
b. demonstrate an understanding of the concept of market efficiency, including the strong form, semi-strong form, and weak form of market efficiency (2.1)
c. describe the role of the credit rating agencies (2.1)
d. demonstrate an understanding of the roles of investment banks, including underwriting, advice, and trading (2.1)
e. define initial public offerings (IPOs) (2.1)
f. define subsequent/secondary offerings (2.1)
g. describe lease financing, explain its benefits and disadvantages, and calculate the net advantage to leasing using discounted cash flow concepts (7.3)
h. define the different types of dividends, including cash dividends, stock dividends, and stock splits (2.6)
i. identify and discuss the factors that influence the dividend policy of a firm (2.6)
j. demonstrate an understanding of the dividend payment process for both common and preferred stock (2.5-2.6)
k. define share repurchase and explain why a firm would repurchase its stock (2.6)
l. define insider trading and explain why it is illegal (2.1)

Part 2 – Section B.4. Working capital management

The candidate should be able to:

Working capital (4.1)

a. define working capital and identify its components
b. calculate net working capital
c. explain the benefit of short-term financial forecasts in the management of working capital

Cash (4.2)

d. identify and describe factors influencing the levels of cash
e. identify and explain the three motives for holding cash
f. prepare forecasts of future cash flows
g. identify methods of speeding up cash collections
h. calculate the net benefit of a lockbox system
i. define concentration banking
j. demonstrate an understanding of compensating balances
k. identify methods of slowing down disbursements
l. demonstrate an understanding of disbursement float and overdraft systems

Marketable securities

m. identify and describe reasons for holding marketable securities (4.3)
n. define the different types of marketable securities, including money market instruments, T-bills, treasury notes, treasury bonds, repurchase agreements, Federal agency securities, bankers' acceptances, commercial paper, negotiable CDs, Eurodollar CDs, and other marketable securities (4.3)
o. evaluate the trade-offs among the variables in marketable security selections, including safety, marketability/liquidity, yield, maturity, and taxability (4.3)
p. demonstrate an understanding of the risk and return trade-off (4.4)

Accounts receivable (4.5)

q. identify the factors influencing the level of receivables
r. demonstrate an understanding of the impact of changes in credit terms or collection policies on accounts receivable, working capital and sales volume
s. define default risk
t. identify and explain the factors involved in determining an optimal credit policy

Inventory

u. define lead time and safety stock; identify reasons for carrying inventory and the factors influencing its level (4.6)
v. identify and calculate the costs related to inventory, including carrying costs, ordering costs and shortage (stockout) costs (4.6)
w. explain how a just-in-time (JIT) inventory management system helps manage inventory (4.6)
x. identify the interaction between high inventory turnover and high gross margin (calculation not required) (6.4, 7.1)
y. demonstrate an understanding of economic order quantity (EOQ) and how a change in one variable would affect the EOQ (calculation not required) (4.6)

Short-term credit and working capital cost management

z. demonstrate an understanding of how risk affects a firm's approach to its current asset financing policy (aggressive, conservative, etc.) (4.1)
aa. identify and describe the different types of short-term credit, including trade credit, short-term bank loans, commercial paper, lines of credit, and bankers' acceptances (7.2)
bb. estimate the annual cost and effective annual interest rate of not taking a cash discount (7.2)
cc. calculate the effective annual interest rate of a bank loan with a compensating balance requirement and/or a commitment fee (7.2)
dd. demonstrate an understanding of factoring accounts receivable and calculate the cost of factoring (4.5)
ee. explain the maturity matching or hedging approach to financing (7.2)
ff. demonstrate an understanding of the factors involved in managing the costs of working capital (7.2)

General

gg. recommend a strategy for managing current assets that would fulfill a given objective (SU 4, 7.2)

Part 2 – Section B.5. Corporate restructuring

The candidate should be able to:

a. demonstrate an understanding of the following:
   i. mergers and acquisitions, including horizontal, vertical, and conglomerate (5.1)
   ii. leveraged buyouts (5.1)
b. identify defenses against takeovers (e.g., golden parachute, leveraged recapitalization, poison pill (shareholders' rights plan), staggered board of directors, fair price, voting rights plan, white knight) (5.1)
c. identify and describe divestiture concepts such as spin-offs, split-ups, equity carve-outs, and tracking stock (5.1)
d. evaluate key factors in a company's financial situation and determine if a restructuring would be beneficial to the shareholders (5.1)
e. validate possible synergies in targeted mergers and acquisitions (5.1)
f. define bankruptcy (5.1)
g. differentiate between reorganization and liquidation (5.1)
h. value a business, a business segment, and a business combination using discounted cash flow method (8.3)
i. evaluate a proposed business combination and make a recommendation based on both quantitative and qualitative considerations (5.1)

<u>Part 2 – Section B.6. International finance</u>

The candidate should be able to:

   a.   demonstrate an understanding of foreign currencies and how foreign currency affects the prices of goods and services (5.2)
   b.   identify the variables that affect exchange rates (5.3)
   c.   calculate whether a currency has depreciated or appreciated against another currency over a period of time, and evaluate the impact of the change (5.2)
   d.   demonstrate how currency futures, currency swaps, and currency options can be used to manage exchange rate risk (5.3)
   e.   calculate the net profit/loss of cross-border transactions, and evaluate the impact of this net profit/loss (5.4)
   f.   recommend methods of managing exchange rate risk and calculate the net profit/loss of your strategy (5.3-5.4)
   g.   identify and explain the benefits of international diversification (5.5)
   h.   identify and explain common trade financing methods, including cross-border factoring, letters of credit, banker's acceptances, forfaiting, and countertrade (5.5)
   i.   demonstrate an understanding of how transfer pricing affects effective worldwide tax rate (5.5)

C. Decision Analysis (20% - Levels A, B, and C)

<u>Part 2 – Section C.1. Cost/volume/profit analysis</u>

The candidate should be able to:

   a.   demonstrate an understanding of how cost/volume/profit (CVP) analysis (breakeven analysis) is used to examine the behavior of total revenues, total costs, and operating income as changes occur in output levels, selling prices, variable costs per unit, or fixed costs (9.2-9.5)
   b.   calculate operating income at different operating levels (9.4)
   c.   differentiate between costs that are fixed and costs that are variable with respect to levels of output (9.1-9.5)
   d.   explain why the classification of fixed vs. variable costs is affected by the timeframe being considered (9.1)
   e.   calculate contribution margin per unit and total contribution margin (9.2-9.5)
   f.   calculate the breakeven point in units and dollar sales to achieve targeted operating income or targeted net income (9.2-9.5)
   g.   demonstrate an understanding of how changes in unit sales mix affect operating income in multiple-product situations (9.5)
   h.   calculate multiple-product breakeven points given percentage share of sales and explain why there is no unique breakeven point in multiple-product situations (9.5)
   i.   define, calculate and interpret margin of safety and margin of safety ratio (9.2-9.3)
   j.   explain how sensitivity analysis can be used in CVP analysis when there is uncertainty about sales (9.2)
   k.   analyze and recommend a course of action using CVP analysis (9.1-9.5)
   l.   demonstrate an understanding of the impact of income taxes on CVP analysis (9.4)

<u>Part 2 – Section C.2. Marginal analysis</u>

The candidate should be able to:

   a.   identify and define relevant costs (incremental, marginal, or differential costs), sunk costs, avoidable costs, explicit and implicit costs, split-off point, joint production costs, separable processing costs, and relevant revenues (10.1, 10.4)
   b.   explain why sunk costs are not relevant in the decision-making process (10.1)
   c.   demonstrate an understanding of and calculate opportunity costs (10.1)
   d.   calculate relevant costs given a numerical scenario (10.1)
   e.   define and calculate marginal cost and marginal revenue (9.1)
   f.   identify and calculate total cost, average fixed cost, average variable cost, and average total cost (9.1)
   g.   demonstrate proficiency in the use of marginal analysis for decisions such as (a) introducing a new product or changing output levels of existing products, (b) accepting or rejecting special orders, (c) making or buying a product or service, (d) selling a product or performing additional processes and selling a more value-added product, and (e) adding or dropping a segment (10.2-10.4)
   h.   calculate the effect on operating income of a decision to accept or reject a special order when there is idle capacity and the order has no long-run implications (10.2)
   i.   identify and describe qualitative factors in make-or-buy decisions, such as product quality and dependability of suppliers (10.3)
   j.   calculate the effect on operating income of a make-or-buy decision (10.3)
   k.   calculate the effects on operating income of a decision to sell or process further; and of a decision to drop or add a segment (10.4)
   l.   identify the effects of changes in capacity on production decisions (10.2)
   m. demonstrate an understanding of the impact of income taxes on marginal analysis (10.1)
   n.   recommend a course of action using marginal analysis (SU 10)

<u>Part 2– Section C.3. Pricing</u>

The candidate should be able to:

a.   identify different pricing methodologies, including market comparables, cost-based, and value-based approaches (10.6)

b.   differentiate between a cost-based approach (cost-plus pricing, mark-up pricing) and a market-based approach to setting prices (10.6)

c.   calculate selling price using a cost-based approach (10.6)

d.   demonstrate an understanding of how the pricing of a product or service is affected by the demand for and supply of the product or service, as well as the market structure within which it operates (9.1, 10.6)

e.   demonstrate an understanding of the impact of cartels on pricing (10.6)

f.   demonstrate an understanding of the short-run equilibrium price for the firm in (1) pure competition; (2) monopolistic competition; (3) oligopoly; and (4) monopoly using the concepts of marginal revenue and marginal cost (9.1)

g.   identify techniques used to set prices based on understanding customers' perceptions of value, competitors' technologies, products and costs (10.6)

h.   define and demonstrate an understanding of target pricing and target costing and identify the main steps in developing target prices and target costs (10.6)

i.   define value engineering (10.6)

j.   calculate the target operating income per unit and target cost per unit (10.6)

k.   define and distinguish between a value-added cost and a nonvalue-added cost (10.6)

l.   define the pricing technique of cost plus target rate of return (10.6)

m.   calculate the price elasticity of demand using the midpoint formula (10.5)

n.   define and explain elastic and inelastic demand (10.5)

o.   estimate total revenue given changes in prices and demand as well as elasticity (10.5)

p.   discuss how pricing decisions can differ in the short-run and in the long-run (10.6)

q.   define product life cycle; identify and explain the four stages of the product life cycle; and explain why pricing decisions might differ over the life of a product (10.6)

r.   evaluate and recommend pricing strategies under specific market conditions (SU 10)

Section D. Risk Management (10% - Levels A, B, and C)

<u>Part 2– Section D.1. Enterprise risk</u>

The candidate should be able to:

a.   identify and explain the different types of risk, including business risk, hazard risks, financial risks, operational risks, and strategic risks (1.6)

b.   demonstrate an understanding of operational risk (1.6)

c.   define legal risk, compliance risk, and political risk (1.6)

d.   demonstrate an understanding of how volatility and time impact risk (1.6)

e.   define the concept of capital adequacy (i.e., solvency, liquidity, reserves, sufficient capital, etc.) (6.7)

f.   explain the use of probabilities in determining exposure to risk and calculate expected loss given a set of probabilities (1.6)

g.   define the concepts of unexpected loss and maximum possible loss (extreme or catastrophic loss) (1.6)

h.   identify strategies for risk response (or treatment), including actions to avoid, retain, reduce (mitigate), transfer (share), and exploit (accept) risks (1.6)

i.   define risk transfer (e.g., purchasing insurance, issuing debt) (1.6)

j.   demonstrate an understanding of the concept of residual risk and distinguish it from inherent risk (1.6)

k.   identify and explain the benefits of risk management (1.6)

l.   identify and describe the key steps in the risk management process (1.6)

m.   explain how attitude toward risk might affect the management of risk (1.6)

n.   demonstrate a general understanding of the use of liability/hazard insurance to mitigate risk (detailed knowledge not required) (1.6)

o.   identify methods of managing operational risk (1.6)

p.   identify and explain financial risk management methods (1.6)

q.   identify and explain qualitative risk assessment tools including risk identification, risk ranking, and risk maps (1.6)

r.   identify and explain quantitative risk assessment tools including cash flow at risk, earnings at risk, earnings distributions, and earnings per share (EPS) distributions (4.4)

s.   identify and explain Value at Risk (VaR) (calculations not required) (4.4)

t.   define enterprise risk management (ERM) and identify and describe key objectives, components and benefits of an ERM program (1.6)

u.   identify event identification techniques and provide examples of event identification within the context of an ERM approach (1.6)
v.   explain the role of corporate governance, risk analytics, and portfolio management in an ERM program (1.6, 4.4)
w.   evaluate scenarios and recommend risk mitigation strategies (1.6)
x.   prepare a cost-benefit analysis and demonstrate an understanding of its uses in risk assessment and decision making (1.6)
y.   demonstrate an understanding of the COSO ERM conceptual framework (1.6)

Section E. Investment Decisions (15% - Levels A, B, and C)

Part 2 – Section E.1. Capital budgeting process (8.1)

The candidate should be able to:

a.   define capital budgeting and identify the steps or stages undertaken in developing and implementing a capital budget for a project
b.   identify and calculate the relevant cash flows of a capital investment project on both a pretax and after-tax basis
c.   demonstrate an understanding of how income taxes affect cash flows
d.   distinguish between cash flows and accounting profits and discuss the relevance to capital budgeting of incremental cash flow, sunk cost, and opportunity cost
e.   explain the importance of changes in net working capital in capital budgeting
f.   discuss how the effects of inflation are reflected in capital budgeting analysis
g.   define hurdle rate
h.   identify and discuss qualitative considerations involved in the capital budgeting decision
i.   describe the role of the post-audit in the capital budgeting process

Part 2 – Section E.2. Discounted cash flow analysis

The candidate should be able to:

a.   demonstrate an understanding of the two main discounted cash flow (DCF) methods, net present value (NPV) and internal rate of return (IRR) (8.3, 8.6)
b.   calculate NPV and IRR (8.3, 8.6)
c.   demonstrate an understanding of the decision criteria used in NPV and IRR analyses to determine acceptable projects (8.3)
d.   compare NPV and IRR focusing on the relative advantages and disadvantages of each method, particularly with respect to independent versus mutually exclusive projects and the "multiple IRR problem" (8.3)
e.   explain why NPV and IRR methods can produce conflicting rankings for capital projects if not applied properly (8.3)
f.   identify assumptions of NPV and IRR (8.3)
g.   evaluate and recommend project investments on the basis of DCF analysis (8.3, 8.6)

Part 2 – Section E.3. Payback and discounted payback

The candidate should be able to:

a.   demonstrate an understanding of the payback and discounted payback methods (8.4)
b.   identify the advantages and disadvantages of the payback and discounted payback methods (8.4)
c.   calculate payback periods and discounted payback periods (8.4, 8.6)

Part 2 – Section E.4. Risk analysis in capital investment (8.2)

The candidate should be able to:

a.   identify alternative approaches to dealing with risk in capital budgeting
b.   distinguish among sensitivity analysis, scenario analysis, and Monte Carlo simulation as risk analysis techniques
c.   explain why a rate specifically adjusted for risk should be used when project cash flows are more or less risky than is normal for a firm
d.   explain how the value of a capital investment is increased if consideration is given to the possibility of adding on, speeding up, slowing up, or discontinuing early
e.   demonstrate an understanding of real options and identify examples of the different types of real options: e.g., abandon, delay, expand, and scale back (calculations not required)

Section F. Professional Ethics (10% - Levels A, B, and C)

Ethics may be tested in conjunction with any topic area.

<u>Part 2 – Section F.1 Ethical considerations for management accounting and financial management professionals</u>

Using the standards outlined in **IMA's Statement of Ethical Professional Practice**, the candidate should be able to:

   a.   identify and describe the four overarching ethical principles (1.1)
   b.   evaluate a given business situation for its ethical implications (1.1-1.3)
   c.   identify and describe relevant standards that may have been violated in a given business situation and explain why the specific standards are applicable (1.1-1.3)
   d.   recommend a course of action for management accountants or financial managers to take when confronted with an ethical dilemma in the business environment (1.1-1.3)
   e.   evaluate and propose resolutions for ethical issues such as fraudulent reporting, manipulation of analyses, results, and budgets (1.1-1.3)

Using the Fraud Triangle model, the candidate should be able to:

   f.   identify the three components of the triangle (1.4)
   g.   use the model to explain how a management accounting and financial management professional can identify and manage the risk of fraud (1.4-1.5)

<u>Part 2 – Section F.2. Ethical considerations for the organization</u>

The candidate should be able to:

   a.   identify the purpose of the U.S. Foreign Corrupt Practices Act (1.2)
   b.   identify the practices that the U.S Foreign Corrupt Practices Act prohibits, and explain how to apply this act to typical business situations (1.2)
   c.   apply relevant provisions of IMA's Statement on Management Accounting, "Values and Ethics: From Inception to Practice" to a business situation (1.3)
   d.   discuss corporate responsibility for ethical conduct (1.3)
   e.   explain why it is important for an organization to have a code of conduct (1.3)
   f.   demonstrate an understanding of the ways ethical values benefit an organization (1.3)
   g.   demonstrate an understanding of the differences between ethical and legal behavior (1.3)
   h.   demonstrate an understanding of role of "leadership by example" or "tone at the top" in determining an organization's ethical environment (1.3)
   i.   explain the importance of human capital to an organization in creating a climate where "doing the right thing" is expected (i.e., hiring the right people, providing them with training, and practicing consistent values-based leadership) (1.3)
   j.   explain how an organization's culture impacts its behavioral values (1.3)
   k.   explain the importance of an organization's core values in explaining its ethical behavior (1.3)
   l.   discuss the importance of employee training to maintaining an ethical organizational culture (1.3)
   m.   describe the following methods to monitor ethical compliance: human performance feedback loop and survey tools (1.3)
   n.   explain the importance of a whistleblowing framework (e.g., ethics helpline) to maintaining an ethical organizational culture (1.3)
   o.   identify the requirements of SOX Section 406 - Code of Ethics for Senior Financial Officers (1.2)
   p.   discuss the issues organizations face in applying their values and ethical standards internationally (1.3)
   q.   demonstrate an understanding of the relationship between ethics and internal controls (1.3)

APPENDIX D
ICMA SUGGESTED READING LIST
(AS PRINTED IN THE ICMA'S 2017 CMA HANDBOOK)

The ICMA suggested reading list that follows is reproduced to give you an overview of the scope of Part 2. You will not have the time to study these texts. Our CMA Review System is complete and thorough and is designed to maximize your study time. Candidates are expected to stay up-to-date by reading articles from journals, newspapers, and professional publications.

NOTE: Edition numbers and publication dates may not be current. Focus entirely on Study Units 1-10 in this book to help you pass Part 2 of the CMA exam.

Part 2 – Financial Decision Making

Financial Statement Analysis

Mackenzie, Bruce, Coetsee, Danie, Njikizana, Tapiwa, Chamboko, Raymond, Colyvas, Blaise, and Hanekom, Brandon, *2012 Interpretation and Application of International Financial Reporting Standards,* John Wiley & Sons, Hoboken, NJ, 2012.

Gibson, Charles H., *Financial Reporting & Analysis*, 13th edition, South-Western Cengage Learning, Mason, OH, 2013.

Subramanyam, K.R., and Wild, John L., *Financial Statement Analysis*, 10th edition, McGraw Hill, New York, NY, 2009.

Corporate Finance

Brealey, Richard A., Myers, Stewart C., and Allen, Franklin, *Principles of Corporate Finance*, 10th edition, McGraw Hill, New York, NY, 2011.

Van Horn, James C., and Wachowicz, John M. Jr., *Fundamentals of Financial Management*, 13th edition, FT/Prentice-Hall, Harlow, England, 2009.

Decision Analysis

Blocher, Edward J., Stout, David E., Juras, Paul E., and Cokins, Gary, *Cost Management: A Strategic Emphasis*, 6th edition, McGraw Hill, New York, NY, 2013.

Horngren, Charles T., Datar, Srikant, Rajan, Madhav, *Cost Accounting: A Managerial Emphasis*, 14th edition, Prentice-Hall, Upper Saddle River, NJ, 2012.

Risk Management

COSO, The Committee of Sponsoring Organizations of the Treadway Commission, 2004, *Enterprise Risk Management – Integrated Framework*.

Moeller, Robert R., *COSO Enterprise Risk Management*, 2nd edition, John Wiley & Sons, Inc., Hoboken, NJ, 2011.

IMA, 2014, *Enterprise Risk Management: Frameworks, Elements, and Integration*, www.imanet.org/insights-and-trends/risk--management/enterprise-risk-management.

IMA, 2007, *Enterprise Risk Management: Tools and Techniques for Effective Implementation*, www.imanet.org/insights-and-trends/risk--management/test.

Investment Decisions

Brealey, Richard A., Myers, Stewart C., and Allen, Franklin, *Principles of Corporate Finance*, 10th edition, McGraw Hill, New York, NY, 2011.

Van Horn, James C., and Wachowicz, John M. Jr., *Fundamentals of Financial Management*, 13th edition, FT/Prentice Hall, Harlow, England, 2009.

Professional Ethics

IMA, 2014, *IMA Statement of Ethical Professional Practice*, www.imanet.org/insights-and-trends/business-leadership-and-ethics/ima-statement-of-ethical-professional-practice.

Association of Certified Fraud Examiners, *The Fraud Triangle*, www.acfe.com/content.aspx?id=6939.

IMA, 2014, *Values and Ethics: From Inception to Practice*, www.imanet.org/insights-and-trends/business-leadership-and-ethics/values-and-ethics---from-inception-to-practice.

United States Department of Justice, *A Resource Guide to the U.S. Foreign Corrupt Practices Act*, www.justice.gov/sites/default/files/criminal-fraud/legacy/2015/01/16/guide.pdf.

INDEX